VOLKSWAGEN | FRONT WHEEL DRIVE
1974-89 REPAIR MANUAL

CHILTON'S

Covers all U.S. and Canadian models of
Volkswagen Cabriolet, Dasher, Fox, Golf, GTI,
Jetta, Quantum, Rabbit, Pick-Up and Scirocco;
gasoline and diesel engines

by **Will Kessler**, A.S.E., S.A.E.

CHILTON *Automotive Books*

PUBLISHED BY **HAYNES NORTH AMERICA. Inc.**

Manufactured in USA
© 1995 Haynes North America, Inc.
ISBN 0-8019-8663-X
Library of Congress Catalog Card No. 94-069446
8901234567 9876543210

Haynes Publishing Group
Sparkford Nr Yeovil
Somerset BA22 7JJ England

Haynes North America, Inc
861 Lawrence Drive
Newbury Park
California 91320 USA

ABCDE
FGHIJ
KL

Contents

Contents

SAFETY NOTICE

Proper service and repair procedures are vital to the safe, reliable operation of all motor vehicles, as well as the personal safety of those performing repairs. This manual outlines procedures for servicing and repairing vehicles using safe, effective methods. The procedures contain many NOTES, CAUTIONS and WARNINGS which should be followed, along with standard procedures to eliminate the possibility of personal injury or improper service which could damage the vehicle or compromise its safety.

It is important to note that repair procedures and techniques, tools and parts for servicing motor vehicles, as well as the skill and experience of the individual performing the work vary widely. It is not possible to anticipate all of the conceivable ways or conditions under which vehicles may be serviced, or to provide cautions as to all possible hazards that may result. Standard and accepted safety precautions and equipment should be used when handling toxic or flammable fluids, and safety goggles or other protection should be used during cutting, grinding, chiseling, prying, or any other process that can cause material removal or projectiles.

Some procedures require the use of tools specially designed for a specific purpose. Before substituting another tool or procedure, you must be completely satisfied that neither your personal safety, nor the performance of the vehicle will be endangered.

Although information in this manual is based on industry sources and is complete as possible at the time of publication, the possibility exists that some car manufacturers made later changes which could not be included here. While striving for total accuracy, the authors or publishers cannot assume responsibility for any errors, changes or omissions that may occur in the compilation of this data.

PART NUMBERS

Part numbers listed in this reference are not recommendations by Haynes North America, Inc. for any product brand name. They are references that can be used with interchange manuals and aftermarket supplier catalogs to locate each brand supplier's discrete part number.

SPECIAL TOOLS

Special tools are recommended by the vehicle manufacturer to perform their specific job. Use has been kept to a minimum, but where absolutely necessary, they are referred to in the text by the part number of the tool manufacturer. These tools can be purchased, under the appropriate part number, from your local dealer or regional distributor, or an equivalent tool can be purchased locally from a tool supplier or parts outlet. Before substituting any tool for the one recommended, read the SAFETY NOTICE at the top of this page.

ACKNOWLEDGMENTS

The publisher expresses appreciation to Volkswagen of America, Inc. for their generous assistance.

1

GENERAL INFORMATION AND MAINTENANCE

HOW TO USE THIS BOOK

Chilton's Total Car Care manual for Volkswagen Front Wheel Drive vehicles is intended to help you learn more about the inner workings of your vehicle while saving you money on its upkeep and operation.

The beginning of the book will likely be referred to the most, since that is where you will find information for maintenance and tune-up. The other sections deal with the more complex systems of your vehicle. Operating systems from engine through brakes are covered to the extent that the average do-it-yourselfer becomes mechanically involved. This book will not explain such things as rebuilding a differential for the simple reason that the expertise required and the investment in special tools make this task uneconomical. It will, however, give you detailed instructions to help you change your own brake pads and shoes, replace spark plugs, and perform many more jobs that can save you money, give you personal satisfaction and help you avoid expensive problems.

A secondary purpose of this book is a reference for owners who want to understand their vehicle and/or their mechanics better. In this case, no tools at all are required.

Where to Begin

Before removing any bolts, read through the entire procedure. This will give you the overall view of what tools and supplies will be required. There is nothing more frustrating than having to walk to the bus stop on Monday morning because you were short one bolt on Sunday afternoon. So read ahead and plan ahead. Each operation should be approached logically and all procedures thoroughly understood before attempting any work.

All sections contain adjustments, maintenance, removal and installation procedures, and in some cases, repair or overhaul procedures. When repair is not considered practical, we tell you how to remove the part and then how to install the new or rebuilt replacement. In this way, you at least save labor costs. "Backyard" repair of some components is just not practical.

Avoiding Trouble

Many procedures in this book require you to "label and disconnect . . ." a group of lines, hoses or wires. Don't be lulled into thinking you can remember where everything goes—you won't. If you hook up vacuum or fuel lines incorrectly, the vehicle may run poorly, if at all. If you hook up electrical wiring incorrectly, you may instantly learn a very expensive lesson.

You don't need to know the official or engineering name for each hose or line. A piece of masking tape on the hose and a piece on its fitting will allow you to assign your own label such as the letter A or a short name. As long as you remember your own code, the lines can be reconnected by matching similar letters or names. Do remember that tape will dissolve in gasoline or other fluids; if a component is to be washed or cleaned, use another method of identification. A permanent felt-tipped marker or a metal scribe can be very handy for marking metal parts. Remove any tape or paper labels after assembly.

Maintenance or Repair?

It's necessary to mention the difference between maintenance and repair. Maintenance includes routine inspections, adjustments, and replacement of parts which show signs of normal wear. Maintenance compensates for wear or deterioration. Repair implies that something has broken or is not working. A need for repair is often caused by lack of maintenance. Example: draining and refilling the automatic transmission fluid is maintenance recommended by the manufacturer at specific mileage intervals. Failure to do this can shorten the life of the transmission/transaxle, requiring very expensive repairs. While no maintenance program can prevent items from breaking or wearing out, a general rule can be stated: MAINTENANCE IS CHEAPER THAN REPAIR.

TOOLS AND EQUIPMENT

▶ **See Figures 1 thru 15**

Naturally, without the proper tools and equipment it is impossible to properly service your vehicle. It would also be virtually impossible to catalog every tool that you would need to perform all of the operations in this book. Of course, It would be unwise for the amateur to rush out and buy an expen-

Two basic mechanic's rules should be mentioned here. First, whenever the left side of the vehicle or engine is referred to, it is meant to specify the driver's side. Conversely, the right side of the vehicle means the passenger's side. Second, screws and bolts are removed by turning counterclockwise, and tightened by turning clockwise unless specifically noted.

Safety is always the most important rule. Constantly be aware of the dangers involved in working on an automobile and take the proper precautions. See the information in this section regarding SERVICING YOUR VEHICLE SAFELY and the SAFETY NOTICE on the acknowledgment page.

Avoiding the Most Common Mistakes

Pay attention to the instructions provided. There are 3 common mistakes in mechanical work:

1. Incorrect order of assembly, disassembly or adjustment. When taking something apart or putting it together, performing steps in the wrong order usually just costs you extra time; however, it CAN break something. Read the entire procedure before beginning disassembly. Perform everything in the order in which the instructions say you should, even if you can't immediately see a reason for it. When you're taking apart something that is very intricate, you might want to draw a picture of how it looks when assembled at one point in order to make sure you get everything back in its proper position. We will supply exploded views whenever possible. When making adjustments, perform them in the proper order. One adjustment possibly will affect another.

2. Overtorquing (or undertorquing). While it is more common for overtorquing to cause damage, undertorquing may allow a fastener to vibrate loose causing serious damage. Especially when dealing with aluminum parts, pay attention to torque specifications and utilize a torque wrench in assembly. If a torque figure is not available, remember that if you are using the right tool to perform the job, you will probably not have to strain yourself to get a fastener tight enough. The pitch of most threads is so slight that the tension you put on the wrench will be multiplied many times in actual force on what you are tightening. A good example of how critical torque is can be seen in the case of spark plug installation, especially where you are putting the plug into an aluminum cylinder head. Too little torque can fail to crush the gasket, causing leakage of combustion gases and consequent overheating of the plug and engine parts. Too much torque can damage the threads or distort the plug, changing the spark gap.

There are many commercial products available for ensuring that fasteners won't come loose, even if they are not torqued just right (a very common brand is Loctite®). If you're worried about getting something together tight enough to hold, but loose enough to avoid mechanical damage during assembly, one of these products might offer substantial insurance. Before choosing a threadlocking compound, read the label on the package and make sure the product is compatible with the materials, fluids, etc. involved.

3. Crossthreading. This occurs when a part such as a bolt is screwed into a nut or casting at the wrong angle and forced. Crossthreading is more likely to occur if access is difficult. It helps to clean and lubricate fasteners, then to start threading the bolt, spark plug, etc. with your fingers. If you encounter resistance, unscrew the part and start over again at a different angle until it can be inserted and turned several times without much effort. Keep in mind that many parts, especially spark plugs, have tapered threads, so that gentle turning will automatically bring the part you're threading to the proper angle. Don't put a wrench on the part until it's been tightened a couple of turns by hand. If you suddenly encounter resistance, and the part has not seated fully, don't force it. Pull it back out to make sure it's clean and threading properly.

Be sure to take your time and be patient, and always plan ahead. Allow yourself ample time to perform repairs and maintenance. You may find maintaining your car a satisfying and enjoyable experience.

sive set of tools on the theory that he/she may need one or more of them at some time.

The best approach is to proceed slowly, gathering a good quality set of those tools that are used most frequently. Don't be misled by the low cost of bargain tools. It is far better to spend a little more for better quality. Forged wrenches, 6 or 12-point sockets and fine tooth ratchets are by far preferable to their less

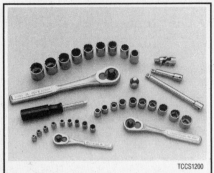

Fig. 1 All but the most basic procedures will require an assortment of ratchets and sockets

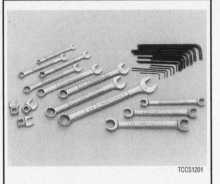

Fig. 2 In addition to ratchets, a good set of wrenches and hex keys will be necessary

Fig. 3 A hydraulic floor jack and a set of jackstands are essential for lifting and supporting the vehicle

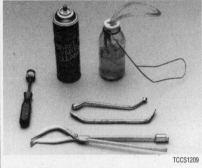

Fig. 4 An assortment of pliers, grippers and cutters will be handy for old rusted parts and stripped bolt heads

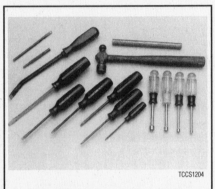

Fig. 5 Various drivers, chisels and prybars are great tools to have in your toolbox

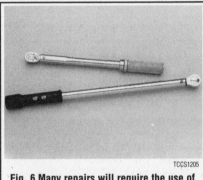

Fig. 6 Many repairs will require the use of a torque wrench to assure the components are properly fastened

Fig. 7 Although not always necessary, using specialized brake tools will save time

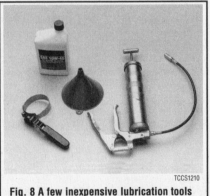

Fig. 8 A few inexpensive lubrication tools will make maintenance easier

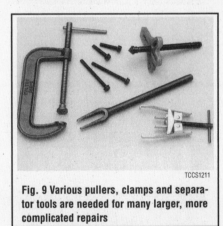

Fig. 9 Various pullers, clamps and separator tools are needed for many larger, more complicated repairs

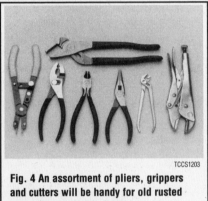

Fig. 10 A variety of tools and gauges should be used for spark plug gapping and installation

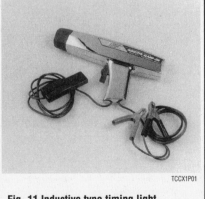

Fig. 11 Inductive type timing light

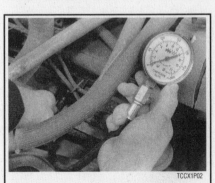

Fig. 12 A screw-in type compression gauge is recommended for compression testing

Fig. 13 A vacuum/pressure tester is necessary for many testing procedures

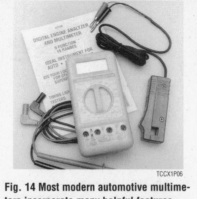

Fig. 14 Most modern automotive multimeters incorporate many helpful features

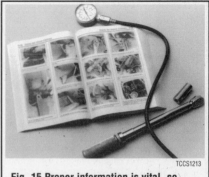

Fig. 15 Proper information is vital, so always have a Chilton Total Car Care manual handy

expensive counterparts. As any good mechanic can tell you, there are few worse experiences than trying to work on a vehicle with bad tools. Your monetary savings will be far outweighed by frustration and mangled knuckles.

Begin accumulating those tools that are used most frequently: those associated with routine maintenance and tune-up. In addition to the normal assortment of screwdrivers and pliers, you should have the following tools:

- Wrenches/sockets and combination open end/box end wrenches in sizes 3mm–19mm $^{13}/_{16}$ in. or $^{5}/_{8}$ in. spark plug socket (depending on plug type).

➡ **If possible, buy various length socket drive extensions. Universal-joint and wobble extensions can be extremely useful, but be careful when using them, as they can change the amount of torque applied to the socket.**

- Jackstands for support.
- Oil filter wrench.
- Spout or funnel for pouring fluids.
- Grease gun for chassis lubrication (unless your vehicle is not equipped with any grease fittings—for details, please refer to information on Fluids and Lubricants, later in this section).
- Hydrometer for checking the battery (unless equipped with a sealed, maintenance-free battery).
- A container for draining oil and other fluids.
- Rags for wiping up the inevitable mess.

In addition to the above items there are several others that are not absolutely necessary, but handy to have around. These include Oil Dry® (or an equivalent oil absorbent gravel—such as cat litter) and the usual supply of lubricants, antifreeze and fluids, although these can be purchased as needed. This is a basic list for routine maintenance, but only your personal needs and desire can accurately determine your list of tools.

After performing a few projects on the vehicle, you'll be amazed at the other tools and non-tools on your workbench. Some useful household items are: a large turkey baster or siphon, empty coffee cans and ice trays (to store parts), ball of twine, electrical tape for wiring, small rolls of colored tape for tagging lines or hoses, markers and pens, a note pad, golf tees (for plugging vacuum lines), metal coat hangers or a roll of mechanic's wire (to hold things out of the way), dental pick or similar long, pointed probe, a strong magnet, and a small mirror (to see into recesses and under manifolds).

A more advanced set of tools, suitable for tune-up work, can be drawn up easily. While the tools are slightly more sophisticated, they need not be outrageously expensive. There are several inexpensive tach/dwell meters on the market that are every bit as good for the average mechanic as a professional model. Just be sure that it goes to a least 1200–1500 rpm on the tach scale and that it

works on 4, 6 and 8-cylinder engines. The key to these purchases is to make them with an eye towards adaptability and wide range. A basic list of tune-up tools could include:

- Tach/dwell meter.
- Spark plug wrench and gapping tool.
- Feeler gauges for valve adjustment.
- Timing light.

The choice of a timing light should be made carefully. A light which works on the DC current supplied by the vehicle's battery is the best choice; it should have a xenon tube for brightness. On any vehicle with an electronic ignition system, a timing light with an inductive pickup that clamps around the No. 1 spark plug cable is preferred.

In addition to these basic tools, there are several other tools and gauges you may find useful. These include:

- Compression gauge. The screw-in type is slower to use, but eliminates the possibility of a faulty reading due to escaping pressure.
- Manifold vacuum gauge.
- 12V test light.
- A combination volt/ohmmeter
- Induction Ammeter. This is used for determining whether or not there is current in a wire. These are handy for use if a wire is broken somewhere in a wiring harness.

As a final note, you will probably find a torque wrench necessary for all but the most basic work. The beam type models are perfectly adequate, although the newer click types (breakaway) are easier to use. The click type torque wrenches tend to be more expensive. Also keep in mind that all types of torque wrenches should be periodically checked and/or recalibrated. You will have to decide for yourself which better fits your pocketbook, and purpose.

Special Tools

Normally, the use of special factory tools is avoided for repair procedures, since these are not readily available for the do-it-yourself mechanic. When it is possible to perform the job with more commonly available tools, it will be pointed out, but occasionally, a special tool was designed to perform a specific function and should be used. Before substituting another tool, you should be convinced that neither your safety nor the performance of the vehicle will be compromised.

Special tools can usually be purchased from an automotive parts store or from your dealer. In some cases special tools may be available directly from the tool manufacturer.

SERVICING YOUR VEHICLE SAFELY

♦ **See Figures 16, 17, 18 and 19**

It is virtually impossible to anticipate all of the hazards involved with automotive maintenance and service, but care and common sense will prevent most accidents.

The rules of safety for mechanics range from "don't smoke around gasoline," to "use the proper tool(s) for the job." The trick to avoiding injuries is to develop safe work habits and to take every possible precaution.

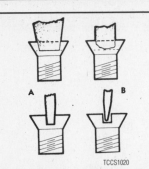

TCCS1020

Fig. 16 Screwdrivers should be kept in good condition to prevent injury or damage which could result if the blade slips from the screw

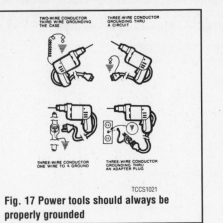

TCCS1021

Fig. 17 Power tools should always be properly grounded

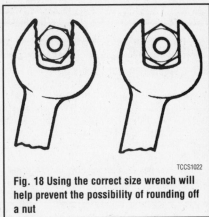

TCCS1022

Fig. 18 Using the correct size wrench will help prevent the possibility of rounding off a nut

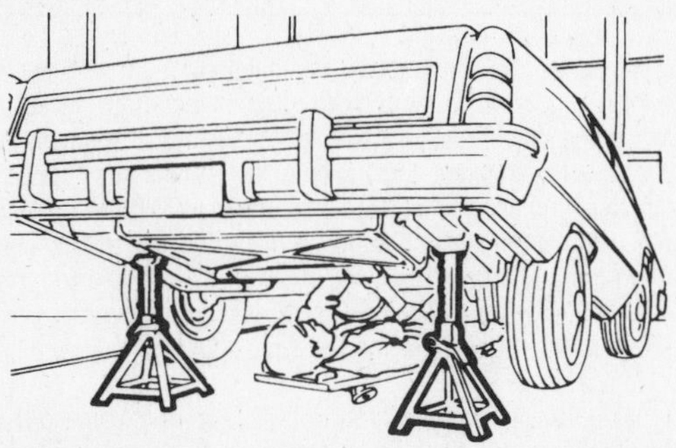

TCCS1023

Fig. 19 NEVER work under a vehicle unless it is supported using safety stands (jackstands)

Do's

• Do keep a fire extinguisher and first aid kit handy.

• Do wear safety glasses or goggles when cutting, drilling, grinding or prying, even if you have 20–20 vision. If you wear glasses for the sake of vision, wear safety goggles over your regular glasses.

• Do shield your eyes whenever you work around the battery. Batteries contain sulfuric acid. In case of contact with the eyes or skin, flush the area with water or a mixture of water and baking soda, then seek immediate medical attention.

• Do use safety stands (jackstands) for any undervehicle service. Jacks are for raising vehicles; jackstands are for making sure the vehicle stays raised until you want it to come down. Whenever the vehicle is raised, block the wheels remaining on the ground and set the parking brake.

• Do use adequate ventilation when working with any chemicals or hazardous materials. Like carbon monoxide, the asbestos dust resulting from some brake lining wear can be hazardous in sufficient quantities.

• Do disconnect the negative battery cable when working on the electrical system. The secondary ignition system contains EXTREMELY HIGH VOLTAGE. In some cases it can even exceed 50,000 volts.

• Do follow manufacturer's directions whenever working with potentially hazardous materials. Most chemicals and fluids are poisonous if taken internally.

• Do properly maintain your tools. Loose hammerheads, mushroomed punches and chisels, frayed or poorly grounded electrical cords, excessively worn screwdrivers, spread wrenches (open end), cracked sockets, slipping ratchets, or faulty droplight sockets can cause accidents.

• Likewise, keep your tools clean; a greasy wrench can slip off a bolt head, ruining the bolt and often harming your knuckles in the process.

• Do use the proper size and type of tool for the job at hand. Do select a wrench or socket that fits the nut or bolt. The wrench or socket should sit straight, not cocked.

• Do, when possible, pull on a wrench handle rather than push on it, and adjust your stance to prevent a fall.

• Do be sure that adjustable wrenches are tightly closed on the nut or bolt and pulled so that the force is on the side of the fixed jaw.

• Do strike squarely with a hammer; avoid glancing blows.

• Do set the parking brake and block the drive wheels if the work requires a running engine.

Don'ts

• Don't run the engine in a garage or anywhere else without proper ventilation—EVER! Carbon monoxide is poisonous; it takes a long time to leave the human body and you can build up a deadly supply of it in your system by simply breathing in a little every day. You may not realize you are slowly poisoning yourself. Always use power vents, windows, fans and/or open the garage door.

• Don't work around moving parts while wearing loose clothing. Short sleeves are much safer than long, loose sleeves. Hard-toed shoes with neoprene soles protect your toes and give a better grip on slippery surfaces. Jewelry such as watches, fancy belt buckles, beads or body adornment of any kind is not safe working around a vehicle. Long hair should be tied back under a hat or cap.

• Don't use pockets for toolboxes. A fall or bump can drive a screwdriver deep into your body. Even a rag hanging from your back pocket can wrap around a spinning shaft or fan.

• Don't smoke when working around gasoline, cleaning solvent or other flammable material.

• Don't smoke when working around the battery. When the battery is being charged, it gives off explosive hydrogen gas.

• Don't use gasoline to wash your hands; there are excellent soaps available. Gasoline contains dangerous additives which can enter the body through a cut or through your pores. Gasoline also removes all the natural oils from the skin so that bone dry hands will suck up oil and grease.

• Don't service the air conditioning system unless you are equipped with the necessary tools and training. When liquid or compressed gas refrigerant is released to atmospheric pressure it will absorb heat from whatever it contacts. This will chill or freeze anything it touches.

• Don't use screwdrivers for anything other than driving screws! A screwdriver used as an prying tool can snap when you least expect it, causing injuries. At the very least, you'll ruin a good screwdriver.

• Don't use an emergency jack (that little ratchet, scissors, or pantograph jack supplied with the vehicle) for anything other than changing a flat! These jacks are only intended for emergency use out on the road; they are NOT designed as a maintenance tool. If you are serious about maintaining your vehicle yourself, invest in a hydraulic floor jack of at least a 1½ ton capacity, and at least two sturdy jackstands.

FASTENERS, MEASUREMENTS AND CONVERSIONS

Bolts, Nuts and Other Threaded Retainers

▶ **See Figures 20, 21, 22 and 23**

Although there are a great variety of fasteners found in the modern car or truck, the most commonly used retainer is the threaded fastener (nuts, bolts, screws, studs, etc.). Most threaded retainers may be reused, provided that they are not damaged in use or during the repair. Some retainers (such as stretch bolts or torque prevailing nuts) are designed to deform when tightened or in use and should not be reinstalled.

Whenever possible, we will note any special retainers which should be replaced during a procedure. But you should always inspect the condition of a

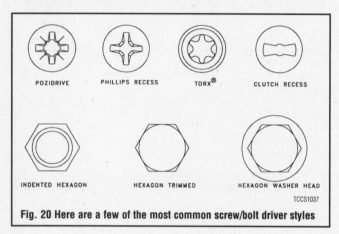

Fig. 20 Here are a few of the most common screw/bolt driver styles

Fig. 21 There are many different types of threaded retainers found on vehicles

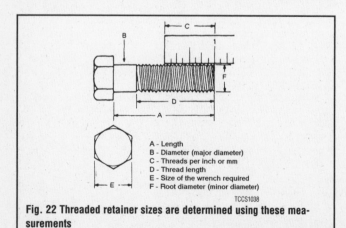

A - Length
B - Diameter (major diameter)
C - Threads per inch or mm
D - Thread length
E - Size of the wrench required
F - Root diameter (minor diameter)

Fig. 22 Threaded retainer sizes are determined using these measurements

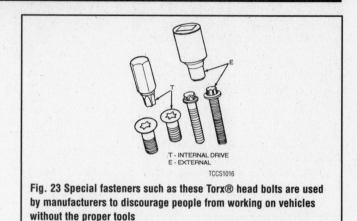

Fig. 23 Special fasteners such as these Torx® head bolts are used by manufacturers to discourage people from working on vehicles without the proper tools

retainer when it is removed and replace any that show signs of damage. Check all threads for rust or corrosion which can increase the torque necessary to achieve the desired clamp load for which that fastener was originally selected. Additionally, be sure that the driver surface of the fastener has not been compromised by rounding or other damage. In some cases a driver surface may become only partially rounded, allowing the driver to catch in only one direction. In many of these occurrences, a fastener may be installed and tightened, but the driver would not be able to grip and loosen the fastener again. (This could lead to frustration down the line should that component ever need to be disassembled again).

If you must replace a fastener, whether due to design or damage, you must ALWAYS be sure to use the proper replacement. In all cases, a retainer of the same design, material and strength should be used. Markings on the heads of most bolts will help determine the proper strength of the fastener. The same material, thread and pitch must be selected to assure proper installation and safe operation of the vehicle afterwards.

Thread gauges are available to help measure a bolt or stud's thread. Most automotive and hardware stores keep gauges available to help you select the proper size. In a pinch, you can use another nut or bolt for a thread gauge. If the bolt you are replacing is not too badly damaged, you can select a match by finding another bolt which will thread in its place. If you find a nut which threads properly onto the damaged bolt, then use that nut to help select the replacement bolt. If however, the bolt you are replacing is so badly damaged (broken or drilled out) that its threads cannot be used as a gauge, you might start by looking for another bolt (from the same assembly or a similar location on your vehicle) which will thread into the damaged bolt's mounting. If so, the other bolt can be used to select a nut; the nut can then be used to select the replacement bolt.

In all cases, be absolutely sure you have selected the proper replacement. Don't be shy, you can always ask the store clerk for help.

✷ WARNING

Be aware that when you find a bolt with damaged threads, you may also find the nut or drilled hole it was threaded into has also been damaged. If this is the case, you may have to drill and tap the hole, replace the nut or otherwise repair the threads. NEVER try to force a replacement bolt to fit into the damaged threads.

Torque

Torque is defined as the measurement of resistance to turning or rotating. It tends to twist a body about an axis of rotation. A common example of this would be tightening a threaded retainer such as a nut, bolt or screw. Measuring torque is one of the most common ways to help assure that a threaded retainer has been properly fastened.

When tightening a threaded fastener, torque is applied in three distinct areas, the head, the bearing surface and the clamp load. About 50 percent of the measured torque is used in overcoming bearing friction. This is the friction between the bearing surface of the bolt head, screw head or nut face and the base material or washer (the surface on which the fastener is rotating). Approximately 40 percent of the applied torque is used in overcoming thread friction. This leaves only about 10 percent of the applied torque to develop a useful clamp load (the force which holds a joint together). This means that friction can account for as much as 90 percent of the applied torque on a fastener.

TORQUE WRENCHES

▶ **See Figures 24, 25, 26 and 27**

In most applications, a torque wrench can be used to assure proper installation of a fastener. Torque wrenches come in various designs and most automotive supply stores will carry a variety to suit your needs. A torque wrench should be used any time we supply a specific torque value for a fastener. A torque wrench can also be used if you are following the general guidelines in the accompanying charts. Keep in mind that because there is no worldwide standardization of fasteners, the charts are a general guideline and should be used with caution. Again, the general rule of "if you are using the right tool for the job, you should not have to strain to tighten a fastener" applies here.

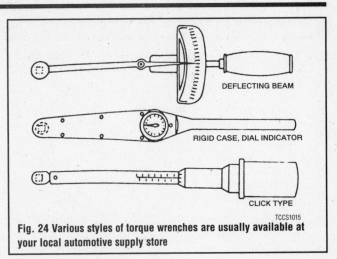

Fig. 24 Various styles of torque wrenches are usually available at your local automotive supply store

Standard Torque Specifications and Fastener Markings

In the absence of specific torques, the following chart can be used as a guide to the maximum safe torque of a particular size/grade of fastener.
- There is no torque difference for fine or coarse threads.
- Torque values are based on clean, dry threads. Reduce the value by 10% if threads are oiled prior to assembly.
- The torque required for aluminum components or fasteners is considerably less.

U.S. Bolts

SAE Grade Number	1 or 2			5			6 or 7		
Number of lines always 2 less than the grade number.									
	Maximum Torque			Maximum Torque			Maximum Torque		
Bolt Size (Inches)—(Thread)	Ft./Lbs.	Kgm	Nm	Ft./Lbs.	Kgm	Nm	Ft./Lbs.	Kgm	Nm
¼—20	5	0.7	6.8	8	1.1	10.8	10	1.4	13.5
—28	6	0.8	8.1	10	1.4	13.6			
⁵/₁₆—18	11	1.5	14.9	17	2.3	23.0	19	2.6	25.8
—24	13	1.8	17.6	19	2.6	25.7			
³/₈—16	18	2.5	24.4	31	4.3	42.0	34	4.7	46.0
—24	20	2.75	27.1	35	4.8	47.5			
⁷/₁₆—14	28	3.8	37.0	49	6.8	66.4	55	7.6	74.5
—20	30	4.2	40.7	55	7.6	74.5			
½—13	39	5.4	52.8	75	10.4	101.7	85	11.75	115.2
—20	41	5.7	55.6	85	11.7	115.2			
⁹/₁₆—12	51	7.0	69.2	110	15.2	149.1	120	16.6	162.7
—18	55	7.6	74.5	120	16.6	162.7			
⅝—11	83	11.5	112.5	150	20.7	203.3	167	23.0	226.5
—18	95	13.1	128.8	170	23.5	230.5			
¾—10	105	14.5	142.3	270	37.3	366.0	280	38.7	379.6
—16	115	15.9	155.9	295	40.8	400.0			
⅞—9	160	22.1	216.9	395	54.6	535.5	440	60.9	596.5
—14	175	24.2	237.2	435	60.1	589.7			
1—8	236	32.5	318.6	590	81.6	799.9	660	91.3	894.8
—14	250	34.6	338.9	660	91.3	849.8			

Metric Bolts

Relative Strength Marking	4.6, 4.8			8.8		
Bolt Markings						
	Maximum Torque			Maximum Torque		
Bolt Size Thread Size x Pitch (mm)	Ft./Lbs.	Kgm	Nm	Ft./Lbs.	Kgm	Nm
6 x 1.0	2–3	.2–.4	3–4	3–6	4–.8	5–8
8 x 1.25	6–8	.8–1	8–12	9–14	1.2–1.9	13–19
10 x 1.25	12–17	1.5–2.3	16–23	20–29	2.7–4.0	27–39
12 x 1.25	21–32	2.9–4.4	29–43	35–53	4.8–7.3	47–72
14 x 1.5	35–52	4.8–7.1	48–70	57–85	7.8–11.7	77–110
16 x 1.5	51–77	7.0–10.6	67–100	90–120	12.4–16.5	130–160
18 x 1.5	74–110	10.2–15.1	100–150	130–170	17.9–23.4	180–230
20 x 1.5	110–140	15.1–19.3	150–190	190–240	26.2–46.9	160–320
22 x 1.5	150–190	22.0–26.2	200–260	250–320	34.5–44.1	340–430
24 x 1.5	190–240	26.2–46.9	260–320	310–410	42.7–56.5	420–550

TCCS1098

Fig. 25 Standard and metric bolt torque specifications based on bolt strengths—WARNING: use only as a guide

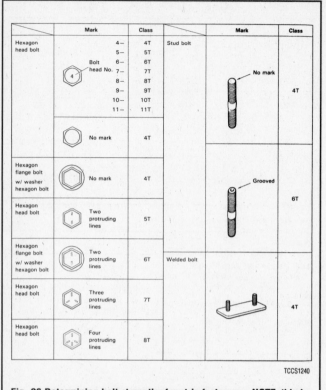

Mark		Class	Mark	Class
Hexagon head bolt	4— 5— 6— Bolt head No. 7— 8— 9— 10— 11—	4T 5T 6T 7T 8T 9T 10T 11T	Stud bolt — No mark	4T
	No mark	4T		
Hexagon flange bolt w/ washer hexagon bolt	No mark	4T	Grooved	6T
Hexagon head bolt	Two protruding lines	5T		
Hexagon flange bolt w/ washer hexagon bolt	Two protruding lines	6T	Welded bolt	4T
Hexagon head bolt	Three protruding lines	7T		
Hexagon head bolt	Four protruding lines	8T		

TCCS1240

Fig. 26 Determining bolt strength of metric fasteners—NOTE: this is a typical bolt marking system, but there is not a worldwide standard

Class	Diameter mm	Pitch mm	Hexagon head bolt			Hexagon flange bolt		
			N·m	kgf·cm	ft·lbf	N·m	kgf·cm	ft·lbf
4T	6	1	5	55	48 in.·lbf	6	60	52 in.·lbf
	8	1.25	12.5	130	9	14	145	10
	10	1.25	26	260	19	29	290	21
	12	1.25	47	480	35	53	540	39
	14	1.5	74	760	55	84	850	61
	16	1.5	115	1,150	83	—	—	—
5T	6	1	6.5	65	56 in.·lbf	7.5	75	65 in.·lbf
	8	1.25	15.5	160	12	17.5	175	13
	10	1.25	32	330	24	36	360	26
	12	1.25	59	600	43	65	670	48
	14	1.5	91	930	67	100	1,050	76
	16	1.5	140	1,400	101	—	—	—
6T	6	1	8	80	69 in.·lbf	9	90	78 in.·lbf
	8	1.25	19	195	14	21	210	15
	10	1.25	39	400	29	44	440	32
	12	1.25	71	730	53	80	810	59
	14	1.5	110	1,100	80	125	1,250	90
	16	1.5	170	1,750	127	—	—	—
7T	6	1	10.5	110	8	12	120	9
	8	1.25	25	260	19	28	290	21
	10	1.25	52	530	38	58	590	43
	12	1.25	95	970	70	105	1,050	76
	14	1.5	145	1,500	108	165	1,700	123
	16	1.5	230	2,300	166	—	—	—
8T	8	1.25	29	300	22	33	330	24
	10	1.25	61	620	45	68	690	50
	12	1.25	110	1,100	80	120	1,250	90
9T	8	1.25	34	340	25	37	380	27
	10	1.25	70	710	51	78	790	57
	12	1.25	125	1,300	94	140	1,450	105
10T	8	1.25	38	390	28	42	430	31
	10	1.25	78	800	58	88	890	64
	12	1.25	140	1,450	105	155	1,600	116
11T	8	1.25	42	430	31	47	480	35
	10	1.25	87	890	64	97	990	72
	12	1.25	155	1,600	116	175	1,800	130

TCCS1241

Fig. 27 Typical bolt torques for metric fasteners—WARNING: use only as a guide

Beam Type

▶ See Figure 28

The beam type torque wrench is one of the most popular types. It consists of a pointer attached to the head that runs the length of the flexible beam (shaft) to a scale located near the handle. As the wrench is pulled, the beam bends and the pointer indicates the torque using the scale.

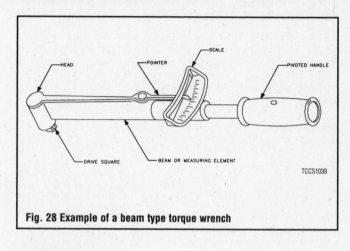

Fig. 28 Example of a beam type torque wrench

Click (Breakaway) Type

▶ See Figure 29

Another popular design of torque wrench is the click type. To use the click type wrench you pre-adjust it to a torque setting. Once the torque is reached, the wrench has a reflex signaling feature that causes a momentary breakaway of the torque wrench body, sending an impulse to the operator's hand.

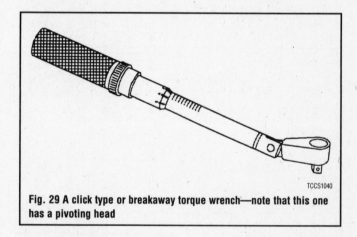

Fig. 29 A click type or breakaway torque wrench—note that this one has a pivoting head

Pivot Head Type

▶ See Figures 29 and 30

Some torque wrenches (usually of the click type) may be equipped with a pivot head which can allow it to be used in areas of limited access. BUT, it must be used properly. To hold a pivot head wrench, grasp the handle lightly, and as you pull on the handle, it should be floated on the pivot point. If the handle comes in contact with the yoke extension during the process of pulling, there is a very good chance the torque readings will be inaccurate because this could alter the wrench loading point. The design of the handle is usually such as to make it inconvenient to deliberately misuse the wrench.

➡ It should be mentioned that the use of any U-joint, wobble or extension will have an effect on the torque readings, no matter what type of wrench you are using. For the most accurate readings, install the socket directly on the wrench driver. If necessary, straight extensions (which hold a socket directly under the wrench driver) will have the least effect

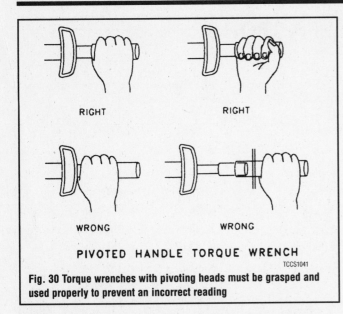

Fig. 30 Torque wrenches with pivoting heads must be grasped and used properly to prevent an incorrect reading

on the torque reading. **Avoid any extension that alters the length of the wrench from the handle to the head/driving point (such as a crow's foot). U-joint or wobble extensions can greatly affect the readings; avoid their use at all times.**

Rigid Case (Direct Reading)

▶ See Figure 31

A rigid case or direct reading torque wrench is equipped with a dial indicator to show torque values. One advantage of these wrenches is that they can be held at any position on the wrench without affecting accuracy. These wrenches are often preferred because they tend to be compact, easy to read and have a great degree of accuracy.

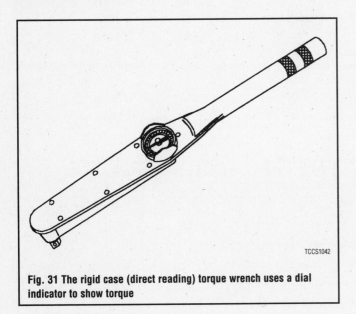

Fig. 31 The rigid case (direct reading) torque wrench uses a dial indicator to show torque

TORQUE ANGLE METERS

▶ See Figure 32

Because the frictional characteristics of each fastener or threaded hole will vary, clamp loads which are based strictly on torque will vary as well. In most applications, this variance is not significant enough to cause worry. But, in certain applications, a manufacturer's engineers may determine that more precise clamp loads are necessary (such is the case with many aluminum cylinder heads). In these cases, a torque angle method of installation would be specified. When installing fasteners which are torque angle tightened, a predetermined seating torque and standard torque wrench are usually used first to remove any compliance from the joint. The fastener is then tightened the specified additional portion of a turn measured in degrees. A torque angle gauge (mechanical protractor) is used for these applications.

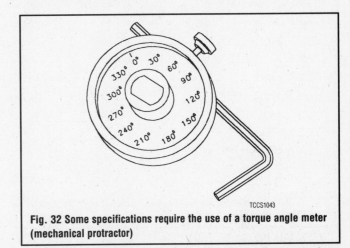

Fig. 32 Some specifications require the use of a torque angle meter (mechanical protractor)

Standard and Metric Measurements

▶ See Figure 33

Throughout this manual, specifications are given to help you determine the condition of various components on your vehicle, or to assist you in their installation. Some of the most common measurements include length (in. or cm/mm), torque (ft. lbs., inch lbs. or Nm) and pressure (psi, in. Hg, kPa or mm Hg). In most cases, we strive to provide the proper measurement as determined by the manufacturer's engineers.

Though, in some cases, that value may not be conveniently measured with what is available in your toolbox. Luckily, many of the measuring devices which are available today will have two scales so the Standard or Metric measurements may easily be taken. If any of the various measuring tools which are available to you do not contain the same scale as listed in the specifications, use the accompanying conversion factors to determine the proper value.

The conversion factor chart is used by taking the given specification and multiplying it by the necessary conversion factor. For instance, looking at the first line, if you have a measurement in inches such as "free-play should be 2 in." but your ruler reads only in millimeters, multiply 2 in. by the conversion factor of 25.4 to get the metric equivalent of 50.8mm. Likewise, if the specification was given only in a Metric measurement, for example in Newton Meters (Nm), then look at the center column first. If the measurement is 100 Nm, multiply it by the conversion factor of 0.738 to get 73.8 ft. lbs.

CONVERSION FACTORS

LENGTH–DISTANCE

Inches (in.)	x 25.4	= Millimeters (mm)	x .0394	= Inches
Feet (ft.)	x .305	= Meters (m)	x 3.281	= Feet
Miles	x 1.609	= Kilometers (km)	x .0621	= Miles

VOLUME

Cubic Inches (in3)	x 16.387	= Cubic Centimeters	x .061	= in3
IMP Pints (IMP pt.)	x .568	= Liters (L)	x 1.76	= IMP pt.
IMP Quarts (IMP qt.)	x 1.137	= Liters (L)	x .88	= IMP qt.
IMP Gallons (IMP gal.)	x 4.546	= Liters (L)	x .22	= IMP gal.
IMP Quarts (IMP qt.)	x 1.201	= US Quarts (US qt.)	x .833	= IMP qt.
IMP Gallons (IMP gal.)	x 1.201	= US Gallons (US gal.)	x .833	= IMP gal.
Fl. Ounces	x 29.573	= Milliliters	x .034	= Ounces
US Pints (US pt.)	x .473	= Liters (L)	x 2.113	= Pints
US Quarts (US qt.)	x .946	= Liters (L)	x 1.057	= Quarts
US Gallons (US gal.)	x 3.785	= Liters (L)	x .264	= Gallons

MASS–WEIGHT

Ounces (oz.)	x 28.35	= Grams (g)	x .035	= Ounces
Pounds (lb.)	x .454	= Kilograms (kg)	x 2.205	= Pounds

PRESSURE

Pounds Per Sq. In. (psi)	x 6.895	= Kilopascals (kPa)	x .145	= psi
Inches of Mercury (Hg)	x .4912	= psi	x 2.036	= Hg
Inches of Mercury (Hg)	x 3.377	= Kilopascals (kPa)	x .2961	= Hg
Inches of Water (H_2O)	x .07355	= Inches of Mercury	x 13.783	= H_2O
Inches of Water (H_2O)	x .03613	= psi	x 27.684	= H_2O
Inches of Water (H_2O)	x .248	= Kilopascals (kPa)	x 4.026	= H_2O

TORQUE

Pounds–Force Inches (in–lb)	x .113	= Newton Meters (N·m)	x 8.85	= in–lb
Pounds–Force Feet (ft–lb)	x 1.356	= Newton Meters (N·m)	x .738	= ft–lb

VELOCITY

Miles Per Hour (MPH)	x 1.609	= Kilometers Per Hour (KPH)	x .621	= MPH

POWER

Horsepower (Hp)	x .745	= Kilowatts	x 1.34	= Horsepower

FUEL CONSUMPTION*

Miles Per Gallon IMP (MPG)	x .354	= Kilometers Per Liter (Km/L)
Kilometers Per Liter (Km/L)	x 2.352	= IMP MPG
Miles Per Gallon US (MPG)	x .425	= Kilometers Per Liter (Km/L)
Kilometers Per Liter (Km/L)	x 2.352	= US MPG

*It is common to covert from miles per gallon (mpg) to liters/100 kilometers (1/100 km), where mpg (IMP) x 1/100 km = 282 and mpg (US) x 1/100 km = 235.

TEMPERATURE

Degree Fahrenheit (°F)	= (°C x 1.8) + 32
Degree Celsius (°C)	= (°F – 32) x .56

TCCS1044

Fig. 33 Standard and metric conversion factors chart

MODEL IDENTIFICATION

Volkswagen's official Vehicle Identification Label is usually mounted somewhere in the luggage compartment, usually on the rear panel or under the carpet. On some models, it may also be found on the crossmember above the grille. It is separate from the federal VIN plate required on all vehicles. The label includes the VIN, a model code, engine and transaxle codes, paint and interior codes and option code numbers. Since the manufacturer sometimes makes production changes in mid-model year, this information is often the most useful when locating parts.

SERIAL NUMBER IDENTIFICATION

Vehicle

◆ See Figures 34, 35 and 36

On 1974–80 models, a 10 digit Vehicle Identification Number (VIN) plate is used. It may be found on the windshield pillar or on top of the dash on the driver's side (both are visible through the windshield). All 1981–89 models have a 17 digit VIN plate usually found on the driver's side of the dashboard, visible through the windshield. On some models, a second plate or imprint may be found on the top of the cowling behind the engine or on the right strut mount.

➡Model years appear in the VIN as the last digit of each particular year (6 is 1976, 8 is 1978, etc.) until 1980 (which is A). This is the final year for the 10 digit code. The 17 digit VIN begins with 1981 (B), and continues 1982 (C) and so on, except letters which may be confused with numbers (I, O and Q are skipped). Because of this, 1987 is represented by (H) while 1988 is (J) and 1989 is (K).

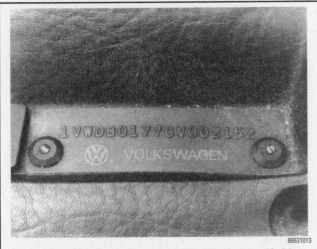

Fig. 34 Most VIN plates are located on top of the dash on the driver's side of the vehicle, and are visible through the windshield

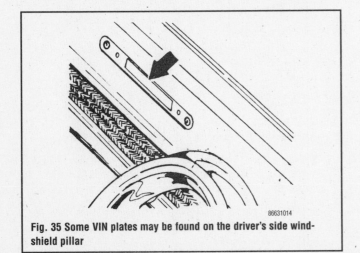

Fig. 35 Some VIN plates may be found on the driver's side windshield pillar

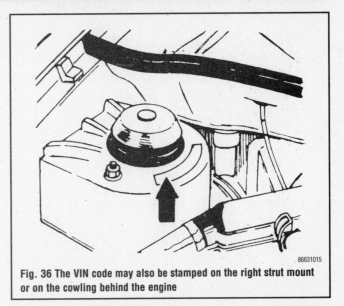

Fig. 36 The VIN code may also be stamped on the right strut mount or on the cowling behind the engine

The VIN will show information on where the vehicle was manufactured, body style, engine type, passenger restraint system, vehicle model, model year and the sequential serial number. This information can be helpful when locating parts or specifications.

Engine

◆ See Figure 37

On gasoline engines, this number may be stamped either into the engine block near the upper coolant hose fitting, between the fuel pump and distributor or on the left side of the engine block just below the cylinder head. On diesel engines, this code can be found stamped on the engine block between the fuel injection pump and the vacuum pump. The first 2 digits represent the engine code, and will be the most useful description of the engine when locating specifications or ordering parts. Although engines share many components, the code indicates differences in engine management systems, emissions specifications, compression ratios, power ratings and other details. The engine code may also appear in large type on the model identification label.

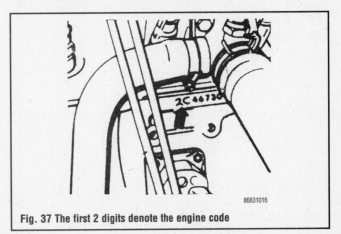

Fig. 37 The first 2 digits denote the engine code

ENGINE IDENTIFICATION

Year	Model	Engine Displacement cu. in. (cc/liter)	Engine Series Identification	No. of Cylinders	Engine Type
1974	Dasher	90.0 (1471/1.5)	XW, XV, XZ, XY	4	SOHC
1975	Dasher	97.0 (1588/1.6)	YG, YH	4	SOHC
	Rabbit	90.0 (1471/1.5)	FC, FG	4	SOHC
	Scirocco	90.0 (1471/1.5)	FC, FG	4	SOHC
1976	Dasher	97.0 (1588/1.6)	YG, YH, YK	4	SOHC
	Rabbit	97.0 (1588/1.6)	EF, EE	4	SOHC
	Scirocco	97.0 (1588/1.6)	EF, EE	4	SOHC
1977	Dasher	97.0 (1588/1.6)	YG, YH, YK	4	SOHC
	Rabbit	97.0 (1588/1.6)	EF, EE	4	SOHC
	Rabbit (Diesel)	90.0 (1471/1.5)	CK	4	SOHC
	Scirocco	97.0 (1588/1.6)	EF, EE	4	SOHC
1978	Dasher	97.0 (1588/1.6)	YG, YH, YK	4	SOHC
	Rabbit	97.0 (1588/1.6)	EF, EE	4	SOHC
	Rabbit (Diesel)	90.0 (1471/1.5)	CK	4	SOHC
	Scirocco	97.0 (1588/1.6)	EF, EE	4	SOHC
1979	Dasher	97.0 (1588/1.6)	YG, YH, YK	4	SOHC
	Dasher (Diesel)	90.0 (1471/1.5)	CK	4	SOHC
	Rabbit	90.0 (1471/1.5)	EH	4	SOHC
	Rabbit (Diesel)	90.0 (1471/1.5)	CK	4	SOHC
	Scirocco	97.0 (1588/1.6)	FX	4	SOHC
1980	Dasher	97.0 (1588/1.6)	YG, YH, YK	4	SOHC
	Dasher (Diesel)	90.0 (1471/1.5)	CK	4	SOHC
	Rabbit	97.0 (1588/1.6)	EH	4	SOHC
	Rabbit (Diesel)	90.0 (1471/1.5)	CK	4	SOHC
	Jetta	97.0 (1588/1.6)	EJ	4	SOHC
	Scirocco	97.0 (1588/1.6)	FX	4	SOHC
1981	Dasher (Diesel)	97.0 (1588/1.6)	CR	4	SOHC
	Jetta	97.0 (1588/1.6)	EJ	4	SOHC
	Jetta	105.0 (1715/1.7)	WT, EN	4	SOHC
	Rabbit	105.0 (1715/1.7)	WT, EN	4	SOHC
	Rabbit (Diesel)	97.0 (1588/1.6)	CR	4	SOHC
	Scirocco	105.0 (1715/1.7)	WT, EN	4	SOHC
1982	Jetta	105.0 (1715/1.7)	WT, EN	4	SOHC
	Jetta (Diesel)	97.0 (1588/1.6)	CR	4	SOHC
	Jetta (Turbo Diesel)	97.0 (1588/1.6)	CR	4	SOHC
	Quantum	105.0 (1715/1.7)	WT, EN	4	SOHC
	Quantum	130.0 (2144/2.2)	WE, KX, KM	5	SOHC
	Quantum (Turbo Diesel)	97.0 (1588/1.6)	CR	4	SOHC
	Rabbit	105.0 (1715/1.7)	WT, EN	4	SOHC
	Scirocco	105.0 (1715/1.7)	WT, EN	4	SOHC

86631300

ENGINE IDENTIFICATION

Year	Model	Engine Displacement cu. in. (cc/liter)	Engine Series Identification	No. of Cylinders	Engine Type
1983	Jetta	105.0 (1715/1.7)	WT, EN	4	SOHC
	Jetta (Diesel)	97.0 (1588/1.6)	JK, CY	4	SOHC
	Jetta (Turbo Diesel)	97.0 (1588/1.6)	JK, CY	4	SOHC
	Quantum	130.8 (2144/2.2)	WE, KX, KM	5	SOHC
	Quantum	105.0 (1715/1.7)	EN, JF, WT	4	SOHC
	Quantum	109.0 (1780/1.8)	JH	4	SOHC
	Quantum (Turbo Diesel)	97.0 (1588/1.6)	JR, MF	4	SOHC
	Rabbit	105.0 (1715/1.7)	WT, EN	4	SOHC
	Rabbit (Conv.)	109.0 (1780/1.8)	JH	4	SOHC
	Rabbit (GTI)	109.0 (1780/1.8)	JH	4	SOHC
	Rabbit (Diesel)	97.0 (1588/1.6)	JK, CY	4	SOHC
	Scirocco	109.0 (1780/1.8)	JH	4	SOHC
	GTI	109.0 (1780/1.8)	JH	4	SOHC
	GLI	109.0 (1780/1.8)	JH	4	SOHC
1984	Jetta	105.0 (1715/1.7)	EN, JF, WT	4	SOHC
	Jetta (Diesel)	97.0 (1588/1.6)	JP, ME	4	SOHC
	Jetta (Turbo Diesel)	97.0 (1588/1.6)	JR, MF	4	SOHC
	Quantum	109.0 (1780/1.8)	UM	4	SOHC
	Quantum	130.8 (2144/2.2)	WE, KX, KM	5	SOHC
	Quantum (Turbo Diesel)	97.0 (1588/1.6)	JR, MF	4	SOHC
	Rabbit	105.0 (1715/1.7)	EN, JF, WT	4	SOHC
	Rabbit (Conv.)	109.0 (1780/1.8)	GX	4	SOHC
	Rabbit (GTI)	109.0 (1780/1.8)	HT	4	SOHC
	Rabbit (Diesel)	97.0 (1588/1.6)	JP, ME	4	SOHC
	Scirocco	109.0 (1780/1.8)	GX	4	SOHC
	GTI	109.0 (1780/1.8)	HT	4	SOHC
	GLI	109.0 (1780/1.8)	—	4	SOHC
1985	Jetta	109.0 (1780/1.8)	GX	4	SOHC
	Jetta (Diesel)	97.0 (1588/1.6)	ME	4	SOHC
	Jetta (Turbo Diesel)	97.0 (1588/1.6)	MF	4	SOHC
	Quantum	109.0 (1780/1.8)	GX	4	SOHC
	Quantum (Turbo Diesel)	97.0 (1588/1.6)	MF	4	SOHC
	Quantum GL5	136.0 (2226/2.2)	WE, KX, KM	5	SOHC
	Scirocco	109.0 (1780/1.8)	JH	4	SOHC
	Cabriolet	109.0 (1780/1.8)	JH	4	SOHC
	GTI	109.0 (1780/1.8)	HT	4	SOHC
	GLI	109.0 (1780/1.8)	HT	4	SOHC
	Golf	109.0 (1780/1.8)	GX	4	SOHC
	Golf (Diesel)	97.0 (1588/1.6)	ME	4	SOHC

86631301

ENGINE IDENTIFICATION

Year	Model	Engine Displacement cu. in. (cc/liter)	Engine Series Identification	No. of Cylinders	Engine Type
1986	Jetta	109.0 (1780/1.8)	GX	4	SOHC
	Jetta (Diesel)	97.0 (1588/1.6)	ME	4	SOHC
	Jetta (Turbo Diesel)	97.0 (1588/1.6)	MF	4	SOHC
	Quantum GL5	136.0 (2226/2.2)	WE, KX	5	SOHC
	Quantum (Turbo Diesel)	97.0 (1588/1.6)	MF	4	SOHC
	Quantum (Syncro)	136.0 (2226/2.2)	JT	5	SOHC
	Cabriolet	109.0 (1780/1.8)	JH	4	SOHC
	Scirocco	109.0 (1780/1.8)	JH	4	SOHC
	GTI	109.0 (1780/1.8)	RD	4	SOHC
	GLI	109.0 (1780/1.8)	RD	4	SOHC
	Golf	109.0 (1780/1.8)	GX	4	SOHC
	Golf (Diesel)	97.0 (1588/1.6)	ME	4	SOHC
1987	Jetta	109.0 (1780/1.8)	RV	4	SOHC
	Jetta GL	109.0 (1780/1.8)	PF	4	SOHC
	Jetta GLI 16V	109.0 (1780/1.8)	PL	4	DOHC
	Quantum GL5	136.0 (2226/2.2)	KX	5	SOHC
	Quantum (Syncro)	136.0 (2226/2.2)	JT	5	SOHC
	Scirocco 16V	109.0 (1780/1.8)	PL	4	DOHC
	Cabriolet	109.0 (1780/1.8)	JH	4	SOHC
	Golf/GL	109.0 (1780/1.8)	RV	4	SOHC
	Golf/GT	109.0 (1780/1.8)	PF	4	SOHC
	Golf GTI 16V	109.0 (1780/1.8)	PL	4	DOHC
	Fox/GL	109.0 (1780/1.8)	UM	4	SOHC
1988	Jetta	109.0 (1780/1.8)	RV	4	SOHC
	Jetta GL	109.0 (1780/1.8)	PF	4	SOHC
	Jetta GLI 16V	109.0 (1780/1.8)	PL	4	DOHC
	Jetta Carat	109.0 (1780/1.8)	PF	4	SOHC
	Quantum GL5	136.0 (2226/2.2)	KX	5	SOHC
	Quantum (Syncro)	136.0 (2226/2.2)	JT	5	SOHC
	Scirocco 16V	109.0 (1780/1.8)	PL	4	DOHC
	Cabriolet	109.0 (1780/1.8)	JH	4	SOHC
	Golf/GL	109.0 (1780/1.8)	RV	4	SOHC
	Golf/GT	109.0 (1780/1.8)	PF	4	SOHC
	Golf GTI 16V	109.0 (1780/1.8)	PL	4	DOHC
	Fox/GL	109.0 (1780/1.8)	UM	4	SOHC

86631302

ENGINE IDENTIFICATION

Year	Model	Engine Displacement cu. in. (cc/liter)	Engine Series Identification	No. of Cylinders	Engine Type
1989	Jetta	109.0 (1780/1.8)	RV	4	SOHC
	Jetta (Diesel)	97.0 (1588/1.6)	ME	4	SOHC
	Jetta GL	109.0 (1780/1.8)	PF	4	SOHC
	Jetta GLI 16V	109.0 (1780/1.8)	PL	4	DOHC
	Jetta Carat	109.0 (1780/1.8)	PF	4	SOHC
	Scirocco 16V	109.0 (1780/1.8)	PL	4	DOHC
	Cabriolet	109.0 (1780/1.8)	JH	4	SOHC
	Golf/GL	109.0 (1780/1.8)	RV	4	SOHC
	Golf/GT	109.0 (1780/1.8)	PF	4	SOHC
	Golf GTI 16V	109.0 (1780/1.8)	PL	4	DOHC
	Fox/GL	109.0 (1780/1.8)	UM	4	SOHC

SOHC: Single Overhead Cam
DOHC: Dual Overhead Cam

8663132X

Transaxle

The transaxle is identified by a letter code that is stamped into the case. The first two or three digits are the transaxle code and the remaining numbers are the build date (day, month and year). The letter code indicates details about the transaxle such as the engine it goes with and the gear ratios. This code may also appear on the model identification label in the luggage compartment. On automatic transaxles, the letter code also describes the valve body and torque converter. When obtaining parts or components for repairing an automatic transaxle, these codes must match.

On manual transaxles, the code letters and date of manufacture are stamped on the top right hand side of the bell housing on 1974–75 Dashers and on top of the transaxle above the axle yokes on 1976 and later Dashers and Quantums. On the Rabbit, Fox, Jetta, Golf and Scirocco, the code is stamped on a pad at the lower center of the bell housing, next to the starter.

On automatic transaxles, the code letters and date of manufacture are stamped on the front of the bell housing next to the dipstick on the Dasher and Quantum and on a pad on the upper center portion of the bell housing on the Rabbit, Jetta, Golf and Scirocco.

TRANSAXLE IDENTIFICATION CHART

Year	Model	Type	Codes
1974	Dasher	4 spd.	ZS
		Auto	EN
1975	Dasher	4 spd.	YZ
		Auto	EO
	Rabbit	4 spd.	GC
		Auto	EQ
	Scirocco	4 spd.	GC
		Auto	EQ
1976	Dasher	4 spd.	YZ, XH
		Auto	ET
	Rabbit	4 spd.	GC
		Auto	EQ
	Scirocco	4 spd.	GC
		Auto	EQ
1977	Dasher	4 spd.	XK
		Auto	ET
	Rabbit	4 spd.	GC
		Auto	EQ
	Scirocco	4 spd.	GC
		Auto	EQ
1978	Dasher	4 spd.	XK
		Auto	ET
	Rabbit	4 spd.	GC
		Auto	EQ
	Scirocco	4 spd.	GC
		Auto	EQ
1979	Dasher	4 spd.	YZ, XH
		Auto	ET
	Rabbit	4 spd.	GC, GP
		5 spd.	FF
		Auto	TB, TC, TF, TG, TH
	Scirocco	4 spd.	GC, GP
		5 spd.	FF
		Auto	EQ, TB

TRANSAXLE IDENTIFICATION CHART

Year	Model	Type	Codes
1980	Dasher	4 spd.	YZ, XH
		Auto	ET
	Jetta	4 spd.	GC, GP
		5 spd.	FF
		Auto	EQ, TB
	Rabbit	4 spd.	GC, GP
		5 spd.	FF
		Auto	TB, TC, TF, TG, TH
	Scirocco	4 spd.	GC, GP
		5 spd.	FF
		Auto	EQ, TB
1981	Jetta	4 spd.	GC, GP
		5 spd.	FF
		Auto	EQ, TB
	Rabbit	4 spd.	GC, GP
		5 spd.	FF
		Auto	TB, TC, TF, TG, TH
	Scirocco	4 spd.	GC, GP
		5 spd.	FF
		Auto	EQ, TB
1982	Jetta	4 spd.	GL, GY
		5 spd.	FR, FN
		Auto	TB, TC, TF, TG, TH
	Quantum	5 spd.	2M, 3M, 5M, 9Q
		Auto	RJ, RU, RAC, RAF
	Rabbit	4 spd.	GL, GY
		5 spd.	FR, FN
		Auto	TB, TC, TF, TG, TH
	Scirocco	4 spd.	GL, GY
		5 spd.	FR, FN
		Auto	TB, TC, TF, TG, TH
1983	Jetta	4 spd.	GL, GY
		5 spd.	FR, FN
		Auto	TB, TC, TF, TG, TH
	Quantum	5 spd.	2M, 3M, 5M, 9Q
		Auto	RJ, RU, RAC, RAF
	Rabbit	4 spd.	GL, GY
		5 spd.	FR, FN
		Auto	TB, TC, TF, TG, TH
	Scirocco	4 spd.	GL, GY
		5 spd.	FR, FN
		Auto	TB, TC, TF, TG, TH

TRANSAXLE IDENTIFICATION CHART

Year	Model	Type	Codes
1984	Jetta	4 spd.	4A
		5 spd.	FN, 2H, 7A, 4K
		Auto	TB, TC, TF, TG, TH, TM, TR, TN
	Quantum	5 spd.	2W, QF, 3Z, 2N, 2M, 3M, 5Q
		Auto	RU, RJ, RAC, RAF, RR, RBB
	Rabbit	4 spd.	GL, GY
		5 spd.	7A, 4R, RN, FR, ZH
		Auto	TCA, TR, TB, TC, TF, TG, TH, TM
	Scirocco	5 spd.	4R, 9A, 2Y, AGB
		Auto	TN, TNA
1985	Cabriolet	5 spd.	9A, ACD, 2Y
		Auto	TNA
	Golf/GTI	5 spd.	9A, ACN, ACH, AGS
		Auto	TJ, TL, TNA
	Jetta	5 spd.	9A, ACH, ACH, AGS
		Auto	TJ, TL, TNA
	Quantum	5 spd.	9Q, 2N, ABV, 3Z, 2M, 5M, 2W, 2N
		Auto	RAC, RAF, RU, RJ, RR, RBB, RBE
	Scirocco	5 spd.	4R, 9A, 2Y, ACB
		Auto	TN, TNA
1986	Cabriolet	5 spd.	9A, ACD, 2Y
		Auto	TNA
	Golf/GTI	5 spd.	9A, ACN, ACH, AGS
		Auto	TJ, TL, TNA
	Jetta	5 spd.	9A, ACH, ACH, AGS
		Auto	TJ, TL, TNA
	Quantum	5 spd.	9Q, 2N, ABV, 3Z, 2M, 5M, 2W, 2N
		Auto	RAC, RAF, RV, RJ, RR, RBB, RBE
	Scirocco	5 spd.	4R, 9A, 2Y, ACB
		Auto	TN, TNA
1987	Cabriolet	5 spd.	9A, ACD, 2Y
		Auto	TNA
	Fox	4 spd.	PW
	Golf/GTI/Jetta	5 spd.	9A, ACN, ACH, AGS
		Auto	TJ, TL, TNA
	Quantum	5 spd.	9Q, 2N, ABV, 3Z, 2M, 5M, 2W, 2N
		Auto	RAC, RAF, RV, RJ, RR, RBB, RBE
	Scirocco	5 spd.	9A, ACD, 2Y
		Auto	TNA

86631305

86631304

TRANSAXLE IDENTIFICATION CHART

Year	Model	Type	Codes
1988	Cabriolet	5 spd.	9A, ACD, 2Y
		Auto	TNA
	Fox	4 spd.	PW
	Golf/GTI/Jetta	5 spd.	9A, ACN, ACH, AGS
		Auto	TJ, TL, TNA
	Quantum	5 spd.	9Q, 2N, ABV, 3Z, 2M, 5M, 2W, 2N
		Auto	RAC, RAF, RV, RJ, RR, RBB, RBE
	Scirocco	5 spd.	9A, ACD, 2Y
		Auto	TNA
1989	Cabriolet	5 spd.	9A, ACD, 2Y
		Auto	TNA
	Fox	4 spd.	PW
	Golf/GTI/Jetta	5 spd.	9A, ACN, ACH, AGS
		Auto	TJ, TL, TNA

8663135X

ROUTINE MAINTENANCE

Volkswagen specifies three types of maintenance groups to be performed at certain intervals. These maintenance intervals are for normal vehicle service. Under severe vehicle service conditions, the same service levels can be used but maintenance should be performed twice as often. Severe service is described as extremely low temperatures, constant dusty or sandy conditions, or probably worst or all, repeated short trips where the engine never fully warms up.

Maintenance Groups

GENERAL MAINTENANCE

The general maintenance procedures are performed most often. They include:
- Change the engine oil and filter.
- Check the transaxle fluid level.
- Drain the water from the fuel filter or water separator on diesel engines.
- Cleaning or replacement of the air filter.
- Test the freeze point of the coolant and check the fluid level.
- Check the battery electrolyte level.
- Check the brake fluid level.

TUNE-UP & EMISSION CONTROL MAINTENANCE

Performing these procedures at the intended interval will help you maintain good engine and emission control equipment performance:
- Check the tension and condition of all drive belts.
- Adjust the valves.
- Perform a cylinder compression test.
- Replace the spark plugs on gasoline engines.
- Replace the ignition condenser and points on gasoline engines without electronic ignition.
- On certain years and models, clean or replace the fuel filter.
- Inspect the ignition wires, distributor cap and rotor on gasoline engines.
- Check the crankcase ventilation hoses for cracks and blockage.
- Check the fuel tank, lines and connections for damage and leaks.
- Check the engine and transaxle for leaks.
- Check the EGR system on gasoline engines.
- If applicable, check and adjust the clutch.

VEHICLE MAINTENANCE

Properly maintaining the vehicle at the specified intervals will contribute to safety and ensure component reliability:

- Inspect the brake system for damage and leaks.
- Inspect the brake shoes and/or pads.
- Check the wheels for distortion and cracks.
- Check the tires for wear and correct pressure.
- Inspect the boots and dust seals on the transaxle for rips or leaks.
- Check for excessive play in the steering.
- Check for proper operation of all lights and accessories.

Air Cleaner

A restrictive, dirty air cleaner filter will cause a reduction in fuel economy and performance and an increase in emissions. The air filter should be replaced according to the maintenance interval chart in this Section, or more often in dusty conditions.

On gasoline engines with CIS or CIS-E fuel injection, the air cleaner is mounted directly under the fuel distributor/airflow sensor assembly. When changing the filter on these engines, the lower portion of the air cleaner housing stays in place and the distributor/sensor assembly is lifted up away from the housing. It is not necessary to disconnect any fuel lines or wires.

On diesel engines, the air cleaner housing is mounted directly to the intake manifold for noise control and ease of maintenance.

REMOVAL & INSTALLATION

▶ See Figures 38, 39, 40, 41 and 42

1. On models with CIS or CIS-E fuel injection, loosen the hose clamps to remove the rubber boot from the top of the airflow sensor.
2. On Digifant engines, loosen the clamp and remove the air duct from the air filter housing.
3. Unsnap the cover retaining clips, starting with the hardest ones to reach. The last clip released will be difficult to unsnap, so it should be the easiest to reach.
4. Lift the cover off and remove the air filter element. On CIS and CIS-E engines, lift the fuel distributor/airflow sensor assembly enough to remove the filter element.
5. With the paper side down, drop the element just a few inches repeatedly on a flat surface to shake out any loose dirt, then examine the element. On CIS and CIS-E engines, there may be fuel stains on the element. Dry stains are not a problem but if the element is wet with fuel, the fuel distributor is probably leaking.
6. Wipe out the housing and install the new element. Make sure the rubber seal fits properly into the groove in the housing.
7. Replace the cover and secure the clips, starting with the least accessible clip.

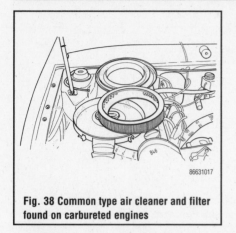

Fig. 38 Common type air cleaner and filter found on carbureted engines

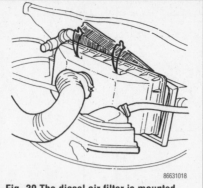

Fig. 39 The diesel air filter is mounted directly on the intake manifold

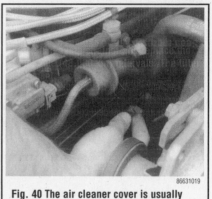

Fig. 40 The air cleaner cover is usually secured by several retaining clips

Fig. 41 On CIS and CIS-E engines, lift the fuel distributor/airflow sensor assembly enough to remove the filter element

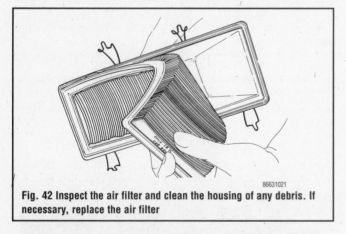

Fig. 42 Inspect the air filter and clean the housing of any debris. If necessary, replace the air filter

8. When installing the boot on the CIS or CIS-E airflow sensor, make sure the boot is fully seated all the way around the lip before tightening the clamp.

Fuel Filter

RELIEVING FUEL SYSTEM PRESSURE

Engines equipped with electric fuel pumps maintain fuel pressure even when the engine has not been run. This residual pressure may remain in the fuel system for several hours after the engine is shut down.

To relieve the fuel system pressure, perform the following:
1. Start the engine and allow it to run at idle speed.
2. Locate the fuel pump electrical connector and disconnect it while the engine is running.
3. Operate the engine until it runs out of fuel and stops.

4. Remove the fuel filler cap.
5. Disconnect the negative battery cable.

➡Have a container ready to catch the fuel that will squirt out when you loosen the clamps or couplings on the fuel system components you are working on. Wrap the connection with a rag and slowly crack the connection to vent any residual pressure from the system. Once all the pressure is relieved, loosen the connection.

6. Proceed with the necessary fuel system component repairs. When finished, engage the fuel pump connector and connect the negative battery cable. Don't forget to install the fuel filler cap.

REMOVAL & INSTALLATION

✳✳ CAUTION

Never smoke when working around gasoline! Avoid all sources of sparks or ignition. Gasoline vapors are EXTREMELY volatile! This procedure will cause a small fuel spill. Make sure the work area is well ventilated and take appropriate fire safety precautions.

Gasoline Engines

Carbureted engines with mechanical fuel pumps have a strainer in the top cover of the fuel pump. Some later models are equipped with an additional inline fuel filter. These filters are small, usually made of plastic and are attached to the fuel line by clamps.

On fuel injected models, the filter removes particulate matter from the fuel system which might clog the fuel distributor or the injectors. The fuel filter is installed on the pressure side of the pump. On some fuel injected models, the fuel filters are large, metal containers. On the other fuel injected models, a small inline filter is used. Arrows on the filter point in the direction of fuel travel (the filter must be installed with the arrows pointing in the direction fuel flow). Some fuel filters are equipped with banjo type fittings, while some use O-ring seals and others may just use hose clamps. Banjo type fittings use metal gaskets to seal the fitting against the filter housing. Always replace these gaskets when replacing the fuel filter. If the fuel filter has O-ring type seals, these must be replaced also.

On 1985–89 models (except 1985–87 Cabriolet), a "lifetime" fuel filter is used. According to the manufacturer, unless the fuel system is damaged or contaminated, the filter is large enough to handle all normal fuel filtering requirements for the life of the engine. However, it is recommended to replace the filter if fuel system contamination is suspected, and to ease the load on the fuel pump on higher mileage vehicles.

CARBURETED MODELS

▶ **See Figures 43 and 44**

➡It is recommended to clean the fuel pump strainer and replace the fuel filter (if equipped) at 30,000 mile (48,000 km) intervals. The filter is located in the engine compartment.

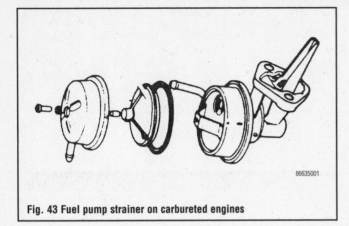

Fig. 43 Fuel pump strainer on carbureted engines

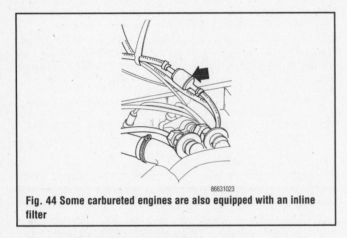

Fig. 44 Some carbureted engines are also equipped with an inline filter

1. Disconnect the negative battery cable.
2. Have a pan ready to catch the fuel that will run out of the fuel pump. Disconnect and plug the hose from the fuel pump cover.
3. Remove the center screw, then remove the cover and strainer.
4. Inspect the strainer for damage, replace if necessary. If it is usable, clean it with compressed air.
5. Install the strainer using new gaskets. On some models, be sure to align the notch in the cover with the groove in the body. Tighten the screw until it is snug.
6. Connect the hose to the pump cover. Use a new clamp if the old one is damaged.
7. If equipped with an inline filter, disconnect and plug the hoses from the filter.
8. Install the new filter in the proper direction (make sure the arrows follow the direction of fuel flow). Use new hose clamps if the old ones are damaged.
9. Wipe any spilled fuel with a rag.
10. Connect the negative battery cable, then start the engine. Check for any leaks.

FUEL INJECTED MODELS—EXCEPT 1985–89 CABRIOLET, FOX, GOLF, GTI AND JETTA

♦ See Figure 45

➡It is recommended for the filter to be replaced at 30,000 mile (48,000 km) intervals except on 1984 Quantum and Scirocco, which is to be replaced at 60,000 mile (96,000 km) intervals. The filter is located in the engine compartment.

1. Relieve the pressure in the system following the procedures outlined in this section.
2. Remove the fuel filter mounting nuts and lift the filter from the mounting bracket.

➡Always use a line or flare nut wrench on the fuel fittings and a back-up wrench to hold the filter, or the fuel lines may become damaged.

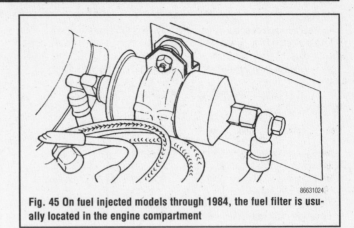

Fig. 45 On fuel injected models through 1984, the fuel filter is usually located in the engine compartment

3. Place a container under the filter to catch the excess fuel and cover the fuel line connections with a rag. Disconnect the fuel lines, then remove the filter.
To install:
4. Position the filter and connect the fuel lines. Torque the fittings (using a crow's foot attachment) to 14 ft. lbs. (20 Nm).
5. Install the filter to the mounting bracket. Tighten the nuts until snug.
6. Wipe any spilled fuel with a rag.
7. Connect the negative battery cable, then start the engine. Check for any leaks.

1985–89 CABRIOLET, FOX, GOLF, GTI AND JETTA

♦ See Figure 46

➡On 1985–87 Cabriolet, replace the filter at 30,000 mile (48,000 km) intervals. All other models are equipped with a "lifetime" filter. It is recommended that these filters be replaced if fuel system contamination is suspected or on high mileage vehicles to ease the load on the fuel pump. The filter is located in the fuel pump assembly, mounted under the vehicle, in front of the fuel tank.

1. Relieve the fuel system pressure following the procedure outlined in this section.
2. Raise and safely support the rear of the vehicle. Have a pan ready to catch the fuel that may run out of the reservoir.
3. Have a rag handy and wear safety glasses when loosening the fittings. The system may be under pressure and fuel could be sprayed.

➡Always use a back-up wrench to hold the filter or the fuel lines may be damaged.

4. Hold the filter with a 19mm or 22mm wrench, then loosen the fittings with a 17mm wrench. Have the catch pan ready.
5. Disconnect the fuel lines, loosen the mounting bracket, then remove the filter.

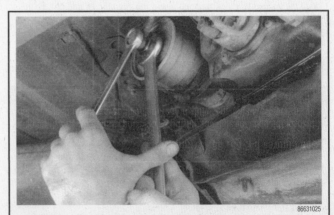

Fig. 46 On fuel injected engines after 1984, the filter can be found under the car just forward of the fuel tank

To install:

6. Install the new filter but do not tighten the mounting bracket yet.

7. Make sure all fittings and sealing surfaces are clean. Install the banjo bolts with new copper gaskets and/or sealing rings. Torque to 14 ft. lbs. (20 Nm).

8. Tighten the mounting bracket nuts until snug. Wipe any spilled fuel with a rag.

9. Lower the vehicle, then connect the negative battery cable. Start the engine and check for leaks.

Diesel Engines

Two styles of fuel filters are used with diesel engines, both are canister types. Depending on the year and model, the filter canister is either threaded onto a mounting base or secured by clamps. Clamp mounted filters are usually found on 1985–89 Golf and Jetta.

The filter is usually mounted on the passenger's side of the vehicle (next to the air cleaner) on the Rabbit, Golf and Jetta, and next to the brake master cylinder on the Dasher and Quantum.

FILTER MOUNTED BELOW BASE

▶ **See Figures 47 and 48**

1. Disconnect the negative battery cable.
2. Open the fuel filler cap to relieve any pressure that may be in the tank.
3. Loosen the drain plug at the bottom of the canister and drain the fuel into a container. Reinstall the drain plug.
4. Use a band wrench to loosen the canister from the base, then remove by hand. Discard the old filter canister.

To install:

5. Pour a small amount of clean diesel fuel into the filter (DO NOT use fuel from the old filter), then apply a thin film of diesel fuel to the mounting gasket.

6. Install the filter and tighten by hand. Wipe any spilled fuel with a rag. Don't forget to tighten the fuel filler cap.

7. Connect the negative battery cable, then start the engine. Accelerate the engine several times until the engine is running smoothly (this will clear the air bubbles in the fuel system). Allow the engine to idle and check for fuel leaks.

CLAMP MOUNTED

▶ **See Figure 49**

1. Disconnect the negative battery cable.
2. Open the fuel filler cap to relieve any pressure that may be in the tank.
3. Disconnect and plug the fuel lines from the filter.

➠**Some models may be equipped with a flow control valve on the filter. Once the two filter lines are disconnected, remove the clip from the control valve (located on top of the filter), then remove the valve leaving the two lines connected. Position the valve and the lines off to the side. This valve is delicate, so be careful during removal and installation.**

4. Loosen the mounting clamp nut/screw, then lift the filter assembly straight up. Discard the old filter.

To install:

5. Install the new filter onto the mounting clamp. If there are arrows indicating fuel flow direction, they point towards the front of the vehicle. Tighten the mounting nut/screw until the filter is secure.

6. On models equipped with a flow control valve, install new control valve O-ring seals. Also, lubricate the seals with clean diesel fuel before installing the valve on the filter. Inspect the retaining clip and replace it if damaged.

7. Connect the fuel lines to the filter. Use new clamps if they are damaged. Don't forget to tighten the fuel filler cap.

8. Connect the negative battery cable, then start the engine. Accelerate the engine a few times (this will clear the air bubbles in the fuel system) and check for fuel leaks.

Diesel Fuel/Water Separator

Although diesel fuel and water do not readily mix, fuel does tend to entrap moisture from the air each time it is moved from one container to another. Eventually every diesel fuel system collects enough water to become a potential hazard. Fortunately, when it's allowed to settle out, the water will always drop to the bottom of the tank or filter housing. Some models are equipped with a fuel filter that has a water drain (a bolt or petcock at the bottom of the housing). Others are equipped with a water separator, located in front of the fuel tank under the right side of the vehicle. It's purpose is to allow water to settle from the fuel right at the tank and to alert the driver when draining is required. When the water level in the separator reaches a certain point, a sensor turns on the glow plug indicator light on the dashboard, causing it to blink continuously.

On models up to and including 1984, water is usually drained from the filter. On most 1985–89 models, water is removed from the fuel system by means of a water separator.

SERVICING

▶ **See Figures 50 and 51**

Fuel Filter

1. Place a pan under the drain to catch the water and fuel.
2. If equipped, loosen the vent bolt/screw on the filter mounting base. If there is no vent, loosen the return line at the injection pump (the line that is not connected to the filter).
3. Loosen the drain bolt or valve. When fuel flows in a clean stream, close the drain and tighten the vent or return line.

Water Separator

1. Raise and safely support the vehicle. Remove the fuel filler cap.
2. At the separator, connect a hose from the separator drain to a catch pan.
3. Open the drain valve (3 turns) and drain the separator until a steady stream of fuel flows from the separator, then close the valve. Don't forget to install the filler cap.

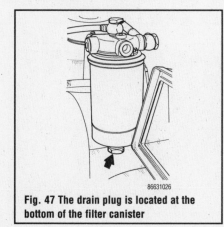

Fig. 47 The drain plug is located at the bottom of the filter canister

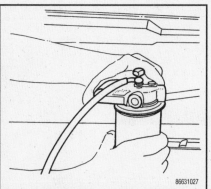

Fig. 48 The filter should be hand tightened only; do not use a strap wrench

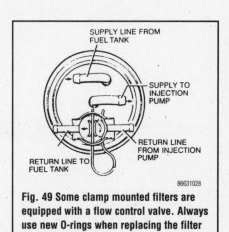

Fig. 49 Some clamp mounted filters are equipped with a flow control valve. Always use new O-rings when replacing the filter

Fig. 50 Some filters are equipped with a vent screw on the mounting base

Fig. 51 Some later model diesels are equipped with a water separator located under the vehicle

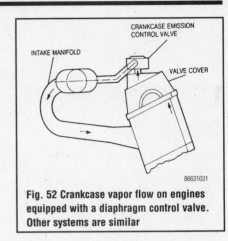

Fig. 52 Crankcase vapor flow on engines equipped with a diaphragm control valve. Other systems are similar

Crankcase Ventilation System

▶ See Figure 52

To send oil fumes and crankcase blow-by gasses into the engine for burning, all engines are equipped with some type of crankcase breather control valve. Volkswagen uses three different types; a simple restrictor orifice, a spring loaded diaphragm or a Positive Crankcase Ventilation (PCV) valve.

SERVICING

On 16 valve engines, a breather is mounted to the side of the engine block near the oil cooler. The breather contains a baffle plate that allows the oil to condense out of the blow-by gasses and drain back to the engine. The large hose connects to the air cleaner so filtered air can be drawn in as required. The small hose connecting to the intake manifold has a built-in restrictor orifice, creating a controlled vacuum leak to the intake manifold. When the throttle opening is small and manifold vacuum is high, crankcase oil fumes are drawn directly into the intake manifold. When the throttle opening is large and manifold vacuum low, some of the oil fumes flow through the large hose to the air cleaner. The hoses should be checked for blockages and for cracks which could cause vacuum leaks.

On engines equipped with diaphragm control valves, the valve is mounted in the top of the cylinder head cover and connects to the intake manifold. The spring and diaphragm maintain a constant balance against manifold vacuum, keeping blow-by vapor flow at a constant percentage of the total intake air volume. Another hose connecting to the air cleaner allows filtered air into the engine as required. The hoses should be checked for blockages and for cracks which could cause vacuum leaks.

Carbureted engines are usually equipped with either a restrictor or a PCV valve in the hose between the camshaft cover and the intake air elbow on the carburetor. The hoses and the restrictor should be checked for blockage and cracks. If equipped, the PCV valve can be checked as follows:

1. Carefully pull the PCV valve from the hose attached to the camshaft cover.

2. Start the engine, then place your finger over the end of the valve. You should feel a strong vacuum and the idle speed should drop slightly.

3. If the valve did not operate properly, it should be replaced (not cleaned). The valve can be replaced by simply disconnecting the hoses attached to the old valve, then connect the hoses to the new valve.

Evaporative Canister

SERVICING

▶ See Figures 53 and 54

All models with gasoline engines are equipped with some form of fuel vapor control device. The evaporative emission control system prevents the escape of raw fuel vapors (unburned hydrocarbons, or HC) into the atmosphere. A carbon (charcoal) canister is used to store fuel tank vapors that accumulate when the engine is not running. On most models, a control valve is used to prevent these vapors from entering the intake manifold when the engine is not running. When the engine is running, these vapors are carried to the intake manifold by allowing fresh air into the bottom of the canister. The canister is usually located in one of the front inner fenders.

Other components of the system include an unvented fuel filler cap, fuel tank expansion chamber and one or more check valves to prevent liquid fuel from entering the canister. On most models, the purge hose must be disconnected at the canister when checking or adjusting air/fuel mixture. Make sure the orifice is still connected to the hose to the intake manifold.

This system does not require any service under normal conditions other than to check for leaks. Check the hoses visually for cracks, breaks, and disconnec-

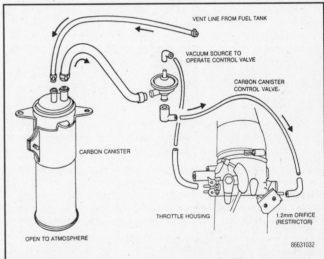

Fig. 53 Most evaporative systems are equipped with a vacuum operated control valve

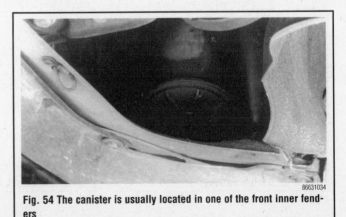

Fig. 54 The canister is usually located in one of the front inner fenders

tions. Also check the seal on the gas tank filler cap. Replace the cap if the is split. If any hoses are in need of replacement, use only hoses marked for fuel system use. These are usually available from your local automotive supply store.

Battery

PRECAUTIONS

Always use caution when working on or near the battery. Never allow a tool to bridge the gap between the negative and positive battery terminals. Also, be careful not to allow a tool to provide a ground between the positive cable/terminal and any metal component on the vehicle. Either of these conditions will cause a short circuit, leading to sparks and possible personal injury.

Do not smoke, have an open flame or create sparks near a battery; the gases contained in the battery are very explosive and, if ignited, could cause severe injury or death.

All batteries, regardless of type, should be carefully secured by a battery hold-down device. If this is not done, the battery terminals or casing may crack from stress applied to the battery during vehicle operation. A battery which is not secured may allow acid to leak out, making it discharge faster; such leaking corrosive acid can also eat away at components under the hood.

Always visually inspect the battery case for cracks, leakage and corrosion. A white corrosive substance on the battery case or on nearby components would indicate a leaking or cracked battery. If the battery is cracked, it should be replaced immediately.

GENERAL MAINTENANCE

♦ **See Figure 55**

A battery that is not sealed must be checked periodically for electrolyte level. You cannot add water to a sealed maintenance-free battery (though not all maintenance-free batteries are sealed); however, a sealed battery must also be checked for proper electrolyte level, as indicated by the color of the built-in hydrometer "eye."

Always keep the battery cables and terminals free of corrosion. Check these components about once a year. Refer to the removal, installation and cleaning procedures outlined in this section.

Keep the top of the battery clean, as a film of dirt can help completely discharge a battery that is not used for long periods. A solution of baking soda and water may be used for cleaning, but be careful to flush this off with clear water. DO NOT let any of the solution into the filler holes. Baking soda neutralizes battery acid and will de-activate a battery cell.

Batteries in vehicles which are not operated on a regular basis can fall victim to parasitic loads (small current drains which are constantly drawing current from the battery). Normal parasitic loads may drain a battery on a vehicle that is in storage and not used for 6–8 weeks. Vehicles that have additional accessories such as a cellular phone, an alarm system or other devices that increase parasitic load may discharge a battery sooner. If the vehicle is to be stored for 6–8 weeks in a secure area and the alarm system, if present, is not necessary, the negative battery cable should be disconnected at the onset of storage to protect the battery charge.

Remember that constantly discharging and recharging will shorten battery life. Take care not to allow a battery to be needlessly discharged.

BATTERY FLUID

Check the battery electrolyte level at least once a month, or more often in hot weather or during periods of extended vehicle operation. On non-sealed batteries, the level can be checked either through the case on translucent batteries or by removing the cell caps on opaque-cased types. The electrolyte level in each cell should be kept filled to the split ring inside each cell, or the line marked on the outside of the case.

If the level is low, add only distilled water through the opening until the level is correct. Each cell is separate from the others, so each must be checked and filled individually. Distilled water should be used, because the chemicals and minerals found in most drinking water are harmful to the battery and could significantly shorten its life.

If water is added in freezing weather, the vehicle should be driven several miles to allow the water to mix with the electrolyte. Otherwise, the battery could freeze.

Although some maintenance-free batteries have removable cell caps for access to the electrolyte, the electrolyte condition and level on all sealed maintenance-free batteries must be checked using the built-in hydrometer "eye." The exact type of eye varies between battery manufacturers, but most apply a sticker to the battery itself explaining the possible readings. When in doubt, refer to the battery manufacturer's instructions to interpret battery condition using the built-in hydrometer.

➡**Although the readings from built-in hydrometers found in sealed batteries may vary, a green eye usually indicates a properly charged battery with sufficient fluid level. A dark eye is normally an indicator of a battery with sufficient fluid, but one which may be low in charge. And a light or yellow eye is usually an indication that electrolyte supply has dropped below the necessary level for battery (and hydrometer) operation. In this last case, sealed batteries with an insufficient electrolyte level must usually be discarded.**

Checking the Specific Gravity

♦ **See Figures 56, 57 and 58**

A hydrometer is required to check the specific gravity on all batteries that are not maintenance-free. On batteries that are maintenance-free, the specific gravity is checked by observing the built-in hydrometer "eye" on the top of the battery case. Check with your battery's manufacturer for proper interpretation of its built-in hydrometer readings.

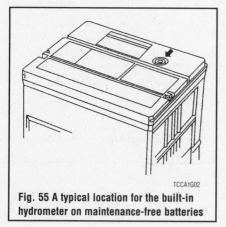

Fig. 55 A typical location for the built-in hydrometer on maintenance-free batteries

TCCA1P07

Fig. 56 On non-maintenance-free batteries, the fluid level can be checked through the case on translucent models; the cell caps must be removed on other models

TCCA1P08

Fig. 57 If the fluid level is low, add only distilled water through the opening until the level is correct

Battery electrolyte contains sulfuric acid. If you should splash any on your skin or in your eyes, flush the affected area with plenty of clear water. If it lands in your eyes, get medical help immediately.

The fluid (sulfuric acid solution) contained in the battery cells will tell you many things about the condition of the battery. Because the cell plates must be kept submerged below the fluid level in order to operate, maintaining the fluid level is extremely important. And, because the specific gravity of the acid is an indication of electrical charge, testing the fluid can be an aid in determining if the battery must be replaced. A battery in a vehicle with a properly operating charging system should require little maintenance, but careful, periodic inspection should reveal problems before they leave you stranded.

As stated earlier, the specific gravity of a battery's electrolyte level can be used as an indication of battery charge. At least once a year, check the specific gravity of the battery. It should be between 1.20 and 1.26 on the gravity scale. Most auto supply stores carry a variety of inexpensive battery testing hydrometers. These can be used on any non-sealed battery to test the specific gravity in each cell.

The battery testing hydrometer has a squeeze bulb at one end and a nozzle at the other. Battery electrolyte is sucked into the hydrometer until the float is lifted from its seat. The specific gravity is then read by noting the position of the float. If gravity is low in one or more cells, the battery should be slowly charged and checked again to see if the gravity has come up. Generally, if after charging, the specific gravity between any two cells varies more than 50 points (0.50), the

battery should be replaced, as it can no longer produce sufficient voltage to guarantee proper operation.

CABLES

▶ **See Figures 59, 60, 61, 62 and 63**

Once a year (or as necessary), the battery terminals and the cable clamps should be cleaned. Loosen the clamps and remove the cables, negative cable first. On batteries with posts on top, the use of a puller specially made for this purpose is recommended. These are inexpensive and available in most auto parts stores. Side terminal battery cables are secured with a small bolt.

Clean the cable clamps and the battery terminal with a wire brush, until all corrosion, grease, etc., is removed and the metal is shiny. It is especially important to clean the inside of the clamp thoroughly (an old knife is useful here), since a small deposit of foreign material or oxidation there will prevent a sound electrical connection and inhibit either starting or charging. Special tools are available for cleaning these parts, one type for conventional top post batteries and another type for side terminal batteries. It is also a good idea to apply some dielectric grease to the terminal, as this will aid in the prevention of corrosion.

After the clamps and terminals are clean, reinstall the cables, negative cable last; DO NOT hammer the clamps onto battery posts. Tighten the clamps securely, but do not distort them. Give the clamps and terminals a thin external coating of grease after installation, to retard corrosion.

Check the cables at the same time that the terminals are cleaned. If the cable insulation is cracked or broken, or if the ends are frayed, the cable should be replaced with a new cable of the same length and gauge.

TCCA1P09

Fig. 58 Check the specific gravity of the battery's electrolyte with a hydrometer

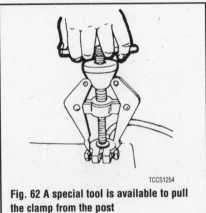

TCCS1206

Fig. 59 Maintenance is performed with household items and with special tools like this post cleaner

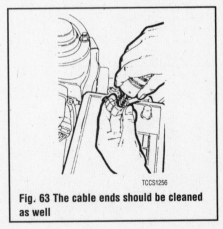

TCCS1207

Fig. 60 The underside of this special battery tool has a wire brush to clean post terminals

TCCS1208

Fig. 61 Place the tool over the battery posts and twist to clean until the metal is shiny

TCCS1254

Fig. 62 A special tool is available to pull the clamp from the post

TCCS1256

Fig. 63 The cable ends should be cleaned as well

CHARGING

⁂ CAUTION

The chemical reaction which takes place in all batteries generates explosive hydrogen gas. A spark can cause the battery to explode and splash acid. To avoid serious personal injury, be sure there is proper ventilation and take appropriate fire safety precautions when connecting, disconnecting, or charging a battery and when using jumper cables.

A battery should be charged at a slow rate to keep the plates inside from getting too hot. However, if some maintenance-free batteries are allowed to discharge until they are almost "dead," they may have to be charged at a high rate to bring them back to "life." Always follow the charger manufacturer's instructions on charging the battery.

REPLACEMENT

When it becomes necessary to replace the battery, select one with an amperage rating equal to or greater than the battery originally installed. Deterioration and just plain aging of the battery cables, starter motor, and associated wires makes the battery's job harder in successive years. The slow increase in electrical resistance over time makes it prudent to install a new battery with a greater capacity than the old.

Belts

INSPECTION

▸ See Figures 64, 65, 66, 67 and 68

Inspect the belts for signs of glazing or cracking. A glazed belt will be perfectly smooth from slippage, while a good belt will have a slight texture of fabric visible. Cracks will usually start at the inner edge of the belt and run outward. All worn or damaged drive belts should be replaced immediately. It is always best to replace all drive belts at one time, as a preventive maintenance measure, during this service operation.

CHECKING TENSION AND ADJUSTMENT

▸ See Figure 69

The belt tension on most driven components is adjusted by moving the component (alternator, power steering pump etc.) within the range of a slotted bracket. Some brackets (toothed) use a rack and pinion mechanism which moves the alternator side-to-side to adjust the belt tension. With this configuration, no prying tools are required. On Quantum (except 5 cylinder) and Fox models, the air conditioner compressor drive belts are adjusted by varying the number of discs (shims) between the halves of the crankshaft pulley. Before adjusting the belt tension on any engine, look at the mounting and determine what kind of bracket is used.

To check belt tension, push in on the drive belt about midway between the crankshaft pulley and the driven component. If the belt is less than 39.4 in. (1m) long, it should deflect between 0.80–0.120 in. (2–5mm). For longer belts, it should deflect between 0.40–0.060 in. (10–15mm). Belt size is usually printed on the back side of the belt. If it can't be read, it's probably time to replace it.

Slotted Brackets

▸ See Figures 70, 71 and 72

1. Loosen the adjustment nut/bolt in the slotted bracket. Slightly loosen the pivot bolt.
2. Pull (don't pry) the component outward to increase tension. Push inward to reduce tension. Tighten the adjusting nut/bolt and the pivot bolt.
3. Components, such as the power steering pump and some air conditioner compressors, may be mounted with a double slotted adjusting bracket using a threaded bolt and locknut to adjust and maintain tension. Loosen the locknut(s) and slightly loosen the bolt(s) in the slotted groove(s). Turn the threaded adjust-

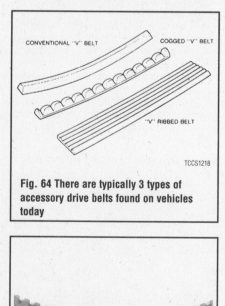

Fig. 64 There are typically 3 types of accessory drive belts found on vehicles today

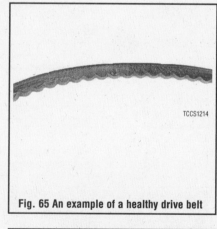

Fig. 65 An example of a healthy drive belt

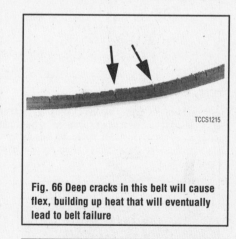

Fig. 66 Deep cracks in this belt will cause flex, building up heat that will eventually lead to belt failure

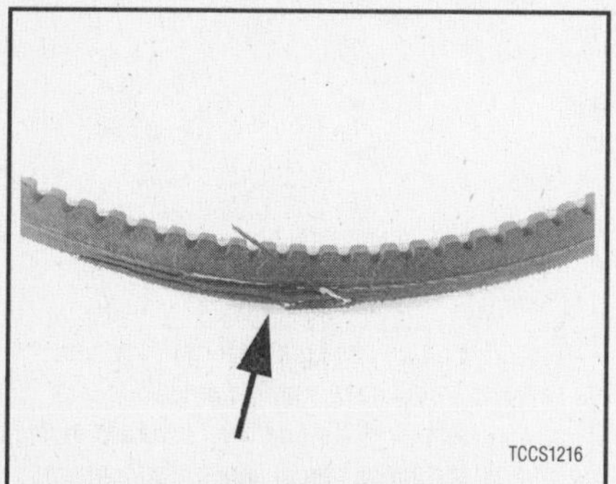

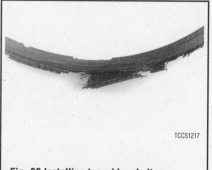

Fig. 67 The cover of this belt is worn, exposing the critical reinforcing cords to excessive wear

Fig. 68 Installing too wide a belt can result in serious belt wear and/or breakage

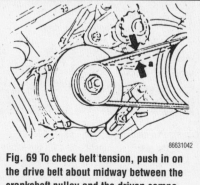

Fig. 69 To check belt tension, push in on the drive belt about midway between the crankshaft pulley and the driven component

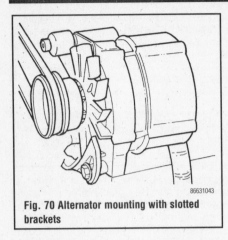

Fig. 70 Alternator mounting with slotted brackets

Fig. 71 Some components use a double slotted adjusting bracket. Loosen the lock-nut (shown) before adjusting the tension bolt

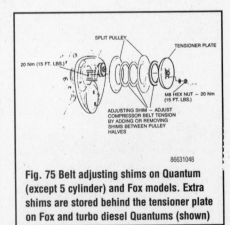

Fig. 72 An extension is helpful when adjusting the tension bolt. Be sure to loosen the nut/bolt on the rear slotted bracket first

ment bolt(s) in or out to gain correct tension. Tighten locknut(s) and slotted bracket bolt(s).

4. Recheck the drive belt tension, readjust if necessary.

Toothed Brackets

▶ **See Figures 73 and 74**

1. Loosen the tension bolt and the alternator pivot bolt. These bolts should be loosened until the alternator swings freely under its own weight.

2. Adjust the V-belt by turning the nut on the tension bolt while checking the belt deflection with your thumb.

3. Once the proper tension is achieved, tighten the tension bolt to 26 ft. lbs. (35 Nm). Tighten the pivot bolt to 15 ft. lbs. (20 Nm).

4. Recheck the drive belt tension, readjust if necessary.

Split Pulley

▶ **See Figure 75**

On Quantum (except 5 cylinder) and Fox models, the air conditioner compressor drive belts are adjusted by varying the number of discs (shims) between the halves of the crankshaft pulley.

1. Remove the nuts/bolts securing the tensioner plate and crankshaft pulley halves.

2. Add or remove the amount of spacer discs between the pulley halves until the belt tension is correct.

➡**If there are any shims left over, do not throw them away. On Fox and turbo diesel Quantum models, store the extra shims in front of the split pulley (behind the tensioner plate). On Quantums with 4 cylinder gas engines, store the extra shims behind the split pulley (in front of the crankshaft hub).**

3. Secure the pulley halves. Torque the pulley nuts or bolts to 15 ft. lbs. (20 Nm).

REMOVAL & INSTALLATION

If a belt must be replaced, the driven unit must be loosened and moved to its extreme loosest position (usually by moving it toward the center of the motor). After removing the old belt, check the pulleys for dirt or built-up material which could affect belt contact. Carefully install the new belt, it may appear to be just a little too small to fit over the pulley flanges. Fit the belt over the largest pulley (usually the crankshaft pulley at the bottom center of the motor) first, then work on the smaller one(s). Gentle pressure in the direction of rotation is helpful. Some belts run around a third or idler pulley, which acts as an additional pivot in the belt's path. It may be possible to loosen the idler pulley as well as the main component, making your job much easier. Depending on which belt(s) you are changing, it may be necessary to loosen or remove other interfering belts to get at the one(s) you want. Some models have a front engine mount installed through the air conditioner compressor belt circle. Support the engine and remove the mount prior to belt removal and installation.

When buying replacement belts, remember that the fit is critical according to the length of the belt, the width of the belt, the depth of the belt and the angle or profile of the V shape (always match up old belt with new belt if possible). The belt shape should exactly match the shape of the pulley; belts that are not an exact match can cause noise, slippage and premature failure.

After the new belt is installed, adjust it for proper tension. This is sometimes a three or four-handed job; you may find an assistant helpful. Make sure that all the bolts you loosened are retightened and that any other loosened belts also have the correct tension. A new belt can be expected to stretch a bit after installation so be prepared to re-adjust your new belt.

➡**After installing a new belt, run the engine for about 5 minutes and then recheck the belt tension.**

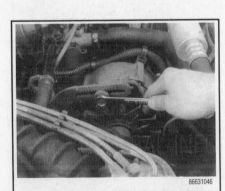

Fig. 73 Loosen the tension bolt (shown) and the alternator pivot bolt until the alternator swings freely under its own weight

Fig. 74 Adjust the V-belt by turning the nut on the tension bolt

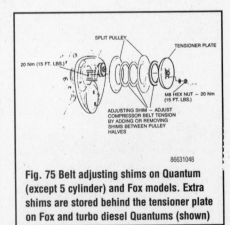

Fig. 75 Belt adjusting shims on Quantum (except 5 cylinder) and Fox models. Extra shims are stored behind the tensioner plate on Fox and turbo diesel Quantums (shown)

Timing Belts

INSPECTION

▶ **See Figures 76 and 77**

✳✳ WARNING

Severe engine damage could occur if the timing belt should break. On some models, Volkswagen uses an "interference" engine design. If the timing belt breaks, the valves could the contact pistons and become damaged.

Volkswagen does not specify an inspection or replacement interval for timing belts. However, since some engines utilize an interference design, it is highly recommended to inspect the timing belt at 60,000 mile (96,000 km) intervals

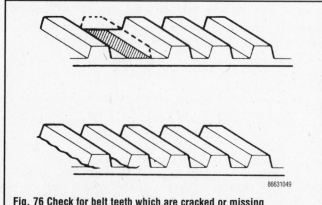

Fig. 76 Check for belt teeth which are cracked or missing

(especially on diesels). It is an even better idea to replace the belt at these intervals. It is far less expensive to replace the belt than to repair the engine damage which could result from the belt breaking.

Inspect the belt for cracks, missing teeth and wear on any of the surfaces. Inspect the sprockets for grease and other deposits. If any of these conditions exist, the belt should be replaced. Please refer to Section 3 for procedures on timing belt removal and installation.

Hoses

INSPECTION

▶ **See Figures 78, 79, 80 and 81**

Upper and lower radiator hoses, along with the heater hoses, should be checked for deterioration, leaks and loose hose clamps. It is also wise to check the hoses periodically in early spring and at the beginning of the fall or winter when you are performing other maintenance. A quick visual inspection could discover a weakened hose which might have left you stranded if it had remained unrepaired.

Whenever you are checking the hoses, make sure the engine and cooling system are cold. Visually inspect for cracking, rotting or collapsed hoses, and replace as necessary. Run your hand along the length of the hose. If a weak or swollen spot is noted when squeezing the hose wall, the hose should be replaced.

REMOVAL & INSTALLATION

▶ **See Figure 82**

✳✳ CAUTION

Disconnect the radiator cooling fan when changing hoses. If the engine is warm, the cooling fan could operate even if the ignition switch is OFF.

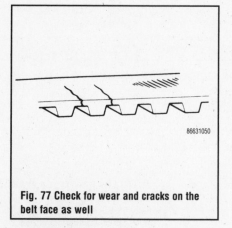

Fig. 77 Check for wear and cracks on the belt face as well

Fig. 78 The cracks developing along this hose are a result of age-related hardening

Fig. 79 A hose clamp that is too tight can cause older hoses to separate and tear on either side of the clamp

Fig. 80 A soft spongy hose (identifiable by the swollen section) will eventually burst and should be replaced

Fig. 81 Hoses are likely to deteriorate from the inside if the cooling system is not periodically flushed

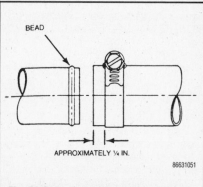

Fig. 82 Correctly positioning the hose and clamp will help prevent coolant leaks

1. Make sure the engine is not hot, then loosen the coolant reservoir cap.

➡**Some early models Rabbits, Dashers and Sciroccos have a petcock at the bottom of the radiator for draining purposes. Check to see if yours is equipped with one. If it is, the system can be drained without disconnecting the lower radiator hose.**

2. Place a large pan under the lower radiator hose, then loosen the clamps on the hose. Carefully disconnect it from the radiator. It makes a mess but it's the only way to drain the system on most models.

3. Remove the clamps from the hose to be replaced, then disconnect it by cutting or twisting it to break its grip on the flange. Be careful not to damage the flange while doing so.

4. Clean all hose connections, then slip the clamps onto the new hose.

5. When installing the new hose, don't overtighten the clamps or the flange may become damaged. Position the hose clamps so that they are about ¼ in. (6mm) from the end of the hose.

6. After the new hose is installed and the cooling system is refilled, run the engine up to operating temperature and check for coolant leaks.

CV-Boots

INSPECTION

♦ **See Figure 83**

The CV (Constant Velocity) boots should should be checked for damage every 15,000 miles (24,000 km) and anytime the vehicle is raised for service. These boots keep water, grime, dirt and other damaging matter from entering the CV joints. Any of these can cause early CV joint failure which can be expensive to repair. Heavy grease thrown around the inside of the front wheel(s) and on the brake caliper/drum can be an indication of a torn boot. Thoroughly check the boots for missing clamps and tears. If the boot is damaged, it should be replaced immediately. Please refer to Section 7 for procedures.

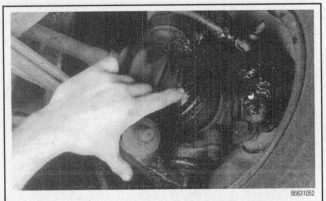

86631052

Fig. 83 The CV-boots should be checked periodically for damage. Note the heavy grease thrown on the brake caliper and the inside of the wheel

Air Conditioning System

SYSTEM SERVICE & REPAIR

➡**It is recommended that the A/C system be serviced by an EPA Section 609 certified automotive technician utilizing a refrigerant recovery/recycling machine.**

The do-it-yourselfer should not service his/her own vehicle's A/C system for many reasons, including legal concerns, personal injury, environmental damage and cost. The following are some of the reasons why you may decide not to service your own vehicle's A/C system.

According to the U.S. Clean Air Act, it is a federal crime to service or repair (involving the refrigerant) a Motor Vehicle Air Conditioning (MVAC) system for money without being EPA certified. It is also illegal to vent R-12 and R-134a refrigerants into the atmosphere. Selling or distributing A/C system refrigerant (in a container which contains less than 20 pounds of refrigerant) to any person who is not EPA 609 certified is also not allowed by law.

State and/or local laws may be more strict than the federal regulations, so be sure to check with your state and/or local authorities for further information. For further federal information on the legality of servicing your A/C system, call the EPA Stratospheric Ozone Hotline.

➡**Federal law dictates that a fine of up to $25,000 may be levied on people convicted of venting refrigerant into the atmosphere. Additionally, the EPA may pay up to $10,000 for information or services leading to a criminal conviction of the violation of these laws.**

When servicing an A/C system you run the risk of handling or coming in contact with refrigerant, which may result in skin or eye irritation or frostbite. Although low in toxicity (due to chemical stability), inhalation of concentrated refrigerant fumes is dangerous and can result in death; cases of fatal cardiac arrhythmia have been reported in people accidentally subjected to high levels of refrigerant. Some early symptoms include loss of concentration and drowsiness.

➡**Generally, the limit for exposure is lower for R-134a than it is for R-12. Exceptional care must be practiced when handling R-134a.**

Also, refrigerants can decompose at high temperatures (near gas heaters or open flame), which may result in hydrofluoric acid, hydrochloric acid and phosgene (a fatal nerve gas).

R-12 refrigerant can damage the environment because it is a Chlorofluorocarbon (CFC), which has been proven to add to ozone layer depletion, leading to increasing levels of UV radiation. UV radiation has been linked with an increase in skin cancer, suppression of the human immune system, an increase in cataracts, damage to crops, damage to aquatic organisms, an increase in ground-level ozone, and increased global warming.

R-134a refrigerant is a greenhouse gas which, if allowed to vent into the atmosphere, will contribute to global warming (the Greenhouse Effect).

It is usually more economically feasible to have a certified MVAC automotive technician perform A/C system service on your vehicle. Some possible reasons for this are as follows:

• While it is illegal to service an A/C system without the proper equipment, the home mechanic would have to purchase an expensive refrigerant recovery/recycling machine to service his/her own vehicle.

• Since only a certified person may purchase refrigerant—according to the Clean Air Act, there are specific restrictions on selling or distributing A/C system refrigerant—it is legally impossible (unless certified) for the home mechanic to service his/her own vehicle. Procuring refrigerant in an illegal fashion exposes one to the risk of paying a $25,000 fine to the EPA.

R-12 Refrigerant Conversion

If your vehicle still uses R-12 refrigerant, one way to save A/C system costs down the road is to investigate the possibility of having your system converted to R-134a. The older R-12 systems can be easily converted to R-134a refrigerant by a certified automotive technician by installing a few new components and changing the system oil.

The cost of R-12 is steadily rising and will continue to increase, because it is no longer imported or manufactured in the United States. Therefore, it is often possible to have an R-12 system converted to R-134a and recharged for less than it would cost to just charge the system with R-12.

If you are interested in having your system converted, contact local automotive service stations for more details and information.

PREVENTIVE MAINTENANCE

♦ **See Figures 84 and 85**

Although the A/C system should not be serviced by the do-it-yourselfer, preventive maintenance can be practiced and A/C system inspections can be performed to help maintain the efficiency of the vehicle's A/C system. For preventive maintenance, perform the following:

• The easiest and most important preventive maintenance for your A/C system is to be sure that it is used on a regular basis. Running the system for five minutes each month (no matter what the season) will help ensure that the seals and all internal components remain lubricated.

➡️Some newer vehicles automatically operate the A/C system compressor whenever the windshield defroster is activated. When running, the compressor lubricates the A/C system components; therefore, the A/C system would not need to be operated each month.

• In order to prevent heater core freeze-up during A/C operation, it is necessary to maintain proper antifreeze protection. Use a hand-held coolant tester (hydrometer) to periodically check the condition of the antifreeze in your engine's cooling system.

➡️Antifreeze should not be used longer than the manufacturer specifies.

• For efficient operation of an air conditioned vehicle's cooling system, the radiator cap should have a holding pressure which meets manufacturer's specifications. A cap which fails to hold these pressures should be replaced.

• Any obstruction of or damage to the condenser configuration will restrict air flow which is essential to its efficient operation. It is, therefore, a good rule to keep this unit clean and in proper physical shape.

➡️Bug screens which are mounted in front of the condenser (unless they are original equipment) are regarded as obstructions.

• The condensation drain tube expels any water which accumulates on the bottom of the evaporator housing into the engine compartment. If this tube is obstructed, the air conditioning performance can be restricted and condensation buildup can spill over onto the vehicle's floor.

SYSTEM INSPECTION

◆ **See Figure 86**

Although the A/C system should not be serviced by the do-it-yourselfer, preventive maintenance can be practiced and A/C system inspections can be performed to help maintain the efficiency of the vehicle's A/C system. For A/C system inspection, perform the following:

The easiest and often most important check for the air conditioning system consists of a visual inspection of the system components. Visually inspect the air conditioning system for refrigerant leaks, damaged compressor clutch,

abnormal compressor drive belt tension and/or condition, plugged evaporator drain tube, blocked condenser fins, disconnected or broken wires, blown fuses, corroded connections and poor insulation.

A refrigerant leak will usually appear as an oily residue at the leakage point in the system. The oily residue soon picks up dust or dirt particles from the surrounding air and appears greasy. Through time, this will build up and appear to be a heavy dirt impregnated grease.

For a thorough visual and operational inspection, check the following:
• Check the surface of the radiator and condenser for dirt, leaves or other material which might block air flow.
• Check for kinks in hoses and lines. Check the system for leaks.
• Make sure the drive belt is properly tensioned. When the air conditioning is operating, make sure the drive belt is free of noise or slippage.
• Make sure the blower motor operates at all appropriate positions, then check for distribution of the air from all outlets with the blower on **HIGH** or **MAX**.

➡️Keep in mind that under conditions of high humidity, air discharged from the A/C vents may not feel as cold as expected, even if the system is working properly. This is because vaporized moisture in humid air retains heat more effectively than dry air, thereby making humid air more difficult to cool.

• Make sure the air passage selection lever is operating correctly. Start the engine and warm it to normal operating temperature, then make sure the temperature selection lever is operating correctly.

Windshield Wipers

ELEMENT (REFILL) CARE & REPLACEMENT

◆ **See Figures 87, 88 and 89**

For maximum effectiveness and longest element life, the windshield and wiper blades should be kept clean. Dirt, tree sap, road tar and so on will cause streaking, smearing and blade deterioration if left on the glass. It is advisable to

Fig. 84 A coolant tester can be used to determine the freezing and boiling levels of the coolant in your vehicle

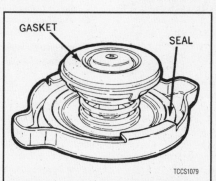

Fig. 85 To ensure efficient cooling system operation, inspect the radiator cap gasket and seal

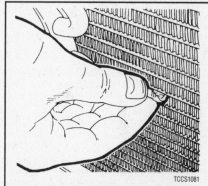

Fig. 86 Periodically remove any debris from the condenser and radiator fins

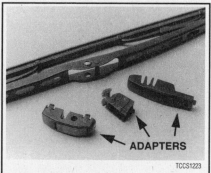

Fig. 87 Most aftermarket blades are available with multiple adapters to fit different vehicles

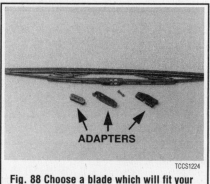

Fig. 88 Choose a blade which will fit your vehicle, and that will be readily available next time you need blades

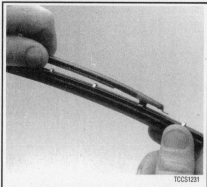

Fig. 89 When installed, be certain the blade is fully inserted into the backing

wash the windshield carefully with a commercial glass cleaner at least once a month. Wipe off the rubber blades with the wet rag afterwards. Do not attempt to move wipers across the windshield by hand; damage to the motor and drive mechanism will result.

To inspect and/or replace the wiper blade elements, place the wiper switch in the **LOW** speed position and the ignition switch in the **ACC** position. When the wiper blades are approximately vertical on the windshield, turn the ignition switch to **OFF**.

Examine the wiper blade elements. If they are found to be cracked, broken or torn, they should be replaced immediately. Replacement intervals will vary with usage, although ozone deterioration usually limits element life to about one year. If the wiper pattern is smeared or streaked, or if the blade chatters across the glass, the elements should be replaced. It is easiest and most sensible to replace the elements in pairs.

If your vehicle is equipped with aftermarket blades, there are several different types of refills and your vehicle might have any kind. Aftermarket blades and arms rarely use the exact same type blade or refill as the original equipment.

Regardless of the type of refill used, be sure to follow the part manufacturer's instructions closely. Make sure that all of the frame jaws are engaged as the refill is pushed into place and locked. If the metal blade holder and frame are allowed to touch the glass during wiper operation, the glass will be scratched.

For maximum effectiveness and longest wiper blade life, the windshield and wiper blades should be kept clean. Dirt, tree sap, road tar and so on will cause streaking, smearing and shorten blade life. It is advisable to clean the windshield carefully with a commercial glass cleaner and paper towels at least once a week. Wipe off the rubber blades with the wet paper towel afterwards. Examine the wiper blades occasionally. If they look cracked, broken or torn, they should be replaced immediately. Replacement intervals will vary with usage, although ozone deterioration usually limits blade life to about one year or less. If the wiper pattern is smeared or streaked, or if the blade chatters across the glass, the blade should be replaced. If that does not fix the problem, the spring in the wiper arm may be weak or the arm may be bent. See Section 6 for more information.

Tires and Wheels

TIRE ROTATION

◆ See Figure 90

To equalize tire wear and increase the mileage you obtain from your tires, rotate them every 7,500 miles (12,000 km). All Volkswagens are designed for radial tires. Radial tires should be rotated by moving the front tires to the rear and the rear tires to the front. You can rotate them diagonally, however, this should not be done unless the tire is exhibiting unusual wear such as feather-edging. Do not rotate studded snow tires or directional tires diagonally.

Common sense and good driving habits will afford maximum tire life. Make sure that you don't overload the vehicle or run with incorrect pressure in the tires. Either of these will increase tread wear. Fast starts, sudden stops and sharp cornering are hard on tires and will shorten their useful life span.

➡**For optimum tire life, keep the tires properly inflated, rotate them often and have the wheel alignment checked periodically.**

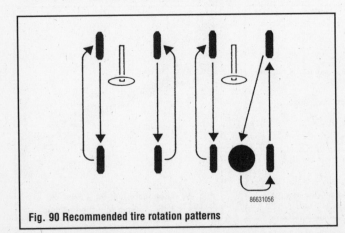

Fig. 90 Recommended tire rotation patterns

Inspect your tires frequently. Be especially careful to watch for bubbles in the tread or sidewall, deep cuts or underinflation. Replace any tires with bubbles in the sidewall. If cuts are so deep that they penetrate to the cords, discard the tire. Any cut in the sidewall of a radial tire renders it unsafe. Also look for uneven tread wear patterns that may indicate the front end is out of alignment or that the tires are out of balance.

TIRE DESIGN

◆ See Figure 91

For maximum satisfaction, tires should be used in sets of four. Mixing of different brands or types (radial, bias-belted, fiberglass belted) should be avoided. In most cases, the vehicle manufacturer has designated a type of tire on which the vehicle will perform best. Your first choice when replacing tires should be to use the same type of tire that the manufacturer recommends.

When radial tires are used, tire sizes and wheel diameters should be selected to maintain ground clearance and tire load capacity equivalent to the original specified tire. Radial tires should always be used in sets of four.

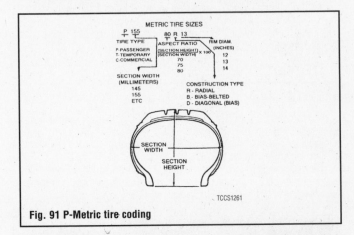

Fig. 91 P-Metric tire coding

❉❉ CAUTION

Radial tires should never be used on only the front axle.

When selecting tires, pay attention to the original size as marked on the tire. Most tires are described using an industry size code sometimes referred to as P-Metric. This allows the exact identification of the tire specifications, regardless of the manufacturer. If selecting a different tire size or brand, remember to check the installed tire for any sign of interference with the body or suspension while the vehicle is stopping, turning sharply or heavily loaded.

Snow Tires

Good radial tires can produce a big advantage in slippery weather, but in snow, a street radial tire does not have sufficient tread to provide traction and control. The small grooves of a street tire quickly pack with snow and the tire behaves like a billiard ball on a marble floor. The more open, chunky tread of a snow tire will self-clean as the tire turns, providing much better grip on snowy surfaces.

To satisfy municipalities requiring snow tires during weather emergencies, most snow tires carry either an M + S designation after the tire size stamped on the sidewall, or the designation "all-season." In general, no change in tire size is necessary when buying snow tires.

Most manufacturers strongly recommend the use of 4 snow tires on their vehicles for reasons of stability. If snow tires are fitted only to the drive wheels, the opposite end of the vehicle may become very unstable when braking or turning on slippery surfaces. This instability can lead to unpleasant endings if the driver can't counteract the slide in time.

Note that snow tires, whether 2 or 4, will affect vehicle handling in all non-snow situations. The stiffer, heavier snow tires will noticeably change the turning and braking characteristics of the vehicle. Once the snow tires are installed, you must re-learn the behavior of the vehicle and drive accordingly.

➡Consider buying extra wheels on which to mount the snow tires. Once done, the "snow wheels" can be installed and removed as needed. This eliminates the potential damage to tires or wheels from seasonal removal and installation. Even if your vehicle has styled wheels, see if inexpensive steel wheels are available. Although the look of the vehicle will change, the expensive wheels will be protected from salt, curb hits and pothole damage.

TIRE STORAGE

If they are mounted on wheels, store the tires at proper inflation pressure. All tires should be kept in a cool, dry place. If they are stored in the garage or basement, do not let them stand on a concrete floor; set them on strips of wood, a mat or a large stack of newspaper. Keeping them away from direct moisture is of paramount importance. Tires should not be stored upright, but in a flat position.

INFLATION & INSPECTION

▶ **See Figures 92 thru 97**

The importance of proper tire inflation cannot be overemphasized. A tire employs air as part of its structure. It is designed around the supporting strength of the air at a specified pressure. For this reason, improper inflation drastically reduces the tire's ability to perform as intended. A tire will lose some air in day-to-day use; having to add a few pounds of air periodically is not necessarily a sign of a leaking tire.

Two items should be a permanent fixture in every glove compartment: an accurate tire pressure gauge and a tread depth gauge. Check the tire pressure (including the spare) regularly with a pocket type gauge. Too often, the gauge on the end of the air hose at your corner garage is not accurate because it suffers too much abuse. Always check tire pressure when the tires are cold, as pressure increases with temperature. If you must move the vehicle to check the tire inflation, do not drive more than a mile before checking. A cold tire is generally one that has not been driven for more than three hours.

A plate or sticker is normally provided somewhere in the vehicle (door post, hood, tailgate or trunk lid) which shows the proper pressure for the tires. Never counteract excessive pressure build-up by bleeding off air pressure (letting some air out). This will cause the tire to run hotter and wear quicker.

✳✳ CAUTION

Never exceed the maximum tire pressure embossed on the tire! This is the pressure to be used when the tire is at maximum loading, but it is rarely the correct pressure for everyday driving. Consult the owner's manual or the tire pressure sticker for the correct tire pressure.

Once you've maintained the correct tire pressures for several weeks, you'll be familiar with the vehicle's braking and handling personality. Slight adjustments in tire pressures can fine-tune these characteristics, but never change the cold pressure specification by more than 2 psi. A slightly softer tire pressure will give a softer ride but also yield lower fuel mileage. A slightly harder tire will give crisper dry road handling but can cause skidding on wet surfaces. Unless you're fully attuned to the vehicle, stick to the recommended inflation pressures.

All automotive tires have built-in tread wear indicator bars that show up as ½ in. (13mm) wide smooth bands across the tire when 1/16 in. (1.5mm) of tread remains. The appearance of tread wear indicators means that the tires should be replaced. In fact, many states have laws prohibiting the use of tires with less than this amount of tread.

TCCS1095

Fig. 92 Tires with deep cuts, or cuts which bulge, should be replaced immediately

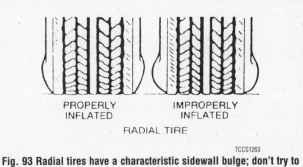

PROPERLY INFLATED | IMPROPERLY INFLATED
RADIAL TIRE
TCCS1263

Fig. 93 Radial tires have a characteristic sidewall bulge; don't try to measure pressure by looking at the tire. Use a quality air pressure gauge

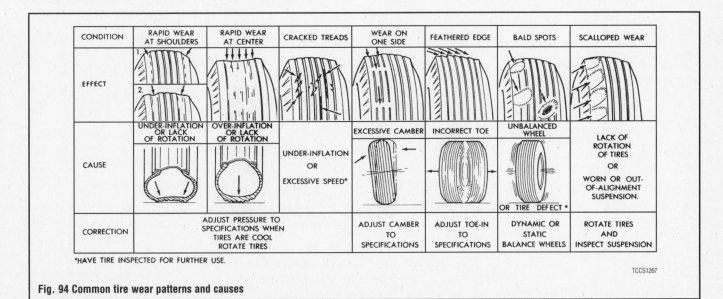

CONDITION	RAPID WEAR AT SHOULDERS	RAPID WEAR AT CENTER	CRACKED TREADS	WEAR ON ONE SIDE	FEATHERED EDGE	BALD SPOTS	SCALLOPED WEAR
EFFECT							
CAUSE	UNDER-INFLATION OR LACK OF ROTATION	OVER-INFLATION OR LACK OF ROTATION	UNDER-INFLATION OR EXCESSIVE SPEED*	EXCESSIVE CAMBER	INCORRECT TOE	UNBALANCED WHEEL OR TIRE DEFECT*	LACK OF ROTATION OF TIRES OR WORN OR OUT-OF-ALIGNMENT SUSPENSION.
CORRECTION		ADJUST PRESSURE TO SPECIFICATIONS WHEN TIRES ARE COOL ROTATE TIRES		ADJUST CAMBER TO SPECIFICATIONS	ADJUST TOE-IN TO SPECIFICATIONS	DYNAMIC OR STATIC BALANCE WHEELS	ROTATE TIRES AND INSPECT SUSPENSION

*HAVE TIRE INSPECTED FOR FURTHER USE.

TCCS1267

Fig. 94 Common tire wear patterns and causes

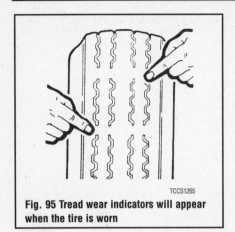

Fig. 95 Tread wear indicators will appear when the tire is worn

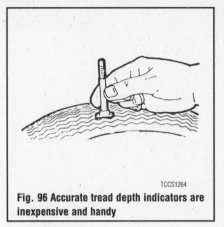

Fig. 96 Accurate tread depth indicators are inexpensive and handy

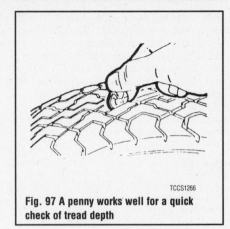

Fig. 97 A penny works well for a quick check of tread depth

You can check your own tread depth with an inexpensive gauge or by using a Lincoln head penny. Slip the Lincoln penny (with Lincoln's head upside-down) into several tread grooves. If you can see the top of Lincoln's head in 2 adjacent grooves, the tire has less than 1/16 in. (1.5mm) tread left and should be replaced. You can measure snow tires in the same manner by using the "tails" side of the Lincoln penny. If you can see the top of the Lincoln memorial, it's time to replace the snow tire(s).

FLUIDS AND LUBRICANTS

Fluid Disposal

Used fluids such as engine oil, transmission/transaxle fluid, antifreeze and brake fluid are considered hazardous waste and must be disposed of properly. Before draining any fluids, check with local authorities. Most states have a recycling program in effect, and many service stations and parts stores accept waste fluids for recycling as long as they are not mixed.

Fuel Requirements

GASOLINE ENGINES

All vehicles sold in the U.S. with gasoline engines are designed to operate on lead-free fuel. The minimum octane ratings required by Volkswagen sometimes vary with where the vehicle was intended for sale and use (high altitude). Octane requirements are listed on the inside of the fuel filler door or on the door jamb. Use of leaded gasoline or certain additives will poison the catalytic converter and in some cases, possibly damage fuel injectors. Volkswagen recommends occasional use of Autobahn Gasoline Additive, VW part no. ZVW 246 001, for keeping injectors clean.

DIESEL ENGINES

The Volkswagen diesel engine is designed to run on Diesel Fuel No. 2. Since diesel fuel is generally available, supply is not usually a problem, though it is wise to check in advance. Several diesel station guides are available from fuel companies and are normally sold at diesel fuel stations. Some U.S states and Canadian provinces require purchasers of diesel fuel to obtain a special permit to buy diesel fuel. Check with your local VW dealer or fuel supplier for regulations in your area.

There is a difference between the refinement levels of diesel fuel and home heating oil. While you may get away with running your diesel on home heating oil for a while, inevitably you will fill your tank with a batch of oil that will leave you stranded. Even though they don't mix, Diesel fuel tends to attract water. This is another reason to stick to mainstream suppliers when filling the tank. Also, never allow diesel fuel to come in contact with any rubber hoses or other parts. It attacks the rubber and causes it to become soft and unstable.

Engine Oil Recommendations

GASOLINE ENGINES

▶ See Figure 98

The SAE (Society of Automotive Engineers) grade number indicates the viscosity of the engine oil, and thus its ability to lubricate at a given temperature. The lower the SAE grade number, the lighter the oil. The lower the viscosity, the easier it is to crank the engine in cold weather. Oil viscosities should be chosen for the lowest anticipated temperatures during the oil change interval. Multi-viscosity oils (10W–30, 20W–50, etc.) offer the important advantage of being adaptable to temperature extremes. They allow easy starting at low temperatures, yet give good protection at high speeds and engine temperatures. This is

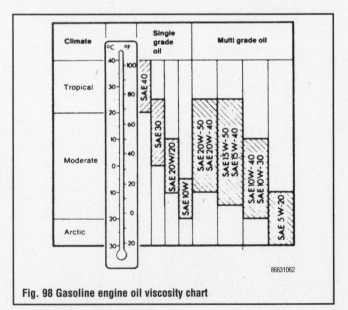

Fig. 98 Gasoline engine oil viscosity chart

a decided advantage in changeable climates or in long distance touring. The API (American Petroleum Institute) designation indicates the classification of engine oil for use under given operating conditions. Oils designated for use Service SF or SG (or a superseding rating) should be used. Oils of the SF or SG type perform a variety of functions inside the engine in addition to the basic function as a lubricant. Through a balanced system of metallic detergents and polymeric dispersants, the oil prevents the formation of high and low temperature deposits, and also keeps sludge and dirt particles in suspension. Acids, particularly sulfuric acid, as well as other by-products of combustion, are neutralized. Both the SAE grade number and the API designation can be found somewhere on the container.

➡ **Non-detergent or straight mineral oils must never be used.**

Oil must be selected with regard to the anticipated temperatures during the period before the next oil change. Using the chart, select the oil viscosity prior to the next oil change for the lowest expected temperature and you will be assured of easy cold starting and sufficient engine protection.

DIESEL ENGINES

◆ **See Figure 99**

Engine oils should be selected from the accompanying chart. The SAE viscosity number should be chosen for the lowest anticipated temperature at which the engine will be required to start, not for the temperature at the time the oil is changed. Use only oils designated by the API (American Petroleum Institute) for service CC or CD (or a superseding rating). The letters should appear somewhere on the oil can for example "SF/CC" or "SG/CD". This indicates that the oil provides protection from rust, corrosion and high temperature deposits in diesel engines in moderate to severe service.

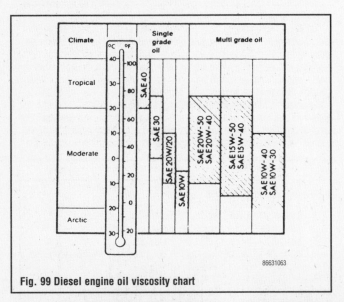

Fig. 99 Diesel engine oil viscosity chart

Engine

OIL LEVEL CHECK

◆ **See Figures 100 and 101**

Engine oil level should be checked weekly. Always check the oil with the vehicle on level ground and after the engine has been shut off for about five minutes. The oil dipstick is either located on the front side of engine or on the driver's side near the fuel pump.

1. Remove the dipstick and wipe it clean.
2. Reinsert the dipstick.
3. Remove the dipstick again. The oil level should be between the two marks. The amount of oil needed to bring the level from the lower mark to the upper mark is approximately 1 quart (0.95L).
4. Add oil through the capped opening on the top of the valve cover. Wipe up any spilled oil.

OIL AND FILTER CHANGE

◆ **See Figures 102, 103, 104, 105 and 106**

Change the oil according to the maintenance interval chart in this section. This interval is only for average driving. Change the oil and filter more frequently if your vehicle is being used under dusty conditions or in mostly stop-and-go city traffic, where acid and sludge buildup is a problem. When draining the oil, warm oil will flow easier and more contaminants will be removed. Dispose of use oil in accordance with state or local regulations.

➡ **Chilton recommends that you replace the filter every time the oil is changed.**

1. Run the engine until it reaches the normal operating temperature.
2. Raise and safely support the front of the vehicle on jackstands.
3. Slide a drain pan under the oil pan drain plug.
4. Loosen the drain plug with a socket or box wrench, and then remove it by hand. Push in lightly on the plug as you turn it out, so that no oil escapes until the plug is completely removed.
5. While the oil is draining, check the condition of the copper gasket on the plug. If it looks split or badly deformed, replace it to avoid an oil leak.
6. After the oil is drained, install the plug and torque it to 22 ft. lbs. (30 Nm).
7. On all models except Dasher, Quantum and Fox, the filter is located on the front of the engine block. On Dasher, Quantum and Fox models, it is located on the left side of the engine block. Reach in and turn the filter off counterclockwise. If it's tight, use a filter strap wrench.
8. Carefully lower the filter from its mounting, direct the filter into the oil pan and drain it before disposal.
9. Clean the oil filter seating area with a clean rag and make sure the old oil filter gasket is not sticking to the mounting base. This is important to avoid a leak.
10. Lightly oil the rubber seal on the new filter and spin it onto the base. When the seal contacts the sealing surface, give it an additional ½ to ¾ turn.

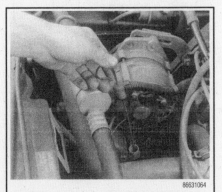

Fig. 100 The engine oil dipstick is usually located on the side of the engine block

Fig. 101 The oil level should be between the high and low marks

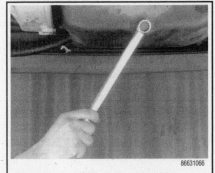

Fig. 102 Loosen the drain plug with a socket or box wrench, then remove it by hand

Fig. 103 Always check the oil cooler for tightness when replacing the oil filter. If necessary, torque the oil cooler retaining nut to 18 ft. lbs. (25 Nm)

Fig. 104 Before installing the new oil filter, coat its rubber gasket with clean oil

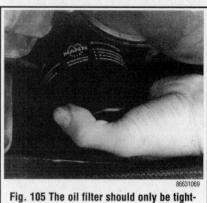

Fig. 105 The oil filter should only be tightened by hand; do not use a strap wrench

Fig. 106 The engine oil should be filled through the uncapped opening in the camshaft cover

Tightening the filter more than this will not improve sealing, but just make it harder to remove the next time.

11. Refill the engine with the specified amount of new oil (refer to the Capacities Chart in this section). The empty containers can be used to return the used oil for recycling.

12. Run the engine and check for leaks.

Manual Transaxle

➡**Volkswagen strongly suggests that manual transaxle maintenance be left to qualified dealers.**

FLUID RECOMMENDATIONS

Manual transaxles use SAE 80W hypoid oil, API service GL-4, Mil-L-2105. The hypoid type is an important specification. Under normal service, changing the oil in a manual transaxle is not really required since there are no combustion by-products to contaminate the oil. A large magnet is fitted in the bottom of the case to attract any gear shavings. If the transaxle has been abused or used most of its life for towing, an oil change may be in order. The most important thing is to make sure the level is correct.

LEVEL CHECK

Dasher, Fox and Quantum

The oil filler plug is located on the driver's side of the transaxle at the rear of the final drive cover. Using the proper size metric Allen wrench, remove the plug, if the fluid is level with the bottom of the hole, it is correct. Add the recommended fluid if necessary.

Rabbit, Scirocco, Cabriolet and 1980–84 Jetta

➡**Both the transaxle and the final drive gears share the same lubricant.**

For Rabbit and Scirocco transaxles up to No. 06 054, check the oil at the oil control plug. Remove the plug with a 5mm Allen wrench. With the vehicle level (the front and rear wheels on level ground or both the front and rear raised the same height off the ground), the oil should just begin to run out of the hole. If not, add the gear oil through the separate filler plug located on the front of the transaxle near the backup light switch. A bulb syringe or an oil squirt can works well here.

For Rabbit and Scirocco transaxles from No. 07 954, you check and fill the transaxle through the oil control plug.

Golf, GTI and 1985–89 Jetta

On Golf, GTI and Jetta transaxles, the oil level is checked by removing the oil filler plug located in the transaxle case.

On transaxles before 08 09 7, position a drain container under the oil filler plug. Remove the oil filler plug and allow the oil to drain from the filler plug opening until the fluid level is even with the edge of the hole. Install and tighten the plug. Disconnect the speedometer cable, then remove the speedometer drive gear from the transaxle. Using a funnel, add approximately 0.5 quart (0.48 L) of gear oil through the speedometer drive gear opening.

On transaxles starting with 08 09 7, remove the filler plug. If the fluid is level with the bottom of the hole, it is correct. The speedometer drive gear does not have to be removed to add oil to these transaxles. On these models, add the required amount gear oil through the filler plug opening using a suction gun.

DRAIN AND REFILL

♦ See Figures 107 and 108

1. Raise and safely support the front of the car on jackstands.
2. Slide a drain pan under the transaxle.
3. Remove the filler plug, then the drain plug.
4. When the oil has been completely drained, install the drain plug. Tighten to 18 ft. lbs. (24 Nm).
5. Refill the gearbox up to the level of the filler plug with the specified amount of gear oil (refer to the Capacities Chart in this section).
6. Install and tighten the filler plug.

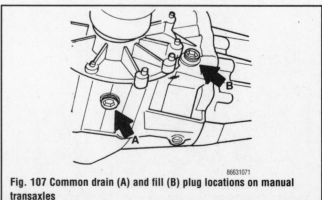

Fig. 107 Common drain (A) and fill (B) plug locations on manual transaxles

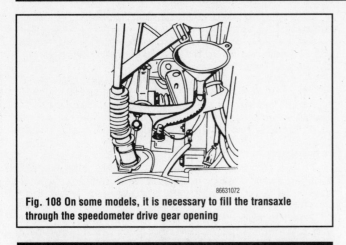

Fig. 108 On some models, it is necessary to fill the transaxle through the speedometer drive gear opening

Automatic Transaxle

FLUID RECOMMENDATIONS

Dexron®II automatic transmission/transaxle fluid is used in automatic transaxles. If this is not available, its superseding fluid type may be used. VW recommends that the fluid be replaced every 30,000 miles (48,000 km).

The final drive section of the automatic transaxle uses SAE 90 hypoid gear oil, API service GL-5, Mil-I-2105B. The final drive unit requires no attention other than an occasional level check.

LEVEL CHECK

▶ **See Figure 109**

On late model VW's, the automatic transaxle dipstick was modified. Old style dipsticks have a fluid level instruction plate attached to the handle. If this type of dipstick is used, the difference between the MIN and MAX marks is 0.35 quarts (0.33 L). When checking the level cold, fill the transaxle to the MIN mark. Warm up the engine to normal operating temperature and check the level again. It should be between the MIN and MAX marks. If not, add fluid as required.

The new style dipstick does not have the instruction plate attached to the handle. In addition to the MIN and MAX marks, there is a 20° mark at the very bottom of the dipstick. The difference between the MIN and MAX marks is 0.24 quarts (0.22 L). When cold, fill the transaxle to the 20° mark. Warm up the engine to normal operating temperature and check the level again. It should be between the MIN and MAX marks. If not, add fluid as required.

1. Idle the engine for a few minutes with the selector in **N**. Apply the parking brake and move the selector lever to **P**.
2. Remove the dipstick, wipe it clean, reinsert it, and withdraw it again.
3. The fluid level should be within the two marks. Top up with Dexron®II (or its superseding fluid type of automatic transmission/transaxle fluid). Bear in mind that the difference between the two marks is less than one pint. Use a

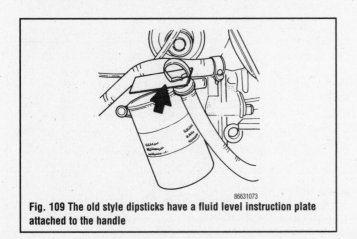

Fig. 109 The old style dipsticks have a fluid level instruction plate attached to the handle

long-necked funnel to add the fluid. Fluid should be drained and replaced at the specified interval in the Maintenance Interval Chart, later in this section.

✳✳ CAUTION

DO NOT overfill the transaxle. Too much fluid can cause damage.

PAN AND FILTER SERVICE

1. Purchase the required amount of automatic transmission/transaxle fluid and a pan gasket.
2. Slide a drain pan under the transaxle. Jack up the front of the vehicle and support it safely on jackstands.
3. Many early models are equipped with drain plugs in the pan. On later models, you must loosen the pan retaining bolts to drain the fluid.
4. On all models, loosen the front pan retaining bolts and remove the rear pan bolts. Lower the pan and drain the oil in the drain container. Once the oil is drained from the pan, remove the front retaining bolts and lower the pan.
5. Discard the old gasket and clean the pan with solvent.
6. On models with circular oil strainers, unscrew the strainer and clean it. On models with rectangular or not perfectly circular oil strainers, the strainer cannot be cleaned and must be replaced. On these models, only replace the oil strainer if the fluid is contaminated.
7. Install the oil strainer, but don't tighten the bolt too much. Specified torque is only 4–14 ft. lbs. (5–19 Nm).
8. Using a long-necked funnel, refill the transaxle with fluid (refer to the Capacities Chart in this section). Check the level with the dipstick. Run the vehicle for a few minutes and check again.

Differential

➡ **This pertains to vehicles with an automatic transaxle only.**

FLUID RECOMMENDATIONS

Use gear oil with API classification GL-5. Viscosity should be:
- SAE 90W above 30°F (–1°C)
- SAE 85W above 0°F (–18°C)
- SAE 80W below –30°F° (–34°C)

LEVEL CHECK

Make sure the vehicle is on level ground. Next to the output flange of the transaxle, remove the filler plug. The oil should be even with the lower edge of the filler hole. Add or drain oil as required. The final drive is filled for life and does not require oil changes.

Cooling System

FLUID RECOMMENDATIONS

All VW's are filled with a mixture of water and special phosphate-free antifreeze at the factory. The antifreeze has corrosion inhibitors that prevent frost, the formation of chalk, and also raise the boiling point of the water. Volkswagen recommends using VW phosphate free antifreeze/coolant part number ZVW237 when replacing or adding coolant. Most brand name antifreeze manufacturers recommend a 50/50 antifreeze-to-water mixture for maximum protection from freezing and overheating. A hydrometer is available at most parts stores that checks the freeze protection of the coolant, much like a battery hydrometer. Don't use a battery hydrometer, though; it's not calibrated for coolant and would no longer be usable for batteries. When deciding on the antifreeze/water mixture for refilling or adding to the system, follow the manufacturer's instructions on the container.

If you intend to switch from an ethylene based antifreeze to a propylene based antifreeze, the cooling system must be flushed several times with clean water. These two different types of antifreeze are not compatible and cannot be mixed together; doing so will neutralize the special properties of a propylene based antifreeze.

LEVEL CHECK

▶ **See Figures 110, 111, 112 and 113**

Make it a habit to periodically check the coolant level in the radiator. Ideally, this should be performed when the engine is cold. When removing the pressure cap, loosen it slightly first. If the coolant begins to boil, tighten the cap again and wait for the engine to cool down. On some models, a gauge plate inside or outside the radiator filler neck aids in level checking. The coolant should be maintained at the bottom of the plate.

Some models are equipped with a coolant reservoir. The reservoir is translucent and can be checked without removing the cap. Some later models have a coolant expansion tank and no radiator cap. The reservoir has low and high level marks. The coolant must be between the two marks when the engine is cold and slightly above the high mark at normal operating temperature. On models with an expansion tank and no radiator cap, observe the same cautions when removing the pressure cap from the expansion tank as with a radiator cap. Wrap it with a heavy rag and open the cap slowly to release the pressure from the cooling system.

Some models are equipped with a light on the dash that flashes until the coolant level is filled to the normal level.

DRAIN AND REFILL

The thermostat must be removed to drain the system. Before draining the coolant, purchase a new thermostat O-ring.

✳ CAUTION

Never attempt to drain the coolant from a hot engine. This is a messy job and there is no way to drain the coolant without getting it on your hands.

1. Raise and safely support the front of the vehicle on jackstands.
2. Place a large drain pan under the engine.

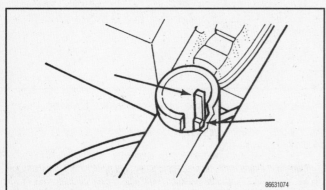

Fig. 110 On some models, there may be a gauge inside the radiator filler neck to check coolant level

86631074

3. On some early models, there is a petcock at the bottom of the radiator. Loosen it to drain the radiator.
4. Loosen the thermostat housing bolts (refer to Section 3). When they are both loose and the housing is pulled slightly away from the water pump assembly, coolant will start to flow.
5. When the coolant stops flowing, there may still be some in the radiator or in the cylinder block. Keep the drain pan in place and remove the thermostat housing from the water pump assembly. It's not necessary to disconnect the lower radiator hose.
6. Remove the thermostat and the radiator/reservoir cap to drain the rest of the coolant.

To refill:

7. Clean and dry the thermostat housing and the rubber O-ring. Examine the O-ring for cracks or damage, replace as necessary.
8. Install the thermostat into the water pump housing on the engine, then fit the O-ring into place.
9. Install the thermostat housing and tighten the bolts evenly. Torque the bolts to 87 inch lbs. (10 Nm). Do not overtorque these bolts or the housing may break.
10. Loosen the upper radiator hose and begin filling the system through the coolant reservoir or radiator. Loosening the upper hose will allow the air to escape and speed the processes.
11. When the system will not take any more coolant, tighten the hose and start the engine. Watch for leaks and add more coolant as required. Don't run the engine too long with the reservoir cap removed or it will boil over.

FLUSHING AND CLEANING THE SYSTEM

The cooling system should be drained and refilled with new coolant at least every 30,000 miles (48,000 km) or 24 months. Other than this service, Volkswagen does not recommend any special cooling system flushing. If you decide to do so, use a system flush made for use with aluminum cooling system components and follow the instructions on the package.

Master Cylinder

FLUID RECOMMENDATIONS

Use a good quality brake fluid that meets or exceeds DOT 3 or DOT 4 specifications. Never try to re-use brake fluid.

LEVEL CHECK

▶ **See Figures 114 and 115**

The brake fluid reservoir is located on the left side of the engine compartment at the firewall. Fluid level can be checked visually without removing the cap on this translucent unit. Brake fluid level will decrease slowly as the brake pads wear thinner. If the level is close to the MIN line, check the brake pads and shoes for wear before adding brake fluid. Also check the hydraulic clutch system (if equipped) for fluid leaks. If necessary, top up with a brand name brake fluid which bears the DOT 3 or DOT 4 marking. This information will be printed on the container.

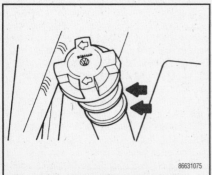

86631075

Fig. 111 On other models, the coolant level indicators are outside the radiator filler neck

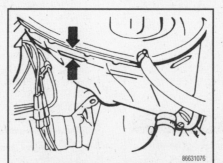

86631076

Fig. 112 A coolant expansion tank is used on some models. Keep in mind that on models with an expansion tank and no radiator cap, the system is under pressure

86631077

Fig. 113 A funnel is helpful when adding coolant to the system

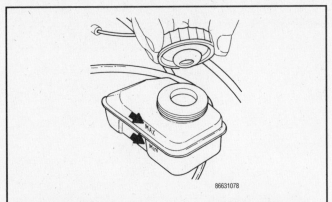

Fig. 114 The fluid level should be between the MIN and MAX marks

Fig. 115 Only use fresh, approved brake fluid when filling the reservoir

Clutch Master Cylinder

FLUID RECOMMENDATIONS

The hydraulic clutch uses fluid from the brake fluid reservoir. Use only new brake fluid that meets or exceeds DOT 3 or DOT 4 specifications.

Power Steering Pump

FLUID RECOMMENDATIONS

Use Dexron®II automatic transmission/transaxle fluid when adding fluid to the power steering reservoir.

LEVEL CHECK

♦ See Figure 116

The reservoir for the power assisted steering is usually located at the rear of the engine compartment on the firewall. The fluid level should be checked at regular intervals. With the engine running, the fluid level should be between the MAX and MIN marks on the outside of the reservoir. If fluid is added, make sure the filler cap is secured.

Steering Gear

The rack and pinion steering gear is filled with lubricant and sealed at the factory. If you notice any leaks, the rack assembly must be repaired or replaced.

Fig. 116 The power steering fluid reservoir is usually located just forward of the transaxle

Chassis Greasing

These vehicles require no chassis greasing and are not equipped with grease nipples. Check the axle shaft and steering rack boots, as well as the tie rod and ball joint rubber boots occasionally for leaking or cracking. At the same time, squirt a few drops of oil on the parking brake equalizer (point where the cables branch off to the rear brakes).

Body Lubrication

Periodic lubrication will prevent squeaky, hard-to-open doors and lids. About every three months, pry the plastic caps off the door hinges (if equipped) and squirt in enough oil to fill the chambers. Press the plug back into the hinge after filling. Lightly oil the door check pivots. Finally, spray graphite lock lubricant onto your key and insert it into the door lock a few times.

Rear Wheel Bearings

➡Please refer to Section 8 for front wheel bearing removal and installation procedures.

REMOVAL, PACKING & INSTALLATION

♦ See Figures 117 thru 126

1. Raise and safely support the vehicle and remove the rear wheels.
2. On drum brakes, insert a small prytool through a wheel bolt hole and push up on the spring tensioned adjusting wedge to slacken the rear brake adjustment.
3. On disc brakes, remove the bolts to remove the caliper. Hang the caliper from the spring with wire, do not let it hang by the hydraulic hose.

Fig. 117 A large pair of pliers can be used to remove the bearing dust cap

Fig. 118 Once the bent ends are cut, grasp the cotter pin and pull it free from the spindle

Fig. 119 Remove the lockcap, then loosen and remove the locknut

Fig. 120 Remove the washer from the spindle

Fig. 121 With the nut and washer out of the way, the outer bearing may be removed from the hub

Fig. 122 Pull the hub and inner bearing assembly from the spindle

Fig. 123 Use a small prytool to remove the old inner bearing seal

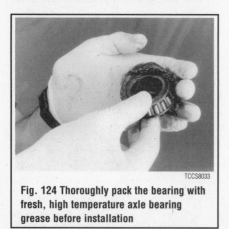

Fig. 124 Thoroughly pack the bearing with fresh, high temperature axle bearing grease before installation

Fig. 125 Apply a thin coat of fresh grease to the new inner bearing seal lip

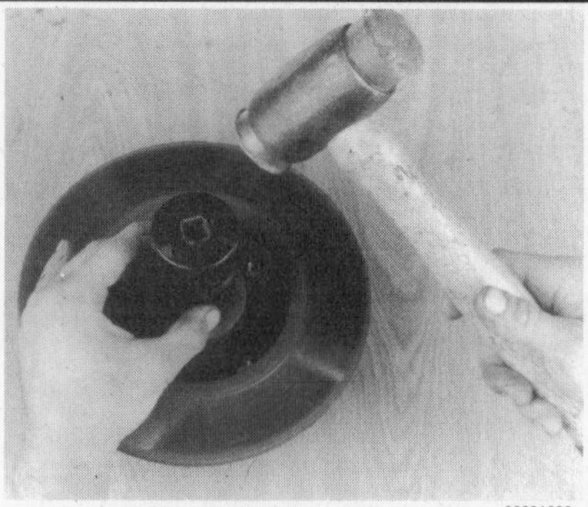

Fig. 126 Use a suitably sized driver to install the inner bearing seal to the hub

4. Pry off the grease cap, remove cotter pin, locking ring, axle nut and thrust washer. Carefully remove the bearing without dropping it.

5. Remove the brake drum or disc and pry the bearing seal out of the hub. The seal will be destroyed, but be careful not to pry on the bearing.

6. Remove the bearing and clean all parts in solvent. Examine the bearings and inner races for wear or damage. If bearings must be replaced, see Section 8.

7. Pack the bearings with new axle bearing grease. If the grease is suitable for use with disc brakes, it's good for all applications.

8. Install the inner bearing and a new wheel seal. Use the old seal or a flat bar across the new seal as an installation tool. The new seal must be driven in straight and seated on the hub.

9. Pack about 1 oz. of grease into the hub and fit the drum or disc onto the axle.

10. Pack the outer bearing with grease and fit the bearing, thrust washer and nut onto the axle. Adjust bearing pre-load and install the locking ring, cotter pin and grease cap.

11. Install the brake caliper, if removed.

ADJUSTMENT

▶ **See Figure 127**

1. Tighten the bearing nut while turning the drum or disc. Torque the nut to 87 inch lbs. (10 Nm) to seat the bearing, then loosen it again.

2. When tightening adjusting the nut again, move the thrust washer side to side with a screwdriver. The thrust washer must still be movable with light effort when adjustment is complete.

3. When installing the locking ring, keep trying different positions of the ring on the nut until the cotter pin goes into the hole. Don't turn the nut to align the locking ring with the hole in the axle. Use a new cotter pin.

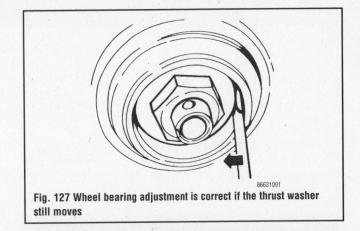

86631091

Fig. 127 Wheel bearing adjustment is correct if the thrust washer still moves

TRAILER TOWING

Factory trailer towing packages are available for most vehicles. However, if you are installing a trailer hitch and wiring on your vehicle, there are a few things that you ought to know.

Trailer Weight

Trailer weight is the first, and most important, factor in determining whether or not your vehicle is suitable for towing the trailer you have in mind. The horsepower-to-weight ratio should be calculated. The basic standard is a ratio of 35:1. That is, 35 pounds of GVW for every horsepower. To calculate this ratio, multiply you engine's rated horsepower by 35, then subtract the weight of the vehicle, including passengers and luggage. The resulting figure is the ideal maximum trailer weight that you can tow.

Hitch Weight

There are three kinds of hitches: bumper mounted, frame mounted, and load equalizing. Bumper mounted hitches are those which attach solely to the vehicle's bumper. Many states prohibit towing with this type of hitch, when it attaches to the vehicle's stock bumper, since it subjects the bumper to stresses for which it was not designed. Aftermarket rear step bumpers, designed for trailer towing, are acceptable for use with bumper mounted hitches. Frame mounted hitches can be of the type which bolts to two or more points on the frame, plus the bumper, or just to several points on the frame. Frame mounted hitches can also be of the tongue type, for Class I towing, or, of the receiver type, for classes II and III. Volkswagens should not be used for towing anything with a Class II or class III rating, as maximum towing capacity for these vehicles is limited to 1000 lbs. gross weight. Load equalizing hitches are usually used for large trailers. Most equalizing hitches are welded in place and use equalizing bars and chains to level the vehicle after the trailer is hooked up. The bolt-on hitches are the most common, since they are relatively easy to install. Check the gross weight rating of your trailer. Tongue weight is usually figured as 10 percent of gross trailer weight. Therefore, a trailer with a maximum gross weight of 2,000 lbs. will have a maximum tongue weight of 200 lbs. Class I trailers fall into this category. Class II trailers are those with a gross weight rating of 2,000–3,500 lbs., while Class III trailers fall into the 3,500–6,000 lb. category. Class IV trailers are those over 6,000 lbs. and are for use with fifth wheel trucks, only. When you've determined the hitch that you'll need, follow the manufacturer's installation instructions, exactly, especially when it comes to fastener torques. The hitch will be subjected to a lot of stress and good hitches come with hardened bolts. Never substitute an inferior bolt for a hardened bolt.

Wiring

Wiring the vehicle for towing is fairly easy. There are a number of good wiring kits available and these should be used, rather than trying to design your own. All trailers will need brake lights and turn signals as well as tail lights and side marker lights. Most states require extra marker lights for oversize trailers. Also, most states have recently required backup lights for trailers (most trailer manufacturers have been building trailers with back-up lights for several years). Additionally, some Class I, most Class II and just about all Class III trailers will have electric brakes. Add to this number an accessories wire, to operate trailer internal equipment or to charge the trailer's battery, and you can have as many as seven wires in the harness. Determine the equipment on your trailer and buy the wiring kit necessary. The kit should contain all the wires needed, plus a plug adapter set which includes the female plug (mounted on the bumper or hitch) and the male plug (wired or plugged into the trailer harness). When installing the kit, follow the manufacturer's instructions. The color coding of the wires is standard throughout the industry. One point to note: some domestic vehicles, and most imported vehicles, have separate turn signals. On most domestic vehicles, the brake lights and rear turn signals operate with the same bulb. For those vehicles with separate turn signals, you can purchase an isolation unit so that the brake lights won't blink whenever the turn signals are operated, or, you can go to your local electronics supply house and buy four diodes to wire in series with the brake and turn signal bulbs. Diodes will isolate the brake and turn signals. The choice is yours. The isolation units are simple and quick to install, but far more expensive than the diodes. The diodes, however, require more work to install properly, since they require the cutting of each bulb's wire and soldering in place of the diode. One, final point, the best kits are those with a spring loaded cover on the vehicle mounted socket. This cover prevents dirt and moisture from corroding the terminals. Never let the vehicle socket hang loosely; always mount it securely to the bumper or hitch.

Engine Cooling

One of the most common, if not THE most common, problems associated with trailer towing is engine overheating. With factory installed trailer towing packages, a heavy duty cooling system is usually included. Heavy duty cooling systems are available as optional equipment on most vehicles, with or without a trailer package. If you have one of these extra capacity systems, you shouldn't have any overheating problems. If you have a standard cooling system, without an expansion tank, you'll definitely need to get an aftermarket expansion tank kit, preferably one with at least a 2 quart capacity. These kits are easily installed on the radiator's overflow hose, and come with a pressure cap designed for expansion tanks. Through the dealer parts network, Volkswagen offers cooling and lubrication system modifications designed for towing.

JUMP STARTING A DEAD BATTERY

▶ See Figure 128

Whenever a vehicle must be jump started, precautions must be followed in order to prevent the possibility of personal injury. Remember that batteries contain a small amount of explosive hydrogen gas which is a by-product of battery charging. Sparks should always be avoided when working around batteries, especially when attaching jumper cables. To minimize the possibility of accidental sparks, follow the procedure carefully.

✳✳ WARNING

NEVER hook the batteries up in a series circuit or the entire electrical system may go up in smoke, including the starter!

Jump Starting Precautions

1. Be sure that both batteries are of the same voltage. Vehicles covered by this manual and most vehicles on the road today utilize a 12 volt charging system.
2. Be sure that both batteries are of the same polarity (have the same ground terminal—in most cases, this is the NEGATIVE terminal).
3. Be sure that the vehicles are not touching, since a short circuit could occur.
4. On serviceable batteries, be sure the vent cap holes are not obstructed.
5. Do not smoke or allow sparks anywhere near the batteries.
6. In cold weather, make sure the battery electrolyte is not frozen. This can occur more readily in a battery that has been in a state of discharge.
7. Do not allow electrolyte to contact your skin or clothing.

Jump Starting Procedure

1. Position the jumping vehicle (with the good battery) so the jumper cables can reach the dead battery and the disabled vehicle's engine. Make sure that the vehicles do NOT touch.
2. Place the transmissions/transaxles of both vehicles in NEUTRAL or PARK, as applicable, then firmly set their parking brakes.

➡ **If necessary for safety reasons, both vehicle's hazard lights may be operated throughout the entire procedure without significantly increasing the difficulty of jumping the dead battery.**

3. Turn all lights and accessories off on both vehicles. Make sure the ignition switches on both vehicles are turned to the **OFF** position.
4. Cover the battery cell caps with a rag, but do not cover the terminals.
5. Make sure the terminals on both batteries are clean and free of corrosion or proper electrical connection will be impeded. If necessary, clean the battery terminals before proceeding.
6. Identify the positive (+) and negative (−) terminals on both battery posts.
7. Connect the first jumper cable to the positive (+) terminal of the dead battery, then connect the other end of that cable to the positive (+) terminal of the booster (good) battery.
8. Connect one end of the other jumper cable to the negative (−) terminal of the booster battery and the other cable clamp to an engine bolt head, alterna-

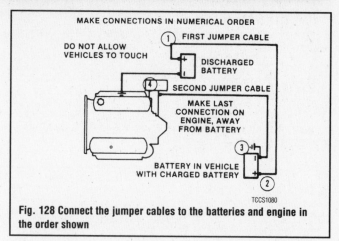

MAKE CONNECTIONS IN NUMERICAL ORDER

DO NOT ALLOW VEHICLES TO TOUCH

① FIRST JUMPER CABLE

DISCHARGED BATTERY

④ SECOND JUMPER CABLE

MAKE LAST CONNECTION ON ENGINE, AWAY FROM BATTERY

③

BATTERY IN VEHICLE WITH CHARGED BATTERY

②

TCCS1080

Fig. 128 Connect the jumper cables to the batteries and engine in the order shown

tor bracket or other solid, metallic point on the dead battery's engine. Try to find a ground on the engine that is positioned away from the battery, in order to minimize the possibility of the two clamps touching should one loosen during the procedure. DO NOT connect this clamp to the negative (−) terminal of the bad battery.

✳✳ CAUTION

Be very careful to keep the jumper cables away from moving parts (cooling fan, belts, etc.) on both engines.

9. Check to make sure that the cables are routed away from any moving parts, then start the donor vehicle's engine. Run the engine at moderate speed for several minutes to allow the dead battery a chance to receive some initial charge.
10. With the donor vehicle's engine still running slightly above idle, try to start the vehicle with the dead battery. Crank the engine for no more than 10 seconds at a time and let the starter cool for at least 20 seconds between tries. If the vehicle does not start in three tries, it is likely that something else is also wrong.
11. Once the vehicle is started, allow it to run at idle for a few seconds to make sure that it is properly operating.
12. Turn on the headlights, heater blower and, if equipped, the rear defroster of both vehicles in order to reduce the severity of voltage spikes and subsequent risk of damage to the vehicles' electrical systems when the cables are disconnected.
13. Carefully disconnect the cables in the reverse order of connection. Start with the negative cable that is attached to the engine ground, then the negative cable on the donor battery. Disconnect the positive cable from the donor battery and finally, disconnect the positive cable from the formerly dead battery. Be careful when disconnecting the cables from the positive terminals not to allow the alligator clips to touch any metal on either vehicle or a short and sparks will occur.

TOWING THE VEHICLE

A flat bed (roll back) truck is the most desirable way to tow your vehicle. The vehicle is safest and the wheels do not have to turn. It is also usually the most expensive way to tow and is not always available.

The second best way to tow your vehicle is with the drive wheels off the ground. Sometimes it may be impossible to tow the vehicle in this way. If this is the case, both manual and automatic models may be flat-towed short distances (provided the transaxle is in working order), but be aware that this is not legal in some states. Attach tow lines to the towing eye on the front suspension or the left or right bumper bracket at the rear. Automatic transaxle equipped vehicles must be towed in Neutral no farther than 30 miles (48 km) and no faster than 30 mph (48 kph), unless the front wheels are off the ground. The steering wheel

must be secured in the straight ahead position. A special clamping device is made for this purpose. Do not use the steering column key lock, as this could cause damage to the lock and steering column.

➡ **Do not flat tow or tow automatic transaxle Quantum Syncro models with the front wheels on the ground. The center and rear differentials must be unlocked on all Quantum Syncro models during towing.**

If the transaxle is known to be damaged, or if an automatic transaxle vehicle must be towed for a long distance, the drive wheels must be dollied and the vehicle towed with the rear wheels off the ground.

JACKING

▶ **See Figures 129 and 130**

Your vehicle is equipped with a single post, crank handle jack which fits the jacking points behind the front wheel and in front of the rear wheel. These are usually marked with triangular sections of the body stamping. Never use the tire changing jack for anything other than that. If you intend to use this book to perform your own maintenance, a good hydraulic floor jack and two sturdy jackstands would be a wise purchase. Always chock the wheels when changing a tire or working beneath the vehicle. This cannot be overemphasized: **CLIMBING UNDER A VEHICLE SUPPORTED ONLY BY THE JACK IS EXTREMELY DANGEROUS!**

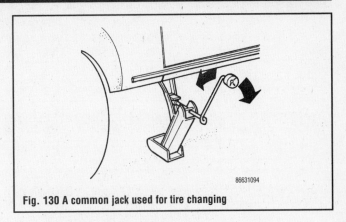

86631094

Fig. 130 A common jack used for tire changing

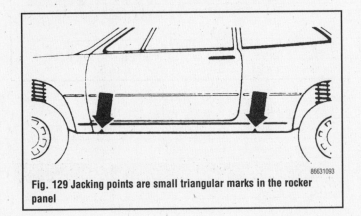

86631093

Fig. 129 Jacking points are small triangular marks in the rocker panel

Follow these points when raising and supporting your vehicle.
1. Always jack the vehicle on a level surface.
2. Set the parking brake, and block the wheels which aren't being raised. This will keep the vehicle from rolling off the jack.
3. During emergency tire changes, at least block the wheel diagonally opposite the one which is being raised.
4. If the vehicle is being raised in order to work underneath it, support it with jackstands. Do not place the jackstands against the sheet metal panels beneath the vehicle, as the panels could become distorted.
5. Do not use a bumper jack to raise the vehicle; the bumpers are not designed for this purpose.
6. Do not use cinder blocks to support a vehicle. They could crumble with little or no warning, dropping the vehicle and possibly causing death or serious injury.

CAPACITIES

Year	Model	Engine Displacement cu. in. (cc)	Engine Crankcase (qts.) with Filter	Engine Crankcase (qts.) without Filter	Transmission (pts.) 4-Spd	Transmission (pts.) 5-Spd	Transmission (pts.) Auto.	Drive Axle (pts)	Fuel Tank (gal.)	Cooling System (qts.)
1974	Dasher	90 (1471)	3.2	2.6	3.2	—	6.4	1.6	12.1	12.6
1975	Dasher	97 (1588)	3.2	2.6	3.2	—	6.4	1.6	11.9	12.6
	Rabbit	97 (1588)	3.7	3.2	2.6	—	6.4	1.6	12.1	9.8
	Scirocco	97 (1588)	3.7	3.2	2.6	—	6.4	1.6	12.1	9.8
1976	Dasher	97 (1588)	3.2	2.6	3.2	—	6.4	1.6	11.9	12.6
	Rabbit	97 (1588)	3.7	3.2	2.6	—	6.4	1.6	12.1	9.8
	Scirocco	97 (1588)	3.7	3.2	2.6	—	64	1.6	12.1	9.8
1977	Dasher	97 (1588)	3.2	2.6	3.4	—	6.4	1.6	11.9	12.6
	Rabbit	97 (1588)	3.7	3.2	2.6	—	6.4	1.6	12.1	9.8
	Rabbit (Diesel)	90 (1471)	3.7	3.2	2.6	—	6.4	1.6	10.6	9.8
	Scirocco	97 (1588)	3.7	3.2	2.6	—	6.4	1.6	12.1	9.8
1978	Dasher	97 (1588)	3.2	2.6	3.4	—	6.4	1.6	11.9	12.6
	Rabbit	89 (1457)	3.7	3.2	2.6	4.2	6.4	1.6	10.5	9.8
	Rabbit (Diesel)	90 (1471)	3.7	3.2	2.6	—	6.4	1.6	10.6	9.8
	Scirocco	89 (1457)	3.2	3.2	2.6	—	6.4	1.6	10.5	9.8
1979	Dasher	97 (1588)	3.2	2.6	3.4	—	6.4	1.6	11.9	12.6
	Dasher (Diesel)	90 (1471)	3.7	3.2	3.2	—	6.4	1.6	11.9	11.8
	Rabbit	89 (1457)	3.7	3.2	2.6	4.2	6.4	1.6	10.5	9.8
	Rabbit (Diesel)	90 (1471)	3.7	3.2	3.2	4.2	6.4	1.6	10.6①	14.6
	Scirocco	97 (1588)	3.7	3.2	3.2	—	6.4	1.6	10.6	9.8
1980	Dasher	97 (1588)	3.2	2.6	3.4	—	6.4	1.6	11.9	12.6
	Dasher (Diesel)	90 (1471)	3.7	3.2	3.2	—	6.4	1.6	11.9	11.8
	Rabbit②	97 (1588)	3.7	3.2	3.2	4.2	6.4	1.6	10.0	9.8③
	Rabbit (Diesel)	90 (1471)	3.7	3.2	3.2	—	6.4	1.6	10.6①	14.6
	Rabbit (Pick-up)	97 (1588)	3.7	3.2	3.2	4.2	6.4	1.6	15.0	14.6
	Jetta②	97 (1588)	3.7	3.2	3.2	—	6.4	1.6	10.5	10.2
	Scirocco	97 (1588)	3.7	3.2	3.2	—	6.4	1.6	10.6	10.2
1981	Dasher (Diesel)	97 (1588)	3.7	3.2	3.2	4.2	—	1.6	12.0	12.2
	Jetta	105 (1715)	4.5	4.0	3.2	4.2	6.4	1.6	10.0	9.8
	Jetta (Diesel)	97 (1588)	4.5	4.0	3.2	4.2	6.4	1.6	10.0	9.8
	Rabbit	105 (1715)	4.5	4.0	3.2	4.2	6.4	1.6	10.0	9.8
	Rabbit (Diesel)	97 (1588)	3.7	3.2	3.2	4.2	—	1.6	10.0	14.3
	Scirocco	105 (1715)	4.5	4.0	3.2	4.2	6.4	1.6	10.0	9.8

86631306

CAPACITIES (cont.)

Year	Model	Engine Displacement cu. in. (cc)	Engine Crankcase (qts.) with Filter	without Filter	Transmission (pts.) 4-Spd	5-Spd	Auto.	Drive Axle (pts.)	Fuel Tank (gal.)	Cooling System (qts.)
1982	Jetta	105 (1715)	4.8	4.3	—	4.2	6.4	1.6	10.5	10.2
	Jetta (Diesel)	97 (1588)	4.8	4.3	—	4.2	6.4	1.6	10.5	13.8
	Jetta (Turbo Diesel)	97 (1588)	4.8	4.3	—	4.2	6.4	1.6	10.5	13.8
	Quantum	105 (1715)	3.6	3.2	—	4.2	6.4	1.6	16.0	11.0
	Quantum	131 (2144)	3.6	3.2	—	4.2	6.4	1.6	16.0	11.0
	Quantum (Turbo Diesel)	97 (1588)	4.0	3.5	—	4.2	6.4	1.6	16.0	13.0
	Rabbit	105 (1715)	4.7	4.2	3.2	4.2	6.4	1.6	10.0	9.8
	Scirocco	105 (1715)	4.8	4.3	—	4.2	6.4	1.6	10.5	10.2
1983	Jetta	105 (1715)	4.3	3.7	—	4.2	6.4	1.6	10.5	5.1
	Jetta (Diesel)	97 (1588)	4.8	4.3	—	4.2	6.4	1.6	10.5	6.9
	Jetta (Turbo Diesel)	97 (1588)	4.8	4.3	—	4.2	6.4	1.6	10.5	6.9
	Quantum (4 cyl.)	105 (1715)	3.6	3.2	—	4.2	6.4	1.6	16.0	5.5
	Quantum (5 cyl.)	109 (1780)	4.0	3.5	—	4.2	6.4	1.6	16.0	5.5
	Quantum (Diesel)	130 (2144)	4.0	3.5	—	4.2	6.4	1.6	16.0	6.5
	Quantum (Turbo Diesel)	97 (1588)	4.8	4.3	—	4.2	6.4	1.6	16.0	6.5
	Rabbit	105 (1715)	4.3	3.7	3.2	4.2	6.4	1.6	10.0	6.9
	Rabbit	109 (1780)	4.3	3.7	3.2	4.2	6.4	1.6	10.0	7.3
	Rabbit (Conv.)	109 (1780)	4.3	3.7	—	4.2	6.2	1.6	10.5	7.3
	Rabbit (Diesel)	97 (1588)	4.8	4.3	3.2	4.2	6.4	1.6	10.0	6.9
	Scirocco	105 (1715)	4.3	3.7	—	4.2	6.4	1.6	10.5	5.1
	Scirocco	109 (1780)	4.3	3.7	—	4.2	6.4	1.6	10.5	6.5
	GTI	109 (1780)	4.3	3.7	3.2	4.2	6.4	1.6	10.0	7.3
	GTI (Diesel)	97 (1588)	4.8	4.3	3.2	4.2	6.4	1.6	11.0	6.5
	GLI	109 (1780)	4.3	3.7	3.2	4.2	—	1.6	14.5	6.5
1984	Jetta	105 (1715)	4.3	3.7	—	4.2	6.4	1.6	10.5	5.1
	Jetta (Diesel)	97 (1588)	4.8	4.3	—	4.2	6.4	1.6	10.5	6.9
	Quantum (4 cyl.)	109 (1780)	3.6	3.2	—	4.2	6.4	1.6	16.0	5.5
	Quantum (5 cyl.)	130 (2144)	4.0	3.5	—	4.2	6.4	1.6	16.0	5.5
	Quantum (Diesel)	97 (1588)	4.0	3.5	—	4.2	6.4	1.6	16.0	6.5
	Rabbit	105 (1715)	4.3	3.7	3.2	4.2	6.4	1.6	10.0	6.9
	Rabbit (Conv.)	109 (1780)	4.3	3.7	—	4.2	6.2	1.6	10.5	7.3
	Rabbit (Diesel)	97 (1588)	4.8	4.3	3.2	4.2	6.4	1.6	10.0	6.9
	Scirocco	109 (1780)	4.3	3.7	—	4.2	6.4	1.6	10.5	6.5
	GTI	109 (1780)	4.3	3.7	3.2	4.2	6.4	1.6	10.0	7.3
	GTI (Diesel)	97 (1588)	4.8	4.3	3.2	4.2	6.4	1.6	11.0	6.5
	GLI	109 (1780)	4.3	3.7	3.2	4.2	—	1.6	14.5	6.5

86631307

CAPACITIES (cont.)

Year	Model	Engine Displacement cu. in. (cc)	Engine Crankcase (qts.) with Filter	Engine Crankcase (qts.) without Filter	Transmission (pts.) 4-Spd	Transmission (pts.) 5-Spd	Transmission (pts.) Auto.	Drive Axle (pts.)	Fuel Tank (gal.)	Cooling System (qts.)
1985	Jetta	105 (1715)	4.3	3.7	—	4.2	6.4	1.6	13.7	7.3
	Jetta (Diesel)	97 (1588)	4.8	4.3	—	4.2	6.4	1.6	13.7	7.3
	Jetta (Turbo Diesel)	97 (1588)	4.8	4.3	—	4.2	6.4	1.6	13.7	7.3
	Quantum (4 cyl.)	109 (1780)	3.6	3.2	—	4.2	6.4	1.6	16.0	5.5
	Quantum (5 cyl.)	136 (2226)	4.0	3.5	—	4.2	6.4	1.6	16.0	6.5
	Quantum (Diesel)	97 (1588)	4.0	3.5	—	4.2	6.4	1.6	16.0	6.9
	Cabriolet	109 (1780)	4.3	3.7	—	4.2	6.4	1.6	13.7	7.3
	Scirocco	109 (1780)	4.3	3.7	—	4.2	6.4	1.6	13.7	6.5
	GTI	109 (1780)	4.3	3.7	—	4.2	—	1.6	14.5	7.3
	GLI	109 (1780)	4.3	3.7	—	4.2	—	1.6	14.5	7.3
	Golf	109 (1780)	4.3	3.7	—	4.2	6.4	1.6	14.5	7.3
	Golf (Diesel)	97 (1588)	4.8	4.3	—	4.2	6.4	1.6	14.5	7.3
1986	Jetta	109 (1780)	4.3	3.7	—	4.2	6.4	1.6	13.7	7.3
	Jetta (Diesel)	97 (1588)	4.8	4.3	—	4.2	6.4	1.6	13.7	7.3
	Jetta (Turbo Diesel)	97 (1588)	4.8	4.3	—	4.2	6.4	1.6	13.7	7.3
	Quantum (4 cyl.)	109 (1780)	3.6	3.2	—	4.2	6.4	1.6	16.0	5.5
	Quantum (5 cyl.)	136 (2226)	4.0	3.5	—	4.2	6.4	1.6	16.0	6.5
	Quantum (Diesel)	97 (1588)	4.0	3.5	—	4.2	6.4	1.6	16.0	6.9
	Cabriolet	109 (1780)	4.3	3.7	—	4.2	6.4	1.6	13.7	7.3
	Scirocco	109 (1780)	4.3	3.7	—	4.2	6.4	1.6	13.7	6.5
	GTI	109 (1780)	4.3	3.7	—	4.2	—	1.6	14.5	7.3
	GLI	109 (1780)	4.3	3.7	—	4.2	—	1.6	14.5	7.3
	Golf	109 (1780)	4.3	3.7	—	4.2	6.4	1.6	14.5	7.3
	Golf (Diesel)	97 (1588)	4.8	4.3	—	4.2	6.4	1.6	14.5	7.3
1987	Jetta	109 (1780)	4.3	3.8	—	4.2	6.4	—	14.5	7.3
	Jetta GL	109 (1780)	4.3	3.8	—	4.2	6.4	—	14.5	7.3
	Jetta GLI 16V	109 (1780)	4.3	3.8	—	4.2	6.4	—	14.5	7.3
	Quantum GL5	136 (2226)	4.0	3.8	—	4.2	6.4	—	15.8	8.5
	Quantum Syncro	136 (2226)	4.0	3.5	—	5.0	6.4	1.2	18.5	8.5
	Scirocco 16V	109 (1780)	4.3	3.8	—	4.2	6.4	—	13.8	5.1
	Cabriolet	109 (1780)	4.3	3.8	—	4.2	6.4	—	13.8	5.1
	Golf GL	109 (1780)	4.3	3.8	—	4.2	6.4	—	14.5	7.3
	Golf GT	109 (1780)	4.3	3.8	—	4.2	6.4	—	14.5	7.3
	Golf GTI 16V	109 (1780)	4.3	3.8	—	4.2	6.4	—	14.5	7.3
	Fox/GL	109 (1780)	3.7	3.2	3.6	—	—	—	12.4	6.9④

86631308

CAPACITIES (cont.)

Year	Model	Engine Displacement cu. in. (cc)	Engine Crankcase (qts.) with Filter	without Filter	Transmission (pts.) 4-Spd	5-Spd	Auto.	Drive Axle (pts.)	Fuel Tank (gal.)	Cooling System (qts.)
1988	Jetta	109 (1780)	4.3	3.8	—	4.2	6.4	—	14.5	7.3
	Jetta GL	109 (1780)	4.3	3.8	—	4.2	6.4	—	14.5	7.3
	Jetta GLI 16V	109 (1780)	4.3	3.8	—	4.2	6.4	—	14.5	7.3
	Jetta Carat	109 (1780)	4.3	3.8	—	4.2	6.4	—	14.5	7.3
	Quantum GL5	136 (2226)	4.0	3.8	—	4.2	6.4	—	15.8	8.5
	Quantum Syncro	136 (2226)	4.0	3.5	—	5.0	6.4	1.2	18.5	8.5
	Scirocco 16V	109 (1780)	4.3	3.8	—	4.2	6.4	—	13.8	5.1
	Cabriolet	109 (1780)	4.3	3.8	—	4.2	6.4	—	13.8	5.1
	Golf GL	109 (1780)	4.3	3.8	—	4.2	6.4	—	14.5	7.3
	Golf GT	109 (1780)	4.3	3.8	—	4.2	6.4	—	14.5	7.3
	Golf GTI 16V	109 (1780)	4.3	3.8	—	4.2	6.4	—	14.5	7.3
	Fox/GL	109 (1780)	3.7	3.2	3.6	—	—	—	12.4	6.9④
1989	Jetta	109 (1780)	4.3	3.8	—	4.2	6.4	—	14.5	7.3
	Jetta (Diesel)	97 (1588)	4.8	4.3	—	4.2	6.4	—	13.7	7.3
	Jetta GL	109 (1780)	4.3	3.8	—	4.2	6.4	—	14.5	7.3
	Jetta GLI 16V	109 (1780)	4.3	3.8	—	4.2	6.4	—	14.5	7.3
	Jetta Carat	109 (1780)	4.3	3.8	—	4.2	6.4	—	14.5	7.3
	Quantum GL5	136 (2226)	4.0	3.8	—	4.2	6.4	—	15.8	8.5
	Quantum Syncro	136 (2226)	4.0	3.5	—	5.0	6.4	1.2	18.5	8.5
	Scirocco 16V	109 (1780)	4.3	3.8	—	4.2	6.4	—	13.8	5.1
	Cabriolet	109 (1780)	4.3	3.8	—	4.2	6.4	—	13.8	5.1
	Golf GL	109 (1780)	4.3	3.8	—	4.2	6.4	—	14.5	7.3
	Golf GT	109 (1780)	4.3	3.8	—	4.2	6.4	—	14.5	7.3
	Golf GTI 16V	109 (1780)	4.3	3.8	—	4.2	6.4	—	14.5	7.3
	Fox/GL	109 (1780)	3.7	3.2	3.6	—	—	—	12.4	6.9④

① Pick-up: 15.0 gals.
② Applies to fuel injected engines. Engines with carburetor, 89 cu. in. (1457cc)
③ Rabbit Convertible: 10.2 pts.
④ Without A/C; with A/C; 6.9 qts.

86631309

Maintenance Interval Chart
(See text for a description of required maintenance)

Thousands of Miles or every 6 months	5	7.5	10	15	20	22.5	25	30	35	37.5	40	45	50
Oil Change & General Maintenance	*	*	*	*	*	*	*	*	*	*	*	*	*
Tune Up & Emission Control	—	—	—	*	—	—	*	—	—	—	—	*	—
Vehicle Maintenance	—	—	—	*	—	—	*	—	—	—	—	*	—
Fuel Injected Engine (FI)	—	FI	—	FI	—	FI	—	FI	—	FI	—	FI	—
Carburetor Engine (C)	—	C	—	C	—	C	—	C	—	C	—	C	—
Diesel Engine (D)	—	D	—	D	—	D	—	D	—	D	—	D	—
Turbo Diesel Engine (TD)	TD	—	TD	TD	TD	—	TD	TD	TD	—	TD	TD	TD

86631095

ENGLISH TO METRIC CONVERSION: MASS (WEIGHT)

Current **mass** measurement is expressed in pounds and ounces (lbs. & ozs.). The metric unit of mass (or weight) is the kilogram (kg). Even although this table does not show conversion of masses (weights) larger than 15 lbs, it is easy to calculate larger units by following the data immediately below.

To convert ounces (oz.) to grams (g): multiply th number of ozs. by 28
To convert grams (g) to ounces (oz.): multiply the number of grams by .035

To convert pounds (lbs.) to kilograms (kg): multiply the number of lbs. by .45
To convert kilograms (kg) to pounds (lbs.): multiply the number of kilograms by 2.2

lbs	kg	lbs	kg	oz	kg	oz	kg
0.1	0.04	0.9	0.41	0.1	0.003	0.9	0.024
0.2	0.09	1	0.4	0.2	0.005	1	0.03
0.3	0.14	2	0.9	0.3	0.008	2	0.06
0.4	0.18	3	1.4	0.4	0.011	3	0.08
0.5	0.23	4	1.8	0.5	0.014	4	0.11
0.6	0.27	5	2.3	0.6	0.017	5	0.14
0.7	0.32	10	4.5	0.7	0.020	10	0.28
0.8	0.36	15	6.8	0.8	0.023	15	0.42

ENGLISH TO METRIC CONVERSION: TEMPERATURE

To convert Fahrenheit (°F) to Celsius (°C): take number of °F and subtract 32; multiply result by 5; divide result by 9

To convert Celsius (°C) to Fahrenheit (°F): take number of °C and multiply by 9; divide result by 5; add 32 to total

Fahrenheit (F)		Celsius (C)		Fahrenheit (F)		Celsius (C)		Fahrenheit (F)		Celsius (C)	
°F	°C	°C	°F	°F	°C	°C	°F	°F	°C	°C	°F
−40	−40	−38	−36.4	80	26.7	18	64.4	215	101.7	80	176
−35	−37.2	−36	−32.8	85	29.4	20	68	220	104.4	85	185
−30	−34.4	−34	−29.2	90	32.2	22	71.6	225	107.2	90	194
−25	−31.7	−32	−25.6	95	35.0	24	75.2	230	110.0	95	202
−20	−28.9	−30	−22	100	37.8	26	78.8	235	112.8	100	212
−15	−26.1	−28	−18.4	105	40.6	28	82.4	240	115.6	105	221
−10	−23.3	−26	−14.8	110	43.3	30	86	245	118.3	110	230
−5	−20.6	−24	−11.2	115	46.1	32	89.6	250	121.1	115	239
0	−17.8	−22	−7.6	120	48.9	34	93.2	255	123.9	120	248
1	−17.2	−20	−4	125	51.7	36	96.8	260	126.6	125	257
2	−16.7	−18	−0.4	130	54.4	38	100.4	265	129.4	130	266
3	−16.1	−16	3.2	135	57.2	40	104	270	132.2	135	275
4	−15.6	−14	6.8	140	60.0	42	107.6	275	135.0	140	284
5	−15.0	−12	10.4	145	62.8	44	112.2	280	137.8	145	293
10	−12.2	−10	14	150	65.6	46	114.8	285	140.6	150	302
15	−9.4	−8	17.6	155	68.3	48	118.4	290	143.3	155	311
20	−6.7	−6	21.2	160	71.1	50	122	295	146.1	160	320
25	−3.9	−4	24.8	165	73.9	52	125.6	300	148.9	165	329
30	−1.1	−2	28.4	170	76.7	54	129.2	305	151.7	170	338
35	1.7	0	32	175	79.4	56	132.8	310	154.4	175	347
40	4.4	2	35.6	180	82.2	58	136.4	315	157.2	180	356
45	7.2	4	39.2	185	85.0	60	140	320	160.0	185	365
50	10.0	6	42.8	190	87.8	62	143.6	325	162.8	190	374
55	12.8	8	46.4	195	90.6	64	147.2	330	165.6	195	383
60	15.6	10	50	200	93.3	66	150.8	335	168.3	200	392
65	18.3	12	53.6	205	96.1	68	154.4	340	171.1	205	401
70	21.1	14	57.2	210	98.9	70	158	345	173.9	210	410
75	23.9	16	60.8	212	100.0	75	167	350	176.7	215	414

TCCS1C01

ENGLISH TO METRIC CONVERSION: LENGTH

To convert inches (ins.) to millimeters (mm): multiply number of inches by 25.4

To convert millimeters (mm) to inches (ins.): multiply number of millimeters by .04

Inches	Decimals	Milli-meters	Inches to millimeters — inches	mm	Inches	Decimals	Milli-meters	Inches to millimeters — inches	mm
1/64	0.051625	0.3969	0.0001	0.00254	33/64	0.515625	13.0969	0.6	15.24
1/32	0.03125	0.7937	0.0002	0.00508	17/32	0.53125	13.4937	0.7	17.78
3/64	0.046875	1.1906	0.0003	0.00762	35/64	0.546875	13.8906	0.8	20.32
1/16	0.0625	1.5875	0.0004	0.01016	9/16	0.5625	14.2875	0.9	22.86
5/64	0.078125	1.9844	0.0005	0.01270	37/64	0.578125	14.6844	1	25.4
3/32	0.09375	2.3812	0.0006	0.01524	19/32	0.59375	15.0812	2	50.8
7/64	0.109375	2.7781	0.0007	0.01778	39/64	0.609375	15.4781	3	76.2
1/8	0.125	3.1750	0.0008	0.02032	5/8	0.625	15.8750	4	101.6
9/64	0.140625	3.5719	0.0009	0.02286	41/64	0.640625	16.2719	5	127.0
5/32	0.15625	3.9687	0.001	0.0254	21/32	0.65625	16.6687	6	152.4
11/64	0.171875	4.3656	0.002	0.0508	43/64	0.671875	17.0656	7	177.8
3/16	0.1875	4.7625	0.003	0.0762	11/16	0.6875	17.4625	8	203.2
13/64	0.203125	5.1594	0.004	0.1016	45/64	0.703125	17.8594	9	228.6
7/32	0.21875	5.5562	0.005	0.1270	23/32	0.71875	18.2562	10	254.0
15/64	0.234375	5.9531	0.006	0.1524	47/64	0.734375	18.6531	11	279.4
1/4	0.25	6.3500	0.007	0.1778	3/4	0.75	19.0500	12	304.8
17/64	0.265625	6.7469	0.008	0.2032	49/64	0.765625	19.4469	13	330.2
9/32	0.28125	7.1437	0.009	0.2286	25/32	0.78125	19.8437	14	355.6
19/64	0.296875	7.5406	0.01	0.254	51/64	0.796875	20.2406	15	381.0
5/16	0.3125	7.9375	0.02	0.508	13/16	0.8125	20.6375	16	406.4
21/64	0.328125	8.3344	0.03	0.762	53/64	0.828125	21.0344	17	431.8
11/32	0.34375	8.7312	0.04	1.016	27/32	0.84375	21.4312	18	457.2
23/64	0.359375	9.1281	0.05	1.270	55/64	0.859375	21.8281	19	482.6
3/8	0.375	9.5250	0.06	1.524	7/8	0.875	22.2250	20	508.0
25/64	0.390625	9.9219	0.07	1.778	57/64	0.890625	22.6219	21	533.4
13/32	0.40625	10.3187	0.08	2.032	29/32	0.90625	23.0187	22	558.8
27/64	0.421875	10.7156	0.09	2.286	59/64	0.921875	23.4156	23	584.2
7/16	0.4375	11.1125	0.1	2.54	15/16	0.9375	23.8125	24	609.6
29/64	0.453125	11.5094	0.2	5.08	61/64	0.953125	24.2094	25	635.0
15/32	0.46875	11.9062	0.3	7.62	31/32	0.96875	24.6062	26	660.4
31/64	0.484375	12.3031	0.4	10.16	63/64	0.984375	25.0031	27	690.6
1/2	0.5	12.7000	0.5	12.70					

ENGLISH TO METRIC CONVERSION: TORQUE

To convert foot-pounds (ft. lbs.) to Newton-meters: multiply the number of ft. lbs. by 1.3

To convert inch-pounds (in. lbs.) to Newton-meters: multiply the number of in. lbs. by .11

in lbs	N-m	in lbs	N-m	in lbs	N-m	in lbs	N-m	in lbs	N-m
0.1	0.01	1	0.11	10	1.13	19	2.15	28	3.16
0.2	0.02	2	0.23	11	1.24	20	2.26	29	3.28
0.3	0.03	3	0.34	12	1.36	21	2.37	30	3.39
0.4	0.04	4	0.45	13	1.47	22	2.49	31	3.50
0.5	0.06	5	0.56	14	1.58	23	2.60	32	3.62
0.6	0.07	6	0.68	15	1.70	24	2.71	33	3.73
0.7	0.08	7	0.78	16	1.81	25	2.82	34	3.84
0.8	0.09	8	0.90	17	1.92	26	2.94	35	3.95
0.9	0.10	9	1.02	18	2.03	27	3.05	36	4.0

2

ENGINE PERFORMANCE AND TUNE-UP

GASOLINE ENGINE TUNE-UP PROCEDURES

The tune-up is a routine maintenance procedure which is essential for the efficient and economical operation of your vehicle's engine. Regular tune-ups will also help prolong the life of the engine. A gasoline engine tune-up should include the following:

- Clean or replace the spark plugs.
- Check the condition of the spark plug wires, distributor cap and rotor.
- Replace the ignition points and condenser.
- Adjust the valve clearance.
- Replace the fuel filter.
- Check the idle speed and mixture.

➡**Volkswagen recommends a tune-up service every 15,000 miles (24,000 km). Keep in mind that not all of these procedures may be applicable to your car and not all procedures are performed at each interval. For example, the valves are not adjustable on all engines and it may not be necessary to replace the fuel filter at every interval. Refer to Section 1 for additional information of the services performed during this maintenance interval.**

During the tune-up, it is a good idea to look around the engine compartment for problem areas and head them off before they get expensive. Look for fuel, oil and coolant leaks, deteriorating radiator and heater hoses, loose and/or frayed belts. These little items have the ability to develop into major headaches.

Spark Plugs

In addition to igniting the air/fuel mixture, the spark plugs in your engine can also serve as useful diagnostic tools. Once removed, compare your spark plugs with the samples illustrated in this section. Typical plug conditions are shown along with their causes and remedies. Most plugs which exhibit only normal wear and deposits can be cleaned, regapped, and installed. However, it is a good practice to replace them at every tune-up.

On some later models, Volkswagen installs Bosch Platinum spark plugs at the factory. These have a center electrode made of platinum wire that is completely sheathed in porcelain. The grounding electrode usually does not wear away as on standard spark plugs and its hard to tell when they are worn. Even though they tend to be more expensive, these and other platinum spark plugs are designed to last at least 30,000 miles (48,000 km). If these plugs are replaced with standard spark plugs, keep in mind that they will not last as long.

REMOVAL, INSPECTION & INSTALLATION

▶ **See Figures 1 thru 6**

➡**The cylinder head is aluminum, which is easily damaged and whose threads are easily stripped. Remove plugs only when the engine is cold.**

1. If compressed air is available, blow any dirt off the cylinder head where the spark plugs seat.
2. On 16-valve engines, pull straight up on the plastic loop attached to one of the spark plug wires. Remove the loop and use it to pull off the remaining wires.
3. On 8-valve engines, disconnect the plug wires by grasping the boot or metal shield, don't pull on the wire. Mark the cylinder number on the boot.
4. Remove the plugs with a spark plug socket and extension. If removal is difficult, loosen the plug slightly and drip a some penetrating oil onto the

Fig. 1 When disconnecting the plug wires, grasp the boot or the metal shield, don't pull on the wire itself

Fig. 2 An extension can be helpful when removing the spark plugs

Fig. 3 Be careful not to let any dirt from around the plug fall in the engine—it's best to clean the area before removal

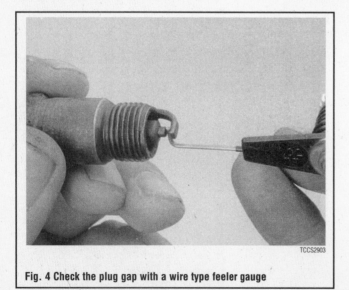

Fig. 4 Check the plug gap with a wire type feeler gauge

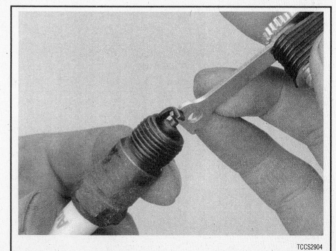

Fig. 5 Adjust the spark plug gap by carefully bending the side electrode

A **normally worn** spark plug should have light tan or gray deposits on the firing tip.

A **physically damaged** spark plug may be evidence of severe detonation in that cylinder. Watch that cylinder carefully between services, as a continued detonation will not only damage the plug, but could also damage the engine.

An **oil fouled** spark plug indicates an engine with worn poston rings and/or bad valve seals allowing excessive oil to enter the chamber.

This spark plug has been **left in the engine too long,** as evidenced by the extreme gap- Plugs with such an extreme gap can cause misfiring and stumbling accompanied by a noticeable lack of power.

A **carbon fouled** plug, identified by soft, sooty, black deposits, may indicate an improperly tuned vehicle. Check the air cleaner, ignition components and engine control system.

A **bridged or almost bridged** spark plug, identified by a build-up between the electrodes caused by excessive carbon or oil build-up on the plug.

TCCA1P40

Fig. 6 Inspect the spark plug to determine engine running conditions

threads. Allow the oil time to work, then unscrew the plug. This will help prevent thread damage in the cylinder head. Examine each spark plug.

To install:

5. If the same plugs are to be installed again, clean them.

6. Check and adjust the gap. This includes both old and new spark plugs. Never rely on "pre-gapped" plugs.

7. When installing a steel spark plug into an aluminum cylinder head, apply a drop of oil to the plug threads. This can help prevent the dissimilar metals from seizing, which would damage the head next time the plugs are removed. Make sure no oil gets on the electrode or porcelain.

8. Torque the spark plugs to 15 ft. lbs. (20 Nm). Do not overtighten or the threads in the head will be damaged.

9. Reconnect the wires in the correct order.

Spark Plug Wires

TESTING

♦ See Figure 7

Visually inspect the spark plug cables for burns, cuts, or breaks in the insulation. Check the spark plug boots and the nipples on the distributor cap and coil. Replace any damaged wiring. If no physical damage is obvious, the wires can be checked with an ohmmeter for excessive resistance.

Remove the distributor cap and leave the wires connected to the cap. Connect one lead of the ohmmeter to the corresponding electrode inside the cap and the other lead to the spark plug terminal (remove it from the spark plug for the test). Replace any wire which shows over 50,000 ohms. Generally speaking, however, resistance should not run over 35,000 ohms and 50,000 ohms should be considered the outer limit of acceptability. It should be remembered that wire resistance is a function of length. The longer the cable, the greater the resistance. Thus, if the cables on your car are longer than the factory originals, resistance will be higher and quite possibly outside of these limits.

REMOVAL & INSTALLATION

If the wires are being replaced, remove one wire and match the length with the new wire. Install the new wire before removing the next old one. If the wires are to be reinstalled, label and remove them one at a time from the distributor cap before disconnecting them from the spark plugs.

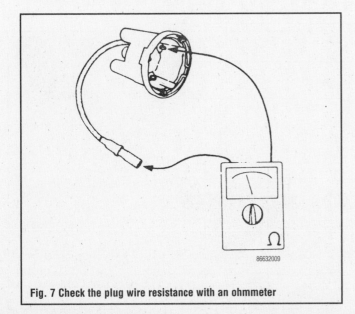

86632009

Fig. 7 Check the plug wire resistance with an ohmmeter

GASOLINE ENGINE TUNE-UP SPECIFICATIONS

Year	Engine ID/VIN	Spark Plugs Gap (In.)	Distributor Dwell (deg.)	Distributor Gap (In.)	Ignition Timing (deg.)	Fuel Pump (psi)	Idle Speed (rpm)	Compression Pressure (psi)	Valve Clearance In.	Valve Clearance Ex.
1983	WE	0.024-0.032	Electronic		6 BTDC [3]	68-78	750-850	145-203	0.008-0.012	0.016-0.020
	KM	0.024-0.032	Electronic		6 BTDC [3]	68-78	730-870	131-174	0.008-0.012	0.016-0.020
	KX, JT	0.024-0.032	Electronic		6 BTDC	75-82	750-850	131-174	0.008-0.012	0.016-0.020
	JH	0.024-0.032	Electronic		6 BTDC	64-74	875-1,000	131-174	0.008-0.012	0.016-0.020
	FX	0.024-0.032	Electronic		7 BTDC	N/A	800-1,000	131-174	0.008-0.012	0.016-0.020
1984	EN	0.024-0.032	Electronic		6 BTDC [2]	64-74	850-1,000	131-174	0.008-0.012	0.016-0.020
	WT	0.024-0.032	Electronic		6 BTDC [2]	68-77	850-1,000	123-174	0.008-0.012	0.016-0.020
	JN	0.024-0.032	Electronic		6 BTDC	75-82	850-1,000	123-174	0.008-0.012	0.016-0.020
	WE	0.024-0.032	Electronic		6 BTDC [3]	68-78	750-850	145-203	0.008-0.012	0.016-0.020
	KM	0.024-0.032	Electronic		6 BTDC [3]	68-78	730-870	131-174	0.008-0.012	0.016-0.020
	KX, JT	0.024-0.032	Electronic		6 BTDC	75-82	750-850	131-174	0.008-0.012	0.016-0.020
	JH	0.024-0.032	Electronic		6 BTDC	64-74	875-1,000	131-174	0.008-0.012	0.016-0.020
1985	JN	0.024-0.032	Electronic		6 BTDC	75-82	850-1,000	123-174	0.008-0.012	0.016-0.020
	KX, JT	0.024-0.032	Electronic		6 BTDC	75-82	850-1,000	131-174	0.008-0.012	0.016-0.020
	JH	0.024-0.032	Electronic		6 BTDC	68-77	850-1,000	131-174	0.008-0.012	0.016-0.020
	GX, MZ	0.024-0.031	Electronic		6 BTDC [4]	68-77	800-1,000	131-174	0.008-0.012	0.016-0.020
1986	HT	0.028-0.032	Electronic		6 BTDC	75-82	800-900	145-189	0.008-0.012	0.016-0.020
	GX, MZ	0.024-0.031	Electronic		6 BTDC [4]	68-77	800-1,000	131-174	0.008-0.012	0.016-0.020
	HT, RD	0.028-0.032	Electronic		6 BTDC	75-82	800-900	145-189	Hyd.	Hyd.
	KX, JT	0.024-0.032	Electronic		6 BTDC	75-82	750-850	131-174	Hyd.	Hyd.
	JN	0.024-0.032	Electronic		6 BTDC	75-82	850-1,000	123-174	Hyd.	Hyd.
	JH	0.024-0.032	Electronic		6 BTDC	68-77	850-1,000	131-174	Hyd.	Hyd.
	PL	0.027-0.035	Electronic		6 BTDC	75-81	800-900	145-189	Hyd.	Hyd.

86632301

GASOLINE ENGINE TUNE-UP SPECIFICATIONS

Year	Engine ID/VIN	Spark Plugs Gap (In.)	Distributor Dwell (deg.)	Distributor Gap (In.)	Ignition Timing (deg.)	Fuel Pump (psi)	Idle Speed (rpm)	Compression Pressure (psi)	Valve Clearance In.	Valve Clearance Ex.
1974	XW, XV, XZ, XY	0.024-0.028	44-50	0.016	3 ATDC	N/A	850-1,000	142-184	0.008-0.012	0.016-0.020
1975	YG, YH, XS, XR	0.024-0.028	44-50	0.016	3 ATDC	N/A	850-1,000	142-184	0.008-0.012	0.016-0.020
	FC, FG	0.024-0.032	44-50	0.016	3 ATDC	N/A	900-1,000	145-188	0.008-0.012	0.016-0.020
1976	YG, YH, YK	0.024-0.028	44-50	0.016	3 ATDC	64-74	850-1,000	142-184	0.008-0.012	0.016-0.020
	FN	0.024-0.032	44-50	0.016	3 ATDC	N/A	875-1,000	145-188	0.008-0.012	0.016-0.020
	EF, EE	0.024-0.032	44-50	0.016	3 ATDC	65-75	875-1,000	145-188	0.008-0.012	0.016-0.020
1977	YG, YH, YK	0.024-0.028	44-50	0.016	3 ATDC	64-74	850-1,000	142-184	0.008-0.012	0.016-0.020
	EF, EE	0.024-0.032	44-50	0.016	3 ATDC	65-75	850-1,000	145-188	0.008-0.012	0.016-0.020
1978	YG, YH, YK	0.024-0.028	44-50	0.016	3 ATDC	64-74	850-1,000	142-184	0.008-0.012	0.016-0.020
	EF, EE	0.024-0.032	44-50	0.016	3 ATDC	65-75	850-1,000	145-188	0.008-0.012	0.016-0.020
1979	YG, YH, YK	0.024-0.028	44-50	0.016	3 ATDC	64-74	850-1,000	142-184	0.008-0.012	0.016-0.020
	EH, EJ	0.024-0.032	44-50	0.016	3 ATDC	65-75	850-1,000	142-184	0.008-0.012	0.016-0.020
	FX	0.024-0.032	44-50	0.016 [1]	7 BTDC	N/A	800-1,000	145-189	0.008-0.012	0.016-0.020
1980	YG, YH, YK	0.024-0.028	44-50	0.016 [1]	3 ATDC	64-74	850-1,000	142-184	0.008-0.012	0.016-0.020
	EH, EJ	0.024-0.032	44-50	0.016 [1]	3 ATDC	65-75	850-1,000	145-189	0.008-0.012	0.016-0.020
	FX	0.024-0.032	44-50	0.016 [1]	7 BTDC	N/A	800-1,000	145-189	0.008-0.012	0.016-0.020
1981	EN, EJ	0.024-0.032	Electronic		3 ATDC	64-74	850-1,000	131-174	0.008-0.012	0.016-0.020
	FX	0.024-0.032	Electronic		7 BTDC	N/A	800-1,000	131-174	0.008-0.012	0.016-0.020
1982	EN, EJ	0.024-0.032	Electronic		3 ATDC	64-74	850-1,000	131-174	0.008-0.012	0.016-0.020
	WT	0.024-0.032	Electronic		3 ATDC	68-77	850-1,000	123-174	0.008-0.012	0.016-0.020
	FX	0.024-0.032	Electronic		7 BTDC	N/A	800-1,000	131-174	0.008-0.012	0.016-0.020
1983	EN	0.024-0.032	Electronic		6 BTDC [2]	64-74	850-1,000	131-174	0.008-0.012	0.016-0.020
	WT	0.024-0.032	Electronic		6 BTDC [2]	68-77	850-1,000	123-174	0.008-0.012	0.016-0.020

86632300

GASOLINE ENGINE TUNE-UP SPECIFICATIONS

Year	Engine ID/VIN	Spark Plugs Gap (in.)	Distributor Dwell (deg.)	Distributor Gap (in.)	Ignition Timing (deg.)	Fuel Pump (psi)	Idle Speed (rpm)	Compression Pressure (psi)	Valve Clearance In.	Valve Clearance Ex.
1987	GX, MZ	0.024-0.031	Electronic		6 BTDC	68-77 [4]	800-1,000	131-174	Hyd.	Hyd.
	RD	0.028-0.032	Electronic		6 BTDC	75-82	800-900	145-189	Hyd.	Hyd.
	KX, JT	0.024-0.032	Electronic		6 BTDC	75-82	750-850	131-174	Hyd.	Hyd.
	JN	0.024-0.032	Electronic		6 BTDC	75-82 [5]	850-1,000 [6]	123-174 [7]	Hyd.	Hyd.
	UM	0.024-0.032	Electronic		6 BTDC	75-82 [5]	800-1,000	131-174	Hyd.	Hyd.
	JH	0.024-0.032	Electronic		6 BTDC	68-77	850-1,000	131-174	Hyd.	Hyd.
	PL	0.027-0.035	Electronic		6 BTDC	75-81	800-900	145-189	Hyd.	Hyd.
1988	RV, PF	0.024-0.032	Electronic		6 BTDC	36	770-870	145-189	Hyd.	Hyd.
	KX, JT	0.024-0.032	Electronic		6 BTDC	75-82	750-850	131-174	Hyd.	Hyd.
	JN	0.024-0.032	Electronic		6 BTDC	75-82 [5]	850-1,000	123-174 [7]	Hyd.	Hyd.
	UM	0.024-0.032	Electronic		6 BTDC	75-82 [5]	800-1,000	131-174	Hyd.	Hyd.
	JH	0.024-0.032	Electronic		6 BTDC	68-77	850-1,000	131-174	Hyd.	Hyd.
	PL	0.027-0.035	Electronic		6 BTDC	75-81	800-900	145-189	Hyd.	Hyd.
1989	RV, PF	0.024-0.032	Electronic		6 BTDC	36	770-870	145-189	Hyd.	Hyd.
	JN	0.024-0.032	Electronic		6 BTDC	75-82 [5]	800-1,000	131-174	Hyd.	Hyd.
	UM	0.024-0.032	Electronic		6 BTDC	75-82 [5]	800-1,000	131-174	Hyd.	Hyd.
	JH	0.024-0.032	Electronic		6 BTDC	68-77	850-1,000	131-174	Hyd.	Hyd.
	PL	0.027-0.035	Electronic		6 BTDC	75-81	800-900	145-189	Hyd.	Hyd.

NOTE: The Vehicle Emission Control Information label often reflects specification changes made during production. The label figures must be used if they differ from those in this chart.

1. California models are equipped with electronic ignition
2. Applies to manual transaxles. Automatic transaxle: 3 ATDC
3. Canada models: 3/3 ATDC
4. Applies to CIS models. CIS-E models: 75-82
5. Applies to CIS-E models. CIS models: 68-78
6. 800-1,000 on Fox
7. 131-174 on Fox

86632302

DIESEL ENGINE TUNE-UP PROCEDURES

The only tune-up procedures for diesel engines are to change the fuel filter, drain the water separator and check engine speed. If the injection pump or timing belt have been removed, pump timing must also be adjusted (see Section 5). See Section 1 for filter and water separator service.

Fuel System Service Precautions

• Do not allow fuel spray or vapors to contact a heating element or open flame. DO NOT smoke while working on the vehicle.

• Always relieve the fuel system pressure prior to disconnecting any fitting or fuel line connection.

• To control spray when relieving system pressure, place a rag around the fitting before loosening it. Ensure that all fuel spillage is quickly wiped up and all fuel soaked rags are deposited into a proper fire safety container.

• Always keep a dry chemical (Class B) fire extinguisher near the work area.

• Always use a backup wrench when loosening/tightening line fittings. Always follow torque specifications.

• Do not re-use fuel system gaskets and O-rings. Do not substitute fuel hose where pipe is installed.

• Cleanliness is absolutely essential. Clean all fittings before opening and maintain a dust free work area.

• Place parts on a clean surface and cover with paper or plastic to keep them clean. Do not cover with rags that may leave fuzz.

DIESEL ENGINE TUNE-UP SPECIFICATIONS

Year	Engine ID/VIN	Engine Displacement Liter (cu. in.)	Valve Clearance Intake (in.)	Valve Clearance Exhaust (in.)	Injection Pump Setting (deg.)	Injection Nozzle Pressure (psi) New	Injection Nozzle Pressure (psi) Used	Idle Speed (rpm)	Cranking Compression Pressure (psi)
1977	CK	1.5 (90)	0.008-0.012	0.016-0.020	Align Marks	1849	1706	770-870	406-493
1978	CK	1.5 (90)	0.008-0.012	0.016-0.020	Align Marks	1849	1706	770-870	406-493
1979	CK	1.5 (90)	0.008-0.012	0.016-0.020	Align Marks	1849	1706	770-870	406-493
1980	CK	1.5 (90)	0.008-0.012	0.016-0.020	Align Marks	1849	1706	770-870	406-493
1981	CK	1.5 (90)	0.008-0.012	0.016-0.020	Align Marks	1849	1706	770-870	406-493
	CR	1.6 (97)	0.008-0.012	0.016-0.020	Align Marks	1885	1740	770-870	406-493
1982	CR	1.6 (97)	0.008-0.012	0.016-0.020	Align Marks	1885	1740	770-870	406-493
	CY	1.6 (97)	0.008-0.012	0.016-0.020	Align Marks	2248-2364	2030-2200	810-950	406-493
1983	CR	1.6 (97)	0.008-0.012	0.016-0.020	Align Marks	1885	1740	810-950	406-493
	JK	1.6 (97)	0.008-0.012	0.016-0.020	Align Marks	1885	1740	810-950	406-493
	CY	1.6 (97)	0.008-0.012	0.016-0.020	Align Marks	2248-2364	2030-2200	810-950	406-493
1984	CR	1.6 (97)	0.008-0.012	0.016-0.020	Align Marks	1885	1740	810-950	406-493
	JK	1.6 (97)	0.008-0.012	0.016-0.020	Align Marks	1885	1740	810-950	406-493
	CY	1.6 (97)	0.008-0.012	0.016-0.020	Align Marks	2248-2364	2030-2200	810-950	406-493
1985	MD	1.6 (97)	0.008-0.012	0.016-0.020	Align Marks	2318	2204	900-980	406-493
	ME	1.6 (97)	0.008-0.012	0.016-0.020	Align Marks	1885-2001	1740	920-980	406-493
	MF	1.6 (97)	0.008-0.012	0.016-0.020	Align Marks	2248-2364	2030	920-980	406-493
1986	ME	1.6 (97)	Hyd.	Hyd.	Align Marks	1885-2001	1740	920-980	406-493
	MF	1.6 (97)	Hyd.	Hyd.	Align Marks	2248-2364	2030	920-980	406-493
1987	ME	1.6 (97)	Hyd.	Hyd.	Align Marks	1885-2001	1740	920-980	406-493
1988	ME	1.6 (97)	Hyd.	Hyd.	Align Marks	1885-2001	1740	920-980	406-493
1989	ME	1.6 (97)	Hyd.	Hyd.	Align Marks	1885-2001	1740	920-980	406-493

NOTE: The Vehicle Emission Control Information label often reflects specification changes made during production. The label figures must be used if they differ from those in this chart

86632303

Engine Speed

ADJUSTMENT

♦ **See Figures 8 and 9**

Diesel engines have both idle and maximum speed adjustments. The maximum speed adjustment prevents the engine from over-revving when the control lever is in the full speed position and there is no load on the engine. No increase in power is available through this adjustment. The adjusters are located side-by-side on top of the injection pump. The screw closest to the engine is for low-idle, the outer screw is for high speed.

Because the diesel engine does not have a conventional ignition system, you may need a special adapter (VW 1324) to use some tachometers. Do not rely on the tachometer in the instrument panel (if so equipped), as they are notorious for being inaccurate. You should check with the manufacturer of your tachometer to see if it is compatible with diesel engines.

1. Connect a suitable diesel engine tachometer as per the manufacturer's instructions.

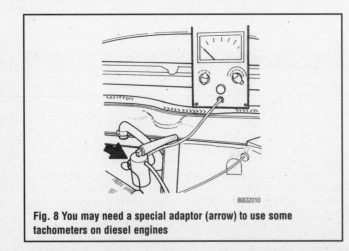

Fig. 8 You may need a special adaptor (arrow) to use some tachometers on diesel engines

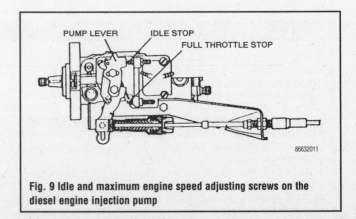

Fig. 9 Idle and maximum engine speed adjusting screws on the diesel engine injection pump

2. Run the engine to normal operating temperature and turn off all electrical accessories.

3. If equipped, make sure the manual cold start knob or idle boost is pushed in all the way.

4. Loosen the locknut and set the low idle to specification (refer to the tune-up chart or the underhood sticker). When set properly, there should be little or no vibration.

5. When tightening the locknut, apply a thread sealer (Loctite® or similar) to prevent the screw from vibrating loose.

6. Advance the control lever (throttle) to full speed. The maximum speed for engines through 1980 is 5,500–5,600 rpm. From 1981 on, the maximum speed is 5,300–5,400 rpm for normally aspirated engines or 5,050–5,150 on turbo engines. If not in this range, loosen the screw and correct the speed (turning the screw clockwise decreases rpm).

7. Lock the adjusting screw nut and apply thread sealer.

➡Do not attempt to squeeze more power out of your engine by raising the maximum speed. This will not increase power, and will more likely result in the need for a major overhaul in the not too distant future.

FIRING ORDERS

▶ See Figures 10 and 11

➡ALWAYS remove the wires one at a time and/or label them for correct installation.

If a distributor is not keyed for installation with only one orientation, it could have been removed previously and rewired. The resultant wiring would hold the

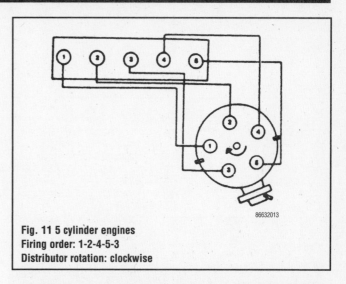

Fig. 11 5 cylinder engines
Firing order: 1-2-4-5-3
Distributor rotation: clockwise

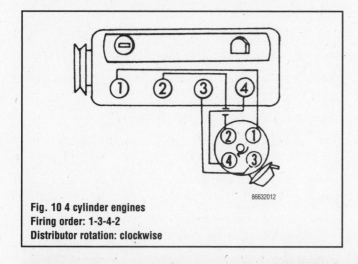

Fig. 10 4 cylinder engines
Firing order: 1-3-4-2
Distributor rotation: clockwise

correct firing order, but could change the relative placement of the plug towers in relation to the engine. For this reason it is imperative that you label all wires before disconnecting any of them. Also, before removal, compare the current wiring with the accompanying illustrations. If the current wiring does not match, make notes in your book to reflect how your engine is wired.

POINT TYPE IGNITION

Description and Operation

▶ See Figures 12 and 13

The points function as a circuit breaker for the primary circuit of the ignition system. The ignition coil must boost the 12 volts of electrical pressure supplied by the battery to as much as 25,000 volts in order to fire the plugs. To do this, the coil depends on the points and the condenser to make a clean break in the primary circuit.

The coil has both primary and secondary circuits. When the ignition is turned **ON**, the battery supplies voltage through the coil and onto the points; which are connected to ground, completing the primary circuit. As the current passes through the coil, a magnetic field is created in the iron center core of the coil. When the cam in the distributor turns, the points open, breaking the primary circuit of the coil which then collapses and cuts through the secondary circuit windings around the iron core. Due to electromagnetic induction, the battery voltage is increased to a level sufficient to fire the spark plugs.

When the points open, the electrical charge in the primary circuit tries to jump the gap created between the two open contacts of the points. If this electrical charge were not transferred elsewhere, the metal contacts of the points would start to wear rapidly. The function of the condenser is to absorb excessive voltage from the points when they open and thus prevent the points from becoming pitted or burned.

There are two ways to check to check breaker point gap: with a feeler gauge or with a dwell meter. Either way you set the points, you are adjusting the amount of time (in degrees of distributor rotation) that the points will remain

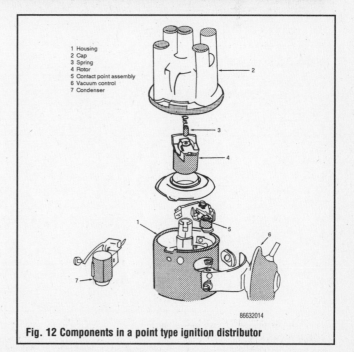

1 Housing
2 Cap
3 Spring
4 Rotor
5 Contact point assembly
6 Vacuum control
7 Condenser

Fig. 12 Components in a point type ignition distributor

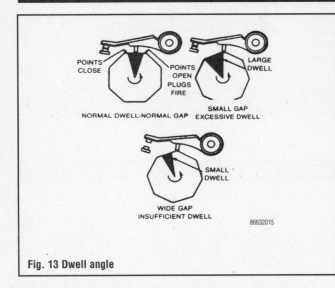

Fig. 13 Dwell angle

open. If you adjust the points with a feeler gauge, you are setting the maximum amount the points will open when the rubber block on the points is on a high point of the distributor cam. When you adjust the points with a dwell meter, you are measuring the number of degrees (of distributor cam rotation) that the points will remain closed before they start to open as a high point of the distributor cam approaches the rubbing block of the points.

There are two rules that should always be followed when adjusting or replacing the points. The points and condenser are a matched set; never replace one without replacing the other. If you change point gap or dwell of the engine, you also change the ignition timing. Therefore, if you adjust the points, you must also adjust the timing.

Testing

IGNITION COIL

▶ **See Figures 14 and 15**

1. Label and disconnect all wires from the ignition coil.
2. With an ohmmeter, measure between terminals 15 and 1 (primary resistance). Check that the ohmmeter reading is between 1.7–2.1 ohms. If not, replace the coil.
3. Measure the resistance between terminals 1 and 4 (secondary resistance). The reading should be between 7,000–12,000 ohms. If not, replace the coil.

BALLAST RESISTOR & RESISTOR WIRE

The ballast resistor was replaced with a resistor wire in 1976. It runs from terminal 15 (+) of the ignition coil to terminal C15 at the back of the fuse block/relay panel. The color of the resistor wire is usually clear with violet stripes.

The old type ballast resistor can also be checked using this method. Before checking, disconnect all wires from the ballast resistor, then measure across the terminals. It should have the same resistance value as those listed for the resistor wire. If not, replace the resistor.

1. Unplug multi-pin connector C from the fuse/relay panel.
2. Unplug the resistor wire from the ignition coil terminal 15.
3. Connect an ohmmeter to each end of the wire (terminal C15 at the fuse/relay panel).
4. The resistance should be between 0.85–0.95 ohms for the Rabbit, Golf, Jetta and Scirocco and approximately 0.9 ohms for Dasher. If not, replace the wire.

Parts Replacement

DISTRIBUTOR CAP

▶ **See Figure 16**

1. Disconnect the negative battery cable.
2. Disconnect the high tension wire which runs between the distributor and the ignition coil.
3. If equipped, remove the metal static shield which is fitted around the distributor cap. Remove the shield by twisting it and pulling it upward and over the cap. It may be necessary to disconnect a ground strap and suppressor lead on some models.
4. Match the position of the new cap with the old cap. Unplug the ignition wires (one at a time) from the old cap and plug them into the new cap.
5. The distributor cap is held down by two spring clips. Insert a screwdriver under their ends and release them. Lift off the cap.

To install:

6. Position the new cap onto the distributor and engage the spring clips.
7. If equipped, install the metal static shield. Connect the ignition coil wire to the cap.
8. Connect the negative battery cable.

ROTOR

1. Remove the distributor cap.
2. Pull the rotor off the distributor shaft.

To install:

3. Slide the new rotor onto the shaft.
4. Install the distributor cap.

BREAKER POINTS AND CONDENSER

▶ **See Figures 17, 18 and 19**

1. Disconnect the negative battery cable.
2. Make sure the ignition switch is in the **OFF** position.
3. Disconnect the high tension wire which runs between the distributor and the ignition coil.

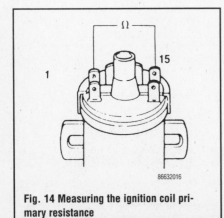

Fig. 14 Measuring the ignition coil primary resistance

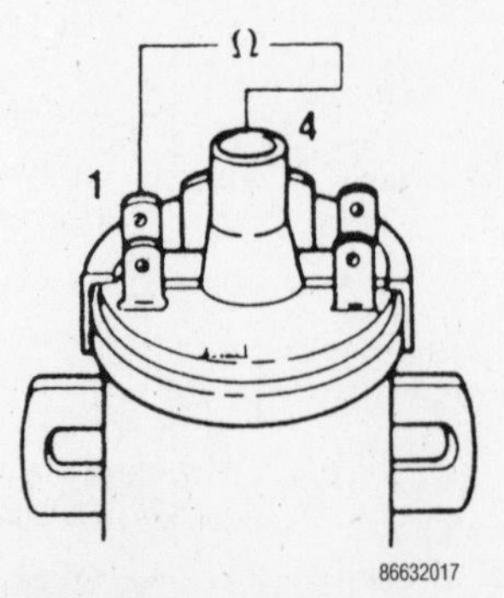

Fig. 15 Measuring the ignition coil secondary resistance

Fig. 16 On some models it will be necessary to remove the static shield—but first remember to disconnect any ground straps or suppressor leads

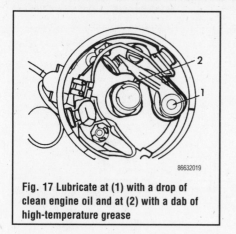

Fig. 17 Lubricate at (1) with a drop of clean engine oil and at (2) with a dab of high-temperature grease

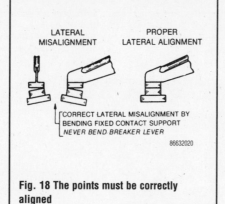

Fig. 18 The points must be correctly aligned

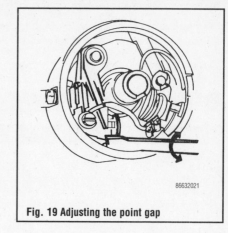

Fig. 19 Adjusting the point gap

4. If equipped, remove the metal static shield which is fitted around the distributor cap. Remove the shield by twisting it and pulling it upward and over the cap.

5. The distributor cap is retained by two spring clips. Insert a screwdriver under their ends and release them. Lift off the cap with the spark plug wires attached. Wipe the inside of the cap clean with a rag and check for burned contacts, cracks or carbon tracks. Carbon tracks are dark lines running from one terminal to another. They cannot be removed, so replace the cap if it has any tracks.

6. Remove the rotor from the distributor shaft by pulling it straight up. Examine the condition of the rotor, if it is cracked or if the metal tip is excessively worn or burned, it should be replaced. If not, clean the tip with a clean cloth.

➡ **Do not file the contact tip on the rotor.**

7. Remove the dust shield, then loosen the screws securing the points (if possible, use a magnetic screwdriver for removal to avoid losing a screw down into the distributor). Slide the point wire connector off of its terminal and remove the point set.

8. The condenser is located on the outside of the distributor body. Pull the wire connector coming from the suppressor off of the condenser terminal. Remove the screw that secures the condenser assembly to the distributor, then remove the assembly.

To install:

9. Before installing the new points and condenser, place a small dab of high-temperature grease on the distributor shaft, then smear it evenly around the cam. Install the new points and condenser. Tighten the condenser mounting screw but leave the points screws loose.

10. Make sure that the faces of the points meet squarely. If not, the fixed mount can be bent slightly with a little force and a pair of needle nose pliers. Do not bend the movable contact.

11. The point gap must be adjusted next. The gap is adjusted with the rubbing block of the points resting on one of the high spots of the distributor cam. To get it there, rotate the engine clockwise with a wrench on the crankshaft pulley bolt.

12. Insert a 0.017 in. (0.43mm) flat feeler gauge between the points. A slight drag should be felt. If no drag can be felt, or if the gauge can't be inserted at all, insert a screwdriver into the notch provided for adjustment and use it to open or close the gap between the points until it is correct.

13. When you feel the gap is set, tighten the points screws and recheck the gap. Sometimes it takes three or four times to get it corrected, so don't feel frustrated if they seem to move around on you a little. It's not easy to feel the correct gap either. To check yourself, use gauges 0.002 in. (0.05mm) larger and smaller than the 0.016 in. (0.40mm) specification as a test. If the points are spread slightly by a 0.018 in. (0.45mm) gauge, but not touched at all by a 0.014 in. (0.35mm) gauge, the testing should be right.

14. After all the adjustments are complete, pull a clean piece of tissue or a piece of white paper between the contacts to clear away any bits of grit.

15. Install the dust cover, the rotor and the distributor cap. Snap on the spring clips, then install the static shield. If you have a dwell meter (using one is recommended for a finer adjustment), your next step should be to set the dwell. Otherwise, go on to set the ignition timing.

IGNITION COIL

1. Label and unplug the wires from the coil.

2. On some models, the coil is secured in a clamp. If so, loosen the screw, then slide the coil out from the clamp. Install the new coil, then tighten the screw until snug.

3. On other models, the coil is secured by bolts. On these models, remove the bolts, then replace the coil. Tighten the bolts until snug.

4. Connect the wires to the coil.

RESISTOR WIRE

1. Cut a new length of resistor wire to $50^{15}/_{16}$ in. (128cm). You must use resistor wire or ignition system damage could result.

2. Remove the bad resistor wire from multi-connector C at the fuse/relay panel.

3. Install the new resistor wire using terminal kit 000 097 002, available at your local VW dealer.

4. Route the new wire and connect it to the terminals.

Adjustments

DWELL

The dwell angle is the number of degrees of distributor cam rotation through which the points remain closed (conducting electricity). Increasing the point gap decreases dwell, while decreasing the gap increases dwell.

The dwell angle may be checked with the distributor cap and rotor installed and the engine running, or with the cap and rotor removed and the engine cranking at starter speed. The meter gives a constant reading with the engine running. With the engine cranking, the meter will fluctuate between zero dwell and the maximum figure for that setting.

❊❊ CAUTION

Keep your hands, hair and clothing clear of the engine fan and pulleys. Be sure the wires from the dwell meter are routed out of the way. If the engine is running, block the front wheels, put the transmission in N or P. Set the parking brake.

1. Connect a meter as per the manufacturer's instructions (usually one lead to the distributor's terminal of the coil and the other lead to a ground). Zero the meter, if necessary.

2. Check the dwell by either the cranking method, or by running the engine. If you are checking the dwell using the cranking method, do not operate the starter for more than 15 seconds at a time. Excessive cranking may cause starter damage. If the setting is not correct, the points must be adjusted.

❊❊ CAUTION

Never attempt to adjust the points when the ignition is ON. You may receive a mild shock.

3. To change the dwell angle, turn the ignition **OFF**. Loosen the points hold-down screw, then adjust the point gap; increase the gap to decrease dwell, and vice-versa. Tighten the hold down screw and check the dwell angle with the engine cranking. If it seems to be correct, install the cap and rotor, then check dwell with the engine running. Readjust as necessary.

4. Run the engine speed up to about 2,500 rpm, then let off on the accelerator pedal. The dwell reading should not change. If it does, a worn distributor shaft, bushing, cam, or breaker plate is indicted. The parts must be inspected and replaced as necessary.

5. After adjusting the dwell angle, go on to adjust the ignition timing.

ELECTRONIC IGNITION

Description and Operation

♦ See Figure 20

Electronic ignition systems offer many advantages over the conventional breaker point ignition system. By eliminating the points, maintenance requirements are greatly reduced. An electronic ignition system is capable of producing much higher voltage which in turn aids starting, reduces spark plug fouling and provides better emission control.

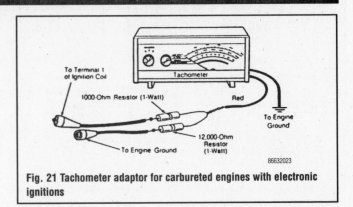

Fig. 21 Tachometer adaptor for carbureted engines with electronic ignitions

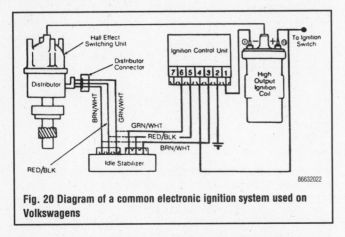

Fig. 20 Diagram of a common electronic ignition system used on Volkswagens

The Hall generator produces a voltage pulse which is sent to the control unit, which in turn switches the primary ignition circuit on and off. Located in the distributor, it consists of a trigger wheel that revolves with the distributor shaft and a stationary unit called the Hall sender. The Hall sender consists of a semiconductor layer positioned on a magnetically conducting element and a permanent magnet, both of which are separated by an air gap. When the trigger wheel shutter enters the air gap, it blocks the magnetic field and the Hall sender is shut off. When this occurs, the control unit will complete the primary circuit and you have the dwell period. When the shutter leaves the air gap, the magnetic field flows again. The Hall sender generates a voltage pulse to the control unit which will then interrupt the primary ignition circuit and ignition will occur.

In 1985, an electronic ignition system with a knock sensor was introduced on some engines. By using a knock sensor input, the ignition timing can be advanced while using a higher compression ratio. The engine can now operate closer to, but not in, the knock threshold where it will operate more efficiently with a higher power output.

Because temperature changes and engine load variations caused by different electrical accessories can affect idle speed, most systems use some type of idle stabilizer. Earlier systems use an electronic idle stabilization system. This system consists of a small control unit between the Hall generator and the Hall control unit. The frequency of the voltage signal sent from the Hall generator gives the idle stabilizer information on engine speed. When the idle stabilizer senses that the engine speed has dropped below a certain rpm, it will advance the timing, causing the idle speed to increase. The use of this electronic idle stabilizer system (which advanced timing to increase idle speed) was eliminated in 1985. On later models, idle stabilization is controlled by idle boost valves and/or idle air stabilizers which bypass additional air around the throttle plate at idle in order to increase engine speed.

Ignition System Precautions

♦ See Figure 21

• Make sure the ignition switch is **OFF** before connecting or disconnecting any wiring or test equipment.

• When cranking the engine without starting, as for a compression test, disconnect the high tension coil wire from distributor and ground it to the engine block or head.
• DO NOT install a standard ignition coil in the system.
• DO NOT connect a condenser/suppressor or powered test light to the negative terminal (1) of the ignition coil.
• DO NOT connect any 12-volt test instruments to the positive terminal (15) of the ignition coil. The electronic control unit will be permanently damaged.
• When jump starting with a booster, DO NOT connect a quick-charger for more than 1 minute, nor exceed 16.5 volts with the booster.
• An adaptor must be used when connecting a conventional tachometer to carbureted engines with electronic ignitions. Use the illustration as a guide to construct your own. The components should be available at your local electronics store. Connect the positive wire of the tachometer to the adapter and the negative wire to ground.
• Always switch the multimeter to the appropriate measuring range BEFORE making the test connections. Use a high-impedance digital multimeter which is designed for testing computerized electrical components.
• Do not use a standard test light (electric bulb type) on electronic circuits. The high electrical consumption of these test lights can lead to electronic component damage.
• Unless otherwise noted, always disconnect the main fuel injection harness on Digifant II engines if you must crank the engine during ignition system testing.

Diagnosis and Testing

➡These components must be tested using the order presented. Keep in mind that not all systems will use all of the components listed.

IGNITION COIL

♦ See Figure 22

Quantum, Fox and 1979–84 Rabbit, Scirocco and Jetta

1. Label and disconnect all wires from the ignition coil.
2. With an ohmmeter, measure between terminals 15 and 1 (primary resistance). Check that the ohmmeter reading is between 0.52–0.76 ohms. If not, replace the coil.
3. Measure the resistance between terminals 1 and 4 (secondary resistance). The reading should be between 2,400–3,500 ohms. If not, replace the coil.

1985–89 Scirocco, Cabriolet, Golf and Jetta

1. Label and disconnect all wires from the ignition coil.
2. With an ohmmeter, measure between terminals 15 and 1 (primary resistance). Check that the ohmmeter reads as follows. If not, replace the coil.

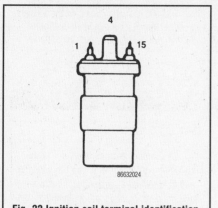

Fig. 22 Ignition coil terminal identification

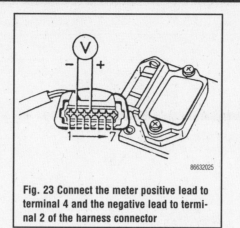

Fig. 23 Connect the meter positive lead to terminal 4 and the negative lead to terminal 2 of the harness connector

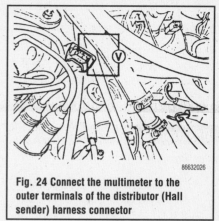

Fig. 24 Connect the multimeter to the outer terminals of the distributor (Hall sender) harness connector

- On CIS 8-valve engines—0.52–0.76 ohms
- On 16-valve engines—0.5–0.8 ohms (yellow and gray labels)
- On Digifant II 8-valve engines—0.6–0.8 ohms (gray label) 0.52–0.76 ohms (green label)

3. Measure the resistance between terminals 1 and 4 on CIS 8-valve engines with knock sensor systems, Measure between 15 and 4 on all others (secondary resistance). The reading should be as follows. If not, replace the coil.

- On CIS 8-valve engines—2,400–3,500 ohms
- On 16-valve engines—6,500–8,500 ohms (yellow label) 6,900–8,500 ohms (gray label)
- On Digifant II 8-valve engines—6,900–8,500 ohms (gray label) 2,400–3,500 ohms (green label)

HALL CONTROL UNIT

Except Digifant II and Knock Sensor Systems

♦ See Figures 23 and 24

1. Unplug the Hall control unit harness connector (at the control unit).
2. Using a digital multimeter switched to the 20V range, connect the meter positive lead to terminal 4 and the negative lead to terminal 2 of the harness connector.
3. Turn the ignition key to the **ON** position. The meter must read approximately battery voltage. If not, check for an open circuit in the wiring.
4. Turn the ignition to the **OFF** position. Reconnect the control unit harness.
5. Unplug the harness connector from the Hall sender at the distributor. Using a digital multimeter switched to the 20V range, connect the meter positive lead to terminal 15 and the negative lead to terminal 1 of the ignition coil.
6. Turn the ignition switch to the **ON** position. The meter must read a 2 volt minimum, then drop to 0 volts after 1–2 seconds. If not, replace the Hall control unit and the ignition coil.
7. Using a jumper wire, briefly touch the center wire of the harness connector to ground. Displayed voltage must rise briefly to 5–6 volts on Quantum and 1979–84 Rabbit, Scirocco and Jetta. Voltage must rise to a 2 volt minimum on other models. If not, determine if there is a open in the center wire.
8. Turn the ignition switch to the **OFF** position. Connect the multimeter to the outer terminals of the distributor (Hall sender) harness connector.
9. Turn the ignition switch **ON**, there must be a minimum of 5 volts.

Knock Sensor Systems

♦ See Figures 25 and 26

1. Unplug the Hall control unit harness connector (at the control unit).
2. Using a digital multimeter switched to the 20V range, connect the meter positive lead to terminal 4 and the negative lead to terminal 2 of the harness connector.
3. Turn the ignition key to the **ON** position. The meter must read approximately battery voltage. If not, check for an open circuit in the wiring.
4. Turn the ignition to the **OFF** position. Check the wire from terminal 1 on the harness connector to terminal 1 of the ignition coil for continuity using an ohmmeter. Reconnect the control unit harness.

5. Unplug the harness connector from the knock sensor control unit. Using a digital multimeter switched to the 20V range, connect the meter positive lead to terminal 15 and the negative lead to terminal 1 of the ignition coil.
6. Turn the ignition switch to the **ON** position. The meter must read a 2 volt minimum, then drop to 0 volts after 1–2 seconds. If not, replace the Hall control unit and inspect the ignition coil for fluid leakage. Replace, if leaking.
7. Using a jumper wire, briefly touch terminal 12 of the harness connector to ground. Displayed voltage must rise briefly to a 2 volt minimum. If not, replace the Hall control unit.

Digifant II

♦ See Figures 27 and 28

Before testing, visually inspect all components of the system. Replace any noticeably damaged parts. Be sure to check the ignition coil and replace if it is leaking fluid.

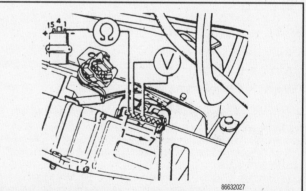

Fig. 25 Terminal identification and multimeter hook-up on the Hall control unit harness connector

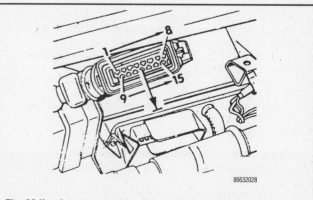

Fig. 26 Knock sensor control unit terminal identification

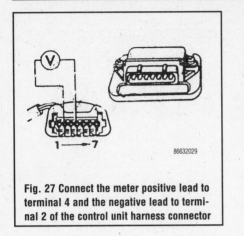

Fig. 27 Connect the meter positive lead to terminal 4 and the negative lead to terminal 2 of the control unit harness connector

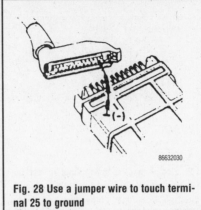

Fig. 28 Use a jumper wire to touch terminal 25 to ground

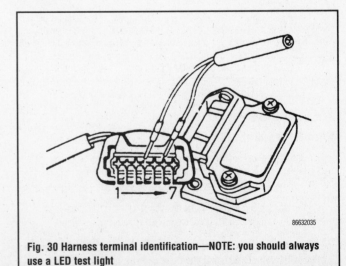

Fig. 29 Connect the positive lead of the multimeter to terminal 6 and the negative lead to terminal 3. Note that the rubber boot is folded back to allow access to the terminals

1. Unplug the Hall control unit harness connector (at the control unit).

2. Using a digital multimeter switched to the 20V range, connect the meter positive lead to terminal 4 and the negative lead to terminal 2 of the harness connector.

3. Turn the ignition key to the **ON** position. The meter must read approximately battery voltage. If not, check for an open circuit in the wiring.

4. Turn the ignition to the **OFF** position. Reconnect the control unit harness.

5. Unplug the harness connector from the Digifant control unit. Using a digital multimeter switched to the 20V range, connect the meter positive lead to terminal 15 and the negative lead to terminal 1 of the ignition coil. If necessary, unplug the wiring from ignition coil terminal 1, then reconnect it so that only the wire to the Hall control unit is engaged.

6. Turn the ignition switch to the **ON** position. The meter must read a 2 volt minimum, then drop to 0 volts after 1–2 seconds. If not, replace the Hall control unit.

7. Using a jumper wire, briefly touch terminal 25 of the Digifant control unit harness connector to ground. Displayed voltage must rise briefly to a 2 volt minimum.

8. Turn the ignition switch to the **OFF** position. Reconnect the control unit harness.

HALL SENDER

CIS and CIS-E Fuel Systems

QUANTUM, FOX AND 1979–84 RABBIT, SCIROCCO AND JETTA

▶ See Figure 29

1. If equipped, unplug the idle stabilizer (ignition advance type) plugs, then connect them together.

2. Unplug the high tension coil wire, then ground it using a jumper wire.

3. Slide the rubber boot away from the back of the Hall control unit harness connector (leave the harness engaged).

4. Using a digital multimeter switched on the 20V scale, connect the positive lead to terminal 6 and the negative lead to terminal 3. Turn the ignition switch **ON**.

5. Turn the engine slowly by hand in the direction of engine rotation. When the engine is rotating, the shutter of the trigger wheel will pass thorough the air gap of the Hall generator.

    a. On the Quantum, and 1979–84 Rabbit, Scirocco and Jetta, when the shutter is outside the air gap voltage should read between 0–0.7 volts. When the shutter is between the air gap, voltage should read from 1.8 volts through battery voltage.

    b. On Fox models, the display must alternate between 0 and 2 volts as the engine is being rotated.

6. If not, replace the Hall sender.

1985–89 GOLF, JETTA, SCIROCCO AND CABRIOLET

▶ See Figure 30

1. Unplug the harness from the Hall control unit.

2. Connect a LED test light to terminals 4 and 6 (on CIS) or 2 and 6 (on CIS-E) of the harness connector.

3. Operate the starter, the LED on the test light must flicker.

4. If not, replace the Hall sender.

Digifant II Fuel Systems

1. Unplug the Hall sender harness connector at the distributor.

2. Using a digital multimeter switched to the 20V range, measure the voltage between the outer terminals of the harness connector.

3. Turn the ignition switch to the **ON** position. There must be a minimum of 10 volts displayed. If not, check for an open circuit in the wiring and low battery voltage. If these are OK, replace the Digifant control unit.

4. Turn the ignition switch **OFF**. Unplug the main fuel injector harness connector. Push up the rubber boot (covering the Hall sender connector) to expose the terminals, then reconnect it to the distributor.

5. Connect a LED test light between the center terminal and either of the outer terminals. When the starter is operated, the LED should flicker, indicating a signal voltage is being generated by the Hall sender. If not, replace the distributor.

6. Connect a LED test light between terminals 1 and 15 of the ignition coil. If necessary, unplug the wiring from ignition coil terminal 1, then reconnect it so that only the wire to the Hall control unit is engaged.

7. When the starter is operated, the LED must flicker. If not, replace the control unit.

KNOCK SENSOR SYSTEMS

Control Unit

▶ See Figures 31, 32 and 33

1. Unplug the harness from the Hall control unit. Turn the ignition switch to the **ON** position.

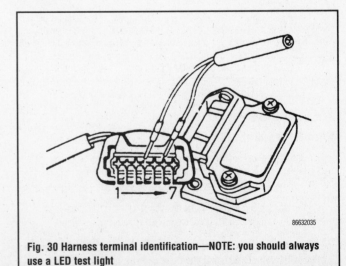

Fig. 30 Harness terminal identification—NOTE: you should always use a LED test light

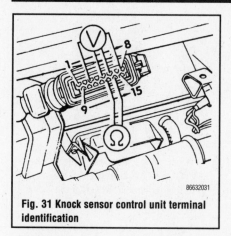

Fig. 31 Knock sensor control unit terminal identification

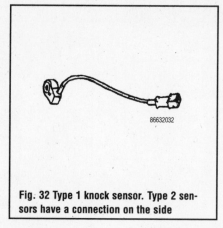

Fig. 32 Type 1 knock sensor. Type 2 sensors have a connection on the side

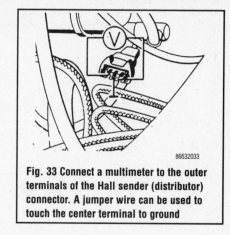

Fig. 33 Connect a multimeter to the outer terminals of the Hall sender (distributor) connector. A jumper wire can be used to touch the center terminal to ground

2. Using a digital multimeter switched on the 20V range, measure the voltage between terminals 3 and 5 of the harness. The meter display should read approximately battery voltage.

3. Measure between terminals 6 and 3. Once again, the display should read approximately battery voltage.

4. Open the throttle valve. The reading must drop to 0 volts. If not, check the throttle valve switch 1 (idle switch) for proper operation.

5. Measure voltage between terminals 8 and 3, while slowly opening the throttle valve. The reading should show approximately battery voltage. If not, check throttle valve switch 2 (full throttle switch).

6. Turn the ignition switch **OFF**. Measure resistance between terminals 13 and 14 with an ohmmeter. If equipped with knock sensor type 1, the meter display should read approximately 300k ohms. On type 2 sensors, the meter should display infinite resistance.

➡Type 1 sensors have a cable connection which is off center (see illustration). On type 2 sensors, the connection is from the side.

7. Reconnect the knock sensor control unit harness. Unplug the harness connector from the Hall sender at the distributor.

8. Connect the multimeter to the outer terminals of the connector. Turn the ignition switch **ON**. The meter display should read a minimum of 5 volts. Turn the ignition **OFF**.

9. Connect the multimeter between terminals 1 and 15 of the ignition coil. Turn the ignition switch **ON**. Use a jumper wire to touch the center terminal of the connector to ground. Voltage value must rise briefly to a minimum of 2 volts. If not, replace the Hall control unit.

Control Unit Vacuum Sensor and Hose

▶ **See Figure 34**

1. Engage a LED test light to test connector 1 (a single connector with a blue/brown lead) and the positive battery cable. The LED must light up.

2. Start the engine. The LED should go out, however a very slight glow is acceptable.

3. Increase the engine speed to over 3,000 rpm one time.

4. Connect a jumper wire from test connector 1 and hold it to ground for at least 3 seconds.

5. After that, the LED must begin blinking. Observe the following patterns:

• Blinking twice in intervals means there is a fault in the knock sensor (this can be due to a break in the wiring, the knock sensor bolt not torqued to specification or a defective knock sensor) or the knock sensor control unit may be defective.

• Blinking three times in intervals means a break in the vacuum hose to the knock sensor control unit or that the vacuum sensor in the knock sensor control unit is defective.

IDLE STABILIZER CONTROL UNIT

▶ **See Figure 35**

➡This applies only to ignition advance type idle stabilizers.

If the engine is difficult to start, does not start or misfires/cuts out, test the idle stabilizer as follows.

1. Disconnect the plugs from the stabilizer, then connect them together. Start the engine. If the troubles are now eliminated, check the contact pins and sockets of both idle stabilizer connectors for damage. If these are OK, the stabilizer control unit is probably defective.

2. Reconnect the plugs to the idle stabilizer. Run the engine until it reaches normal operating temperature. With all accessories off, make sure engine speed is below 1,000 rpm. Check the ignition timing and make a note of the reading.

3. Turn all electrical accessories ON except the air conditioning. Check the timing and compare it to the first reading. It must be advanced, if not, replace the stabilizer control unit.

➡On 1979–82 models, the idle speed must drop below 940 rpm for the idle stabilizer to advance timing. On 1983 and later models, the idle speed must drop below 840 rpm. If the idle speed is not brought down by the increased electrical load to below these specifications, the stabilizer will not advance the timing.

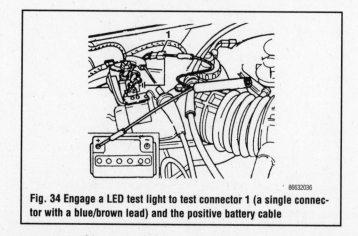

Fig. 34 Engage a LED test light to test connector 1 (a single connector with a blue/brown lead) and the positive battery cable

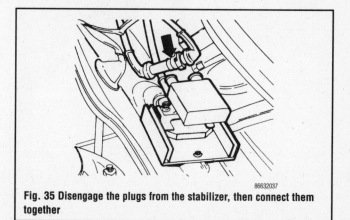

Fig. 35 Disengage the plugs from the stabilizer, then connect them together

Parts Replacement

DISTRIBUTOR CAP

1. Disconnect the negative battery cable.
2. Label each spark plug wire and terminal on the old distributor cap.
3. Disengage the spark plug wires from the distributor cap.
4. Release the retaining clips securing the distributor/suppression cap.
5. Remove the cap from the distributor, then separate the suppression cap from the distributor cap.

To install:

6. Slip the suppression cap over the new distributor cap, then install the assembly on the distributor. Engage the retaining clips.
7. Match the position of the old distributor cap to the new cap, then connect the spark plug wires to their appropriate terminals.
8. Connect the battery cable.

ROTOR

▶ **See Figure 36**

1. Disconnect the negative battery cable.
2. Disengage the retaining clips securing the distributor/suppression cap. Pull the assembly away from the distributor, then lay it aside with the spark plug wires attached.
3. Pull the rotor off of the distributor shaft. On 16-valve engines, the rotor is "glued" to the shaft. If you cannot pull it off the shaft, use a pair of pliers to break it. Clean the remaining pieces from the shaft.

➡ **Do not hit the rotor with a hammer or similar tool. The impact could damage other components including the distributor itself. Grasp the rotor with a pair of pliers and carefully break the pieces off.**

To install:

4. Install a new rotor onto the shaft. On 16-valve engines, use Loctite® 325 speed bonder to secure the rotor on the shaft. The rotor must be bonded to the shaft on these engines.
5. Install the distributor cap, then engage the retaining clips.
6. Connect the battery cable.

IGNITION COIL

▶ **See Figure 37**

1. Disconnect the negative battery cable.
2. Label and unplug the wires from the coil.
3. On some models, the coil is secured in a clamp. If so, loosen the screw,

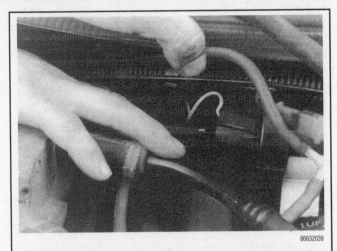

Fig. 37 Label wires before unplugging them—Note the white connector above the vacuum tee (On some models it is used to check the idle air stabilizer duty cycle during idle speed adjustment

then slide the coil out from the clamp. Install the new coil, then tighten the screw until snug.
4. On other models, the coil is secured by bolts. On these models, remove the bolts, then replace the coil. Tighten the bolts until snug.
5. Connect the wires to the coil.
6. Connect the battery cable.

HALL CONTROL UNIT

▶ **See Figure 38**

On models equipped with an ignition advance type idle stabilizer, the Hall control unit is located under the stabilizer in the engine compartment. On other models, the Hall control unit is located in the cowling above the firewall in the engine compartment.

1. Disconnect the negative battery cable.
2. Make sure the ignition key is in the **OFF** position.
3. On models equipped with an ignition advance type idle stabilizer, remove the stabilizer. On other models, remove the rubber weatherstrip seal from the firewall. Carefully pull the plastic cover from the cowling.
4. Unplug the connector from the Hall control unit.
5. Loosen and remove the screws securing it to the heat sink/bracket assembly.
6. Remove the Hall control unit.

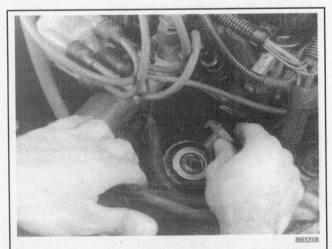

Fig. 36 Except for 16-valve engines (on which the rotor is glued in place) the rotor may be pulled from the shaft once the distributor cap is removed

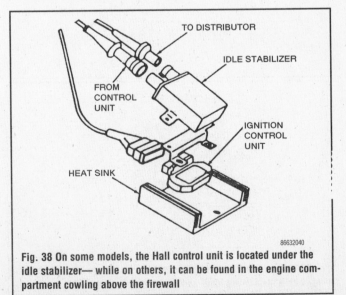

Fig. 38 On some models, the Hall control unit is located under the idle stabilizer— while on others, it can be found in the engine compartment cowling above the firewall

To install:

7. Clean the mating surface of the heat sink/bracket and the bottom of the Hall control unit. These surfaces must be free of any debris. This will provide a good contact surface for the control unit to dissipate heat. Failure to do so may result in early control unit failure.

8. Position the new Hall control unit on the heat sink/bracket, then tighten the screws until snug.

9. Engage the electrical connection.

10. Install the idle stabilizer or plastic cowling cover and weatherstrip seal as applicable.

11. Connect the battery cable.

HALL SENDER

▶ **See Figures 39 and 40**

The Hall sender is located inside the distributor.

1. Disconnect the negative battery cable.

2. Make sure the ignition switch is **OFF** and remove the distributor cap/suppression shield as a unit. It is not necessary to remove the spark plug wires from the cap.

3. Remove the rotor and dust shield. On 16-valve engines, the rotor is glued onto the distributor and may have to be broken apart with pliers to remove it. Carefully crush the lower portion, remove the rotor and clean off all the old adhesive.

4. On 8-valve engines, remove the snapring holding the trigger wheel in place.

5. Pry the trigger wheel off carefully using a pair of small prytools. Be careful not to lose the locating pin that indexes the wheel to the shaft. DO NOT distort the trigger wheel by using excessive force.

6. Unplug the Hall sender connector, then loosen and remove the screw(s) to remove the sender from the base plate.

To install:

7. Install the new Hall sender. Use a magnetic screwdriver to start the screw.

8. When fitting the trigger wheel into place, make sure the locating pin and wheel are correctly aligned on the shaft. On 8-valve engines, install the snapring.

9. Install the dust shield and rotor. On 16-valve engines, use Loctite® 325 speed bonder when installing the rotor.

10. Install the cap and suppressor shield. Check the ignition timing.

11. Connect the battery cable.

KNOCK SENSOR CONTROL UNIT

▶ **See Figure 41**

The knock sensor control unit is located in the cowling above the firewall in the engine compartment.

1. Disconnect the negative battery cable.

2. Make sure the ignition key is in the **OFF** position.

3. Remove the rubber weatherstrip seal from the firewall. Carefully pull the plastic cover from the cowling.

4. Unplug the electrical harness connector and the vacuum hose from the knock sensor control unit.

5. Loosen and remove the screws securing the control unit to the bracket assembly.

6. Remove the knock sensor control unit.

To install:

7. Position the control unit on the bracket, then tighten the screws until snug.

8. Engage the electrical and vacuum hose connections.

9. Install the plastic cowling cover and weatherstrip seal.

10. Connect the battery cable.

DIGIFANT II CONTROL UNIT

The Digifant II control unit is located in the cowling above the firewall in the engine compartment.

1. Disconnect the negative battery cable.

2. Make sure the ignition key is in the **OFF** position.

3. Remove the rubber weatherstrip seal from the firewall. Carefully pull the plastic cover from the cowling.

4. Unplug the electrical harness connector from the control unit.

5. Loosen and remove the nuts securing the control unit bracket assembly.

6. Turn the bracket assembly upside down, then remove the screws securing the control unit to the bracket.

7. Remove the control unit.

To install:

8. Position the control unit on the bracket, then tighten the screws until snug.

9. Install the bracket assembly, then tighten the nuts to 15 inch lbs. (1.7 Nm).

10. Engage the electrical connection.

11. Install the plastic cowling cover and weatherstrip seal.

12. Connect the battery cable.

IDLE STABILIZER

1. Disconnect the wire plugs from the idle stabilizer.

2. Remove the mounting screws, then remove the unit.

To install:

3. Install the idle stabilizer, tighten the screws until snug.

4. Connect the wire plugs to the stabilizer.

KNOCK SENSOR

1. Disconnect the negative battery cable. This must be done before loosening or tightening the knock sensor securing bolt to avoid short circuiting the alternator.

2. Unplug the knock sensor electrical connection.

3. Loosen and remove the bolt securing the knock sensor.

To install:

4. Install the sensor, then thread the bolt in by hand first. Do not use any washers.

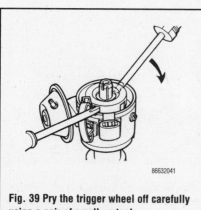

Fig. 39 Pry the trigger wheel off carefully using a pair of small prytools

Fig. 40 The sending unit is usually secured by small screws

Fig. 41 The knock sensor control unit is located in the engine compartment cowling above the firewall

5. On CIS-E engines with type 1 sensors, tighten the bolt to 9 ft. lbs. (12 Nm). On CIS-E engines with type 2 sensors and on Digifant II systems, tighten the bolt to 18 ft. lbs. (25 Nm).

➡Type 1 sensors have a cable connection which is off center (see illustration in this section). On type 2 sensors, the connection is from the side. Tightening torque must be strictly observed as it affects the function of the knock sensor.

6. Engage the electrical connection, then connect the negative battery cable.

IGNITION TIMING

♦ See Figures 42, 43 and 44

The timing mark is on the flywheel and can be viewed through a window in the bellhousing on the transaxle. On some models, there is a plastic cap that can be pulled out. It's easier to see the marks if the cover is removed completely by unscrewing it with an Allen wrench (most are 27mm).

Two marks appear on the flywheel: Top Dead Center (TDC) of cylinder No. 1 is usually indicated with a "0". The only other machined mark on the flywheel is the correct timing mark for that engine. On some flywheels the mark is a machined groove, on others it will appear as a raised lug.

Timing Procedures

❊❊ CAUTION

When performing this or any other operation with the engine running, be very careful of the alternator belt and pulleys. Make sure that your timing light wires don't interfere with the belt.

INSPECTION AND ADJUSTMENT

Breaker Point Ignition Systems

1. Attach a timing light and a dwell/tachometer.
2. Locate the timing mark opening in the bellhousing of the transaxle. The "OT" mark stands for TDC or zero advance. There is another mark which designates the correct timing position. DON'T disconnect the vacuum line at the distributor.
3. Start the engine and allow it to reach the normal operating temperature. The engine should be running at normal idle speed.
4. Shine the timing light at the marks.
5. The timing mark and the V-shaped pointer should be aligned.
6. If not, loosen the distributor hold-down bolt and rotate the distributor very slowly to align the marks.
7. Tighten the mounting nut when the ignition timing is correct.
8. Recheck the timing when the distributor is tight.

Electronic Ignition Systems

1979–84 MODELS

1. Run the engine to operating temperature. Connect a tachometer.

➡On carbureted models with electronic ignition, a special adaptor must be used to connect a tachometer to the engine. Refer to the electronic ignition precautions in this section for a description on how to construct your own. Failure to use an adaptor on these engines may cause ignition system damage.

2. Stop the engine. If equipped, disconnect the idle stabilizer plugs at the control unit and plug them together. On carbureted Rabbits, disconnect and plug the vacuum advance/retard hoses.
3. Switch all electrical accessories to the OFF position.
4. Start the engine and check the idle speed. Adjust, if it is out of specification.
5. With your timing light, check that the pointer lines up with the notch in the flywheel. To adjust the timing, loosen the distributor hold-down bolt and rotate the distributor very slowly to align the marks.
6. On carbureted Rabbits, connect the vacuum hose(s). Idle speed should drop to 600–750 rpm.
7. Stop the engine, then reconnect the plugs at the control unit. On carbureted Rabbits, start the engine and accelerate it a few times. The idle speed should now be 850–950 rpm.

1985–89 8 VALVE ENGINES

♦ See Figure 45

1. Run the engine for a few minutes to allow it reach normal operating temperature. Wait for the cooling fan to come on once. Make sure all electrical accessories are in the OFF position. On Digifant II engines, raise the idle speed to a minimum of 2,100 rpm four times to cancel the (computer controlled) hot start idle speed increase function, then allow the engine to idle normally. If you don't do this step, the hot re-start program stored in the computer will cause the engine idle speed to run higher than normal and affect the timing adjustment.
2. Stop the engine.
3. If equipped, disconnect the vacuum hose from the distributor and plug it. On Digifant II engines, unplug the coolant temperature sensor connector. The connector is usually blue and is attached directly to the coolant temperature sensor.
4. Connect a timing light and tachometer.
5. Start the engine and check the timing. The pointer must line up with the notch in the flywheel. On Digifant II engines, briefly raise the engine speed to 3,000 rpm 3 times, then check idle speed and timing again.
6. If the timing is not as specified, loosen the distributor base clamp and rotate the distributor clockwise or counterclockwise until the timing is within specs.
7. Tighten the distributor clamp and clamp base bolt.

Fig. 42 On some models, there is a plastic cap that can be pulled out to view the timing marks

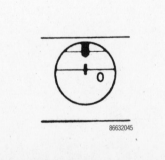

86632045

Fig. 43 On some models the timing mark is a machined groove, on others it will appear as a raised lug

86632046

Fig. 44 Shine the timing light at the viewing window. If necessary, adjust the timing by turning the distributor

86632047

...gifant II engines

8. Once the clamp base bolt is tight, check the timing again.
9. Check the idle speed and adjust if necessary.
10. Stop the engine, then disconnect the timing light and tachometer. Connect the wiring for the coolant temperature sensor or connect the distributor vacuum line (if required).

16 VALVE ENGINES

1. Run the engine for a few minutes to allow it reach normal operating temperature. Wait for the cooling fan to come on once.
2.. Stop the engine, then connect a timing light and tachometer.
3. Start the engine and check the timing. The pointer in the hole must line up with the notch in the flywheel.
4. If the timing is not as specified, remove the cap that covers the head of the distributor base clamp bolt (if installed). Loosen the distributor base clamp and rotate the distributor clockwise or counterclockwise until the timing is within specification.
5. Tighten the distributor clamp and clamp base bolt.
6. Once the clamp base bolt is tight, check the timing again.
7. Check the idle speed and adjust if necessary.
8. Stop the engine, disconnect the timing light and tachometer.

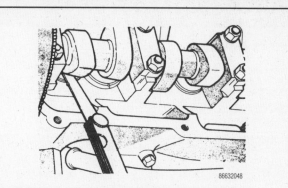

86632048

Fig. 46 Check the valve clearance with a feeler gauge—the camshaft lobe should not apply pressure on the valve disc

... valve lifters. No
... draulic lifters. A
... identify the type of
... is equipped. The
... valve lash is or is

... the intake and
... is too large, part of
... ssive clearance,
... ill effects; one, the
valve gear will become noisy as the excess clearance is taken up and, two, the engine will perform poorly. This is because intake valves which don't open the full distance will admit less air/fuel mixture into the cylinders. Exhaust valves which aren't opening the full amount create a greater back pressure in the cylinder which also prevents the proper air/fuel mixture from entering the cylinder.

If the valve clearance is too small, the intake and exhaust valves will not fully seat on the cylinder head when they close. When a valve seats on the cylinder head it does two things; it seals the combustion chamber so that none of the gases in the cylinder can escape and it cools itself by transferring some of the heat absorbed from the combustion process through the cylinder head and into the cooling system. Therefore, if the valve clearance is too small, the engine will run poorly (due to gases escaping from the combustion chamber), and the valves will overheat and eventually warp (since they cannot properly transfer heat unless they fully seat on the cylinder head). While all valve adjustments must be as accurate as possible, it is better to have the valve adjustment slightly loose than tight.

ADJUSTMENT

♦ See Figures 46 and 47

The overhead cam acts directly on the valves through cam followers which fit over the springs and valves. Adjustment is made with an adjusting disc which fits into the cam follower. Different thickness discs result in changes in valve clearance.

➡VW recommends that two special tools be used to remove and install the adjustment discs. One is a pry bar to compress the valve springs and the other a pair of special pliers to grasp the disc. Ask your local VW dealer for current tool part numbers. If the purchase of these tools is not possible, a flat metal plate can be used to compress the valve springs if you are careful not to gouge the camshaft lobes. The cam follower (lifter) has two slots which permit the disc to be lifted out. Again, you may improvise by using a thin bladed tool. An assistant to pry the

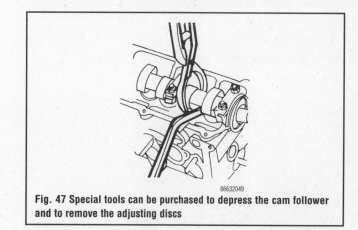

86632049

Fig. 47 Special tools can be purchased to depress the cam follower and to remove the adjusting discs

spring down while you remove the disc would be the ideal way to perform the operation if you must improvise your own tools.

Valve clearance is checked with the engine moderately warm (coolant temperature should be about 95°F (35°C).

1. Disconnect the accelerator linkage (if equipped with automatic transmission). Remove the upper drive belt cover (if necessary), the air cleaner and any hoses or lines which may be in the way. When disconnecting the accelerator cable, do not allow the cable to become kinked or twisted. Route the cable neatly off to side and out of the way.
2. Remove the camshaft cover and gasket. Valve clearance is checked in

the firing order 1–3–4–2 for 4 cylinder engines and 1–2–4–5–3 for 5 cylinder engines, with the piston of the cylinder being checked at TDC of the compression stroke. Both valves will be closed at this position and the cam lobes will be pointing upward.

➡**When adjusting the clearances on the diesel engines, the pistons must NOT be at TDC. Turn the crankshaft ¼ turn past TDC so that the valves do not contact the pistons when the tappets are depressed.**

3. Turn the crankshaft pulley bolt with a socket wrench to position the camshaft for checking. There is a hole behind the front license plate, on Dasher models, through which a wrench can be used.

※※ CAUTION

Do not turn the camshaft by the camshaft mounting bolt, this will stretch the drive belt. When turning the crankshaft pulley bolt, turn CLOCKWISE ONLY.

4. With the No. 1 piston at TDC (¼ turn past for the diesel) of the compression stroke, determine the clearance with a feeler gauge. Compare this reading with the correct clearance from the tune-up charts in this section or from the underhood label.

5. Continue to check the other cylinders in the firing order, turning the crankshaft to bring each particular piston to the top of the compression stroke (¼ turn past for the diesel). Record the individual clearances as you go along.

6. If measured clearance is within tolerance levels, it is not necessary to replace the adjusting discs.

7. If adjustment is necessary, the discs will have to be removed and replaced with thicker or thinner ones which will yield the correct clearance. Discs are available in 0.002 in. (0.05mm) increments.

➡**The thickness of the adjusting discs are etched on one side. When installing, the marks must face the cam followers. Discs can be can be reused if they are not worn or damaged.**

8. To remove the discs; turn the cam followers so that the grooves are accessible when the pry bar is depressed.

9. Press the cam follower down with the pry bar and remove the adjusting discs with the special pliers or a similar tool.

10. Replace the adjustment discs as necessary to bring the clearance within the tolerance level. If the measured clearance is larger than the given tolerance, remove the existing disc and insert a thicker one to bring the clearance up to specification. If it is smaller, insert a thinner one.

11. Recheck all valve clearances after adjustment.

12. Install the cylinder head cover with a new gasket.

13. Install the accelerator linkage, the upper drive belt cover and any wires or lines which were removed.

IDLE SPEED AND MIXTURE ADJUSTMENTS

◆ **See Figure 48**

➡**Changes are often made during a production run, which will be reflected on the underhood emissions label. If the information in the procedures differs from the values given on the underhood emission control label, use the data on the label.**

Carbureted Engines

The Dasher carburetor is a Solex 32/35 DIDTA 2-barrel unit through 1974, and a Zenith 2B3 in 1975. Both have vacuum operated secondary barrels. The 1975–76 Rabbit and Scirocco use a Zenith 2B2 carburetor with a vacuum operated secondary barrel and dual floats. Some 1978 and 1980 Rabbits are equipped with the 34 PICT-5 single barrel carburetor. Some 1982 and later models use a Carter TYF feedback carburetor.

IDLE ADJUSTMENT

Solex 32/35 DIDTA, Zenith 2B2 and 2B3 Carburetors

◆ **See Figure 49**

1. Start the engine and run it until the normal operating temperature is reached. Make sure the ignition timing is correct.

2. Hook up a tachometer to the engine and observe the idle speed.

3. If not as specified, turn the idle speed adjusting screw to correct it.

Solex 34 PICT-5 Carburetor

◆ **See Figures 50, 51 and 52**

1. The engine must be at normal operating temperature. Make sure the ignition timing is correct.

2. Disconnect the two hoses from the carburetor air intake elbow, then plug the two inlets on the elbow (it sits right on top of the carburetor).

3. Remove both of the air injection hoses at the air injection valves. Plug the valves.

4. Shut off all electrical equipment, including the air conditioner (if equipped).

5. Connect a tachometer to the engine.

➡**On models with electronic ignition, a special adaptor must be used to connect a tachometer to the engine. Refer to the electronic ignition precautions in this section for a description on how to construct your own. Failure to use an adaptor on these engines may cause ignition system damage.**

6. Start the engine. On models with electronic ignition, accelerate the engine a few times to activate the idle stabilizer.

7. Check the idle speed (refer to the underhood sticker or to the tune-up chart in this section).

8. If the idle speed is not correct on models with breaker point ignitions, turn the idle adjusting screw until the correct specification is reached.

9. If the idle speed is not correct on models with electronic ignition:

Fig. 48 Always follow the specifications and any special instructions found on the underhood emissions label

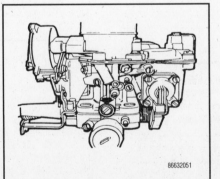

Fig. 49 Idle speed adjusting screw (arrow at center)

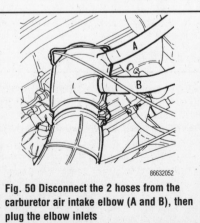

Fig. 50 Disconnect the 2 hoses from the carburetor air intake elbow (A and B), then plug the elbow inlets

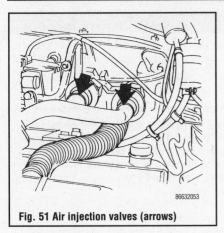

Fig. 51 Air injection valves (arrows)

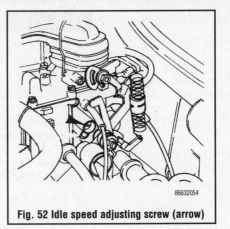

Fig. 52 Idle speed adjusting screw (arrow)

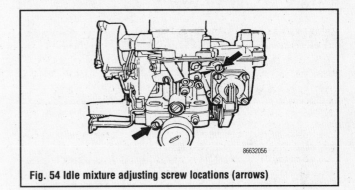

Fig. 53 On models without air conditioning, adjust the idle at screw (A). If equipped with air conditioning, adjust the idle at screw (A) and hex nut (B)

a. Disconnect the wire plugs at the idle stabilizer control unit, then connect them together.

b. Disconnect and plug the vacuum advance and retard hoses.

c. Adjust the idle speed to 800–1000 rpm at the adjustment screw.

d. Check the timing and adjust, if necessary. If the timing was off, recheck the idle speed.

e. Reconnect the advance/retard hoses and the idle stabilizer control unit. Accelerate the engine briefly to reactivate idle stabilizer. Idle speed should be 850–950 rpm.

10. Reconnect the hoses to the air intake elbow and the air injection valves.

Carter TYF

▶ See Figure 53

1. Run the engine until normal operating temperature is reached. Make sure the ignition timing is correct.

2. Remove the breather hose from the side of the camshaft cover. Shut off all electrical equipment including the air conditioner (if so equipped).

3. Connect a tachometer to the engine. Start the engine and run it at 2,000 rpm for 5 seconds. Check the idle speed, it should be 850–1000 rpm.

➡On models with electronic ignition, a special adaptor must be used to connect a tachometer to the engine. Refer to the electronic ignition precautions in this section for a description on how to construct your own. Failure to use an adaptor on these engines may cause ignition system damage.

4. If necessary, adjust the idle speed as follows:

a. Disconnect both idle stabilizer plugs (if equipped), then connect them together.

b. Disconnect and plug the vacuum hoses at the distributor.

c. On models without air conditioning, adjust the speed to 820–900 rpm by turning the idle adjusting screw on the throttle lever.

d. On air conditioned cars, set the controls to MAX cold and FAST fan speed. Set the speed to 820–900 rpm by turning the idle adjusting screw on the throttle lever. Turn the air conditioning OFF, then set the speed to 820–900 rpm by turning the hex nut on the SOLVAC (throttle kicker) unit.

5. Stop the engine. Reconnect the idle stabilizer plugs, vacuum hoses and the breather hose.

MIXTURE ADJUSTMENT

➡The air/fuel mixture is measured by sampling the exhaust gas with a CO meter, except on models equipped with a Carter TYF carburetor (a dwell meter may be used on these). If this equipment is not available, the mixture should be adjusted at a properly equipped shop.

On some models, there may be CO test point near the back of the engine compartment (a metal tube with a cap). Make sure the test probe is a tight fit and will not draw in outside air. Others models may be tested at the tailpipe. Always follow any special instructions on the underhood emissions label. If this label is missing from your vehicle, you should be able to order it through your local dealer. Keep in mind that ignition timing and idle speed must be correct before checking and/or adjusting the fuel mixture.

Dasher

▶ See Figure 54

1. Run the engine until it reaches normal operating temperature. Make sure that the ignition timing and idle speed settings are correct.

2. If equipped with an air injection pump, disconnect the hoses at the pump, then plug them.

3. Using a CO meter, check the air/fuel mixture. On 1974 models, check the reading at the tailpipe. The 1975 models should have a CO test point in the engine compartment. Compare the reading with the specification listed on the underhood emission label.

4. If adjustment is necessary, turn the mixture adjustment screw until it is within specification. Readjust the idle speed, if necessary.

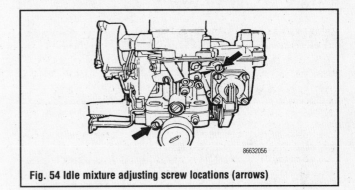

Fig. 54 Idle mixture adjusting screw locations (arrows)

Rabbit and Scirocco

EXCEPT CARTER TYF

▶ See Figure 55

1. Run the engine until it reaches normal operating temperature. Make sure that the ignition timing and idle speed settings are correct.

Fig. 55 Idle mixture adjusting screw

2.. Disconnect the hoses from the air cleaner duct, then plug the openings on the duct.

3. Disconnect the air injection hoses at the check valves, then plug the valves.

4. Using a CO meter, check the air/fuel mixture. On Canada models, check the reading at the tailpipe. On U.S models, there should be a CO test point in the engine compartment. Compare the reading with the specification listed on the underhood emission label.

5. If adjustment is necessary, turn the mixture adjustment screw until it is within specification.

6. If necessary, readjust the idle speed.

CARTER TYF

♦ See Figure 56

1. Make sure the engine is at normal operating temperature. The ignition timing and idle speed settings must be correct.

2. Remove the PCV valve or breather hose from the camshaft cover. Shut off all electrical accessories, including the air conditioner.

3. Connect a duty cycle or dwell meter to the test lead on the strut tower.

4. Start the engine, then increase the engine speed to 2,000 rpm for 5 seconds.

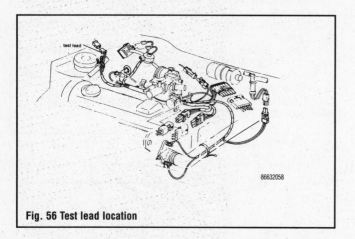

Fig. 56 Test lead location

5. Check the reading on the meter. It should be fluctuating between 20–50 percent (duty cycle meter) or 18–45 degrees (dwell meter).

6. If the reading is not within specification, remove the carburetor from the vehicle, then remove the tamper-proof plug from the mixture adjusting screw. Reinstall the carburetor, then perform the previous steps to check the meter reading again.

7. Adjust the mixture screw until the correct meter reading is reached. Turn the screw slowly in small increments. This will allow the meter to stabilize between adjustments.

8. Recheck the idle speed and install a new tamper-proof plug over the mixture screw.

CIS Fuel Injection

CIS fuel injection vehicles can be identified by the absence of electrical connections on the fuel distributor. Also, the fuel distributor is usually painted black on these models.

IDLE ADJUSTMENT

➡**Certain 1.8 Liter engines are equipped with a manual pre-heat valve located on the air cleaner housing. The valve is marked "S" (summer) and "W" (winter). When adjusting the idle speed, position the valve to S (unless work area is below freezing). After servicing, return the valve to the position that matches climate conditions.**

Four Cylinder Engines

1976–80 MODELS

♦ See Figure 57

1. Run the engine until normal operating temperature is reached. Make sure the ignition timing is set correctly. Read the underhood emission sticker for any special instructions which differ from these procedures.

2. On some models, it may be necessary to bypass the idle stabilizer. Disconnect the plugs from the stabilizer, then connect them together.

3. Turn the headlamps on high beam (except 1979–80 Canadian Rabbit, Scirocco and all models equipped with an oxygen sensor). All other electrical accessories must be OFF.

4. Connect a tachometer to the engine. Start the vehicle and check the idle speed. Compare it to the specifications shown in the tune-up chart (in this section) or the underhood sticker.

5. If necessary, adjust by turning the idle speed screw on the side of the throttle body. Turning the screw in reduces idle speed, turning it out increases idle speed.

1981–84 MODELS

♦ See Figures 58 and 59

1. The engine must be at normal operating temperature. Make sure the ignition timing is set correctly. Read the underhood emission sticker for any special instructions which differ from these procedures.

2. Disconnect the crankcase breather hoses. Plug them on models through 1982. On 1983 and later models, allow hose to be opened to air. On 1982 Rabbit, Scirocco and Jetta without an oxygen sensor, disconnect the charcoal canister hose from the air inlet boot. On Quantum models, remove the plastic cap from the T-connector at the air inlet boot.

3. Disconnect the two plugs from the idle stabilizer control unit (if equipped) and connect them together. Make sure all electrical accessories are turned OFF.

4. Connect a tachometer to the engine. Start the vehicle and check the idle speed. Compare it to the specifications shown in the tune-up chart (in this section) or the underhood sticker.

5. If necessary, adjust the idle speed using the adjustment screw on the side of the throttle body.

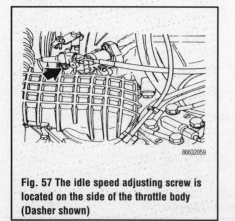

Fig. 57 The idle speed adjusting screw is located on the side of the throttle body (Dasher shown)

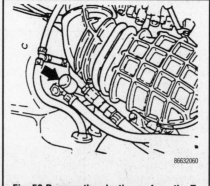

Fig. 58 Remove the plastic cap from the T-connector on Quantum models

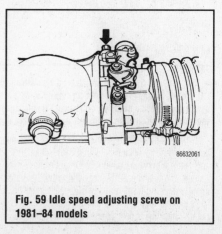

Fig. 59 Idle speed adjusting screw on 1981–84 models

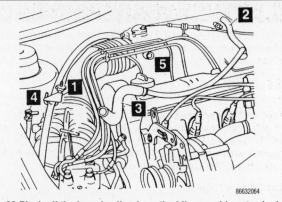

Fig. 60 Pinch off the hose leading from the idle speed boost valve(s) with a clamp (1)
Disconnect the crankcase ventilation hoses (2 and 3)
The T-connector location (4)
The idle speed adjusting screw (5)

1985–89 EXCEPT FOX

▶ See Figure 60

1. Run the engine until normal operating temperature is reached. Make sure the ignition timing is set correctly. Read the underhood emission sticker for any special instructions which differ from these procedures.

2. Pinch off the hose leading from the idle speed boost valve(s) with a clamp. Disconnect the crankcase ventilation hoses.

3. On Cabriolet and Scirocco, disconnect the carbon canister hose from the T-connector on the air intake boot.

4. On Golf, Jetta and GTI, remove the T-connector at the air intake boot. Rotate the connector 90 degrees, then insert the blank side with the 0.059 in. (1.5mm) restrictor into the air intake boot opening. Some engines may not be equipped with this type of restrictor T-connector. This plug is available from your Volkswagen dealer as part number 026 133 382D.

5. Connect a tachometer to the engine. Start the engine and check the idle speed. Compare it to the specifications shown in the tune-up chart (in this section) or the underhood sticker.

6. If necessary, adjust by turning the idle speed screw on the side of the throttle body. Turning the screw in reduces idle speed, turning it out increases idle speed.

1986–1989 FOX

1. The engine must be at normal operating temperature. Make sure the ignition timing is set correctly. Read the underhood emission sticker for any special instructions which differ from these procedures.

2. Disconnect the crankcase ventilation hose.

3. Loosen the clamp which connects the T-connector with the restrictor to the charcoal canister, then disconnect the line.

4. Turn OFF all electrical accessories.

5. Connect a tachometer to the engine. Start the vehicle and check the idle speed. Compare it to the specifications shown in the tune-up chart (in this section) or the underhood sticker.

6. If necessary, adjust the idle speed using the adjusting screw located on the side of the throttle body.

5-Cylinder Engines

▶ See Figures 61, 62 and 63

1. The engine must be at normal operating temperature. Make sure the ignition timing is set correctly. Read the underhood emission sticker for any special instructions which differ from these procedures.

2. Remove the plastic cap from the T-connector at the air intake boot.

3. Disconnect both crankcase breather hoses, then plug them.

4. If equipped, disconnect both plugs at the idle stabilizer, then plug the connectors together to bypass the unit. Make sure the connectors are tight.

5. Turn OFF all electrical accessories.

6. Connect a tachometer to the engine. Start the vehicle and check the idle

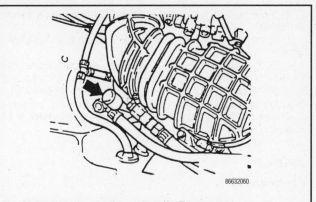

Fig. 61 Remove the plastic cap from the T-connector

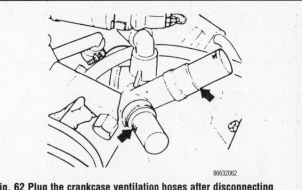

Fig. 62 Plug the crankcase ventilation hoses after disconnecting them

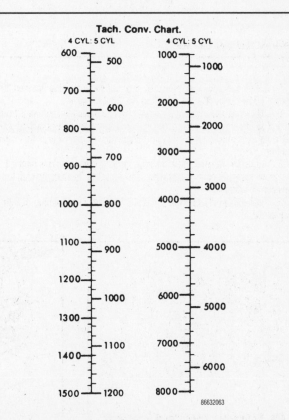

Fig. 63 Use this chart to convert a 4-cylinder tachometer reading to the actual idle speed on 5-cylinder engines

speed. Compare it to the specifications shown in the tune-up chart (in this section) or the underhood sticker.

7. If necessary, adjust the idle speed using the adjusting screw located on the side of the throttle body.

MIXTURE ADJUSTMENT

➡**The air/fuel mixture is measured by sampling the exhaust gas with a CO meter. If this equipment is not available, the mixture should be adjusted at a properly equipped shop.**

Most models have a CO test point near the back of the engine compartment (a metal tube with a cap). Make sure the probe is a tight fit and will not draw in outside air. Others may have to be tested at the tailpipe. Always follow any special instructions on the underhood emissions label. If this label is missing from the vehicle, you should be able to order it through your local dealer. Keep in mind that ignition timing and idle speed must be correct before checking and/or adjusting the fuel mixture.

On 1981 and later models, the fuel mixture adjusting screw is covered by a tamper resistant plug to prevent adjustment of the factory setting. The mixture adjustment is not a normal maintenance or tune-up procedure on these models. Refer to Section 5 for procedures.

1976–80 Models

▸ **See Figure 64**

With the engine at normal operating temperature, check the CO level at the test point. If adjustment is needed, follow these steps.

1. Disconnect the charcoal filter hose from the air cleaner. Turn the headlights on high beam (except 1979 Canadian Rabbit/Jetta/Scirocco). On 1980 models, unplug the oxygen sensor connector (if equipped).

2. The removable plug covering the mixture adjusting screw has a wire loop attached to it. Remove the plug by pulling it straight up. Insert tool VW-P377 or a 3mm hex wrench in the hole. Turn the adjusting tool clockwise (in) to raise the percentage of CO and counter-clockwise (out) to lower the percentage of CO.

❋❋ CAUTION

Do not push down on the adjusting tool or accelerate the engine with the tool in place.

3. Remove the tool after each adjustment. Accelerate the engine briefly, then check the CO reading after the engine has stabilized.

CIS-E Fuel Injection

CIS-E fuel injected vehicles can be identified by the aluminum color of the fuel distributor. Unlike CIS fuel injected vehicles, there are electrical connections on the fuel distributor.

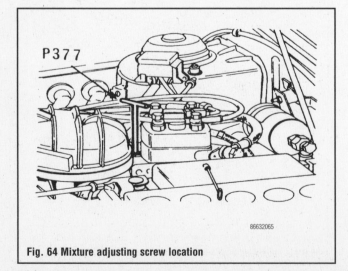

86632065

Fig. 64 Mixture adjusting screw location

IDLE ADJUSTMENT

➡**Certain 1.8L engines are equipped with a manual pre-heat valve located on the air cleaner housing. The valve is marked "S" (summer) and "W" (winter). When adjusting the idle speed, position the valve to S (unless work area is below freezing). After servicing, return the valve to the position that matches climate conditions.**

Fox

1. The engine must be at normal operating temperature. Make sure the ignition timing is set correctly. Read the underhood emission sticker for any special instructions which differ from these procedures.

2. Unplug the connector from the idle speed boost valves.

3. Disconnect the crankcase ventilation hose from the camshaft cover.

4. Disconnect the suction line from the charcoal canister.

5. Turn OFF all electrical accessories.

6. Connect a tachometer to the engine. Start the vehicle and check the idle speed. Compare it to the specifications shown in the tune-up chart (in this section) or the underhood sticker.

7. If necessary, adjust the idle speed using the adjusting screw located on the side of the throttle body.

Quantum

FOUR CYLINDER ENGINES

▸ **See Figure 61**

1. Run the engine until normal operating temperature is reached. Make sure the ignition timing is set correctly. Read the underhood emission sticker for any special instructions which differ from these procedures.

2. Pinch off the hose leading from the idle speed boost valve(s) with a clamp. Disconnect the crankcase ventilation hoses (do not plug them).

3. Remove the plastic cap from the T-connector at the air intake boot.

4. Connect a tachometer to the engine. Start the engine and check the idle speed. Compare it to the specifications shown in the tune-up chart (in this section) or the underhood sticker.

5. If necessary, adjust by turning the idle speed screw on the side of the throttle body. Turning the screw in reduces idle speed, turning it out increases idle speed.

FIVE CYLINDER ENGINES

▸ **See Figures 61, 62 and 63**

1. The engine must be at normal operating temperature. Make sure the ignition timing is set correctly. Read the underhood emission sticker for any special instructions which differ from these procedures.

2. Remove the plastic cap from the T-connector at the air intake boot.

3. Disconnect then crankcase breather hoses, then plug them.

4. Turn OFF all electrical accessories.

5. Connect a duty cycle or dwell meter to the test connector in the wiring harness near the right strut tower (positive lead of the meter to the test connector and the negative lead to ground).

6. Start the engine and check the meter reading. The display should read 26–30 percent (with a duty cycle meter) or 23–27 degrees (with a dwell meter).

7. If necessary, adjust the idle speed using the adjusting screw located on the side of the throttle body.

Golf, Jetta and Scirocco

GX ENGINES

▸ **See Figure 60**

1. Run the engine until normal operating temperature is reached. Make sure the ignition timing is set correctly. Read the underhood emission sticker for any special instructions which differ from these procedures.

2. Pinch off the hose leading from the idle speed boost valve(s) with a clamp. Disconnect the crankcase ventilation hoses (do not plug them).

3. Remove the T-connector from the carbon canister at the air intake boot. Rotate the connector 90 degrees, then insert the blank side with the 0.059 in. (1.5mm) restrictor into the air intake boot opening. Some engines may not be

equipped with this type of restrictor T-connector. This plug is available from your Volkswagen dealer as part number 026 133 382D.

4. Connect a tachometer to the engine. Start the engine and check the idle speed. Compare it to the specifications shown in the tune-up chart (in this section) or the underhood sticker.

5. If necessary, adjust by turning the idle speed screw on the side of the throttle body. Turning the screw in reduces idle speed, turning it out increases idle speed.

HT, RD AND PL ENGINES

▶ **See Figures 65, 66, 67 and 68**

1. Run the engine until normal operating temperature is reached. Make sure the ignition timing is set correctly. Read the underhood emission sticker for any special instructions which differ from these procedures.

2. Disconnect the crankcase ventilation hoses (do not plug them).

3. Remove the T-connector from the carbon canister at the air intake boot. Rotate the connector 90 degrees, then insert the blank side with the 0.059 in.

(1.5mm) restrictor into the air intake boot opening. Some engines may not be equipped with this type of restrictor T-connector. This plug is available from your Volkswagen dealer as part number 026 133 382D.

4. Connect a duty cycle or dwell meter to the test connector in the wiring harness near the ignition coil (positive lead of the meter to the test connector and the negative lead to ground).

5. Start the engine and check the meter reading. For HT and RD engines, the display should read 26–30 percent (with a duty cycle meter) or 23–27 degrees (with a dwell meter). On PL engines, the display should read 23–27 percent (duty cycle meter) or 21–24 degrees (dwell meter).

6. If necessary, adjust by turning the idle speed screw on the side of the throttle body.

MIXTURE ADJUSTMENT

The fuel mixture is screw is plugged to prevent tampering with the factory setting. The mixture adjustment is not a normal maintenance or tune-up procedure on these models. Refer to Section 5 for procedures.

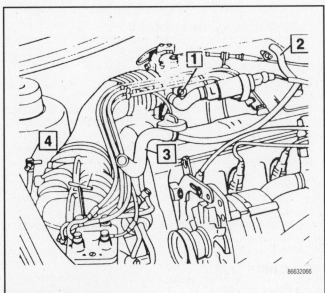

86632066

Fig. 65 8-valve engines:
The idle speed adjusting screw (1)
Disconnect the crankcase ventilation hoses (2 and 3)
The T-connector location (4)

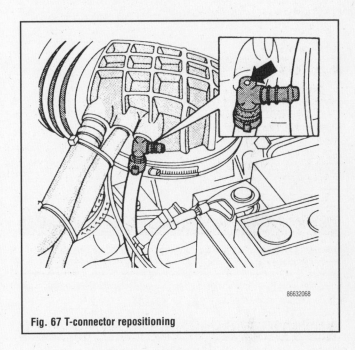

86632068

Fig. 67 T-connector repositioning

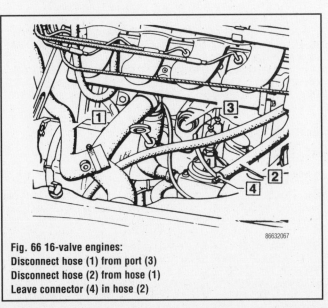

86632067

Fig. 66 16-valve engines:
Disconnect hose (1) from port (3)
Disconnect hose (2) from hose (1)
Leave connector (4) in hose (2)

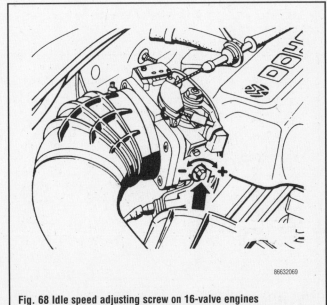

86632069

Fig. 68 Idle speed adjusting screw on 16-valve engines

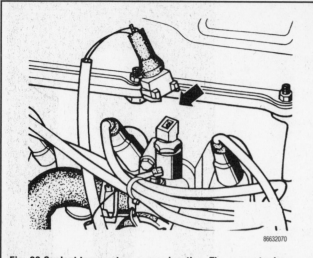

Fig. 69 Coolant temperature sensor location. The connector is usually blue

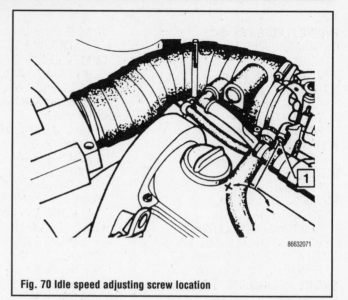

Fig. 70 Idle speed adjusting screw location

Digifant II

IDLE ADJUSTMENT

▶ **See Figures 69 and 70**

1. Run the engine until normal operating temperature is reached. Make sure the ignition timing is set correctly. Read the underhood emission sticker for any special instructions which differ from these procedures.
2. Connect a tachometer to the engine.
3. Make sure the idle stabilizer valve is operating. With the ignition **ON** (engine not running), the valve should vibrate or hum slightly.
4. Start the vehicle, then accelerate the engine to over 2,100 rpm at least four times. Allow the idle speed to stabilize. This cancels the hot-start idle function of the computer.

5. Make sure the crankcase ventilation hoses are connected and the engine oil dipstick is fully seated in its tube.
6. Unplug the coolant temperature sensor connector. This connector is usually blue.
7. Check the idle speed. It should be between 900–1000 rpm. If not, adjust the idle speed screw on the side of the throttle body until idle speed is between 925–975 rpm.
8. Engage the coolant temperature sensor connector. Idle speed should drop to 750–850 rpm.

MIXTURE ADJUSTMENT

The fuel mixture is screw is plugged to prevent tampering with the factory setting. The mixture adjustment is not a normal maintenance or tune-up procedure on these models. Refer to Section 5 for procedures.

3

ENGINE AND ENGINE OVERHAUL

ENGINE ELECTRICAL

Distributor

REMOVAL

▶ See Figures 1, 2 and 3

1. Remove the distributor cap (leave the spark plug wires attached). Label and disconnect any electrical connections on the distributor.
2. At the front crankshaft pulley bolt, turn the engine to Top Dead Center (TDC) on No. 1 piston. It's easier to turn the engine with the spark plugs removed.
3. The rotor should point to the No. 1 reference mark on the distributor housing. If not, turn the engine one full turn to align the mark.
4. Make a chalk or paint mark on the engine where the rotor points to the rim of the distributor.
5. On 8-valve engines, remove the bolt and hold-down flange, then lift the distributor straight out of the engine.
6. On 16-valve engines, remove the 2 bolts, then pull the distributor straight out of the cylinder head. Note which holes the bolts came from to make sure the timing can be adjusted correctly.

INSTALLATION

▶ See Figure 4

Engine Not Rotated

If the engine was not rotated while the distributor was removed, follow these procedures.
1. Check the condition of the O-ring on the distributor housing, replace it if necessary.

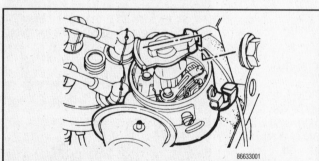

Fig. 1 Align the rotor with the notch on the distributor housing. Make sure the engine is at TDC on the compression stroke; if not, rotate the engine one revolution until the rotor aligns with the notch once again

➡Note the drive at the bottom of the distributor shaft. The lug is offset to one side on some models.

2. Align the rotor with the mark on the rim of the distributor.
3. Carefully fit the distributor into place and gently push while turning the rotor side–to–side. The lug will drop into place on the shaft.
4. Make sure the mark on the distributor aligns with the mark you make on the block or head and install the hold down flange or bolts.
5. Install the cap, connect the wires and check ignition timing.

Engine Rotated

Follow these procedures if the engine was rotated while the distributor was removed.
1. Check the condition of the O-ring on the distributor housing, replace it if necessary.
2. Turn the crankshaft so that the No. 1 piston is on its compression stroke and the TDC timing mark on the flywheel is aligned.
3. On 8-valve engines, the oil pump drive slot must be parallel with the crankshaft. This can be turned with a screw driver if necessary.
4. On 16-valve engines, look into the mounting hole and note the position of the slot in the crankshaft.
5. Turn the distributor so that the rotor points to the mark on the rim of the housing.
6. Install the distributor, making sure the drive lug engages the slot. On 8-valve engines, the distributor may turn as it is pushed down all the way.
7. Make sure the mark on the distributor aligns with the mark you make on the block or head, then install the hold-down flange and bolt(s).
8. Install the cap, connect the wires and check ignition timing.

Alternator

All Volkswagens are equipped with either a Bosch or Motorola alternator. The voltage regulator is mounted on the back of the alternator housing and includes the brushes. No adjustments are possible but the regulator can be replaced separately.

ALTERNATOR PRECAUTIONS

- Always disconnect the battery cables when removing or disconnecting the alternator.
- Disconnect the battery cables before using a fast charger. The charger has a tendency to force current "backwards" through the diodes and burn them out.
- Never disconnect the battery cables or alternator while the engine is running.
- Do not attempt to polarize an alternator.
- Never reverse battery connections. Do not connect the battery in series with another without disconnecting it from the charging system.
- When jump starting from another vehicle, try to avoid running the other vehicle's engine. Do not allow alternators from two different charging systems to be running and connected with jumper cables.

Fig. 2 Remove the bolt and hold-down flange. Make sure all electrical connections are unplugged from the distributor

Fig. 3 Pull the distributor out from the engine block. This may be difficult on some engines due to corrosion

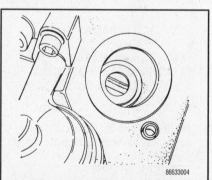

Fig. 4 On 8-valve engines, the oil pump drive slot must be parallel with the crankshaft

- Do not ground the alternator output terminal.
- Disconnect the battery cables before using an electric arc welder on the vehicle.

TESTING

There are several possible ways in which the charging system can malfunction. The first thing to do is to see if the discharge warning lamp on the dashboard illuminates when the ignition switch is turned **ON**. If it does not, check for blown fuses, a burned out bulb, or bad connections.

If the warning lamp does light with the ignition switch **ON**, but stays on with the engine running, check for the following:
- Proper electrolyte level (specific gravity) in the battery
- Loose or missing alternator belt
- Loose or corroded battery cable
- A blown fuse or fusible link
- A shorted or open wire

If everything checks out OK, but the charge lamp is still on, the alternator itself is probably to blame. This does not mean the entire alternator needs to be replaced. Many times the voltage regulator may be faulty and cause a no charge condition. Check the charging system by performing the following tests.

Current Drain Test

➡**Perform this test first to be sure there is not a shorted circuit or component which is constantly draining the battery.**

1. Turn the ignition switch to the **OFF** position. Make sure all electrical accessories are OFF.
2. Disconnect the negative battery cable. Connect a test light between the battery cable and the battery post.
3. If it lights up, something is either switched ON, or a wire/component is shorted and is draining the battery. To isolate the problem circuit, remove the fuses from the fuse/relay panel one at a time until the test light goes out.
4. Repair or replace any wires/components as necessary.

Alternator Output and Voltage Regulator Test

1. Connect an alternator/regulator tester according to the manufacturer's instructions. Volkswagen recommends a Sun VAT-40 or 60 model. If this equipment is not available to you, further charging system testing should be performed by a repair facility which is properly equipped for charging system diagnosis.
2. Start the engine. Make sure all electrical accessories are OFF.
3. Run the engine at 3,000 rpm, then adjust the load to the maximum ammeter reading (do not allow the voltage to go below 12 volts). The maximum ammeter reading should be equal to the alternator rated output minus 16–20 amps. If the reading is below this specification, replace the voltage regulator and retest. If it is still too low, the alternator is defective.

4. Leave the alternator/regulator tester connected (a voltmeter connected to the battery terminals and set it to the 20 volt scale may be used instead of the alternator/regulator tester). Make sure all electrical accessories are OFF.
5. Run the engine at 3,000 rpm. The voltmeter should display between 13.5–14.5 volts.
6. If the voltage is not as indicated, the voltage regulator is probably defective.
7. Remove the alternator/regulator tester. Repair or replace any components as necessary.

REMOVAL & INSTALLATION

▶ **See Figure 5**

Before purchasing a replacement alternator, read the specification plate on the housing. The number 14V will appear to indicate maximum voltage rating. On the same line will be two more digits followed by the letter **A**. This is the maximum amperage output. Be sure to purchase an alternator with the same rating. The regulator can be replaced without removing the alternator.

1. Disconnect the negative battery cable.
2. Disconnect the wiring from the alternator.
3. Loosen the bolts, then remove the belt from the alternator pulley.
4. Remove the mounting bolts and remove the alternator.

To install:
5. Position the alternator and install the mounting bolts.
6. Tension the drive belt, then torque the bolts to 20 ft. lbs. (27 Nm).
7. Connect the wiring to the alternator and the negative battery cable.
8. Start the engine and check for proper charging system operation.

Voltage Regulator

REMOVAL & INSTALLATION

▶ **See Figures 6 and 7**

The voltage regulator is attached to the rear of the alternator and includes the brushes. Since no adjustment can be performed on the regulator, it is serviced by replacement only.

1. Disconnect the negative battery cable.
2. Remove the mounting screws, then remove the regulator.
3. Measure the free length of the brushes. If they are less than 7/32 in. (5mm) in length, the regulator must be replaced.

To install:
4. Position the regulator on the alternator, then tighten the screws.
5. Connect the negative battery cable.

Fig. 5 Make sure the battery cable is disconnected before removing any electrical connections from the alternator

Fig. 6 Loosen and remove the screws securing the voltage regulator

Fig. 7 After the screws are removed, pull the regulator out of the alternator

Battery

REMOVAL & INSTALLATION

▶ **See Figure 8**

✳✳ CAUTION

Battery electrolyte (acid) is highly corrosive and can damage both you and the paint work. Be careful when lifting the battery in and out of the engine compartment.

1. Disconnect the battery cables, negative cable first.
2. Remove the bolt and the retaining plate/clamp.
3. If equipped, disconnect the small electrical lead for the computer.
4. Lift the battery carefully out of the tray.

To install:

5. Clean all corrosion deposits from the battery tray and the retaining plate with a baking soda and water solution to neutralize the acid.
6. When dry, spray the tray and retaining plate with rust preventive paint.
7. Install the battery and the retaining plate with the bolt. Clean the inside of the cables and coat them with grease or silicone compound after installation.

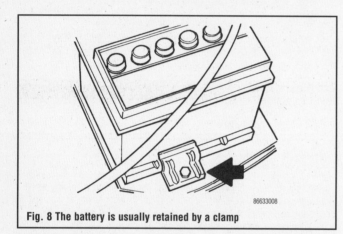

Fig. 8 The battery is usually retained by a clamp

Starter

TESTING

▶ **See Figure 9**

✳✳ CAUTION

Make sure the vehicle is NOT in gear and block the wheels from turning. You will be standing in front of or lying under the vehicle to test the starter. Wear safety glasses and make sure there are no fuel leaks. This procedure may produce sparks.

1. Make sure the battery and all connections are in good condition.
2. Disconnect the small wire from terminal 50 on the solenoid.
3. With the ignition switch **OFF**, briefly touch a jumper wire from the solenoid terminal to the large battery wire on the starter. The starter should operate.
4. If the starter turns slowly or not at all, the starter is faulty.
5. If the starter runs at normal speed, the problem is between the ignition switch and starter terminal 50. This could include the wiring, the neutral safety switch on the automatic transaxle or the seat belt interlock system on some models.

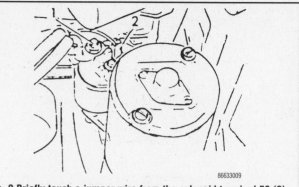

Fig. 9 Briefly touch a jumper wire from the solenoid terminal 50 (2) to the large battery wire (1) on the starter

REMOVAL & INSTALLATION

Dasher with Diesel Engines; Fox with A/C

▶ **See Figure 10**

1. Disconnect the battery ground cable.
2. Support the weight of the engine with either special tool 10-222 or use a jack with a block of wood under the oil pan. Don't jack the engine too high; just take the weight off the motor mounts. Be careful not to bend the oil pan.
3. On Dasher models, remove the engine/transaxle cover plate, then unbolt and remove the starter side motor mount and carrier. On Fox models, remove the mounting bolts from the engine mount support, rubber engine mount lower nut and clamp screw. Then, remove the engine mount support and mount.
4. Label and disconnect the starter wiring.
5. Remove the bolts securing the starter and remove the starter.

Fig. 10 On Dasher models, remove the engine/transaxle cover plate, then unbolt and remove the starter side motor mount and carrier (arrows)

To install:

6. Install the starter and tighten the nuts/bolts to 14 ft. lbs. (19 Nm).
7. Connect the starter solenoid wires. Make sure that the wires are connected to the proper terminals and the wire nuts are tight.
8. Install the engine mounts and related components.
9. Lower the engine or remove the engine support.
10. Connect the battery cable.

Other Models

▶ **See Figures 11, 12, 13 and 14**

1. Disconnect the battery ground cable.
2. Raise and safely support the front of the vehicle with jackstands.

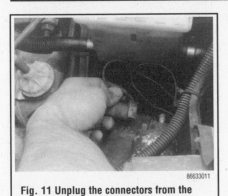

Fig. 11 Unplug the connectors from the starter solenoid. Label them to ease installation later

Fig. 12 Remove the nut securing the large cables to the solenoid

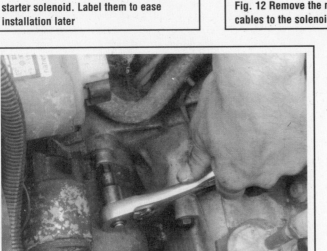

Fig. 13 A box end wrench can be used to remove the standard bolt(s)

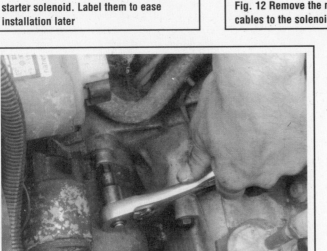

Fig. 14 Use a special socket to remove the Allen head bolts

3. If necessary, label the small wires before disconnecting them.

4. Disconnect the large cable, which is the positive battery cable, from the solenoid.

5. Remove the top bolt first, then remove the bottom bolt while supporting the weight of the starter.

6. Pull the starter straight out.

7. On vehicles with manual transaxles, there is a bushing where the starter shaft fits into the bellhousing. If the shaft or bushing are worn or if the starter has been jamming, the bushing should be replaced. There is a special bushing removal tool available but a small inside bearing removal tool is usually sufficient.

To install:

8. If the bushing was removed, carefully drive the new bushing in until it is flush with the case.

9. Lift the starter into place and install the top bolt first. On 1.6L and 1.8L Golf, GTI and Jetta engines with manual transaxles, torque the starter mounting bolts to 43 ft. lbs. (58 Nm). On other models, torque the starter mounting bolts to 14 ft. lbs. (19 Nm).

10. Connect the wires. Be careful not to overtighten the battery cable connection. The metal is soft and the threads will strip easily.

ENGINE MECHANICAL

Description

GASOLINE ENGINES

The engine in all models is a water cooled inline 4-cylinder with a cast iron block and an aluminum alloy cylinder head. The crankshaft is supported in five plain main bearings and the center bearing includes a 4-piece thrust bearing. The oil pump is mounted below the crankshaft and driven by the intermediate

SOLENOID REPLACEMENT

1. Remove the starter.

2. Remove the nut which secures the connector strip on the end of the solenoid.

3. Take out the two retaining screws on the mounting bracket and withdraw the solenoid after it has been unhooked from the operating lever.

4. Installation is the reverse of removal. In order to facilitate engagement of the lever, the pinion should be pulled out as far as possible when inserting the solenoid.

Sending Units and Sensors

REMOVAL & INSTALLATION

Oil Pressure Switch

The oil pressure switch can be found on top of the oil filter mounting flange and/or threaded into the back of the cylinder head (on the transaxle side). Use a deep socket or a wrench to remove the switch. Before installing the switch, apply a sealer to the threads. Torque the switch to 87 inch lbs. (10 Nm) on models through 1984 (except Quantum). On other models, torque the switch to 18 ft. lbs. (25 Nm).

Water Temperature Sensor

The water temperature sensor can usually be found either on the coolant inlet or outlet housing on the cylinder head. A deep socket or a wrench can be used to remove the sensor. Apply a sealant to the threads before installing the sensor. Torque to 5 ft. lbs. (7 Nm).

Cooling Fan (Thermo) Switch

The cooling fan switch can be found near the bottom of the radiator. A deep socket or a wrench can be used to remove the switch. Always replace the seal if the switch is loosened or removed. Torque to 22 ft. lbs. (30 Nm) on models through 1984 (except Quantum). On other models, torque to 18 ft. lbs. (25 Nm).

shaft. The 16-valve engine has additional oil passages and spray nozzles for cooling the under side of the pistons. On 8-valve engines, the oil pump drive shaft includes an extension that engages the drive lugs on the distributor.

The cylinder head is lightweight aluminum alloy. The intake and exhaust manifolds are mounted on the same side of the cylinder head. The valves are opened and closed by the camshaft lobes operating on cupped cam followers which fit over the valves and springs. This design results in lighter valve train weight and fewer moving parts. The intermediate shaft and the camshaft are driven by a steel-reinforced toothed belt. The valves move in alloy guides that can be replaced when worn. The bearing surfaces for the camshafts and lifters are machined directly into the cylinder head and cannot be serviced.

On 16-valve engines, there are two overhead camshafts that operate two intake valves and two exhaust valves per cylinder. The exhaust camshaft is driven by the belt and the intake camshaft is driven by a chain connecting the two camshafts. The 4-valve per cylinder design allows a central spark plug location for a more controlled and symmetrical combustion. This allows a higher compression ratio for more power and cleaner combustion with the same fuel consumption. The intake and exhaust manifolds are on opposite sides of the cylinder head to improve the engine's ability to "breathe" over the entire rpm range.

The Quantum 5-cylinder engine is an inline engine with a single overhead camshaft and fuel injection. The engine is installed in the straight ahead manner and tilted to the right. The crankshaft runs in six main bearings, the cylinder block is made of cast iron and the cylinder head is light weight aluminum alloy. The oil pump is driven by the crankshaft, while the distributor is camshaft driven.

DIESEL ENGINES

VW introduced the diesel engine option on 1977 Rabbit models. The key difference between the gasoline and diesel engine is that the diesel does not use a carburetor or electrical ignition system. There are no plugs, points or coil to replace. Combustion occurs when a fine mist of diesel fuel is sprayed into hot compressed air (1,650°F/899°C) under high pressure (850 psi). The air is heated by the compression as the piston moves up on the compression stroke. The diesel engine has a compression ratio of 23.5:1 compared to an average gasoline engine's compression ratio of 8.2:1.

VW's diesel block, flywheel, bearings and crankshaft are identical to those in the gasoline engine. The connecting rod wrist pins were strengthened and new pistons and cylinder head, made of aluminum for lightness, were designed.

The cylinder head has an overhead camshaft to actuate the valves and the cam is driven by a flexible toothed belt which also operates the fuel injection pump. This engine has a spherical pre-combustion chamber in which combustion begins. The burning fuel/air mixture is given a swirl pattern by the chamber's shape. The swirl promotes more complete combustion as the combustion process continues in the main combustion chamber. Using the swirl chamber has other advantages: it reduces the peak load which the force of combustion would normally exert on pistons, rods, bearings and crankshaft, enabling VW to use many standard components.

The turbo diesel engine shares the basic design and principals of the normally aspirated diesel, however various modifications have been made to suit the special requirements of turbocharging.

Modifications include a new cylinder head alloy, as well as new materials in the valves, valve seats and swirl chambers—all of which improve heat resistance. A new cylinder head gasket is used to provide better heat resistance and sealing. The engine block has been reinforced to accept 12mm stretch type cylinder head bolts. Piston cooling jets have been installed in the block to provide a spray of oil to help cool the pistons and internal temperatures. The pistons have been modified and strengthened, while the piston rings have been redesigned to provide better sealing and wear characteristics. The surface of the crankshaft connecting rod journals have been hardened to increase torsional rigidity and the front crank pulley size has been increased to help reduce vibration.

Engine Overhaul Tips

Most engine overhaul procedures are fairly standard. In addition to specific parts replacement procedures and complete specifications for your individual engine, this section also is a guide to accepted rebuilding procedures. Examples of standard rebuilding practice are shown and should be used along with specific details concerning your particular engine.

Competent and accurate machine shop services are a must any time an engine is rebuilt. Procedures requiring close tolerance measurements should be performed by a competent machine shop, and are provided so that you will be familiar with the procedures necessary to perform a successful overhaul.

In most instances it is more profitable for the do-it-yourself mechanic to remove, clean and inspect the component, buy the necessary parts and deliver these to a shop for actual machine work. On the other hand, much of the final assembly of the new and machined components is well within the scope of the do-it-yourself mechanic.

TOOLS

The tools required for an engine overhaul or parts replacement will depend on the depth of your involvement. With a few exceptions, they will be the normal hand tools found in a mechanic's tool kit (see Section 1). More in-depth work will require any or all of the following:

- A dial indicator (reading in thousandths) mounted on a universal base
- Micrometers and telescope gauges
- Jaw and screw-type pullers
- Scraper
- Valve spring compressor
- Ring groove cleaner
- Piston ring expander and compressor
- Ridge reamer
- Cylinder hone or glaze breaker
- Plastigage®
- Engine stand

Use of most of these tools is illustrated in this section. Many can be rented for a one-time use from a local parts jobber or tool supply house specializing in automotive work. Occasionally, the use of special tools is called for. See the information on Special Tools and Safety Notice in the front of this book before substituting another tool.

INSPECTION TECHNIQUES

Procedures and specifications are given in this section for inspecting, cleaning and assessing the wear limits of most major components. Other procedures such as Magnaflux® and Zyglo® can be used to locate material flaws and stress cracks. Magnaflux® is a magnetic process applicable only to ferrous materials. The Zyglo® process coats the material with a fluorescent dye penetrant and can be used on any material. Checks for suspected surface cracks can be more readily made using spot check dye. The dye is sprayed onto the suspected area, wiped off and the area sprayed with a developer. Cracks will show up brightly.

OVERHAUL TIPS

Aluminum has become extremely popular for use in engines, due to its low weight. Observe the following precautions when handling aluminum parts:

- Never hot tank aluminum parts (the caustic hot-tank solution will eat the aluminum.
- Remove all aluminum parts (identification tag, etc.) from engine parts prior to cleaning in a hot tank.
- Always coat threads lightly with engine oil or anti-seize compounds before installation, to prevent seizure.
- Never over-torque bolts or spark plugs especially in aluminum threads.

Stripped threads in any component can be repaired using any of several commercial repair kits (Heli-Coil®, Microdot®, Keenserts®, etc.).

When assembling the engine, prelube all power-pack components (pistons, bearings, bearing caps, thrust washers, etc.) to provide lubrication at initial start-up. There are many products specifically formulated for this purpose, but clean engine oil is sufficient. When permanent installation of bolts or nuts is desired, threads should be cleaned and coated with Loctite® or other similar, commercial thread locking compound. When used properly, fasteners will not vibrate loose but can still be removed with tools.

REPAIRING DAMAGED THREADS

▶ **See Figures 15, 16, 17, 18 and 19**

Several methods of repairing damaged threads are available. Heli-Coil® (shown here), Keenserts® and Microdot® are among the most widely used. All involve basically the same principle—drilling out stripped threads, tapping the hole and installing a prewound insert—making welding, plugging and oversize fasteners unnecessary.

Two types of thread repair inserts are usually supplied: a standard type for most inch coarse, inch fine, metric course and metric fine thread sizes and a spark lug type to fit most spark plug port sizes. Consult the individual manufacturer's catalog to determine exact applications. Typical thread repair kits will contain a selection of prewound threaded inserts, a tap (corresponding to the outside diameter threads of the insert) and an installation tool. Spark plug

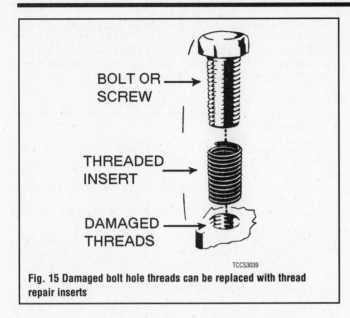

Fig. 15 Damaged bolt hole threads can be replaced with thread repair inserts

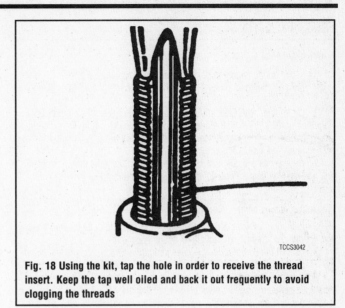

Fig. 18 Using the kit, tap the hole in order to receive the thread insert. Keep the tap well oiled and back it out frequently to avoid clogging the threads

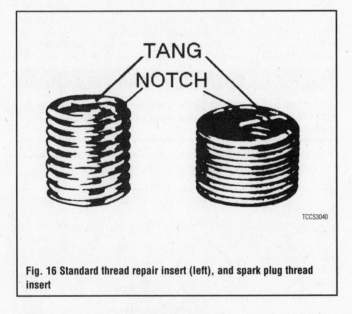

Fig. 16 Standard thread repair insert (left), and spark plug thread insert

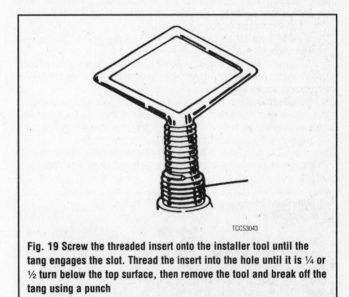

Fig. 19 Screw the threaded insert onto the installer tool until the tang engages the slot. Thread the insert into the hole until it is ¼ or ½ turn below the top surface, then remove the tool and break off the tang using a punch

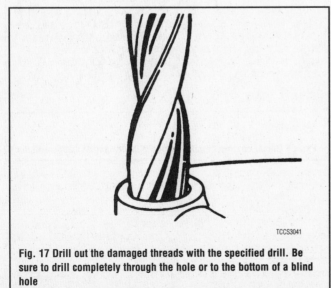

Fig. 17 Drill out the damaged threads with the specified drill. Be sure to drill completely through the hole or to the bottom of a blind hole

inserts usually differ because they require a tap equipped with pilot threads and a combined reamer/tap section. Most manufacturers also supply blister-packed thread repair inserts separately in addition to a master kit containing a variety of taps and inserts plus installation tools.

Before attempting to repair a threaded hole, remove any snapped, broken or damaged bolts or studs. Penetrating oil can be used to free frozen threads. The offending item can be removed with locking pliers or using a screw/stud extractor. After the hole is clear, the thread can be repaired, as shown in the series of accompanying illustrations and in the kit manufacturer's instructions.

Checking Engine Compression

A noticeable lack of engine power, excessive oil consumption and/or poor fuel mileage measured over an extended period are all indicators of internal engine wear. Worn piston rings, scored or worn cylinder bores, blown head gaskets, sticking or burnt valves and worn valve seats can all effect engine compression and will show up in a compression test.

This test will provide useful information only if the battery and starter are in good condition and capable of turning the engine at normal cranking speed. As mentioned in Section 1, a screw-in type compression gauge is more accurate and the job can be done with only one person.

GASOLINE ENGINES

▶ **See Figure 20**

1. Warm up the engine to normal operating temperature.
2. Remove the spark plugs. Note their color and location for later diagnosis.
3. On engines with CIS/CIS-E fuel injection, disconnect the air duct boot from the throttle body. On all models, disconnect the wiring from the primary side of the coil and the Hall sender (if equipped). This will prevent operation of both ignition and fuel injection systems.
4. On engines with Digifant fuel injection, disconnect the ignition control unit and the Hall sender. This will prevent operation of both ignition and fuel injection systems.
5. Screw the compression gauge into the No. 1 spark plug hole until the fitting is snug.
6. Inside the vehicle, depress the accelerator pedal to open the throttle fully and operate the starter continuously for about 3 seconds.
7. Record the compression gauge reading, release the pressure and test the remaining cylinders. Be sure to write down each reading.
8. Compare the readings to the tune-up chart in Section 2. The maximum difference between cylinders must be no more than 44 psi.
9. If a cylinder is unusually low, a "wet test" may isolate the problem. Pour about a tablespoon of clean engine oil into the cylinder through the spark plug hole and test that cylinder again.
10. Interpret the test results:

   a. If the compression comes up when oil is added, the rings and/or cylinder bore are worn.

   b. If compression in any two adjacent cylinders is low, and if the addition of oil doesn't help the compression, there is leakage past the head gasket indicating a warped head.

   c. If there is little or no change when oil is added, there is probably a leaking valve or head gasket or even a cracked cylinder head. Look for oil in the coolant, coolant in the oil, signs of coolant in the exhaust system or one spark plug with a significantly different color from the others.

   d. If all cylinders are low but within the allowable spread, repeat the test with oil in all cylinders. It will probably increase, indicating worn rings.

11. Any time the compression test shows a big difference between cylinders, a cylinder leak-down test can provide more information. This requires a special tool with a gauge and fittings to apply air pressure to the cylinder. The rate of cylinder leakage can determine the extent of wear or damage but the only way to really know what's wrong is to remove the cylinder head.

DIESEL ENGINES

▶ **See Figure 21**

Under each injector is a washer to protect the injector tip from heat and form a good seal. These can be used only one time. Have new heat shield washers on hand before removing the injectors.

1. Carefully remove all the injection lines from the pump and the injectors. Use a back-up wrench when loosening the lines from the pump.
2. Cap all the fittings to prevent dirt from getting into the pump or injectors.
3. Remove the injector leak-off tubes and remove the injectors. Remove the heat shield washers under each injector.
4. Disconnect the fuel shut-off solenoid wire from the injection pump so fuel will not squirt out of the pump during the test.
5. Screw the compression gauge into the No. 1 injector hole until the fitting is snug.
6. Inside the vehicle, operate the starter continuously for about 3 seconds.
7. Record the compression gauge reading, release the pressure and test the remaining cylinders. Be sure to write down each reading.
8. Compare the reading to the tune-up chart in Section 2. The maximum difference between cylinders must be no more than 73 psi.

❊❊ CAUTION

Do not add oil to a cylinder when checking diesel engine compression. The compression generates enough heat to ignite the oil in the cylinder.

9. Except for the added-oil compression test, interpreting compression test results for diesel engines is the same as for gasoline engines.

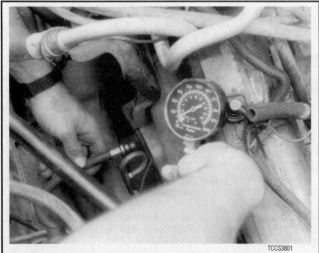

Fig. 20 A screw-in type compression gauge is more accurate and can be used without the aid of an assistant

TCCS3801

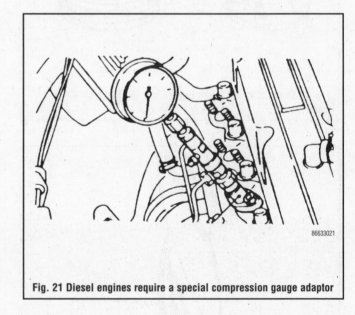

86633021

Fig. 21 Diesel engines require a special compression gauge adaptor

GENERAL ENGINE SPECIFICATIONS

Year	Engine ID/VIN	Engine Displacement Liters (cc)	Fuel System Type	Net Horsepower @ rpm	Net Torque @ rpm (ft. lbs.)	Bore x Stroke (in.)	Compression Ratio	Oil Pressure @ rpm
1983	JF	1.7 (1715)	Carb.	65 @ 5000	88 @ 2800	3.13 x 3.40	8.2:1	28 @ 2000
	CR	1.6 (1588)	Diesel	52 @ 4800	72 @ 3000	3.01 x 3.40	23.0:1	28 @ 2000
	CY	1.6 (1588)	Turbo Diesel	68 @ 4500	98 @ 2800	3.01 x 3.40	23.0:1	74 @ 5000
1984	JK	1.6 (1588)	Diesel	52 @ 4800	97 @ 2700	3.13 x 3.40	23.0:1	28 @ 2000
	EN	1.7 (1715)	CIS	74 @ 5000	90 @ 3000	3.13 x 3.40	8.2:1	28 @ 2000
	JH	1.8 (1780)	CIS	90 @ 5500	100 @ 3000	3.19 x 3.40	9.0:1	28 @ 2000
	JN	1.8 (1780)	CIS-E	88 @ 5500	96 @ 3250	3.19 x 3.40	8.5:1	28 @ 2000
	KM	2.2 (2226)	CIS	100 @ 5100	112 @ 3000	3.19 x 3.40	8.5:1	28 @ 2000
	KX, JT	2.2 (2226)	CIS-E	110 @ 5500	122 @ 2500	3.19 x 3.40	8.5:1	28 @ 2000
	CR	1.6 (1588)	Diesel	52 @ 4800	72 @ 3000	3.01 x 3.40	23.0:1	28 @ 2000
	CY	1.6 (1588)	Turbo Diesel	68 @ 4500	98 @ 2800	3.01 x 3.40	23.0:1	74 @ 5000
1985	JK	1.6 (1588)	Diesel	52 @ 4800	97 @ 2700	3.01 x 3.40	23.0:1	28 @ 2000
	GX	1.8 (1780)	CIS/CIS-E	85 @ 5250	96 @ 3000	3.19 x 3.40	9.0:1	28 @ 2000
	MZ	1.8 (1780)	CIS	90 @ 5500	98 @ 3250	3.19 x 3.40	9.0:1	28 @ 2000
	JH	1.8 (1780)	CIS	90 @ 5500	100 @ 3000	3.19 x 3.40	9.0:1	28 @ 2000
	HT	1.8 (1780)	CIS-E	100 @ 5500	105 @ 3000	3.19 x 3.40	10.0:1	28 @ 2000
	JN	1.8 (1780)	CIS-E	88 @ 5500	96 @ 3250	3.19 x 3.40	9.0:1	28 @ 2000
	KX, JT	2.2 (2226)	CIS-E	110 @ 5500	122 @ 2500	3.19 x 3.40	8.5:1	28 @ 2000
	MD	1.6 (1588)	Turbo Diesel	68 @ 4500	98 @ 2800	3.01 x 3.40	23.0:1	74 @ 5000
	ME	1.6 (1588)	Diesel	52 @ 4800	71 @ 2500	3.01 x 3.40	23.0:1	28 @ 2000
1986	MF	1.6 (1588)	Turbo Diesel	68 @ 4500	98 @ 2500	3.01 x 3.40	23.0:1	74 @ 5000
	GX	1.8 (1780)	CIS/CIS-E	85 @ 5250	96 @ 3000	3.19 x 3.40	9.0:1	28 @ 2000
	MZ	1.8 (1780)	CIS	90 @ 5500	98 @ 3250	3.19 x 3.40	9.0:1	28 @ 2000
	JH	1.8 (1780)	CIS	90 @ 5500	100 @ 3000	3.19 x 3.40	9.0:1	28 @ 2000
	RD	1.8 (1780)	CIS-E	102 @ 5250	110 @ 3250	3.19 x 3.40	10.0:1	28 @ 2000
	HT	1.8 (1780)	CIS-E	100 @ 5500	105 @ 3000	3.19 x 3.40	10.0:1	28 @ 2000
	JN	1.8 (1780)	CIS/CIS-E	85 @ 5500	96 @ 3250	3.19 x 3.40	9.0:1	28 @ 2000
	KX, JT	2.2 (2226)	CIS-E	110 @ 5500	122 @ 2500	3.19 x 3.40	8.5:1	28 @ 2000
	PL	1.8 (1780)	CIS-E	123 @ 5800	120 @ 4250	3.19 x 3.40	10.0:1	28 @ 2000
	ME	1.6 (1588)	Diesel	52 @ 4800	71 @ 2500	3.01 x 3.40	23.0:1	28 @ 2000
1987	MF	1.6 (1588)	Turbo Diesel	68 @ 4500	98 @ 2500	3.01 x 3.40	23.0:1	74 @ 5000
	GX	1.8 (1780)	CIS/CIS-E	85 @ 5250	96 @ 3000	3.19 x 3.40	9.0:1	28 @ 2000
	MZ	1.8 (1780)	CIS	90 @ 5500	98 @ 3250	3.19 x 3.40	9.0:1	28 @ 2000
	JH	1.8 (1780)	CIS	90 @ 5500	100 @ 3000	3.19 x 3.40	9.0:1	28 @ 2000
	JN	1.8 (1780)	CIS/CIS-E	88 @ 5500	96 @ 3250	3.19 x 3.40	9.0:1	28 @ 2000
	RD	1.8 (1780)	CIS-E	102 @ 5250	110 @ 3250	3.19 x 3.40	10.0:1	28 @ 2000
	KX, JT	2.2 (2226)	CIS-E	110 @ 5500	120 @ 2500	3.19 x 3.40	8.5:1	28 @ 2000
	PL	1.8 (1780)	CIS-E	123 @ 5800	120 @ 4250	3.19 x 3.40	10.0:1	28 @ 2000
	UM	1.8 (1780)	CIS-E	81 @ 5500	93 @ 3250	3.19 x 3.40	10.0:1	28 @ 2000
	ME	1.6 (1588)	Diesel	52 @ 4800	71 @ 2500	3.01 x 3.40	23.0:1	28 @ 2000
1988	RV	1.8 (1780)	Digifant II	105 @ 5400	109 @ 3800	3.19 x 3.40	10.0:1	28 @ 2000
	PF	1.8 (1780)	Digifant II	105 @ 5400	114 @ 3800	3.19 x 3.40	10.0:1	28 @ 2000
	PL	1.8 (1780)	CIS-E	123 @ 5800	120 @ 4250	3.19 x 3.40	10.0:1	28 @ 2000
	KX, JT	2.2 (2226)	CIS-E	110 @ 5500	122 @ 2500	3.19 x 3.40	8.5:1	28 @ 2000
	JN	1.8 (1780)	CIS/CIS-E	96 @ 5250	96 @ 3250	3.19 x 3.40	9.0:1	28 @ 2000
	UM	1.8 (1780)	CIS-E	81 @ 5500	93 @ 3250	3.19 x 3.40	10.0:1	28 @ 2000
	JH	1.8 (1780)	CIS	90 @ 5500	100 @ 3000	3.19 x 3.40	9.0:1	28 @ 2000
	ME	1.6 (1588)	Diesel	52 @ 4800	71 @ 2500	3.01 x 3.40	23.0:1	28 @ 2000

86633301

GENERAL ENGINE SPECIFICATIONS

Year	Engine ID/VIN	Engine Displacement Liters (cc)	Fuel System Type	Net Horsepower @ rpm	Net Torque @ rpm (ft. lbs.)	Bore x Stroke (in.)	Compression Ratio	Oil Pressure @ rpm
1974	XW, XV, XZ, XY	1.5 (1471)	Carb.	78 @ 5800	81 @ 4000	3.01 x 3.15	8.5:1	40 @ 2500
1975	FC, FG	1.5 (1471)	Carb.	70 @ 6000	81 @ 3500	3.01 x 3.15	8.2:1	40 @ 2500
	XS, XR	1.5 (1471)	Carb.	71 @ 5600	82 @ 3300	3.01 x 3.15	8.2:1	40 @ 2500
	YG	1.6 (1588)	CIS	77 @ 5500	90 @ 3300	3.13 x 3.15	8.0:1	40 @ 2500
	YH	1.6 (1588)	CIS	79 @ 5500	90 @ 3300	3.13 x 3.15	8.0:1	40 @ 2500
1976	YH, YK	1.6 (1588)	CIS	79 @ 5500	90 @ 3300	3.13 x 3.15	8.0:1	40 @ 2500
	YG	1.6 (1588)	CIS	77 @ 5500	90 @ 3300	3.13 x 3.15	8.0:1	40 @ 2500
	EE	1.6 (1588)	CIS	78 @ 5500	90 @ 3300	3.13 x 3.15	8.0:1	40 @ 2500
	EF	1.6 (1588)	CIS	76 @ 5500	90 @ 3300	3.13 x 3.15	8.0:1	40 @ 2500
	FN	1.6 (1588)	Carb.	71 @ 5600	82 @ 3300	3.13 x 3.15	8.2:1	40 @ 2500
1977	YH, YK	1.6 (1588)	CIS	79 @ 5500	90 @ 3300	3.13 x 3.15	8.0:1	40 @ 2500
	YG	1.6 (1588)	CIS	77 @ 5500	90 @ 3300	3.13 x 3.15	8.0:1	40 @ 2500
	EE	1.6 (1588)	CIS	78 @ 5500	90 @ 3300	3.13 x 3.15	8.0:1	40 @ 2500
	EF	1.6 (1588)	CIS	76 @ 5500	90 @ 3300	3.13 x 3.15	8.0:1	40 @ 2500
	CK	1.5 (1457)	Diesel	48 @ 5000	57 @ 3000	3.01 x 3.15	23.5:1	28 @ 2000
1978	YH, YK	1.6 (1588)	CIS	79 @ 5500	90 @ 3300	3.13 x 3.15	8.0:1	40 @ 2500
	YG	1.6 (1588)	CIS	77 @ 5500	90 @ 3300	3.13 x 3.15	8.0:1	40 @ 2500
	EE	1.6 (1588)	CIS	78 @ 5500	90 @ 3300	3.13 x 3.15	8.0:1	40 @ 2500
	EF	1.6 (1588)	CIS	76 @ 5500	90 @ 3300	3.13 x 2.89	8.0:1	40 @ 2500
	FX	1.5 (1457)	Carb.	62 @ 5800	77 @ 3000	3.13 x 2.89	8.0:1	28 @ 2000
	CK	1.5 (1457)	Diesel	48 @ 5000	57 @ 3000	3.01 x 3.15	23.5:1	28 @ 2000
1979	YH, YK	1.6 (1588)	CIS	79 @ 5500	90 @ 3300	3.13 x 3.15	8.0:1	40 @ 2500
	YG	1.6 (1588)	CIS	77 @ 5500	90 @ 3300	3.13 x 3.15	8.0:1	40 @ 2500
	EH	1.5 (1457)	CIS	71 @ 5800	73 @ 3500	3.13 x 2.89	8.0:1	28 @ 2000
	EJ	1.6 (1588)	CIS	78 @ 5500	84 @ 3200	3.13 x 3.15	8.0:1	28 @ 2000
	FX	1.5 (1457)	Carb.	62 @ 5400	77 @ 3000	3.13 x 2.89	8.0:1	28 @ 2000
	CK	1.5 (1471)	Diesel	48 @ 5000	57 @ 3000	3.01 x 3.15	23.5:1	40 @ 2500
1980	YH, YK	1.6 (1588)	CIS	77 @ 5500	90 @ 3300	3.01 x 3.15	8.0:1	40 @ 2500
	YG	1.6 (1588)	CIS	77 @ 5500	90 @ 3300	3.13 x 3.15	8.0:1	40 @ 2500
	EH	1.5 (1457)	CIS	71 @ 5800	73 @ 3500	3.13 x 2.89	8.0:1	28 @ 2000
	EJ	1.6 (1588)	CIS	78 @ 5500	84 @ 3200	3.13 x 3.15	8.0:1	28 @ 2000
	FX	1.5 (1457)	Carb.	62 @ 5400	57 @ 3000	3.13 x 2.89	8.0:1	28 @ 2000
	CK	1.6 (1588)	Diesel	48 @ 5000	72 @ 3000	3.01 x 3.15	23.5:1	28 @ 2000
1981	EJ	1.6 (1588)	CIS	74 @ 5000	90 @ 3000	3.13 x 3.15	8.2:1	28 @ 2000
	EN	1.7 (1715)	CIS	65 @ 5500	88 @ 2800	3.13 x 3.40	8.2:1	28 @ 2000
	JF	1.7 (1715)	Diesel	52 @ 4800	72 @ 3000	3.01 x 3.40	23.0:1	28 @ 2000
	CR	1.6 (1588)	Diesel	52 @ 4800	72 @ 3000	3.01 x 3.40	23.0:1	28 @ 2000
	CY	1.6 (1588)	Turbo Diesel	68 @ 4500	98 @ 2800	3.01 x 3.40	23.0:1	74 @ 5000
1982	EN	1.7 (1715)	CIS	74 @ 5000	90 @ 3000	3.13 x 3.40	8.2:1	28 @ 2000
	WT	1.7 (1715)	CIS	74 @ 5000	96 @ 3250	3.13 x 3.40	8.2:1	28 @ 2000
	CR	1.6 (1588)	Diesel	52 @ 4800	72 @ 3000	3.01 x 3.40	23.0:1	28 @ 2000
	CY	1.6 (1588)	Turbo Diesel	68 @ 4500	98 @ 2800	3.01 x 3.40	23.0:1	74 @ 5000
1983	EN	1.7 (1715)	CIS	74 @ 5000	90 @ 3000	3.13 x 3.40	8.2:1	28 @ 2000
	WT	1.7 (1715)	CIS	74 @ 5000	90 @ 3000	3.13 x 3.40	8.2:1	28 @ 2000
	WE	2.2 (2226)	CIS	100 @ 5100	112 @ 3000	3.19 x 3.40	8.5:1	28 @ 2000
	JH	1.8 (1780)	CIS	90 @ 5500	100 @ 3000	3.19 x 3.40	8.5:1	28 @ 2000

86633300

CAMSHAFT INSPECTION
All measurements given in inches.

Year	Engine	Run-Out	Bearing Clearance	Camshaft End-Play
1974	Gasoline	0.0004	0.001-0.002	0.006
1975	Gasoline	0.0004	0.001-0.002	0.006
1976	Gasoline	0.0004	0.001-0.002	0.006
1977	Gasoline	0.0004	0.001-0.002	0.006
1978	Gasoline	0.0004	0.001-0.002	0.006
1979	Gasoline	0.0004	0.001-0.002	0.006
1979	Diesel	0.0004	0.004	0.006
1980	Gasoline	0.0004	0.001-0.002	0.006
1980	Diesel	0.0004	0.004	0.006
1981	Gasoline	0.0004	0.001-0.002	0.006
1981	Diesel	0.0004	0.004	0.006
1982	Gasoline	0.0004	0.001-0.002	0.006
1982	Diesel	0.0004	0.004	0.006
1983	Gasoline	0.0004	0.001-0.002	0.006
1983	Diesel	0.0004	0.004	0.006
1984	Gasoline	0.0004	0.001-0.002	0.006
1984	Diesel	0.0004	0.004	0.006
1985	Gasoline	0.0004	0.001-0.002	0.006
1985	Diesel	0.0004	0.004	0.006
1986	Gasoline	0.0004	0.001-0.002	0.006
1986	Diesel	0.0004	0.004	0.006
1987	Gasoline	0.0004	0.001-0.002	0.006
1987	Diesel	0.0004	0.004	0.006
1988	Gasoline	0.0004	0.001-0.002	0.006
1988	Diesel	0.0004	0.004	0.006
1989	Gasoline	0.0004	0.001-0.002	0.006
1989	Diesel	0.0004	0.004	0.006

NOTE: End-play and oil clearance measurements are checked with the cam followers (lifters) removed. On end-play measurements, only the first and last bearing caps are installed.

86633304

GENERAL ENGINE SPECIFICATIONS

Year	Engine ID/VIN	Engine Displacement Liters (cc)	Fuel System Type	Net Horsepower @ rpm	Net Torque @ rpm (ft. lbs.)	Bore x Stroke (in.)	Compression Ratio	Oil Pressure @ rpm
1989	RV	1.8 (1780)	Digifant II	100 @ 5400	109 @ 3800	3.19 x 3.40	10.0:1	28 @ 2000
	PF	1.8 (1780)	Digifant II	105 @ 5400	114 @ 3800	3.19 x 3.40	10.0:1	28 @ 2000
	PL	1.8 (1780)	CIS-E	123 @ 5800	120 @ 4250	3.19 x 3.40	10.0:1	28 @ 2000
	JN	1.8 (1780)	CIS/CIS-E	88 @ 5500	96 @ 3250	3.19 x 3.40	9.0:1	28 @ 2000
	UM	1.8 (1780)	CIS-E	81 @ 5500	93 @ 3250	3.19 x 3.40	9.0:1	28 @ 2000
	JH	1.8 (1780)	CIS	90 @ 5500	100 @ 3000	3.19 x 3.40	9.0:1	28 @ 2000
	ME	1.6 (1588)	Diesel	52 @ 4800	71 @ 2500	3.01 x 3.40	23.0:1	28 @ 2000

86633302

VALVE SPECIFICATIONS

Year	Seat Angle (deg.)	Face Angle (deg.)	Spring Test Pressure (lbs. @ in.)	Spring Installed Height (in.)	Stem-to-Guide Clearance (in.) Intake [2]	Stem-to-Guide Clearance (in.) Exhaust [2]	Stem Diameter (in.) Intake	Stem Diameter (in.) Exhaust
1974	45	45	N/A	N/A	0.039 MAX [1]	0.051 MAX [1]	0.3140	0.3130
1975	45	45	N/A	N/A	0.039 MAX [1]	0.051 MAX [1]	0.3140	0.3130
1976	45	45	N/A	N/A	0.039 MAX [1]	0.051 MAX [1]	0.3140	0.3130
1977	45	45	N/A	N/A	0.039 MAX [1]	0.051 MAX [1]	0.3140	0.3130
1978	45	45	N/A	N/A	0.039 MAX [1]	0.051 MAX [1]	0.3140	0.3130
1979	45	45	N/A	N/A	0.039 MAX [1]	0.051 MAX [1]	0.3140	0.3130
1980	45	45	N/A	N/A	0.039 MAX [1]	0.051 MAX [1]	0.3140	0.3130
1981	45	45	N/A	N/A	0.039 MAX [1]	0.051 MAX [1]	0.3140	0.3130
1982	45	45	N/A	N/A	0.039 MAX [1]	0.051 MAX [1]	0.3140	0.3130
1983	45	45	N/A	N/A	0.039 MAX [1]	0.051 MAX [1]	0.3140	0.3130
1984	45	45	N/A	N/A	0.039 MAX [1]	0.051 MAX [1]	0.3140	0.3130
1985	45	45	N/A	N/A	0.039 MAX [1]	0.051 MAX [1]	0.3140	0.3130
1986	45	45	N/A	N/A	0.039 MAX [1]	0.051 MAX [1]	0.3140	0.3130
1987	45	45	N/A	N/A	0.039 MAX [1]	0.051 MAX [1]	0.3140	0.3130
1988	45	45	N/A	N/A	0.039 MAX [1]	0.051 MAX [1]	0.3140	0.3130
1989	45	45	N/A	N/A	0.039 MAX [1]	0.051 MAX [1]	0.3140	0.3130

1 Diesels: 0.051 MAX.
2 Values listed are maximum wear limit. Measure with a dial indicator touching the valve face. Measure with dial indicator touching the valve face, valve stem end flush with guide

86633303

PISTON AND RING SPECIFICATIONS

All measurements are given in inches.

Year	Engine	Piston Clearance	Ring Gap Top Compression	Ring Gap Bottom Compression	Ring Gap Oil Control	Ring Side Clearance Top Compression	Ring Side Clearance Bottom Compression	Ring Side Clearance Oil Control
1974	Gasoline	0.001-0.003	0.012-0.018	0.012-0.018	0.010-0.016	0.0008-0.002	0.0008-0.002	0.0008-0.002
1975	Gasoline	0.001-0.003	0.012-0.018	0.012-0.018	0.010-0.016	0.0008-0.002	0.0008-0.002	0.0008-0.002
1976	Gasoline	0.001-0.003	0.012-0.018	0.012-0.018	0.010-0.016	0.0008-0.002	0.0008-0.002	0.0008-0.002
1977	Gasoline	0.001-0.003	0.012-0.018	0.012-0.018	0.010-0.016	0.0008-0.002	0.0008-0.002	0.0008-0.002
	Diesel	0.001-0.003	0.012-0.020	0.012-0.020	0.010-0.016	0.002-0.004	0.002-0.003	0.001-0.002
1978	Gasoline	0.001-0.003	0.012-0.018	0.012-0.018	0.010-0.016	0.0008-0.002	0.0008-0.002	0.0008-0.002
	Diesel	0.001-0.003	0.012-0.020	0.012-0.020	0.010-0.016	0.002-0.004	0.002-0.003	0.001-0.002
1979	Gasoline	0.001-0.003	0.012-0.018	0.012-0.018	0.010-0.016	0.0008-0.002	0.0008-0.002	0.0008-0.002
	Diesel	0.001-0.003	0.012-0.020	0.012-0.020	0.010-0.016	0.002-0.004	0.002-0.003	0.001-0.002
1980	Gasoline	0.001-0.003	0.012-0.018	0.012-0.018	0.010-0.016	0.0008-0.002	0.0008-0.002	0.0008-0.002
	Diesel	0.001-0.003	0.012-0.020	0.012-0.020	0.010-0.016	0.002-0.004	0.002-0.003	0.001-0.002
1981	Gasoline	0.001-0.003	0.012-0.018	0.012-0.018	0.010-0.016	0.0008-0.002	0.0008-0.002	0.0008-0.002
	Diesel	0.001-0.003	0.012-0.020	0.012-0.020	0.010-0.016	0.002-0.004	0.002-0.003	0.001-0.002
1982	Gasoline	0.001-0.003	0.012-0.018	0.012-0.018	0.010-0.016	0.0008-0.002	0.0008-0.002	0.0008-0.002
	Diesel	0.001-0.003	0.012-0.020	0.012-0.020	0.010-0.016	0.002-0.004	0.002-0.003	0.001-0.002
1983	Gasoline	0.001-[1] 0.003	0.012-[2] 0.018	0.012-[2] 0.018	0.012-[2] 0.018	0.0008-[3] 0.002	0.0008-[3] 0.002	0.0008-[3] 0.002
	Diesel	0.001-0.003	0.012-0.020	0.012-0.020	0.010-0.016	0.002-0.004	0.002-0.003	0.001-0.002
1984	Gasoline	0.001-[1] 0.003	0.012-[2] 0.018	0.012-[2] 0.018	0.012-[2] 0.018	0.0008-[3] 0.002	0.0008-[3] 0.002	0.0008-[3] 0.002
	Diesel	0.001-0.003	0.012-0.020	0.012-0.020	0.010-0.016	0.002-0.004	0.002-0.003	0.001-0.002
1985	Gasoline	0.001-[1] 0.003	0.012-[2] 0.018	0.012-[2] 0.018	0.012-[2] 0.018	0.0008-[3] 0.002	0.0008-[3] 0.002	0.0008-[3] 0.002
	Diesel	0.001-0.003	0.012-0.020	0.012-0.020	0.010-0.016	0.002-0.004	0.002-0.003	0.001-0.002
1986	Gasoline	0.001-[1] 0.003	0.012-[2] 0.018	0.012-[2] 0.018	0.012-[2] 0.018	0.0008-[3] 0.002	0.0008-[3] 0.002	0.0008-[3] 0.002
	Diesel	0.001-0.003	0.012-0.020	0.012-0.020	0.010-0.016	0.002-0.004	0.002-0.003	0.001-0.002

86633306

CRANKSHAFT AND CONNECTING ROD SPECIFICATIONS

All measurements are given in inches.

Year	Engine	Crankshaft Main Brg. Journal Dia.	Crankshaft Main Brg. Oil Clearance	Crankshaft Shaft End-play	Crankshaft Thrust on No.	Connecting Rod Journal Diameter	Connecting Rod Oil Clearance	Connecting Rod Side Clearance
1974	4-Cylinder	2.126	0.001-0.003	0.003-0.007	3	1.811	0.001-0.003	0.015
1975	4-Cylinder	2.126	0.001-0.003	0.003-0.007	3	1.811	0.001-0.003	0.015
1976	4-Cylinder	2.126	0.001-0.003	0.003-0.007	3	1.811	0.001-0.003	0.015
1977	4-Cylinder	2.126	0.001-0.003	0.003-0.007	3	1.811	0.001-0.003	0.015
1978	4-Cylinder	2.126	0.001-0.003	0.003-0.007	3	1.811	0.001-0.003	0.015
1979	4-Cylinder	2.126	0.001-0.003	0.003-0.007	3	1.811	0.001-0.003	0.015
1980	4-Cylinder	2.126	0.001-0.003	0.003-0.007	3	1.811	0.001-0.003	0.015
1981	4-Cylinder	2.126	0.001-0.003	0.003-0.007	3	1.811 [1]	0.001-0.003	0.015
1982	4-Cylinder	2.126	0.001-0.003	0.003-0.007	3	1.811	0.001-0.003	0.015
1983	4-Cylinder	2.126	0.001-0.003	0.003-0.007	3	1.811 [1]	0.001-0.003	0.015
	5-Cylinder	2.2822	0.0006-0.0030	0.003-0.0070	4	1.811	0.0006-0.0020	0.016
1984	4-Cylinder	2.126	0.001-0.003	0.003-0.007	3	1.811 [1]	0.001-0.003	0.015
	5-Cylinder	2.2822	0.0006-0.0030	0.003-0.0070	4	1.811	0.0006-0.0020	0.016
1985	4-Cylinder	2.126	0.001-0.003	0.003-0.007	3	1.881	0.001-0.003	0.015
	5-Cylinder	2.2822	0.0006-0.0030	0.003-0.0070	4	1.811	0.0006-0.0020	0.016
1986	4-Cylinder	2.126	0.001-0.003	0.003-0.007	3	1.881	0.001-0.003	0.015
	5-Cylinder	2.2822	0.0006-0.0030	0.003-0.0070	4	1.811	0.0006-0.0020	0.016
1987	4-Cylinder	2.126	0.001-0.003	0.003-0.007	3	1.881	0.001-0.003	0.015
	5-Cylinder	2.2822	0.0006-0.0030	0.003-0.0070	4	1.811	0.0006-0.0020	0.016
1988	4-Cylinder	2.126	0.001-0.003	0.003-0.007	3	1.881	0.001-0.003	0.015
	5-Cylinder	2.2822	0.0006-0.0030	0.003-0.0070	4	1.811	0.0006-0.0020	0.016
1989	4-Cylinder	2.126	0.001-0.003	0.003-0.007	3	1.881	0.001-0.003	0.015

1 1.8L Engine: 1.881

86633305

PISTON AND RING SPECIFICATIONS
All measurements are given in inches.

Year	Engine	Piston Clearance	Ring Gap Top Compression	Ring Gap Bottom Compression	Ring Gap Oil Control	Ring Side Clearance Top Compression	Ring Side Clearance Bottom Compression	Ring Side Clearance Oil Control
1987	Gasoline	0.001-0.003 [1]	0.012-0.018 [2]	0.012-0.020 [2]	0.012-0.018 [2]	0.0008-0.002 [3]	0.0008-0.002	0.0008-0.002 [3]
	Diesel	0.001-0.003	0.012-0.018	0.012-0.020	0.010-0.018	0.002-0.004	0.002-0.003	0.001-0.002
1988	Gasoline	0.001-0.003 [1]	0.012-0.018 [2]	0.012-0.020 [2]	0.012-0.018 [2]	0.0008-0.002 [3]	0.0008-0.002	0.0008-0.002 [3]
	Diesel	0.001-0.003	0.012-0.018	0.012-0.020	0.010-0.018	0.002-0.004	0.002-0.003	0.001-0.002
1989	Gasoline	0.001-0.003 [1]	0.012-0.018 [2]	0.012-0.020 [2]	0.012-0.018 [2]	0.0008-0.002	0.0008-0.002	0.001-0.002
	Diesel	0.001-0.003	0.012-0.018	0.012-0.020	0.010-0.018	0.002-0.004	0.002-0.003	0.001-0.002

1 5 cylinder: 0.0011
2 5 cylinder: 0.010-0.020
3 5 cylinder: 0.0008-0.003

8663307

TORQUE SPECIFICATIONS
All readings in ft. lbs.

Year	Engine	Cylinder Head Bolts	Main Bearing Bolts	Rod Bearing Bolts	Crankshaft Sprocket Bolt	Flywheel Bolts	Manifold Intake	Manifold Exhaust	Spark Plugs	Lug Nut
1974	Gasoline	54 [1]	48	33 [3]	58 [4]	55 [8]	18	18	22	81
1975	Gasoline	54 [1]	48	33 [3]	58 [4]	55 [8]	18	18	22	81
1976	Gasoline	54 [1]	48	33 [3]	58 [4]	55 [8]	18	18	22	81
1977	Gasoline	54 [1]	48	33 [3]	58 [4]	55 [8]	18	18	22	81
	Diesel	2	48	33 [3]	58 [6]	55 [8]	18	18	N/A	81
1978	Gasoline	54 [1]	48	33 [3]	58 [4]	55 [8]	18	18	22	81
	Diesel	2	48	33 [3]	58 [6]	55 [8]	18	18	N/A	81
1979	Gasoline	54 [1]	48	33 [3]	58 [4]	55 [8]	18	18	14	81
	Diesel	2	48	33 [3]	58 [6]	55 [8]	18	18	N/A	81
1980	Gasoline	54 [1]	48	33 [3]	58 [4]	55 [8]	18	18	14	81
	Diesel	2	48	33 [3]	58 [6]	55 [8]	18	18	N/A	81
1981	Gasoline	54 [1]	48	33 [3]	58 [4]	55 [8]	18	18	14	81
	Diesel	2	48	33 [3]	58 [6]	55 [8]	18	18	N/A	81
1982	Gasoline	54 [1]	48	33 [3]	58 [4]	55 [8]	18	18	14	81
	Diesel	2	48	33 [3]	58 [6]	55 [8]	18	18	N/A	81
1983	Gasoline	54 [1]	48	33 [3]	58 [4]	55 [8]	18	18	14	81
	Diesel	2	48	33 [3]	58 [6]	55 [8]	18	18	N/A	81
1984	Gasoline	54 [1]	48	33 [3]	58 [4]	55 [8]	18	18	14	81
	Diesel	2	48	33 [3]	58 [6]	55 [8]	18	18	N/A	81
1985	Gasoline	54 [1]	48	33 [3]	145 [5]	55 [8]	18	18	14	81
	Diesel	2	48	33 [3]	7	55 [8]	18	18	N/A	81
1986	Gasoline	54 [1]	48	33 [3]	145 [5]	55 [8]	18 [9]	18	14	81
	Diesel	2	48	33 [3]	7	55 [8]	18	18	N/A	81
1987	Gasoline	54 [1]	48	33 [3]	145 [5]	55 [8]	18 [9]	18	14	81
	Diesel	2	48	33 [3]	7	55 [8]	18	18	N/A	81
1988	Gasoline	54 [1]	48	33 [3]	145 [5]	55 [8]	18 [9]	18	14	81
	Diesel	2	48	33 [3]	7	55 [8]	18	18	N/A	81
1989	Gasoline	54 [1]	48	33 [3]	145 [5]	55 [8]	18 [9]	18	14	81
	Diesel	2	48	33 [3]	7	55 [8]	18	18	N/A	81

1 Applies to 6-point bolts. On carbureted engines with 12-point bolts, tighten to 54 ft. lbs., plus an additional 1/4 turn. On fuel injected engines, first tighten to 29 ft. lbs., then 43 ft. lbs., plus an additional 1/2 turn. See text for details.

2 On 6-point bolts, first tighten to 35 ft. lbs., then 50 ft. lbs., then 65 ft. lbs. On 12-point bolts, first tighten to 29 ft. lbs., then 43 ft. lbs., plus an additional 1/2 turn. See text for details.

3 Applies to 4-cylinder models without stretch-type bolts. On 5-cylinder models without stretch-type bolts, tighten to 37 ft. lbs. On all models with stretch-type bolts, tighten to 22 ft. lbs., plus an additional 1/4 turn. See text for details.

4 Applies to 12mm bolts. Tighten 14 mm bolts to 145 ft. lbs. On 5-cylinder models, tighten to 258 ft. lbs. with tools VW 2084 and 2079 only.

5 On 5-cylinder models, tighten to 258 ft. lbs. with tools VW 2084 and 2079 only.

6 Applies to 12mm bolts (usually found on 1.5 L models). Tighten 14mm bolts to 108 ft. lbs. (usually found on 1.6L models).

7 These models use a 12-sided bolt which must be replaced any time it is removed. First tighten to 66 ft. lbs., then an additional 1/2 turn.

8 Applies to bolts without shoulders. Tighten bolts with shoulders to 74 ft. lbs. and stretch-type bolts to 22 ft. lbs. plus an additional 1/4 turn. Bolts with shoulders and stretch-type bolts cannot be reused. See text for details.

9 On 16-valve engines, tighten the lower manifold bolts to 18 ft. lbs. Tighten the upper bolts to 15 ft. lbs.

8663308

Engine

REMOVAL & INSTALLATION

▶ **See Figure 22**

On some models, some of the front body work must be removed, but removing the hood is not necessary unless it interferes with the lifting equipment. Some components can be removed without disconnecting hydraulic or coolant hoses. Cover the front fenders so components can be hung over them. Before beginning the job, make sure you have some way of labeling the wires, lines and hoses so they can be reconnected correctly. On some engines, special tools are required to remove and install the exhaust pipe–to–manifold spring clamps (VW tool numbers 3140/1 and 3140/2). These are available at your dealer and some larger parts stores.

Fig. 22 Be sure to label hoses, wires and vacuum lines to ensure correct installation later

Dasher With Gasoline Engine

▶ **See Figures 23, 24 and 25**

1. Disconnect the battery cables, negative cable first. On fuel injected engines, release the fuel system pressure.
2. Remove the exhaust manifold heater hose and breather hose from the air cleaner.
3. Remove the air cleaner assembly.
4. On carbureted models, pull the clip off the accelerator cable and detach the cable. On fuel injected models, disconnect the electrical connectors/wiring harnesses and detach the control pressure regulator lines.
5. Loosen the upper adjustment nut on the clutch cable and detach it. Move the cable off to the side and out of the way.
6. On carbureted models only, disconnect the fuel line from the fuel pump, drain it, plug it, and place it out of the way. On fuel injected models, disconnect the air duct. Remove the cold start valve. Remove the fuel injectors from the cylinder head (protect the ends with caps) and the accelerator cable. Remove the airflow sensor with the fuel distributor and place out of the way.
7. Detach emission control hoses. Remove power steering pump (if equipped) and V-belts.
8. Disconnect the wiring from the alternator.
9. Detach the clip and remove the heater cable.

❋❋ CAUTION

Do not disconnect refrigerant lines on vehicles equipped with air conditioning.

10. On cars with air conditioning:
    a. Remove the horn and the bolts/nuts securing the compressor and condenser assemblies.
    b. Move the compressor and condenser out of the way, without disconnecting the refrigerant lines.
    c. Disconnect the vacuum hoses and brake booster hose, if equipped.
11. Disconnect the front engine mounts and remove the mount bracket.

❋❋ CAUTION

When draining the coolant, keep in mind that cats and dogs are attracted by ethylene glycol antifreeze, and are quite likely to drink any that is left in an uncovered container or in puddles on the ground. This will prove fatal in sufficient quantity. Always drain the coolant into a sealable container.

12. Drain the coolant from the radiator. The plug is located near the lower hose, or remove the hose on models without the drain plug. Drain the cylinder block at the plug near the starter.
13. Disconnect the electrical wire from the coil and distributor, oil pressure and temperature sending units, fan and the thermal switch on the radiator.
14. Disconnect the radiator and heater hoses from the engine. Detach the heater valve cable.
15. Loosen the radiator shroud retainers. Remove the mounting bolts and nuts and lift out the radiator and fan from the engine compartment.
16. Raise the front of the vehicle and safely support it.
17. Remove the starter.
18. Disconnect the exhaust pipe from the manifold.
19. Detach the engine side mounts.
20. Loosen the upper engine-to-transaxle bolts. Remove the lower bolts. If the car is equipped with an automatic transaxle, remove the three torque converter-to-flywheel bolts by working through the starter hole. Use a bar or locking device to hold the flywheel. Also disconnect the automatic transaxle vacuum hose.
21. Support the transaxle with a floor jack.
22. Lower the car until the wheels are on the ground.
23. Attach the hoist to the engine lift points. Make sure the lifting bracket fasteners are tight before connecting the hoist.
24. Raise the engine/transaxle until the transaxle touches the steering rack.
25. Adjust your jack or support so that the transaxle is held firmly.
26. Remove the upper engine-to-transaxle bolts.
27. Pry the engine and transaxle apart and remove the intermediate plate.

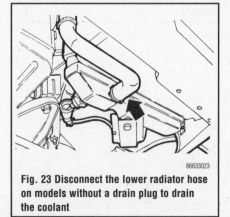

Fig. 23 Disconnect the lower radiator hose on models without a drain plug to drain the coolant

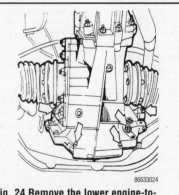

Fig. 24 Remove the lower engine-to-transaxle bolts (arrows)

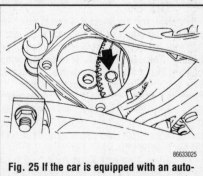

Fig. 25 If the car is equipped with an automatic transaxle, remove the torque converter-to-flywheel bolts by working through the starter hole

Install a bar or cable to the torque converter housing on automatic transaxle equipped cars to prevent the converter from falling out.

28. Remove the engine by slowly lifting and turning simultaneously.

❊❊ WARNING

Do this very carefully to avoid damaging the halfshafts or transaxle.

To install:

29. Lower the engine into the vehicle. Be careful not to damage the input shaft of the transaxle during installation.

30. Install the upper engine-to-transaxle bolts. Torque the bolts to 40 ft. lbs. (54 Nm).

31. Install the engine-to-transaxle (manual) or torque converter (automatic) bolts. Use new bolts. Torque the torque converter bolts to 25 ft. lbs. (34 Nm), engine-to-transaxle bolts to 40 ft.lbs. (54 Nm).

32. Install the engine side mount bolts and torque them to 32 ft. lbs. (44 Nm).

33. Connect the exhaust pipe to the manifold. Use new gaskets as required.

34. Install the starter and connect the wiring.

35. Lower the car.

36. Install the radiator and fan.

37. Connect the heater cable, heater hoses and radiator hoses.

38. Connect the thermal switch, cooling fan, temperature sending unit and distributor wires.

39. Install the coolant drain plugs and fill the cooling system.

40. Install the front engine mounts and bracket.

41. On cars equipped with air conditioning, connect the brake booster and vacuum hoses. Mount the compressor and condenser units.

42. Connect the heater cable and install the cable clip.

43. Connect the alternator wiring. Make sure the wire nuts are tight.

44. Connect the emission control hoses. If equipped, install the power steering pump and V-belt. Tension the belt.

45. On fuel injected engines, install the airflow sensor/fuel distributor, fuel injectors, accelerator cable and air duct. On carbureted engines, connect the fuel line to the fuel pump.

46. Connect and adjust the clutch cable.

47. On fuel injected engines, connect the control pressure regulator lines, frequency valve, cold start valve and fuel injector wiring. On carbureted engines, connect and adjust the accelerator cable. Secure the cable with the cable clip.

48. Install the air cleaner assembly and the exhaust manifold heater and breather hoses.

49. Connect the battery cables.

Dasher With Diesel Engine

▶ **See Figures 23, 24 and 25**

1. Disconnect the battery cables, negative cable first.

2. Set the heat control to HOT. Remove the lower radiator hose and remove the thermostat to drain the coolant. Remove the thermo-switch electrical connector and the radiator brace at the bottom of the radiator. Remove the top radiator shroud, upper hose, radiator mounting bolts, then remove the radiator and fan.

❊❊ CAUTION

When draining the coolant, keep in mind that cats and dogs are attracted by ethylene glycol antifreeze, and are quite likely to drink any that is left in an uncovered container or in puddles on the ground. This will prove fatal in sufficient quantity. Always drain the coolant into a sealable container. Coolant should be reused unless it is contaminated or several years old.

3. Remove the supply and return lines from the injection pump. Disconnect the throttle cable from the pump and remove the cable mounting bracket. Disconnect the cold start cable at the pin and remove the electrical connector from the fuel shut-off solenoid.

4. Unplug the electrical connectors from the oil pressure switch, coolant temperature sensor and glow plugs. Remove the radiator hose from the cylinder head and the vacuum hose from the vacuum pump.

5. Loosen the clutch cable adjusting nuts.

6. Disconnect the clutch cable from the lever.

7. Remove the hose from the water pump.

8. Loosen the right engine mount.

9. Remove the alternator.

10. Remove the front engine mounts.

11. Disconnect the exhaust pipe from the manifold, and the pipe bracket from the transaxle.

12. Loosen the left engine mount.

13. Remove the starter.

14. Remove the engine-to-transaxle bolts, and the flywheel cover bolts.

15. Attach a lifting chain to the engine and raise the engine until the transaxle touches the steering rack. Make sure the lifting bracket fasteners are tight before connecting the hoist. Remove the left engine mount.

16. Support the transaxle with a floor jack and raise and turn the engine at the same time to remove.

To install:

17. Lower the engine into the vehicle and install the flywheel cover bolts and the engine-to-transaxle bolts. Install the left engine mount. Tighten the engine-to-transaxle bolts to 40 ft. lbs. (54 Nm) and the engine mount bolts to 29 ft. lbs. (39 Nm).

18. Install the starter.

19. Mount the exhaust pipe bracket to the transaxle and connect the exhaust pipe to the manifold. Use new gaskets as required. Torque the exhaust manifold nuts to 18 ft. lbs. (24 Nm).

20. Install the front engine mounts and torque the bolts to 29 ft. lbs. (39 Nm).

21. Install the alternator.

22. Connect the water pump hose.

23. Install the right engine mount and torque the bolts to 29 ft. lbs. (39 Nm).

24. Connect the clutch cable to the adjusting lever and adjust it.

25. Connect the vacuum pump hose and the radiator hose to the cylinder head.

26. Engage the glow plug, coolant temperature sensor and oil pressure switch electrical connectors.

27. Connect the fuel shut-off solenoid wiring. Connect the throttle cable to the mounting bracket and the fuel injection pump. Attach the injection pump supply and return lines. Adjust the throttle and cold start cables.

28. Install the radiator and fan and connect the wiring and hoses. Install the thermostat with a new gasket.

29. Connect the battery cables. Refill the cooling system and adjust the belt tension.

4-Cylinder Quantum Gasoline Engine

▶ **See Figures 23, 24 and 25**

1. Relieve the fuel system pressure. Disconnect the battery cables, negative cable first.

2. Set the heater control to HOT. Remove the radiator cap and drain the cooling system. Remove the radiator hoses from the engine.

❊❊ CAUTION

When draining the coolant, keep in mind that cats and dogs are attracted by ethylene glycol antifreeze, and are quite likely to drink any that is left in an uncovered container or in puddles on the ground. This will prove fatal in sufficient quantity. Always drain the coolant into a sealable container.

3. If equipped, remove the power steering mounting bolts and the drive belt, then move the pump aside leaving the hoses attached.

4. Unplug the electrical connectors from the thermo-time switch, the alternator and the control pressure regulator.

5. Disconnect the distributor vacuum hoses from the distributor.

6. Remove the control pressure regulator bolts, then move the regulator aside with the fuel lines attached.

7. Disconnect the radiator fan wires. Remove the radiator bolts and the radiator assembly with the air duct.

8. Remove the clip on the clutch cable and disconnect the cable. Position the cable off to the side and out of the way.

9. Remove the left engine mount nut.

10. Unplug the coolant temperature sender wire, oxygen sensor, thermo-switch, Hall sending unit and the coil wire from the distributor.

11. Unplug the electrical connectors from the auxiliary air regulator, the cold start and frequency valves.

12. Remove the emissions canister hose from the air duct.

13. Remove the preheater hose and the cold start valve (leave the fuel line attached).

14. Disconnect the distributor vacuum hose from the intake manifold. Remove the accelerator cable, the crankcase breather hose and the brake booster hose.

15. Remove the fuel injectors (protect them with caps), the fuel distributor (leave the lines attached) and move them aside.

16. If equipped with air conditioning, remove the throttle body housing, the auxiliary air regulator, the horn bracket, the crankcase pulley nuts and the drive belt. Loosen and remove the compressor and condenser mounting nuts/bolts. Position and tie the compressor and the condenser off to the side and out of the way. DO NOT open the refrigerant lines.

17. Remove the right engine mount nuts.

18. Remove the exhaust pipe at the manifold.

19. Remove the starter wiring and the starter. Remove the lower engine-to-transaxle bolts and the flywheel cover plate.

20. If equipped with an automatic transaxle, remove the torque converter-to-driveplate bolts. Attach the engine support tool VW 785/1B or an equivalent support tool to the transaxle.

21. Loosen the nuts on the outer half of the damper pulley and remove the drive belt.

22. Attach tool US-1105 or an equivalent sling to the engine. Support it with a vertical hoist and lift the engine slightly, then remove the right engine mount.

23. Remove the upper engine-to-transaxle bolts, then separate the engine from the transaxle. Lift and turn the engine to remove it from the vehicle.

➡**If equipped with an automatic transaxle, secure the torque converter to the transaxle to keep it from falling out.**

To install:

24. Lower the engine into the vehicle and install the engine-to-transaxle bolts. Torque the bolts to 40 ft. lbs. (54 Nm).

25. Install the right engine mount and torque the bolts to 25 ft. lbs. (34 Nm).

26. Slip the drive belt onto the damper pulley and tighten the outer pulley half nuts.

27. If equipped with automatic transaxle, install the torque converter-to-flywheel bolts and torque them to 22 ft. lbs. (30 Nm).

28. Install the lower engine-to-transaxle bolts and torque them to 40 ft. lbs. (54 Nm).

29. Install the starter and connect the wiring.

30. Connect the exhaust pipe to the exhaust manifold and torque the nuts to 30 ft. lbs. (41 Nm). Use a new gasket as required.

31. Install the right engine mount nuts and torque them to 25 ft. lbs. (34 Nm).

32. Mount the air conditioning compressor and install all related components. Torque the upper air conditioning compressor mounting bolts to 22 ft. lbs. (30 Nm) and the lower bolts to 18 ft. lbs. (24 Nm).

33. Install the fuel distributor and fuel injectors.

34. Connect the crankcase and brake booster hoses. Connect and adjust the accelerator cable. Connect the distributor vacuum hose to the intake manifold.

35. Install the cold start valve and connect the pre-heater hose.

36. Connect the emissions canister hose to the air duct.

37. Plug in the frequency valve, cold start and auxiliary air regulator connectors.

38. Connect the Hall sending unit and coil wire to the distributor. Connect the oxygen sensor, thermo-switch and temperature sending unit wires.

39. Install the left engine mount. Torque the nuts to 25 ft. lbs. (34 Nm).

40. Connect and adjust the clutch cable. Install the cable clip.

41. Install the radiator and fan assembly with the air duct. Plug in the radiator fan wires.

42. Install the control pressure regulator.

43. Connect the distributor vacuum advance hose.

44. Connect the wires to the control pressure regulator, alternator and the thermo-time switch.

45. Mount the power steering pump and torque the bolts to 15 ft. lbs. (20 Nm).

46. Connect the radiator hoses.

47. Connect the battery cables. Refill the cooling system and adjust the belt tension.

5-Cylinder Quantum Engine

▶ **See Figures 23 thru 28**

1. Disconnect the negative battery cable, negative cable first.

2. Move the heater control valve to the HOT position. Remove the radiator cap from the expansion tank.

3. At the power steering pump, remove the drive belt cover, the drive belt, the mounting bolts and the pump. Move the pump aside with the hoses connected.

4. Remove the grille and the radiator cover.

5. Remove the lower radiator hose and drain the coolant.

6. Remove the front bumper with the energy absorbers.

7. Remove the vacuum hoses from the intake manifold, the upper radiator hose, the radiator hose from the thermostat housing and the heater hose (drain the remaining coolant).

8. Unplug the electrical connectors from the oil pressure switch, the control pressure regulator and the thermo-time switches.

9. Remove the cylinder head cover ground wire.

10. Remove the control pressure regulator (leave the lines attached) and the ball joint circlip (disconnect it at the pushrod).

11. Remove the alternator drive belt, the bracket bolts and the alternator assembly.

12. Remove the air duct and the front engine stop.

13. Unplug the electrical connectors from the cold start valve, the frequency valve and the throttle switch. Disconnect the electrical leads at the idle stabilizer valve, the Hall sender at the distributor and the oxygen sensor.

14. Remove the accelerator cable circlip, then disconnect the cable rod from the throttle body.

15. Remove the distributor cap, the cold start valve and the vacuum hose from the thermo-valve.

16. Remove the fuel injection cooling hose.

17. Remove the fuel injectors from the intake manifold (leave the fuel lines connected).

Fig. 26 Front bumper and energy absorber attaching bolts (arrows)

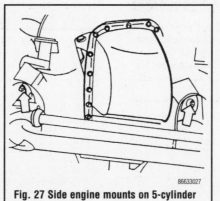

Fig. 27 Side engine mounts on 5-cylinder models (arrows)

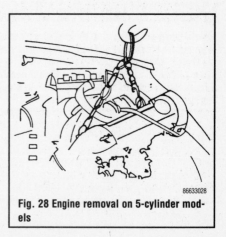

Fig. 28 Engine removal on 5-cylinder models

➡**When removing the fuel injectors and the cold start valve, place caps on the ends to protect them from damage.**

18. Remove the air filter housing bolts and the filter.

➡**If equipped with an automatic transaxle, disconnect (and plug) the oil cooler hoses.**

19. Remove the heater hoses. Remove the exhaust pipe bracket from the engine and transaxle assembly.

20. If equipped with air conditioning, remove the drive belt, the electrical connector at the compressor, the compressor bracket to engine bolts and the compressor assembly. Move it off to the side and out of the way. Tie the compressor to some convenient point in the engine compartment. DO NOT disconnect the lines or allow the compressor to hang by the pressure hoses.

21. Remove the crankshaft damper bolt, refer to the crankshaft damper procedure in this section (do not remove the damper, only the bolt).

22. Of the four crankshaft pulley bolts, remove two and loosen two. To remove the pulley, tap lightly on the remaining bolts. Remove the bolts and the pulley.

➡**When removing the pulley from the crankshaft, leave the drive belt sprocket attached to the crankshaft.**

23. Remove the front engine mount and the subframe-to-body bolts. Remove the exhaust pipe from the exhaust manifold and the support bracket.

24. Disconnect the starter cables and remove the starter.

25. Remove the torque converter-to-flywheel bolts, the bolts can be removed through the starter hole. Remove the lower engine-to-transaxle bolts. Unhook the shift rod clip and disconnect the rod.

26. Remove the rubber plugs from the left side frame member. Using tool VW 785/1 or an equivalent support tool, connect it to the transaxle and to the frame member, then adjust to make contact with the transaxle.

27. Remove both engine mount nuts and the upper engine-to-transaxle bolts (leave one bolt in place).

28. Attach tool US 1105 or an equivalent engine support tool to the engine and a vertical hoist.

➡**If equipped with an automatic transaxle, secure the torque converter before removing the engine from the transaxle.**

29. Remove the last engine-to-transaxle bolt and lift the engine while prying the engine apart from the transaxle. Remove the engine from the vehicle.

To install:

30. Lower the engine into the vehicle and install a engine-to-transaxle bolt to hold the engine in place. Install the remaining bolts and also the engine mount nuts. Torque the transaxle-to-engine bolts to 22 ft. lbs. (30 Nm) for 8mm bolts, 32 ft. lbs. (44 Nm) for 10mm bolts and 43 ft. lbs. (58 Nm) for 12mm bolts. Torque the engine mount nuts to 32 ft. lbs. (44 Nm).

31. Install the left frame side member rubber plugs, then remove the support fixtures from the engine.

32. Connect the shift rod and install a new circlip.

33. Install the lower engine-to-transaxle bolts. Torque to 22 ft. lbs. (30 Nm) for 8mm bolts, 32 ft. lbs. (44 Nm) for 10mm bolts and 43 ft. lbs. (58 Nm) for 12mm bolts. Install the converter-to-flywheel bolts (working through the starter hole) and torque them to 22 ft. lbs. (30 Nm).

34. Install the starter and connect the starter wiring.

35. Connect the exhaust pipe using a new gasket. Torque the manifold nuts to 18 ft. lbs. (24 Nm).

36. Install the front engine mounts and subframe-to-body bolts. Torque the subframe-to-body bolts to 28 ft. lbs. (38 Nm), then tighten them an additional ¼ turn (90 degrees). Torque the mount nuts to 33 ft. lbs. (45 Nm).

37. When installing the crankshaft bolt, coat the threads with Loctite® 573. Using tools VW 2084 and 2079, torque the damper pulley center bolt to 258 ft. lbs. (350 Nm). These tools must be used to torque the damper bolt (refer to the crankshaft damper procedure in this section). Tighten the crankshaft pulley bolts to 14 ft. lbs. (19 Nm).

38. Install the air conditioning compressor, drive belt and connect the electrical wiring. Torque the mounting bolts to 29 ft. lbs. (39 Nm).

39. Mount the exhaust pipe bracket to the engine and transaxle. Torque the mounting bolts to 22 ft. lbs. (30 Nm).

40. Connect the heater hoses.

41. If equipped with automatic transaxle, unplug and connect the transaxle cooler lines.

42. Install the air filter housing and filter.

43. Install the fuel injectors and connect the fuel injector cooling hose.

44. Connect the vacuum hose to the thermo-valve. Install the distributor cap and cold start valve.

45. Plug in the oxygen sensor, Hall sender unit (at the distributor), idle stabilizer valve, frequency valve (at the throttle switch) and cold start valve electrical connectors.

46. Install the front engine stop and torque the bolts to 33 ft. lbs. (45 Nm). Connect the air inlet duct.

47. Install the alternator.

48. Install the ball joint circlip and the control pressure regulator.

49. Attach the cylinder head cover ground wire.

50. Plug in the thermo-time, control regulator and oil pressure switch electrical connectors.

51. Connect the heater, thermostat and upper radiator, and install the manifold (vacuum) hoses.

52. Install the energy absorber and front bumper assemblies.

53. Connect the lower radiator hose.

54. Install the radiator cover and grille.

55. Install the power steering pump, drive belt and and drive belt cover. Torque the power steering pump mounting bolts to 15 ft. lbs. (20 Nm).

56. Connect the battery cables, fill the cooling system and adjust the drive belt tension.

Quantum Turbo Diesel

◗ **See Figures 23, 24 and 25**

1. Disconnect the battery cables, negative cable first.

2. Remove the horn and the cover plates of the engine and the transaxle.

3. Move the heater control lever to the HOT position, then remove the radiator cap.

4. Remove the two lower hoses of the thermostat housing and drain the coolant.

5. Unplug the electrical connections from the fan, the thermo-switch and the series resistor near the alternator.

6. Remove the radiator to engine coolant hose, the radiator bolts, the right fan connector and the radiator.

7. Remove the fuel supply and the return lines at the fuel injectors. Cap the lines to prevent the entry of dirt into the fuel system.

8. Disconnect the accelerator cable from the fuel injection pump and from the support bracket.

9. Disconnect the cold start cable.

10. Unplug the electrical connector at the fuel shut-off solenoid and remove the gear shift indicator switch with the wiring from the bracket.

11. Remove the air filter-to-turbocharger (air filter) hose.

12. Unplug the electrical connector from the oil pressure switch, the coolant temperature sensors and the glow plugs.

13. Remove the power steering bracket bolts (leave the lines attached) and move the pump off to the side and out of the way.

14. Disconnect the hose from the vacuum pump.

15. Remove the clutch cable lock plate and unhook the cable.

16. Remove the two nuts from both engine mounts and the engine torque support bolts at the front of the engine.

17. Remove the alternator and the front engine stop.

➡**If equipped with air conditioning, remove the pulley nuts from the compressor, the drive belt and the compressor bracket bolts. Position and tie the compressor off to the side and out of the way so that the hoses are not under strain. DO NOT disconnect the lines or allow the compressor to hang freely by the hoses.**

18. Disconnect the exhaust pipe and oil lines (supply and return) from the turbocharger. Remove the turbocharger from its mounting bracket. Cap the ends of the oil lines to prevent leakage and dirt from entering.

19. Unplug the electrical connectors and remove the starter. Place the starter on the engine subframe.

20. Remove the two bottom engine-to-transaxle bolts and the flywheel cover plate bolts.

➡**If equipped with an automatic transaxle, remove the cover plate and the torque converter mounting bolts.**

21. Install tool VW 785/1B or an equivalent support bar under the front of the transaxle and support it.

22. Attach tool US 1105 or an equivalent engine sling and a vertical lift to the engine. Lift the engine and transaxle assembly free of the engine mounts.

23. Adjust the support bar under the transaxle.

24. Remove the three upper transaxle-to-engine bolts and pry the engine from the transaxle.

➡**If equipped with an automatic transaxle, secure the torque converter to the transaxle to keep it from falling out.**

25. Lift the engine from the engine compartment.

To install:

➡**Before installing the engine, place the starter on the subframe.**

26. Lower the engine into the engine compartment and shake the engine until it seats on the transaxle housing.

27. Install the three upper engine-to-transaxle bolts and torque them to 40 ft. lbs. (54 Nm).

28. If equipped with automatic transaxle, install the torque converter and cover plate bolts. Torque the converter bolts to 22 ft. lbs. (30 Nm) and the cover plate bolts to 7 ft. lbs. (10 Nm).

29. Install the flywheel cover plate bolts (manual transaxles) and torque them to 7 ft. lbs. (10 Nm). Install the two bottom engine-to-transaxle bolts and torque them to 40 ft. lbs. (54 Nm).

30. Remove the engine support bars.

31. Mount the starter and connect the starter wiring. Torque the starter mounting bolts to 15 ft. lbs. (20 Nm).

32. Install the turbocharger with an new gasket. Connect the oil lines and exhaust pipe (with a new gasket) to the turbo. Torque the turbo-to-manifold bolts to 30 ft. lbs. (41 Nm) and exhaust pipe nuts to 18 ft. lbs. (24 Nm).

33. Mount the air conditioning compressor, install the drive belt and pulley nuts. Torque the 8mm bracket bolts to 18 ft. lbs. (24 Nm) and the 12mm bolts to 59 ft. lbs. (80 Nm).

34. Install the engine mount nuts and the torque support bolts. Torque the mount nuts to 25 ft. lbs. (34 Nm).

35. Connect the clutch cable and install the lock plate.

36. Connect the vacuum pump hose.

37. Install the power steering pump and torque the mounting bolts to 15 ft. lbs. (20 Nm).

38. Engage the glow plug, coolant temperature sensor and oil pressure switch electrical connectors.

39. Connect and adjust the cold start and accelerator cables.

40. Connect the fuel lines to the injection pump.

41. Install the radiator and plug in the fan wire. Connect the coolant hose.

42. Plug in the alternator series resistor, thermo-switch and fan electrical connectors.

43. Install the cover plates and the horn.

44. Connect the battery cables. Fill the cooling system and adjust the drive belt tension.

1975–84 Rabbit, Jetta and Scirocco (Gasoline Engines)

◆ **See Figure 23**

The engine and transaxle assembly is removed from the vehicle with the transaxle attached. If the vehicle is carbureted, ignore any procedures that pertain to fuel injection.

1. On 1979 fuel injected vehicles equipped with air conditioning, turn the ignition **ON** and the air conditioning control (engine not running) to engage the compressor clutch. Remove the compressor clutch bolt and press the clutch from the air conditioning compressor shaft (using a ⅝ in.×18 UNF bolt). Turn **OFF** the ignition and the air conditioning. Disconnect the compressor clutch wire.

2. Disconnect the battery cables, negative cable first. Remove the battery from the engine compartment.

3. Remove the fuel tank cap and relieve the pressure in the fuel system.

➡**If equipped with an automatic transaxle, place the selector lever in the PARK position.**

4. Remove the air intake duct between the fuel distributor and the throttle housing.

5. Remove the radiator cap. Turn the heater temperature control valve to the HOT position. Place a container under the thermostat housing, remove the thermostat flange and drain the coolant.

6. Remove the upper radiator and heater hoses from the engine. Unplug the electrical connector from the radiator fan motor and the thermo-switch.

7. Remove the radiator mounting nuts, the upper radiator clamp clip, the clamp and the radiator.

8. Disconnect the alternator, thermo-switch, oil pressure switch, warm-up regulator and distributor wiring.

9. Turn the A/C belt tensioner until a 10mm Allen key can be inserted through one the holes in the tensioner to remove its bolts. Remove the alternator, the timing belt cover and the compressor mounting bracket bolts (under the timing cover). Disconnect the pre-heat hose. Remove the diagonal braces, the support brace and the compressor bracket. Move and tie the compressor off to the side and out of the way. DO NOT disconnect the refrigerant hoses and do not allow the compressor to hang freely by the hoses.

10. Remove the pre-heat tube from the rear of the engine.

11. Remove the distributor vacuum hoses and the EGR temperature valve.

12. Remove the coil and the coolant temperature sensor wires.

13. Place a suitable container (to catch the fuel) under the cold start valve, then remove the fuel line and the warm-up regulator.

14. Remove the electrical connectors from the cold start valve and the auxiliary air regulator.

15. At the throttle body (fuel injected engines), remove the vacuum lines of the brake booster and the vacuum amplifier (if equipped).

16. Remove the PCV hose from the cylinder head cover.

17. At the throttle body (fuel injected engines), pull back the accelerator cable clip and disconnect the cable from the ball. Loosen the accelerator cable locknut and remove the cable from the cylinder head cover. Position the cable off the side and out of the way.

18. On fuel injected engines, remove the fuel injector rail, then position the entire assembly aside. Cover the fuel injector openings with masking tape to prevent the entry of dirt. Move the fuel and vacuum lines off to the side and out of the way. On Scirocco, remove the intake manifold.

19. Unplug the electrical connectors from the starter, the back-up light switch and the ground cable from the transaxle.

20. If equipped with a manual transaxle, loosen the locknut (at the clutch cable), then remove the clip from under the clutch lever and the cable. If equipped with an automatic transaxle, disconnect the selector cable from the transaxle and the bracket. On Scirocco and Cabriolet with automatic transaxle, loosen the accelerator pedal cable and disconnect it from the operating rod and the bracket.

21. Remove the speedometer cable clamp and the cable.

22. Remove the upper starter bolts and the starter.

23. Remove the nuts from the exhaust flex-pipe and the relay shaft. Disconnect the lever from the relay shaft.

24. Remove the driveshafts from the mounting flanges.

25. Remove the horn (move aside), the front mount cup bolts, the cup and the front mount.

26. At both front wheels, remove the axle nuts.

27. At both steering knuckles, remove the ball joint lock bolts. Using a large prybar, pry the ball joints from the steering knuckle.

28. Swing the wheel and strut assembly away from the vehicle. Remove the drive axles from the wheel hubs.

➡**With the driveshafts removed, reconnect the ball joints and lock bolts so that the vehicle may be lowered on its wheels.**

29. Remove the entire rear mount and the right front wheel and tire assembly.

30. Attach tool US 1105, 2024A or an equivalent sling to the engine and an overhead hoist. Lift the engine slightly.

31. On manual transaxles, remove the clip from the gearshift lever rod. Remove the rod from the selector shaft lever and the relay shaft with the gearshift lever rod attached. Open the clip on the front of the selector rod and remove the rod from the relay lever.

32. Remove the right and left side engine mount-to-body bolts.

33. Slide an engine dolly under the vehicle.

34. Carefully lower the engine and transaxle assembly onto the dolly.

35. Raise the vehicle and slide the engine and transaxle assembly clear of the vehicle.

To install:

36. With the engine/transaxle positioned on the dolly, slide the engine under the vehicle and re-connect the crane to the lifting brackets.

37. Carefully, raise the engine and transaxle into the vehicle and align as follows: Move the engine from side to side until the rear mount is straight. Then, move the engine assembly in the front to rear direction until the left and right mounts are centered in their brackets. Tighten the right, left and rear mount bolts to 25–30 ft. lbs. (34–41 Nm). Position the front mount cup until the rubber core is centered in the cup. Now, torque the cup bolts to 38 ft. lbs. (52 Nm). On all models, make sure that the exhaust system is aligned properly before completing the rest of the installation procedure. Re-align the exhaust system if necessary.

38. On manual transaxles: Insert the selector rod into the relay lever. Spread the ends of the circlip and install it in the groove at the front of the selector rod. Insert the gearshift lever rod (with selector lever and relay shaft attached) into the selector shaft and install the circlip.

39. Mount the right front wheel and tire assembly. Install the transaxle mounting nuts.

40. Bolt the drive axles to the wheel hubs. Center the wheel and strut assembly.

41. Connect the ball joints to the steering knuckles and install the ball joint lock bolts. Torque the bolts to 36 ft. lbs. (49 Nm).

42. Install the axle nuts and torque to 174 ft. lbs. (237 Nm).

43. Install the horn.

44. Connect the driveshafts to the mounting flanges on the transaxle. Torque the mounting bolts to 30–33 ft. lbs. (41–45 Nm).

45. Connect the relay shaft lever and install the relay shaft and exhaust flex pipe nuts.

46. Install the starter. Torque the starter mounting bolts to 14 ft. lbs. (19 Nm).

47. Connect the speedometer cable to the transaxle and install the cable clamp.

48. If equipped with an automatic transaxle, connect and adjust the selector cable. If equipped with a manual transaxle, connect the clutch cable to the selector lever, install the cable clip and adjust the locknut.

49. Connect the ground wire to the transaxle. Connect the back-up light switch and starter wiring.

50. On fuel injected engines, install the fuel injectors. Position the accelerator cable onto the cylinder head cover and install the cable locknut. Pull the cable tight and connect the cable end to the locking ball by depressing the ball spring, then secure the cable with the cable clip.

51. Connect the PCV hose to the cylinder head cover.

52. On fuel injected engines, connect the vacuum amplifier and brake booster vacuum lines to the throttle body.

53. Plug in the cold start valve and auxiliary air regulator electrical connectors.

54. Install the warm up regulator and connect the fuel line to the cold start valve.

55. Connect the coolant temperature and coil wires.

56. Install the EGR valve and connect the distributor vacuum hoses.

57. Connect the pre-heat tube to the rear of the engine.

58. On vehicles equipped with air conditioning, install the compressor bracket, support brace and diagonal braces, then mount the compressor. Slip the drive belt onto the pulley. Install the alternator adjusting bracket and snug the bolts to tension the belt. Once the belt is tensioned properly, torque the alternator bracket bolts to 20 ft. lbs. (25 Nm). Install the alternator and timing belt covers.

59. Connect the distributor, warm-up regulator, oil pressure switch, thermoswitch and alternator wiring.

60. Install the radiator and connect the fan motor wiring.

61. Connect the upper radiator and heater hoses to the engine.

62. Install the thermostat flange with a new gasket.

63. Connect the air intake duct to the fuel distributor and throttle housing.

64. Connect the battery cables.

65. On 1979 fuel injected vehicles equipped with air conditioning, position the compressor clutch on the compressor shaft and install the clutch bolt. Connect the clutch wire.

66. Fill the cooling system and connect the battery cables.

1977–84 Rabbit and Jetta (Diesel/Turbo Diesel Engines)

◆ **See Figures 23 and 29**

The engine and transaxle assembly is removed from the vehicle with the transaxle attached.

1. Disconnect the battery cables, negative cable first.

2. Turn the heater control to the HOT position. Remove the radiator cap and the radiator hose at the thermostat housing to drain the cooling system. Remove the thermostat flange.

3. Remove the fuel filter. Cap the fuel line connections to prevent leakage.

4. Remove the radiator hoses.

5. Disconnect the wiring from the radiator fan motor and the thermoswitch. Remove the radiator mounting nuts and upper clamp. Lift the radiator out of the vehicle.

6. Disconnect the brake booster hose from the vacuum pump.

7. Remove the alternator.

8. Unplug the electrical connectors at the fuel shut-off solenoid, the glow plugs, the oil pressure switch and the coolant temperature sensor.

9. Remove the heater and the expansion tank hoses.

10. At the injection pump, disconnect the accelerator cable with the bracket and remove the fuel supply and the return lines from the injection pump. Cap the ends of the lines to prevent leakage and the entry of dirt into the system.

11. Disconnect the cold start cable.

12. If equipped with air conditioning:

   a. Remove the timing belt cover, loosen the timing belt tensioner, and remove the timing belt from the injection pump sprocket.

   b. Using tool US 4484 or a suitable puller, remove the injection pump sprocket from the shaft of the pump. Remove the injection pump mounting plate bolts, then support and remove the pump (the fuel lines should already have been disconnected).

   c. Remove the air conditioning belt tensioner, water pump pulley and belt. Remove the windshield washer reservoir and set it off to the side out of the way.

   d. Remove the air conditioning drive belt, the electrical connector at the compressor and the compressor bracket-to-engine bolts. Move the compressor off to the side and support it with wire leaving the hoses connected. DO NOT disconnect the lines or allow the compressor to hang freely by the hoses.

13. If equipped with power steering, remove the belt and the bracket bolts (leave the lines attached), then tie the assembly off to the side out of the way. DO NOT allow the pump to hang freely by the hoses.

14. Unplug the electrical connectors from the starter, back-up switch and the transaxle mount ground wire.

15. If equipped with a manual transaxle, disconnect the clutch cable and route it out of the way.

16. Remove the speedometer cable clamp, then disconnect the speedometer cable from the transaxle.

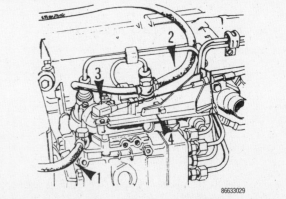

Fig. 29 Disconnect/remove the following from the injection pump. Fuel supply line (1), return line (2), accelerator cable (3) and bracket (4)

86633029

17. Remove the upper starter bolt.
18. On non-turbocharged engines, remove the exhaust pipe nuts or spring clips and disconnect the exhaust pipe from the manifold.

✳✳ CAUTION

If the exhaust pipe is secured to the manifold with spring clamps, use the proper tools and procedures for removal and installation. The springs are under heavy tension and can cause serious injury if mishandled.

19. To remove the spring clamps:
  a. Push the pipe to one side to expand the opposite clamp. Insert a wedge into the expanded clamp.
  b. Push the pipe to the other side and insert a wedge into the clamp.
  c. Push the pipe the other way again to expand the clamp further. It should be possible to grab the wedge with locking pliers and pry the clamp off the pipe flange.
  d. Leave the wedges in the clamps and put them in a box so they won't be disturbed and fly apart.
20. If equipped with a turbocharger, remove the turbocharger-to-exhaust manifold bolts, the turbocharger-to-transaxle bracket, the air intake ducts and the oil lines. Remove the turbocharger from the engine. Cap the oil lines to prevent leakage and dirt entry.
21. Disconnect the relay shaft lever.
22. Unbolt and disconnect the halfshafts from the drive flanges.
23. Remove the lower starter bolt and remove the starter.
24. Remove the horn and set it off to the side.
25. Remove the front mount cup bolts and remove the cup and the front mount.
26. Drain the oil and unscrew the oil filter.
27. Remove the axle hub nuts and disconnect the lower ball joints from the steering knuckles.
28. Raise the vehicle, swing the strut assemblies away from the vehicle and pull out the drive shafts.
29. Reconnect the ball joints so that the vehicle may be lowered to the ground.
30. Remove the rear engine mount and the right front wheel.
31. Attach tool US 1105 (or an equivalent engine sling) and a vertical hoist to the engine, then lift it slightly.

➡**If equipped with a manual transaxle, make sure the relay shaft and the gearshift lever rods are removed.**

32. Remove both side engine mount to body bolts.
33. Slide an engine dolly under the vehicle.
34. Lower the engine and transaxle assembly onto the dolly. Raise the vehicle and slide the dolly from under the vehicle.

To install:
35. With the engine/transaxle positioned on the dolly, slide the engine under the vehicle and re-connect the crane to the lifting brackets.
36. Carefully, raise the engine and transaxle into the vehicle and align as follows:
  a. Move the engine from side to side until the rear mount is straight. Then, move the engine assembly in the front to rear direction until the left and right mounts are centered in their brackets.
  b. Tighten the right, left and rear mount bolts to 25–30 ft. lbs. (34–41 Nm). Position the front mount cup until the rubber core is centered in the cup. Now, torque the cup bolts to 38 ft. lbs. (52 Nm).
  c. On all models, make sure that the exhaust system is aligned properly before completing the rest of the installation procedure. Re-align the exhaust system if necessary.
37. Mount the right front wheel.
38. Disconnect the ball joints and raise the front end.
39. Swing the strut assemblies away from the vehicle and insert the drive shafts.
40. Attach the ball joint to the wheel bearing housing and torque the locknut to 36 ft. lbs. (49 Nm). Install the axle nuts and torque them to 174 ft. lbs. (237 Nm).
41. Install a new oil filter.
42. Mount the horn.
43. Mount the starter and install the lower starter bolt. Do not tighten at this time.

44. Connect the halfshafts to the drive flanges and torque the mounting bolts to 30 ft. lbs. (41 Nm).
45. Connect the relay shaft lever.
46. If equipped, install the turbocharger onto the engine, connect the oil lines and attach the exhaust pipe. Use new gaskets.
47. On non-turbocharged engines, connect the exhaust flex pipe to the manifold. Torque the nuts to 18 ft. lbs. (25 Nm).
48. Install the upper starter bolts and torque to 14 ft. lbs. (19 Nm).
49. Connect the speedometer to the transaxle and install the cable clamp.
50. On manual transaxle, connect and adjust the clutch cable.
51. Connect the transaxle ground, back-up switch and starter wiring.
52. If equipped with power steering, install the power steering pump and the drive belt.
53. If equipped with air conditioning:
  a. Attach the compressor bracket to the engine block and torque the mounting bolts to 18 ft. lbs. (25 Nm). Mount the compressor and tensioner on the bracket.
  b. Install the windshield washer bottle. Place the alternator drive belt onto the compressor clutch pulley, and do the same for the air conditioning drive belt. Install the water pump pulley and torque the pulley bolts to 14 ft. lbs. (19 Nm). Adjust the belt tension, then tighten the compressor mounting and tensioning bolts to 22 ft. lbs. (30 Nm).
  c. Install the injection pump, sprocket and timing belt as described later in this section. Install the timing belt cover cover with a new gasket.
54. Connect the cold start cable.
55. Connect the fuel lines to the injection pump. Do not mix up the supply and return lines. The return lines are marked with OUT to prevent this from happening.
56. Connect the expansion tank and heater hoses.
57. Connect the temperature sensor, oil pressure switch, glow plug and fuel shut-off solenoid wires.
58. Install the radiator and connect the thermo-switch and fan motor wiring.
59. Install the radiator hoses.
60. Install a new fuel filter.
61. Install the thermostat flange with a new gasket.
62. Connect the negative battery cable, fill the cooling system and crankcase. Adjust the belt tension and injection pump timing.

1985–89 Golf, GTI, Jetta, Scirocco and Cabriolet (Gasoline Engines)

▶ **See Figures 23, 30, 31, 32 and 33**

The engine and transaxle assembly are removed from the vehicle together.
1. Disconnect the battery cables (negative cable first) and remove the battery.
2. Relieve the fuel system pressure.

➡**If equipped with an automatic transaxle, place the selector lever in the PARK position.**

3. Remove the air intake duct between the fuel distributor and the throttle housing.
4. Remove the radiator cap. Turn the heater temperature control valve to the HOT position. Place a container under the thermostat housing, remove the thermostat flange and drain the coolant.

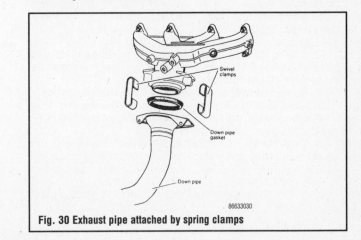

Fig. 30 Exhaust pipe attached by spring clamps

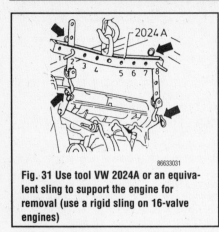

Fig. 31 Use tool VW 2024A or an equivalent sling to support the engine for removal (use a rigid sling on 16-valve engines)

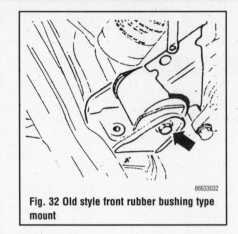

Fig. 32 Old style front rubber bushing type mount

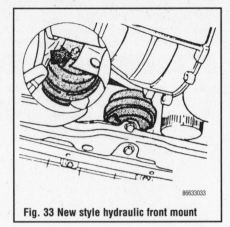

Fig. 33 New style hydraulic front mount

5. Remove the upper radiator and heater hoses from the engine. Unplug the electrical connector from the radiator fan motor. Remove the radiator mounting nuts, the upper radiator clamp and clip. Remove the radiator shroud and the radiator.

6. On Golf/GTI and Jetta, the front body section of the vehicle must be removed:

  a. Unplug the headlight electrical connectors, then disconnect the hood release cable from the hood latch assembly.

  b. Remove the lower valance and the front grille.

  c. Remove the front apron.

➡ **If equipped with power steering, remove the drive belt and the pump mounting bolts. Remove the power steering pump and move it aside. DO NOT disconnect the power steering pressure lines and DO NOT allow the pump to hang freely by the hoses.**

7. Unplug the electrical connector(s) from the alternator, the thermoswitch, the oil pressure switch, the warm-up regulator and the distributor.

8. If equipped with air conditioning, remove the nuts/bolts securing the compressor and the condenser. Tie the compressor and condenser off to the side and out of the way. DO NOT disconnect the refrigerant hoses or allow the compressor to hang freely by the hoses.

9. Remove the pre-heat tube from the rear of the engine.

10. Remove the distributor vacuum hoses and the EGR temperature valve.

11. Disconnect the ignition coil, coolant temperature sensor, Lambda (oxygen) sensor and the knock sensor wires.

✳✳ CAUTION

Use care when disconnecting the fuel lines. The fuel may still be under some pressure in the lines and if sprayed, may cause fire or personal injury.

12. Place a container under the cold start valve, then remove the fuel line and the warm-up regulator.

13. Unplug the electrical connectors from the cold start valve and the auxiliary air regulator.

14. At the throttle body, remove the hoses of the brake booster and the vacuum amplifier (if equipped).

15. Remove the PCV hose from the cylinder head cover.

16. At the throttle body, pull back the accelerator cable clip and disconnect the cable from the ball. Loosen the accelerator cable locknut, then remove the cable from the cylinder head cover.

17. Remove the fuel injectors, then position the entire assembly aside. Cover the fuel injector openings with masking tape to prevent the entry of dirt.

18. Unplug the electrical connectors from the starter, the back-up light switch and the ground cable from the transaxle.

19. If equipped with a manual transaxle, loosen the locknut (at the clutch cable). Remove the clip from under the clutch lever and remove the cable. If equipped with an automatic transaxle, disconnect the selector cable from the transaxle and the bracket.

20. Remove the speedometer cable clamp and the cable. Remove the upper starter bolts and the starter.

21. If equipped with a manual transaxle, remove the transaxle and upshift indicator vacuum switches. If equipped with an automatic transaxle and CIS-E fuel injection, position the wiring harness aside.

➡ **On the GTI/GLI models, remove the idle stabilizer control valve, the throttle plate switch and the knock sensor.**

22. Remove the nuts from the relay shaft. Disconnect the lever from the relay shaft.

23. Remove the driveshafts from the mounting flanges.

24. Unbolt the exhaust pipe from the manifold or remove the spring clamps holding the exhaust pipe to the manifold and lower the pipe.

✳✳ CAUTION

If the exhaust pipe is secured to the manifold with spring clamps, use the proper tools and procedures for removal and installation. The springs are under heavy tension and can cause serious injury if mishandled.

25. To remove the spring clamps:

  a. Push the pipe to one side to expand the opposite clamp. Insert a wedge into the expanded clamp.

  b. Push the pipe to the other side and insert a wedge into the clamp.

  c. Push the pipe the other way again to expand the clamp further. It should be possible to grab the wedge with locking pliers and pry the clamp off the pipe flange.

  d. Leave the wedges in the clamps and put them in a box so they won't be disturbed and fly apart.

26. Remove the horn (move aside) and the front mount cup bolts. Remove the cup and the front mount. There are two kinds of front mounts. Earlier mounts are the rubber bushing type which were replaced with a hydraulic mount in January of 1985. To remove the rubber bushing type front mount, remove the mounting bolt and disengage the transaxle from the mount by turning it slightly side to side. Hydraulic mounts are removed in the same manner except that they are held in place by an acorn nut instead of a bolt.

27. Remove the rear engine mounting nuts.

➡ **On vehicles equipped with the 16-valve engine, the intake manifold will have to be removed in order to remove the engine.**

28. Attach tool VW 2024A or an equivalent sling to the engine (use a rigid sling on 16-valve engines). Using an overhead hoist, lift the engine slightly.

29. On manual transaxles, remove the clip from the gearshift lever rod, the rod from the selector shaft lever and the relay shaft with the gearshift lever rod. Open the clip on the front of the selector rod and remove the rod from the relay lever.

30. Remove the right and left side engine mount to body bolts.

31. Slightly lower and tilt the engine and transaxle. Lift the engine/transaxle assembly, turning it slightly, out of the vehicle.

To install:

32. Lower the engine/transaxle assembly into the vehicle and install the right and left engine mount-to-body bolts. Torque to 33 ft. lbs. (45 Nm) for 10mm bolts or 54 ft. lbs. (73 Nm) for 12mm bolts.

33. On manual transaxles, insert the selector rod into the relay lever. Spread the ends of the circlip and install it in the groove at the front of the selector rod.

Insert the gearshift lever rod (with selector lever and relay shaft attached) into the selector shaft and install the circlip.

34. Install the rear engine mounting nuts. On 16-valve engines, install the intake manifold with a new gasket.

35. Install the front engine mounts. Lubricate the bolt threads with engine oil prior to installation. For the old style rubber bushing type mounts, torque the bolt to 37 ft. lbs. (50 Nm). On the new hydraulic mounts, torque the acorn nut to 22 ft. lbs. (30 Nm).

36. Install the horn.

37. Connect the driveshafts to the mounting flanges. Torque the bolts to 30–33 ft. lbs. (40–45 Nm) Torque the ball joint-to-steering knuckle bolt to 36 ft. lbs. (49 Nm) and the drive axle nut to 174 ft. lbs. (237 Nm).

38. Connect the relay shaft lever.

39. Connect the exhaust pipe. On 16-valve engines use new self-locking nuts to secure the flange and torque to 30 ft. lbs. (41 Nm).

40. On GLI/GTI models, install the knock sensor, throttle plate switch and idle stabilizer control valve.

41. On CIS-E engines with automatic transaxles, position the wiring harness and make sure that it is routed neatly. On manual transaxles, install the upshift indicator and transaxle switches.

42. Install the starter, connect the speedometer cable and install the cable clamp.

43. Connect the selector (automatic transaxle) or clutch (manual transaxle) cables.

44. Connect the transaxle ground, back-up light switch and starter wiring.

45. Install the fuel injectors.

46. Position the accelerator cable onto the cylinder head cover and install the cable locknut. Pull the cable tight and connect the cable end to the locking ball by depressing the ball spring, then secure the cable with the cable clip.

47. Connect the PCV hose to the cylinder head cover.

48. Connect the vacuum amplifier (if equipped) and brake booster vacuum lines to the throttle body.

49. Plug in the cold start valve and auxiliary air regulator electrical connectors.

50. Install the warm up regulator and connect the fuel line to the cold start valve.

51. Connect the coolant temperature, coil, oxygen sensor, knock sensor wires.

52. Install the EGR valve and connect the distributor vacuum hoses.

53. Connect the pre-heat tube to the rear of the engine.

54. If equipped with air conditioning, install the compressor and mounting bracket, then tighten the mounting bolts. Connect the air flow assembly and the idle boost vacuum hose. Install the air duct work, lower apron and trim panel.

55. Engage the distributor wiring and plug in the warm-up regulator, oil pressure switch, thermo-switch and alternator connectors.

56. Install the power steering pump and drive belt. Torque the mounting bolts to 15 ft. lbs. (20 Nm).

57. Connect the hood release cable to the hood latch.

58. Plug in the headlight connectors.

59. Install the front grille, trim and apron.

60. Install the radiator and connect the fan wiring. Install the upper radiator and heater hoses.

61. Install the thermostat flange with a new gasket.

62. Connect the air intake duct.

63. Install the battery and connect the battery cables.

64. Fill the cooling system and adjust the drive belt tension.

1985–89 Jetta and Golf (Diesel/Turbo Diesel Engines)

▶ **See Figures 23 and 30**

1. Remove the battery.

2. Turn the heater temperature control to maximum. Remove the radiator cap and the radiator hose at the thermostat housing and drain the cooling system. Remove the thermostat flange.

3. Disconnect the wiring from the radiator fan motor and the thermo-switch. Remove the upper radiator mounting brackets and lift the radiator and fan out of the vehicle.

4. Remove the fuel filter and base. Cap the fuel line connections to prevent leakage.

5. Disconnect the brake booster hose from the vacuum pump.

6. Remove the alternator.

7. Disconnect the wiring to the fuel shut-off solenoid, the glow plugs, the oil pressure switch and the coolant temperature sensor.

8. Disconnect the heater and the expansion tank hoses.

9. At the injection pump, disconnect the accelerator cable and the cold start cable.

10. Disconnect the fuel supply and the return lines from the injection pump. Plug the openings in the pump and cap the ends of the lines to prevent the entry of dirt into the system.

11. If equipped with air conditioning, the injection pump must be removed to remove the compressor. See Section 5 for instructions on removing the pump. To remove the compressor:

a. Remove the air conditioning belt tensioner, water pump pulley and drive belt.

b. Disconnect the wiring from the compressor and the pressure switches.

c. Remove the condenser and compressor mounting bolts/nuts.

d. Secure the compressor and condenser out of the way. Do not let them hang by the coolant hoses.

12. The front body section must be removed:

a. Disconnect the headlight electrical connectors and the hood release cable from the hood latch assembly.

b. Remove the lower valance and the front grille.

c. Remove the front apron

13. If equipped with power steering, remove the pump without disconnecting the hydraulic hoses. Secure the pump out of the way, do not let it hang by the hoses.

14. Disconnect the wiring from the starter, back-up light switch and the transaxle mount ground wire.

15. If equipped with a manual transaxle, disconnect the clutch cable and shift linkage.

16. If equipped with an automatic transaxle, place the selector lever in the **P** position and disconnect the shifter cable at the transaxle.

17. Remove the speedometer cable from the transaxle and plug the hole in the case.

18. If not already done, raise and safely support the vehicle on jack stands. Unbolt the halfshafts from the flanges and hang them from the body with wire. DO NOT let the halfshafts hang by the outer CV joint or the joint may fall apart.

✳✳ CAUTION

The exhaust pipe is secured to the manifold with spring clamps. Use the proper tools and procedures for removal and installation. The springs are under heavy tension and can cause serious injury if mishandled.

19. To remove the exhaust pipe spring clamps:

a. Push the pipe to one side to expand the opposite clamp. Insert a wedge into the expanded clamp.

b. Push the pipe to the other side and insert a wedge into the clamp.

c. Push the pipe the other way again to expand the clamp further. It should be possible to grab the wedge with locking pliers and pry the clamp off the pipe flange.

d. Leave the wedges in the clamps and put them in a box so they won't be disturbed and fly apart.

20. Check carefully to make sure all necessary wiring, hoses and linkages have been disconnected. Attach a chain yoke and a hoist to the engine, then lift it slightly.

21. Unbolt the engine mounts, tilt the assembly down at the transaxle side and carefully lift the engine and transaxle out.

To install:

22. See Section 7 for information on assembling the engine and transaxle. Make sure all mount brackets are securely bolted to the engine/transaxle. Fit the assembly into the engine bay and install the mounts, starting at the rear. Start all nuts and bolts that secure the mounts to the body but don't tighten them yet.

23. With all mounts installed and the engine safely in the vehicle, allow some slack in the lifting equipment. With the vehicle safely supported, shake the engine/transaxle as a unit to settle it in the mounts. Torque all mounting bolts, starting at the rear and working forward. Torque to 33 ft. lbs. (41 Nm) for 10mm bolts or 54 ft. lbs. (73 Nm) for 12mm bolts.

24. Install the starter and torque the bolts to 14 ft. lbs. (19 Nm).

25. Connect the halfshafts to the flanges and torque the bolts to 33 ft. lbs. (45 Nm).

26. Connect the exhaust pipe.

27. Connect the shift linkage and the clutch cable. Adjust the clutch and shift linkage as required.

28. Install the front apron and connect the wiring.

29. Install the air conditioner compressor and condenser.

30. Install the fuel injection pump as described in Section 5.

31. Install the power steering pump. Install and adjust all accessory drive belts.

32. Install the radiator, fan and heater hoses. Use a new O-ring on the thermostat and torque the thermostat housing bolts to 7 ft. lbs. (10 Nm).

33. Install the remaining components and connect all remaining wiring and vacuum hoses. Check carefully to make sure all components are correctly installed and connected.

34. Fill and bleed the cooling system. Check the adjustment of the accelerator cable.

Fox

▶ **See Figures 23, 34 and 35**

The engine is lifted out of the vehicle after separation from the transaxle.

1. Disconnect the battery cables (negative cable first), then remove the battery.

❊❊ CAUTION

The battery tub located on the right side of the engine may contain a small amount of battery electrolyte which contains sulfuric acid. When removing the battery, wear protective gloves and goggles to prevent personal injury.

2. Turn the heater lever to the HOT position, and remove the cap on the coolant expansion tank. Drain the coolant by removing the hoses. Unplug the electrical connector from the radiator fan.

❊❊ CAUTION

When draining the coolant, keep in mind that cats and dogs are attracted by ethylene glycol antifreeze, and are quite likely to drink any that is left in an uncovered container or in puddles on the ground. This will prove fatal in sufficient quantity. Always drain the coolant into a sealable container.

➡ **Do not disconnect or loosen any refrigerant hose connections during engine removal on cars equipped with air conditioning.**

3. On cars equipped with air conditioning, remove the bolts/nuts securing the condenser to the radiator. Loosen and remove the compressor support bolts. Tie the air conditioning compressor and condenser off to the side and out of the way without disconnecting any refrigerant lines. DO NOT allow the compressor to hang freely by the hoses.

4. Disconnect the radiator thermo-switch and remove the radiator cover. Disconnect the motor mount and remove the rubber bushing. Remove the radiator with the air ducts and fan.

5. Disconnect the clutch cable.

6. Disconnect the alternator, oil pressure switches and oxygen sensor wiring.

7. Disconnect the wiring harnesses at the thermostat flange, auxiliary air regulator and cold start valve.

8. Disconnect the throttle cable from the throttle body. Route the cable off to the side and out of the way.

9. Disconnect the vacuum hoses from the intake manifold and the throttle body.

10. From the distributor, disconnect the ignition coil wire, vacuum advance hoses and Hall effect sender wire.

11. Remove the fuel injectors. Cover the injector openings with masking tape to prevent the entry of dirt.

12. Unbolt and remove the cold start valve (leave the fuel line connected).

13. Loosen the charcoal canister clamp and move the canister to the rear of the engine so that it out of your way.

14. Remove the engine stop.

15. Disconnect the air intake duct from the intake manifold and move it off to the side.

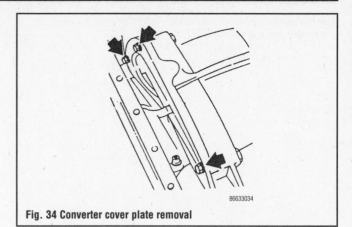
Fig. 34 Converter cover plate removal

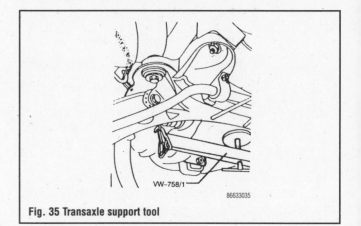
Fig. 35 Transaxle support tool

16. Remove the right and left engine mounting nuts.

17. Disconnect the starter wiring and remove the starter from the engine.

18. Remove the two lower engine to transaxle bolts. Then remove the cover plate bolts and the cover plate.

19. Disconnect the exhaust pipe from the manifold at the flange. Remove the bolt from the exhaust pipe support and remove the exhaust pipe from the manifold.

20. Install tool VW-758/1 or an equivalent transaxle support bar, with a slight amount of preload.

21. Install tool US-1105 or an equivalent sling on the engine lifting eyes, located on the left side of the cylinder head.

22. Lift the engine until its weight is taken off the engine mounts.

23. Adjust the support bar to contact the transaxle.

24. Separate the engine and transaxle.

25. Carefully lift the engine out of the engine compartment so as not to damage the transaxle main shaft, clutch and body.

To install:

➡ **When installing a replacement block on Fox, the oil pump drive bushing does not come with the new block. You must purchase one. Before installing the new block, make sure to install the oil pump drive bushing between the oil pump shaft and the distributor drive gear. If this bushing is not installed, the engine will have little oil pressure or none at all.**

26. Lubricate the clutch release bearing and transaxle main shaft splines with a high-temperature synthetic grease. Do not lubricate the guide sleeve or the clutch release bearing.

27. Carefully guide the engine into the vehicle and attach to the transaxle while keeping weight off the motor mounts.

28. Install and tighten the upper engine-to-transaxle bolts.

29. Remove the transaxle support bar and lower the engine onto the engine mounts. Install the upper engine-to-transaxle bolts and torque them to 40 ft. lbs. (54 Nm). Install the cover plate and torque the mounting bolts to 7 ft. lbs. (10 Nm). Install the engine mount nuts and snug them.

➡️**The engine mounts and subframe bracket bolts will will be torqued later with the engine running at idle speed.**

30. Connect the exhaust pipe to the manifold with a new gasket and torque the pipe nuts to 18 ft. lbs. (24 Nm). Attach the pipe to the support bracket and torque the support bolt to 18 ft. lbs. (25 Nm).

31. Install the starter and connect the starter wiring. Torque the starter mounting bolts to 18 ft. lbs. (24 Nm).

32. Connect the air intake duct to the intake manifold.

33. Install the engine stop.

34. Move the charcoal canister back to the front of the engine and tighten the mounting clamp.

35. Install the cold start valve and torque the mounting bolts to 7 ft. lbs. (10 Nm).

36. Install the fuel injectors.

37. Connect the Hall effect sender wire, vacuum unit hose and the ignition coil wire to the distributor.

38. Connect the intake manifold and throttle body vacuum hoses.

39. Connect and adjust the throttle cable.

40. Connect the cold start valve, auxiliary regulator, thermostat flange, oxygen sensor, oil pressure and alternator wiring.

41. Connect and adjust the clutch cable.

42. Install the radiator, fan and duct assemblies. Install the radiator cover and connect the thermo-switch.

43. If equipped with air conditioning, mount the compressor and install the drive belt. Install the condenser onto the radiator.

44. Connect the radiator fan wire and install the radiator hoses.

45. Refill the cooling system and adjust the accessory belt tension. Install the battery and connect the battery cables.

46. Run the engine at idle speed and torque the engine mount nuts to 30 ft. lbs. (41 Nm), the body-to-engine front mounting carrier fasteners to 47 ft. lbs. (64 Nm) and the block front mounting bracket to 22 ft. lbs. (30 Nm).

Engine Mounts

ADJUSTMENT

▶ **See Figures 36 and 37**

If there is excessive engine vibration, an engine alignment procedure may cure the problem. Loosen all the bolts that go into the rubber mounts. Do not loosen engine or body mounting brackets. With the vehicle safely supported, shake the engine/transaxle as a unit to settle it in the mounts. Retorque all mounting bolts, starting at the rear and working forward. If engine vibration is not reduced, check for torn rubber mounts. The mount at the timing belt end usually fails first.

Camshaft (Valve) Cover

REMOVAL & INSTALLATION

Except 16-Valve Engines

▶ **See Figures 38 thru 45**

1. Disconnect the negative battery cable.

2. Disconnect the throttle cable, crankcase ventilation hose and any other components in the way.

3. Remove the nut at the front of the upper camshaft belt cover. If necessary, remove the cover.

4. Remove the nuts securing the cover, then lift the cover from the engine.

5. Discard the old gaskets. This is also a good time to clean the inside of the camshaft cover and oil baffle plate of any sludge deposits.

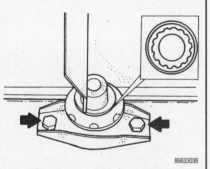

Fig. 36 On Rabbit, Jetta and Scirocco through 1984, align the front mount so the rubber core is centered in the housing

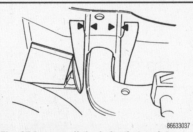

Fig. 37 Loosen all the bolts that go into the rubber mounts. With the vehicle safely supported, shake the engine/transaxle as a unit to settle it in the mounts. The clearance should be about the same on both sides of the mount

Fig. 38 Remove any components which will interfere with the removal of the camshaft cover (crankcase ventilation hose shown)

Fig. 39 It will be helpful to use an extension to reach the nuts securing the cover

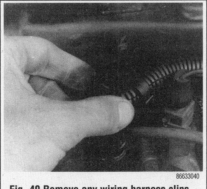

Fig. 40 Remove any wiring harness clips which may be attached to the cover studs

Fig. 41 Be careful not to lose or damage the camshaft cover support plates

Fig. 42 Carefully lift the cover from the engine. If necessary, gently tap the cover with a soft faced hammer to loosen it; never pry on the cover

Fig. 43 Remove and discard the old gaskets

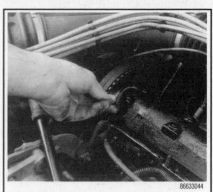

Fig. 44 Don't forget the seal next to the camshaft sprocket

Fig. 45 It is a good idea to clean the inside of the camshaft cover and the oil baffle plate of any sludge deposits when the cover is removed

To install:

6. Install the cover on the engine. Use a new gasket without using any additional sealer. Torque the nuts to 87 inch lbs. (10 Nm).

7. Connect the throttle cable and any other components necessary. Connect the negative battery cable.

8. Start the engine and check for leaks.

16-Valve Engines

1. Disconnect the negative battery cable.
2. Remove the spark plug wires and the intake air duct.
3. Disconnect the wiring and vacuum lines from the throttle body.
4. Remove the support bracket and the 5 nuts to remove the upper intake manifold.
5. Remove the bolts securing the camshaft cover, then remove the cover.

To install:

6. Install the cover. Use a new gasket without using any additional sealer. Torque the cover bolts to 87 inch lbs. (10 Nm)

7. Install the intake manifold with a new gasket and tighten the nuts to 15 ft. lbs. (20 Nm).

8. Connect all other wires/cables/hoses.

9. Start the engine and check for leaks.

Thermostat

REMOVAL & INSTALLATION

◆ **See Figures 46 thru 51**

1. The thermostat is in the bottom of the water pump housing and the lower radiator hose connects to the thermostat housing. Place a large drain pan under the thermostat housing. On some models, it will be necessary to position the power steering pump aside.

2. Remove the radiator cap and drain the cooling system.

Fig. 46 If necessary, remove the power steering pump

Fig. 47 Hang the pump with a wire and position it aside

Fig. 48 The thermostat housing is secured by two bolts

Fig. 49 Slowly pull the housing away from the engine. Stand back and allow any residual coolant to drain into a pan

Fig. 50 Pull the thermostat out of the water pump housing. Once again, stand back to allow any left over coolant to drain

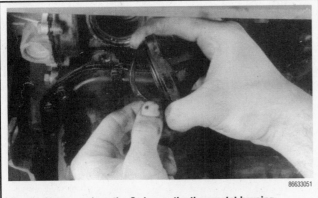

Fig. 51 Always replace the O-ring on the thermostat housing

3. Loosen one bolt at a time until coolant begins to flow. Allow this residual coolant to drain into a pan.

4. Remove both bolts, then remove the thermostat. It's not necessary to disconnect the radiator hose.

5. Discard the O-ring on the thermostat housing.

To install:

6. Place the thermostat into the water pump housing, then install the new O-ring. Install the housing and torque the bolts to 7 ft. lbs. (10 Nm).

7. Fill the cooling system. Start the engine and check for leaks.

Intake Manifold

REMOVAL & INSTALLATION

Carbureted Engines

1. Disconnect the negative battery cable.
2. Remove the air cleaner. Drain the cooling system.
3. Disconnect the accelerator cable.
4. Label and disconnect the EGR valve connections.
5. Label and unplug all electrical leads.
6. Disconnect the coolant hoses.
7. Disconnect the fuel line from the carburetor.
8. Label and disconnect the vacuum hoses from the carburetor.
9. Loosen and remove the retaining bolts, then lift the manifold off the engine.

To install:

10. Install a new gasket. Fit the manifold and tighten the bolts from the center working outwards. Tightening torque is 18 ft. lbs. (25 Nm).

11. Connect the vacuum hoses to the carburetor.
12. Connect the fuel line to the carburetor.
13. Connect the coolant hoses.
14. Connect all electrical leads.
15. Connect the EGR valve.

16. Connect the accelerator cable.
17. Install the air cleaner and refill the cooling system. Start the engine and check for leaks.

CIS/CIS-E Fuel Injected Engines (Except 16-Valve)

▶ See Figures 52, 53 and 54

1. Disconnect the negative battery cable.
2. Disconnect the air duct from the throttle valve body. Drain the cooling system.
3. Disconnect the accelerator cable.
4. If necessary, remove the injectors and position them aside. Cap the injectors to prevent any entry of dirt. Disconnect the line from the cold start valve. Have a small plastic container handy to catch the excess fuel.
5. Disconnect all coolant hoses.
6. Disconnect all vacuum and emission control hoses. Label all hoses for ease of installation.

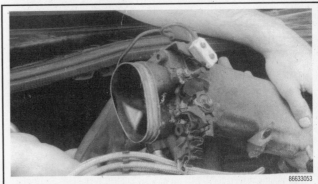

Fig. 52 On some models, it will be necessary to use a special Allen head socket to remove the manifold attaching bolts

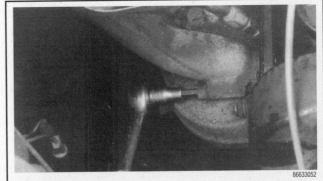

Fig. 53 Carefully lift the manifold from the engine. Be careful not to damage any components

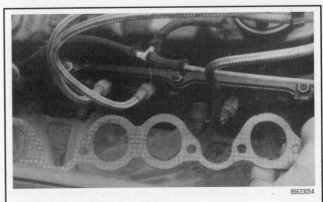

Fig. 54 Always discard the old gasket

7. Remove the auxiliary air regulator.

8. Unplug all electrical connectors. Label all wires for installation.

9. Disconnect the EGR line from the exhaust manifold.

10. Loosen and remove the retaining bolts and lift off the manifold with the throttle body attached. It is easier to remove the throttle body with the intake manifold off the engine. Clean the intake manifold gasket mating surfaces thoroughly. Make sure that all traces of the old gasket material are removed. Inspect the intake manifold for cracks and the gasket surfaces for warpage. If the manifold is damaged, replace it.

To install:

11. Install a new gasket. Install the manifold and tighten the bolts to 18 ft. lbs. (25 Nm).

12. Connect the EGR valve to the exhaust manifold.

13. Plug in all electrical connectors.

14. Install the auxiliary air regulator with a new gasket.

15. Connect all vacuum and emission control hoses.

16. Connect the coolant hoses.

17. Install the cold start valve with a new gasket. If applicable, install the fuel injectors using new injector O-ring seals.

18. Connect and adjust the accelerator cable.

19. Fill the cooling system and connect the air intake duct to the throttle body.

Digifant II Engines

1. Disconnect the negative battery cable and remove the air duct from the throttle body.

2. Disconnect the accelerator cable and the wiring from the throttle switches.

3. Remove the idle stabilizer valve and disconnect the wiring from the fuel injector harness. Disconnect the fuel supply and return lines.

4. Remove the 2 bolts to remove the fuel rail and injectors as an assembly.

5. Label and disconnect the vacuum hoses and any remaining wiring as required.

6. Remove the bolts and remove the manifold from the cylinder head.

To install:

7. Use a new gasket and fit the manifold into place. Torque the bolts to 18 ft. lbs. (25 Nm).

8. Install the fuel injector assembly.

9. Connect fuel system hoses and vacuum lines.

10. Connect the wiring and throttle cable. Install the air duct and battery.

11. Run the engine to check idle speed and ignition timing.

16-Valve Engines

♦ See Figure 55

1. Disconnect the negative battery cable and remove the air duct from the throttle body.

2. Disconnect the accelerator cable and the wiring from the throttle switches. Disconnect any vacuum lines at the throttle body.

3. Remove the idle stabilizer valve and disconnect the spark plug wires. On California models, disconnect the vacuum line and wiring from the EGR valve.

4. Remove the bolts to remove the upper intake manifold.

5. To remove the lower intake manifold, pull the injectors straight out and put caps on the tips to protect them. Do not disconnect the lines.

6. Remove the nuts and remove the manifold.

To install:

7. Use a new gasket and fit the manifold into place. Torque the bolts to 18 ft. lbs. (25 Nm). Install the fuel injectors with new O-ring seals.

8. Use a new gasket and install the upper intake manifold. Torque the bolts to 15 ft. lbs. (20 Nm).

9. Connect the wiring and vacuum lines.

10. Install the idle stabilizer valve.

11. Connect the throttle cable. Install the air duct and battery.

12. Run the engine to check idle speed and ignition timing.

Diesel Engines

1. Disconnect the negative battery cable.

2. Drain the cooling system.

3. Disconnect the hose that runs between the air duct and the turbocharger (turbo-diesel only).

4. Remove the air cleaner.

5. Disconnect and plug all lines coming from the brake booster vacuum pump and remove the pump.

6. Disconnect the PCV line.

7. Disconnect and remove the blow-off valve and then disconnect the hose which runs from the intake manifold to the turbocharger (turbo-diesel only).

8. Remove the intake manifold from the engine. Clean the intake manifold gasket mating surfaces thoroughly. Make sure that all traces of the old gasket material are removed. Inspect the intake manifold for cracks and the gasket surfaces for warpage. If the manifold is damaged, replace it.

To install:

9. Install the manifold onto the engine with a new gasket. Tighten the bolts from the center towards the ends to 18 ft. lbs. (25 Nm).

10. Connect the intake manifold-to-turbocharger hose (turbo-diesels only). Install the blow-off valve.

11. Connect the PCV line.

12. Install the brake booster vacuum pump and connect the vacuum lines.

13. Install the air cleaner.

14. On turbo diesel engines, connect the air duct-to-turbocharger hose.

15. Fill the cooling system.

16. Connect the negative battery cable.

Exhaust Manifold

REMOVAL & INSTALLATION

♦ See Figures 56, 57, 58 and 59

➡Some diesel and gasoline engines use two spring clamps to connect the exhaust pipe to the manifold. If spring clips are used, they require the use of a special wedge tool kit 3140 for removal and installation.

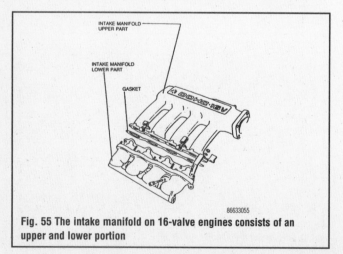

Fig. 55 The intake manifold on 16-valve engines consists of an upper and lower portion

Fig. 56 The exhaust manifold nuts can be accessed after the intake manifold is removed

Fig. 57 An extension is helpful for removing the lower attaching nuts

Fig. 58 Carefully remove the exhaust manifold from the engine. Be careful not to damage any components

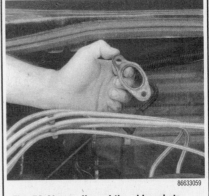

Fig. 59 Always discard the old gaskets

1. Disconnect the EGR tube from the exhaust manifold (if equipped).
2. Remove the air pump components or any other type of interference which would prevent access to the exhaust manifold.
3. Remove the air cleaner hose from the exhaust manifold.
4. Disconnect the intake manifold and support (if equipped). Raise and support the front end.
5. Separate the front exhaust pipe from the manifold or turbocharger and remove any heat shields. If the front exhaust pipe is in the way, unbolt it from the converter and remove it completely. On Scirocco with automatic transaxle, remove the starter motor heat shield, starter wiring and remove the starter. To expand the spring clamp:

   a. Push the exhaust pipe to one side and insert the longer starter wedge into the clamp all the way up to the shoulder.

   b. Push the pipe to the other side and install a wedge into the opposite clamp. Continue to work the pipe side to side while pushing the wedges into the clamps. The wedge must be inserted all the way to its shoulder.

   c. Push the pipe to one side again, grasp the opposite clamp and wedge with locking pliers and remove them together. Do not remove the wedge if the same clamp is to be installed again.

6. Unplug the connector from the oxygen sensor (if equipped), then unscrew the sensor from the exhaust manifold.
7. If equipped, remove the CO probe tube and tube clamp from the manifold.
8. Remove the turbocharger (turbo diesels).
9. Remove the nuts/bolts securing the manifold, then remove it from the engine. Clean the cylinder head and manifold mating surfaces. Make sure that all traces of the old gasket material are removed. Inspect the intake manifold for cracks and the gasket surfaces for warpage. If the manifold is damaged, replace it.

To install:

10. Using a new gasket, install the exhaust manifold. Tighten the nuts to 18 ft. lbs. (24 Nm). Start from the center and work outwards.
11. On turbo diesels, install the turbocharger.
12. Connect the CO probe tube to the manifold and install the tube clamp (if equipped).
13. If equipped, screw the oxygen sensor into the exhaust manifold with a new gasket and plug in the connector. Lubricate the threads of the sensor with high temperature sealant and torque the sensor nut to 37 ft. lbs. (50 Nm). Make sure that the sealant is applied only to the threads of the nut and not the slots of the sensor.
14. Connect the front exhaust pipe to the turbocharger or manifold using a new gasket. On Scirocco with automatic transaxle, install the starter, wiring and starter heat shield.

➡Some exhaust systems use nuts to connect the exhaust pipe to the manifold, while others use spring clamps. If spring clamps are used, the gasket (which looks like a donut) is reusable unless it was leaking or damaged.

15. Install the heat deflector shield and intake manifold support. Torque the heat deflector shield fasteners to 7 ft. lbs. (10 Nm).
16. Connect the air cleaner hose to the manifold.
17. Install any interfering component that was removed to gain access to the exhaust manifold.
18. Connect the EGR tube (if equipped).

Turbocharger

REMOVAL & INSTALLATION

◆ See Figure 60

1. Disconnect the negative battery cable. Drain the engine oil and remove the oil filter.

➡Whenever the turbocharger is replaced, especially in cases of a turbo failure, it is good practice to change the oil and filter. If the turbo failed, metal particles from the compressor shaft bearings will have contaminated the old engine oil. Not changing the oil and filter may allow these particles to wipe the compressor shaft bearings of the new turbocharger and destroy it. The amount of money spent on oil and a filter is relatively cheap insurance to ensure successful and sustained operation of the turbo.

2. If applicable, remove the engine and transaxle cover shield to gain access to the turbocharger.
3. If equipped, loosen the stabilizer bar clamps on both sides of the stabilizer and push the bar down out of the way.
4. Remove the turbocharger heat shield mounting nuts. Disconnect the oil return line adapter flange at the bottom of the turbo. On Quantum models, also remove the side bolt. Plug the end of the line to prevent leakage. Have a container ready to catch any oil.
5. Remove the turbocharger-to-intake manifold and air cleaner hoses.
6. Loosen and remove the oil supply line to the turbocharger.
7. Remove the exhaust pipe-to-turbocharger mounting bolts.

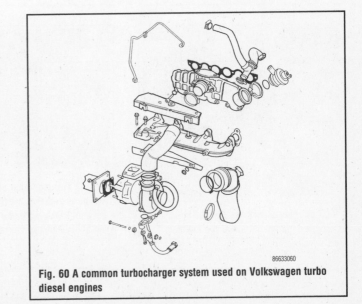

Fig. 60 A common turbocharger system used on Volkswagen turbo diesel engines

8. Remove the turbocharger exhaust manifold mounting bolts, then remove the turbocharger.

To install:

9. Coat the threads of turbocharger mounting bolts with an anti-seize compound.

10. Position the turbocharger on the exhaust manifold and hand tighten the mounting bolts.

11. Attach the oil return line adapter to the bottom of the turbo with a new O-ring seal. Hand tighten the mounting bolts.

12. Connect the exhaust pipe to the turbocharger and hand tighten the mounting bolts.

13. Tighten the turbo-to-exhaust manifold bolts to 30 ft. lbs. (41 Nm). Tighten the oil return line adaptor bolts to 22 ft. lbs. (30 Nm) on all models except Quantum. On Quantum models, tighten the bolts attaching the return line to the turbocharger to 18 ft. lbs. (30 Nm), then tighten the side bolt to 18 ft. lbs. (30 Nm). Tighten the exhaust pipe bolts to 18 ft. lbs. (30 Nm).

14. Fill the upper oil supply connection on the turbocharger with oil. This ensures proper bearing pre-lube during start up. Connect the supply line and tighten until snug.

15. Connect the turbocharger-to-air intake manifold and air cleaner hoses.

16. Install the heat shields.

17. Raise the stabilizer bar to its original position and install the stabilizer bar clamps.

18. Install the engine and transaxle covers.

19. Connect the negative battery cable. Install a new oil filter and fill the crankcase to the proper level.

20. When installation is complete, start the engine and allow to idle for several minutes. Do not increase engine speed above idle until the turbocharger oil supply system has had a chance to fill.

Radiator and Fan

REMOVAL & INSTALLATION

4-Cylinder Gasoline Engines

♦ **See Figures 61 thru 71**

1. Disconnect the negative battery cable and drain the cooling system.

2. Remove the inner shroud mounting bolts and any clamps secured to the shroud.

3. Disconnect the lower radiator hose.

4. Disconnect the thermo-switch lead and fan motor wiring. If possible at this point, unbolt and remove the fan(s) and shroud from the radiator. This will make removing the radiator easier. On some vehicles equipped with air conditioning, it will be necessary to remove the condenser from the radiator (leaving lines connected) and position it off to the side.

5. Remove the lower radiator shroud.

6. Remove the lower radiator mounting bolts.

➡**Various late models have the radiator retained by locating tabs at the bottom and two mounting brackets at the top.**

7. Disconnect the upper radiator hose.

8. Detach the upper radiator shroud, air duct work and support braces.

9. Disconnect the heater and intake manifold hoses.

10. Remove the side mounting bolts and top clips. Lift the radiator and fan(s) out as an assembly from the mounts.

11. On Golf/GTI and Jetta, it may be necessary to remove the front body section the vehicle for clearance:

Fig. 61 A common radiator and fan mounting found on Dasher, Quantum and Fox models

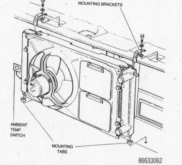

Fig. 62 Radiator and fan mounting found on many late model Golf, GTI and Jetta models

Fig. 63 Remove any clamps which may be secured to the shroud

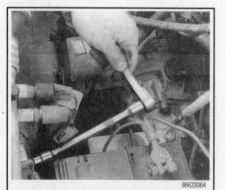

Fig. 64 If necessary, remove the bolts securing the fan shroud to the radiator

Fig. 65 For additional clearance, remove the bolts securing the fan to the shroud, then slide the fan motor forward. Be careful not to damage the radiator fins

Fig. 66 Carefully lift the fan and shroud assembly from the engine bay

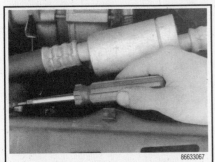

Fig. 67 Disconnect the hoses from the radiator. This is a good time to check the condition of the hoses. Replace them if necessary

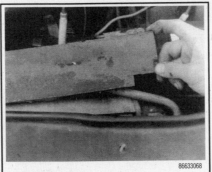

Fig. 68 On some models, remove the heavy paper board covering the radiator/condenser

Fig. 69 Remove the bolts securing the radiator mounting clips

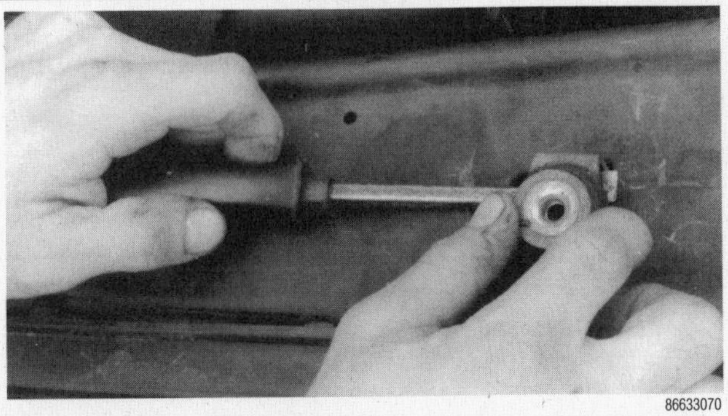

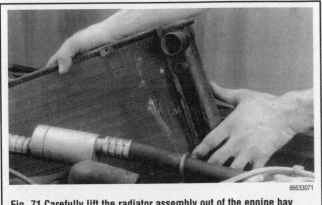

Fig. 70 A small prybar can be used to remove the radiator mounting clips

Fig. 71 Carefully lift the radiator assembly out of the engine bay

   a. Unplug the headlight electrical connectors, then disconnect the hood release cable from the hood latch assembly.
   b. Remove the lower valance and the front grille.
   c. Remove the front apron.
To install:
  12. Set the radiator and fan(s) assembly onto the mounts and install the mounting bolts and toe clips.
  13. If applicable, install the front body section.
  14. Connect the heater and intake manifold hoses.
  15. Attach the support braces, air duct work and the upper radiator shroud.
  16. Connect the upper radiator hose.
  17. Install the lower radiator mounting bolts.
  18. Install the lower radiator mounting shroud.
  19. Connect the thermo-switch lead and fan motor wiring. If the fan(s) were removed, install them at this time. Mount the condenser if equipped with air conditioning.

  20. Connect the lower radiator hose.
  21. Install the inner shroud mounting bolts.
  22. Fill the cooling system and connect the negative battery cable. Start the engine, allow it to warm up check for coolant leaks.

5-Cylinder Engines

  1. Drain the cooling system and disconnect the negative battery cable.
  2. Remove the three pieces of the radiator cowl.
  3. Disconnect the fan motor wiring and remove the fan motor assembly. Take care in removing the fan motor connectors to avoid bending them.
  4. Remove the upper and lower radiator hoses and the coolant tank supply hose.
  5. Disconnect the coolant temperature switch located on the lower right side of the radiator.
  6. Remove the radiator mounting bolts and lift out the radiator.
To install:
  7. Lower the radiator into the engine compartment and install the mounting bolts.
  8. Connect the coolant temperature switch.
  9. Connect the coolant supply, lower and upper radiator hoses.
  10. Install the fans and connect the fan motor wiring.
  11. Install the three radiator cowl pieces.
  12. Fill the cooling system and connect the negative battery cable. Start the engine, allow it to warm up check for coolant leaks.

Diesel Engines

➡**The Quantum turbo diesel has two cooling fans on the radiator.**

  1. Drain the cooling system and disconnect the negative battery cable.
  2. Remove the inner shroud mounting bolts.
  3. Disconnect the lower radiator hose.
  4. Disconnect the thermo-switch lead.
  5. Remove the lower radiator shroud.
  6. Remove the lower radiator mounting bolts.
  7. Disconnect the upper radiator hose.
  8. Detach the upper radiator shroud.
  9. Remove the side mounting bolts and lift the radiator and fan out as an assembly.
To install:
  10. Lower the radiator into the engine compartment and install the side mounting bolts.
  11. Install the upper radiator shroud.
  12. Connect the upper radiator hose.
  13. Install the lower mounting bolts.
  14. Install the lower radiator shroud.
  15. Connect the thermo-switch lead.
  16. Connect the lower radiator hose.
  17. Install the inner shroud mounting bolts.
  18. Fill the cooling system and connect the negative battery cable. Start the engine, allow it to warm up check for coolant leaks.

Oil Cooler

REMOVAL & INSTALLATION

1. Disconnect the negative battery cable.
2. Remove the thermostat to drain the cooling system.
3. Remove the oil filter.
4. Disconnect the hoses from the cooler.
5. Remove the nut holding the cooler to the oil filter base and remove the cooler.

To install:

6. Position the oil cooler, then connect the coolant hoses. Tighten the nut to 18 ft. lbs. (25 Nm).
7. Install the oil filter and the thermostat.
8. Fill the cooling system and connect the negative battery cable. Start the engine, allow it to warm up check for coolant leaks.

Water Pump

REMOVAL & INSTALLATION

✳✳ CAUTION

When draining the coolant, keep in mind that cats and dogs are attracted by ethylene glycol antifreeze, and are quite likely to drink any that is left in an uncovered container or in puddles on the ground. This will prove fatal in sufficient quantity. Always drain the coolant into a sealable container.

4-Cylinder Gasoline Engines

◆ **See Figures 72, 73, 74, 75 and 76**

1. Disconnect the negative battery cable and drain the cooling system.
2. If required, remove the alternator and drive belt for additional access.
3. Remove the timing belt covers.
4. Remove the pump pulley. If the water pump is to be reused, matchmark it to the pump pulley first.
5. Disconnect the lower radiator hose, engine hose, and heater hose from the water pump.
6. Remove the metal plate covering the water pump, then remove the pump-to-housing retaining bolts. Make a note of where the different length bolts are located.
7. Turn the pump slightly, then lift it out of the pump housing. If the pump is stubborn, tap around the edges of the pump with a rubber mallet to loosen it, then separate the pump from the pump housing. Clean the pump housing gasket surface to remove all traces of the gasket material.

To install:

8. Install a new O-ring seal into the pump. Make sure the seal seats evenly in the groove. Lubricate the seal with a liberal coat of silicone compound prior to installation.
9. Place the new pump gasket onto the pump housing, then install the pump. Install one of the mounting bolts to hold the pump and gasket in place. Make sure all the gasket bolt holes are aligned properly with the holes in the housing before installing the remaining bolts. Torque the bolts to 7 ft. lbs. (10 Nm). Torque the pulley bolts to 15 ft. lbs. (20 Nm), then adjust the belt tension.

➡ **On 1985–89 Golf models, install the water pump pulley with the word "Klima" facing outward.**

10. Connect the radiator and heater hoses.
11. Install the timing belt cover.

Fig. 72 If the water pump is to be reused, matchmark the pump pulley to allow installation in the same position

Fig. 73 Remove the bolts securing the metal plate which covers the water pump

Fig. 74 Access to the water pump bolts is much easier with the pump pulley removed

Fig. 75 Turn the pump slightly, then lift it out of the pump housing

Fig. 76 Always discard the old gasket

12. If removed, install the alternator and adjust the drive belt tension.

13. Fill the cooling system. Start the engine and check for leaks.

5-Cylinder Engines

→Some replacement water pumps for five cylinder engines have a larger O-ring seal groove that does not accept the standard 4mm O-ring seal. Instead, an oversized 5mm seal must be used. Pumps that require a 5mm seal are stamped with a "5" on the water pump bolt flange area. Make sure that you use the proper O-ring seal when installing the water pump.

1. Disconnect the negative battery cable and drain the cooling system.

2. Loosen the three water pump pulley retaining bolts.

3. Remove the V-belts, timing belt covers and timing belt as outlined in this section.

4. Unscrew the three water pump pulley retaining bolts, then remove the pulley.

5. Remove the intermediate shaft drive sprocket retaining bolt, then remove the sprocket.

6. Unscrew the water pump retaining bolts and remove the pump from its housing. If the pump is stubborn, tap around the edges of the pump with a rubber mallet to loosen it, then separate the pump from the pump housing. Clean the pump housing gasket surface to remove all traces of the gasket material. Remove the pump pulley and transfer it to the new pump.

To install:

7. Install a new O-ring seal into the pump. Make sure the seal seats evenly in the groove. Lubricate the seal with a liberal coat of silicone compound prior to installation.

8. Place the new pump gasket onto the pump housing and install the pump onto the gasket. Install one of the mounting bolts to hold the pump and gasket in place. Make sure all the gasket bolt holes are aligned properly with the holes in the housing before installing the remaining bolts. Torque the bolts to 15 ft. lbs. (20 Nm). Torque the pulley bolts to 15 ft. lbs. (20 Nm). It will be easier to torque the pulley bolts after the belt has been installed and tensioned.

9. Mount the intermediate drive shaft sprocket and install the retaining bolt.

10. Install the timing belt, timing belt covers and drive belts. Adjust the drive belt tension.

11. Refill the cooling system and connect the negative battery cable. Start the engine and check for leaks.

Diesel Engine

→Some replacement water pumps for Quantum turbo diesel engines have a larger O-ring seal groove that does not accept the standard 4mm O-ring seal. Instead, an oversized 5mm seal must be used. Pumps that require a 5mm seal are stamped with a "5" on the water pump bolt flange area. Make sure that you use the proper O-ring seal when installing the water pump.

1. Drain the cooling system.

2. Remove the alternator and drive belt.

3. Remove the timing belt cover.

4. Disconnect the lower radiator hoses, engine hose and heater hose from the water pump.

5. Remove the pump retaining bolts. Note where the different length bolts are located, for installation.

6. Turn the pump slightly and lift it out of the engine block. If the pump is stubborn, tap around the edges of the pump with a rubber mallet to loosen it, then separate the pump from the pump housing. Clean the pump housing gasket surface to remove all traces of the gasket material. Remove the pump pulley and transfer it to the new pump.

To install:

7. Install a new O-ring seal into the pump. Make sure the seal seats evenly in the groove. Lubricate the seal with a liberal coat of silicone compound prior to installation.

8. Place the new pump gasket onto the pump housing and install the pump onto the gasket. Install one of the mounting bolts to hold the pump and gasket in place. Make sure all the gasket bolt holes are aligned properly with the holes in the housing before installing the remaining bolts. Torque the bolts to 7 ft. lbs. (10 Nm). Torque the pulley bolts to 15 ft. lbs. (20 Nm). It will be easier to torque the pulley bolts after the belt has been installed and tensioned.

9. Connect the heater, radiator and engine hoses.

10. Install the timing belt cover.

11. Install the alternator and adjust the drive belt tension.

12. Fill the cooling system and connect the negative battery cable. Start the engine and check for leaks.

Cylinder Head

REMOVAL & INSTALLATION

▶ **See Figures 77 thru 86**

Carbureted Engines

The engine should be cold before the cylinder head can be removed. The head is retained by ten socket head bolts and can be removed without removing the intake and exhaust manifolds.

→Beginning in approximately July 1977, 12-point socket head bolts were used in place of the older 6-point version. These should be used in complete sets only and do not need to be retorqued after a mileage interval.

1. Rotate the crankshaft to set the No. 1 cylinder at TDC. Disconnect the negative battery cable.

2. Drain the cooling system.

3. Remove the air cleaner. Disconnect the fuel line from the carburetor.

4. Disconnect the radiator, heater, and choke hoses.

5. Label and unplug all electrical wires and emission control vacuum hoses. Remove the spark plug wires. The spark plugs can be left in the head if you choose to do so.

6. Remove the air conditioner compressor with lines attached and secure it out of the way. DO NOT disconnect any hoses or allow the unit to hang freely by the hoses.

7. Separate the exhaust manifold from the exhaust pipe.

8. Disconnect the EGR line from the exhaust manifold. Remove the EGR valve and filter from the intake manifold.

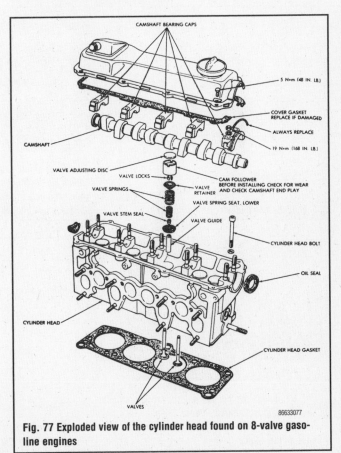

Fig. 77 Exploded view of the cylinder head found on 8-valve gasoline engines

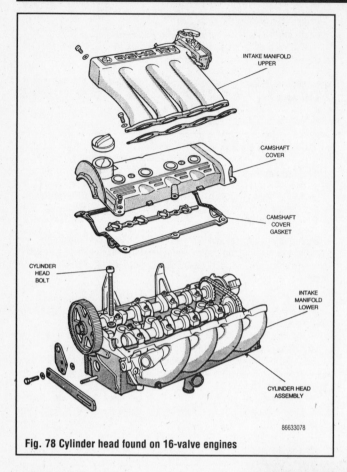

Fig. 78 Cylinder head found on 16-valve engines

Labels in figure: INTAKE MANIFOLD UPPER, CAMSHAFT COVER, CAMSHAFT COVER GASKET, CYLINDER HEAD BOLT, INTAKE MANIFOLD LOWER, CYLINDER HEAD ASSEMBLY

9. Remove the carburetor from the intake manifold.
10. Disconnect the air pump fittings.
11. Remove the timing belt cover and belt. Remove the camshaft cover and gasket.
12. Loosen the cylinder head bolts in the reverse order of the tightening sequence (refer to the illustration).
13. Remove the bolts and lift the cylinder head straight off.
14. Clean the head and block surfaces thoroughly and check the flatness of the cylinder block with a feeler gauge and a metal straight edge. Refer to the cleaning and inspection procedures in this section.

To install:

15. Install the new cylinder head gasket. If printed with the words TOP or OBEN, make sure these are facing upwards. Lower the head onto the gasket.
16. Install bolts 10 and 8 first. These holes are smaller and will properly position the gasket and cylinder head.
17. Install the remaining bolts. Tighten them in three stages using the tightening sequence shown in the illustration. Cylinder head tightening torque is 54 ft. lbs. (75 Nm). If equipped with 12-point bolts, tighten to 54 ft. lbs. (73 Nm), then tighten them ¼ turn more.
18. Install and tension the timing belt. Install the timing belt and camshaft covers. Use a new gasket on the camshaft cover.
19. Connect the air pump fittings.
20. Install the carburetor with a new gasket.
21. Install the EGR valve and filter on the intake manifold. Connect the EGR valve line.
22. Connect the exhaust pipe to the exhaust manifold with a new gasket.
23. Mount the air conditioning compressor.
24. Connect the spark plug wires. Connect all the vacuum hoses and electrical wires.
25. Connect the choke, radiator and heater hoses.
26. Connect the fuel line to the carburetor. Install the air cleaner.
27. Fill the cooling system.
28. Connect the negative battery cable. Start the engine and check for leaks. Adjust the ignition timing and the idle speed.

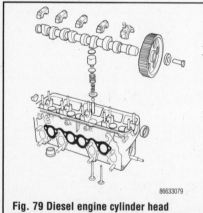

Fig. 79 Diesel engine cylinder head

Fig. 80 A small extension can be used to reach the cylinder head bolts. The extra leverage of a breaker bar is also useful for loosening the bolts

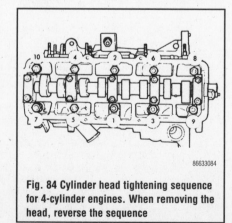

Fig. 81 After the bolts have been removed, carefully lift the cylinder head from the engine block

Fig. 82 Always discard the old gasket. On diesel engines, make a note as to the number of identification notches on the edge of the gasket

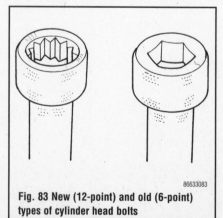

Fig. 83 New (12-point) and old (6-point) types of cylinder head bolts

Fig. 84 Cylinder head tightening sequence for 4-cylinder engines. When removing the head, reverse the sequence

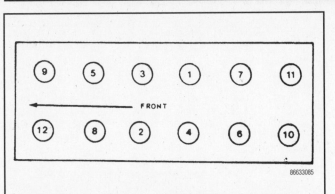

Fig. 85 Cylinder head tightening sequence for 5-cylinder engines. When removing the head, reverse the sequence

Fig. 86 Always torque the cylinder head bolts using the proper sequence, to the correct specification

➡**After approximately 1000 miles, the 6-point cylinder head bolts must be retorqued. Loosen them approximately 30 degrees, then tighten them to 54 ft. lbs. (75 Nm) on cold engines or 61 ft. lbs. (85 Nm) on hot engines (operating temperature). This is applicable to 6-point bolts only, 12-point bolts do not have to be retorqued.**

Fuel Injected Engines

Special tools (VW 3140/1 and 2) are required for removing and installing the spring clamps securing the exhaust pipe to the manifold. This is a set of different sized wedges for spreading the spring clamps in steps. The installed spring clamp has considerable tension and could cause damage or injury if not properly removed. Clamps with wedges installed are under high tension and should be handled carefully.

➡**Most fuel injected engines use 12-point socket head bolts in place of the older style 6-point bolts and do not require retorquing after any mileage interval. On Fox models, the head bolts may only be used once and should be replaced any time they are loosened or removed.**

1. Rotate the crankshaft until the No. 1 cylinder is at TDC. Disconnect the negative battery cable.
2. Drain the cooling system.
3. Remove all the accessory drive belts.
4. Remove the alternator and, if required, the alternator mounting bracket.
5. Disconnect the air inlet ductwork from the throttle body assembly.
6. Label and disconnect all the emission control vacuum lines.
7. Disconnect the throttle cable from the throttle body assembly. On the 16-valve engines, remove the upper half of the intake manifold.
8. On vehicles with CIS/CIS-E fuel injection, remove the injectors and the cold start valve without disconnecting the fuel lines, then cap them. Secure all the lines aside.
9. On vehicles with Digifant II fuel injection, the injectors and fuel rail assembly may be left on the head. Disconnect the fuel supply and return lines and the wiring harness for the injectors.
10. Disconnect the radiator and heater hoses.

11. Remove the camshaft cover and gasket.
12. If equipped, remove the auxiliary air regulator from the intake manifold.
13. Label and unplug all electrical connections on the cylinder head. Remove the spark plugs.
14. Remove the bolts securing the air conditioner compressor, then tie it off to the side and out of the way. DO NOT disconnect any lines or allow the compressor to hang freely.
15. On 16-valve engines, remove the distributor with the cap and wires as an assembly.
16. Disconnect the exhaust pipe from the exhaust manifold. If the pipe is secured to the manifold with spring clamps:
    a. Push the exhaust pipe to one side and insert the longer starter wedge into the opposite clamp.
    b. Push the pipe to the other side and install a wedge into the opposite clamp. Continue to work the pipe side to side while pushing the wedges into the clamps. The wedge must be inserted all the way to its shoulder.
    c. Push the pipe to one side again, grasp the opposite clamp and wedge at the same time with locking pliers and remove them together. Leave the wedge in the clamp if it is going to be reinstalled. Place the clamps (with wedges installed) in a box until needed again.
17. Remove the EGR line from the exhaust manifold, if equipped.
18. Remove the intake manifold.
19. Remove the timing belt covers and belt.
20. Loosen the cylinder head bolts in the reverse order of the tightening sequence (refer to the illustration).
21. Remove the bolts and lift the head straight off. Remove the old cylinder head gasket.
22. Clean the head and block surfaces thoroughly and check the flatness of the cylinder block with a feeler gauge and a metal straight edge. Refer to the cleaning and inspection procedures in this section.

To install:

23. Install the new cylinder head gasket. If printed with the words TOP or OBEN, make sure these are facing upwards. Lower the head onto the gasket.
24. Install bolts 10 and 8 first. These holes are smaller and will properly position the gasket and cylinder head.
25. Install the remaining bolts. Tighten them in three stages using the tightening sequence shown in the illustration. Cylinder head tightening torque is 54 ft. lbs. (75 Nm) for 6-point bolts. If equipped with 12-point bolts, the bolts should be tightened first to 29 ft. lbs. (40 Nm), then 43 ft. lbs. (60 Nm)., then an additional 180 degree turn (two 90 degree turns are permissible).
26. Install the timing belt and adjust the belt tension. Install the timing belt covers.
27. Install the intake manifold with new gaskets.
28. Connect the EGR pipe to the exhaust manifold, if equipped.
29. Connect the exhaust pipe to the manifold. On 16-valve engines, use new gaskets and self-locking nuts. Torque to 18 ft. lbs. (25 Nm). On models with spring clamps, push the pipe to one side and install the clamp. Push the pipe the other way to install the other clamp and continue to work the pipe side to side to remove the wedges.
30. Install the air conditioning compressor.
31. Connect all electrical wires. Install the spark plugs.
32. Install the auxiliary air regulator onto the intake manifold, if equipped.
33. Install the camshaft cover with a new gasket.
34. Connect all emission control vacuum lines.
35. Connect the radiator and heater hoses.
36. Install the fuel injection equipment and connect the wiring.
37. On 16-valve engines, install the upper intake manifold and the distributor.
38. Connect and adjust the throttle cable.
39. Connect the air inlet ductwork to the throttle body.
40. Install the alternator mounting bracket and alternator as required.
41. Install the accessory drive belts and adjust the belt tension.
42. Fill the cooling system.
43. Connect the negative battery cable. Start the engine and check for leaks. Adjust the ignition timing and the idle speed.

➡**After approximately 1000 miles, the 6-point cylinder head bolts must be retorqued. Loosen them approximately 30 degrees, then tighten them to 54 ft. lbs. (75 Nm) on cold engines or 61 ft. lbs. (85 Nm) on hot engines (operating temperature). This is applicable to 6-point bolts only; 12-point bolts do not have to be retorqued.**

Diesel and Turbo Diesel Engines

The engine should be cold when the head is removed to avoid chances of warpage. Diesel cylinder heads cannot be resurfaced. The older 6-point socket head bolts are not interchangeable with the newer 12-point head bolts nor are their major engine components (engine block, cylinder head and gasket). The 6-point bolts were used up to March of 1982 and the 12-point bolts were used intermittently starting in April of 1981. The 12-point head bolts are not reusable and must always be replaced anytime they are removed.

1. Disconnect the negative battery cable.
2. Drain the cooling system.
3. Remove the air cleaner and duct.
4. Disconnect the fuel (injector) lines. Cap the ends of the lines to prevent the entry of dirt into the fuel system.
5. Label and disconnect all electrical wires and leads.
6. If equipped, disconnect and plug all lines coming from the brake booster vacuum pump, then remove the pump.
7. Disconnect the air supply tubes (turbo diesels only), then unbolt and remove the intake manifold.
8. Disconnect and plug all lines coming from the power steering pump, then remove the pump.
9. On turbo diesels, disconnect and remove the oil supply and return lines from the turbocharger.
10. Remove the exhaust manifold heat shields (if equipped). Remove the glow plugs and the fuel injectors.
11. Separate the exhaust pipe from the exhaust manifold or turbocharger, then remove the manifold.
12. Disconnect all radiator and heater hoses where they are attached to the cylinder head, then position them out of the way.
13. Remove the timing belt cover and the timing belt. Refer to the procedures in this section.
14. Remove the PCV hose.
15. Remove the camshaft cover.
16. Loosen the cylinder head bolts in the reverse order of the tightening sequence.
17. Remove the bolts and lift the cylinder head straight off.

➡ **If the head sticks, tap it upward with a soft rubber mallet. Do not force anything between the head and the engine block to pry it upward; this may result in damage to the gasket seating surfaces.**

18. Clean the head and block surfaces thoroughly and check the flatness of the cylinder block with a feeler gauge and a metal straight edge. Refer to the cleaning and inspection procedures in this section.

To install:

On these engines, the pistons actually project above the deck of the block. Depending upon the piston height, there are gaskets of different thicknesses which can be used to adjust piston-to-valve clearance. The gasket thickness is determined by the number of identification notches in the gasket. Be sure that the new gasket has the same number of notches as the gasket being replaced. If the pistons were removed or if the old gasket is not available, the piston height must be measured and a gasket selected from the measurement. Refer to the piston and connecting rod procedures in this section.

19. Install the new cylinder head gasket. If printed with the words TOP or OBEN, make sure these are facing upwards. Lower the head onto the gasket.
20. Turn the crankshaft to TDC, then turn the crankshaft back until all the pistons are nearly equal height in the cylinders.
21. Place the cylinder head on the engine block and turn the camshaft gear so that the cam lobes for the No.1 cylinder point upwards. Install bolts No. 8 and 10 first. These holes are smaller and will properly locate the head on the engine block.

➡ **Keep in mind that 12-point bolts cannot be reused. Always replace them!**

22. Install and hand tighten the remaining bolts.
23. On 6-point bolts, tighten the bolts using this procedure:
    a. Tighten the head bolts in numerical sequence to 35 ft. lbs. (50 Nm).
    b. Tighten the head bolts in numerical sequence to 50 ft. lbs. (70 Nm).
    c. Tighten the head bolts in numerical sequence to 65 ft. lbs. (90 Nm).
24. On 12-point bolts, use this procedure to tighten the bolts:

a. Tighten the head bolts in numerical sequence to 29 ft. lbs. (40 Nm).
    b. Tighten the head bolts in numerical sequence to 43 ft. lbs. (60 Nm).
    c. Finally, turn each head bolt an additional ½ (180 degree) turn in numerical sequence. Two ¼ (90 degree) turns are permissible.
25. Install the camshaft cover and the PCV hose.
26. Install the timing belt and its covers.
27. Connect all necessary heater and radiator hoses to the engine.
28. Connect the exhaust pipe to the turbocharger or the exhaust manifold.
29. Install the exhaust heat shields. Install the fuel injectors and glow plugs.
30. Connect the oil supply and return lines to the turbocharger. Refer to the turbocharger procedures in this section.
31. Install the power steering pump.
32. Install the intake manifold. Connect the air supply tubes on turbo diesels.
33. Connect all necessary wires and vacuum hoses.
34. Connect the fuel injector lines.
35. Install the air cleaner and duct. Fill the cooling system.
36. Change the engine oil and replace the oil filter.
37. Connect the negative battery cable. Start the engine and run it to normal operating temperature. Check for leaks.

➡ **Be sure the engine is at normal operating temperature when retightening the bolts.**

38. Remove the camshaft cover. On 6-point bolts, retighten the head bolts in numerical order to 65 ft. lbs. (90 Nm). On 12-point bolts, turn the bolts in numerical order an additional ¼ turn (90 degrees). The bolts should be tightened in one movement without loosening them first. This applies to both 6 and 12-point bolts.
39. Install the camshaft cover. Correct any leaks observed earlier.

➡ **After 1,000 miles (1,609 km), the cylinder head bolts must be retorqued. The engine may be cold or warm. On 6-point bolt heads, loosen the bolts in the reverse of the tightening sequence about 30 degrees, then tighten them to 65 ft. lbs. (90 Nm). On 12-point bolt heads, tighten the bolts an additional ¼ (90 degrees) in numerical order (do not loosen them first). The bolts should be tightened in one movement.**

CLEANING AND INSPECTION

◆ **See Figures 87 and 88**

1. Remove the manifolds and all other items that can be unbolted or unscrewed.
2. Place the head on wooden blocks and remove the camshaft, cam followers and end seals.

➡ **Keep the cam followers and bearing shells in order. Tag them so they can be installed in the same location.**

3. Working in a clean area, use spray solvent or brush cleaning solvent on the cylinder head top, sides and combustion chamber surfaces to remove any grease, dirt or oil, and help soften carbon deposits. After cleaning with solvent, wash the head with hot water and wipe dry.

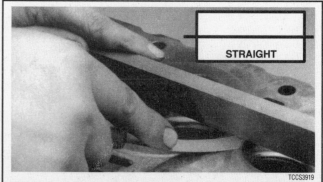

TCCS3919

Fig. 87 Checking the cylinder head flatness along the length of the head

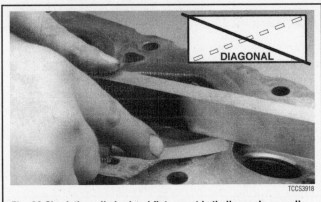

Fig. 88 Check the cylinder head flatness at both diagonals as well

4. Turn the head so the combustion chambers are facing up.

5. Before removing any carbon, examine the chambers and valve faces for obvious damage such as burnt valves or cracks. If one chamber is very clean, this usually indicates a coolant leak into that cylinder.

6. Mount a rotary wire carbon cleaning brush in an electric drill and clean the combustion chambers and valve heads. Be careful not to remove any aluminum or make deep scratches that may look like cracks. A complete inspection of the cylinder head (combustion chambers, valves, guides etc.) can be done after the valves and springs are removed.

7. To check the head for warping:

a. Place a straight edge along the length of the head and attempt to slip a 0.004 inch (0.01mm) feeler gauge between them. Move the gauge the full length of the head and look for high or low spots.

b. Move the straight edge diagonally across the head and use the feeler gauge again.

c. If the head is warped more than allowed, use thicker feeler gages to determine how much and record the results. This information is needed to determine how much material to remove during resurfacing.

RESURFACING

▶ **See Figure 89**

If the cylinder head is warped more than 0.004 inches (0.01mm), it must be resurfaced. Diesel cylinder heads cannot be resurfaced because the relationship between the pre-chambers, injectors and head surface would be changed. If warped beyond specifications, diesel cylinder heads must be replaced.

To determine how much material can be removed from the cylinder head, measure the thickness of the head between the valve cover and head gasket surfaces. On 8-valve engines, the minimum cylinder head height is 5.22 inches (132.6mm). On 16-valve engines, minimum head height is 4.650 inches (118.1mm). Measure this dimension at several different points to determine the average thickness. These measurements are often best left for the machinist.

If required, cylinder head resurfacing can be performed by most automotive machine shops.

Valves

REMOVAL & INSTALLATION

1. Number the valves in the head with a permanent marker for reinstallation identification.

2. Loosen each cam bearing nut about 1 turn at a time to prevent bending the camshaft. Remove the bearing caps and lift off the camshaft. Remove the lifters. Keep hydraulic lifters upside down to prevent leak-down. Lifters MUST be reinstalled in their original location.

3. Block the head on wooden supports in a position that permits use of the type of valve spring removing tool you are going to use. Volkswagen uses tool VW 541, although you should be able to perform the job with several other available removers (the locking C-clamp type is popular).

4. Compress the valve springs and remove the stem locks and retainers. Remove the valve springs. Keep the parts and each valve separate and in order for reinstallation. It is important that the valves are installed back in their same location. Remove the lower valve spring seats and valve stem oil seals. Remove the valves, keep them in order in case the identification marking wears off.

5. Clean valve faces, tips and combustion chambers with a rotary wire brush or bench grinder wire wheel. Do not wire brush the valve stems, take care not to damage the valve seats. Remove the carbon, do not just burnish. If a stubborn carbon deposit is encountered, use a blunt drift to break the carbon loose. Again use caution around the valve seat.

6. Inspect the valves and guides as described later. Measure valve guide clearance.

7. If a water leak is suspected, or the valve seats, guides or valves need machine work, take the head and parts to the machine shop. Now is also a good time to have the head super cleaned in a cold parts cleaner, the machine shop can handle the job. However, never allow the aluminum head to be hot tanked, this will damage the head and make replacement necessary.

8. After all machine work has been done and all the new parts are on hand, install the valves with new oil seals.

9. Install the camshaft (refer to the procedure in this section).

INSPECTION

▶ **See Figures 90, 91 and 92**

Check the sealing face of the valves and seats. They may be uneven and worn but there must be a distinct ring around the valve showing where it sealed against the seat. If there is any gap or signs of burning, the valve must be replaced and the seat reground.

To check the valve guides, place a new valve in the guide with the end of the stem flush with the camshaft end of the guide. Set a dial indicator against the valve head and rock the valve side-to-side. If the free-play is more than 0.039 inches (1.0mm) on gasoline engines or 0.051 inches (1.3mm) on diesel engines, the guides should be replaced. The guides are pressed out from the camshaft side of the head.

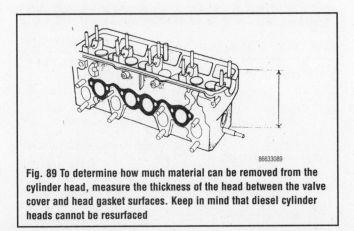

Fig. 89 To determine how much material can be removed from the cylinder head, measure the thickness of the head between the valve cover and head gasket surfaces. Keep in mind that diesel cylinder heads cannot be resurfaced

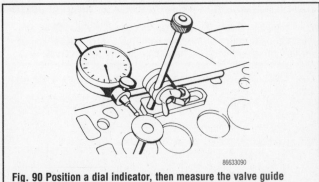

Fig. 90 Position a dial indicator, then measure the valve guide clearance with the end of the valve stem flush with the camshaft end of the guide

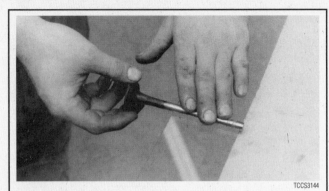

Fig. 91 Valve stems may be rolled on a flat surface to check for bends

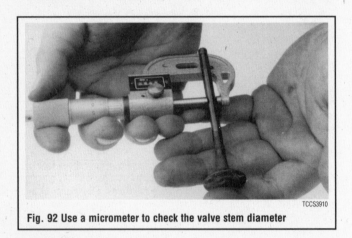

Fig. 92 Use a micrometer to check the valve stem diameter

REFACING VALVES

On all engines, machining the intake valves is not recommended, they should only be hand-lapped. See the valve chart in this section for information on face angles and dimensions. To hand lap the valves:

1. Invert the cylinder head, lightly lubricate the valve stem and install the valves in the head as numbered.
2. Moisten the suction cup on the lapping tool and attach to the valve head.
3. Slightly raise the valve from the seat and apply a small amount of valve grinding compound to the seat.
4. Rotate the lapping tool and valve between the palms of your hands while gently pushing the valve into the seat. Lift the tool often and turn the valve to a new position to prevent grooving.
5. Continue until a smooth polished surface is evident on the valve and valve seat. Remove the valve from the head and clean away all traces of lapping compound, especially from the guide.

✳✳ CAUTION

The exhaust valves in the 16-valve engine are sodium-filled and must not be machined. Improper handling or disposal can cause serious personal injury. To dispose of sodium-filled valves:

6. Wear protective gloves and goggles. Sodium reacts violently with water; make sure the work area is dry.
7. Clamp the valve in a vise and saw the head off with a hack saw. Do not use power tools.
8. Throw the valve pieces into a bucket of water and stand back. When the reaction is complete, the valves can be safely thrown away.

Valve Stem Seals

REPLACEMENT

▶ **See Figure 93**

Cylinder Head Removed

1. With the valve springs removed, hold the valve in place and slip the protector sleeve over the valve stem.
2. Lightly oil the seal and fit it over the protector sleeve.
3. Push the seal into place with the installation tool.
4. Install the valve springs.

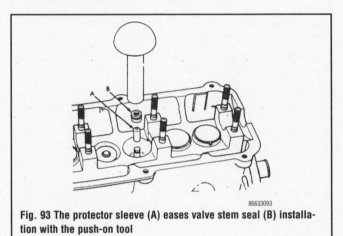

Fig. 93 The protector sleeve (A) eases valve stem seal (B) installation with the push-on tool

Cylinder Head Installed

This procedure requires an air adaptor fitting that threads into a spark plug hole. Also required is the special valve spring tool, VW 541.

1. Remove the camshaft.
2. Remove the spark plug and make sure the piston is at the bottom of the stroke.
3. Install an air adaptor fitting into the spark plug hole and apply 85 psi of air pressure to the cylinder.
4. Install the valve spring tools onto the cylinder head and press down on the handle. The upper seat should move down on the stem so the keepers can be removed.
5. With the valve spring and old oil seal removed, hold the valve in place and slip the protector sleeve over the valve stem.
6. Lightly oil the seal and fit it over the protector sleeve.
7. Push the seal into place with the installation tool.
8. Install the valve springs, upper seat and keepers.
9. Install the camshaft.

Valve Springs

REMOVAL & INSTALLATION

▶ **See Figure 94**

1. Remove the camshaft.
2. If the cylinder head is still on the engine:
   a. Remove the spark plug and make sure the piston is at the bottom of the stroke.
   b. Install an air adaptor fitting into the spark plug hole and apply 87 psi of air pressure to the cylinder.

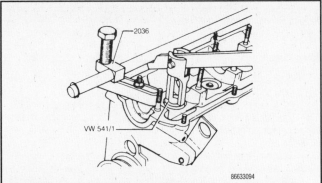

Fig. 94 These tools can be used to remove the valve springs with the cylinder head on or off the engine

3. Install the valve spring compressor tools onto the cylinder head and press down on the handle. The upper seat should move down on the stem so the keepers can be removed with a magnet.

4. Remove the keepers, upper seat and valve spring. If necessary, replace the oil seal.

To install:

5. Install the valve spring and upper seat. Compress the spring and install the keepers.

6. If applicable, remove the air adaptor fitting.

7. Install the camshaft.

INSPECTION

♦ **See Figure 95**

Free length, installed height and force specifications are not available from Volkswagen. If the free length or squareness of the spring varies more

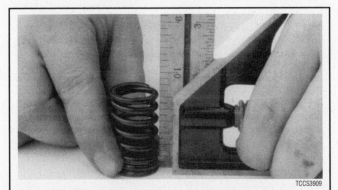

Fig. 95 The valve spring can be checked for squareness and free length with a carpenter's square

than 1/16 inches (1.5mm) from side to side, the pair of springs must be replaced.

Valve Seats

RECONDITIONING

♦ **See Figures 96, 97 and 98**

Valve seats cannot be replaced but can be refaced with either grinding stones or cutting tools. There is a limit to how much material can be removed. To determine how much of the seat can be cut on Quantums equipped with 4-cylinder CIS-E (1.8L) engines and 1985–89 Jetta, Golf, GTI, Scirocco, Cabriolet and Fox:

1. Insert the valve and make sure it is flat against the seat.

2. Place a straight edge across the valve cover gasket surface. Make sure the surface is clean and all gasket material is removed.

3. Measure the distance from the straight edge to the valve stem.

4. The final measurement after cutting the valve seat must be no less than the following dimensions. If not, the cylinder head must be replaced.

- 8-valve gasoline engines: Intake—1.331 in. (33.8mm) Exhaust—1.343 in. (34.1mm)
- 16-valve engines: Intake—1.354 in. (34.4mm) Exhaust—1.366 in. (34.7mm)
- Diesel engines: Intake—1.409 in. (35.8mm) Exhaust—1.421 in. (36.1mm)

To determine how much of the seat can be cut on Quantums equipped with 5-cylinder CIS/CIS-E and 4-cylinder CIS (1.7L) engines and 1974–84 Dasher, Rabbit, Scirocco and Jetta:

5. Invert the cylinder head so that the combustion chambers are facing upwards, then insert the valves in the head.

6. Place a straight edge across cylinder head surface. Make sure the surface is clean and all gasket material is removed.

7. Measure the distance from the straight edge to the valve.

8. The final measurement after cutting the valve seat must not be greater than the following dimensions. If not, the cylinder head must be replaced.

- Gasoline engines, except 1.8L JH engines: Intake—0.354 in. (9mm) Exhaust—0.378 in. (9.6mm)
- 1.8L JH engines: Intake—0.362 (9.2mm) Exhaust—0.378 in. (9.6mm)
- Diesel engines: Intake and Exhaust—0.059 in. (1.5mm)

Valve Guides

REMOVAL & INSTALLATION

Worn valve guides should be replaced by the automotive machine shop. The job requires a press and special cutting/reaming tools. In some cases a worn valve guide can be knurled which is a process where metal is displaced and raised, thereby reducing clearance. Consult a machine shop for advice.

Fig. 96 Measure from the valve stem tip to the valve cover gasket surface to determine how much of the seat can be cut— Quantums equipped with 4-cylinder CIS-E (1.8L) engines, as well as 1985–89 Jetta, Golf, GTI, Scirocco, Cabriolet and Fox models

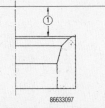

Fig. 97 Measure between the cylinder head gasket surface and valve, as indicated by dimension (1)— Quantums equipped with 5-cylinder CIS/CIS-E and 4-cylinder CIS (1.7L) engines, as well as 1974–84 Dasher, Rabbit, Scirocco and Jetta models

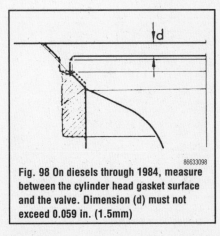

Fig. 98 On diesels through 1984, measure between the cylinder head gasket surface and the valve. Dimension (d) must not exceed 0.059 in. (1.5mm)

Valve Lifters

REMOVAL & INSTALLATION

▶ **See Figure 99**

The adjusting discs and cam follower/lifters can be removed once the camshaft is removed. Hydraulic lifters should be kept upside down when not in their bore to prevent oil loss. The lifter must be returned to the same bore. They cannot be repaired or rebuilt and must be replaced if worn or damaged.

Fig. 99 A hydraulic lifter used on Volkswagen engines. Always return lifters to their original bores

Oil Pan

REMOVAL & INSTALLATION

▶ **See Figures 100, 101 and 102**

Dasher, Fox and Quantum Models

1. Raise and safely support the vehicle on jack stands.
2. Drain the engine oil. Loosen the bolts/nuts securing motor mounts.
3. Support and slightly raise the engine with an overhead hoist.
4. Gradually loosen the engine crossmember mounting bolts. Remove the left and right side engine mounts.
5. Lower the crossmember very carefully.
6. Remove the oil pan. If it is stuck, tap the sides with a mallet. Do not pry against the gasket surfaces. Clean the gasket mating surfaces.
   To install:
7. Install the pan using a new gasket and sealer.
8. Tighten the retaining bolts in a crisscross pattern. Tighten the hex head bolts to 14 ft. lbs. (19 Nm), or the Allen head bolts to 7 ft. lbs. (10 Nm).

9. Raise the crossmember. Tighten the crossmember bolts to 42 ft. lbs. (57 Nm) and the engine mounting bolts to 32 ft. lbs. (44 Nm).
10. Refill the engine with oil. Start the engine and check for leaks.

Other Models

1. Raise and safely support the vehicle on jack stands.
2. Drain the engine oil.
3. Loosen and remove the socket or Allen head oil pan retaining bolts.
4. Lower the pan from the car. If it is stuck, tap the sides with a mallet. Do not pry against the gasket surfaces.
   To install:
5. Clean all the gasket surfaces thoroughly and coat the block surface with sealant before installing the gasket.
6. Install the pan using a new gasket.
7. Tighten the hex headed bolts to 14 (19 Nm), or Allen bolts to 7 ft. lbs. (10 Nm) in a crisscross pattern.
8. Refill the engine with oil. Start the engine and check for leaks.

Oil Pump

REMOVAL

4-Cylinder Engines

1. Remove the oil pan.
2. Remove the two mounting bolts that hold the pump to the block. Note that one bolt is longer than the other.
3. Pull the oil pump down and out of the engine.

5-Cylinder Engines

1. Remove the timing belt cover and remove the timing belt.
2. Remove the drive belt sprocket from the crankshaft.
3. Remove the oil dip stick and drain the engine oil.
4. Remove the oil pan.
5. Remove the oil pickup tube bolts and the tube.
6. Remove the oil pump to engine bolts and the oil pump.

INSPECTION

4-Cylinder Engines

▶ **See Figures 103 and 104**

1. With the oil pump on the bench and the bottom cover removed, insert a feeler gauge between the gear teeth. A new pump will have 0.002 inch (0.05mm) clearance, the wear limit is 0.008 inches (0.20mm).
2. Place a straight edge across the gears and the pump housing. Use a feeler gauge to measure the distance between the gears and the straight edge. The axial play of the gears should be no more than 0.004 inches (0.15mm).
3. The pressure relief valve is in the lower housing. Note position of the piston when removing.

Fig. 100 An extension is helpful for reaching the bolts securing the oil pan

Fig. 101 Lowering the pan from the car. If it is stuck, gently tap the sides with a soft mallet. Do not pry against the gasket surfaces

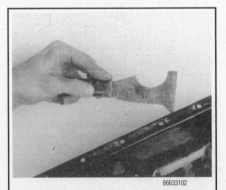

Fig. 102 A gasket scraper can be used to thoroughly clean the gasket mating surfaces

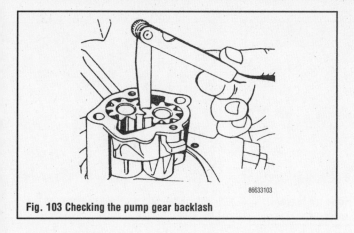

Fig. 103 Checking the pump gear backlash

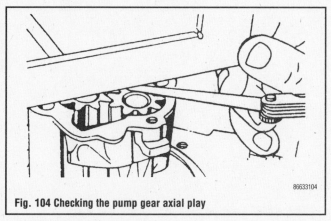

Fig. 104 Checking the pump gear axial play

4. Service parts for VW oil pumps are not available. If the measurements do not meet specification, replace the pump.

5-Cylinder Engines

1. At the rear of the oil pump, remove the end cover bolts and the cover. Check the cover for scoring or other damage. If necessary, replace it.

2. Check the pump gears for wear and/or damage, replace the parts if necessary. Remove the pressure relief valve, clean it in solvent and check the relief spring for wear. Torque the relief valve to 26 ft. lbs. (35 Nm).

➡**Install the pump gears with the marks facing the end cover.**

3. Pack the pump with petroleum jelly, then reassemble.

INSTALLATION

4-Cylinder Engines

1. Position the oil pump and a new gasket onto the block. Install the mounting bolts. Torque the long bolt to 15 ft. lbs. (20 Nm) and the short one to 7 ft. lbs. (10 Nm).

2. Install the oil pan.

5-Cylinder Engines

1. Mount the oil pump with a new gasket to the block and install the mounting bolts. Torque the pump-to-engine bolts to 14 ft. lbs. (19 Nm).

2. Attach the oil pump pick-up tube to the pump using new gaskets. Torque the mounting bolts to 7 ft. lbs. (10 Nm).

3. Install the oil pan.

4. Refill the engine with oil.

5. Install the drive belt sprocket onto the crankshaft.

6. Install the drive belt and drive belt covers.

7. Start the engine and check for leaks.

Crankshaft Damper

REMOVAL & INSTALLATION

This special procedure is applicable to 5-cylinder Quantum models only.

1. Disconnect the negative battery cable.

2. Remove the accessory drive belts.

3. Remove the timing belt cover.

4. Turn the engine until cylinder No. 1 is at TDC on the compression stroke. You can turn the engine by using a socket on the damper bolt.

5. Attach VW tool 2084 to the damper, then loosen the damper center bolt.

6. Slacken the timing belt tension (refer to the timing belt procedures).

7. Remove the damper bolt, then use a puller to remove the damper from the crankshaft.

   To install:

8. Install the damper onto the crankshaft.

9. Install the timing belt (refer to the timing belt procedures). Make sure the timing marks are aligned and the belt is properly tensioned.

10. Coat the threads of the damper bolt with Loctite® or a similar thread locking compound. Thread the damper bolt onto the crankshaft.

11. Install VW tools 2084 and 2079. These tools must be used to torque the damper bolt. Tighten the bolt to 258 ft. lbs. (350 Nm)

12. Install the timing belt cover and all accessory drive belts.

13. Connect the negative battery cable.

Timing Belt Cover

REMOVAL & INSTALLATION

♦ **See Figures 105, 106, 107 and 108**

1. Remove the accessory drive belts.

2. To remove the crankshaft accessory drive pulley, hold the center crankshaft sprocket bolt with a socket and loosen the pulley bolts.

3. The cover is now accessible. It comes off in 2 pieces, remove the upper half first. Take note of any special spacers or other hardware.

4. Installation is the reverse of removal.

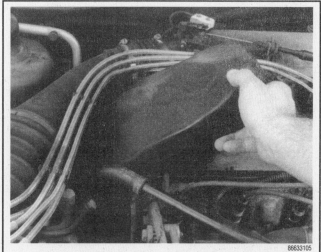

Fig. 105 Remove the bolts securing the upper timing belt cover, then carefully remove it from the engine

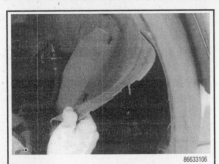

Fig. 106 To make access to the lower timing belt cover easier, remove the screws securing the splash shield, then position it aside

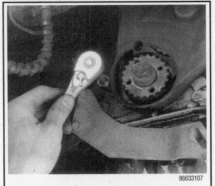

Fig. 107 Use a short extension to reach the lower timing belt cover bolts

Fig. 108 An Allen wrench can be used to remove the "hidden screw"

Timing Belt

Timing belts are designed to last 60,000–75,000 miles (96,000–120,000 km). If the vehicle has been stored for long periods (2 years or more), the belt should be changed before returning the vehicle to service.

REMOVAL & INSTALLATION

▶ See Figures 109 thru 116

✳✳ WARNING

Do not turn the engine or camshaft with the timing belt removed. The pistons may contact the valves and cause internal engine damage.

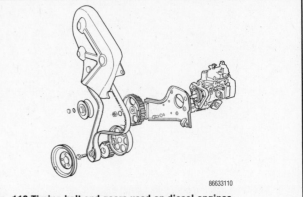

Fig. 110 Timing belt and gears used on diesel engines

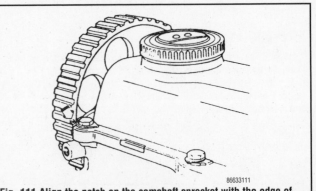

Fig. 111 Align the notch on the camshaft sprocket with the edge of the cylinder head on 8-valve engines

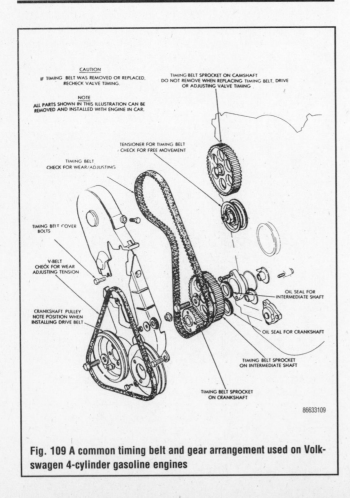

Fig. 109 A common timing belt and gear arrangement used on Volkswagen 4-cylinder gasoline engines

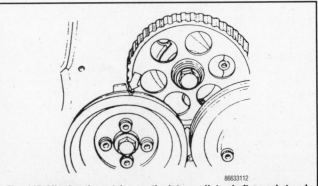

Fig. 112 Aligning the notches on the intermediate shaft sprocket and crankshaft pulley

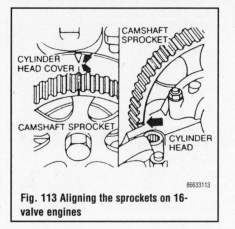

Fig. 113 Aligning the sprockets on 16-valve engines

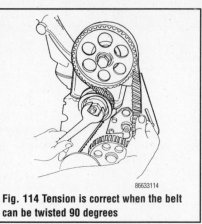

Fig. 114 Tension is correct when the belt can be twisted 90 degrees

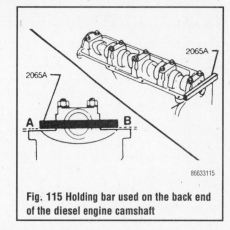

Fig. 115 Holding bar used on the back end of the diesel engine camshaft

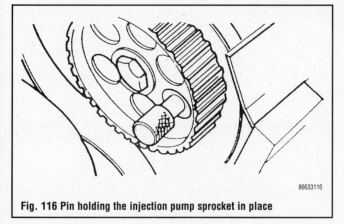

Fig. 116 Pin holding the injection pump sprocket in place

Dasher, Fox, Quantum and 1975–84 Rabbit, Scirocco and Jetta

→Timing belt installation will be less confusing if the engine is set for TDC (Top Dead Center) of cylinder No. 1 prior to belt removal or replacement.

1. Remove front belt cover(s).
2. Turn the engine until the 0 or TDC mark on the flywheel is aligned with the stationary pointer on the bell housing. On 4-cylinder engines, turn the camshaft until the mark on the rear of the sprocket is aligned with the upper edge of the rear drive belt cover at the left side of the engine. On 5-cylinder engines, turn the camshaft until the mark on the sprocket lines up with the left side edge of the camshaft housing. The notch on the crankshaft pulley should align with the dot on the intermediate shaft sprocket. Remove the distributor cap; the distributor rotor should be pointing toward the mark on the rim of the distributor housing.
3. Remove the crankshaft pulley(s).
4. On 4-cylinder engines, hold the large nut on the tensioner pulley and loosen the smaller pulley lock nut. Turn the tensioner counterclockwise to relieve the tension on the timing belt.
5. On 5-cylinder engines, loosen the water pump bolts and turn the pump clockwise to relieve timing belt tension.
6. Slide the timing belt from the pulleys.
   To install:
7. Install timing belt and retension the belt by the turning the pulley or water pump. Reinstall the crankshaft pulley(s). Recheck alignment of timing marks. Torque the tensioner nut to 33 ft. lbs. (45 Nm).
8. Check the timing belt tension. The tension is correct when the belt can be twisted 90 degrees with the thumb and index finger. Check this along the straight run between the camshaft sprocket and the water pump.
9. Turn the engine two complete revolutions (clockwise rotation) and align the flywheel mark at TDC. Recheck belt tension and timing marks. Readjust as required.
10. Reinstall the cam belt cover and drive belts.

11. If the belt is too tight, there will be a growling noise that rises and falls with engine speed.

✴✴ WARNING

If the timing marks are not correctly aligned with the No. 1 piston at TDC of the compression stroke and the belt is installed, valve timing will be incorrect. Poor performance and possible engine damage can result from improper valve timing.

1985–89 Golf, GTI, Jetta, Cabriolet and Scirocco

1. Disconnect the negative battery cable and remove the accessory drive belts, crankshaft pulley and the timing belt cover(s).
2. Temporarily reinstall the crankshaft pulley bolt and turn the crankshaft to TDC of No. 1 piston. The mark on the camshaft sprocket should be aligned with the mark on the inner timing belt cover or the edge of the cylinder head.
3. With the distributor cap removed, the rotor should be pointing toward the No. 1 mark on the rim of the distributor housing. On 8-valve engines, the notch on the crankshaft pulley should align with the dot on the intermediate shaft sprocket.
4. Loosen the locknut on the tensioner pulley and turn the tensioner counterclockwise to relieve the tension on the timing belt.
   To install:
5. Check the alignment of the timing marks. On 16-valve engines, the mark on the tooth should align with the mark on the rear belt cover.
6. Install the new timing belt. Engage the flats of the large pulley nut with an open end wrench and loosen the smaller pulley locknut. Tension the belt by turning the tensioner in a clockwise direction. The belt should be able to be twisted 90 degrees at the middle of its longest section, between the camshaft and intermediate sprockets.

→On some engines, the tensioner may not have the large pulley nut. Instead, a spanner wrench is used to engage the 2 holes in the tensioner.

7. Recheck the alignment of the timing marks and, if correct, turn the engine 2 full revolutions to return to TDC of No. 1 piston. Recheck belt tension and timing marks. Readjust as required. Torque the tensioner nut to 33 ft. lbs. (45 Nm).
8. Install the belt cover and accessory drive belts.
9. If the belt is too tight, there will be a growling noise that rises and falls with engine speed.

Diesel Engines

Some special tools are required. A flat bar, VW tool no. 2065A, is used to secure the camshaft in position. A pin, VW tool no. 2064, is used to fix the pump position while the timing belt is removed. The camshaft and pump work against spring pressure and will move out of position when the timing belt is removed. It is not difficult to find substitutes, but do not remove the timing belt without these tools.

Do not turn the engine or camshaft with the timing belt removed. The pistons will contact the valves and cause internal engine damage.

1. Disconnect the negative battery cable and remove the accessory drive belts, crankshaft pulley and the timing belt cover(s). Remove the camshaft cover and rubber plug at the back end of the camshaft.

2. Temporarily reinstall the crankshaft pulley bolt and turn the crankshaft to TDC of No. 1 cylinder. The mark on the camshaft sprocket should be aligned with the mark on the inner timing belt cover or the edge of the cylinder head.

3. With the engine at TDC, insert the bar (VW 2065A) into the slot at the back of the camshaft. The bar rests on the cylinder head to will hold the camshaft in position.

4. Insert the pin (VW 2064) into the injection pump drive sprocket to hold the pump in position.

5. Loosen the locknut on the tensioner pulley and turn the tensioner counterclockwise to relieve the tension on the timing belt. Slide the timing belt from the sprockets.

To install:

6. Install the new timing belt and adjust the tension so the belt can be twisted 45 degrees at a point between the camshaft and pump sprockets. Torque the tensioner nut to 33 ft. lbs. (45 Nm).

7. Remove the holding tools.

8. Turn the engine 2 full revolutions to return to TDC of No. 1 piston. Recheck belt tension and timing mark alignment, readjust as required.

9. Install the belt cover and accessory drive belts.

10. If the belt is too tight, there will be a growling noise that rises and falls with engine speed.

Timing Sprockets

REMOVAL & INSTALLATION

▶ **See Figures 117, 118 and 119**

➡The 12-point crankshaft sprocket bolt is meant to be used one time only and must be replaced when removed.

Depending on the year and model, the timing sprockets are located on the shaft by a key, a self-contained drive lug, or in the case of early diesel engine camshaft, a tapered fit. All sprockets are retained by a bolt. To remove any or all sprockets, removal of the timing belt cover(s) and belt is required. The old hex head washered style bolt on many engine crankshaft sprockets has been replaced with a new 12-point stretch bolt that does not have a washer. If removed, this bolt must be thrown away and replaced. The crankshaft threads can accept the new style bolts, however, washers must not be used.

➡When removing the crankshaft pulley, it is not necessary to remove the four bolts which hold the outer component drive pulley to the timing belt sprocket. Remove the component drive belt, center retaining bolt and crankshaft pulley. To remove the crankshaft sprocket on 5-cylinder models, refer to the crankshaft damper procedure in this section.

1. Remove the timing belt covers and the timing belt. The crankshaft sprocket should slide off easily when the center bolt is removed. Don't lose the Woodruff key.

2. Remove the cylinder head cover.

3. Use a wrench to hold the camshaft on the flat section and remove the sprocket retaining bolt.

4. Gently pull or tap the sprocket off the shaft with a soft mallet. If the sprocket will not easily slide off the shaft, use a gear puller. Do not hammer on the sprocket or damage to the sprocket or bearings could occur.

On 16-valve engines, make sure the camshaft sprockets are installed so that the curved portion of the sprocket key faces the surface of the engine block. If the sprocket is installed incorrectly, the timing will be advanced and cause the valves to hit the pistons.

To install:

5. Install the sprockets. On crankshaft sprockets, oil the threads before installing the bolt. Torque the bolts as follows:

    a. Camshaft sprocket on gasoline engines (except 16-valve)—59 ft. lbs. (80 Nm).

    b. Camshaft sprocket on 16-valve engines—48 ft. lbs. (65 Nm).

    c. Camshaft sprocket on diesel engines—33 ft. lbs. (45 Nm)

    d. Refer to the torque specifications chart in this section for crankshaft sprockets.

6. Install the timing belt and adjust the belt tension. Install the covers.

Camshaft and Bearings

REMOVAL & INSTALLATION

▶ **See Figures 120 thru 126**

Except 16-Valve Engines

1. Disconnect the negative battery cable. Remove the timing belt cover(s), the timing belt, cylinder head cover and the camshaft sprocket (if necessary).

2. Number the bearing caps from front to back. If the cap does not already have one, scribe an arrow pointing towards the front of the engine. The caps are offset and must be installed correctly. Factory numbers on the caps are not always on the same side.

3. Remove the front and rear bearing caps. Loosen the remaining bearing cap nuts a little at a time to avoid bending the camshaft. Start from the outside caps near the ends of the head and work toward the center.

4. Remove the bearing caps and the camshaft.

To install:

5. Install a new oil seal and end plug in the cylinder head. Lubricate the camshaft bearing journals and lobes and set the camshaft in place.

6. Install the bearing caps in the correct position with the arrow pointing towards the front of the engine. Tighten the cap nuts diagonally and in several steps until they are torqued to 15 ft. lbs. (20 Nm). Do not over torque. Camshaft shaft end-play should be about 0.006 inches (0.15mm).

Fig. 117 A breaker bar is essential for loosening the timing sprocket bolts

Fig. 118 Gently pull or tap the sprocket off the shaft with a soft mallet

Fig. 119 Oil the threads of the crankshaft sprocket bolt before installing it

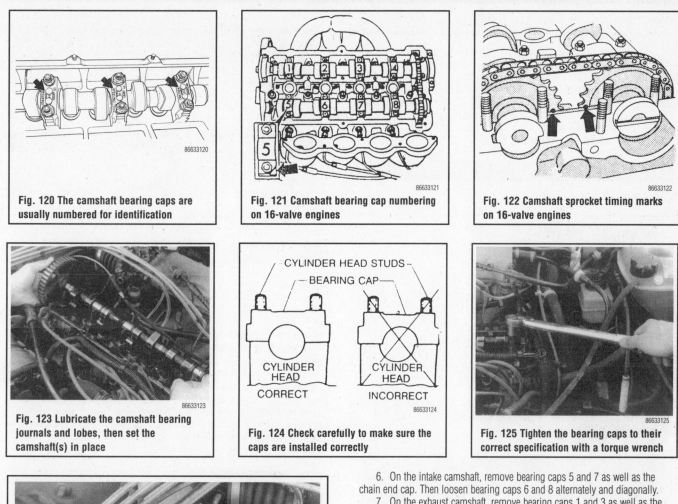

Fig. 120 The camshaft bearing caps are usually numbered for identification

Fig. 121 Camshaft bearing cap numbering on 16-valve engines

Fig. 122 Camshaft sprocket timing marks on 16-valve engines

Fig. 123 Lubricate the camshaft bearing journals and lobes, then set the camshaft(s) in place

Fig. 124 Check carefully to make sure the caps are installed correctly

Fig. 125 Tighten the bearing caps to their correct specification with a torque wrench

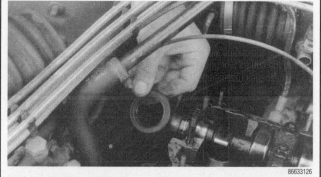

Fig. 126 It will be necessary to remove the camshaft sprocket to replace the camshaft oil seal

7. Install the drive sprocket and timing belt. Wait at least ½ hour after installing camshaft shaft before starting the engine to allow the lifters to leak down.

16-Valve Engines

1. Remove the timing belt cover.
2. Remove the bolts from the upper intake manifold and remove the manifold and gasket.
3. Remove the bolts from the cylinder head cover and remove the cover and gaskets.
4. Turn the engine to TDC on cylinder No. 1, then loosen and remove the timing belt.
5. If necessary, remove the camshaft sprocket. Matchmark the intake sprocket to the drive chain with a felt-tip marker or equivalent before removal. DO NOT scratch, inscribe or punch the drive chain in any way.

6. On the intake camshaft, remove bearing caps 5 and 7 as well as the chain end cap. Then loosen bearing caps 6 and 8 alternately and diagonally.
7. On the exhaust camshaft, remove bearing caps 1 and 3 as well as the end caps. Then loosen bearing caps 2 and 4 alternately and diagonally.
8. Remove the remaining bearing cap bolts, then remove the camshafts.
   To install:
9. Lubricate the camshaft bearing journals and lobes and set the camshafts in place. Install the camshaft drive chain so the marks on the chain sprockets are matched at the base of the cylinder head, directly across from each other.

➡ **When installing the bearing caps, make sure the notch points towards the intake side of the head.**

10. On the intake camshaft, install and tighten bearing caps 6 and 8 alternately and diagonally to 11 ft. lbs. (15 Nm).
11. Install and tighten the remaining intake bearing caps to 11 ft. lbs. (15 Nm).
12. On the exhaust camshaft, tighten bearing caps 2 and 4 alternately and diagonally to 11 ft. lbs. (15 Nm).
13. Install and tighten the remaining exhaust bearing caps to 11 ft. lbs. (15 Nm). Camshaft shaft end play on both camshafts should be about 0.006 inches (0.15mm).
14. If necessary, position and install the camshaft sprocket.

❊❊ WARNING

Make sure the camshaft sprockets are installed so that the curved portion of the sprocket key faces the surface of the engine block. If the sprocket is installed incorrectly, the timing will be advanced and cause the valves to hit the pistons.

15. Install the drive belt and adjust the timing.
16. Install the remaining components. Wait at least ½ hour after installing camshaft shafts before starting the engine to allow the hydraulic lifters to leak down.

INSPECTION

Degrease the camshaft using a safe solvent. Visually inspect the cam lobes and bearing journals for excessive wear. If a lobe is questionable or a bearing journal scored, the camshaft should be replaced. Check the lobes and journals with a micrometer. Measure the lobes from nose to heel. If all intake or all exhaust lobes do not measure the same, replace the camshaft. If the lobes and journals appear intact, place the front and rear journals in V-blocks. Position a dial indicator on the center journal and rotate the camshaft. If deviation exceeds 0.0004 in. (0.01mm) replace the camshaft.

Intermediate Shaft

REMOVAL & INSTALLATION

▶ **See Figures 127, 128 and 129**

1. Remove timing belt cover(s), timing belt and intermediate shaft drive sprocket.
2. On 8-valve gasoline engines, remove the distributor. On carbureted engines, remove the fuel pump.
3. Remove the mounting flange retaining bolts. Thread the sprocket bolt onto the shaft finger-tight, then remove the flange and shaft by pulling on the sprocket bolt.
4. Remove flange from the intermediate shaft and install a new oil seal.

To install:

5. Lubricate the oil seal lips with oil. When installing the mounting flange, be sure the oil return hole is at the bottom. Tighten the flange mounting bolts to 18 ft. lbs. (25 Nm).
6. Install the sprocket. Tighten the bolt to 58 ft. lbs. (79 Nm) on 8-valve engines, 48 ft. lbs. (65 Nm) on 16-valve engines and 33 ft. lbs. (45 Nm) on diesel engines.

Fig. 127 Remove the bolt securing the intermediate shaft sprocket, then remove the sprocket

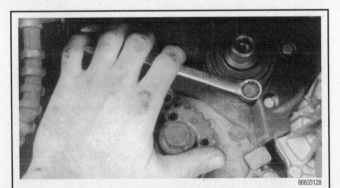

Fig. 128 The intermediate shaft seals can be replaced without removing the shaft. Remove the bolts securing the flange, then pull the flange from the engine block

Fig. 129 Replace both the O-ring and the lip seal on the flange

Pistons and Connecting Rods

REMOVAL

▶ **See Figures 130, 131, 132, 133 and 134**

➤These procedures may be performed with the engine in the vehicle. If additional overhaul work is to be performed, it will be easier if the engine is removed and mounted on an engine stand. Most stands allow the block to be rotated, giving easy access to both the top and bottom. These procedures require certain hand tools which may not be in your tool box. A cylinder ridge reamer, a numbered punch set, piston ring expander, snaping tools and piston installation tool (ring compressor) are all necessary for correct piston and rod repair. These tools are commonly available from retail tool suppliers; you may be able to rent them from larger automotive supply houses.

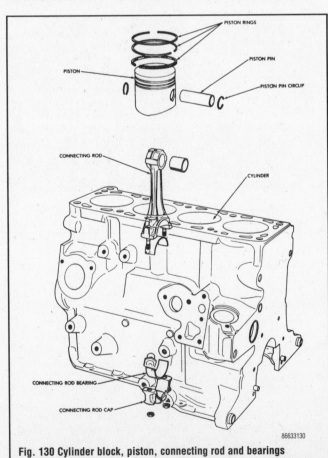

Fig. 130 Cylinder block, piston, connecting rod and bearings

Fig. 131 If the connecting rod cap cannot pulled off easily, tap it gently with a soft faced hammer to loosen it

Fig. 132 Removing the ridge from the cylinder bore using a ridge cutter

Fig. 133 Place lengths of rubber hose over the connecting rod studs in order to protect the crankshaft and cylinders from damage

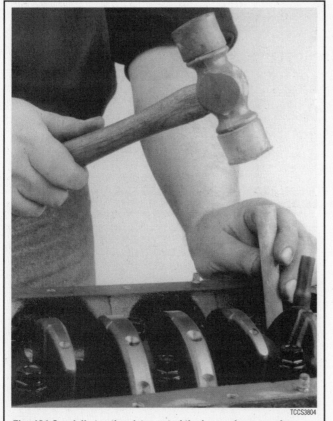

Fig. 134 Carefully tap the piston out of the bore using a wooden dowel

1. If the engine is still in the vehicle, the pistons and rods can be removed without removing the crankshaft. Remove the cylinder head and oil pan.

2. Turn the crankshaft until the piston to be removed is at the bottom of its travel.

3. Matchmark the connecting rod and cap on the same side to indicate the cylinder number and so they can be reassembled the same way. Remove the connecting rod cap and bearing insert.

4. Mark the top of the piston to indicate the cylinder number and an arrow pointing towards the timing belt. This will allow you to make sure the pistons are installed in their original cylinder and facing the correct direction.

5. Place a rag down the cylinder bore on the head of the piston to be removed. Remove the cylinder top ridge and carbon deposits with a ridge reamer, following the instructions of the reamer's manufacturer.

➡Do not cut too deeply or remove more than 0.15mm (0.006 inches) from the ring travel area when removing the ridge.

6. Remove the rag and metal shavings from the cylinder bore. The cylinder bore must be free of metal shavings before attempting remove the piston.

7. Use a short pieces of hose to cover the bolt threads. This protects the bolt, the crankshaft and the cylinder walls during removal. Push the connecting rod up the bore slightly and remove the upper bearing insert.

8. Push the connecting rod and piston assembly up and out of the cylinder with a hammer handle or wooden dowel.

9. Wipe any dirt or oil from the connecting rod bearing saddle and rod cap. Install the bearing inserts (if to be reused) in the connecting rod and cap to protect them from damage. Install cap, then finger-tighten the rod bolts.

10. If necessary, remove the rest of the rod and piston assemblies.

CLEANING AND INSPECTION

▶ See Figures 135 thru 140

Pistons

After removing the piston and rod assemblies from the engine, clamp the connecting rod into a vise with the lower edge of the piston just resting on the vise jaws. Use a ring expanding tool and remove the piston rings from the piston. Clean the top of the piston with a dull scraper or wire wheel. Use care not to gouge the piston when removing the carbon deposits. Clean the ring grooves using an appropriate groove cleaning tool. A broken piston ring can be used if a groove cleaner is not available. Once again, use care not to cut too deeply or gouge the ring seat. After all the pistons have had the rings removed and grooves cleaned, soak them in safe solvent. Do not use a caustic solvent on the pistons.

❋❋ CAUTION

Wear goggles during this cleaning; the solvent is very strong and can cause eye damage.

After the pistons have been cleaned and wiped dry inspect them for scuffing, scoring, cracks, pitting or excessive ring groove wear. If wear is evident, the piston must be replaced. Hold the connecting rod in one hand, grasp the piston in the other hand and twist the piston and rod in opposite directions. If excessive clearance (looseness) is detected, the piston pin, connecting rod bushing or piston and rod may require replacement. An automotive machine shop can perform this job for you. If you are not sure of the extent of wear present or what component needs replacing, take the assemblies to the machine shop and have them checked.

Measure, or have the machine shop measure the piston with a micrometer. Turn the piston upside down and take a measurement at a point ⅝ in. (16mm) below the lower edge of the piston, 90 degrees away from the piston pin holes. Measure the cylinder bore at three places to see if the cylinder is still round and straight. Measurements should be taken at a number of places in each cylinder (at the top, middle and bottom at two points at each location) that is at a point 90 degrees from the crankshaft, as well as a point parallel to the crankshaft. The difference between the greatest measurement of the cylinder wall and the diameter measurement of the piston is the piston-to-cylinder wall clearance. If the difference is greater than 0.0028 inches (0.03mm), the clearance is too great and the cylinders should be machined to accept the next oversize piston. If any one

Fig. 135 Use a ring expander tool to remove the piston rings

Fig. 136 Clean the piston grooves using a ring groove cleaner

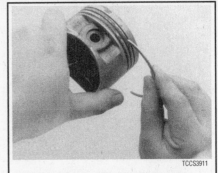

Fig. 137 You can use a piece of an old ring to clean the ring grooves, but be careful, the ring is sharp

Fig. 138 Measure the piston's outer diameter using a micrometer

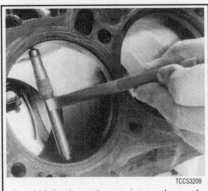

Fig. 139 A telescoping gauge may be used to measure the cylinder bore diameter

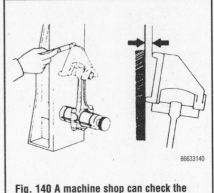

Fig. 140 A machine shop can check the connecting rods for bends and cracks

cylinder is more than 0.0016 inches (0.04mm) out of round, all cylinders should be bored out to the next oversize. The machine shop or dealer parts department can provide information about what piston sizes are available.

Connecting Rods

The connecting rods must be free from wear, cracking and bending. Visually examine the rod, particularly at its upper and lower ends. Look for any sign of metal stretching or wear. The piston pin should fit cleanly and tightly through the upper end, allowing no side-play wobble. The bottom end should also be an exact ½ circle, with no deformity of shape. The bolts must be parallel.

The rods may be taken to a machine shop for exact measurement of twist or bend. This is easier and cheaper than purchasing a seldom used rod-alignment tool.

CYLINDER HONING

♦ **See Figures 141 and 142**

Most inspection and service work on the cylinder block should be handled by a machinist or professional engine rebuilding shop. Included in this work are bearing alignment checks, line boring, deck resurfacing, hot-tanking and cylinder block boring. Any or all of this work requires that the block be completely stripped of all components and transported to the shop. A block that has been checked and properly serviced will last much longer than one whose owner cut corners during a repair.

Cylinder de-glazing (honing) can be performed by the owner/mechanic who is careful and takes time to be accurate. The cylinder bores become glazed during normal operation of the engine as the rings ride up and down constantly. This shiny glaze must be removed in order for a new set of piston rings to seat properly.

Cylinder hones are available at most auto tool stores and parts jobbers. Install the hone into the chuck of a variable speed drill (preferred in place of a constant speed drill). With the piston, rod and crankshaft assemblies removed from the block, insert the hone into the cylinder. If the crankshaft is not being

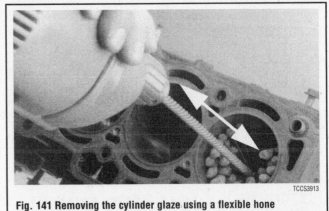

Fig. 141 Removing the cylinder glaze using a flexible hone

Fig. 142 A properly cross-hatched cylinder bore

removed from the block, cover it completely with oil soaked rags to prevent grit from collecting on it.

→**Make sure the drill and hone are kept square to the cylinder bore during the entire honing procedure.**

Start the drill and move the hone up and down in the cylinder at a rate which will produce approximately a 60 degree cross-hatch pattern. DO NOT extend the hone below the bottom of the cylinder bore. After the crosshatched pattern is established, remove the hone.

Wash the cylinder with a solution of detergent and water to remove the honing and cylinder grit. Wipe the bores out several times with a clean rag soaked in fresh engine oil. If applicable, carefully remove the rags from the crankshaft and check closely to see that NO grit has found its way onto the crankshaft.

PISTON PIN REPLACEMENT

Make sure the piston, connecting rod and rod cap are marked with the number of the cylinder the assembly came from. Remove the piston from the connecting rod by inserting a small blunt drift in the small cutout provided on each side of the piston at the piston pin ends. Pry upward on the circlip to compress, and remove both circlips. Use a blunt drift slightly smaller than the diameter of the piston pin to gently drive the pin out. If resistance is encountered when removing the piston pin, submerge the pistons in hot water (140°F/60°C) to expand the metal, then carefully drive the pin out. Inspect the piston pin, connecting rod bushing and piston pin bore for galling, scoring or excessive wear. If wear is evident, consult the machine shop for advice as to what repair will be necessary.

PISTON RING REPLACEMENT

▶ **See Figures 143 and 144**

After the cylinder bore has been finish honed, or determined to be in satisfactory condition, ring end gap clearance can be checked. Compress one of the piston rings to be used into the cylinder. Press the ring down the bore to a point about 1 in. (25mm) below the top with an inverted piston. Measure the distance between the two ends (ring gap) of the ring with feeler gauges and compare to specifications. Carefully pull the ring from the cylinder, and if necessary, file the ends with a fine file to gain required clearance. Roll the outside of the ring around the piston groove it will be installed in to check for burrs or unremoved carbon deposits. Dress the groove with a fine file if necessary. Hold the ring in the groove and measure between top of ring and groove with a set of feeler gauges to check side clearance. If clearance is excessive, a new piston may be required. Consult the machine shop for their advice.

Install the piston rings on the piston starting with the lower oil control ring. Always refer to the ring manufacturer's instruction sheet for guidance. Be sure, when installing a three piece expander type oil ring, that the ends of the expander are butted together and do not overlap. Hold the butted edges together and install the lower rail first. Install with the ring gap about 19mm (¾ inches) away from the butted point of the expander. Install the upper rail on the opposite side, 3/4 away from the butted point of the expander. Use a ring expander and install the compression rings, lower ring first. Most compression rings will have a top mark of some kind, be sure the mark is facing up.

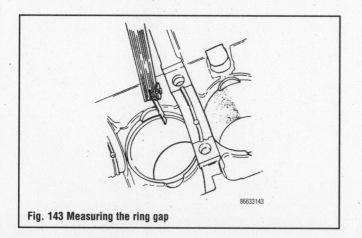

Fig. 143 Measuring the ring gap

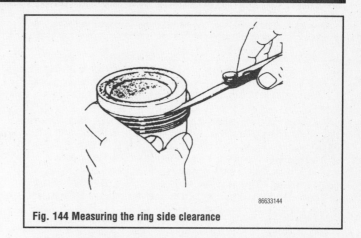

Fig. 144 Measuring the ring side clearance

Before installing the piston ring compressor, be sure the piston ring gaps are staggered 60 degrees apart from each other. The gaps should be at three equal spacings, never in a straight line. Avoid installing the rings with their ends in line with the piston pin bosses and the thrust direction. Always refer to the ring manufacturer's instruction sheet for guidance.

ROD BEARING REPLACEMENT

▶ **See Figure 145**

Connecting rod bearings on all engines consist of two halves or shells which are not interchangeable in the rod and cap. When the shells are in position, the ends extend slightly beyond the rod and cap surfaces so that when the bolts are tightened, the shells will be clamped tightly in place. This insures a positive seating and prevents turning. A small tang holds the shells in place within the cap and rod housings.

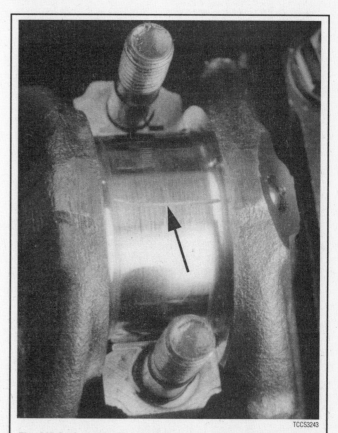

Fig. 145 Apply a strip of gauging material to the bearing journal, then install the cap. After the bearing cap is once again removed, use the gauge supplied with the material to check the clearances

➡The ends of the bearing shells must never be filed flush with the mating surface of the rod or cap.

If a rod becomes noisy or is worn so that its clearance on the crankshaft is out of specification, a new bearing of the correct undersize must be selected and installed. There is no provision for adjustment. Under no circumstances should the rod end or cap be filed to compensate for wear, nor should shims of any type be used.

Inspect the rod bearings while the rods are out of the engine. If the shells are scored or show flaking they should be replaced. Measuring the clearance between the connecting rod bearings and the crankshaft (oil clearance) is done with a plastic measuring material such as Plastigage® or similar product.

1. Remove the rod cap with the bearing shell. Completely clean the cap, bearing shells and the journal on the crankshaft. Blow any oil from the oil hole in the crank. The plastic measuring material is soluble in oil and will begin to dissolve if the area is not totally free of oil.

2. Place a piece of the measuring material lengthwise along the bottom center of the lower bearing shell. Install the cap and shell. Tighten to:

    a. 37 ft. lbs. (50 Nm) on 5-cylinder engines without stretch-type bolts.

    b. 33 ft. lbs. (45 Nm) on 4-cylinder engines (gas and diesel) without stretch-type bolts.

    c. 22 ft. lbs. (30 Nm) on all engines with stretch-type bolts.

➡Do not turn the crankshaft with the measuring material installed.

3. Remove the bearing cap with the shell. The flattened plastic material will be found sticking to either the bearing shell or the crank journal. DO NOT remove it yet.

4. Use the scale printed on the packaging for the measuring material to measure the flattened plastic at its widest point. The number within the scale which is closest to the width of the plastic indicates the bearing clearance in thousandths of an inch.

5. Check the specifications chart for the proper clearance. If there is any measurement approaching the maximum acceptable value, replace the bearing.

DIESEL PISTON PROJECTION

▶ See Figure 146

On diesel engines, the top of the piston actually protrudes above the top of the cylinder deck when the piston is at TDC. This piston "pop-up" must be measured before installing the cylinder head.

A spacer (VW385/17) and bar with dial indicator (VW 382/7) are necessary, and should be set up as shown in the illustration to measure the maximum amount of piston projection above the deck height. To measure the piston height of particular cylinder, bring the piston up so that the top of the piston is dead flush with the surface of the block. Mount the indicator and spacer onto the cylinder deck. Slide the indicator over and zero the indicator stylus on the top of the piston. Now, very slowly rotate the crankshaft until a deflection is read on the indicator. This can be a very tricky reading, because you have to catch the indicator deflection before the piston starts on the downward travel. Take several readings per cylinder to get an average.

After piston height has been determined, a head gasket of suitable thickness must be used. Head gasket thickness is coded by the number of notches located on the edge and by a part number on the gasket near the notches. If the same parts are being used over again, install a new gasket with the same number of notches as the one removed. The following shows the piston height with its corresponding notch number:

Dasher
- 0.017–0.025 in. (0.43–0.63mm)—2 notches
- 0.025–0.032 in. (0.63–0.82mm)—3 notches
- 0.032–0.036 in. (0.82–0.92mm)—4 notches
- 0.036–0.040 in. (0.92–1.023mm)—5 notches

Quantum
- 0.026–0.031 in. (0.67–0.80mm)—1 notch
- 0.032–0.035 in. (0.81–0.90mm)—2 notches
- 0.036–0.040 in. (0.91–1.02mm)—3 notches

1977–78 Rabbit
- 0.021–0.027 in. (0.53–0.68mm)—2 notches
- 0.027–0.032 in. (0.68–0.80mm)—3 notches

1979–84 Rabbit and Jetta
- 0.025–0.032 in. (0.63–0.82mm)—3 notches on 1979–80 1.5 L or 1 notch on 1981–84 1.6 L
- 0.033–0.036 in. (0.83–0.92mm)—4 notches on 1979–80 1.5 L or 2 notches on 1981–84 1.6 L
- 0.037–0.040 in. (0.93–1.02mm)—5 notches on 1979–80 1.5 L or 3 notches on 1981–84 1.6 L

1985–86 Golf and Jetta (Mechanical Lifters)
- 0.026–0.031 in. (0.67–0.80mm)—1 notch
- 0.032–0.035 in. (0.81–0.90mm)—2 notches
- 0.036–0.040 in. (0.91–1.02mm)—3 notches

1985–89 Golf and Jetta (Hydraulic Lifters)
- 0.026–0.034 in. (0.66–0.86mm)—1 notch
- 0.034–0.036 in. (0.87–0.90mm)—2 notches
- 0.036–0.040 in. (0.91–1.02mm)—3 notches

INSTALLATION

▶ See Figures 147, 148, 149 and 150

➡Connecting rod bolts with a conical head and six notches on the nuts are stretch-type bolts and cannot be reused. The bolts must be replaced when the connecting rod is disassembled.

1. After the piston and connecting rod have been cleaned, inspected and prepared for installation, use new oil to lubricate the piston, rings, cylinder walls and crankshaft journal.

2. Lubricate the upper rod bearing saddle and fit the new bearing into place.

3. Install a piston ring compressor over the rings and top of the piston. Before tightening the ring compressor, be sure the ring gaps are staggered 60 degrees apart.

4. Lower the piston and rod assembly into the cylinder bore with the arrow on the piston head facing the front of the engine. When the ring compressor contacts the top of the engine block, check to make sure the connecting rod is properly aligned with the crankshaft journal. Use a wooden hammer handle to gently tap the piston into the bore.

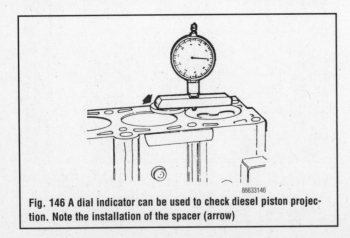

Fig. 146 A dial indicator can be used to check diesel piston projection. Note the installation of the spacer (arrow)

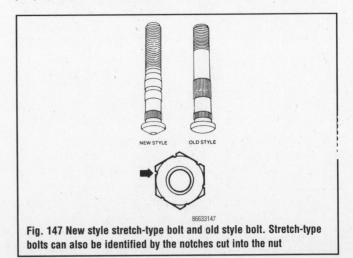

Fig. 147 New style stretch-type bolt and old style bolt. Stretch-type bolts can also be identified by the notches cut into the nut

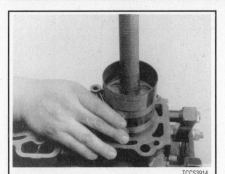

Fig. 148 Installing the piston into the block using a ring compressor and a wooden hammer handle

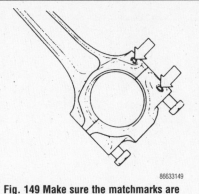

Fig. 149 Make sure the matchmarks are aligned when installing the cap

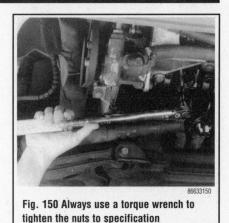

Fig. 150 Always use a torque wrench to tighten the nuts to specification

→ **If unusual resistance is encountered when starting the piston into the cylinder bore, the piston may be cocked or a ring has slipped out of the compressor and is caught at the top of the cylinder. Remove the piston and reinstall compressor. Forcing the piston in will break the rings.**

5. Carefully guide the connecting rod down the cylinder bore and over the crankshaft journal, taking care not to score the wall or crankshaft.

6. Fit the lower bearing insert into the bearing cap. Lubricate the insert and mount the cap on the rod with matchmarks aligned.

7. Install rod nuts and torque carefully to the following:

a. 37 ft. lbs. (50 Nm) on 5-cylinder engines without stretch-type bolts.

b. 33 ft. lbs. (45 Nm) on 4-cylinder engines (gas and diesel) without stretch-type bolts.

c. 22 ft. lbs. (30 Nm), then an additional ¼ turn on all engines with stretch-type bolts.

8. Lubricate the cylinder wall and turn the crankshaft to make sure the rod bearing is properly installed. If the crankshaft will not turn, remove the bearing cap and check bearing alignment.

9. If removed, install the oil spray nozzle. Apply a thread locking compound to the threads, then tighten the bolt to 7 ft. lbs. (10 Nm).

10. Install remaining piston and rod assemblies. Turn the crankshaft each time so the crank journal of the piston being installed is at the bottom of travel.

Freeze Plugs

REMOVAL & INSTALLATION

▶ **See Figures 151 and 152**

The freeze plugs can be loosened and removed using a punch and a hammer. Or, drill a small hole in the middle of the freeze plug, then thread a large sheet metal screw into the hole. Remove the plug with a slide hammer. When installing, coat the freeze plugs with sealer. Tap into position using a piece of pipe, slightly smaller than the plug, as a driver.

Main Oil Seals

REMOVAL & INSTALLATION

▶ **See Figures 153, 154, 155 and 156**

The front crankshaft oil seal retainer can be removed and a new seal installed after the pulley and drive sprocket have been removed. The rear main oil seal is located in a housing on the rear of the cylinder block. To replace the seal, the engine and transaxle must be separated. The transaxle can be removed without removing the engine.

1. Remove the transaxle and flywheel.

2. Remove the oil pan, then remove the bolts securing the rear main oil seal support ring.

3. Using a small prytool or VW seal remover tool, very carefully pry or pull the old seal out of the support ring. Discard the old gasket.

To install:

4. Carefully tap the new seal into the support ring with a small plastic or rubber faced hammer. Be sure the seal is being driven in evenly, do not cock it to the side.

5. Lubricate the seal lip with clean engine oil.

6. Install a VW seal installation tool or a similar protective cover on the crankshaft to avoid damaging the seal. Install the seal, be careful not to damage the seal or score the crankshaft. Tighten the bolts in a crisscross pattern until they are snug. Remove the installation tool or protective cover.

7. Install the flywheel and transaxle.

Fig. 151 The freeze plug can be loosened in the block with a punch and hammer

Fig. 152 Once the freeze plug has been loosened, it can be removed from the block

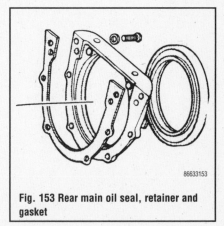

Fig. 153 Rear main oil seal, retainer and gasket

Fig. 154 A small prybar can be used to remove the oil seal (front seal shown)

Fig. 155 A large socket can be used to drive the front seal into the retainer

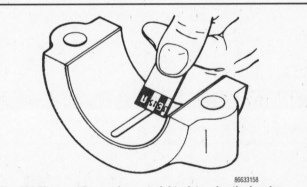

Fig. 156 A rear main oil seal protector (arrow) is necessary when installing the new seal

Crankshaft and Main Bearings

REMOVAL & INSTALLATION

▶ **See Figure 157**

1. Remove the engine from the vehicle and remove the cylinder head.
2. Remove the oil pan, oil pump, flywheel and the front and rear main seals.
3. Remove the piston and rod assemblies.
4. If not already identified, mark the main bearing caps for location and direction. They must face the same direction when installed.
5. Loosen all the bolts and remove the main bearing caps.
6. Remove the crankshaft and bearing inserts. Clean and inspect the engine block. If this is a high mileage engine, a machine shop should check the main bearing bore alignment.

To install

7. After all parts are fully prepared for assembly and the bearing oil clearance has been checked, lubricate the upper main bearing inserts with new engine oil and fit them into the engine block.
8. If the engine uses a 6-piece center bearing, install the upper thrust bearing washers.

9. Lubricate the bearing inserts and the crankshaft journals. Slowly and carefully lower the crankshaft into position.
10. Lubricate and fit the bearing inserts into the bearing caps and set the caps into place. Don't forget the thrust washers on the center bearing.
11. Start all the bolts and torque them in 3 steps to 48 ft. lbs. (65 Nm). Turn the crankshaft between each step to make sure there is no binding.

CLEANING AND INSPECTION

▶ **See Figures 158, 159 and 160**

With the crankshaft removed from the engine, clean the crank, bearings and block areas thoroughly. Visually inspect each crankshaft section for any sign of wear or damage, paying close attention to the main bearing journals. Any scoring or ridges on the crankshaft means the crankshaft should be repaired or replaced. Using a micrometer, measure the diameter of each journal on the crankshaft and record the measurements. The acceptable specifications for both

Fig. 158 Measure the gauging material to determine the bearing clearance

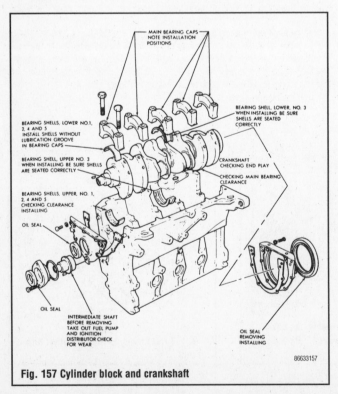

Fig. 157 Cylinder block and crankshaft

Fig. 159 A dial indicator can be used to check crankshaft end-play

Fig. 160 Carefully pry the shaft back and forth while reading the dial for play

connecting rod and main journals are found in the Crankshaft and Connecting Rod specifications chart in this section. If any journal is beyond the acceptable range, the crank must be repaired or replaced. Repair is possible by having the crankshaft machined to a standard undersize. In most cases, however, some thought should be given to replacing the damaged crankshaft with a reground shaft kit. A reground crankshaft kit contains the necessary main and rod bearings for installation. The shaft has been ground and polished to undersize specifications and will usually hold up well if installed correctly. Most automotive machine shops are able to provide this service.

Check the bearing oil clearance. The procedure described here assumes the engine is out of the vehicle. The oil clearance can be checked with the engine installed to help determine main bearing and crankshaft condition. Follow the same procedure but remove only one main bearing cap at a time.

1. With the upper bearing inserts and the crankshaft installed, wipe the oil from the main journal on the crankshaft so it is dry.

2. Lay a piece of Plastigage® on the crankshaft and install the bearing cap with the bearing. Make sure the bearing is dry and torque the cap bolts to 48 ft. lbs. (65 Nm).

3. Remove the bolts and cap. The Plastigage® may not stick to the crankshaft, so don't drop it when removing the cap.

4. Use the gauge and conversion table printed on the package to determine the bearing clearance.

The crankshaft end-play and connecting rod side clearance should also be checked. Place a prybar between a main bearing cap and crankshaft casting taking care not to damage any journals. Pry backward and forward and measure the distance between the thrust bearing and crankshaft with a feeler gauge. Compare reading with specifications. If too great a clearance is determined, a larger thrust bearing or crank machining may be required. Connecting rod clearance between the rod and crank throw casting can be checked with a feeler gauge. Pry the rod carefully to one side as far as possible and measure the distance on the other side of the rod. If the clearance is excessive, the connecting rods may have to be replaced. Consult an automotive machine shop for their advice.

BEARING REPLACEMENT

♦ See Figures 161 and 162

➡The bearing oil clearances should be checked to determine if replacement is required. If the bearing inserts are replaced, recheck the oil clearance to be sure the correct bearings were installed.

Engine Installed

Main bearings may be replaced while the engine is still in the vehicle by rolling them out. Special roll-out pins are available from automotive parts houses or can be fabricated from a cotter pin (see illustration). The roll out pin fits in the oil hole of the main bearing journal. When the crankshaft is rotated opposite the direction of the bearing lock tab, the pin engages the end of the bearing and rolls out the insert.

1. Remove main bearing cap and roll out the upper bearing insert. Remove the insert from main bearing cap. Clean the inside of the bearing cap and crankshaft journal.

To install:

➡Main bearing inserts with the lubrication grooves must be installed in the block. Inserts without grooves are installed in the bearing caps.

2. Lubricate and roll upper insert into position, make sure the lock tab is anchored and the insert is not cocked. Install the lower bearing insert into the cap, then lubricate and install it on the engine. Make sure the main bearing cap is installed facing in the correct direction, then torque the bolts in 3 steps to 48 ft. lbs. (65 Nm).

Engine Removed

1. Remove the piston and rod assemblies. Remove the main bearing caps after marking them for position and direction.

2. Remove the crankshaft and bearing inserts. Clean the engine block and cap bearing saddles.

To install:

➡The main bearing inserts with lubrication grooves must be installed in the block. Inserts without grooves are installed in the bearing caps.

3. Install the main bearing upper inserts into the engine block.

4. Lubricate the bearing inserts and the crankshaft journals. Slowly and carefully lower the crankshaft into position.

5. Install the bearing inserts into the bearing caps, then install the caps. Torque cap bolts in 3 steps to 48 ft. lbs. (65 Nm).

Flywheel

REMOVAL & INSTALLATION

♦ See Figures 163, 164 and 165

➡For Rabbit, Scirocco, Golf and Jetta models equipped with manual transaxles, please refer to the clutch procedures in Section 7 for flywheel removal and installation.

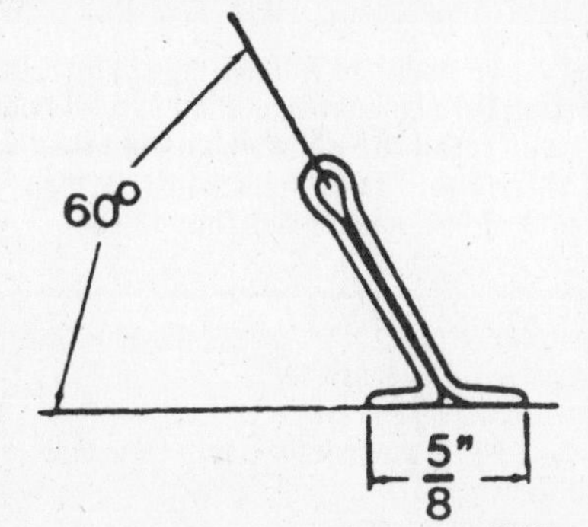

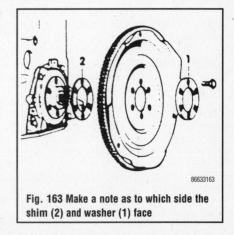

Fig. 161 Home made bearing roll-out pin

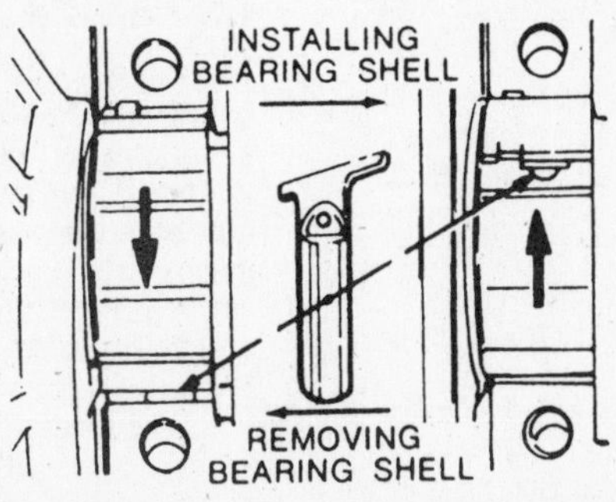

Fig. 162 Remove or install the upper bearing insert using a roll-out pin

Fig. 163 Make a note as to which side the shim (2) and washer (1) face

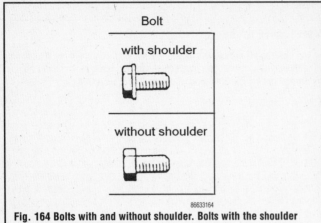

Fig. 164 Bolts with and without shoulder. Bolts with the shoulder must always be replaced

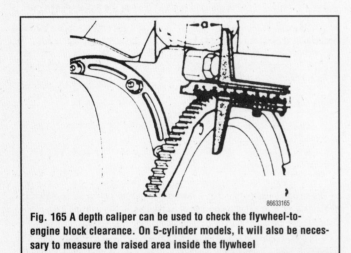

Fig. 165 A depth caliper can be used to check the flywheel-to-engine block clearance. On 5-cylinder models, it will also be necessary to measure the raised area inside the flywheel

1. Remove the transaxle from the vehicle.
2. Mark the flywheel so it can be installed in the same position. As you are removing the flywheel, also make a note as to which side the shim and washer faces. These shims/washers may either have notches cut into them or have a chamfered edge and must be installed correctly.
3. The flywheel bolts are secured with a thread locking compound and can be difficult to remove. VW tool 558 or an equivalent flywheel locking tool can be used to keep the flywheel from turning.
4. Remove the bolts, then remove the flywheel. Clean the thread locking compound out of the bolt holes in the crankshaft with a tap.

➡Bolts with a raised shoulder and stretch-type bolts must be replaced anytime they are removed. Be sure to install new ones.

To install:

5. On Quantum, Fox and Dasher models equipped with manual transaxles, coat the threads of the flywheel bolts with Loctite® or a similar thread locking compound. Tighten to 55 ft. lbs. (75 Nm) for bolts without shoulders or 74 ft. lbs. (100 Nm) for bolts with shoulders. Remember, shoulder bolts cannot be reused, always replace them.
6. On automatic transaxle models, the flywheel-to-engine block clearance must be checked:
   a. Temporarily install the flywheel with only 2 bolts.
   b. On 4-cylinder models, use a depth caliper to measure the distance between the outer face of the ring gear and the cylinder block. The distance must be 1.20–1.28 inches (30.6–32.0mm). Remove the flywheel and change the shims as required.
   c. On 5-cylinder models, use a depth caliper to measure the distance between the raised rim above the ring gear and the cylinder block on both sides. This is the outside measurement. Now use the depth caliper to measure from the raised rim (above the ring gear) to the raised area inside the flywheel. This is the inside measurement. Subtract the outside measurement from the inside measurement. It should be between 0.677–0.741 inches (17.2–18.8mm). If not, remove the flywheel and change the shim as required.
7. Install the flywheel and apply Loctite® or a similar thread locking compound to the bolts. On 1985 and later Jetta and Golf models, stretch-type bolts are used. Tighten them to 22 ft. lbs. (30 Nm) plus an additional ¼ turn. On other models, tighten the bolts without shoulders to 55 ft. lbs. (75 Nm) and the bolts with shoulders to 74 ft. lbs. (100 Nm). Once again, keep in mind that shoulder bolts and stretch-type bolts cannot be reused, always replace them.
8. Install the transaxle.

EXHAUST SYSTEM

General Information

♦ **See Figures 166, 167, 168 and 169**

➡Safety glasses should be worn at all times when working on or near the exhaust system. Older exhaust systems will almost always be covered with loose rust particles which will shower you when disturbed. These particles are more than a nuisance and could injure your eyes.

Whenever working on the exhaust system always keep the following in mind:
1. Check the complete exhaust system for open seams, holes, loose connections, or other deterioration which could permit exhaust fumes to seep into the passenger compartment.
2. The exhaust system is usually supported by free-hanging rubber mountings which permit some movement of the exhaust system, but does not permit transfer of noise and vibration into the passenger compartment. Do not replace the rubber mounts with solid ones.
3. Before removing any component of the exhaust system, ALWAYS squirt a liquid rust dissolving agent onto the fasteners for ease of removal. A lot of knuckle skin will be saved by following this rule. It may even be wise to spray the fasteners and allow them to sit overnight.
4. Annoying rattles and noise vibrations in the exhaust system are usually caused by misalignment of the parts. When aligning the system, leave all bolts and nuts loose until all parts are properly aligned, then tighten, working from front to rear.
5. When installing exhaust system parts, make sure there is enough clearance between the hot exhaust parts and pipes and hoses that would be

adversely affected by excessive heat. Also make sure there is adequate clearance from the floor pan to avoid possible overheating of the floor.

Front Pipe

REMOVAL & INSTALLATION

Pipes Secured With Spring Clamps

✳✳ CAUTION

The exhaust pipe is secured to the manifold with spring clamps. Do not attempt to remove or install the clamps without the correct tools or serious personal injury could result. Do not work on the exhaust system of a vehicle that is still warm. The catalytic converter operates at temperatures in excess of 950°F and takes time to cool down.

Special tools are required to remove and install the exhaust pipe–to–manifold spring clamps, VW tool numbers 3140/1 and 3140/2.
1. Disconnect the oxygen sensor wiring.
2. Push the pipe to one side to expand the opposite clamp. Insert the starter wedge into the expanded clamp.
3. Push the pipe to the other side and insert a wedge into the clamp.
4. Push the pipe the other way again to expand the clamp further. It should

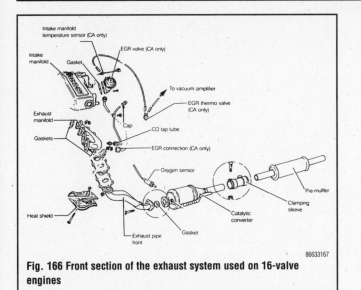

Fig. 166 Front section of the exhaust system used on 16-valve engines

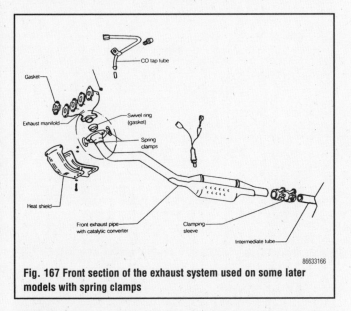

Fig. 167 Front section of the exhaust system used on some later models with spring clamps

be possible to grab the wedge with locking pliers and pry the clamp off the pipe flange.

5. Leave the wedges in the clamps and put them in a box so they won't be disturbed and fly apart.

6. To remove the wedge from the clamp, set the clamp in the partially open jaws of a vise. Carefully drive the long starter wedge in to spread the clamp further (there will be 2 wedges in the clamp).

7. Turn the clamp over and carefully drive the short wedge out, then the longer wedge.

❊❊ CAUTION

The wedges will be forced out with considerable force and could cause serious injury. Position the clamp so the wedge will fly into a container.

To install:

8. If new clamps are to be used, set the clamp on the vise and use the starter wedge to spread it far enough to install the short wedge. Remove the starting wedge.

9. Fit the pipe and gasket into place. Tilt the pipe to one side to install the clamp, then push it to the other side to install the other clamp.

10. Push the pipe side—to—side as necessary to expand the clamps enough to remove the wedges.

Pipes Secured With Bolts

1. Disconnect the oxygen sensor wiring and remove the heat shield.
2. Disconnect the catalytic converter from the exhaust pipe.
3. Remove the nuts to remove the pipe from the manifold.
4. Installation is the reverse of removal. Use new gaskets and self-locking nuts. Torque the pipe-to-manifold nuts to 18 ft. lbs. (24 Nm) on Quantum (5-cylinder and diesel) and Fox or 30 ft. lbs. (41 Nm) on others. Tighten the front pipe-to-catalytic converter nuts to 18 ft. lbs. (24 Nm).

Rear Section

REMOVAL & INSTALLATION

To remove the rubber rings, support the exhaust system and pry the rings from the hangers on the body. When installing the system, leave all bolts and nuts loose until the rings are installed and all parts are properly aligned, then tighten the clamps from front to rear.

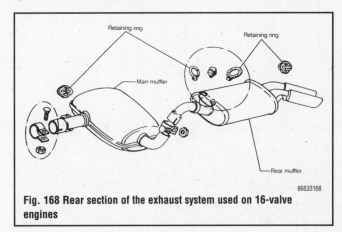

Fig. 168 Rear section of the exhaust system used on 16-valve engines

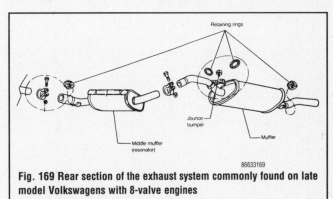

Fig. 169 Rear section of the exhaust system commonly found on late model Volkswagens with 8-valve engines

TORQUE SPECIFICATIONS

Component	US	Metric
Alternator bolts	20 ft. lbs.	25 Nm
Camshaft (valve) cover	7 ft. lbs.	10 Nm
Camshaft bearing caps		
Except 16-Valve	15 ft. lbs.	20 Nm
16-Valve	11 ft. lbs.	15 Nm
Camshaft sprocket		
Gasoline (except 16-valve)	59 ft. lbs.	80 Nm
16-Valve	48 ft. lbs.	65 Nm
Diesel	33 ft. lbs.	45 Nm
Cooling fan (thermo) switch		
1974-1984 (except Quantum)	22 ft. lbs.	30 Nm
Others	18 ft. lbs.	25 Nm
Engine mounts		
Dasher		
Gasoline	32 ft. lbs.	44 Nm
Diesel	29 ft. lbs.	39 Nm
Quantum		
4-Cylinder	25 ft. lbs.	34 Nm
5-Cylinder	33 ft. lbs.	45 Nm
Fox	30 ft. lbs.	41 Nm
Other 1975-1984 models		
Front mount	38 ft. lbs.	52 Nm
Other mounts	25-30 ft. lbs.	34-41 Nm
Other 1985-1989 models		
Front mount		
Rubber	37 ft. lbs.	50 Nm
Hydraulic	22 ft. lbs.	30 Nm
Other mounts		
10mm	33 ft. lbs.	45 Nm
12mm	54 ft. lbs.	73 Nm
Intermediate shaft		
Flange	18 ft. lbs.	25 Nm
Sprocket		
Gasoline (except 16-valve)	58 ft. lbs.	79 Nm
16-Valve	48 ft. lbs.	65 Nm
Diesel	33 ft. lbs.	45 Nm
Oil cooler	18 ft. lbs.	25 Nm
Oil pan		
Hex head bolts	14 ft. lbs.	19 Nm
Allen head bolts	7 ft. lbs.	10 Nm
Oil pressure switch		
1974-1984 (except Quantum)	7 ft. lbs.	10 Nm
Others	18 ft. lbs.	25 Nm
Oil pump		
4-Cylinder		
Short bolt	7 ft. lbs.	10 Nm
Long bolt	15 ft. lbs.	20 Nm
5-Cylinder		
Pump	14 ft. lbs.	19 Nm

8663309

Component	US	Metric
Starter		
Pickup	7 ft. lbs.	10 Nm
1.6/1.8L Golf, Jetta, GTI (manual trans.)	43 ft. lbs.	58 Nm
Others	14 ft. lbs.	19 Nm
Thermostat cover	7 ft. lbs.	10 Nm
Timing belt tensioner	33 ft. lbs.	45 Nm
Turbocharger		
Attaching bolts	30 ft. lbs.	41 Nm
Oil return line bolts		
Quantum	18 ft. lbs.	25 Nm
Others	22 ft. lbs.	30 Nm
Water pump		
4-Cylinder	7 ft. lbs.	10 Nm
5-Cylinder	15 ft. lbs.	20 Nm
Water pump pulley	15 ft. lbs.	20 Nm
Water temperature sensor	5 ft. lbs.	7 Nm

8663310

4

EMISSION CONTROLS

VOLKSWAGEN EMISSION CONTROLS

Crankcase Ventilation System

▶ **See Figures 1 and 2**

OPERATION

The purpose of the crankcase ventilation system is two-fold. It keeps harmful vapor by-products of combustion from escaping into the atmosphere and prevents the building of crankcase pressure which in turn causes gasket failure and oil leaks. Crankcase vapors are recirculated from the camshaft cover through a hose to the air cleaner. Here they are mixed with the air/fuel mixture and burned in the combustion chamber.

86634002

Fig. 1 The crankcase ventilation hoses should be removed and checked for clogging at every tune-up

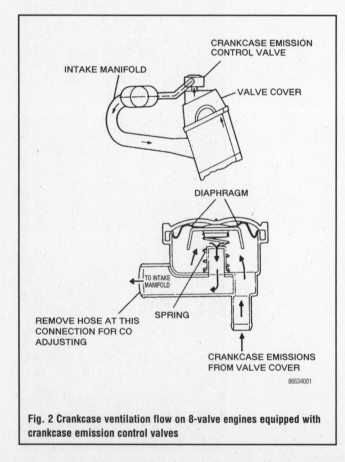

86634001

Fig. 2 Crankcase ventilation flow on 8-valve engines equipped with crankcase emission control valves

SERVICE

The crankcase ventilation system should be inspected at the interval suggested in Section 1. Remove the crankcase ventilation valve (if so equipped) and examine both the valve and hoses and for clogging or deterioration. Replace any components as necessary.

REMOVAL & INSTALLATION

To remove the Positive Crankcase Ventilation (PCV) or crankcase emission control valve, simply pull it out of the camshaft cover and its hose. On models not equipped with these valves, remove the PCV hoses by twisting and pulling them from their ports. Always check the hoses for clogging, breaks and deterioration.

Evaporative Emission Controls

OPERATION

▶ **See Figures 3 and 4**

This system prevents the escape of raw fuel vapors. It consists of a sealed carburetor (when applicable), an unvented fuel tank cap, a tank expansion chamber, a filter canister and connector hoses. Vapors which reach the filter deposit hydrocarbons on the charcoal element. Fresh air enters the filter with the engine running and forces hydrocarbons to the air cleaner where they join the air/fuel mixture and are burned. Many 1979 and later models use a charcoal filter valve which prevents vapors from escaping when the engine is **OFF**.

SERVICE

Maintenance of the system consists of checking the condition of the various connector hoses and the charcoal filter. All worn or damaged components should be replaced.

REMOVAL & INSTALLATION

Removal and installation of the evaporative emission control system components consists of labeling and disconnecting hoses, loosening retaining screws and removing the part which is to be replaced from its mounting point.

➡ **When replacing any EVAP system hoses, always use hoses that are fuel-resistant or are marked EVAP. Use of hoses which are not fuel-resistant will lead to premature hose failure.**

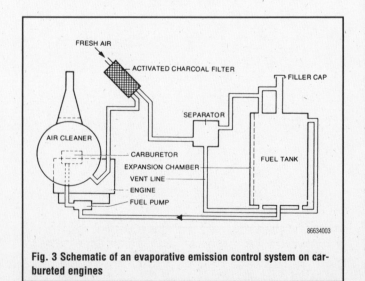

86634003

Fig. 3 Schematic of an evaporative emission control system on carbureted engines

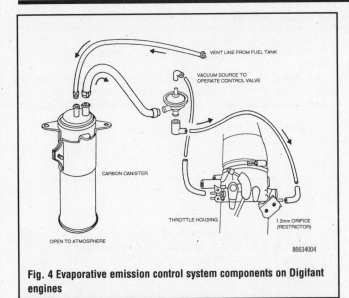

Fig. 4 Evaporative emission control system components on Digifant engines

Exhaust Gas Recirculation (EGR) System

OPERATION

▶ **See Figures 5, 6 and 7**

To reduce NOx (oxides of nitrogen) emissions, metered amounts of exhaust gases are added to the air/fuel mixture. The recirculated exhaust gas lowers the peak flame temperature during combustion to cut the output of oxides of nitrogen. On some early models, the exhaust gas from the manifold passes through a filter where it is cleaned. The EGR valve controls the amount of this exhaust gas which is allowed into the intake manifold. There is no EGR flow at idle, partial at slight throttle and full EGR flow at mid-throttle.

The 1974–75 models have an EGR filter and a 2-stage EGR valve. The first stage is controlled by the temperature valve. The second stage is controlled by the microswitch on the carburetor throttle valve.

The EGR filter was discontinued on 1976 and later models but the 2-stage EGR valve was retained. On Federal vehicles, only the first stage is connected; California vehicles use both stages. The first stage is controlled by engine vacuum and coolant temperature. The second stage is controlled by temperature, engine vacuum and a microswitch on the carburetor throttle valve.

The EGR valve on other models is controlled by a temperature valve and a vacuum amplifier.

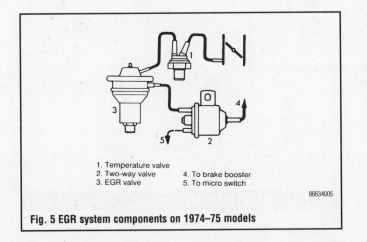

1. Temperature valve
2. Two-way valve
3. EGR valve
4. To brake booster
5. To micro switch

Fig. 5 EGR system components on 1974–75 models

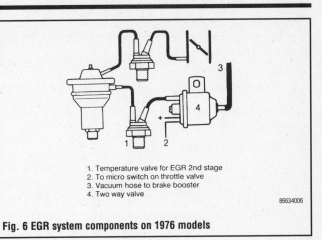

1. Temperature valve for EGR 2nd stage
2. To micro switch on throttle valve
3. Vacuum hose to brake booster
4. Two way valve

Fig. 6 EGR system components on 1976 models

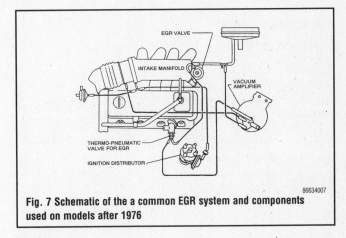

Fig. 7 Schematic of the a common EGR system and components used on models after 1976

TESTING

EGR Valve

1974–76 MODELS

▶ **See Figure 8**

To test the first stage:
1. Disconnect the vacuum line from the end of the EGR valve.
2. Disconnect the vacuum hose from the distributor vacuum unit and extend hose.

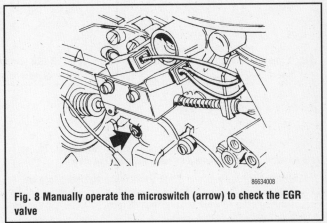

Fig. 8 Manually operate the microswitch (arrow) to check the EGR valve

3. Start the engine and allow it to idle.

4. Connect the line from the anti-backfire valve to the EGR valve. The engine should stumble or stall.

5. If the idle stays even, the EGR line is clogged or the EGR valve is defective. If equipped, the EGR filter may be clogged.

To test the second stage, manually operate the microswitch (on the carburetor) with the engine at idle. If the engine speed drops or the engine stalls, the system is operating correctly. If not, check the microswitch, the EGR filter and the EGR return lines for blockage.

1977 AND LATER MODELS

Be sure the vacuum lines are not leaking. Replace any that are leaking or cracked.

1. Warm the engine to normal operating temperature.
2. Run the engine at idle.
3. Disconnect the vacuum hose from the EGR valve.
4. Apply vacuum to the EGR valve using a hand vacuum pump
5. If the engine speed does not change, the EGR valve is clogged or damaged.

EGR Temperature Valve

1974–76 MODELS

▶ See Figure 9

1. Remove the temperature valve.
2. Apply vacuum to the angled connection. With the valve temperature below approximately 120°F (49°C), it should hold a vacuum.
3. Heat the temperature valve in a hot water bath to over 120°F (49°C). When vacuum is applied to the angled connection, it should not hold a vacuum.

1977 AND LATER MODELS

▶ See Figure 10

Warm the engine to normal operating temperature. With the engine at idle, attach a vacuum gauge between the EGR temperature valve and the EGR valve. The temperature valve should be replaced if the gauge shows less than 2 in. Hg. (14 kPa).

EGR Vacuum Amplifier

1. Run the engine at idle.
2. Connect a vacuum gauge between the vacuum amplifier and the throttle valve port.
3. The gauge should read between 0.2–0.3 in. Hg. (1.4–2.1 kPa). If not, check the throttle plate for correct position or check the port for obstruction.
4. Connect a vacuum gauge between the vacuum amplifier and the temperature valve.
5. Replace the vacuum amplifier if the gauge reads less than 2 in. Hg. (14 kPa).

REMOVAL & INSTALLATION

EGR Valve

1. Disconnect the negative battery cable.
2. Disconnect the vacuum hose from the EGR valve.
3. Unbolt the EGR line fitting on the opposite side of the valve.
4. Remove the two retaining bolts and lift the EGR valve from the intake manifold.
To install:
5. Install the EGR valve with a new gasket. Tighten the bolts to 7 ft. lbs. (10 Nm).
6. Connect the vacuum hose to the EGR valve.
7. Connect the battery cable.

EGR Filter

1. Disconnect the EGR filter line fittings.
2. Remove the filter and discard.
To install:
3. Position the new filter into the EGR lines, then securely tighten the fittings.

Temperature Valve

1. Disconnect the negative battery cable.
2. Label and disconnect the vacuum hoses from the valve.

		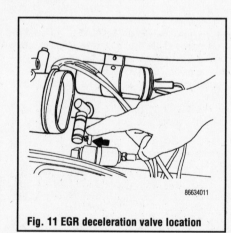

Fig. 9 Angled connection on the EGR temperature valve

Fig. 10 EGR temperature valve location on fuel injected engines

Fig. 11 EGR deceleration valve location

EGR Deceleration Valve

▶ See Figure 11

➡The deceleration valve was first used on some models in 1976. No automatic transaxle Volkswagens have deceleration valves.

1. Remove the hose leading to the air intake duct from the deceleration valve. Plug the hose.
2. Run the engine for a few seconds at 3,000 rpm.
3. Snap the throttle valve closed.
4. With your finger, check for suction at the hose connection.
5. Unplug the hose from the vacuum fitting.
6. Run the engine at about 3,000 rpm. No suction should be felt.

3. Remove the valve using a wrench or deep socket.
To install:
4. Thread the valve in by hand, then tighten until snug.
5. Connect the hoses to the valve.
6. Connect the battery cable.

Air Injection/Air Suction Systems

OPERATION

The air injection system is used on carbureted engines, except 1978 and 1980 models with 34 PICT-5 carburetors and later models equipped with a

Carter TYF carburetor. This system includes a belt driven air pump, filter, check valve, anti-backfire valve (or gulp valve), and connecting hoses. Reduction of exhaust emissions is achieved by pumping fresh air to the exhaust manifold or directly behind the exhaust valves where it combines with the hot exhaust gas to burn away excess hydrocarbons and reduce carbon monoxide.

The air suction system used on 1978 and later carbureted models does not utilize an air pump. Instead, air is drawn from the air cleaner through a silencer and into two check valves. This system uses the same principle as the air injection system to reduce emissions.

TESTING

Air Pump and Hoses

♦ See Figure 12

1. Disconnect the hose from the check valve and plug the valve opening.
2. With the engine idling, check for air flow from the hose (make sure the hoses are not kinked or damaged). If no air flows from the hose, either the diverter valve or the air pump is defective. These cannot be repaired, only replaced.

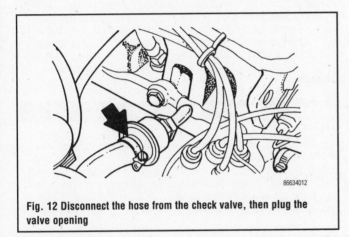

Fig. 12 Disconnect the hose from the check valve, then plug the valve opening

Anti-Backfire Valve

♦ See Figure 13

A defective anti-backfire valve could be indicated by the engine backfiring while coasting.
1. Disconnect the bottom hose from the valve.
2. Start the engine and run it briefly at higher than normal fast idle.
3. Snap the throttle valve closed. As the throttle snaps shut, suction should be felt at the valve for about 1-3 seconds. If not, the hoses could be kinked/blocked or the valve is defective.

Fig. 13 Disconnect the bottom hose from the anti-backfire valve

Check Valves

♦ See Figure 14

On air injection systems, disconnect the hose from the check valve. Start the engine. If you feel exhaust gases coming out of the check valve, it must be replaced.

On air suction systems, if the check valves are discolored with a blue tint, they must be replaced. This condition indicates that the valves were overheated due to the back-flow of exhaust gases.

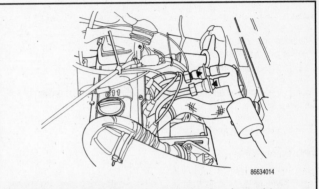

Fig. 14 On air suction systems, if the check valves (arrows) turn blue, they must be replaced

REMOVAL & INSTALLATION

Air Pump

1. Disconnect the negative battery cable.
2. Label and disconnect the hoses from the air pump.
3. Remove the air pump drive belt.
4. Loosen and remove the bolts securing the air pump.
5. Remove the pump from the vehicle.

To install:

6. Position the air pump, then install the mounting bolts finger-tight.
7. Install the drive belt and tighten the pump mounting bolts until snug.
8. Tension the belt, then tighten the lock bolt.
9. Connect the hoses to the air pump.
10. Connect the battery cable.

Anti-Backfire Valve

1. Disconnect the negative battery cable.
2. Label and disconnect the hoses from the valve.
3. Remove the nuts/bolts securing the valve, then remove it from the vehicle.

To install:

4. Position the valve, then tighten the nuts/bolts until snug.
5. Connect the hoses to the valve.
6. Connect the battery cable.

Check Valves

1. Disconnect the negative battery cable.
2. Disconnect the hoses from the check valves.
3. Loosen and remove the check valve. If the valve is difficult to remove, spray some penetrating oil on the threads and allow it to soak.

To install:

4. Thread the check valve in by hand first, then tighten until snug. Do not over-tighten the valve or the pipe could become distorted.
5. Connect the hoses to the check valve.
6. Connect the battery cable.

Catalytic Converter

Many models are equipped with catalytic converters located in the exhaust system. This device contains noble metals acting as catalysts to convert hydrocarbons and carbon monoxide into harmless water and carbon dioxide. On earlier models, a warning light on the dash will glow STEADILY when inspection of the converter is required. Once the converter is inspected, the warning light can be be reset.

Many models are also equipped with a converter heat sensor. On models so equipped, damage and overheating of the catalytic converter, is indicated by a FLICKERING warning light. Damage or overheating can be caused by the following:

- Engine misfire
- Improper ignition timing
- Incorrect fuel mixture
- Faulty air pump diverter valve
- Faulty temperature sensor
- Engine under strain caused by trailer hauling, high speed driving in hot weather, etc

A faulty converter can be indicated by one of the following symptoms:

- Poor engine performance
- The engine stalls
- Rattling in the exhaust system
- A high CO reading at the tail pipe

✳✳ CAUTION

Never attempt to remove the converter from a just-run or warm engine. Catalytic temperatures can reach 1,900°F (1,038°C), be careful!

INSPECTION

➡**Do not drop or strike the converter assembly or damage to the ceramic insert will result.**

Check the converter as follows:
1. If equipped, disconnect the temperature sensor from the converter.
2. Loosen and remove the bolts holding the converter to the exhaust system and the chassis.
3. Remove the converter.
4. Hold the converter up to a strong light and look through both ends, checking for blockages. If the converter is blocked, replace it.

Maintenance Reminder Lights

➡**Not all VW's are equipped with maintenance reminder lights.**

RESETTING

▶ **See Figures 15, 16 and 17**

On some models, there is an EGR warning lamp that is located in the instrument cluster. Every 15,000 miles (24,000 km), the EGR warning lamp will light. This tells the driver that the EGR and emission systems should be inspected and checked for proper operation.

The CAT warning light used on some models should come on at 30,000 mile (48,000 km) intervals to remind you to have the catalytic converter serviced.

Also on some models, there is an oxygen sensor (OXS) light located in the instrument cluster. This indicates when the oxygen sensor should be replaced. Once the system has been serviced, reset the light(s) as follows:

Locate the mileage counter found under the hood. It is mounted near the firewall, inline with the speedometer cable. To locate the counter, follow the speedometer cable up from the transmission towards the firewall. Once the counter is located, push in the reset button marked EGR, OXS or CAT. These buttons are located right on the face of the mileage counter.

Some Rabbits and Pick-Ups are not equipped with the firewall mounted mileage counter. If so, remove the instrument panel cover trim plate. Locate the mileage counter rest arms at the top left corner of the speedometer housing. Pull the release arms to reset the mileage counter. The left arm is used to reset the EGR warning light and the right arm is used to reset the oxygen sensor warning light.

Oxygen Sensor

This sensor is used to report the concentration of oxygen in the exhaust. It consists of a tube coated with platinum on the outside and zirconia on the inside. The tube is protected with a slotted outer shield. The platinum side is exposed only to exhaust gas. If there is any oxygen in the exhaust, a voltage is generated across the dissimilar metals that the engine control unit can read. The sensor operates only when it is above about 600°F (315°C). Some sensors include a built-in heater for faster response when the engine is started cold.

TESTING

➡**An exhaust gas analyzer is required to test the oxygen sensor.**

1. Disconnect the wiring at the sensor. If there is a brown wire, it is ground for the sensor heater. The green wire is for the sensor itself, the other wire is for

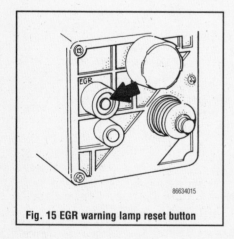

Fig. 15 EGR warning lamp reset button

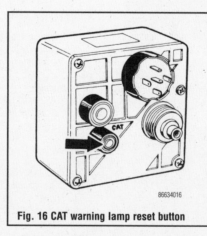

Fig. 16 CAT warning lamp reset button

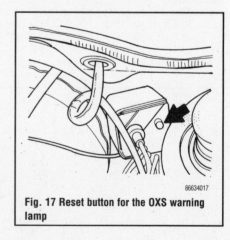

Fig. 17 Reset button for the OXS warning lamp

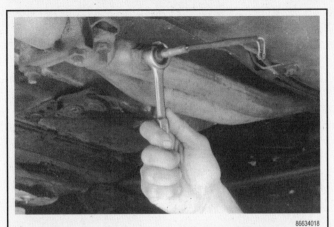

Fig. 18 The oxygen sensor may be threaded into the catalytic converter or the exhaust pipe

voltage to the heater. On the wiring harness side of the connector, there should be 12 volts at the heater wire terminal with the ignition switch **ON**.

2. Turn the ignition switch **OFF** and connect an ohmmeter to the heater wire on the sensor connector. There should be 3–15 ohms resistance between the sensor heater and ground.

3. To test the sensor output, reconnect the wiring and warm the engine to normal operating temperature.

4. Remove the plastic cap from the exhaust gas sample tap and insert the probe of an exhaust gas analyzer. With the engine at idle, disconnect the fuel pressure regulator vacuum hose from the intake manifold and plug the port. The CO reading should increase momentarily, then return to the original value. If it does not, the sensor or the engine control unit may be faulty.

REMOVAL & INSTALLATION

▶ **See Figure 18**

The sensor is threaded into the catalytic converter or the exhaust pipe. An anti-seize compound is used on the threads. When replacing it, be careful not to get anti-seize in the slots of the outer shield. Torque to 37 ft. lbs. (50 Nm).

ELECTRONIC ENGINE CONTROLS

CIS/CIS-E Engine Controls

TESTING

Control Pressure Regulator

▶ **See Figures 19 and 20**

The control pressure regulator is designed to provide a richer fuel mixture during cold engine operation. When the engine is cold, the valve in the regulator is open. This reduces the pressure on the control plunger in the fuel distributor, which in turn provides a richer mixture. As the engine is running, the bi-metallic strip is warmed by a heating element in the regulator. This will eventually close the valve in the regulator and increase the pressure on the control plunger. As pressure on the plunger increases, the mixture leans out. The control pressure regulator is found only on CIS equipped engines.

1. Unplug the electrical connector from the regulator.
2. Measure the resistance across the terminals of the regulator (not the connector). It should read approximately 22 ohms. If not, replace the regulator.
3. On vehicles without electronic ignition, unplug the center wire from the distributor and ground it. On models with electronic ignition, unplug the connector from the Hall sending unit on the distributor. This will disable the ignition system.
4. Measure the voltage across the connector terminals while an assistant cranks the engine. There should be at least 8 volts displayed. If not, check the wiring for shorts or opens.

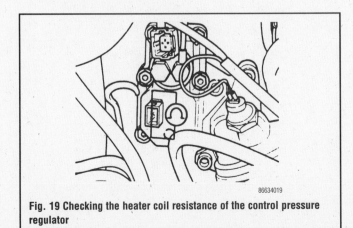

Fig. 19 Checking the heater coil resistance of the control pressure regulator

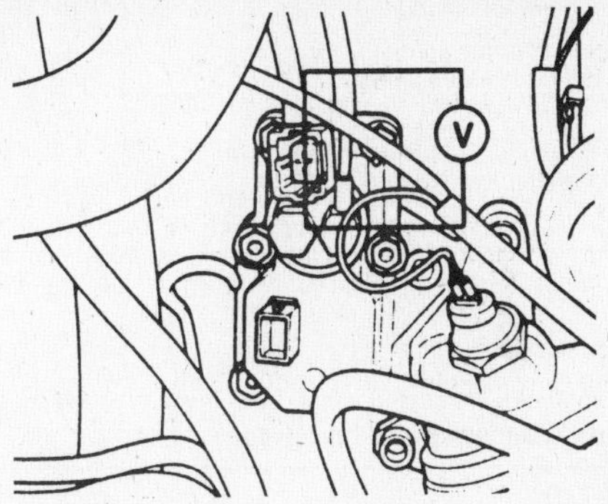

Fig. 20 Checking the voltage supply to the control pressure regulator

Throttle Switches

The throttle switches are used on CIS-E systems and are mounted on the throttle body. They send a signal to the control unit when the throttle valve is at an idle or wide-open throttle position.

1. Unplug the connectors from the throttle switches.
2. Connect an ohmmeter to the idle switch terminals. With the throttle closed, there should be continuity. With the throttle valve open, there should be no continuity.
3. Connect an ohmmeter to the full-throttle switch terminals. With the throttle closed, there should be no continuity. With the throttle valve approaching wide-open throttle, there should be continuity.

Coolant Temperature Sensor

▶ **See Figure 21**

The coolant temperature sensor is found on CIS-E systems. Since its resistance value changes with temperature, it allows the control unit to determine if the engine is cold or warm.

1. Unplug the coolant temperature sensor connector.
2. Connect an ohmmeter across the sensor terminals.
3. Compare the reading with the graph.

Thermo-Time Switch

▶ **See Figure 22**

The thermo-time switch, used on CIS and CIS-E systems, determines the amount of time the cold-start injector is on.

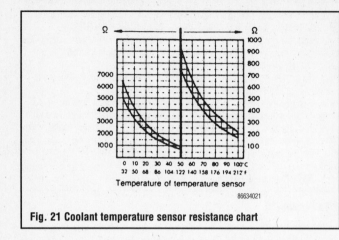

Fig. 21 Coolant temperature sensor resistance chart

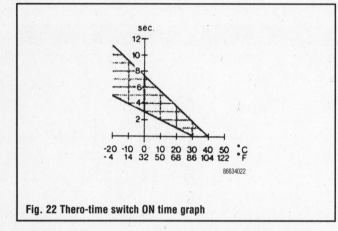

Fig. 22 Thero-time switch ON time graph

1. Make sure the engine is cold. The coolant temperature must be below 86°F (30°C).
2. On vehicles without electronic ignition, unplug the center wire from the distributor and ground it. On models with electronic ignition, unplug the connector from the Hall sending unit on the distributor. This will disable the ignition system.
3. Unplug the connector from the cold-start injector. Connect a test light across the terminals of the connector.
4. While an assistant cranks the engine, record the amount of time the test light stays on. Compare the time to the graph.

Idle Air Controls

Volkswagen uses different types of idle air control systems. Most CIS and some early CIS-E systems use an idle boost valve and/or an auxiliary air regulator. The boost valve increases idle speed when the engine is under load at idle. Models with air conditioning will have another boost valve which is used when the air conditioning is turned on. The auxiliary air regulator is used to bypass additional air around the throttle plate to increase idle speed when the engine is cold.

Most CIS-E systems use an idle air stabilizer valve which constantly adjusts idle speed under all conditions.

➡ Some early Volkswagen engines use an ignition advance type of idle speed control. Refer to Section 2 for testing procedures of these systems.

IDLE BOOST VALVES

1. Run the engine until normal operating temperature is reached.
2. Turn all electrical accessories ON, except the air conditioner (if equipped).
3. Lower the idle speed by turning the adjusting screw. At about 750 rpm, the boost valve should turn on and increase the idle speed.

4. Pinch the hose from the idle boost valve(s) shut with a clamp. The idle speed should drop.
5. Adjust the idle speed (with hose from the boost valve pinched shut) to 875–925 rpm.
6. Remove the clamp from the hose. The idle speed should increase. At about 1050 rpm, the boost valve should turn off and the idle speed should drop to specification.

On models with air conditioning, perform these additional steps:
7. Run the engine until normal operating temperature is reached.
8. Make sure all electrical accessories are OFF, including the air conditioner.
9. Pinch the hose from the boost valves shut with a clamp. The idle speed should not drop.
10. Turn the air conditioning ON, the idle speed should drop.

AUXILIARY AIR REGULATOR

1. The engine must be cold (coolant temperature below 86°F (30°C), and the ignition key must NOT have been in the **ON** position for at least an hour.
2. Unplug the connector from the auxiliary air regulator.
3. Start the engine and pinch the hose leading from the auxiliary air regulator to the intake manifold shut with a clamp. The idle speed should drop.
4. Engage the connector to the regulator and remove the clamp. Run the engine to normal operating temperature.
5. When the engine is warm, pinch the hose shut with the clamp again. This time the idle speed should not drop.

IDLE AIR STABILIZER

1. With the ignition **ON** (engine not running), you should feel the stabilizer vibrate or hum. If not, continue with the test.
2. The ignition switch should still be in the **ON** position (engine not running). Unplug the connector from the stabilizer valve.
3. Check the stabilizer valve with an ohmmeter. There should be continuity between the center terminal and each of the outer terminals.
4. Connect the positive lead of a voltmeter to the center terminal of the connector (not the valve) and the negative lead to ground. The voltmeter should display approximately 12 volts. With the positive lead still connected to the center terminal, connect the negative lead to outer terminals (one at a time). There should be 10 volts present at each of the outer terminals.

Airflow Sensor Potentiometer

▶ See Figure 23

The airflow sensor potentiometer sends a signal of the sensor plate position to the control unit.
1. Remove the air intake boot.
2. Unplug the connector from the potentiometer.
3. Connect an ohmmeter to terminals 1 and 2 of the potentiometer. There should be more than 4,000 ohms present.

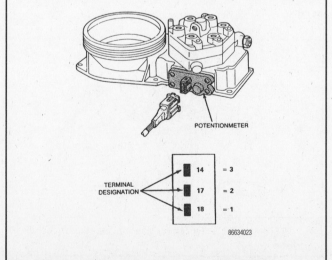

Fig. 23 Airflow sensor potentiometer terminal identification

4. Connect an ohmmeter to terminals 2 and 3 of the potentiometer. There should be less than 1,000 ohms present.

5. With the ohmmeter still connected to terminals 2 and 3 of the potentiometer, slowly lift the sensor plate through its entire range of travel. The resistance should rise evenly to over 4,000 ohms.

Differential Pressure Regulator

The control unit regulates the air/fuel ratio by adjusting the pressure in the lower chambers of the fuel distributor. The differential pressure regulator is attached to the side of the fuel distributor. It consists of a plate with an electromagnet on either side. The control unit regulates the current to the magnets, moving the plate side-to-side, which controls the size of the opening to the lower chamber. When the lower chamber pressure is high, the diaphragms are pushed up towards the outlets of the upper chamber, making the outlets smaller and reducing fuel flow. This provides for very fine adjustment of fuel flow (to the injectors) while maintaining the same pressure (at the injectors).

To test the differential pressure regulator, please refer to the fuel pressure tests in Section 5.

Digifant II Engine Controls

TESTING

Airflow Sensor

▶ **See Figure 24**

This unit converts air flow to a voltage signal. Air enters and moves a spring-loaded vane which is attached to a potentiometer. The potentiometer then modulates a voltage sent from the control unit and the return signal represents the mass of air flowing to the intake manifold. Air temperature is also measured and reported to the control unit. Adjustment of the air/fuel mixture is accomplished by means of a bypass screw which is also contained in this unit. This screw allows a certain amount of air to bypass the vane and enter the engine unmeasured. More unmeasured air means a leaner mixture.

1. With the ignition **OFF**, unplug the sensor connector and measure the resistance across the of the sensor terminals. At 60°F (15°C), there should be about 3000 ohms. At 80°F (27°C), there should be about 1900 ohms.

2. The resistance between terminals 3 and 4 should be 500–1000 ohms when the flap is in the rest position.

3. Connect the ohmmeter between the center terminals 2 and 3, then move the vane inside the sensor. The resistance change should be smooth and linear as the vane is moved. There is a strong return spring on the flap but it should move smoothly with no binding.

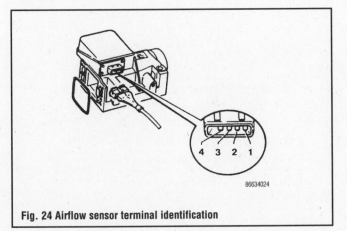

Fig. 24 Airflow sensor terminal identification

Throttle Position Switches

There are 2 switches on the throttle body, one above and one below. The lower switch signals the ECU when the throttle is at idle and the upper switch signals full throttle. This information is used to calculate fuel shut-off and igni-

tion timing during deceleration, idle stabilizer valve operation and full throttle enrichment. If there is a problem with any of these functions, check these switches first.

1. Locate the switches on the throttle body and unplug the connector.

2. Connect an ohmmeter to the idle switch and make sure it is closed when the throttle is against the stop. Open the throttle, position a 0.024 inch (0.60mm) feeler gauge against the stop and let the throttle close on the gauge. The switch must remain open. DO NOT adjust the throttle stop screw.

3. Connect the ohmmeter to the full throttle switch. Open the throttle all the way to the stop and make sure the switch closes. The switch should open when the throttle is allowed to close 10 degrees from the stop.

4. Turn the ignition switch **ON** and use a voltmeter to check for 5 volts at each switch connector. This signal comes directly from the ECU.

Idle Stabilizer Valve

▶ **See Figure 25**

The idle stabilizer is a linear motor solenoid valve that is operated by the ECU. The linear motion moves a plunger to control an opening in the valve which meters the amount of air that bypasses the throttle. This design allows very precise control of idle speed regardless of engine temperature or load. The voltage supplied to the valve can't really be measured because it is not constant. To test the duty cycle of the valve in operation, a special adapter (available at your dealer) is required which allows connection of a multi-meter that reads milliamps while the wiring is still connected to the valve.

1. With the ignition **ON** but the engine not running, the valve should vibrate to the touch. If not, make sure the idle switch on the throttle body is working properly and that the throttle is fully closed.

2. If there is no vibration at the valve, turn the ignition **OFF** and unplug the connector. Use an ohmmeter to check the resistance across the terminals on the valve. There should be about 2–10 ohms resistance.

3. Connect the adapter so a multi-meter can be connected. With the engine at operating temperature and idling, the current to the valve should fluctuate from 390–460 milliamps. With the blue temperature sensor wiring disconnected, the current should be steady.

4. If the current is not correct, remove the valve and check for visual signs of sticking. Do not lubricate the valve. If no other problem is found, check the continuity of the wiring between the valve and the ECU with the ignition **OFF**.

5. If the idle stabilizer valve seems to work properly but engine idle is out of specification, check for a vacuum leak, a faulty coolant temperature sensor or some other problem with the engine control system.

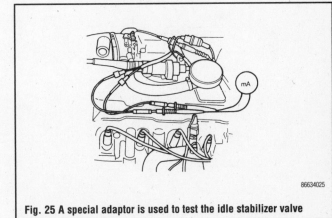

Fig. 25 A special adaptor is used to test the idle stabilizer valve

Temperature Sensors

There are two coolant temperature sensors mounted in the upper radiator hose–to–engine flange. The black connector is for the gauge on the instrument panel. The blue connector is for the ECU.

There is also an air temperature sensor at the inlet end of the air flow sensor. Both the coolant and air temperature sensors operate with the same resistance values.

1. Unplug the sensor connector.

2. Using an ohmmeter, check the sensor resistance.

3. Compare the test values to the specifications listed. If resistance is out of specification, replace the sensor.
- 55°F (13°C)—3000–3800 ohms
- 65°F (18°C)—2200–3000 ohms

- 75°F (24°C)—1800–2500 ohms
- 85°F (29°C)—1500–2100 ohms
- 150°F (65°C)—400–550 ohms
- 200°F (93°C)—200–270 ohms

VACUUM DIAGRAMS

Following is a listing of vacuum diagrams for most of the engine and emissions package combinations covered by this manual. Because vacuum circuits will vary based on various engine and vehicle options, always refer first to the vehicle emission control information label, if present. Should the label be missing, or should vehicle be equipped with a different engine from the origi-

nal equipment, refer to the diagrams below for the same or similar configuration.

If you wish to obtain a replacement emissions label, most manufacturers make the labels available for purchase. The labels can usually be ordered from a local dealer.

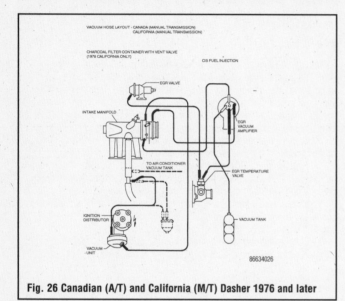

Fig. 26 Canadian (A/T) and California (M/T) Dasher 1976 and later

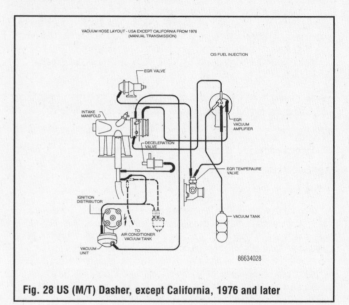

Fig. 28 US (M/T) Dasher, except California, 1976 and later

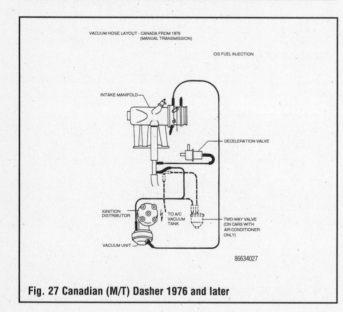

Fig. 27 Canadian (M/T) Dasher 1976 and later

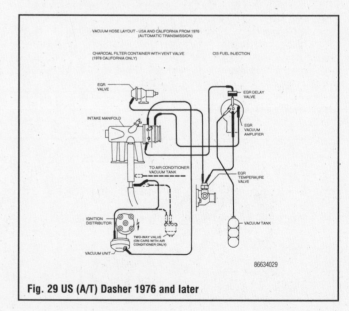

Fig. 29 US (A/T) Dasher 1976 and later

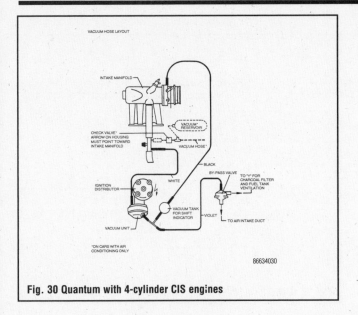

Fig. 30 Quantum with 4-cylinder CIS engines

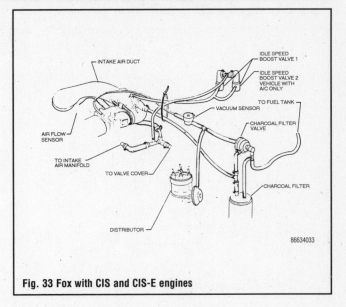

Fig. 33 Fox with CIS and CIS-E engines

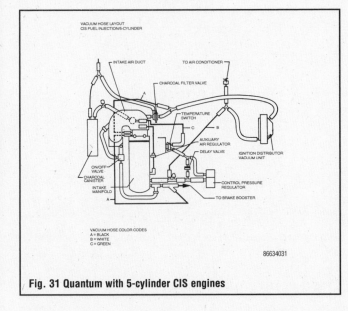

Fig. 31 Quantum with 5-cylinder CIS engines

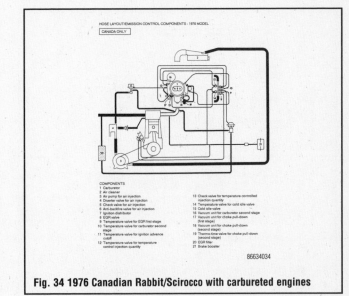

Fig. 34 1976 Canadian Rabbit/Scirocco with carbureted engines

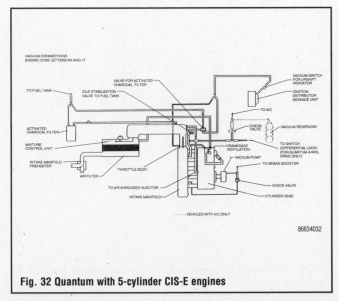

Fig. 32 Quantum with 5-cylinder CIS-E engines

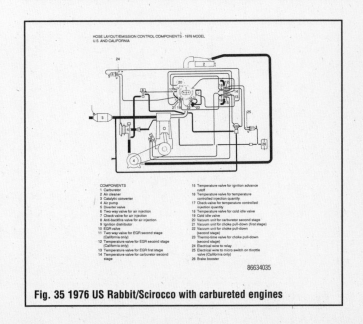

Fig. 35 1976 US Rabbit/Scirocco with carbureted engines

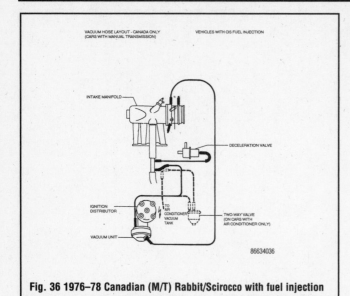

Fig. 36 1976–78 Canadian (M/T) Rabbit/Scirocco with fuel injection

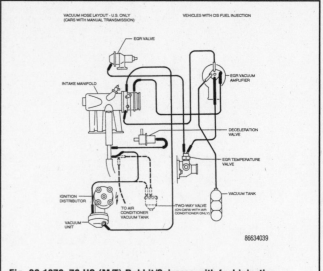

Fig. 39 1976–78 US (M/T) Rabbit/Scirocco with fuel injection

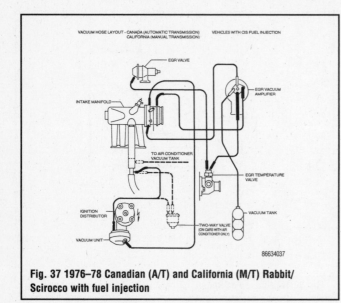

Fig. 37 1976–78 Canadian (A/T) and California (M/T) Rabbit/Scirocco with fuel injection

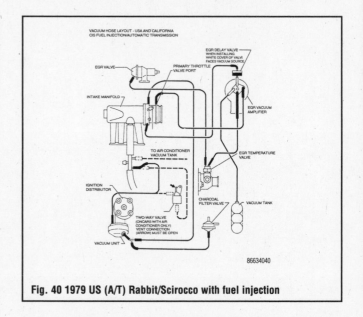

Fig. 40 1979 US (A/T) Rabbit/Scirocco with fuel injection

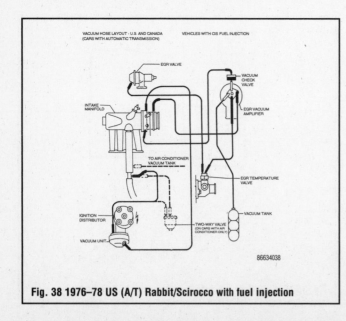

Fig. 38 1976–78 US (A/T) Rabbit/Scirocco with fuel injection

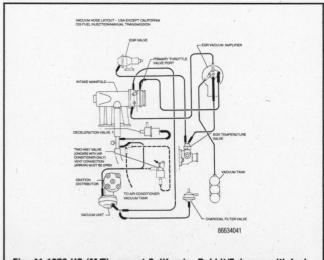

Fig. 41 1979 US (M/T), except California, Rabbit/Scirocco with fuel injection

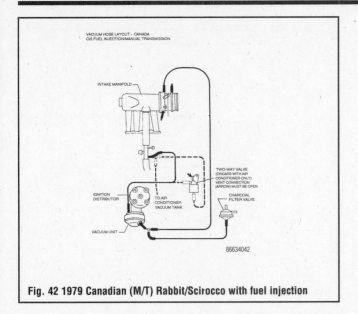

Fig. 42 1979 Canadian (M/T) Rabbit/Scirocco with fuel injection

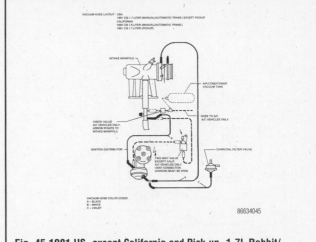

Fig. 45 1981 US, except California and Pick-up, 1.7L Rabbit/ Scirocco with fuel injection; 1980 California 1.6L Rabbit/Scirocco with fuel injection; 1981 California 1.7L Pick-up with fuel injection

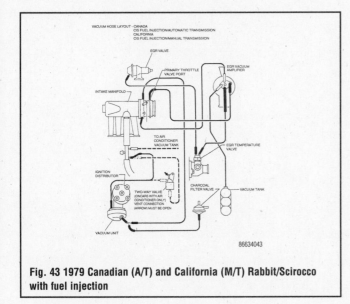

Fig. 43 1979 Canadian (A/T) and California (M/T) Rabbit/Scirocco with fuel injection

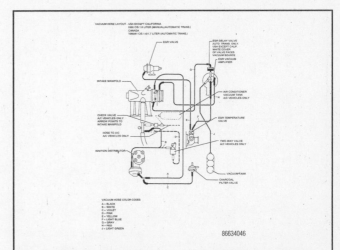

Fig. 46 1980 US, except California, 1.6L Rabbit/Scirocco with fuel injection; 1980–81 Canadian (A/T) 1.6/1.7L Rabbit/Scirocco with fuel injection

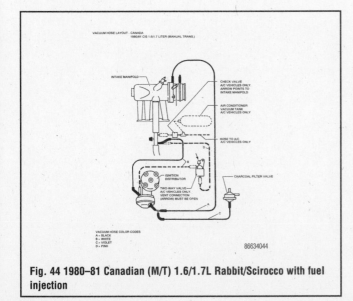

Fig. 44 1980–81 Canadian (M/T) 1.6/1.7L Rabbit/Scirocco with fuel injection

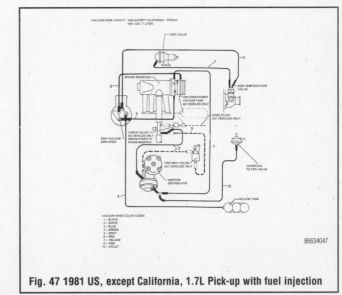

Fig. 47 1981 US, except California, 1.7L Pick-up with fuel injection

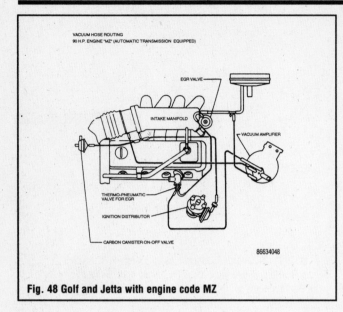

Fig. 48 Golf and Jetta with engine code MZ

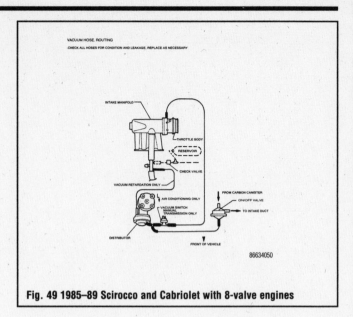

Fig. 49 1985–89 Scirocco and Cabriolet with 8-valve engines

5

FUEL
SYSTEM

CARBURETED FUEL SYSTEM

Mechanical Fuel Pump

REMOVAL & INSTALLATION

♦ **See Figure 1**

1. Disconnect the negative battery cable.
2. Disconnect and plug both fuel lines.
3. Remove the two socket head retaining bolts.
4. Remove the fuel pump and its plastic flange.

To install:

5. Install the pump using a new flange seal. Tighten the bolts 14 ft. lbs. (19 Nm).
6. Connect the fuel lines to the carburetor.
7. Connect the battery cable.
8. Start the engine and check for leaks.

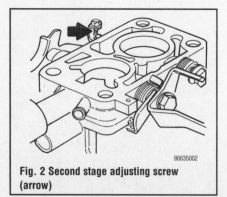

Fig. 1 Exploded view of the fuel pump showing the filter screen

Carburetor

The 1974 Dasher uses a Solex 32/35 DIDTA two barrel carburetor with a vacuum operated secondary throttle. The 1975 Dasher uses a Zenith 2B3 two barrel carburetor. It, too, has a vacuum operated secondary throttle. The Rabbit and Scirocco carburetor is a Zenith 2B2 two barrel which also has a vacuum operated secondary throttle.

Some 1978 and 1980 Rabbits are equipped with a single barrel Solex 34 PICT–5 carburetor. Some 1982 and later carburetor equipped models use a Carter TYF feedback model.

ADJUSTMENTS

Solex 32/35 DIDTA Carburetor

THROTTLE GAP (BASIC SETTING)

♦ **See Figure 2**

This adjustment is made at the adjuster screw located in the linkage on the carburetor, below and to the right of the automatic choke unit.

1. Open the choke and close the throttle.

2. Turn the first stage adjusting screw out until there is a gap between it and its stop. The first stage throttle valve should be fully closed now.
3. Turn the adjusting screw in until it just touches its stop.
4. Turn the screw in ¼ turn more and lock it.
5. The second stage throttle (secondary) should only be adjusted when it is definitely out of adjustment.
   a. Loosen the adjusting screw until the secondary throttle closes.
   b. Turn the screw in 12 turns and lock it.
   c. Adjust the idle mixture after this adjustment.

FUEL LEVEL

This adjustment is made with the carburetor installed on the engine. Incorrect fuel level can cause stalling or high speed miss.

1. Remove the air cleaner.
2. Remove the five carburetor cover mounting screws.
3. Plug the fuel inlet with a finger and lift off the carburetor cover and gasket. Set them to the side, leaving the linkages attached.
4. On models with the original equipment float (which is shaped like a child's top), with the float in the up or closed position, the distance from the edge of the float rim to the carburetor surface (minus the gasket) should be 0.59–0.63 in. (16–17mm).
5. Adjust the float by varying the thickness of the fiber sealing ring under the float needle valve.
6. On models with an aftermarket float (which is more rectangular in shape), with the float in the up or closed position, measure from the top edge of the float closest to the throttle chambers down to the carburetor surface (minus the gasket). The distance should be 1.46–1.54 in. (37–39mm).
7. Adjust the float by bending the tab that contacts the needle valve.

➡For added accuracy, when measuring the float level, make all measurements with the carburetor top at a 45 degree angle so that the stop ball in the needle valve is not pushed down by the weight of the float.

FAST IDLE

♦ **See Figure 3**

It will be necessary to remove the carburetor from the engine to perform this operation.

1. Turn the carburetor upside down and drain the fuel from it.
2. With the carburetor upside down, close the choke tightly and measure the gap between the lower edge of the throttle valve and the housing wall with a drill. The measurement should be:
   - All Except Calif. Manual Trans.—0.030–0.034 in. (0.80–0.85mm)
   - Calif. Manual Trans.—0.024–0.028 in. (0.60–0.70mm)
3. Adjust the fast idle speed at the eyebolt fitted in the choke lever attachment.

CHOKE VALVE GAP

♦ **See Figure 4**

1. Remove the automatic choke cover with the water hoses still attached.
2. Push the plunger rod down into its seat, then move the choke valve toward the fully closed position.

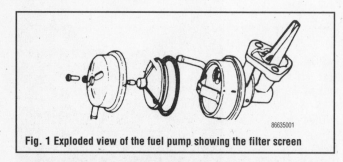

Fig. 2 Second stage adjusting screw (arrow)

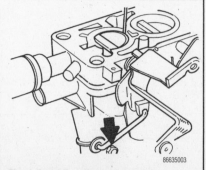

Fig. 3 Fast idle adjuster (arrow)

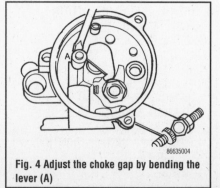

Fig. 4 Adjust the choke gap by bending the lever (A)

3. With an appropriate size drill bit, measure the gap between the choke valve and the carburetor housing. It should be 0.142–0.154 in. (3.5–4.0mm) on all except California models and 0.134–0.146 in. (3.5–3.7mm) on California models.

4. Adjust the choke gap by bending the lever arm attached to the plunger rod.

➡When installing the choke spring inside the choke cover, the loop in the spring must go over the protruding choke lever. Insert the spring so that it uncoils in a clockwise direction (facing you).

AUTOMATIC CHOKE

Align the mark on the automatic choke cover with the mark on the carburetor by loosening the three retaining screws and turning the choke cover with the hoses still attached.

DASHPOT

▶ See Figure 5

The purpose of the dashpot is to keep the throttle from snapping shut and stalling the engine. The dashpot has a plunger that extends when the throttle is closed suddenly. The plunger contacts a tab on the throttle lever and holds the throttle open slightly for a second, then closes the throttle slowly over the period of another second or so.

➡Not all models have dashpots.

1. Close the throttle valve and make sure the choke is fully open. You may have to run the car up to operating temperature.
2. Press the dashpot plunger in as far as it will go.
3. Measure the gap between the plunger and its striking surface. It should be 0.04 in. (1mm).
4. Adjust by loosening the lock nut and moving the dashpot on its threads.

Zenith 2B3 Carburetor

THROTTLE GAP

▶ See Figures 6 and 7

To adjust first stage throttle gap:
1. The choke must be open and the first stage (primary) throttle closed.
2. Turn the first stage throttle valve stop screw until there is a gap between it and the lever moves.
3. Turn the screw in until it just touches the lever.
4. Turn screw in ¼ turn more.
5. Adjust the idle speed and fuel mixture.
To adjust the second stage (secondary) throttle gap, proceed as follows:
6. The choke must be open and the first stage throttle must be closed.
7. Turn the second stage (secondary) adjusting screw until there is no clearance in the lever it is mounted on.
8. From this position, turn the screw out ¼ turn. There should be noticeable clearance at the lever.

FUEL LEVEL

▶ See Figure 8

Remove the top of the carburetor. You may not have to remove the entire carburetor from the engine to perform this operation.
1. With the carburetor top upside down and canted at a 45 degree angle (to prevent the damping ball in the needle valve from settling too deeply due to the weight of the float), measure from the highest tip of the first stage float to the carburetor surface (minus the gasket). The distance for the first stage float should be 1.08–1.12 in. (27.5–28.5mm)
2. Adjust the second stage float in the same manner. The distance for the second stage float should be 1.18–1.22 in. (29.5–30.5mm).
3. Adjust the float level by bending the float bracket.

➡If the float height must be adjusted, remove the float from the carburetor to prevent damage to the needle valve.

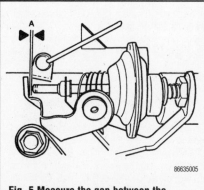

Fig. 5 Measure the gap between the plunger and its striking surface

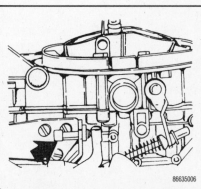

Fig. 6 First stage throttle gap adjustment point (arrow)

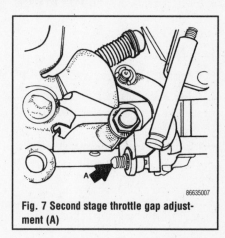

Fig. 7 Second stage throttle gap adjustment (A)

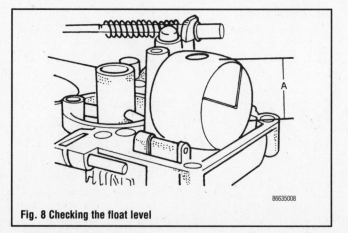

Fig. 8 Checking the float level

FAST IDLE

▶ See Figure 9

It will be necessary to remove the carburetor from the engine to perform this procedure.
1. Turn the carburetor upside down and drain the fuel from it.
2. With the carburetor upside down, close the choke tightly and measure the gap between the lower edge of the throttle valve and the housing wall with a drill. The measurement should be 0.018–0.020 in. (0.45–0.50mm).
3. Adjust the gap at the adjusting screw (beside the first stage valve) which is facing up when the carburetor is upside down.

CHOKE VALVE GAP

▶ See Figures 10 and 11

1. Remove the automatic choke cover. You should be able to remove the cover without unfastening the water hoses.

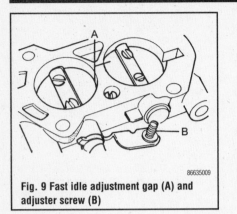

Fig. 9 Fast idle adjustment gap (A) and adjuster screw (B)

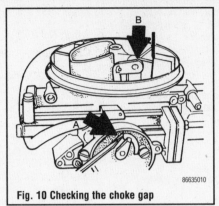

Fig. 10 Checking the choke gap

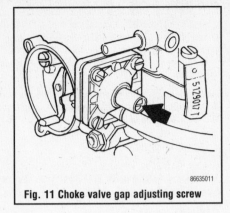

Fig. 11 Choke valve gap adjusting screw

2. Open and close the choke to make sure its internal spring is working. If not, remove the vacuum cover at the side of the choke assembly and check the spring.

3. Push the choke lever to its stop (arrow A) and hold the rod there with a rubber band.

4. Equalize the bushing and lever clearances by pushing the choke valve slightly open (arrow B).

5. Check the choke gap with an appropriate size drill. The gap should be between 0.152–0.168 in. (3.8–4.2mm).

6. Adjust the choke valve gap by turning the screw in the end of the vacuum unit at the side of the choke assembly. Lock the adjusting screw by dabbing a little paint or thread sealant over its end.

➡**When installing the automatic choke cover, the choke lever (protruding part) must fit in the loop on the coiled spring.**

AUTOMATIC CHOKE

Align the mark on the automatic choke cover with the mark on the carburetor by loosening the three retaining across and turning the choke with the hoses still attached.

DASHPOT

♦ **See Figure 12**

The purpose of the dashpot is to keep the throttle from snapping shut and stalling the engine. The dashpot has a plunger that extends when the throttle is closed suddenly. The plunger contacts a tab on the throttle lever and holds the throttle open slightly for a second, then closes the throttle slowly over the period of another second or so.

➡**Not all models are equipped with dashpots.**

1. Close the throttle valve and make sure the choke is fully open. You may have to run the car up to the operating temperature.

2. Push the plunger in as far as it will go and measure the gap between the end of the plunger and its striking surface. The gap should be 0.122 in. (3mm).

3. Adjust by loosening the lock nut and moving the dashpot on its threads.

Zenith 2B2 Carburetor

THROTTLE GAP

See the Zenith 2B3 section for throttle gap adjustment procedures.

FUEL LEVEL

This fuel level adjustment procedure is the same as that for the Zenith 2B3 carburetor.

FAST IDLE—1975

See the 2B3 carburetor section for fast idle gap adjustment on 1975 models.

FAST IDLE—1976

♦ **See Figure 13**

On these models it is not necessary to remove the carburetor. The engine must be at normal operating temperature.

1. Set the ignition timing.
2. Disconnect and plug the hose from the choke pull-down unit.
3. Open the throttle valve slightly and close the choke valve.
4. Close the throttle valve. The choke valve should be fully open again.
5. Set the stop screw of the fast idle cam on the highest step. Start the engine.
6. Adjust the speed with the screw (arrow) to 3,150–3,250 rpm on manual transaxles, or 3,350–3,450 rpm on automatic transaxles.

CHOKE GAP

♦ **See Figure 14**

1. Remove the automatic choke cover.
2. Close the choke valve and push the choke rod to the stop (arrow).
3. Hold the choke in position with a rubber band (a).
4. Push the choke lever (b) down slightly to equalize the clearances.
5. Check the choke gap between the edge of the carburetor wall and the edge of the valve with a drill. It should be:
   • 1975—0.19 in. (4.8mm) with vacuum delay valve
   • 1976—0.14 in. (3.5mm) with primary activated; 0.20 in. (5.0mm) with secondary activated
6. Adjust the gap by turning the screw on the choke vacuum unit in to decrease the gap or out to increase the gap.

AUTOMATIC CHOKE

Align the mark on the automatic choke cover with the mark on the carburetor.

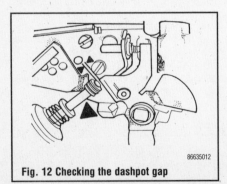

Fig. 12 Checking the dashpot gap

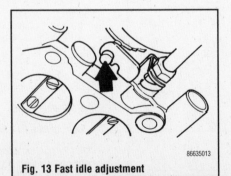

Fig. 13 Fast idle adjustment

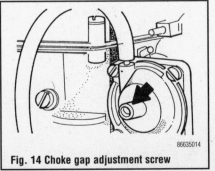

Fig. 14 Choke gap adjustment screw

AUTOMATIC CHOKE TEMPERATURE SWITCH

The temperature switch must be removed from the carburetor and checked with an ohmmeter. Connect an ohmmeter across the 2 terminals. It should read 0 ohms below 107°F (42°C), and infinite resistance above 136°F (58°C).

DASHPOT

Dashpot adjustments are the same as those for Zenith 2B3 carburetor.

Solex 34 PICT–5—1978 Models

THROTTLE VALVE (BASIC SETTING)

▶ See Figure 15

You need a vacuum gauge to set the throttle valve. The stop screw is set at the factory, and should not be moved. If the screw is accidentally turned, proceed as follows.
1. Run the engine at idle.
2. Remove the vacuum advance hose at the carburetor and connect a vacuum gauge.
3. Remove the plastic screw cap and turn the stop screw in until the gauge indicates vacuum.
4. Turn the stop screw out until the gauges indicates no vacuum. Turn the screw an additional ¼ turn and install the plastic cap.
5. Adjust the idle and fuel mixture.

CHOKE VALVE

▶ See Figure 16

1. Remove the cover from the automatic choke and fully close the choke.
2. Push the choke rod in the direction of the arrow (1) and check the gap between the choke valves and the air horn wall. It should be 0.11–0.13 in. (2.8–3.3mm).
3. If necessary, change the gap by turning the adjusting screw (2).

4. Reassemble the choke cover. There is an index mark on the choke housing and another on the choke cover.

FAST IDLE

▶ See Figure 17

The engine should be at normal operating temperature.
1. Run the engine with the screw on the 3rd step of the fast idle cam. The speed should be 2,350–2,450 rpm. Adjust this speed with the adjusting screw.
2. Stop the engine. Open the choke valve fully and check the gap between the adjusting screw and fast idle cam (arrow). It should be 0.008 in. (0.20mm).

ALTITUDE CORRECTION

▶ See Figure 18

Cars that are generally operated 3,600 feet (1,097 meters) above sea level may require altitude correction, which is made by backing out the two screws (arrows) until they are flush with the carburetor body. Adjust the idle and fuel mixture.

Solex 34 PICT–5—1980 Models

▶ See Figures 19 and 20

PART THROTTLE HEATER

This carburetor is equipped with a heating element which partly pre-heats the throttle channel while the engine temperature is below 167°F (75°C). This allows the engine to run smoother during warm-up time and prevents excessive use of the choke valve.

To test the part throttle heater, disconnect its wire and connect a test light between the throttle heater lead and the positive battery terminal. The heating element is working if the test light lights up. If the light fails to light, the element is bad and must be replaced.

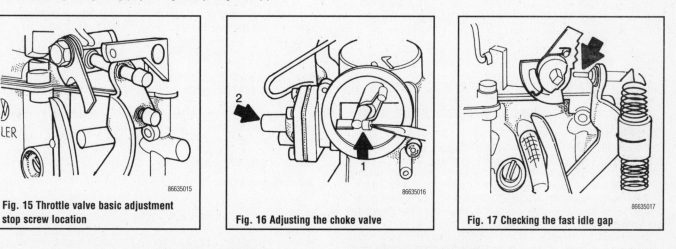

Fig. 15 Throttle valve basic adjustment stop screw location

Fig. 16 Adjusting the choke valve

Fig. 17 Checking the fast idle gap

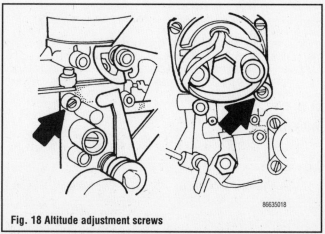

Fig. 18 Altitude adjustment screws

MAIN JET SHUT-OFF SYSTEM

The shut-off valve is vacuum activated by the vacuum control unit, located on the fender inside the engine compartment next to the brake master cylinder. A relay is activated via terminal 15 of the fuse panel and shuts off the fuel flow to the main jet if voltage is less than 5 volts at terminal 15 or when the ignition is cut-off. Test the system as follows:
1. Run the engine at idle and disconnect the electrical connector from the front of the vacuum control unit.
2. The engine should stall. If not, check the vacuum tubes for blockage and check the vacuum control unit. If these are not the problem, replace the main jet cut-off valve.

IDLE SHUT-OFF VALVE

1. Run the engine at idle.
2. Pull the electrical connector from the idle shut-off valve.
3. The engine should stall. If not, replace the idle shutoff valve.

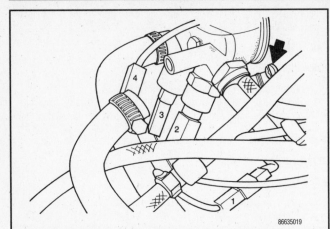

Fig. 19 Part throttle heater connection (1), thermoswitch 1 (2), thermoswitch 2 (3), choke heater connection (4). Arrow indicates the idle jet

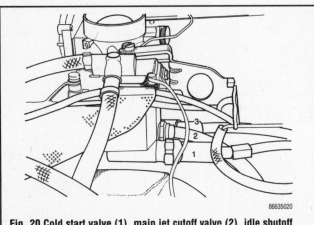

Fig. 20 Cold start valve (1), main jet cutoff valve (2), idle shutoff valve (3)

AUTOMATIC CHOKE

The automatic choke is operated by the electrical heating element inside the choke and coolant temperature. When coolant temperature is below 61°F (16°C), the electrical heating element in the choke receives current from thermoswitch 1 and the resistor wire. Approximately 9 volts of current is applied at this point.

When the engine temperature (coolant) is between 61°F (16°C) and 167°F (75°C), the resistor wire is bypassed by thermoswitch 2 and the heating element in the choke receives full battery voltage (12 volts).

When the coolant temperature exceeds 167°F (75°C), all electrical activation of the choke valve is switched off, thermoswitch 1 opens interrupting the current to the heating element while the choke fully opens. To test the choke system, proceed as follows:

1. Unplug the choke heating element connector and connect the positive lead of a voltmeter to the female part of the connector (part leading into the wiring harness). Connect the negative lead of the voltmeter to the carburetor ground wire. Turn the ignition **ON**.
2. With the coolant temperature below 59°F (15°C), record the voltage.
3. Run the engine up above 131°F (55°C) and check the voltage again. Compare the two readings. The first reading should be one or two volts below the second reading.
4. With the engine at operating temperature (the cooling fan must have come on at least once), the voltmeter should have no reading. If it does, check the thermoswitches.

To test the thermoswitches, remove the switches and connect an ohmmeter between the terminals on each thermoswitch. Thermoswitch 1 opens when the temperature reaches 167°F (75°C) and closes when the temperature drops to 149°F (65°C). Thermoswitch 2 closes when the temperature reaches 131°F (55°C) and opens when the temperature drops to 61°F (16°C).

CHOKE VALVE GAP

1. Set the cold idle speed adjuster screw in its upper notch.
2. Connect a manually operated vacuum pump to the connection on the pulldown unit and build up vacuum.
3. Close the choke valve by hand with the lever and check the choke valve gap with a drill. The gap should be 0.123–0.146 in. (3.0–3.7mm).
4. Adjust the gap using the adjusting screw on the pulldown unit. After adjusting, lock the screw with sealant or a dab of paint.

FAST IDLE SPEED

1. Run the engine up to operating temperature and make sure the ignition setting and the idle adjustment are correct.
2. Run the engine at idle and set the adjusting screw on its third notch on the choke valve lever.
3. Open the choke valve fully by hand using the choke valve lever.
4. Connect a tachometer and check the rpm.

➡ **See Electronic Ignition Precautions in Section 2 for warning about connecting tachometers to electronic ignition systems.**

5. The fast idle speed should be between 2,350–2,450 rpm. If not, adjust with fast idle adjustment screw. Lock screw with safety cap after adjustment.

COLD START VALVE

The cold start valve enriches the air/fuel mixture when engine temperature is below 60°F (15°C) by injecting fuel into the throttle chamber through a passage parallel to the main jet. Test the valve for continuity with an ohmmeter. The ohmmeter should display approximately 80 ohms. If it reads infinite resistance, replace the valve.

THROTTLE KICKER

The throttle kicker increases the idle speed to prevent stalling when the air conditioner is engaged. To test, proceed as follows:

1. Run the engine up to operating temperature and check the ignition timing. Unplug the ignition advance idle stabilizer and connect the two plugs together (if equipped). Remove the retard and advance vacuum hoses and plug them. Make sure the basic idle speed and mixture adjustments are correct.
2. Reconnect the advance and retard hoses and reconnect the plugs for the idle stabilizer.
3. Rev the engine to start the idle stabilizer and note the ignition timing at idle.
4. Switch on the air conditioner (coldest temperature setting, highest fan speed), the ignition timing should not change.
5. If the timing changes, adjust the throttle kicker screw where it contacts the throttle valve lever until the correct setting (no timing change) is reached. Seal the screw with Loctite® or equivalent sealant.

VACUUM CONTROL UNIT

◆ **See Figures 21 and 22**

The vacuum control unit has two functions. It houses both the relay for the main jet cutoff valve and the relay for the throttle kicker on air conditioner equipped vehicles.

To test the main jet cutoff valve relay, perform the steps under the heading Main Jet Cutoff Valve. If the engine continues to run and you are sure the vacuum lines are not clogged and the valve is working replace the relay inside the vacuum control unit.

To test the throttle kicker relay, run the engine and turn the air conditioner on and then turn it off. The kicker should move in and out. If it doesn't connect the vacuum retard hose from the distributor to the throttle kicker vacuum connector. If the kicker moves, replace the relay. If the kicker does not move, replace the throttle kicker.

Carter TYF Carburetors

THROTTLE GAP

Throttle gap is set at the factory and should not be tampered with.

FAST IDLE

1. Run the engine until it reaches normal operating temperature. Make sure that the timing and idle speed are set to specifications.
2. Run the engine at idle and set the fast idle adjustment screw to the second step of the fast idle cam.

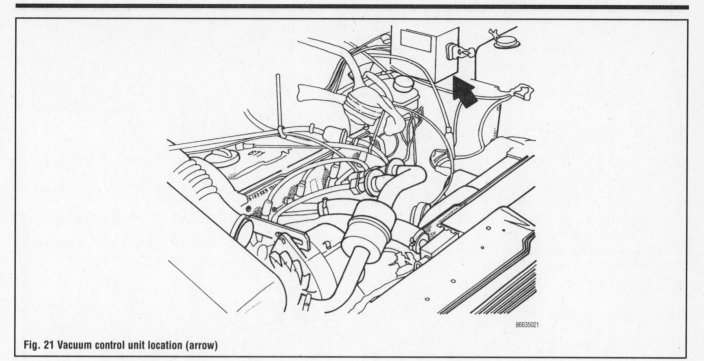

Fig. 21 Vacuum control unit location (arrow)

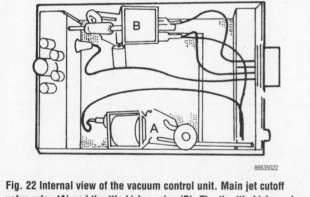

Fig. 22 Internal view of the vacuum control unit. Main jet cutoff valve relay (A) and throttle kicker relay (B). The throttle kicker relay is used on air conditioned cars

3. Disconnect the purge valve. Disconnect and plug the vacuum hose at the EGR valve.

4. Connect a tachometer as per the manufacturer's instructions and check that the engine speed is 2,800–3,200 rpm. If not, turn the fast idle screw until it is.

5. Reconnect the purge valve and the vacuum hose at the EGR valve.

CHOKE GAP

1. Set the cold idle speed adjuster screw in its upper notch.

2. Connect a manually operated vacuum pump to the connection on the pulldown unit and build up vacuum.

3. Close the choke valve by hand with the lever and check the choke valve gap with a drill. The gap should be 0.154 in. (4.0mm) for 1982 models and 0.165 in. (4.2mm) for 1983 models.

4. Adjust the gap using the adjusting screw in the end of the vacuum unit at the side of the choke unit. After adjusting, lock the screw with sealant.

THROTTLE LINKAGE ADJUSTMENT

All Carbureted Models

Throttle linkage adjustments are not normally required. However, it is a good idea to make sure that the throttle valve(s) in the carburetor open all the way when the accelerator pedal is held in the wide-open position. Only the primary (first stage) throttle valve will open when the pedal is pushed with the engine

off: the secondary throttle on Volkswagen 2-barrel carburetors is vacuum operated. Make note of the following:

1. Always be careful not to kink or twist the cables during installation or adjustment. This can cause rapid wear and binding.

2. On the Rabbits and Sciroccos, the accelerator cable will only bend one way; make sure you install it with the bends in the right positions.

3. On 1974–75 Dashers, when installing new accelerator cable, the hole in the firewall must be enlarged to ⅝ in. (16mm). Adjust these cables at the pedal clamp.

➡️**When installing new cables, all bends should be as wide as possible, and fittings between which the inner cable is exposed must be aligned.**

REMOVAL & INSTALLATION

1. Disconnect the negative battery cable.
2. Remove the air cleaner.
3. Disconnect and plug the fuel lines.
4. Drain the coolant to below the level of the choke hoses, then disconnect them.
5. Disconnect and label all vacuum lines.
6. Disconnect and label all electrical leads.
7. Remove the clip which secures the throttle linkage to the carburetor. Detach the linkage, being careful not to lose any washers or bushings.
8. Unbolt the carburetor from the manifold and remove it. If the carburetor is to be left off the engine for any length of time, cover the intake manifold opening with masking tape to prevent anything from falling into the engine.
   To install:
9. Clean the carburetor and intake manifold surfaces and lay the new gasket onto the intake manifold. ALWAYS use a new gasket.
10. Set the carburetor on top of the gasket and tighten the nuts in a crisscross pattern until snug. Don't overtighten.
11. Connect and adjust the throttle linkage.
12. Connect the electrical leads and vacuum lines.
13. Connect the choke hoses.
14. Connect the fuel lines.
15. Install the air cleaner and fill the cooling system to the proper level.
16. Connect the battery cable.

OVERHAUL

▶️ **See Figures 23 and 24**

➡️**Specific directions and specifications for carburetor overhaul are usually contained in the rebuilding kit.**

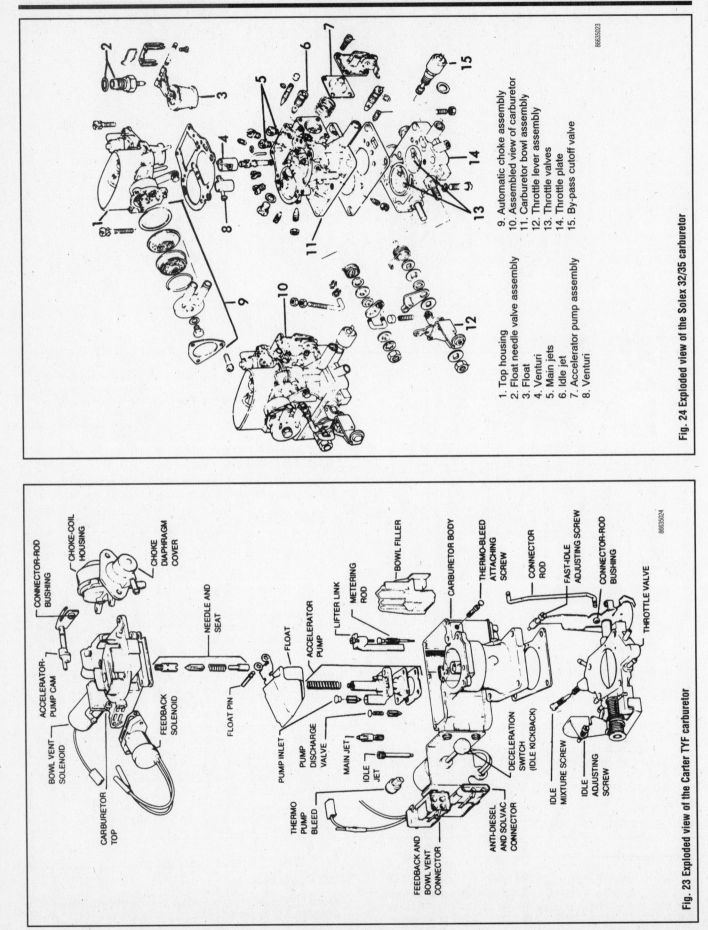

1. Top housing
2. Float needle valve assembly
3. Float
4. Venturi
5. Main jets
6. Idle jet
7. Accelerator pump assembly
8. Venturi
9. Automatic choke assembly
10. Assembled view of carburetor
11. Carburetor bowl assembly
12. Throttle lever assembly
13. Throttle valves
14. Throttle plate
15. By-pass cutoff valve

Fig. 24 Exploded view of the Solex 32/35 carburetor.

CONNECTOR-ROD BUSHING
CHOKE-COIL HOUSING
CHOKE DIAPHRAGM COVER
ACCELERATOR-PUMP CAM
BOWL VENT SOLENOID
FEEDBACK SOLENOID
CARBURETOR TOP
FEEDBACK AND BOWL VENT CONNECTOR
NEEDLE AND SEAT
FLOAT PIN
FLOAT
PUMP INLET
ACCELERATOR PUMP
THERMO PUMP BLEED
PUMP DISCHARGE VALVE
MAIN JET
IDLE JET
ANTI-DIESEL AND SOLVAC CONNECTOR
LIFTER LINK
METERING ROD
BOWL FILLER
CARBURETOR BODY
DECELERATION SWITCH (IDLE KICKBACK)
IDLE MIXTURE SCREW
THERMO-BLEED ATTACHING SCREW
CONNECTOR ROD
FAST-IDLE ADJUSTING SCREW
CONNECTOR-ROD BUSHING
THROTTLE VALVE
IDLE ADJUSTING SCREW

Fig. 23 Exploded view of the Carter TYF carburetor

Efficient carburetion depends greatly on careful cleaning and inspection during overhaul since dirt, gum, water, or varnish in or on the carburetor parts are often responsible for poor performance.

Overhaul your carburetor in a clean, dust-free area. Carefully disassemble the carburetor, referring often to the exploded views. Keep all similar and look-alike parts segregated during disassembly and cleaning to avoid accidentally interchange during assembly. Make a note of all jet sizes.

When the carburetor is disassembled, wash all parts (except diaphragms, electric choke units, pump plunger, and any other plastic, leather, fiber, or rubber parts) in clean carburetor solvent. Do not leave parts in the solvent any longer than is necessary to sufficiently loosen the deposits. Excessive cleaning may remove the special finish from the float bowl and choke valve bodies, leaving these parts unfit for service. Rinse all parts in clean solvent and blow them dry with compressed air or allow them to air dry. Wipe clean all cork, plastic, leather, and fiber parts with a clean, lint-free cloth.

Blow out all passages and jets with compressed air and be sure that there are no restrictions or blockages. Never use wire or similar tools to clean jets, fuel passages, or air bleeds. Clean all jets and valves separately to avoid accidental interchange.

Check all parts for wear or damage. If wear or damage is found, replace the defective parts. Especially check the following:

1. Check the float needle and seat for wear. If wear is found, replace the complete assembly.

2. Check the float hinge pin for wear and the float(s) for dents or distortion. Replace the float if fuel has leaked into it.

3. Check the throttle and choke shaft bores for wear or an out-of-round condition. Damage or wear to the throttle arm, shaft, or shaft bore will often require replacement of the throttle body. These parts require a close tolerance of fit. Wear may allow air leakage, which could adversely affect starting and idling.

4. Inspect the idle mixture adjusting needles for burrs or grooves. Any such condition requires replacement of the needle, since you will not be able to obtain a satisfactory idle.

5. Test the accelerator pump check valves. They should pass air one way but not the other. Test for proper seating by blowing and sucking on the valve.

Replace the valve if necessary. If the valve is satisfactory, wash the valve again to remove breath moisture.

6. Check the bowl cover for warped surfaces with a straightedge.

7. Closely inspect the valves and seats for wear and damage, replacing as necessary.

8. After the carburetor is assembled, check the choke valve for freedom of operation.

Carburetor overhaul kits are recommended for each overhaul. These kits contain all gaskets and new parts to replace those that deteriorate most rapidly. Failure to replace all parts supplied with the kit (especially gaskets) can result in poor performance later.

Some carburetor manufacturers supply overhaul kits of three basic types: minor repair, major repair and gasket kits. Basically, they contain the following:

Minor Repair Kits
- All gaskets
- Float needle valve
- All diaphragms
- Spring for the pump diaphragm

Major Repair Kits
- All jets and gaskets
- All diaphragms
- Float needle valve
- Pump ball valve
- Float
- Complete intermediate rod
- Intermediate pump lever
- Some cover hold-down screws and washers

Gasket kits contain all gaskets.

After cleaning and checking all components, reassemble the carburetor, using new parts and referring to the exploded view. When reassembling, make sure that all screws and jets are tight in their seats, but do not overtighten, as the tips will be distorted. Tighten all screws gradually, in rotation. Do not tighten needle valves into their seats; uneven jetting will result. Always use new gaskets. Be sure to adjust the float level when reassembling.

CARBURETOR SPECIFICATIONS

Year	Model	Type	Main Jet Primary	Main Jet Secondary	Air Correction Jet Primary	Air Correction Jet Secondary	Idle Fuel Jet Primary	Idle Fuel Jet Secondary	Idle Air Jet Primary	Idle Air Jet Secondary	Accelerator Pump Discharge (cm3/stroke) Fast	Accelerator Pump Discharge (cm3/stroke) Slow
1974	Dasher (Calif. M/T)	Solex 32/35	x122.5	x142.5	130	140	g45	g45	180	180	0.3-0.5	0.75-1.05
	Dasher (Calif. A/T)	Solex 32/35	x120	x145	140	140	g45	g45	180	180	0.3-0.5	0.75-1.05
	Dasher (Fed. M/T)	Solex 32/35	x135	x140	150	150	g52.5	g52.5	180	180	0.3-0.5	0.75-1.05
	Dasher (Fed. A/T)	Solex 32/35	x130	x140	140	140	g52.5	g52.5	180	180	0.3-0.5	0.75-1.05
1975	Dasher	Zenith 2B3	x117.5	x137.5	140	92.5	52.5	65	130	110	-	0.75-1.05
	Rabbit	Zenith 2B2	x115	x115	140	92.5	52.5	70	135	100	-	0.75-1.05
	Scirocco	Zenith 2B2	x115	x115	140	92.5	52.5	70	135	100	-	0.75-1.05
1976	Rabbit	Zenith 2B2	x117.5	x110	130	92.5	52.5	65	135	140	1.3-1.7 ①	0.6-0.9 ②
	Scirocco	Zenith 2B2	x117.5	x110	130	92.5	52.5	65	135	140	1.3-1.7 ①	0.6-0.9 ②
1977	Rabbit	Zenith 2B2	x117.5	x110	130	92.5	52.5	65	135	140	1.3-1.7 ①	0.6-0.9 ②
1978	Rabbit	34 PICT-5	x127.5	-	120 Z	-	52.5	-	120	-	3	3
1980	Rabbit	34 PICT-5	x127.5	-	120 Z	-	4	-	120	-	5	5

1 Cold
2 Warm
3 Rate given as 0.85-1.15 cm3/stroke
4 Come in sizes 50/55/57.5 The jet size is stamped on the float housing next to the plug in front of the carburetor
5 Rate given as 0.8-1.2 cm3/stroke
NOTE: Refer to the instruction sheet in the carburetor rebuilding kit for specifications on 1981 and later Carter TYF carburetors.

CONTINUOUS INJECTION SYSTEMS (CIS/CIS-E)

Description of System

▶ **See Figures 25 and 26**

The Continuous Injection System (CIS) is an independent mechanical system. The basic operating principle is to continuously inject fuel into the intake side of the engine by means of an electric pump. The amount of fuel delivered is metered by an air flow measuring device. Since CIS is a mechanical system, there is no electronic "brain" deciding when or how much fuel to inject.

The primary fuel circuit consists of an electric pump, which pulls fuel from the tank. Fuel then passes through an accumulator. The accumulator is basically a container in the fuel line. It houses a spring-loaded diaphragm that provides fuel damping and delays pressure build-up when the engine is first started.

When the engine is shut down, the expanded chamber in the accumulator keeps the system under enough pressure for good hot restarts with no vapor locking. Fuel flows through a large, paper element filter to the mixture control assembly.

The mixture control assembly is the heart of the CIS system. It houses the airflow sensor and the fuel distributor. The air sensor is a round plate attached to a counterbalanced lever. The plate and lever are free to move up-and-down on a fulcrum. Accelerator pedal linkage connects to a throttle butterfly, which is upstream (closer to the manifold and intake valves) of the air sensor. Stepping on the accelerator pedal opens the throttle valve. Increased air, demanded by the engine, is sucked through the air cleaner and around the air sensor plate.

In the air funnel, where the air sensor plate is located, the quantity of intake air lifts the plate until an equilibrium is reached between air flow and hydraulic counter-pressure acting on the lever through a plunger. This is the control

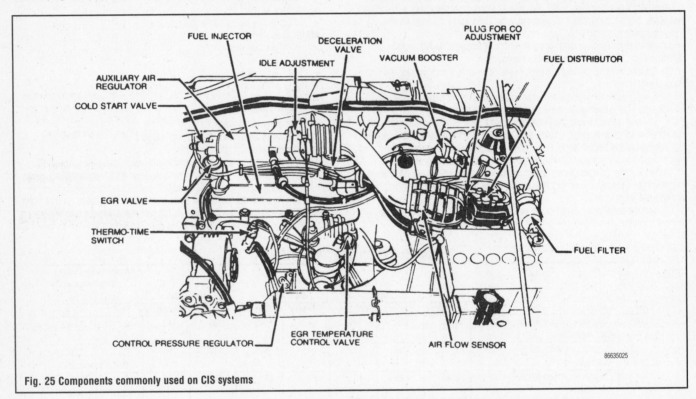

Fig. 25 Components commonly used on CIS systems

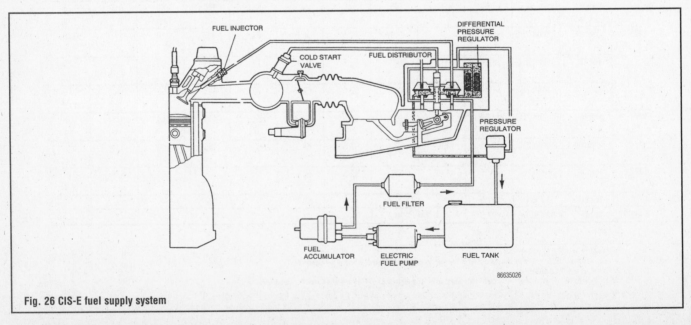

Fig. 26 CIS-E fuel supply system

plunger. In this balanced position, the plunger stays at a level in the fuel distributor to open small metering slits, one for each cylinder in the engine. Fuel under controlled pressure from the pump goes through the slits to the injectors' supply opening. The slit meters the right amount of fuel.

In order to maintain a precise fuel pressure, a pressure regulator, or pressure relief valve, is located in the primary fuel circuit of the fuel distributor. Excess fuel is diverted back to the tank through a return line. To make sure the amount of fuel going through the control plunger slits depends only on their area, an exact pressure differential must always be maintained at the openings. This pressure is controlled by a differential-pressure valve. There's one valve for each cylinder. The valve consists of a spring loaded steel diaphragm and an outlet to the injectors. The diaphragm separates the upper and lower chambers.

The valve keeps an exact pressure differential of 1.42 psi between upper chamber pressure and lower chamber pressure. Both pressures act on the spring loaded steel diaphragm which opens the outlet to the injectors. The size of the outlet opening is always just enough to maintain that 1.42 psi pressure differential at the metering slit. The diaphragm opens more if a larger amount of fuel flows. If less fuel enters the upper chamber, the diaphragm opens less and less fuel goes to the injectors. An exact pressure differential between upper and lower chamber is kept constant. Diaphragm movement is actually only a thousandths of an inch (few hundreths of a millimeter).

The control pressure regulator can alter the pressure on the control plunger according to engine and outside air temperature. For warm-up running, it lowers the pressure so that the air sensor plate can go higher for the same air flow. This exposes more metering slit area, and more fuel flows for a richer mixture. For cold starts, a separate injector is used to squirt fuel into the intake manifold. This injector is electronically controlled. A thermo-time switch, screwed into the engine, limits the amount of time the valve is open and at higher temperatures, cuts it off.

CIS-E is an electronically controlled continuous fuel injection system. This system utilizes the basic CIS mechanical system for injection, with electrically controlled correction functions. The electronic portion of the system consists of an airflow sensor position indicator, coolant temperature sensor, throttle valve switches, idle air stabilizer and the differential pressure regulator.

When the ignition switch is turned **ON**, the electric fuel pump is activated causing pressurized fuel to move from the tank to the accumulator. Fuel pulsations exerted by the fuel pump are then damped or smoothed out by the accumulator. The pressurized fuel is directed through the fuel filter and to the fuel distributor. A differential pressure regulator located on the side of fuel distributor is used to control the air/fuel mixture. The control pressure regulator is not used in the CIS-E fuel injection system. The system pressure regulator valve has been removed from the fuel distributor and replaced by an external, diaphragm type, pressure regulator. This regulator contains an additional port which is used to return fuel from the differential pressure regulator.

The differential pressure regulator is an electro-magnetic operated pressure regulator. It receives an electronic signal in milliamps from the control unit. The higher the milliamp signal the higher the differential between the upper and lower chamber pressures, resulting in a richer mixture. The lower the milliamp signal the lower the differential pressure resulting in a leaner mixture.

In the CIS-E fuel injection system, system pressure is always present in the upper chamber of the fuel distributor. The metering slit in the control plunger regulates the amount of fuel delivered to the upper chamber depending on the airflow sensor position and control plunger position. The amount of fuel delivered to the injectors and consequently fuel mixture, is adjusted by the differential pressure regulator.

Relieving Fuel System Pressure

Engines equipped with electric fuel pumps maintain fuel pressure even when the engine has not been run. This residual pressure may remain in the fuel system for several hours after the engine is shut down.

To relieve the fuel system pressure, perform the following:
1. Start the engine and allow it to run at idle speed.
2. Locate the fuel pump electrical connector and disconnect it while the engine is running.
3. Operate the engine until it runs out of fuel and stops.
4. Remove the fuel filler cap.
5. Disconnect the negative battery cable.

➡**Have a container ready to catch the fuel that will squirt out when you loosen the clamps or couplings on the fuel system components you are working on. Wrap the connection with a rag and slowly crack the connection to vent any residual pressure from the system. Once all the pressure is relieved, loosen the connection.**

6. Proceed with the necessary fuel system component repairs. When finished, engage the fuel pump connector and connect the negative battery cable. Don't forget to install the fuel filler cap.

Electric Fuel Pump

REMOVAL & INSTALLATION

▶ **See Figure 27**

CIS Models Except Quantum

1. Raise the vehicle and support it on jackstands. Disconnect the battery negative cable.
2. Remove the right rear wheel on all cars. On the Rabbit Pick-up truck, it will probably be easier if you raise all four wheels off the ground and support the vehicle on jackstands.

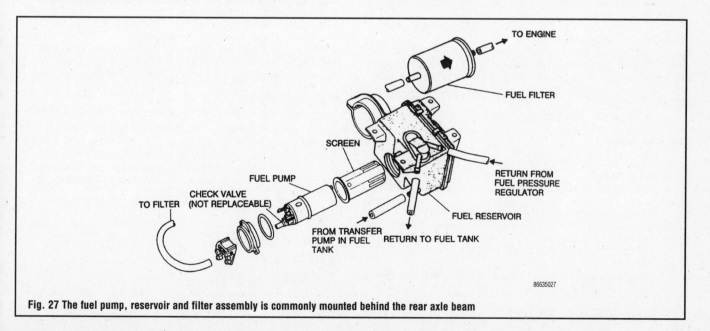

Fig. 27 The fuel pump, reservoir and filter assembly is commonly mounted behind the rear axle beam

3. Remove the gas tank filler cap to release the fuel pressure.

4. Clamp off the line between the fuel pump and the fuel tank with a pair of soft jawed vise grips or other suitable lock pliers. Don't clamp the line too tightly or you may damage it.

5. Disconnect the clamped line from the fuel pump. There's bound to be a little gas in the line, so be careful.

6. If your vehicle has an accumulator mounted next to the fuel pump, disconnect the fuel lines from the accumulator. Disconnect the wiring from the fuel pump and remove all other lines after marking them for assembly.

7. Loosen and remove the retaining nuts and remove the fuel pump on Dashers and pre-1979 Rabbits and Sciroccos. On 1979 and later Rabbits, Jettas, Golfs and Sciroccos (including the Rabbit Pick-up), remove the nuts on the lower bracket, loosen the nut on the upper slotted bracket where it connects to the body and slide the pump out.

To install:

8. Slide the fuel pump into the mounting bracket and install the pump/bracket fasteners.

9. Connect the fuel lines and wiring to the pump. Make sure that the new seal washers are installed on the fuel discharge line.

10. Lower the vehicle. Start the engine and check for leaks.

CIS-E Models Except Quantum

1. Disconnect the negative battery cable.
2. Relieve the fuel system pressure.

➡**When replacing the old fuel pump with a new pump, the new pump may have a positive lock connector that differs from the earlier pumps. The electrical connectors of the fuel pump wiring harness must be changed when installing this newer pump.**

3. Raise the vehicle and support it safely.
4. Unplug the electrical connector from the fuel pump.
5. Remove both wire terminals from the connector housing.
6. Discard the old connector and protective boot.
7. Install the new protective boot over the wires and insert the wire terminals into the new connector.
8. Slide the protective boot over the connector.
9. Disconnect fuel line from the fuel pump. Wrap a cloth around the connection to catch any escaping fuel.
10. Remove the lower pump cover (if equipped), pump mounting bolts and remove the pump.

To install:

11. Position the fuel pump it place and secure it with the mounting bolts. Make sure the tabs in the pump housing catch in the retaining ring recess.

12. Install new O-ring seals when connecting the fuel lines to the pump. Lubricate the O-rings with clean fuel prior to installation.

13. Connect the electrical connector to the fuel pump.

14. Lower the vehicle.

15. Connect the negative battery cable. Turn the ignition switch on and off several times to pressurize the system.

16. Start the engine and observe for fuel leaks. When the engine is started after a fuel pump replacement, you may here knocking or clunking noises from the rear of the vehicle for about 5–20 seconds. This is normal due to fuel filling the accumulator under pressure from the pump. Do not attempt to remedy this situation if it occurs.

17. Shut the engine off and lower the vehicle.

Quantum Models

1. Pull up carpet under rear cargo area, revealing the fuel pump access plate.
2. Remove the plate.
3. Detach fuel return hose, fuel supply hose, and vent hose from top of fuel pump.
4. Disconnect electrical wire from sending unit and fuel pump.
5. Loosen fuel pump attaching screws and pull fuel pump out in one motion.

To install:

6. Slide the fuel pump into the mounting bracket and install the pump/bracket fasteners.

7. Connect the fuel lines and wiring to the pump. Make sure that the new seal washers are installed on the fuel discharge line.

8. Connect the negative battery cable.

9. Start the engine and check for leaks.

TESTING

Operating Test

1. Have an assistant operate the starter. Listen near the fuel pump location to determine if the pump is running.

2. If the pump is not running, check the wiring and the fuse on the front of the fuel pump relay.

3. If the fuse is good, replace the fuel pump relay.

4. If the fuel pump still does not operate, and you're sure there are no loose connections in the wiring, the fuel pump is faulty and must be replaced.

Delivery Rate Test

CIS SYSTEMS

1. Check the condition of the fuel filter. Make sure it is clean and is able to flow fuel freely. The best way to do this is to replace it.

2. Disconnect the return fuel line and hold it in a measuring container with a capacity of more than 1 liter.

3. Locate and remove the fuel pump relay on the main fuse panel. Install tool US 4480/3 in the fuel pump relay socket. This is essentially a jumper wire with a switch used to turn on the fuel pump. The fuel pump will run any time the switch is ON.

The minimum allowable flow for the 1975–78 Rabbit and Scirocco is 750cc in 30 seconds; 900cc in 30 seconds for 1979–84 Rabbits, Jettas and Sciroccos; 760cc in 30 seconds for 1985 and later Golfs and Jettas.

For Dashers with the type A fuel pump (identified by the fuel inlet and outlet ports being at opposite end of the pump), the pump must delivery 1 liter of fuel in 32 seconds. For Dashers with the type B fuel pump (identified by the inlet and outlet ports forming a 90 degree angle through the center of the pump), the pump must delivery 1 liter of fuel in 40 seconds. Quantum fuel pumps must deliver 700cc of fuel in 30 seconds.

➡**For the above test, the battery must be fully charged. Also, make sure you have plenty of fuel in the tank.**

If your pump fails its specific test, check for a dirty fuel filter, blocked lines or blocked fuel tank strainer (if so equipped). If all of these are in good condition, replace the pump.

CIS-E SYSTEMS

1. Check the condition of the fuel filter. Make sure it is clean and is able to flow fuel freely. The best way to do this is to replace it.

2. Disconnect the fuel return line at the fuel distributor.

3. Place the return line in a 1 quart capacity measuring container.

4. Locate and remove the fuel pump relay on the main fuse panel. Install tool US 4480/3 in the fuel pump relay socket. This is essentially a jumper wire with a switch used to turn on the fuel pump. The fuel pump will run any time the switch is ON.

5. Operate the fuel pump for exactly 30 seconds.

6. Delivery quantity should be 675cc in 30 seconds. This is the maximum flow rate with 12 volts available at the fuel pump.

7. If the fuel pump delivery is incorrect, check for fuel line leaks, blocked fuel lines, fuel filter or fuel tank screen and the voltage at the fuel pump (with the pump operating). If all systems are in good order, replace the fuel pump.

FUEL PRESSURE TESTS

A fuel pressure gauge with a T-fitting and shut-off valve (VW 1318) is required to perform these fuel pressure tests. On CIS-E systems, you will also need an ammeter and tools VW 1490 and 1315 A/1. Tool VW 1490 is a 15,000 ohm resistor which plugs into the coolant temperature sensor connector, and tool VW 1315 A/1 is a jumper wire harness which allows you to connect an ammeter to the differential pressure regulator.

CIS Systems

GAUGE INSTALLATION

▶ **See Figure 28**

1. Relieve the fuel system pressure.

2. Disconnect the fuel line on the top of the fuel distributor from the control pressure regulator.

3. Connect the pressure gauge inline between the control pressure regulator and the fuel distributor.

4. Start the engine. Bleed the pressure gauge by holding the gauge down and move the shut-off valve several times from the open (A) and closed (B) positions.

SYSTEM PRESSURE

▶ **See Figure 29**

1. Set the shut-off valve lever to the closed position (fuel flow from the control pressure regulator is shut off).

2. Start the engine and let it idle.

3. Read the system pressure displayed on the gauge. Compare the reading to the specifications listed on the tune-up charts in Section 2.

4. Turn the engine off.

5. If the reading is not within specification, check for a clogged fuel filter, crushed or blocked fuel lines and the fuel pump delivery rate. If these are OK, the fuel pressure can be adjusted to specification by adding or subtracting the shims on the pressure regulating valve.

6. To adjust the pressure:

a. Relieve the fuel system pressure.

b. Remove the pressure regulating valve from the side of the fuel distributor.

c. If the system pressure was too high, reduce the number of the shim(s), or use a thinner shim.

➡**Removing a 0.020 in. (0.50mm) shim will decrease the pressure about 4.2 psi. Removing a 0.040 in. (1mm) shim will reduce the pressure about 8.5 psi.**

d. If the system pressure was too low, increase the number of the shim(s), or use a thicker shim.

➡**Adding a 0.020 in. (0.50mm) shim will increase the pressure about 4.2 psi. Adding a 0.040 in. (1mm) shim will increase the pressure about 8.5 psi.**

e. Install the pressure regulator valve using a new sealing washer and O-rings. Lubricate the O-rings with gasoline before installing.

7. Check the system pressure again. Readjust the pressure as necessary.

CONTROL PRESSURE

▶ **See Figure 30**

➡**The engine should be cold when checking the control pressure.**

1. Turn the shut-off valve on the pressure gauge to the open position (allow the fuel to flow from the pressure regulator).

2. Unplug the electrical connector on the control pressure regulator.

3. Determine the ambient temperature around the control pressure regulator.

4. Start the engine and take a pressure reading.

a. On Quantums and 1985–89 Golf and Jetta (except engine code MZ) compare the reading to the graph.

b. On 1985–89 Golf and Jetta with engine code MZ, the control pressure should be 14.5–19.3 psi at 68°F (20°C); 17.4–24.7 psi at 77°F (25°C) and 18.8–27.6 psi at 86°F (30°C).

c. On Fox models, the control pressure should be 15–20 psi at 50°F (10°C); 17–25 psi at 68°F (20°C) and 19–28 psi at 86°F (30°C).

d. On 1980 California models with regulator part number 035 133 4038, the control pressure should be 23–29 psi at 68°F (20°C); 26–33 psi at 77°F (25°C) and 29–36 psi at 86°F (30°C).

e. On other 1975–1984 models, the control pressure should be 19–25 psi at 68°F (20°C); 22–29 psi at 77°F (25°C) and 25–32 psi at 86°F (30°C).

5. Engage the electrical connection on the control pressure regulator. Allow the engine to run until the control pressure stabilizes. The reading should be 49–55 psi. If the reading is too low, the fuel return line is probably blocked. If the reading is too high, the fuel filter may be clogged or the pressure regulator is defective.

RESIDUAL PRESSURE

1. After performing the control pressure test, leave the gauge lever in the open position and shut the engine off. The vehicle must pass the control pressure test to proceed.

2. After about 10 minutes, check the gauge reading. On 1975 to early 1980 models, the pressure must not drop below 25 psi. On other models, it must be at least 38 psi.

3. If residual pressure is low, look for leaks at the fuel distributor O-ring under the plunger. This will appear as fuel dripping onto the air filter. Other possibilities are the fuel pump check valve, the fuel accumulator, a leaking injector, the fuel pressure regulator or improper free-play between the airflow sensor arm and the plunger in the fuel distributor. This is only likely if the fuel distributor has been removed.

CIS-E Systems

GAUGE INSTALLATION

▶ **See Figure 31**

1. Relieve the fuel system pressure.

2. Disconnect the fuel supply line to the cold start injector, then connect it to the shut-off valve side of the pressure gauge. Connect the hose from the pressure gauge to the lower chamber test port on the fuel distributor.

SYSTEM PRESSURE

1. Locate and remove the fuel pump relay on the main fuse panel. Install tool US 4480/3 in the fuel pump relay socket. This is essentially a jumper wire with a switch used to turn on the fuel pump. The fuel pump will run any time the switch is ON.

2. Open the valve on the fuel pressure gauge.

3. Unplug the electrical connector from the differential pressure regulator (except 16-valve engines).

4. Turn the fuel pump ON and read the system pressure. Compare the reading to the specification listed in the tune-up chart in Section 2.

5. Turn the fuel pump OFF.

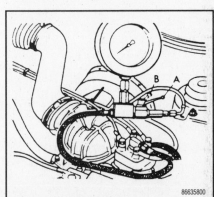

Fig. 28 Fuel pressure gauge connection on CIS systems. In position (A), the shut-off valve is open; in position (B), the valve is closed

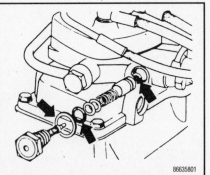

Fig. 29 Adjust the fuel system pressure, if necessary, by adding or removing shims from the pressure regulating valve. Be sure to use a new sealing washer and O-rings (as indicated by the arrows)

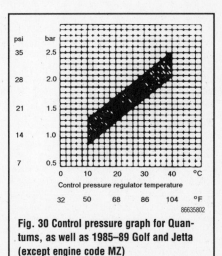

Fig. 30 Control pressure graph for Quantums, as well as 1985–89 Golf and Jetta (except engine code MZ)

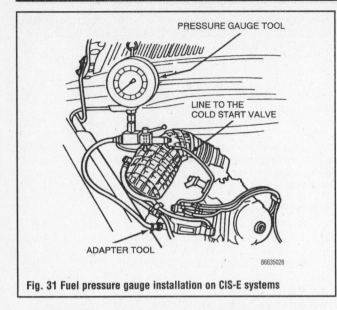

Fig. 31 Fuel pressure gauge installation on CIS-E systems

6. If the reading is below specification, check the delivery rate of the fuel pump. If the delivery quantity is OK, replace the diaphragm pressure regulator.

7. If the pressure is above specification, relieve the fuel system pressure, then disconnect the fuel return line from the diaphragm pressure regulator. Direct the end of the return line into a container, then repeat the test. If the system pressure is now OK, the return line is blocked. If it is still too high, replace the diaphragm pressure regulator.

DIFFERENTIAL PRESSURE

1. Close the valve on the fuel pressure gauge.
2. The connector on the differential pressure regulator should be unplugged.
3. Turn the fuel pump ON and read the differential pressure. It should be between 2.9–7 psi less than the system pressure. If not:
   a. Turn the fuel pump OFF and relieve the fuel system pressure. Disconnect the small fuel line from the diaphragm pressure regulator.
   b. Plug the fuel line opening in the diaphragm pressure regulator, then hold the open fuel line into a measuring container.
   c. Turn the fuel pump ON for 1 minute. Fuel flow quantity should be between 30–150cc. If quantity is OK, replace the differential pressure regulator. If it is not OK, replace the fuel distributor.
4. Connect the test lead harness (VW 1315 A/1) to the differential pressure regulator. Switch the ammeter to the DC 200 mA scale.
5. Unplug the coolant temperature sensor connector. Plug tool VW 1490 into the connector.
6. Turn the fuel pump and the ignition **ON**. The differential pressure must be 10–17.5 psi less than the system pressure. The ammeter should display between 50–80 mA (50–70 mA on Fox and 16-valve engines).
7. If the pressure is not OK, but the current reading is OK, replace the differential pressure regulator.
8. If the pressure and current readings are not OK, check the resistance between the terminals of the differential pressure regulator with an ohmmeter. It should be between 17.5–21.5 ohms. If not, replace it. If it is OK, check the ground wire of the temperature sensor to the cold start injector. If it is OK, check the power supply fuse. If the fuse is OK, check the connectors on the control unit for damage or corrosion. If they are OK, replace the control unit.

RESIDUAL PRESSURE

1. Open the valve on the fuel pressure gauge.
2. Turn the fuel pump ON for 30 seconds, then turn it OFF.
3. After about 10 minutes, check the gauge reading. It must be at least 38 psi.
4. If residual pressure is low, look for leaks at the fuel distributor O-ring under the plunger. This will appear as fuel dripping onto the air filter. Other possibilities are the fuel pump check valve, the fuel accumulator, a leaking injector, the fuel pressure regulator or improper free-play between the airflow sensor arm and the plunger in the fuel distributor. This is only likely if the fuel distributor has been removed.

REMOVAL & INSTALLATION

1. Disconnect the negative battery cable.
2. Remove the air intake hose from the throttle body.
3. Label and disconnect the vacuum hoses from the throttle body.
4. Disconnect the accelerator cable from the throttle body.
5. Remove the bolts securing the throttle body, then remove it.
6. Clean the gasket mating surface and discard the old gasket.

To install:

7. Install the throttle body with a new gasket.
8. Thread the bolts in by hand first, then tighten them to 14 ft. lbs. (20 Nm).
9. Connect the vacuum hoses and accelerator cable to the throttle body.
10. Adjust the throttle valve basic setting and the throttle cable.
11. Install the air intake hose.
12. Connect the battery cable.
13. Adjust the idle speed.

ADJUSTMENTS

Basic Setting

1. On 5-cylinder models, disconnect the accelerator cable from the throttle body.
2. Back the throttle valve adjusting screw out until a gap occurs between the screw and the throttle stop.
3. Slide a thin piece of paper between the screw and the throttle stop. Turn the screw in until the paper will not slide out, plus an additional ½ turn.
4. On 5-cylinder models, connect the accelerator cable.
5. Adjust the accelerator cable.

Accelerator Cable

1985–89 SCIROCCO AND CABRIOLET (8-VALVE/AUTOMATIC TRANSAXLE)

1. Place the selector lever in the **P** position.
2. Loosen the accelerator cable adjusting nut and disconnect the accelerator cable from the throttle lever.
3. Loosen the throttle cable adjusting nut and locknut.
4. Pull the throttle cable out until all play is removed from the cable. While doing this the throttle valves must remain closed and the transaxle operating lever must be in the closed position.
5. When the play is removed from the cable tighten the adjusting nut against the cable bracket and tighten the locknut.
6. Connect the accelerator pedal cable.
7. Have an assistant press the accelerator cable until the operating lever on the transaxle lever contacts the kick-down stop. Turn the adjusting nut to hold the cable in this position and tighten the locknut.

QUANTUM 5-CYLINDER

If the linkage is out of adjustment, the transaxle will shift poorly. The adjustment is correct when the throttle valve and transaxle operating lever rest against the stop in the idle position. If not, adjust as follows.

1. Remove the circlips at the ball sockets.
2. Remove the pushrod at the ball pin.
3. Move the throttle linkage against the idle stop, then push the linkage against the bracket stop.
4. Adjust the length of the pushrod so that the ball socket will drop onto the ball without moving the linkage off the stop or tensioning the cable.
5. Install the ball socket circlips.

1985–89 GOLF AND JETTA (8-VALVE/AUTOMATIC TRANSAXLE)

1. Warm up the engine to normal operating temperature, then shut it off.
2. Place the shifter lever in the Park position.
3. Loosen the accelerator pedal adjustment nut and set the cable off to the side.
4. Loosen the nuts on the cable jacket.
5. Pull the cable jacket out until all play is removed from the cable. While doing this the throttle plates must remain closed and the transaxle linkage must stay in the no-throttle position.

6. When all the play is removed, tighten the jacket nuts.
7. Connect the accelerator cable and have an assistant depress the gas pedal all the way down.
8. Turn the cable adjusting nut until the transaxle accelerator linkage contacts the kick-down stop. Tighten the cable locknut.

1985–89 GOLF, JETTA AND FOX (8-VALVE/MANUAL TRANSAXLE)

To check the throttle cable adjustment, have an assistant press the gas pedal all the way to the floor. Open the hood and make sure the throttle valve just reaches the full throttle position. There should be approximately 0.04 in. (1mm) clearance between the throttle valve and the throttle valve stop. If not, adjust the throttle cable as follows:
1. Pull the throttle cable adjusting grommet out of the adjusting bracket.
2. Remove the positioning clip until the throttle valve just reaches the full throttle position.
3. Install the positioning clip.
4. Push the grommet back into the retaining bracket. Re-check the gap and adjust as necessary.

➡Remember, if there is no play in the cable the throttle lever will bottom out and stretch the cable. If there is too much play, transaxle performance will be reduced.

16-VALVE ENGINES

On the 16-valve engine, the accelerator cable is adjusted by moving the retainer clip on the notched cable housing. The cable is properly adjusted when the gas pedal is fully depressed, there is about 0.039 in. (1mm) of play before contacting the stop at the wide open throttle position.

OTHER MODELS

1. Check that the throttle valve is closed (in the idle position).
2. If adjustment is necessary, loosen locknut and turn the adjusting nut until the throttle cable is free of slack or tension.

➡On automatic transaxle models, make sure the throttle cable levers on the transaxle are moved the whole way into their rest positions. Some models do not use transaxle cables.

Fuel Injectors

REMOVAL & INSTALLATION

♦ **See Figures 32, 33 and 34**

1. Disconnect the negative battery cable.
2. Relieve the pressure from the system.
3. Using a small prytool, pry the injectors up out of the head. A spray lubricant can help release stuck injectors.
4. Hold the fuel line fitting with a line wrench and unscrew the injector.
5. Discard the old rubber rings.
To install:
6. Lightly lubricate the rubber rings.
7. Screw the injector onto the fuel line fitting. Tighten until snug.
8. Push the injectors straight into the head.
9. Connect the battery cable.

TESTING

♦ **See Figures 35, 36 and 37**

The injectors in all CIS systems are purely mechanical and open at a predetermined pressure. All injectors are open when the engine is running, injecting fuel to the intake ports continuously. The spray pattern is critical to good atomization of the fuel, which will affect power and emissions. The injectors can be tested for spray pattern and leakage with tool US 4480 or equivalent. This is a set of clear, graduated cylinders that allow viewing the spray pattern and measuring the fuel flow.

✳✳ CAUTION

The following procedure will produce fuel vapors. Make sure there is proper ventilation and take the appropriate fire safety precautions. Fuel will be sprayed from the injectors at high pressure. Do not point the injector at anything except the test tube.

Fig. 32 A small prytool can be used to remove the injectors

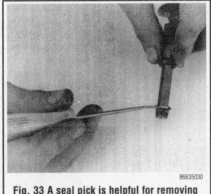

Fig. 33 A seal pick is helpful for removing the small O-ring

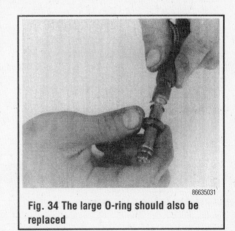

Fig. 34 The large O-ring should also be replaced

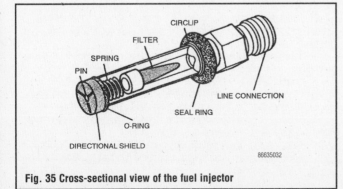

Fig. 35 Cross-sectional view of the fuel injector

1. Remove the injectors by prying them out of the head. Inspect the injectors for signs of leakage. They should not be wet.
2. Carefully route the fuel lines so the injectors can be inserted into the tubes.
3. Locate and remove the fuel pump relay on the main fuse panel. Install tool US 4480/3 in the fuel pump relay socket. This is essentially a jumper wire with a switch used to turn on the fuel pump. The fuel pump will run any time the switch is ON.
4. Remove the airflow sensor boot and insert a 0.020–0.040 inch (0.50–1.0mm) feeler gauge between the airflow sensor plate and the housing so the plate is slightly lifted.
5. Operate the fuel pump and observe the spray pattern. It should be a narrow conical pattern, even all the way around. Move the sensor plate up higher to see how the pattern changes. Any irregularity in the pattern indicates a partially clogged injector. Raising the sensor plate all the way may clear it.

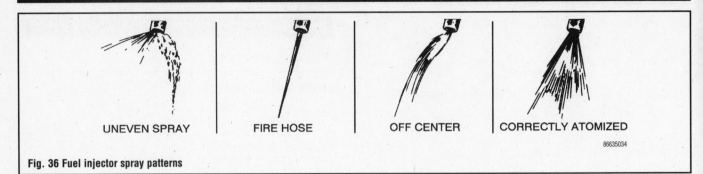

UNEVEN SPRAY | FIRE HOSE | OFF CENTER | CORRECTLY ATOMIZED

86635034

Fig. 36 Fuel injector spray patterns

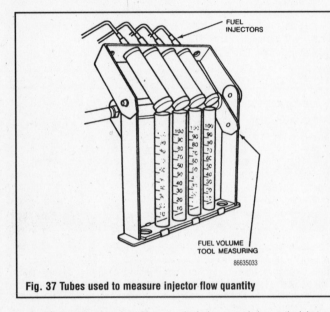

Fig. 37 Tubes used to measure injector flow quantity

6. After one tube has about 20cc, stop the fuel pump and observe the injectors. Note the quantity of fuel in each tube; they should all be within 2cc of each other.

7. Repeat the test with the sensor plate all the way up to flow about 80cc of fuel. The flows should all be within 8cc.

8. If an injector flows high or low, move it to another line and flow test them again. If the incorrect flow follows the injector, the injector is faulty. If the incorrect flow stays with the same fuel line, the line or the fuel distributor is faulty.

9. To leak test the injectors, remove the feeler gauge so the sensor plate is resting on its stop and run the fuel pump. There should be no fuel dripping from any injector. Any injector with a bad spray pattern, leak or incorrect flow quantity must be replaced.

Fuel Distributor

REMOVAL & INSTALLATION

▶ **See Figure 38**

1. Disconnect the negative battery cable.
2. Relieve the fuel system pressure.
3. Clean any dirt away from the fuel fittings.
4. Mark the fuel lines in the top of the distributor so that you will be able to put them back in their correct positions.
5. Remove the fittings and disconnect the fuel lines from the fuel distributor. Have a rag ready to catch the fuel that escapes.
6. Remove the screws to lift the distributor from the airflow sensor housing.

➡**When removing the fuel distributor on CIS engines, be sure the control plunger does not fall out from underneath.**

To install:

7. On CIS-E engines, check the stop screw adjustment if a new fuel distributor is being installed.

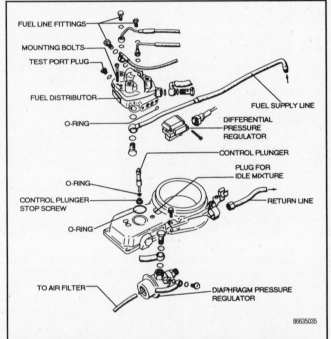

Fig. 38 The fuel distributor is mounted on top of the airflow sensor

8. Install the fuel distributor on the airflow sensor housing with a new O-ring. If the control plunger has been removed, moisten it with gasoline before installing. The small shoulder on the plunger is inserted first. Tighten the screws until snug.

9. Use new sealing washers and connect the fuel lines to the distributor. Torque the smaller fittings to 7 ft. lbs. (10 Nm). and the larger fittings to 15 ft. lbs. (20 Nm).

10. Connect the battery cable.

ADJUSTMENT

▶ **See Figure 39**

➡**These adjustments are only necessary on CIS-E engines.**

1. Use a depth caliper to measure the distance from the shoulder of the gland nut to the stop screw. Distance (a) should be about 0.024 inches (0.6mm).

2. Turn the stop screw in or out as required. Turning the screw in ¼ turn will increase the installed free-play by 0.050 inches. (1.3mm).

3. Install the fuel distributor.

4. Remove the air inlet boot from the sensor plate and operate the starter for about 10 seconds to build fuel system pressure. The engine will not start.

5. Measure the distance from the top of the airflow sensor housing to the sensor plate at the point nearest the fuel distributor.

6. Use a magnet on the sensor plate bolt to lift the plate until resistance is felt. There should be a minimum of at least some free-play movement to a maximum of 0.074 in. (2mm).

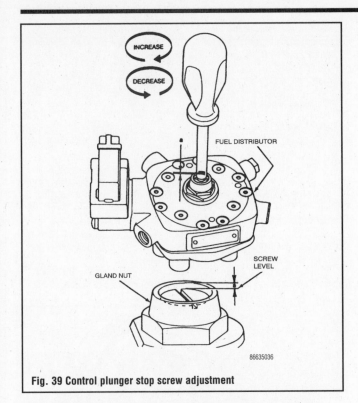

Fig. 39 Control plunger stop screw adjustment

7. If the free-play is not as specified, remove the fuel distributor and check the sensor plate lever basic adjustment. This can be measured with a depth caliper between the fuel distributor contact surface and the roller on the sensor lever. On 4-cylinder models, the specification is approximately 0.748 in. (19mm), on 5-cylinder models it is approximately 0.827 in. (21mm). If adjustment is necessary, remove the mixture adjusting screw plug and adjust as follows:

    a. Center-punch the mixture adjusting screw plug.

    b. Drill a 3/32 in. (2.5mm) hole approximately 5/32 in. (4mm) deep in the center of the plug. It is helpful to apply a small amount of grease to the drill bit to catch the metal shavings.

    c. Thread a 1/8 in. (3mm) sheet metal screw into the hole.

    d. Remove the plug using a pair of pliers.

    e. Insert tool P377 or a 3mm Allen wrench into the hole, then adjust the sensor plate lever basic setting until it is within specification. Drive a new mixture adjusting screw plug into the hole.

8. If the sensor plate basic adjustment was correct, adjust the free-play with the stop screw on the bottom of the fuel distributor. Turn it clockwise to increase free-play or counterclockwise to decrease free-play. A 1/4 turn will change free-play by about 0.050 in. (1.3mm).

Control Pressure Regulator

REMOVAL & INSTALLATION

1. Disconnect the negative battery cable.
2. Relieve the fuel system pressure.
3. Unplug the electrical connection on the control regulator.
4. Remove the union bolts securing the fuel lines to the regulator. Have a rag ready to catch the fuel that escapes.
5. Remove the bolts securing the regulator, then remove it from the engine block.

To install:

6. Install the pressure regulator to the engine block. Tighten the bolts to 15 ft. lbs. (20 Nm).
7. Connect the fuel lines to the regulator using new seal washers. Tighten the large union bolt to 15 ft. lbs. (20 Nm) and the small bolt to 7 ft. lbs. (10 Nm).
8. Engage the electrical connection.
9. Connect the battery cable.

Differential Pressure Regulator

REMOVAL & INSTALLATION

▶ See Figure 40

1. Disconnect the negative battery cable.
2. Unplug the electrical connector from the regulator.
3. Clean any dirt away from the regulator.
4. Remove the screws securing the regulator, then remove the regulator from the fuel distributor.

To install:

5. Install the pressure regulator with new O-rings. If the screws must be replaced, make sure they are made of a non-magnetic material.
6. Tighten the screws until snug. Engage the electrical connection on the regulator.
7. Connect the battery cable.

Fig. 40 The differential pressure regulator is secured to the side of the fuel distributor with screws. Also note the location of the diaphragm pressure regulator positioned to the right of it

Diaphragm Pressure Regulator

REMOVAL & INSTALLATION

1. Disconnect the negative battery cable.
2. Relieve the fuel system pressure.
3. Disconnect the vacuum hose and fuel lines from the diaphragm pressure regulator, then remove the regulator from the vehicle.

To install:

4. Connect the fuel lines to the regulator. Always use new sealing washers.
5. Connect the vacuum hose to the regulator.
6. Connect the battery cable.

Airflow Sensor Potentiometer

REMOVAL & INSTALLATION

1. Disconnect the negative battery cable.
2. Unplug the electrical connection from the potentiometer.
3. Remove the screws securing the potentiometer, then remove it from the airflow sensor assembly.

To install:

4. Install the potentiometer on the airflow sensor. Thread the screws in, but they should still be loose.

5. Engage the electrical connection.
6. Adjust the potentiometer.
7. Connect the battery cable.

ADJUSTMENT

4-Cylinder Models

▶ **See Figures 41, 42 and 43**

1. Lift the sensor plate up to the lower edge (on the fuel distributor side) of the airflow sensor. This can be done with tool VW 1348/1.
2. Connect jumper harness VW 1501 between the potentiometer and the connector. Connect a voltmeter to terminals 2 and 3 on 16-valve engines and to terminal 2 and ground on other models. Switch the meter to the DC 20 volt range.

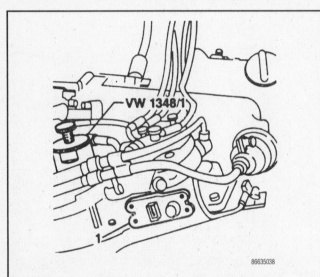

Fig. 41 Tool VW 1348/1 can be used to lift the sensor plate

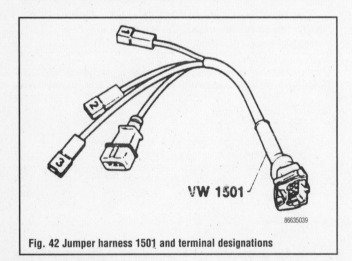

Fig. 42 Jumper harness 1501 and terminal designations

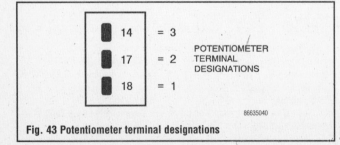

		POTENTIOMETER TERMINAL DESIGNATIONS
14	= 3	
17	= 2	
18	= 1	

Fig. 43 Potentiometer terminal designations

3. Turn the ignition **ON**. Adjust the potentiometer so that the meter displays between 0.02–0.2 volts on 16-valve engines and 0.2–0.3 volts on other models, then tighten the screws.
4. Lift the sensor plate up to its stop. The meter should display approximately 7 volts. Lock the screws with a sealing compound or paint.

5-Cylinder Models

▶ **See Figure 44**

1. Place tool VW 1348/1 centrally on the edge of the airflow sensor assembly. Pointer (3) faces the center of the fuel distributor.
2. Push the adjusting slide (2) down onto its stop. Turn setting screw (1) clockwise until the magnetic end contacts the airflow sensor plate retaining bolt.
3. Connect jumper harness VW 1501 between the potentiometer and the connector. Connect a voltmeter to terminals 2 and 3 of the harness. Switch the meter to the DC 20 volt range.
4. Turn the ignition **ON**. Pull slide (2) of the adjusting device into the first detent (idle position). Adjust the potentiometer until 0.2–0.5 volts is displayed. Tighten the potentiometer adjusting screws.
5. Pull slide (2) into the second detent (full throttle position). The meter should display 4–4.5 volts. Lock the screws with a sealing compound or paint.

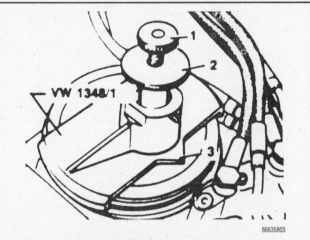

Fig. 44 Using tool VW 1348/1 to adjust the airflow sensor potentiometer on 5-cylinder engines

Idle Air Controls

REMOVAL & INSTALLATION

▶ **See Figures 45 and 46**

The idle boost valves and auxiliary air regulator (on CIS systems), as well as the idle air stabilizer (on CIS-E and Digifant systems), can be removed using the same basic procedure.
1. Disconnect the negative battery cable.
2. Label and disconnect the hoses and the electrical connection from the valve.
3. Remove the nuts/bolts securing the valve, then remove the valve.
4. Installation is the reverse of removal.

Cold Start Injector

▶ **See Figure 47**

REMOVAL & INSTALLATION

1. Disconnect the negative battery cable.
2. Relieve the fuel system pressure.
3. Unplug the electrical connector from the injector.

Fig. 45 Unplug the necessary hoses and electrical connections, then remove any nuts/bolts securing the valve (CIS-E idle air stabilizer shown)

Fig. 46 Removing the idle air stabilizer from the engine

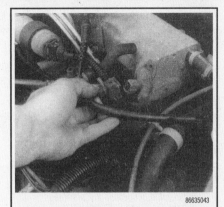

Fig. 47 Unplugging the electrical connection from the cold start injector

4. Disconnect the fuel line from the injector.
5. Remove the bolts securing the injector, then remove it from the intake manifold.

To install:
6. Using new gaskets, connect the fuel line to the injector and install it in the intake manifold. Tighten the fuel line bolt and injector securing bolts to 7 ft. lbs. (10 Nm).
7. Engage the electrical connector on the injector.
8. Connect the battery cable.

Airflow Sensor

REMOVAL & INSTALLATION

1. Disconnect the negative battery cable.
2. Remove the air intake boot from the top of the airflow sensor.
3. Remove the fuel distributor.
4. Remove the screws securing the airflow sensor to the air filter housing, then remove the sensor assembly.

To install:
5. Position the airflow sensor on top of the air filter housing with a new gasket. Tighten the screws until snug.
6. Install the fuel distributor with a new gasket.
7. Install the air intake boot on the sensor assembly. If the sensor assembly is equipped with a protective screen, make sure the dome points upwards towards the air intake boot, not towards the sensor plate.
8. Connect the battery cable.

TESTING & ADJUSTMENT

▶ **See Figures 48 and 49**

➡For the sensor plate lever basic adjustment procedure, refer to the fuel distributor adjustment procedures. This adjustment should be checked anytime the fuel distributor or airflow sensor is replaced.

1. On vehicles without electronic ignition, unplug the center wire from the distributor and ground it. On models with electronic ignition, unplug the connector from the Hall sending unit on the distributor. This will disable the ignition system.
2. Remove the air intake boot from the sensor assembly.
3. Crank the engine for about 10 seconds. This will pressurize the fuel system.

➡The sensor plate must be centered in the air cone. If it is not, loosen the centering bolt slightly, then run a 0.004 in. (0.10mm) feeler gauge around the perimeter of the air gap (between the sensor plate and air cone). Retighten the bolt.

4. Lift the sensor plate with a magnet. Over its entire travel, an even resistance should be felt. Move the sensor plate quickly from the raised position to its rest. No resistance should be felt. If resistance is felt, the airflow sensor must

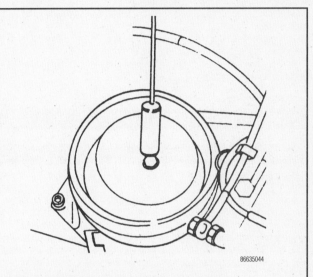

Fig. 48 A magnet can be used to lift the sensor plate

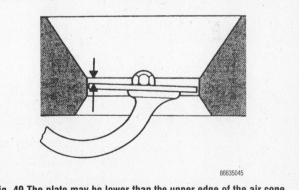

Fig. 49 The plate may be lower than the upper edge of the air cone, but not more than 0.019 in. (0.5mm)

be replaced. If the plate is hard to move upwards, but moves freely downwards, the control plunger in the fuel distributor is sticking. Replace the fuel distributor.
5. Install the air intake boot.
6. Enable the ignition system, then run the engine to normal operating temperature.
7. Once again, disable the ignition system, then operate the starter for 10 seconds. Remove the air intake boot from the sensor assembly.
8. Check the sensor plate rest position. The upper edge of the sensor plate must be flush with the edge of the air cone.

9. If it is too high, adjust the air sensor plate position. The plate may be lower than the upper edge of the air cone, but not more than 0.019 in. (0.5 mm). To adjust the sensor plate:

a. Carefully lift the sensor plate.

b. Adjust the plate by bending the wire, NOT the small leaf spring.

10. Install the air intake boot and enable the ignition system.

11. Adjust the idle speed.

Air/Fuel Mixture Adjustment

ADJUSTMENT

The air/fuel mixture is measured by sampling the exhaust with a CO meter. If this equipment is not available, no checking or adjustment is possible. Since adjusting the mixture is not part of a normal tune-up, the adjusting screw is protected with a tamper-proof plug. If the air/fuel ratio is obviously incorrect (lean miss, sooty spark plugs and tail pipe), or if the CO measurement is out of specification, look for other problems such as a vacuum leak, bad sensors, loose electrical connections, and correct any faults before deciding to adjusting the mixture.

1. With the engine at normal operating temperature, make sure the ignition timing and idle speed are correct. Stop the engine.

2. Disconnect the crank case breather hose and move it so only fresh air can enter.

3. Insert the CO meter probe into the CO test point at the back of the engine compartment, a metal tube with a plastic cap. Make sure the probe is a tight fit and will not draw in outside air.

4. Start the engine and turn OFF all lights and accessories. If any fuel injection lines have been disconnected, rev the engine to 3000 rpm, 2–3 times to clear any air from the system.

5. The CO reading should be between 0.2–1.2 percent. Stop the engine.

6. If the CO reading is not correct, remove the mixture adjusting screw plug as follows:

a. Center-punch the mixture adjusting screw plug.

b. Drill a 3/32 in. (2.5mm) hole approximately 5/32 in. (4mm) deep in the center of the plug. It is helpful to apply a small amount of grease to the drill bit to catch the metal shavings.

c. Thread a 1/8 in. (3mm) sheet metal screw into the hole.

d. Remove the plug using a pair of pliers.

❋❋ WARNING

DO NOT accelerate the engine with the adjusting tool in place. Damage to the airflow sensor unit will result.

7. Start the engine and run it at idle, then insert tool P377 or a 3mm Allen wrench into the hole. Adjust the screw slightly (clockwise increases the CO reading), then remove the adjusting tool. Briefly accelerate the engine and check the CO reading again. Continue adjusting until the CO reading is within specification.

8. Drive a new mixture adjusting screw plug into the hole.

DIGIFANT II FUEL INJECTION SYSTEM

General Description

▶ **See Figure 50**

The Digifant system is all electronic, using electric injectors at a relatively low injection pressure. All injectors are operated by the Electronic Control Unit (ECU), so injector opening timing and duration can be closely controlled for reduced emissions and improved fuel mileage. During deceleration above about 1500 rpm, the injectors are shut off to save fuel and reduce emissions. The system uses an air vane and potentiometer type airflow sensor and an inlet air temperature sensor to calculate air flow into the engine. An idle stabilizer valve is used to control idle speed. This is a motorized rotary valve that controls the amount of air allowed to bypass the throttle plate.

The fuel pump is mounted in a reservoir under the vehicle along with the filter. The reservoir holds about 1 liter of fuel and is supplied by a small transfer pump in the fuel tank. The transfer pump is part of the fuel gauge sending unit assembly but it can be replaced separately.

The electric fuel injectors are secured in place by the fuel rail, which also houses the wiring. All injectors are wired together in parallel and are operated at the same time. Power is supplied to all injectors any time the ECU is receiving an rpm signal.

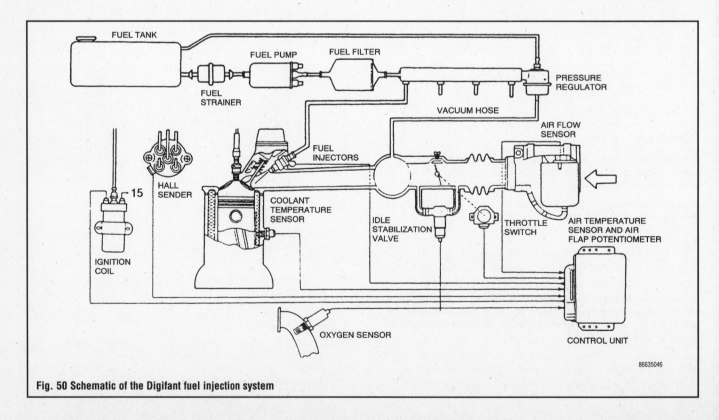

Fig. 50 Schematic of the Digifant fuel injection system

86635046

Other components in the Digifant system include the oxygen sensor, a coolant temperature sensor, a throttle position switch, the idle air stabilizer valve, the fuel system pressure regulator and the ignition system.

Relieving Fuel System Pressure

Before working on any components of the fuel system, any residual pressure should be relieved first to limit the possibility of injury or fire. This can be done by loosening the service port bolt at the end of the fuel rail. Hold a rag at the fitting to catch the spray, loosen the fuel line bolt, then tighten it again. Do not over tighten the fitting or the copper sealing washer will split.

❊❊ CAUTION

Most of the following procedures will produce fuel vapors. Make sure there is proper ventilation and take the appropriate fire safety precautions.

Fuel Pumps

REMOVAL & INSTALLATION

Transfer Pump

1. Disconnect the negative battery cable.
2. Remove the rear seat and the access cover.
3. Disconnect the wiring and hoses, then unscrew the lock ring.
4. Carefully lift out the pump and gauge sending unit assembly.
5. Installation is the reverse of removal. When installing the assembly, use a new seal.

Main Pump

▶ **See Figure 51**

1. Disconnect the negative battery cable.
2. Relieve the fuel system pressure.
3. Raise and safely support the rear of the vehicle on jackstands.
4. Disconnect the wiring from the pump. Clean any dirt away from the fuel line fitting.

5. Use locking pliers to pinch off the fuel line from the transfer pump to the main pump. If the fuel line is metal, remove the rear seat and access panel, then disconnect the line at the transfer pump.
6. Place a pan under the pump and disconnect the fuel line fitting from the pump.
7. Remove the retaining ring screws and slide the pump out of the reservoir.
   To install:
8. Moisten the pump O-ring with a little fuel, then slide it into the reservoir. Install the retaining ring screws.
9. When connecting the fittings, use new copper washers and torque the fittings to 15 ft. lbs. (20 Nm).
10. Connect the battery cable.

TESTING

Operating Test

1. Have an assistant operate the starter. Listen near the fuel pump location to determine if the pump is running.
2. If the pump is not running, check the wiring and the fuse on the front of the fuel pump relay.
3. If the fuse is good, replace the fuel pump relay.
4. If the fuel pump still does not operate, and you're sure there are no loose connections in the wiring, the fuel pump is faulty and must be replaced.

Pressure and Delivery Test

1. Connect tool VW 1318 or an equivalent fuel pressure gauge to the fuel line T-piece. If equipped, the fuel shut-off lever on the gauge must be in a closed position.
2. Locate and remove the fuel pump relay. Install tool US 4480/3 in the fuel pump relay socket. This is essentially a jumper wire with a switch used to turn on the fuel pump. The fuel pump will run any time the switch is ON.
3. Run fuel pump and observe the pressure reading. It must be a minimum of 36 psi. Shut the fuel pump OFF, then relieve the fuel system pressure.
4. Be sure that the fuel tank is at least half full of fuel. Disconnect fuel return line at pressure regulator.
5. Disconnect the fuel return line at the pressure regulator, then plug it with the cap from the CO measuring tube or any other suitable plug.

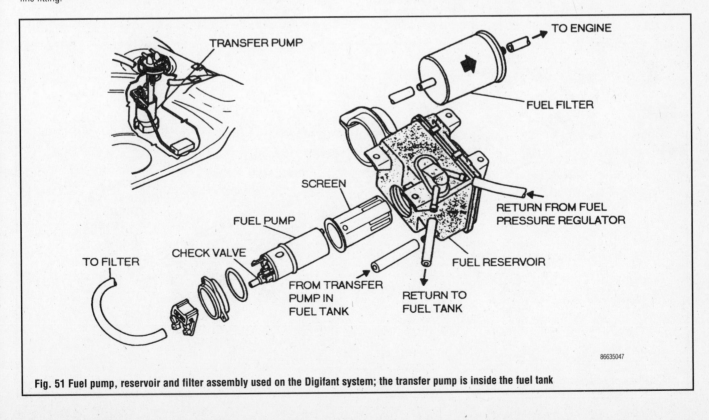

Fig. 51 Fuel pump, reservoir and filter assembly used on the Digifant system; the transfer pump is inside the fuel tank

6. Attach a 4 ft. (123cm) length of fuel line to the return port of the pressure regulator. Place other end of the fuel line into a 1 liter measuring container.

7. Run the fuel pump for exactly 30 seconds. Delivery quantity should be at least 300cc.

8. If delivery quantity is not within specification, check the fuel flow from the tank before and after the fuel filters.

Throttle Body

REMOVAL & INSTALLATION

1. Disconnect the negative battery cable.
2. Remove the air intake hose from the throttle body.
3. Label and disconnect the vacuum hoses from the throttle body.
4. Disconnect the accelerator cable from the throttle body.
5. Remove the bolts securing the throttle body, then remove it.
6. Clean the gasket mating surface and discard the old gasket.

To install:

7. Install the throttle body with a new gasket.
8. Thread the bolts in by hand first, then tighten them to 15 ft. lbs. (20 Nm).
9. Connect the vacuum hoses and accelerator cable to the throttle body.
10. Adjust the throttle valve basic setting and the throttle cable.
11. Install the air intake hose.
12. Adjust the idle speed.
13. Connect the battery cable.

ADJUSTMENTS

Basic Setting

1. Unplug the vacuum hose from the carbon canister control valve on the throttle body. Install a vacuum gauge to the fitting on the throttle body.
2. Start the engine and let it idle. At idle, there should be 0 inches of Hg; however up to 1 inch is acceptable. If it is greater than this, the throttle valve must be adjusted.
3. Back the throttle valve adjusting screw out until a gap occurs between the screw and the throttle stop.
4. Slide a thin piece of paper between the screw and the throttle stop. Turn the screw in until the paper will not slide out, plus an additional ½ turn.
5. Repeat the vacuum test.

Accelerator Cable

Refer to the accelerator cable adjustments outlined in the CIS/CIS-E systems.

Fuel Injectors

REMOVAL & INSTALLATION

▶ **See Figure 52**

1. Disconnect the negative battery cable.
2. Remove the fuel rail assembly.
3. Remove the retaining clip securing the injector to the fuel rail.
4. Pull the injector out of the fuel rail assembly.

To install:

5. Replace the O-rings on the injector. Coat them lightly with gasoline.
6. Carefully push the injector into the fuel rail assembly.
7. Secure the injector with the retaining clip.
8. Connect the battery cable.

Fuel Rail

REMOVAL & INSTALLATION

▶ **See Figure 52**

1. Disconnect the negative battery cable and relieve the pressure from the fuel system.
2. Disconnect the fuel supply and return lines.
3. Dismount the idle stabilizer valve and lay it aside.
4. Unplug the wiring harness end connector and pry wiring guide away from its retainers.
5. Remove the fuel rail securing bolts, then remove the rail, wiring guide, pressure regulator and injectors as an assembly.

To install:

6. Install new O-rings on the injectors and coat them lightly with gasoline.
7. Install the fuel rail assembly on the engine. Tighten the securing bolts to 7 ft. lbs. (10 Nm).
8. Engage the wiring guide into the retainers, then connect the wiring harness.
9. Mount the idle stabilizer valve.

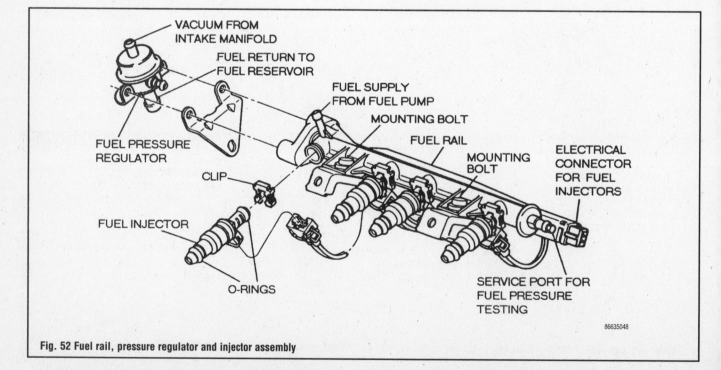

Fig. 52 Fuel rail, pressure regulator and injector assembly

86635048

10. Connect the fuel lines and the negative battery cable.
11. Start the engine and check for leaks.

Pressure Regulator

REMOVAL & INSTALLATION

▶ **See Figure 52**

The regulator can be removed without removing the fuel rail assembly. When installing the regulator, use a new O-ring and hose clamp.

1. Disconnect the negative battery cable and relieve the fuel system pressure.
2. Disconnect the vacuum hose from the pressure regulator.
3. Slide the spring clamps up the hose (away from the connections), then disconnect the hoses from the pressure regulator. Discard the clamps.
4. Remove the bolts securing the pressure regulator, then pull it out from the fuel rail. Discard the O-ring.

To install:

5. Install a new O-ring on the pressure regulator. Lightly coat the O-ring with gasoline.
6. Carefully push the pressure regulator into the fuel rail. Tighten the securing bolts to 11 ft. lbs. (15 Nm).
7. Connect the fuel hoses to the pressure regulator using new clamps.
8. Connect the vacuum hose to the pressure regulator and the negative battery cable.
9. Start the engine and check for leaks.

Airflow Sensor

REMOVAL & INSTALLATION

1. Disconnect the negative battery cable.
2. Disconnect the air intake hose from the airflow sensor.
3. Unplug the electrical connection on the side of the airflow sensor.
4. Disconnect the vacuum hoses from the air filter housing cover, then remove the cover/sensor assembly.
5. Remove the bolts securing the sensor to the cover. Discard the seal.

To install:

6. Using a new seal, install the sensor on the cover. Tighten the bolts until snug.

➡**Do not overtighten the bolts as this may damage the sensor and/or the cover.**

7. Install the cover/sensor assembly on the air filter housing. Connect the vacuum hoses to the cover.
8. Engage the electrical connection on the side of the sensor.
9. Connect the air intake hose to the airflow sensor.
10. Connect the battery cable.

Throttle Switches

REMOVAL & INSTALLATION

The throttle switches are held in place with screws and are slotted for adjustment. Make sure the idle switch is closed when the throttle in in idle position. The full throttle switch should be closed for the last 10 degrees of throttle movement.

Idle Air Stabilizer

REMOVAL & INSTALLATION

▶ **See Figures 45 and 46**

1. Disconnect the negative battery cable.
2. Label and disconnect the hoses and the electrical connection from the valve.
3. Remove the nuts/bolts securing the valve, then remove the valve.
4. Installation is the reverse of removal.

Air/Fuel Mixture Adjustment

ADJUSTMENT

The air/fuel mixture is measured by sampling the exhaust with a CO meter. If this equipment is not available, no checking or adjustment is possible. Since adjusting the mixture is not part of a normal tune-up, the adjusting screw is protected with a tamper-proof plug. If the air/fuel ratio is obviously incorrect (lean miss, sooty spark plugs and tailpipe), or if the CO measurement is out of specification, look for other problems such as a vacuum leak, bad sensors, loose electrical connections, and correct any faults before deciding to adjusting the mixture.

1. With the engine at normal operating temperature, make sure the ignition timing and idle speed are correct. Stop the engine.
2. Unplug the blue coolant temperature sensor connector.
3. Raise the dipstick slightly to allow for crankcase ventilation. Clamp the crankcase breather hose near its control valve.
4. Start the engine and measure the CO content; it must read 0.3–1.1 percent. If adjustment is necessary, remove the mixture adjusting screw plug as follows:
   a. Center-punch the mixture adjusting screw plug.
   b. Drill a 3/32 in. (2.5mm) hole approximately 5/32 in. (4mm) deep in the center of the plug. It is helpful to apply a small amount of grease to the drill bit to catch the metal shavings.
   c. Thread a 1/8 in. (3mm) sheet metal screw into the hole.
   d. Remove the plug using a pair of pliers.
5. Insert a 5mm Allen wrench in the hole. Adjust the CO to the proper level following the graph.
6. When adjustment is completed, carefully drive a new plug into the adjusting hole.

DIESEL FUEL SYSTEM

The diesel fuel system is an extremely complex and sensitive system. Very few repairs or adjustments are possible by the owner. Any service other than that listed here should be referred to an authorized VW dealer or diesel specialist. Injection pump repair requires experience, very expensive calibration/test equipment and a large number of special tools. This type of work should be referred to a shop that specializes in diesel engine injection pump overhaul.

Any work performed to the diesel fuel injection system should be done with absolute cleanliness. Even the smallest specks of dirt will have a disastrous effect on the injection system.

The fuel in the system is also under tremendous pressure (1,700–1,850 psi), so it's not wise to loosen any lines with the engine running. Exposing your skin to the spray from the injector at working pressure can cause fuel to penetrate the skin.

Fuel System Service Precautions

- Do not allow fuel spray or fuel vapors to come into contact with a heating element or open flame. Do not smoke while working on the fuel system.

• To control fuel spills, place a shop towel around the fitting prior to loosening to catch the spray. Ensure that all fuel spillage is quickly wiped up and that fuel soaked rags are deposited into a fire safe container.

• Always use a backup wrench when loosening and tightening fuel line fittings. Always follow the proper torque specifications.

• Do not re-use fuel system gaskets and O-rings; replace with new ones. Do not substitute fuel hose where fuel pipe is installed.

• Cleanliness is absolutely essential. Clean all fittings before opening them and maintain a dust free work area while the system is open.

• Place removed parts on a clean surface and cover with paper or plastic to keep them clean. Do not cover with rags that can leave fuzz on the parts.

Fuel Injection Lines

REMOVAL & INSTALLATION

1. Disconnect the negative battery cable.
2. The lines should be removed as a set. Loosen the fittings at each injector with a line or flare nut wrench.
3. Use a back-up wrench to loosen the lines from the injection pump.
4. Remove the lines as a set and cap the injectors and pump fittings immediately.

To install:

5. Make sure the flares on the lines are not split or flattened. If so, the line should be replaced. They can be purchased or made up separately but are usually replaced as a set.
6. Fit the lines into place and start all the nuts. Use a back-up wrench and torque the line nuts at the pump to 18 ft. lbs. (25 Nm). Do not over torque the nuts or the flares will split and the line will leak.

➡It will be necessary to use a crow's foot attachment on the torque wrench to properly tighten the fittings.

7. Torque the nuts at the nozzle end to 18 ft. lbs. (25 Nm).
8. Connect the battery cable.

Injectors

REMOVAL & INSTALLATION

▶ **See Figures 53 and 54**

1. Disconnect the negative battery cable.
2. Loosen the injector lines using a line or flare nut wrench.

➡Remove the injector lines as a complete set. DO NOT attempt to bend or alter the configuration of the lines in any way. These lines are preformed for precise flow.

3. Remove the injectors from the cylinder head using tool US 2775 or an equivalent deep socket.
4. Remove the injector heat shields from the cylinder head. This should be done as part of an injector replacement.

To install:

5. Install new heat shields into the head with the concave portion facing down (as shown in the illustration).
6. Install the injectors into the head, then torque to 51 ft. lbs. (70 Nm).
7. Connect the injector lines and torque the line nuts to 18 ft. lbs. (25 Nm). It will be necessary to use a crow's foot attachment on the torque wrench to properly tighten the fittings.
8. Connect the battery cable.

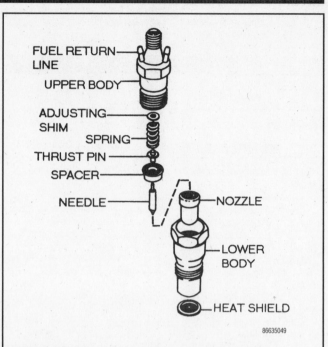

Fig. 53 Exploded view of an injector used on diesel engines

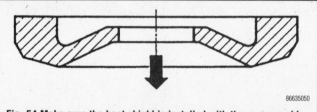

Fig. 54 Make sure the heat shield is installed with the concave side down

Fuel Supply Pump

REMOVAL & INSTALLATION

1. Disconnect the negative battery cable.
2. Remove the rear seat and the access cover. If there is no access cover, it will be necessary to remove the fuel tank to access the pump.
3. Disconnect the wiring and hoses and unscrew the lock ring.
4. Carefully lift out the pump and gauge sending unit assembly.
5. Installation is the reverse of removal. When installing the assembly, use a new seal.

Diesel Injection Pump

REMOVAL & INSTALLATION

▶ **See Figure 55**

➡Read through this entire procedure before proceeding. Special tools are required for injection pump installation. Do not remove the pump without these tools on hand.

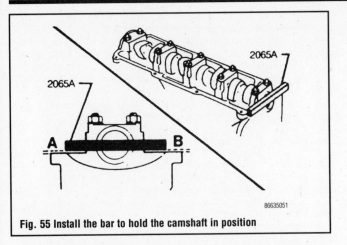

Fig. 55 Install the bar to hold the camshaft in position

1. Disconnect the negative battery cable and remove the air cleaner, cylinder head cover and timing belt cover.

2. Turn the engine to TDC of No. 1 cylinder and insert a setting bar into the slot on the rear of the camshaft, VW tool 2065A or equivalent, to hold the camshaft in place. Remove the timing belt. Be careful to not turn the engine while the belt is removed.

3. Loosen the pump drive sprocket nut but don't remove it yet. Install a puller on the sprocket and apply moderate tension.

4. Rap the puller bolt with light hammer taps until the sprocket jumps off the tapered shaft, then remove the puller and sprocket. Be careful not to lose the Woodruff key.

5. Hold the pump fittings with a wrench and using a line wrench, remove the injection lines from the pump. Cap the pump fittings to keep dirt out. It may be easier to remove the lines from the injectors also and set them aside as an assembly. Cap the injector fittings to keep dirt out.

6. Disconnect the control cables, fuel solenoid wire and fuel supply and return lines.

7. Remove the pump mounting bolts and lift the pump from the vehicle.

To install:

8. When reinstalling, align the marks on the top of the mounting flange and the pump and torque the mounting bolts to 18 ft. lbs. (25 Nm).

9. Install the Woodruff key and sprocket and torque the nut to 33 ft. lbs. (45 Nm).

10. When reinstalling the supply and return lines, be sure the fitting marked OUT is used for the return line. This fitting has an orifice and must be in the correct place. Use new gaskets.

11. Turn the pump sprocket so the mark aligns with the mark on the side of the mounting flange and insert a pin through the hole in the sprocket to hold it in place.

12. Install the camshaft drive sprocket and belt and set the belt tension. Tension the drive belt by turning the tensioner pulley clockwise until belt can be flexed ½ in. (13mm) between the camshaft and the pump sprockets. Remove the pin.

13. Remove the camshaft holding bar. Turn the engine through 2 full turns, return to TDC of No. 1 cylinder and recheck the belt tension and camshaft timing.

14. Reinstall the injection lines, wiring and control cables. Torque the line nuts to 18 ft. lbs. (25 Nm).

15. Connect the battery cable.

ADJUSTMENTS

Accelerator Cable

The ball pin on the pump lever should be pointing up and be aligned with the mark in the slot. The accelerator cable should be attached at the upper hole in the bracket. With the pedal in the full throttle position, adjust the cable so that the pump lever contacts the stop without any binding or strain.

Cold Start Cable

♦ See Figure 56

When the cold start knob on the dash is pulled out, the fuel injection pump timing is advanced 2.5 degrees. This improves cold starting and running until the engine warms up.

1. Insert the washer on the cable.

2. Insert the cable in the bracket with the rubber bushing. Install the cable in the pin.

3. Install the lockwasher.

4. Move the lever to the zero position (direction of arrow). Pull the inner cable taut and tighten the clamp screw.

INJECTION PUMP TIMING

♦ See Figure 57

1. Turn the engine to TDC of the No. 1 cylinder.

2. Make sure the pump control lever is fully against the low idle stop. If equipped with a manual cold start knob, make sure the knob is all the way in against the stop.

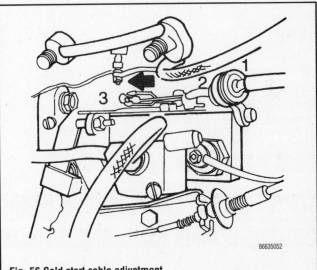

Fig. 56 Cold start cable adjustment

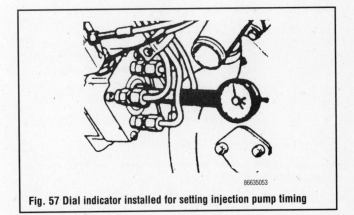

Fig. 57 Dial indicator installed for setting injection pump timing

3. Remove the center plug on the pump head, then install tool VW 2066 or an equivalent adaptor tool, and a dial indicator. Preload the dial indicator to 2.5mm.

4. Slowly turn the engine counterclockwise until the dial gauge stops moving, then zero the dial indicator. This is the bottom of the pump stroke.

5. Turn the engine clockwise until the TDC mark on the flywheel aligns with the pointer on the bell housing.

6. The dial indicator should read 0.036–0.038 in. (0.90–0.95mm) for diesel engines or 0.038–0.040 in. (0.95–1.00mm) for turbo-diesel engines.

7. If adjustment is required, remove the timing belt cover and loosen the pump mounting bolts without turning the engine.

8. Turn the pump body until the dial indicator reads the correct value.

9. Torque the mounting bolts to 18 ft. lbs. (25 Nm) and turn the engine backwards about 1 turn. Turn the engine forwards to TDC of No. 1 cylinder and recheck the dial indicator.

10. When the correct setting is reached on the dial indicator, reinstall the belt cover and the center plug on the pump. Use a new copper gasket.

Glow Plugs

The 1982 and later diesels (except Turbo models) have a new "quick-glow" system. Nominal glow time is seven seconds. Although the wiring for this system is the same as the earlier system, the glow plugs and relay cannot be paired or interchanged with earlier parts or vice versa, except on 1978 Dashers. On these Dasher models, you can convert from the old type system to the new type by simply exchanging the old style plugs and relay with the new type.

TESTING

System Check

Quick-glow system plugs are identified by a brass nut on the plug wire terminals and by red lettering on the glow plug relay. Normal-glow system plugs are identified by an aluminum nut and white lettering.

1. Connect a test light between the No. 4 cylinder glow plug and a suitable engine ground. The glow plugs are connected by a flat, coated busbar (located near the bottom of the cylinder head).

2. Unplug the wire from the engine temperature sensor.

3. Turn the ignition key to the heating position for no more than 15 seconds. The test light should light.

4. There should be voltage to the glow plug for approximately five seconds after the glow plug indicator lamp goes out. Voltage is applied as a normal part of the controlled pre-heat period. If not, possible problems include the glow plug relay, ignition switch, glow plug fuse or a break in the wire to the relay terminal.

5. If the test lamp lights, perform the individual glow plug checks as described below.

Individual Glow Plug Test

1. Remove the wire and busbar from the glow plugs.
2. Connect a test light to the battery positive terminal.
3. Touch the test light probe to each glow plug in turn.
4. If the test lamp lights, the plug is good. If the test light does not light, replace the plug.

A common cause of glow plug failure is worn glow plug tips. This is due to faulty injector operation in the related cylinder. This type of condition has nothing to do with the operation of the glow plugs. If you find that you are constantly replacing glow plugs, and have eliminated all possible electrical faults, check the fuel injector(s) for damage or have the injectors pressure and leak tested by a diesel injector repair shop.

REMOVAL & INSTALLATION

1. Disconnect the negative battery cable.
2. Loosen the nut and disconnect the wire from the glow plug terminal.
3. Using the proper size deep socket, remove the plug from engine.
4. Install the new plug, then tighten it to 29 ft. lbs. (40 Nm) on Quantum, Rabbit and Dasher models, or 22 ft. lbs. (30 Nm) on Golf and Jetta models.

✳ WARNING

Do not exceed the specified torque when installing the glow plug. Doing so will close the plug ring gap and cause premature failure.

5. Connect the wire to the glow plug terminal, then tighten the nut until snug.
6. Connect the battery cable.

FUEL TANK

Tank Assembly

REMOVAL & INSTALLATION

Rabbit (Except Pick-up), Golf, Jetta and 1975–84 Scirocco

1. Disconnect the battery.
2. Remove the drain plug and empty the tank. Disconnect the remove fuel pump if removal of the pump is necessary to gain clearance to remove the tank.
3. Disconnect the parking brake cables at the parking brake lever.
4. If required, disconnect and plug the rear brake lines.
5. If required, remove the rear axle mounting nuts and pull the rear axle down.
6. Disconnect the sending unit ground wire, gauge wire and transfer pump wiring.
7. Loosen the clamps and pull off the fuel line(s).

➡**If more than one fuel line attaches to the sending unit, mark the lines to avoid confusion when assembly.**

8. Disconnect any other breather lines. Disconnect the filler pipe.

9. Remove the rubber exhaust hangers if they hinder removal of the fuel tank.

10. Remove the fuel tank straps and allow the tank to come down far enough to see if there are any other vent hoses to be disconnected.

11. After removing all vent hoses, remove the tank.

➡**Many earlier models do not have these vent lines.**

To install:

12. Raise and support the tank. If you have to connect any vent lines, do so at this time, before securing the tank straps. Make sure that all breather and vent lines are not kinked. Use new clamps on all connections.

13. Install the rubber exhaust hangers, if they were removed.
14. Connect the filler pipe and any breather lines.
15. Connect the fuel lines. Use new clamps on all connections.
16. Connect the transfer pump, gauge and sending unit wires.
17. Install the rear axle and tighten the rear axle nut to specification.
18. Connect the rear brake lines and bleed the brakes.
19. Connect the parking brake cables to the lever and adjust.
20. Install the fuel pump.
21. Install the drain plug and fill the tank.
22. Connect the negative battery cable.

Rabbit Pick-up

▶ **See Figure 58**

The fuel tank is located to the rear of the cab.
1. Disconnect the battery.
2. Drain the fuel from the tank using a conventional siphon.
3. Remove and match mark all hoses from the tank, except for the breather hose in the sending unit.
4. Remove the wires from the sending unit.
5. Loosen the straps holding the tank and unhook them from their brackets.
6. Lower the tank and unhook the vent hose in the sending unit.
7. Remove the fuel tank.

To install:
8. Raise and support the tank. Connect the vent hose and the sending unit wire. Connect and tighten the tank straps.
9. Connect the sending unit wires.
10. Connect the hoses to the tank.
11. Fill the tank and connect the negative battery cable.

Dasher and Quantum

1. Disconnect the negative battery cable.
2. Remove the trunk floor mat.
3. Drain the fuel tank.
4. Disconnect and label the fuel and overflow lines.

5. Disconnect the electrical plugs from the fuel tank gauge sending unit.
6. Detach the vent line from the tank.
7. Remove all the retaining bolts from the trunk floor.
8. Detach the filler tube from the tank filler neck and lower the tank.

To install:
9. Raise and support the tank. Connect the filler tube to the filler neck.
10. Install the trunk floor retaining bolts.
11. Connect the vent line to the tank.
12. Connect the fuel tank gauge sending unit wiring.
13. Connect the fuel lines. Use new clamps.
14. Install the trunk floor mat.
15. Fill the tank and connect the negative battery cable.
16. Reseal the edge of the lower trunk floor to prevent leaks.

Fox

1. Disconnect the negative battery cable.
2. Remove the luggage compartment cover.
3. Remove the access cover to the fuel gauge sending unit.
4. Disconnect the supply line to the main fuel pump.
5. Disconnect the return line to the fuel tank.
6. Unplug the fuel gauge and transfer pump connectors.
7. Using VW tool US 2021A or equivalent spanner wrench, unscrew the fuel gauge sending unit from the tank.
8. Siphon the fuel from the fuel gauge sending unit opening.
9. Raise the rear of the vehicle and support safely.

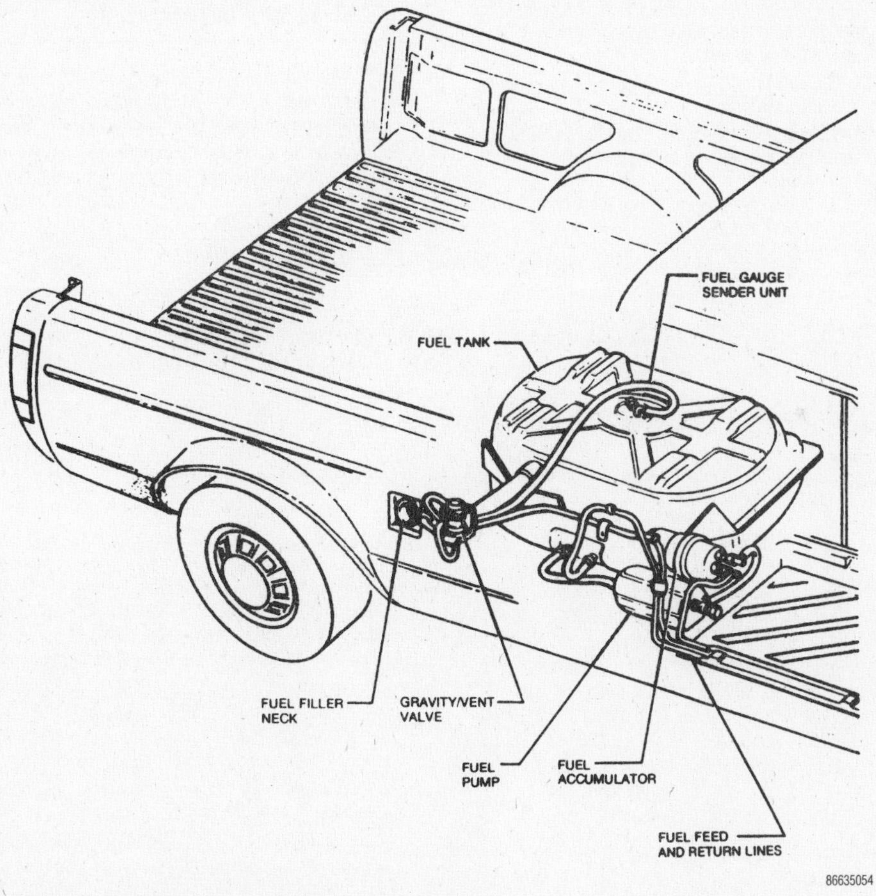

FUEL GAUGE SENDER UNIT

FUEL TANK

FUEL FILLER NECK

GRAVITY/VENT VALVE

FUEL PUMP

FUEL ACCUMULATOR

FUEL FEED AND RETURN LINES

86635054

Fig. 58 Fuel tank assembly used on the Rabbit Pick-up. Other models are similar

10. Place a support or stand under the fuel tank.
11. Remove the clamp that connects the filler pipe to the tank.
12. Remove the fuel tank strap nuts.
13. Work the filler pipe hose from the tank.
14. Disconnect the breather hoses and lower the tank.

To install:

15. Raise and support the tank, while connecting the breather hoses. Use new hose clamps as required.
16. Connect the filler pipe hose to the tank.
17. Lower the vehicle.
18. Screw the fuel gauge sending unit into the tank.
19. Plug in the fuel gauge and transfer pump connectors.
20. Connect the fuel tank return and fuel pump supply lines.
21. Install the fuel gauge sending unit access cover.
22. Install the luggage compartment cover.
23. Fill the tank and connect the negative battery cable.

1985–89 Scirocco and Cabriolet

1. Disconnect the negative battery cable and drain the fuel tank.
2. Remove the rear right wheel housing cover.
3. Disconnect the large breather hose from the filler neck.
4. Pull the gravity valve down leaving the hoses connected.
5. Unbolt the fuel pump bracket from the body and lower the pump.
6. Remove the fuel tank screw.
7. Disconnect the fuel pump hose and pull the blue hose from the return line.
8. Disconnect the brake hoses from both sides of the rear axle and plug them.
9. Disconnect the rear axle from both sides of the body and allow it to swing down and rest on the handbrake cable guides.
10. Unhook the rear muffler support lugs.
11. Disconnect the filler hose from the tank.
12. Support the tank, remove the tank fasteners and lower the tank enough to disconnect the fuel gauge sending unit wires and breather hoses.
13. Remove the fuel tank.

To install:

➡**If installing a new or used tank, make note of where the old foam strips were installed, and install new foam strips on the replacement tank in the same locations.**

14. Raise and support tank. Connect the small breather hoses and fuel gauge sending unit wires. Install the tank fasteners.

➡**When connecting the breather hoses, position the hose clips so that they do not make contact with the body.**

15. Connect the filler hose to the tank and connect the rear muffler support lugs.
16. Raise the rear axle off the handbrake cable guides and install.
17. Connect the brake hoses and bleed the brakes.
18. Connect the return line and fuel pump hose.
19. Install the fuel tank screw.
20. Raise the fuel pump and attach the fuel pump bracket to the body.
21. Put the gravity valve back into its original (raised) position.
22. Connect the large breather hose to the filler neck.

➡**When connecting the breather hose, position the hose clip so that it does not make contact with the body.**

23. Install the right rear wheel housing cover.
24. Fill the tank and connect the negative battery cable.

Sending Unit

REMOVAL & INSTALLATION

On some models, the sending unit can be reached through the access panel under the rear seat. If it is not equipped with an access panel, it will be necessary to remove the fuel tank. Disconnect the wiring, unscrew the locking ring and lift the sending unit (also the pump on some models) straight out. Before installing the unit, check the condition of the O-ring; replace it if necessary.

6

CHASSIS ELECTRICAL

UNDERSTANDING AND TROUBLESHOOTING ELECTRICAL SYSTEMS

Basic Electrical Theory

♦ See Figure 1

For any 12 volt, negative ground, electrical system to operate, the electricity must travel in a complete circuit. This simply means that current (power) from the positive (+) terminal of the battery must eventually return to the negative (-) terminal of the battery. Along the way, this current will travel through wires, fuses, switches and components. If, for any reason, the flow of current through the circuit is interrupted, the component fed by that circuit will cease to function properly.

Perhaps the easiest way to visualize a circuit is to think of connecting a light bulb (with two wires attached to it) to the battery—one wire attached to the negative (-) terminal of the battery and the other wire to the positive (+) terminal. With the two wires touching the battery terminals, the circuit would be complete and the light bulb would illuminate. Electricity would follow a path from the battery to the bulb and back to the battery. It's easy to see that with longer wires on our light bulb, it could be mounted anywhere. Further, one wire could be fitted with a switch so that the light could be turned on and off.

The normal automotive circuit differs from this simple example in two ways. First, instead of having a return wire from the bulb to the battery, the current travels through the frame of the vehicle. Since the negative (-) battery cable is attached to the frame (made of electrically conductive metal), the frame of the vehicle can serve as a ground wire to complete the circuit. Secondly, most automotive circuits contain multiple components which receive power from a single circuit. This lessens the amount of wire needed to power components on the vehicle.

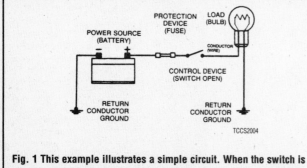

TCCS2004

Fig. 1 This example illustrates a simple circuit. When the switch is closed, power from the positive (+) battery terminal flows through the fuse and the switch, and then to the light bulb. The light illuminates and the circuit is completed through the ground wire back to the negative (-) battery terminal. In reality, the two ground points shown in the illustration are attached to the metal frame of the vehicle, which completes the circuit back to the battery

HOW DOES ELECTRICITY WORK: THE WATER ANALOGY

Electricity is the flow of electrons—the subatomic particles that constitute the outer shell of an atom. Electrons spin in an orbit around the center core of an atom. The center core is comprised of protons (positive charge) and neutrons (neutral charge). Electrons have a negative charge and balance out the positive charge of the protons. When an outside force causes the number of electrons to unbalance the charge of the protons, the electrons will split off the atom and look for another atom to balance out. If this imbalance is kept up, electrons will continue to move and an electrical flow will exist.

Many people have been taught electrical theory using an analogy with water. In a comparison with water flowing through a pipe, the electrons would be the water and the wire is the pipe.

The flow of electricity can be measured much like the flow of water through a pipe. The unit of measurement used is amperes, frequently abbreviated as amps (a). You can compare amperage to the volume of water flowing through a pipe. When connected to a circuit, an ammeter will measure the actual amount of current flowing through the circuit. When relatively few electrons flow through a circuit, the amperage is low. When many electrons flow, the amperage is high.

Water pressure is measured in units such as pounds per square inch (psi);

The electrical pressure is measured in units called volts (v). When a voltmeter is connected to a circuit, it is measuring the electrical pressure.

The actual flow of electricity depends not only on voltage and amperage, but also on the resistance of the circuit. The higher the resistance, the higher the force necessary to push the current through the circuit. The standard unit for measuring resistance is an ohm. Resistance in a circuit varies depending on the amount and type of components used in the circuit. The main factors which determine resistance are:

• Material—some materials have more resistance than others. Those with high resistance are said to be insulators. Rubber materials (or rubber-like plastics) are some of the most common insulators used in vehicles as they have a very high resistance to electricity. Very low resistance materials are said to be conductors. Copper wire is among the best conductors. Silver is actually a superior conductor to copper and is used in some relay contacts, but its high cost prohibits its use as common wiring. Most automotive wiring is made of copper.

• Size—the larger the wire size being used, the less resistance the wire will have. This is why components which use large amounts of electricity usually have large wires supplying current to them.

• Length—for a given thickness of wire, the longer the wire, the greater the resistance. The shorter the wire, the less the resistance. When determining the proper wire for a circuit, both size and length must be considered to design a circuit that can handle the current needs of the component.

• Temperature—with many materials, the higher the temperature, the greater the resistance (positive temperature coefficient). Some materials exhibit the opposite trait of lower resistance with higher temperatures (negative temperature coefficient). These principles are used in many of the sensors on the engine.

OHM'S LAW

There is a direct relationship between current, voltage and resistance. The relationship between current, voltage and resistance can be summed up by a statement known as Ohm's law.

Voltage (E) is equal to amperage (I) times resistance (R): $E = I \times R$

Other forms of the formula are $R = E/I$ and $I = E/R$

In each of these formulas, E is the voltage in volts, I is the current in amps and R is the resistance in ohms. The basic point to remember is that as the resistance of a circuit goes up, the amount of current that flows in the circuit will go down, if voltage remains the same.

The amount of work that the electricity can perform is expressed as power. The unit of power is the watt (w). The relationship between power, voltage and current is expressed as:

Power (w) is equal to amperage (I) times voltage (E): $W = I \times E$

This is only true for direct current (DC) circuits; The alternating current formula is a tad different, but since the electrical circuits in most vehicles are DC type, we need not get into AC circuit theory.

Electrical Components

POWER SOURCE

Power is supplied to the vehicle by two devices: The battery and the alternator. The battery supplies electrical power during starting or during periods when the current demand of the vehicle's electrical system exceeds the output capacity of the alternator. The alternator supplies electrical current when the engine is running. Just not does the alternator supply the current needs of the vehicle, but it recharges the battery.

The Battery

In most modern vehicles, the battery is a lead/acid electrochemical device consisting of six 2 volt subsections (cells) connected in series, so that the unit is capable of producing approximately 12 volts of electrical pressure. Each subsection consists of a series of positive and negative plates held a short distance apart in a solution of sulfuric acid and water.

The two types of plates are of dissimilar metals. This sets up a chemical reaction, and it is this reaction which produces current flow from the battery when its positive and negative terminals are connected to an electrical load .

The power removed from the battery is replaced by the alternator, restoring the battery to its original chemical state.

The Alternator

On some vehicles there isn't an alternator, but a generator. The difference is that an alternator supplies alternating current which is then changed to direct current for use on the vehicle, while a generator produces direct current. Alternators tend to be more efficient and that is why they are used.

Alternators and generators are devices that consist of coils of wires wound together making big electromagnets. One group of coils spins within another set and the interaction of the magnetic fields causes a current to flow. This current is then drawn off the coils and fed into the vehicles electrical system.

GROUND

Two types of grounds are used in automotive electric circuits. Direct ground components are grounded to the frame through their mounting points. All other components use some sort of ground wire which is attached to the frame or chassis of the vehicle. The electrical current runs through the chassis of the vehicle and returns to the battery through the ground (-) cable; if you look, you'll see that the battery ground cable connects between the battery and the frame or chassis of the vehicle.

➡**It should be noted that a good percentage of electrical problems can be traced to bad grounds.**

PROTECTIVE DEVICES

♦ **See Figures 2 and 3**

It is possible for large surges of current to pass through the electrical system of your vehicle. If this surge of current were to reach the load in the circuit, the

86636001

Fig. 3 Fusible links can be found routed in the engine compartment wiring harness

surge could burn it out or severely damage it. It can also overload the wiring, causing the harness to get hot and melt the insulation. To prevent this, fuses, circuit breakers and/or fusible links are connected into the supply wires of the electrical system. These items are nothing more than a built-in weak spot in the system. When an abnormal amount of current flows through the system, these protective devices work as follows to protect the circuit:

- Fuse—when an excessive electrical current passes through a fuse, the fuse "blows" (the conductor melts) and opens the circuit, preventing the passage of current.
- Circuit Breaker—a circuit breaker is basically a self-repairing fuse. It will open the circuit in the same fashion as a fuse, but when the surge subsides, the circuit breaker can be reset and does not need replacement.
- Fusible Link—a fusible link (fuse link or main link) is a short length of special, high temperature insulated wire that acts as a fuse. When an excessive electrical current passes through a fusible link, the thin gauge wire inside the link melts, creating an intentional open to protect the circuit. To repair the circuit, the link must be replaced. Some newer type fusible links are housed in plug-in modules, which are simply replaced like a fuse, while older type fusible links must be cut and spliced if they melt. Since this link is very early in the electrical path, it's the first place to look if nothing on the vehicle works, yet the battery seems to be charged and is properly connected.

✳✳ CAUTION

Always replace fuses, circuit breakers and fusible links with identically rated components. Under no circumstances should a component of higher or lower amperage rating be substituted.

SWITCHES & RELAYS

♦ **See Figures 4 and 5**

Switches are used in electrical circuits to control the passage of current. The most common use is to open and close circuits between the battery and the various electric devices in the system. Switches are rated according to the amount of amperage they can handle. If a sufficient amperage rated switch is not used in a circuit, the switch could overload and cause damage.

Some electrical components which require a large amount of current to operate use a special switch called a relay. Since these circuits carry a large amount of current, the thickness of the wire in the circuit is also greater. If this large wire were connected from the load to the control switch, the switch would have to carry the high amperage load and the fairing or dash would be twice as large to accommodate the increased size of the wiring harness. To prevent these problems, a relay is used.

Relays are composed of a coil and a set of contacts. When the coil has a current passed though it, a magnetic field is formed and this field causes the contacts to move together, completing the circuit. Most relays are normally open, preventing current from passing through the circuit, but they can take any elec-

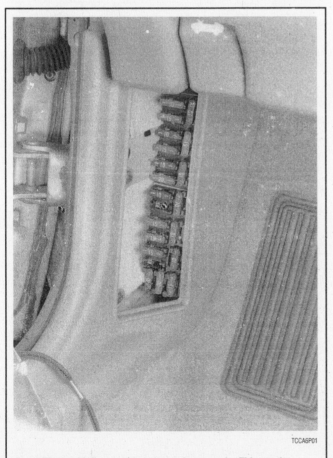
TCCA6P01

Fig. 2 Most vehicles use one or more fuse panels. This one is located on the driver's side kick panel

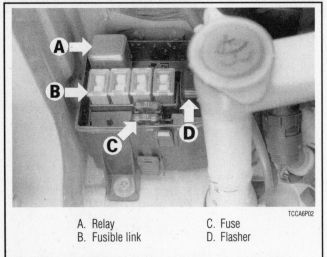

A. Relay   C. Fuse
B. Fusible link   D. Flasher

TCCA6P02

Fig. 4 The underhood fuse and relay panel usually contains fuses, relays, flashers and fusible links

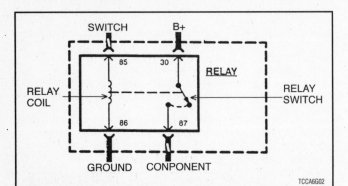

TCCA6G02

Fig. 5 Relays are composed of a coil and a switch. These two components are linked together so that when one operates, the other operates at the same time. The large wires in the circuit are connected from the battery to one side of the relay switch (B+) and from the opposite side of the relay switch to the load (component). Smaller wires are connected from the relay coil to the control switch for the circuit and from the opposite side of the relay coil to ground

trical form depending on the job they are intended to do. Relays can be considered "remote control switches." They allow a smaller current to operate devices that require higher amperages. When a small current operates the coil, a larger current is allowed to pass by the contacts. Some common circuits which may use relays are the horn, headlights, starter, electric fuel pump and other high draw ciruits.

LOAD

Every electrical circuit must include a "load" (something to use the electricity coming from the source). Without this load, the battery would attempt to deliver its entire power supply from one pole to another. This is called a "short circuit." All this electricity would take a short cut to ground and cause a great amount of damage to other components in the circuit by developing a tremendous amount of heat. This condition could develop sufficient heat to melt the insulation on all the surrounding wires and reduce a multiple wire cable to a lump of plastic and copper.

WIRING & HARNESSES

The average vehicle contains meters and meters of wiring, with hundreds of individual connections. To protect the many wires from damage and to keep them from becoming a confusing tangle, they are organized into bundles,

enclosed in plastic or taped together and called wiring harnesses. Different harnesses serve different parts of the vehicle. Individual wires are color coded to help trace them through a harness where sections are hidden from view.

Automotive wiring or circuit conductors can be either single strand wire, multi-strand wire or printed circuitry. Single strand wire has a solid metal core and is usually used inside such components as alternators, motors, relays and other devices. Multi-strand wire has a core made of many small strands of wire twisted together into a single conductor. Most of the wiring in an automotive electrical system is made up of multi-strand wire, either as a single conductor or grouped together in a harness. All wiring is color coded on the insulator, either as a solid color or as a colored wire with an identification stripe. A printed circuit is a thin film of copper or other conductor that is printed on an insulator backing. Occasionally, a printed circuit is sandwiched between two sheets of plastic for more protection and flexibility. A complete printed circuit, consisting of conductors, insulating material and connectors for lamps or other components is called a printed circuit board. Printed circuitry is used in place of individual wires or harnesses in places where space is limited, such as behind instrument panels.

Since automotive electrical systems are very sensitive to changes in resistance, the selection of properly sized wires is critical when systems are repaired. A loose or corroded connection or a replacement wire that is too small for the circuit will add extra resistance and an additional voltage drop to the circuit.

The wire gauge number is an expression of the cross-section area of the conductor. Vehicles from countries that use the metric system will typically describe the wire size as its cross-sectional area in square millimeters. In this method, the larger the wire, the greater the number. Another common system for expressing wire size is the American Wire Gauge (AWG) system. As gauge number increases, area decreases and the wire becomes smaller. An 18 gauge wire is smaller than a 4 gauge wire. A wire with a higher gauge number will carry less current than a wire with a lower gauge number. Gauge wire size refers to the size of the strands of the conductor, not the size of the complete wire with insulator. It is possible, therefore, to have two wires of the same gauge with different diameters because one may have thicker insulation than the other.

It is essential to understand how a circuit works before trying to figure out why it doesn't. An electrical schematic shows the electrical current paths when a circuit is operating properly. Schematics break the entire electrical system down into individual circuits. In a schematic, usually no attempt is made to represent wiring and components as they physically appear on the vehicle; switches and other components are shown as simply as possible. Face views of harness connectors show the cavity or terminal locations in all multi-pin connectors to help locate test points.

CONNECTORS

♦ See Figures 6 and 7

Three types of connectors are commonly used in automotive applications—weatherproof, molded and hard shell.

TCCA6P03

Fig. 6 Hard shell (left) and weatherproof (right) connectors have replaceable terminals

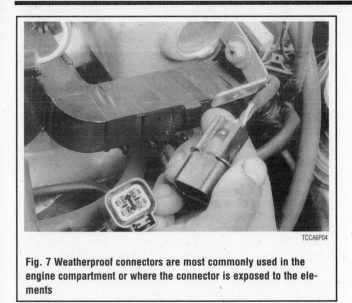

Fig. 7 Weatherproof connectors are most commonly used in the engine compartment or where the connector is exposed to the elements

TCCA6P04

• Weatherproof—these connectors are most commonly used where the connector is exposed to the elements. Terminals are protected against moisture and dirt by sealing rings which provide a weathertight seal. All repairs require the use of a special terminal and the tool required to service it. Unlike standard blade type terminals, these weatherproof terminals cannot be straightened once they are bent. Make certain that the connectors are properly seated and all of the sealing rings are in place when connecting leads.

• Molded—these connectors require complete replacement of the connector if found to be defective. This means splicing a new connector assembly into the harness. All splices should be soldered to insure proper contact. Use care when probing the connections or replacing terminals in them, as it is possible to create a short circuit between opposite terminals. If this happens to the wrong terminal pair, it is possible to damage certain components. Always use jumper wires between connectors for circuit checking and NEVER probe through weatherproof seals.

• Hard Shell—unlike molded connectors, the terminal contacts in hard-shell connectors can be replaced. Replacement usually involves the use of a special terminal removal tool that depresses the locking tangs (barbs) on the connector terminal and allows the connector to be removed from the rear of the shell. The connector shell should be replaced if it shows any evidence of burning, melting, cracks, or breaks. Replace individual terminals that are burnt, corroded, distorted or loose.

Test Equipment

Pinpointing the exact cause of trouble in an electrical circuit is most times accomplished by the use of special test equipment. The following describes different types of commonly used test equipment and briefly explains how to use them in diagnosis. In addition to the information covered below, the tool manufacturer's instructions booklet (provided with the tester) should be read and clearly understood before attempting any test procedures.

JUMPER WIRES

✱✱ CAUTION

Never use jumper wires made from a thinner gauge wire than the circuit being tested. If the jumper wire is of too small a gauge, it may overheat and possibly melt. Never use jumpers to bypass high resistance loads in a circuit. Bypassing resistances, in effect, creates a short circuit. This may, in turn, cause damage and fire. Jumper wires should only be used to bypass lengths of wire or to simulate switches.

Jumper wires are simple, yet extremely valuable, pieces of test equipment. They are basically test wires which are used to bypass sections of a circuit.

Although jumper wires can be purchased, they are usually fabricated from lengths of standard automotive wire and whatever type of connector (alligator clip, spade connector or pin connector) that is required for the particular application being tested. In cramped, hard-to-reach areas, it is advisable to have insulated boots over the jumper wire terminals in order to prevent accidental grounding. It is also advisable to include a standard automotive fuse in any jumper wire. This is commonly referred to as a "fused jumper". By inserting an in-line fuse holder between a set of test leads, a fused jumper wire can be used for bypassing open circuits. Use a 5 amp fuse to provide protection against voltage spikes.

Jumper wires are used primarily to locate open electrical circuits, on either the ground (-) side of the circuit or on the power (+) side. If an electrical component fails to operate, connect the jumper wire between the component and a good ground. If the component operates only with the jumper installed, the ground circuit is open. If the ground circuit is good, but the component does not operate, the circuit between the power feed and component may be open. By moving the jumper wire successively back from the component toward the power source, you can isolate the area of the circuit where the open is located. When the component stops functioning, or the power is cut off, the open is in the segment of wire between the jumper and the point previously tested.

You can sometimes connect the jumper wire directly from the battery to the "hot" terminal of the component, but first make sure the component uses 12 volts in operation. Some electrical components, such as fuel injectors or sensors, are designed to operate on about 4 to 5 volts, and running 12 volts directly to these components will cause damage.

TEST LIGHTS

◗ See Figure 8

The test light is used to check circuits and components while electrical current is flowing through them. It is used for voltage and ground tests. To use a 12 volt test light, connect the ground clip to a good ground and probe wherever necessary with the pick. The test light will illuminate when voltage is detected. This does not necessarily mean that 12 volts (or any particular amount of voltage) is present; it only means that some voltage is present. It is advisable before using the test light to touch its ground clip and probe across the battery posts or terminals to make sure the light is operating properly.

✱✱ WARNING

Do not use a test light to probe electronic ignition, spark plug or coil wires. Never use a pick-type test light to probe wiring on computer controlled systems unless specifically instructed to do so. Any wire insulation that is pierced by the test light probe should be taped and sealed with silicone after testing.

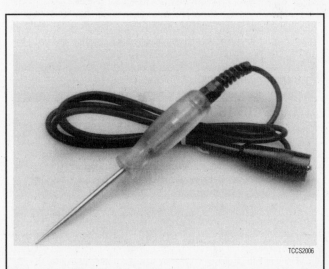

TCCS2006

Fig. 8 A 12 volt test light is used to detect the presence of voltage in a circuit

Like the jumper wire, the 12 volt test light is used to isolate opens in circuits. But, whereas the jumper wire is used to bypass the open to operate the load, the 12 volt test light is used to locate the presence of voltage in a circuit. If the test light illuminates, there is power up to that point in the circuit; if the test light does not illuminate, there is an open circuit (no power). Move the test light in successive steps back toward the power source until the light in the handle illuminates. The open is between the probe and a point which was previously probed.

The self-powered test light is similar in design to the 12 volt test light, but contains a 1.5 volt penlight battery in the handle. It is most often used in place of a multimeter to check for open or short circuits when power is isolated from the circuit (continuity test).

The battery in a self-powered test light does not provide much current. A weak battery may not provide enough power to illuminate the test light even when a complete circuit is made (especially if there is high resistance in the circuit). Always make sure that the test battery is strong. To check the battery, briefly touch the ground clip to the probe; if the light glows brightly, the battery is strong enough for testing.

➡ **A self-powered test light should not be used on any computer controlled system or component. The small amount of electricity transmitted by the test light is enough to damage many electronic automotive components.**

MULTIMETERS

Multimeters are an extremely useful tool for troubleshooting electrical problems. They can be purchased in either analog or digital form and have a price range to suit any budget. A multimeter is a voltmeter, ammeter and ohmmeter (along with other features) combined into one instrument. It is often used when testing solid state circuits because of its high input impedance (usually 10 megaohms or more). A brief description of the multimeter main test functions follows:

➡ Voltmeter—the voltmeter is used to measure voltage at any point in a circuit, or to measure the voltage drop across any part of a circuit. Voltmeters usually have various scales and a selector switch to allow the reading of different voltage ranges. The voltmeter has a positive and a negative lead. To avoid damage to the meter, always connect the negative lead to the negative (-) side of the circuit (to ground or nearest the ground side of the circuit) and connect the positive lead to the positive (+) side of the circuit (to the power source or the nearest power source). Note that the negative voltmeter lead will always be black and that the positive voltmeter will always be some color other than black (usually red).

• Ohmmeter—the ohmmeter is designed to read resistance (measured in ohms) in a circuit or component. Most ohmmeters will have a selector switch which permits the measurement of different ranges of resistance (usually the selector switch allows the multiplication of the meter reading by 10, 100, 1,000 and 10,000). Some ohmmeters are "auto-ranging" which means the meter itself will determine which scale to use. Since the meters are powered by an internal battery, the ohmmeter can be used like a self-powered test light. When the ohmmeter is connected, current from the ohmmeter flows through the circuit or component being tested. Since the ohmmeter's internal resistance and voltage are known values, the amount of current flow through the meter depends on the resistance of the circuit or component being tested. The ohmmeter can also be used to perform a continuity test for suspected open circuits. In using the meter for making continuity checks, do not be concerned with the actual resistance readings. Zero resistance, or any ohm reading, indicates continuity in the circuit. Infinite resistance indicates an opening in the circuit. A high resistance reading where there should be none indicates a problem in the circuit. Checks for short circuits are made in the same manner as checks for open circuits, except that the circuit must be isolated from both power and normal ground. Infinite resistance indicates no continuity, while zero resistance indicates a dead short.

⚙✳ WARNING

Never use an ohmmeter to check the resistance of a component or wire while there is voltage applied to the circuit.

• Ammeter—an ammeter measures the amount of current flowing through a circuit in units called amperes or amps. At normal operating voltage, most circuits have a characteristic amount of amperes, called "current draw" which can be measured using an ammeter. By referring to a specified current draw rating, then measuring the amperes and comparing the two values, one can determine what is happening within the circuit to aid in diagnosis. An open circuit, for example, will not allow any current to flow, so the ammeter reading will be zero. A damaged component or circuit will have an increased current draw, so the reading will be high. The ammeter is always connected in series with the circuit being tested. All of the current that normally flows through the circuit must also flow through the ammeter; if there is any other path for the current to follow, the ammeter reading will not be accurate. The ammeter itself has very little resistance to current flow and, therefore, will not affect the circuit, but it will measure current draw only when the circuit is closed and electricity is flowing. Excessive current draw can blow fuses and drain the battery, while a reduced current draw can cause motors to run slowly, lights to dim and other components to not operate properly.

Troubleshooting Electrical Systems

When diagnosing a specific problem, organized troubleshooting is a must. The complexity of a modern automotive vehicle demands that you approach any problem in a logical, organized manner. There are certain troubleshooting techniques, however, which are standard:

• Establish when the problem occurs. Does the problem appear only under certain conditions? Were there any noises, odors or other unusual symptoms? Isolate the problem area. To do this, make some simple tests and observations, then eliminate the systems that are working properly. Check for obvious problems, such as broken wires and loose or dirty connections. Always check the obvious before assuming something complicated is the cause.

• Test for problems systematically to determine the cause once the problem area is isolated. Are all the components functioning properly? Is there power going to electrical switches and motors. Performing careful, systematic checks will often turn up most causes on the first inspection, without wasting time checking components that have little or no relationship to the problem.

• Test all repairs after the work is done to make sure that the problem is fixed. Some causes can be traced to more than one component, so a careful verification of repair work is important in order to pick up additional malfunctions that may cause a problem to reappear or a different problem to arise. A blown fuse, for example, is a simple problem that may require more than another fuse to repair. If you don't look for a problem that caused a fuse to blow, a shorted wire (for example) may go undetected.

Experience has shown that most problems tend to be the result of a fairly simple and obvious cause, such as loose or corroded connectors, bad grounds or damaged wire insulation which causes a short. This makes careful visual inspection of components during testing essential to quick and accurate troubleshooting.

Testing

OPEN CIRCUITS

♦ **See Figure 9**

This test already assumes the existence of an open in the circuit and it is used to help locate the open portion.

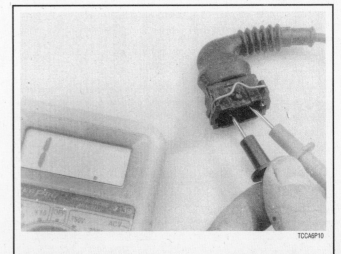

TCCA6P10

Fig. 9 The infinite reading on this multimeter indicates that the circuit is open

1. Isolate the circuit from power and ground.
2. Connect the self-powered test light or ohmmeter ground clip to the ground side of the circuit and probe sections of the circuit sequentially.
3. If the light is out or there is infinite resistance, the open is between the probe and the circuit ground.
4. If the light is on or the meter shows continuity, the open is between the probe and the end of the circuit toward the power source.

SHORT CIRCUITS

➡**Never use a self-powered test light to perform checks for opens or shorts when power is applied to the circuit under test. The test light can be damaged by outside power.**

1. Isolate the circuit from power and ground.
2. Connect the self-powered test light or ohmmeter ground clip to a good ground and probe any easy-to-reach point in the circuit.
3. If the light comes on or there is continuity, there is a short somewhere in the circuit.
4. To isolate the short, probe a test point at either end of the isolated circuit (the light should be on or the meter should indicate continuity).
5. Leave the test light probe engaged and sequentially open connectors or switches, remove parts, etc. until the light goes out or continuity is broken.
6. When the light goes out, the short is between the last two circuit components which were opened.

VOLTAGE

This test determines voltage available from the battery and should be the first step in any electrical troubleshooting procedure after visual inspection. Many electrical problems, especially on computer controlled systems, can be caused by a low state of charge in the battery. Excessive corrosion at the battery cable terminals can cause poor contact that will prevent proper charging and full battery current flow.

1. Set the voltmeter selector switch to the 20V position.
2. Connect the multimeter negative lead to the battery's negative (-) post or terminal and the positive lead to the battery's positive (+) post or terminal.
3. Turn the ignition switch **ON** to provide a load.
4. A well charged battery should register over 12 volts. If the meter reads below 11.5 volts, the battery power may be insufficient to operate the electrical system properly.

VOLTAGE DROP

▶ **See Figure 10**

When current flows through a load, the voltage beyond the load drops. This voltage drop is due to the resistance created by the load and also by small resistances created by corrosion at the connectors and damaged insulation on the wires. The maximum allowable voltage drop under load is critical, especially if there is more than one load in the circuit, since all voltage drops are cumulative.

1. Set the voltmeter selector switch to the 20 volt position.
2. Connect the multimeter negative lead to a good ground.
3. Operate the circuit and check the voltage prior to the first component (load).
4. There should be little or no voltage drop in the circuit prior to the first component. If a voltage drop exists, the wire or connectors in the circuit are suspect.
5. While operating the first component in the circuit, probe the ground side of the component with the positive meter lead and observe the voltage readings. A small voltage drop should be noticed. This voltage drop is caused by the resistance of the component.
6. Repeat the test for each component (load) down the circuit.
7. If a large voltage drop is noticed, the preceding component, wire or connector is suspect.

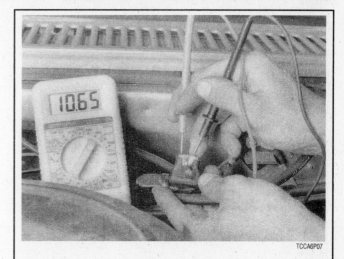

TCCA6P07

Fig. 10 This voltage drop test revealed high resistance (low voltage) in the circuit

RESISTANCE

▶ **See Figures 11 and 12**

❊❊ **WARNING**

Never use an ohmmeter with power applied to the circuit. The ohmmeter is designed to operate on its own power supply. The normal 12 volt electrical system voltage could damage the meter!

1. Isolate the circuit from the vehicle's power source.
2. Ensure that the ignition key is **OFF** when disconnecting any components or the battery.
3. Where necessary, also isolate at least one side of the circuit to be checked, in order to avoid reading parallel resistances. Parallel circuit resistances will always give a lower reading than the actual resistance of either of the branches.
4. Connect the meter leads to both sides of the circuit (wire or component) and read the actual measured ohms on the meter scale. Make sure the selector

TCCA6P08

Fig. 11 Checking the resistance of a coolant temperature sensor with an ohmmeter. Reading is 1.04 kilohms

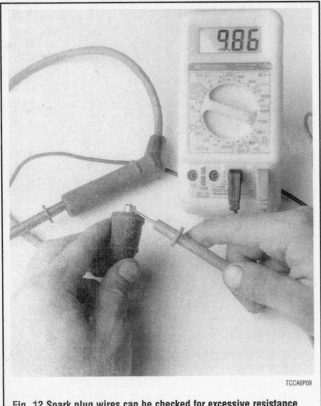

Fig. 12 Spark plug wires can be checked for excessive resistance using an ohmmeter

TCCA6P09

switch is set to the proper ohm scale for the circuit being tested, to avoid misreading the ohmmeter test value.

Wire and Connector Repair

Almost anyone can replace damaged wires, as long as the proper tools and parts are available. Wire and terminals are available to fit almost any need. Even the specialized weatherproof, molded and hard shell connectors are now available from aftermarket suppliers.

Be sure the ends of all the wires are fitted with the proper terminal hardware and connectors. Wrapping a wire around a stud is never a permanent solution and will only cause trouble later. Replace wires one at a time to avoid confusion. Always route wires exactly the same as the factory.

➡**If connector repair is necessary, only attempt it if you have the proper tools. Weatherproof and hard shell connectors require special tools to release the pins inside the connector. Attempting to repair these connectors with conventional hand tools will damage them.**

HEATING AND AIR CONDITIONING

The heater core and blower on most models are contained in the heater box (fresh air housing) located in the center of the passenger compartment under the dashboard. On most air conditioned models, the evaporator is located in the heater box. On air conditioned Dashers and most Quantums the evaporator is located under the hood separate from the heater box.

The blower fan on non-air conditioned models before 1977 is open bladed, much like an airplane propeller. The blower fan on all air conditioned models and non-air conditioned models after 1977 is of the turbine type.

On some models, the fan and core can be removed without removing the heater box. The fan should be accessible from under the hood on these models, while the heater core is accessible from inside the passenger compartment.

Blower Motor

REMOVAL & INSTALLATION

Models Through 1977

▶ **See Figure 13**

1. Disconnect the negative battery cable.
2. Remove the heater box following the procedure outlined in this section.
3. On Rabbit and Scirocco, remove the screws holding the heater cover in place, then remove the heater cover. Remove the circular cutoff flap by unhooking it from its hinge. On Dashers, remove the heater cover by pulling out its pins.
4. On the Rabbit and Scirocco, the heater blower should pull right out of the assembly.
5. On Dashers, remove the clips holding the heater box halves together and separate the halves. The fan should just pull out.
6. Installation is the reverse of removal.

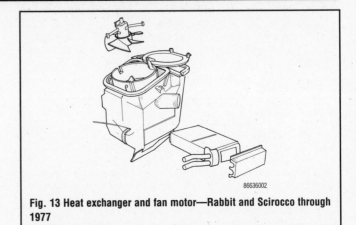

Fig. 13 Heat exchanger and fan motor—Rabbit and Scirocco through 1977

86636002

➡**On the Dasher, when installing the fan in the heater box halves, make sure the wiring connections on the fan face the wiring harness on the heater box. Also, when joining the housing halves, make sure there is no side to side play in the blower motor.**

1978 and Later Models, Except Fox and 1985–89 Golf/Jetta

1. Disconnect the negative battery cable.
2. Remove the heater box following the procedure outlined in this section.
3. Remove the screws holding the cover on the heater box, then remove the cover. Remove the blower motor cover, if so equipped.
4. After matchmarking to insure you assemble them in the correct order, unplug the electrical connections from the blower motor.
5. Remove the clamp or screws holding the motor in place, then remove the motor.
6. Installation is the reverse of removal.

Fox

◆ **See Figure 14**

1. Disconnect the negative battery cable.
2. Remove the front cover sealing gasket.
3. Remove the water deflector.
4. Loosen the fresh air housing cover retaining clips, then remove the front fresh air housing cover.
5. If equipped with air conditioning, undo the lock and disconnect the air distribution flap levers.
6. Remove the rear fresh air housing cover.
7. If equipped with air conditioning, label and disconnect the vacuum servo motor hoses and hoses from the grommets in the lower portion of the fresh air housing covers.
8. Remove the thermal resistor and thermal circuit breaker from the support.
9. Loosen the blower motor mounting screw and disconnect the blower wiring connectors.
10. Remove the lower fresh air covers.
11. Maneuver the fan and motor towards the front of the car, then remove it from the fresh air (blower) housing.

To install:

12. Install the fan and motor assembly into the fresh air (blower) housing.
13. Install the lower fresh air covers.
14. Connect the blower wiring and install the blower motor mounting screw.
15. Attach the thermal circuit breaker and thermal resistor to the support.
16. Connect the hoses to the lower fresh air housing covers and connect the vacuum servo motor hoses.
17. Install the rear fresh air housing cover.
18. If equipped with air conditioning, connect the air distribution flap levers and engage the lock.
19. Install the front fresh air housing cover and lock the retaining clips.
20. Install the water deflector.
21. Connect the negative battery cable and check the blower operation at all speeds.

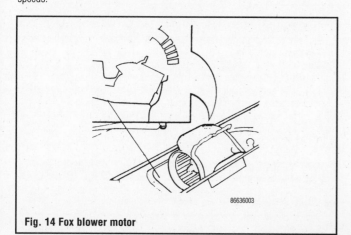

Fig. 14 Fox blower motor

1985–89 Golf and Jetta

◆ **See Figures 15, 16 and 17**

➡The blower motor is located behind the glove box and it may be necessary to remove the glove box to gain access to the motor.

WITHOUT AIR CONDITIONING

1. Disconnect the negative battery cable.
2. Unplug the wires at the blower motor.
3. At the blower motor flange near the cowl, disengage the retaining lug (pull down on the lug).
4. Turn the motor in the clockwise direction to release it from its mount, then lower it from the plenum.
5. To install, reverse the removal procedures. Use a new gasket or sealant as required.

WITH AIR CONDITIONING

◆ **See Figures 18, 19, 20 and 21**

1. Disconnect the negative battery cable.
2. Unplug the wires and the motor vent tube from the blower motor.
3. Remove the three mounting screws and pull the motor from the plenum.
4. To install, reverse the removal procedures. Use a new gasket or sealant as required.

Heater Core

REMOVAL & INSTALLATION

❋❋ CAUTION

When draining the coolant, keep in mind that cats and dogs are attracted by ethylene glycol antifreeze, and are quite likely to drink any that is left in an uncovered container or in puddles on the ground. This will prove fatal in sufficient quantity. Always drain the coolant into a sealable container. Coolant should be reused unless it is contaminated or several years old.

Except Fox

◆ **See Figures 22 and 23**

1. Disconnect the negative battery cable.
2. Drain the cooling system.
3. Remove the two heater inlet hoses at the firewall.

➡On some 1977 and later models, it is possible to remove the heater core without removing the heater case. To determine if this is possible on your vehicle, remove the center console side panels (if equipped). Locate the heater core cover positioned on the side of the case. Remove

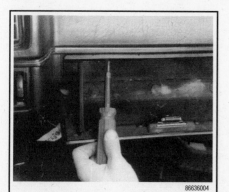

Fig. 15 Remove the screws securing the top of the glove box

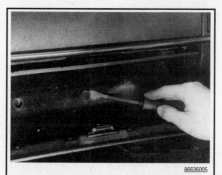

Fig. 16 A small prytool can be used to remove the cover concealing the lower screws—then unthread the lower screws

Fig. 17 Pull the glove box out, then unplug the electrical connection

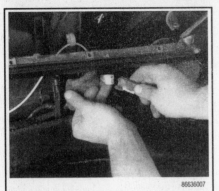

Fig. 18 Unplug the wiring connector for the blower motor

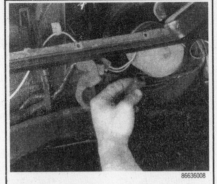

Fig. 19 It will also be necessary to unplug the air vent for the motor

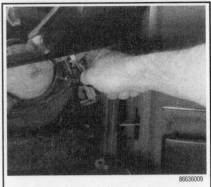

Fig. 20 A nutdriver can be used to remove the screws securing the blower motor

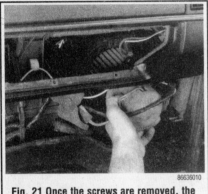

Fig. 21 Once the screws are removed, the motor can be extracted from the housing

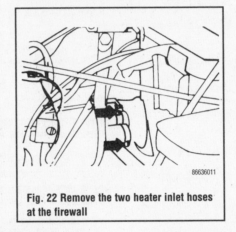

Fig. 22 Remove the two heater inlet hoses at the firewall

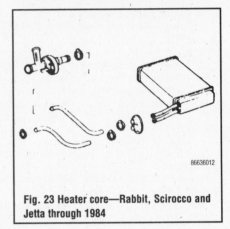

Fig. 23 Heater core—Rabbit, Scirocco and Jetta through 1984

the screws or unclip the cover, then remove the cover for access. If there is sufficient clearance to pull the core out without damaging the heater tubes, remove the core from the case and you may skip the rest of the removal procedure.

4. Remove the heater case (refer to the procedure in this section). Locate the heater core cover located on the side of the case. Remove the screws or unclip the cover, then remove it.

5. The heater core can now be slid out from the case. If the retaining clips break off, don't worry, they can be replaced with screws.

To install:

6. Insert the heater core into the case. Install the heater core cover, making sure that the gasket on the cover is properly fitted.

7. If applicable, install the heater case.

8. Connect the heater hoses at the firewall. Make sure the seal fits tightly without any gaps. Fill the cooling system to the proper level.

Fox

1. Disconnect the negative battery cable.

2. Drain the engine coolant.

3. Disconnect the heater inlet hoses at the firewall.

4. Inside the vehicle, remove the center console side panels. Disconnect the temperature control cables at the heater case.

5. Remove the left and right air distribution ducts.

6. In the engine compartment, remove the cowl cover and remove the air distribution housing cover.

7. Inside the vehicle, remove the lower housing retaining clips and remove the housing.

➡On vehicles equipped with A/C the heater box also contains the A/C system evaporator mounted in the lower housing cover. When removing the lower cover on these models lay the cover and evaporated aside WITHOUT disconnecting the refrigerant lines.

8. Remove the bolts retaining the heater case and remove the case.

9. Remove the clips holding the case together and split the case, the heater core can now be removed.

To install:

10. Insert the heater core into the case, then reassemble it.

11. Install the case into the vehicle. Attach the lower heater case cover to the heater case. Install the air distribution ducts and the control cables.

12. Install the center console side panels. Reconnect the heater inlet hoses. Install the air distribution housing cover and the cowl.

13. Fill the cooling system to the proper level.

Control Head and Cables

REMOVAL & INSTALLATION

1. Disconnect the negative battery cable.

2. Remove the bezel in order to gain access to the control head.

3. Remove the screws that fasten the control head to the instrument panel. Remove the control panel and disconnect the blower switch wiring.

4. Pry the cable clips free and disconnect the cables from the control levers to remove the control head.

5. Release the clips to disconnect the cables from the heater. Take note of the cable routing.

To install:

6. Fit the cables into place but don't install the retaining clips yet.

7. Connect the self-adjusting clip to the door crank and secure the cable.

8. Connect the upper end of the cable to the control head.

9. Place the temperature lever on the coolest side of its travel. Allowing the self-adjusting clip to slide on the cable, rotate the door counterclockwise by hand until it stops.

10. Cycle the lever back and forth a few times to make sure the cable moves freely.

ADJUSTMENT

1. Move the temperature control lever to the full cold position.
2. With the control cable attached to the air mix door link, pull the cable housing out and push the inner cable in the opposite direction.
3. Secure the cable in this position with the retaining clamp.
4. Operate the temperature control lever and check freedom of movement at the full stroke range.

Heater Case/Box

REMOVAL & INSTALLATION

Without Center Console

▶ **See Figures 24, 25 and 26**

1. Disconnect the battery ground cable.
2. Drain the cooling system.

3. Remove the windshield washer container (from its mounts) and/or the ignition coil, but only if they prevent access to the heater components under the hood.
4. Disconnect the two hoses from the heater core connections at the firewall.
5. Unplug the blower fan electrical connectors. Some models are equipped with an external series resistor mounted on the heater box. Do not try to remove the wires from the resistor.
6. Remove the heater control knobs on the dash.
7. Remove the two retaining screws and remove the controls from the dash complete with brackets.
8. Some models have a cable attached to a lever which is operated by a round knob on the dashboard. Remove the cable from the lever.
9. Remove either the clips or the screws holding the heater box in place and remove the heater box with the heater controls.

To install:

10. When installing the new type of housing in Rabbits and Sciroccos originally equipped with the older style heater box, proceed as follows:
   a. Make a hole by cutting along the line "W".
   b. Clip the connections after installing the new air outlet pipe and seal the joint with a suitable adhesive.
11. Mount and install the heater box (with controls) and install the retaining clips or screws.
12. On those models with cable operated lever, connect the cable to the lever.
13. Mount the controls to the dash and secure with the two retaining screws.
14. Install the heater control knobs.
15. Plug in the blower fan connectors.
16. Connect the hoses to the heater core at the fire wall.
17. Install the ignition coil and windshield washer reservoir if they were removed.

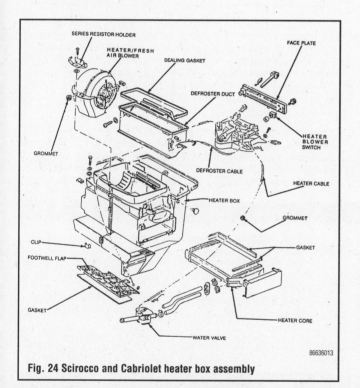

Fig. 24 Scirocco and Cabriolet heater box assembly

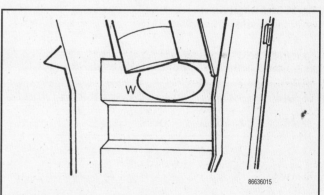

Fig. 26 Cut along line (W) for Rabbits and Sciroccos originally equipped with the older style heater box

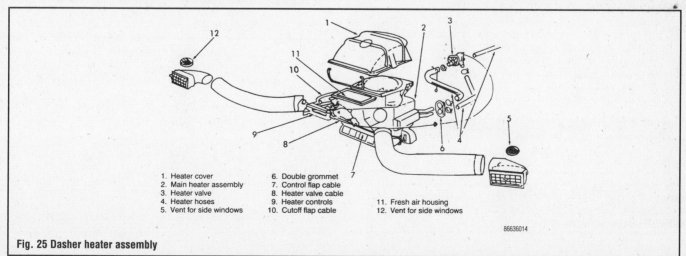

1. Heater cover	6. Double grommet
2. Main heater assembly	7. Control flap cable
3. Heater valve	8. Heater valve cable
4. Heater hoses	9. Heater controls
5. Vent for side windows	10. Cutoff flap cable
	11. Fresh air housing
	12. Vent for side windows

Fig. 25 Dasher heater assembly

18. Fill the cooling system to the proper level.
19. Connect the negative battery cable.

With Center Console

1. Disconnect the negative battery cable.
2. Drain the engine coolant.
3. Trace the heater hoses coming from the firewall and disconnect them. One leads to the back of the cylinder head and the other leads to the heater valve located above and behind the oil filter.
4. Detach the cable for the heater valve.
5. Remove the center console.
6. Remove the left and right covers below the instrument panel.
7. Pull off the fresh air/heater control knobs.
8. Pull off the trim plate.
9. Remove the screws for the controls.
10. Remove the center cover mounting screws and remove the cover.
11. Detach the right, left and center air ducts.
12. Remove the heater housing retaining spring.
13. Remove the cowl for the air plenum which is located under the hood in front of the windshield.
14. Remove the heater housing mounting screws and remove the heater housing. The mounting screws are under the hood where the air plenum was. Remove all the old sealing material and replace.
   To install:
15. Mount the heater housing and install the mounting screws.
16. Install the air plenum cowl.
17. Install the heater housing retaining spring.
18. Connect the right, left and center air ducts.
19. Install the center cover.
20. Install the control assembly screws.
21. Mount the trim plate.
22. Install the fresh air/heater control knobs.
23. Install the lower left and right instrument panel covers.
24. Install the center console.

25. Connect the heater cable valve.
26. Connect the heater hoses.
27. Fill the cooling system to the proper level.
28. Connect the negative battery cable.

Blower Switch

REMOVAL & INSTALLATION

1. Disconnect the negative battery cable.
2. Remove the control head and unplug the electrical connector on the blower switch.
3. Remove the screws securing the switch or disengage its retaining clips.
4. Installation is the reverse of removal.

Air Conditioning Components

REMOVAL & INSTALLATION

Repair or service of air conditioning components is not covered by this manual, because of the risk of personal injury or death, and because of the legal ramifications of servicing these components without the proper EPA certification and experience. Cost, personal injury or death, environmental damage, and legal considerations (such as the fact that it is a federal crime to vent refrigerant into the atmosphere), dictate that the A/C components on your vehicle should be serviced only by a Motor Vehicle Air Conditioning (MVAC) trained, and EPA certified automotive technician.

➡ **If your vehicle's A/C system uses R-12 refrigerant and is in need of recharging, the A/C system can be converted over to R-134a refrigerant (less environmentally harmful and expensive). Refer to Section 1 for additional information on R-12 to R-134a conversions, and for additional considerations dealing with your vehicle's A/C system.**

CRUISE CONTROL

Control Switch

REMOVAL & INSTALLATION

1. Disconnect the negative battery cable.
2. Remove the horn pad.
3. Mark the position of the steering wheel to the shaft and remove the wheel.
4. Remove the combination switch retaining screws. Carefully remove the switch from the steering column.
5. Remove the screws retaining the cruise control switch to combination switch and remove the cruise control switch.
   To install:
6. Assemble the cruise control switch to the combination switch.
7. Install the combination switch and connect the wiring.
8. Align the marks made for the steering wheel-to-column position and install the steering wheel. Torque the nut to 30 ft. lbs. (40 Nm).
9. Install the horn pad.
10. Connect the battery cable.

Speed Sensor

REMOVAL & INSTALLATION

1. Disconnect the negative battery cable.
2. Remove the instrument cluster assembly.

3. From behind the cluster, disconnect the harness connector at the speedometer.
4. Unscrew the sensor from the instrument cluster and remove it.
   To install:
5. Position the sensor in place and screw it in securely.
6. Connect the wiring to the sensor and instruments, then install the instrument cluster.
7. Connect the negative battery cable. Road test the vehicle and check the cruise control operation.

Control Unit

REMOVAL & INSTALLATION

1. Disconnect the negative battery cable.
2. On models with the 16-valve engine, the control unit is in the center console. On other models, the control unit is usually under the right side of the dashboard.
3. Disengage the electrical connector from the control unit.
4. Remove the bracket retaining screw and remove the control unit.
   To install:
5. Plug in the electrical connector to the control unit.
6. Secure the control unit in place with the retaining screw.
7. Connect the negative battery cable. Road test the vehicle and check the cruise control operation.

86636019

Fig. 27 Unplug the vacuum line and remove the nuts securing the servo

Vacuum Servo

REMOVAL & INSTALLATION

▶ **See Figures 27 and 28**

1. Disconnect the negative battery cable.
2. If necessary, remove the air cleaner.
3. Disconnect the vacuum line from the servo.

86636020

Fig. 28 Disconnect the rod, then remove the servo from the engine

4. Remove the nut(s), then disconnect the rod and remove the servo from the engine.
5. Installation is the reverse of removal.

ADJUSTMENT

1. Disengage the connecting rod from the throttle lever ball socket.
2. Make sure the throttle is fully closed against the stop screw.
3. Adjust the length of the rod to fit exactly between the servo and the throttle, then turn the ball socket out one more turn to lengthen the rod.
4. Make sure the idle speed is correct and check the throttle for smooth movement.

CRUISE CONTROL TROUBLESHOOTING

Problem	Possible Cause
Will not hold proper speed	Incorrect cable adjustment
	Binding throttle linkage
	Leaking vacuum servo diaphragm
	Leaking vacuum tank
	Faulty vacuum or vent valve
	Faulty stepper motor
	Faulty transducer
	Faulty speed sensor
	Faulty cruise control module
Cruise intermittently cuts out	Clutch or brake switch adjustment too tight
	Short or open in the cruise control circuit
	Faulty transducer
	Faulty cruise control module
Vehicle surges	Kinked speedometer cable or casing
	Binding throttle linkage
	Faulty speed sensor
	Faulty cruise control module
Cruise control inoperative	Blown fuse
	Short or open in the cruise control circuit
	Faulty brake or clutch switch
	Leaking vacuum circuit
	Faulty cruise control switch
	Faulty stepper motor
	Faulty transducer
	Faulty speed sensor
	Faulty cruise control module

Note: Use this chart as a guide. Not all systems will use the components listed.

TCCA6C01

ENTERTAINMENT SYSTEMS

Radio

REMOVAL & INSTALLATION

♦ See Figure 29

Except Heidleberg V and VI Radios

1. Disconnect the negative battery cable.
2. Remove the knobs from the radio.
3. Remove the nuts from the radio control shafts.
4. Detach the antenna lead from the jack on the radio case.

✳ WARNING

Never operate the radio without a speaker; severe damage to the output transistor will result. If the speaker must be replaced, use a speaker of the correct impedance (ohms) or else the output transistors will be damaged and require replacement.

5. Detach the power and speaker leads.
6. Remove the radio support nuts and bolts.
7. Withdraw the radio from beneath the dashboard.

To install:

8. Insert the radio into the dashboard, then install the radio support fasteners.
9. Connect the power and speaker leads.
10. Connect the antenna leads.
11. Install the control shafts and knobs.
12. Connect the battery cable.

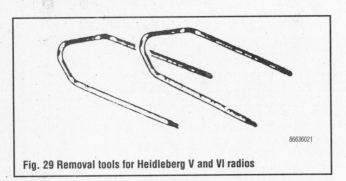

86636021

Fig. 29 Removal tools for Heidleberg V and VI radios

Heidleberg V

The Heidleberg V radio is equipped with an electronic locking circuit to deter radio theft. Whenever the radio is removed or the battery is disconnected, the locking circuit code must be entered in order for the radio to operate. There are 2 codes that can be entered, the first is the original factory code. The second is the programmed personal code entered by the vehicle owner. If the codes are not entered the radio will not operate. If the correct code is not entered in 6 tries, the radio becomes electronically locked-up and must be replaced.

The Heidleberg V radio is retained in the instrument panel by means of lock clips at the sides of the radio body. To remove the radio from its mounting posi-

tion two special removal pins are required. Insert the tools, into the holes, in the side of the radio face plate. The tools will "click" into position. With the tools installed the radio can be pulled from the instrument panel. Disconnect the electrical leads to complete the removal. When installing the radio, be sure to connect the electrical leads in their proper position.

Heidleberg VI

The Heidleberg VI fix-coded radio is equipped with an electronic locking circuit to deter radio theft. The Heidelberg radio is assigned a fixed four digit security code when it leaves the factory. Unlike the Heidelberg V system, this code cannot be changed. The Heidleberg VI radio is identified by white lettering on the faceplate and separate knobs for the fader, bass and treble controls. After two attempts at entering the security code, the radio will lock-up electronically for about one hour. This is indicated by a "SAFE" display. Unlike the previous generation, the radio will not permanently lock-up no matter how many incorrect coding attempts are made. The reactivation procedure can be repeated indefinitely.

The Heidleberg VI radio is retained in the instrument panel by means of lock clips at the sides of the radio body. To remove the radio from its mounting position, two special removal pins are required. Insert the tools, into the holes, in the side of the radio face plate. The tools will "click" into position. With the tools installed the radio can be pulled from the instrument panel. Disconnect the electrical leads to complete the removal. When installing the radio, be sure to connect the electrical leads in their proper position.

Speakers

REMOVAL & INSTALLATION

➡**Always disconnect the negative battery cable before attempting to remove the speakers.**

Dash Mounted

Dash mounted speakers can be accessed after removing the appropriate trim panel. These panels are usually retained by screws and clips. Be sure you have removed all of the attaching screws before prying the panel from the dash. Do not use excessive force on the panel as this will only lead to damage. Once the panel has been removed, loosen the speaker attaching bolts/screws, then pull the speaker from the dash and unplug the electrical connection.

Door Mounted

Door mounted speakers can be accessed after removing the door panel. These panels are usually retained by screws and clips. Be sure you have removed all of the attaching screws before prying the panel from the door. A special tool can be purchased for this purpose. Do not use excessive force on the panel as this will only lead to damage. Once the panel has been removed, loosen the speaker attaching bolts/screws, then pull the speaker from its mount and unplug the electrical connection.

Rear Speakers

Removing the rear speakers involves basically the same procedure as the front speakers. Remove the appropriate trim panel, then remove the speaker. The rear speakers on some models can be accessed from inside the trunk.

WINDSHIELD WIPERS AND WASHERS

Blade and Arm

REMOVAL & INSTALLATION

♦ See Figures 30, 31 and 32

➡**There are two different styles of wiper arms. On the first, the arm pivot attaching nut is covered with a plastic cap that pulls off. On the**

second, the arm pivot is covered by a spring-loaded metal cap that slips back off the nut.

1. Lift the blade and arm up off the windshield.
2. Simultaneously push the arm down and lift the smaller end cap up, or pull the plastic cap off, to expose the retaining nut.
3. Remove the retaining nut and lift the arm off the shaft.
4. Install the arm in the reverse order of removal. When properly installed, the blade-to-windshield molding clearance should be as follows. Blade clear-

Fig. 30 Pull the cap to expose the retaining nut, then remove the nut

Fig. 31 Lift the arm off the shaft, then remove it from the vehicle

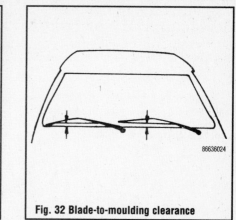

Fig. 32 Blade-to-moulding clearance

ance is adjusted by holding the base of the wiper arm with pliers and bending the arm at the point where it connects to the blade.
- Fox—1.8 in. (45.5mm) for both arms
- Scirocco with single blade—2.2 in. (55.5mm)
- Scirocco with double blade and Cabriolet—Front right: 1.4 in. (35mm) Left front: 2.5 in. (63.5mm) Rear: 1.2 in. (30mm)
- 1979–84 Rabbit, Jetta and Pick-Up—Right arm: 1.2 in. (30mm) Left arm: 2.5 in. (63.5mm)
- 1985–89 Golf and Jetta—Right and left front arms: 2.4 in. (61mm) Rear arm: 0.4 in. (10mm) from the bottom and 0.8 in. (20mm) from the window center line
- Dasher: 1.2 in. (30mm) for both arms

Front Wiper Motor

REMOVAL & INSTALLATION

Dasher and Quantum

▶ See Figures 33 and 34

➡ Do not remove the wiper drive crank from the wiper motor shaft. If it must be removed for any reason, matchmark the shaft, motor and crank for installation.

1. Disconnect the negative battery cable.
2. Unplug the multiconnector from the wiper motor.
3. Remove the motor-to-linkage bracket retaining screws.

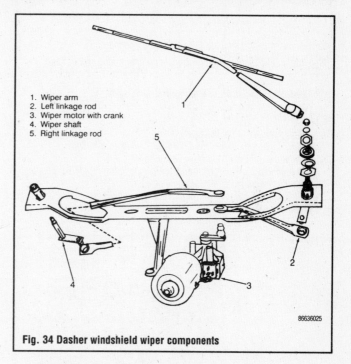

1. Wiper arm
2. Left linkage rod
3. Wiper motor with crank
4. Wiper shaft
5. Right linkage rod

Fig. 34 Dasher windshield wiper components

4. Carefully pry the motor crank out of the two linkage arms.
5. Remove the motor from the car.
6. Install the motor in the reverse order of removal. The crank arm should be at a right angle to the motor.

Rabbit, Scirocco and Jetta Through 1984

▶ See Figure 35

When removing the wiper motor, leave the mounting frame in place. On all models with two front wiper arms, do not remove the wiper drive crank from the motor shaft.

On Sciroccos with one front wiper arm, matchmark the drive crank and motor arm, then remove the arm.

➡ If, for any reason you must remove the wiper drive crank from the motor shaft on two wiper arm models, matchmark both parts for reassembly.

1. Access is with the hood open. Disconnect the battery ground cable.
2. Detach the connecting rods or motor crank arm from the motor.
3. Pull off the wiring plug.
4. Remove the four mounting bolts. You may have to energize the motor for access to the top bolt.
5. Remove the motor. Reverse the procedure for installation.

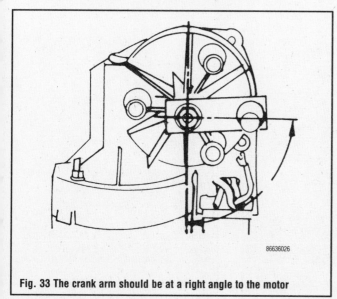

Fig. 33 The crank arm should be at a right angle to the motor

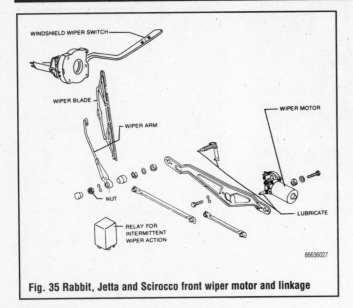

Fig. 35 Rabbit, Jetta and Scirocco front wiper motor and linkage

1985–89 Golf, Fox, Jetta, Scirocco and Cabriolet

♦ **See Figures 36, 37, 38 and 39**

1. Disconnect the negative battery cable.
2. Remove the cowl cover and seal to access the wiper motor.
3. Unplug the electrical connector to the wiper motor.
4. Disconnect the crank arm from the wiper arm assembly. Make a note or drawing of the crank arm installation angle before removing.
5. If necessary for clearance, remove the retaining nut and the crank arm from the wiper motor shaft.

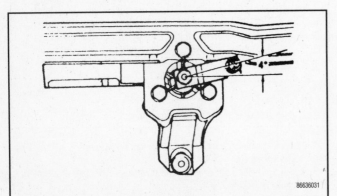

Fig. 36 To install the crank arm on the Golf and Jetta, raise the right side 4 degrees from horizontal, then connect it to the motor shaft

6. Remove the motor mounting bolts and the motor from the vehicle.

To install:

7. Run the motor and turn it off (it will stop in the PARK position). If necessary, the motor may be connected to the vehicle wiring harness and the battery may be temporarily connected for this.
8. Install the motor.
9. On Golf and Jetta to install the crank arm, raise it 4 degrees from horizontal on the right side and connect it to the motor shaft. On all other models, set the crank at the original angle.
10. To complete the installation, connect the crank arm to the wiper assembly and reverse the removal procedures.

Rear Wiper Motor

REMOVAL & INSTALLATION

♦ **See Figure 40**

There are 2 kinds of rear wiper motors used on Rabbits. Until 1976, a gear housing with a smooth cover plate was used; later models used a ribbed gear housing. Parts are different and cannot be combined between the two systems (except that the new style wiper motor bracket can be installed on earlier models). Scirocco motors are totally interchangeable, and their linkage remains unchanged.

Dasher, Fox and Quantum station wagons are also equipped with rear windshield wipers (optional). Golf models also have a rear wiper.

➡ **On all models, do not interchange the wires of terminal 53 and 53a on the rear wiper switch. Damage to the motor will result.**

1. Disconnect the negative battery cable.
2. Remove the inside trim panel from the hatch.
3. Disconnect the relay rod from the drive crank on the motor.
4. Remove the bolts securing the motor bracket to the body and move the assembly so the wiring can be disconnected.
5. Remove the assembly and separate the motor from the mounting bracket.
6. Installation is the reverse of removal. Before connecting the relay rod, run the motor for about 1 minute, then turn the switch OFF. When the motor stops at the park position, install the relay rod and make sure the wiper arm is in the correct position.

Wiper Linkage

REMOVAL & INSTALLATION

1. Disconnect the negative battery cable.
2. Remove the wiper arms and the motor.
3. Remove the relay rods.
4. Remove the nut that secures the wiper shaft to the body and push it out of the frame.
5. Installation is the reverse of removal.

Fig. 37 Remove the cowl cover and seal to access the wiper motor

Fig. 38 Be careful not to break the lock tab on the connector

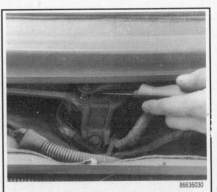

Fig. 39 A small prybar can be used to disconnect the crank from the arm assembly

Windshield Washer Pump/Reservoir

REMOVAL & INSTALLATION

The reservoir is usually held in place with a single nut that can be reached with a long extension and socket. It may be easier to remove the nut and lift the reservoir out to disconnect the pump wiring and hose. The pump is held in place with a grommet and can be easily pulled out.

Rear Window Washer Pump/Reservoir

REMOVAL & INSTALLATION

The reservoir is usually behind the trim panel in the right side of the luggage compartment. Remove the screws, then pull the reservoir out to disconnect the wiring and hose. The pump is held to the reservoir with a grommet.

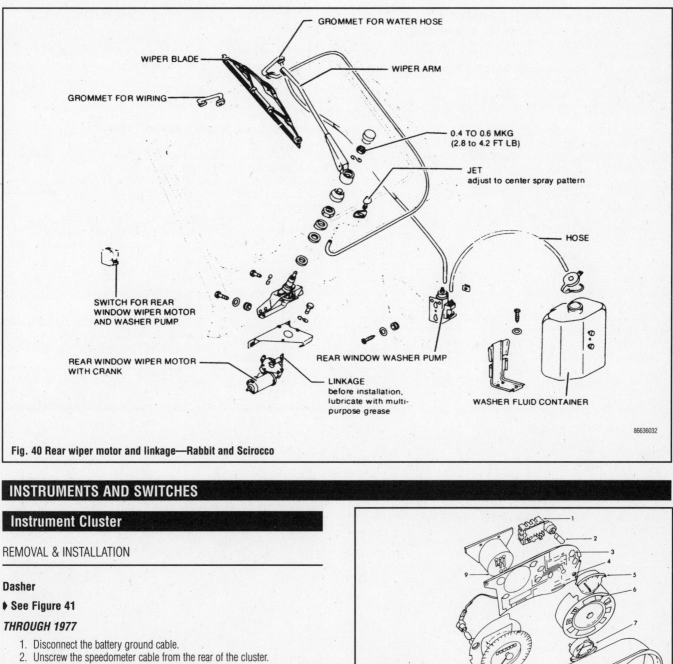

Fig. 40 Rear wiper motor and linkage—Rabbit and Scirocco

INSTRUMENTS AND SWITCHES

Instrument Cluster

REMOVAL & INSTALLATION

Dasher

▸ **See Figure 41**

THROUGH 1977

1. Disconnect the battery ground cable.
2. Unscrew the speedometer cable from the rear of the cluster.
3. Using needle-nosed pliers, detach the retaining springs on either side of the cluster.
4. Pivot the instrument cluster out of the dash.
5. Disengage the multi-connector plug at the rear of the cluster.
6. Remove the cluster from the dash.
To install:
7. Support the cluster and engage the multi-plug connector.
8. Mount the cluster to the dash and connect the side cluster retaining springs.

1. Voltage stabilizer
2. Bulb
3. Printed circuit board
4. Washer
5. Fuel gauge
6. Trim plate
7. Coolant temperature gauge
8. Instrument cluster
9. Cover

Fig. 41 Dasher instrument panel

9. Connect the speedometer cable to the speedometer at the rear of the cluster.

10. Connect the negative battery cable.

1978 AND LATER

1. Disconnect the negative battery cable.
2. Remove the radio or shelf.
3. Pull the knobs off the fresh air control and fan switch.
4. Remove the six instrument cluster-to-dashboard retaining screws.
5. Snap out the light, emergency flasher and rear window defogger switches.
6. Disengage the air fan switch electrical connector.
7. Remove the instrument cluster, then disconnect the speedometer cable and the multi-point connector from the back of the cluster.

To install:

8. Support the cluster, then connect the multi-point plug and speedometer cable to the rear of the cluster.
9. Plug in the air fan switch connector.
10. Push the rear window defogger, emergency and light switches into the cluster.
11. Install the cluster-to-dash retaining screws.
12. Mount the fan switch and fresh air control knobs.
13. Mount the radio or shelf.
14. Connect the battery cable.

1975–81 Scirocco and Pre-1985 Rabbit and Jetta

1. Disconnect the battery ground cable.
2. Remove the fresh air controls trim plate.
3. Remove the radio and glove box.
4. Unscrew the speedometer drive cable from the back of the speedometer. Detach the electrical plug.
5. Remove the attaching screw inside the radio/glove box opening.
6. Remove the instrument cluster.

To install:

7. Mount the instrument cluster and install the attaching screw through the radio/glove box opening.
8. Connect the electrical plug and speedometer cable.
9. Install the radio and glove box.
10. Mount the fresh air controls trim plate.
11. Connect the negative battery cable.

1982–84 Scirocco

1. Disconnect battery ground cable.
2. Remove the two Phillips head screws on the inner top surface of the instrument compartment.
3. Start to pull down on the instrument cluster and remove the screws in the top of the cluster.
4. Tip out the top of the instrument cluster.
5. Remove the speedometer cable by twisting the tabs of the plastic fixture around the end of the cable. On some vehicles, the speedometer cable is attached by a nut.
6. Unplug the multi-point connector, then remove instrument cluster.

To install:

7. Support the cluster and connect the multi-point plug connector.
8. Connect the speedometer cable.
9. Mount the cluster and install the lower retaining screws.
10. Install the two Phillips head screws on the inner top surface of the instrument compartment.
11. Connect the negative battery cable.

Quantum

1. Disconnect battery ground strap.
2. Carefully pry off switch trim below instruments.
3. Pull the heater control knobs off and press out the heater control trim.
4. Remove the Phillips head screws holding heater control trim to panel.
5. Remove the Phillips screws around perimeter of instrument cluster.
6. Disconnect all wiring to switches and warning lamps. Remove all trim panels.

7. Start to pull down on the instrument cluster and remove the screws in the top of the cluster.
8. Tip out the top of the instrument cluster.
9. Remove the speedometer cable by twisting the tabs of the plastic fixture around the end of the cable. On some vehicles, the speedometer cable is attached by a nut.
10. Unplug the multi-point connector and remove instrument cluster.

To install:

11. Support the cluster and connect the multi-point plug connector.
12. Connect the speedometer cable.
13. Mount the cluster and install the lower retaining screws.
14. Install the two Phillips head screws on the inner top surface of the instrument compartment.
15. Install the trim panels and connect all switch wiring.
16. Install the Phillips heads screws around the cluster perimeter.
17. Install the heater control-to-trim panel screws.
18. Press in the heater control trim and mount the heater control knobs.
19. Mount the lower instrument trim.
20. Connect the negative battery cable.

1985–89 Golf, Fox, Jetta, Scirocco and Cabriolet

▶ See Figure 42

1. Disconnect the negative battery cable.
2. Pull off all of the temperature control knobs and levers.
3. Unclip the control lever trim plate, unplug the electrical connectors and remove the plate.
4. Remove the retaining screws and the instrument panel trim plate.
5. Remove the retaining screws and pull out the instrument panel.
6. Squeeze the clips on the speedometer cable head and remove the cable from the instrument cluster.
7. Unplug all of the vacuum hose and the electrical connections.

To install:

8. Support the cluster, then engage the electrical and vacuum connections.
9. Connect the speedometer cable.
10. Mount the instrument panel and install the panel retaining screws.
11. Install the trim plate with retaining screws.
12. Install the control lever trim plate and plug in the electrical connectors. Secure the plate with the clip.
13. Mount the temperature control knobs and levers.
14. Connect the battery cable.

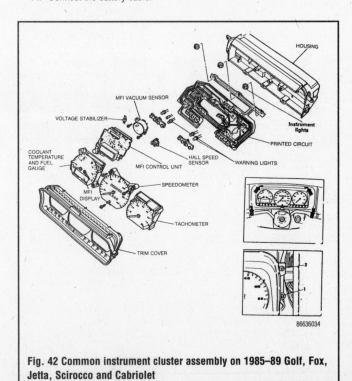

Fig. 42 Common instrument cluster assembly on 1985–89 Golf, Fox, Jetta, Scirocco and Cabriolet

Speedometer, Tachometer and Gauges

REMOVAL & INSTALLATION

Once the instrument cluster has been removed, the speedometer, tachometer and gauges can usually be replaced using the same basic procedure. In most cases, removal of the gauges involves disassembling the printed circuit board and front lens from the meter. The gauges are normally secured by a series of small screws or bolts. Be careful not to damage the indicator needles and gauge faces when disassembling the meter.

Speedometer Cable

REMOVAL & INSTALLATION

The speedometer cable should not be kinked or greased. When installing the Scirocco speedometer cable, attach the cable to the bracket so the speedometer cable will not contact the clutch cable.

➡**On models with EGR elapsed mileage counters, there are two cables. One section runs from the transaxle to the EGR counter and a shorter section runs from the counter to the instrument cluster.**

1. On 1 cable vehicles (or if replacing the shorter piece on 2 cable vehicles) reach in behind the instrument cluster from below and detach the speedometer cable from the rear of the cluster. Either unscrew the cable end or squeeze the retaining tabs while pulling the cable end from the instrument cluster.
2. If equipped, unscrew the speedometer cable attachments from the EGR elapsed mileage counter.
3. Unless you are only replacing the longer piece on a 2 cable system, unsnap the rubber grommet from the dash panel support and the firewall. Pull the speedometer cable through the hole.
4. If applicable, use pliers to unscrew the cable from the transaxle. Remove the cable(s) from the vehicle.
5. Installation is the reverse of removal.

Printed Circuit Board

REMOVAL & INSTALLATION

The printed circuit board is attached to the back of the instrument cluster. It is usually secured by a series of screws/nuts and by the bulb sockets. These

LIGHTING

Headlights

REMOVAL & INSTALLATION

▶ **See Figures 43, 44, 45 and 46**

Dasher

SINGLE HEADLIGHT MODELS

1. Disconnect the negative battery cable.
2. Remove the grille. The retaining screws are located on the left of the VW insignia and one each between the VW and the headlight.
3. Remove the three headlight retaining ring screws.

➡**Do not disturb the two headlight aiming screws or it will be necessary to re-aim the headlights. This requires special tools and you will likely have to take it to a service station.**

4. Remove headlight retaining ring.
5. Pull the headlight out of the housing and unplug the multi-connector.
6. Replace the new bulb in the reverse order of removal. Make sure that the three lugs on the bulb engage the slots in the housing.

sockets are normally removed by first twisting, then pulling them from the meter. Do not force any components as they are easily damaged

Windshield Wiper/Washer Switch

REMOVAL & INSTALLATION

1. Disconnect the negative battery cable.
2. Pull off the steering wheel cover/horn pad.
3. Remove the steering wheel lock nut and spacer.
4. Using a steering wheel puller, remove the steering wheel.
5. Remove the retaining screws, then remove the combination turn signal/headlight switch.
6. Remove the windshield wiper/washer switch from the steering column.
To install:
7. Install the windshield wiper/washer switch onto the steering column.
8. Install the combination turn signal/headlight switch.
9. Install the steering wheel, lock nut and spacer. Torque the nut to 30 ft. lbs. (40 Nm).
10. Install the steering wheel cover.
11. Connect the battery cable.

Headlight Switch

REMOVAL & INSTALLATION

➡**A modified headlight switch has been installed on 1989 Cabriolets and Jettas produced from Novembr . of 1988. The new component includes two additional terminals. The new switch is NOT interchangeable with the old one.**

1. Disconnect the negative battery cable.
2. Remove the steering wheel.
3. Remove the retaining screws, then remove the combination turn signal, headlight switch.
4. Installation is the reverse of the removal procedure. Torque the steering wheel nut to 30 ft. lbs. (40 Nm).

Back-Up Light Switch

The back-up light switch is mounted on the transaxle. For removal and installation procedures, please refer to Section 7.

86636035

Fig. 43 Remove the screws securing the trim ring (arrows). Do not disturb the headlight aiming screws

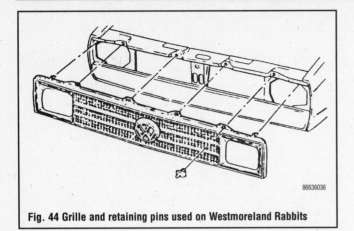

Fig. 44 Grille and retaining pins used on Westmoreland Rabbits

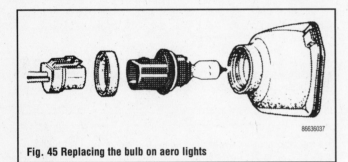

Fig. 45 Replacing the bulb on aero lights

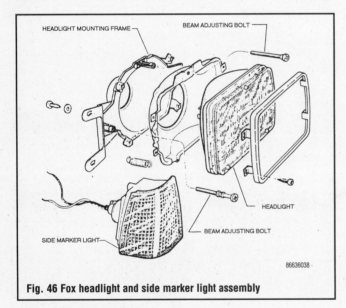

Fig. 46 Fox headlight and side marker light assembly

DUAL HEADLIGHT MODELS

1. Disconnect the negative battery cable.
2. Remove the radiator grille. Pry up the two retaining clips, one located at each end of the top of the grille. Unsnap the four plastic tabs along the top of the grille and remove it.
3. Remove the three small screws and remove the retaining ring. Don't fiddle with the spring loaded adjusting screws or you will need to have the light re-aimed (likely at a shop with the proper equipment). Pull the light out and unhook it.
4. When installing new headlight, be aware that the outside lights have both high beam and low beam filaments while the inside lights have only high beam filaments. Be sure to mention which one you need when buying replacement.
5. When the light is in position, make sure the glass lugs on the light engage in the support ring.

Scirocco

1975–81 MODELS

1. Disconnect the negative battery cable.
2. Remove the grille. There are about fourteen screws located inside the grids of the grille. Remove these, then remove the grille.
3. Remove the small screws (usually 3) and remove the retaining ring. Don't fiddle with the spring loaded adjusting screws or you will need to have the light re-aimed (likely at a shop with the proper equipment). Pull the light out and unhook it.
4. When installing new headlight, be aware that the outside lights have both high beam and low beam filaments while the inside lights have only high beam filaments. Be sure to mention which one you need when buying replacement.
5. When the light is in position, make sure the glass lugs on the light engage in the support ring.

1982 AND LATER MODELS

1. Disconnect the negative battery cable.
2. Remove the black moldings below the headlights.
3. Remove the screws retaining the headlamp mounting bracket.
4. Gently pull the headlamp from the support, unplug the connector from the back of the unit and remove the sealed beam.
5. Install in the reverse order.

Rabbit

MODELS THROUGH 1980

1. Disconnect the negative battery cable.
2. Remove the grille.
   a. On Westmoreland Rabbits (those made in the U.S., with square headlamps), the radiator grille is retained by two snap tabs and four fasteners on earlier models and by four screws along the top of the grille on later models. Both early and late model grilles use an additional 4 fasteners at each headlight. On the earlier models, remove the 4 fasteners along the top of the grille (not the ones at the headlights) with a small punch.

➡During grille installation for early model Westmorelant rabbits, new fasteners will be needed to replace the four which were removed using the punch.

   b. On Rabbits equipped with round headlights, remove the screws and clips along the top and sides of the grille.
3. Remove the headlight on all models by removing the 3 retaining ring screws (round headlights) or 4 screws (square headlights), then by removing the ring and the light. Unhook the electrical connector.
4. When installing new light, be sure to align the lugs in the light with their positions in the frame.

1981 AND LATER—ROUND SEALED BEAM

1. Disconnect the negative battery cable.
2. Remove the screws and clips along the top and side of the grille, then remove it from the vehicle.
3. Remove the three retaining screws that hold the headlamp mounting bracket.
4. Gently pull the headlamp from the support, unplug the connector from the back of the unit and remove the sealed beam.
5. Install in the reverse order.

1981 AND LATER—RECTANGULAR SEALED BEAM

1. Disconnect the negative battery cable.
2. Remove the four screws located around the headlamp trim cover, then remove the cover from the vehicle.
3. Remove the four screws retaining the headlamp mounting bracket.
4. Gently pull the headlamp from the support, unplug the connector from the back of the unit and remove the sealed beam.
5. Install in the reverse order.

Cabriolet

1. Disconnect the negative battery cable.
2. Remove the grille. If equipped with dual headlights, loosen the grille for access, then disengage the driving lamp harness and remove the grille completely.

3. Remove the 2 retaining screws which secure the outer grille trim, then remove the trim piece.

4. Unplug the connector from the back of the headlight.

5. Remove the 3 retainer ring screws and remove the light.

6. Installation is the reverse of the removal procedure.

1980–84 Jetta

1. Disconnect the negative battery cable.

2. Remove the 2 retaining nuts which secure the marker light on the side of the headlight assembly which is being removed. These nuts are accessed from the engine compartment.

3. Remove the screws retaining the center grille section, then remove the center grille from the vehicle.

4. Remove the screws retaining the side grille/headlight cover, then remove the grille/cover.

5. Loosen and remove the 4 retaining ring screws, then support the headlight and remove the ring.

➡The inner and outer sealed beams of the headlight assembly ARE NOT interchangeable. The inner is a high beam unit only, while the outer is for both high and low beams.

6. Unplug the electrical connector and remove the headlight from the vehicle.

7. Installation is the reverse of removal.

1985–89 Jetta and Golf

STANDARD LIGHTS

Disconnect the negative battery cable. Remove the grille by removing the two screws and the clip, swinging the side grille forward and lifting it out of the lower support holders. Remove the four screws and tensioner spring (Golf) in the face of the ring and remove the headlight after unhooking its electrical connector. When inserting a new light, make sure the lugs in the light align with their supports in the ring.

AERO LIGHTS

1. Disconnect the negative battery cable.

2. Pull the connector off the bulb at the back of the headlight.

3. Push down on the clip to disengage it.

4. Pull the headlight bulb out of the housing. If it is difficult to remove, gently rock it up and down.

5. Be careful not to touch the glass part of the bulb. Any oil or dirt even from clean hands will cause a hot spot on the glass during operation and the bulb will break.

6. To ease installation, spray some silicone lubricant on your finger and rub it onto the rubber O-ring. Do not spray directly on the O-ring because it will also get on the bulb.

7. Install the bulb, snap the clip into place and connect the wiring.

Quantum

1. Disconnect the negative battery cable.

2. Open the hood. Loosen the lower parking/signal lamp retaining screws until the cover lens can be removed.

3. Remove the 3 screws (two lower and one upper) that retain the headlamp trim housing.

4. Remove the four screws that mount the headlamp retaining bracket.

5. Gently pull the headlamp from the support and unplug the connector from the back of the sealed beam.

6. Install in the reverse order.

Fox

1. Disconnect the negative battery cable.

2. Remove the two clips from the top of the headlight frame using a small prytool.

3. Remove the headlight frame.

4. Remove the four screws at each corner of the headlight.

5. Gently pull the headlamp from the support and unplug the connector from the back of the sealed beam.

6. Install in the reverse order.

AIMING

The procedure outlined here is intended to provide a basic adjustment only. Most states have aiming specifications or require the job be done by licensed technicians with specialized aiming equipment. Always check with your local authorities before attempting to adjust your head-lights.

1. Park the vehicle on a level surface 25 feet (7.62 meters) from a vertical wall. There must be a horizontal reference point, such as a line on the pavement or another wall, at a right angle to the aiming wall. The fuel tank should be about 1/2 full, tire pressures must be correct and there must be a person in the driver's seat.

2. Measure the distance from the floor to the center of each headlight. Mark these heights on the wall and draw a line between them.

3. Measure the horizontal distance from the reference point to the center of each headlight. Make reference marks on the wall so that X marks the center of each headlight.

4. With the headlights on low beam, the high intensity zone of the light beam should be immediately below the line and about 2 inches to the right of the center of each headlight.

5. If adjustment is required, remove the grille and use a Phillips screwdriver to turn the adjuster screws.

Signal and Marker Lights

REMOVAL & INSTALLATION

➡Always disconnect the negative battery cable before attempting to remove any signal or marker lights.

Front Turn Signal and Parking Lights

1985–89 GOLF AND JETTA

▶ See Figures 47 and 48

On the front turn signal and side marker lights, the bulb can be removed after removing the lens. Inspect the condition of the lens seal and replace if required before installing the new bulb.

RABBIT AND SCIROCCO

To remove the front turn signal and marker light, open the hood, then pull the rubber cap covering the bulb holder. Squeeze the lug on the bulb holder (if equipped), then remove it from the lens assembly. Press the bulb into the holder slightly, then turn it left and take it out.

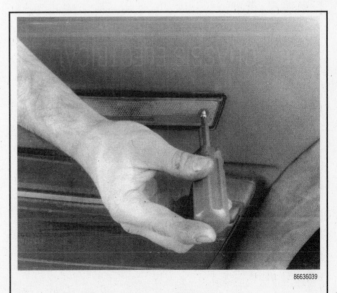

Fig. 47 Remove the screw securing the lens. . .

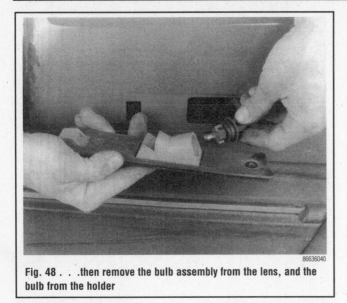

Fig. 48 . . .then remove the bulb assembly from the lens, and the bulb from the holder

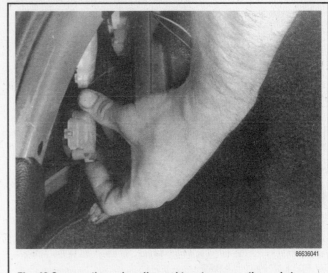

Fig. 49 Squeeze the spring clips and turn to remove the socket

QUANTUM

To replace the turn signal bulb, remove the screws securing the lens assembly, then pull it out. Press the bulb in slightly, then turn it left. To replace the side marker light, pry the bulb holder off with a small prytool. Pull the bulb out of the holder.

FOX AND PRE-1985 JETTA

To remove the front marker lights, open the hood, then pull the rubber cap covering the bulb holder. Squeeze the lug on the bulb holder (if equipped), then remove it from the lens assembly. Press the bulb into the holder slightly, then turn it left and take it out.

For the turn signal bulbs, remove the screws securing the lens, then pull it out of the bumper. Push the bulb in slightly, then turn it and take it out.

DASHER

To remove the front turn signal and side marker lights, remove the screws securing the lens, then remove it. Push the bulb in slightly, then turn it and take it out.

Rear Turn Signal, Brake and Parking Lights

EXCEPT PICK-UP AND DASHER WAGON

▶ See Figures 49 and 50

The rear light bulbs can be reached from inside the luggage compartment. Except on Golf, Rabbit and pre-1984 Scirocco, the entire light bulb panel can be removed by squeezing the clips. On Golf and Rabbit, squeeze the spring clips and turn to remove the socket. On pre-1984 Scirocco, remove the knurled screw inside the trunk, then remove the lens. Squeeze the spring clips and turn to remove the socket.

PICK-UP AND DASHER WAGON

Remove the screws securing the lens, then remove it. Push the bulb in slightly, then turn it and take it out.

High-Mount Brake Light

▶ See Figures 51 and 52

Squeeze the retaining clips on both sides, then pull out the lens/bulb housing assembly. Pull out the defective bulb and replace it. Reinstall the lens/bulb housing assembly.

License Plate Lights

▶ See Figure 53

Remove the screws securing the lens assembly, then pull it off. Some bulbs can be removed by pushing the bulb in slightly, then turning and taking it out. Others can be removed by simply pulling it out.

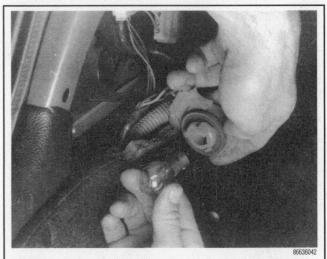

Fig. 50 Push the bulb in slightly, then turn it to remove it from the socket

Fig. 51 Squeeze the retaining clips on both sides, then pull out the lens/bulb housing assembly

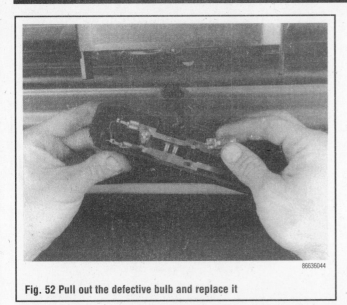

Fig. 52 Pull out the defective bulb and replace it

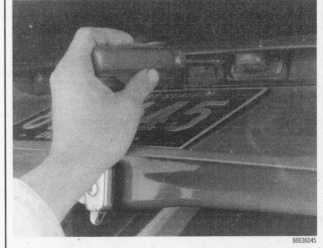

Fig. 53 Remove the screws securing the lens assembly, then pull it off for access to the bulb

TRAILER WIRING

Wiring the car for towing is fairly easy. There are a number of good wiring kits available and these should be used, rather than trying to design your own.

All trailers will need brake lights and turn signals as well as tail lights and side marker lights. Most states require extra marker lights for overwide trailers. Also, most states have recently required back-up lights for trailers, and most trailer manufacturers have been building trailers with back-up lights for several years.

Additionally, some Class I, most Class II and just about all Class III trailers will have electric brakes. Add to this number an accessories wire, to operate trailer internal equipment or to charge the trailer's battery, and you can have as many as seven wires in the harness.

Determine the equipment on your trailer and buy the wiring kit necessary. The kit will contain all the wires needed, plus a plug adapter set which included the female plug, mounted on the bumper or hitch, and the male plug, wired into, or plugged into the trailer harness.

When installing the kit, follow the manufacturer's instructions. The color cod-ing of the wires is usually standard throughout the industry. One point to note: some domestic vehicles, and most imported vehicles, have separate turn signals. On most domestic vehicles, the brake lights and rear turn signals operate with the same bulb. For those vehicles with separate turn signals, you can purchase an isolation unit so that the brake lights won't blink whenever the turn signals are operated, or, you can go to your local electronics supply house and buy four diodes to wire in series with the brake and turn signal bulbs. Diodes will isolate the brake and turn signals. The choice is yours. The isolation units are simple and quick to install, but far more expensive than the diodes. The diodes, however, require more work to install properly, since they require the cutting of each bulb's wire and soldering in place of the diode.

One, final point, the best kits are those with a spring loaded cover on the vehicle mounted socket. This cover prevent dirt and moisture from corroding the terminals. Never let the vehicle socket hang loosely; always mount it securely to the bumper or hitch.

LIGHT BULB AND FUSE APPLICATIONS

All fuses are found in the main fuse/relay panel to the left of the steer-ing column, except on the Dasher, which locates its panel under the hood on the driver's side fender. The panel's cover has a label to identify each fuse. Additionally, the current rating of each fuse is printed on the fuse itself.

For information on access to the light bulbs for replacement, please refer to the procedures found earlier in this section.

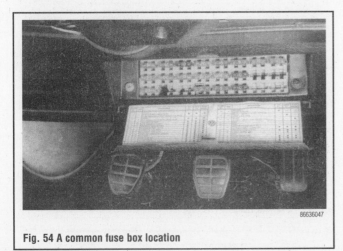

Fig. 54 A common fuse box location

LIGHT BULB APPLICATION CHART

Light Bulbs	Bulb No.
1974-1981 Dasher	
Dual headlights	
Inner	4001
Outer	4000
Single headlights	-
Front turn signals	1073
Parking lights	1816
Side marker lights	1816
Rear turn signals	1073
Stop lights	1073
Tail lights	67
Back-up Lights	1073
License plate lights	1816
Interior light	211
Luggage compartment light	211

LIGHT BULB APPLICATION CHART

Quantum	
Light Bulbs	**Bulb No.**
Headlights	
Outer	4656
Inner	4651
Front turn signal/parking lights	1157
Front side marker lights	168
Tail lights	67
Rear side marker lights	168
Rear turn signals	1073
Stop lights	1073
Center stop light	168
Back-up lights	1073
License plate lights	1816
Interior light	211
Reading light	
Wagon	211
Sedan	168
Luggage compartment light	211
Glove compartment light	211

86636201

LIGHT BULB APPLICATION CHART

Fox	
Light Bulbs	**Bulb No.**
Headlights	6054
Front turn signal/parking light	1157
Side marker lights	194
Rear turn signals	1156
Tail/stop lights	1157
Back-up lights	1156
Reading lamp	168
Center stop light	168
License plate lights	1816

86636202

LIGHT BULB APPLICATION CHART

1975-1984 Scirocco	
Light Bulbs	**Bulb No.**
Headlights	
Inner	4001
Outer	4000
Front turn signal/parking lights	1034
Rear side marker lights	1816
Rear turn signals	1073
Stop lights	1073
Tail lights	67
Back-up Lights	1073
License plate lights	1816
Interior light	211
Luggage compartment light	211

86636203

LIGHT BULB APPLICATION CHART

Rabbit/Pick-Up	
Light Bulbs	**Bulb No.**
Headlights	H6054
Front turn signal/parking lights	1034
Rear side marker lights	194
Rear turn signals	1073
Stop lights	1034
Tail lights	1034
Back-up Lights	1073
License plate lights	1816
Interior light	211
Luggage compartment light	-

86636204

LIGHT BULB APPLICATION CHART

1979-1984 Jetta	
Light Bulbs	**Bulb No.**
Headlights	
High beam	4651
Low beam	4652
Front turn signal/parking lights	1034
Front side marker lights	-
Rear turn signals	1073
Stop lights	1073
Tail lights	67
Back-up Lights	1073
License plate lights	1816
Interior light	211
Luggage compartment light	211

86636205

LIGHT BULB APPLICATION CHART

Rabbit Convertible/Cabriolet	
Light Bulbs	**Bulb No.**
Headlights	H6014
Front turn signal/parking lights	1034
Side marker lights	1816
Rear turn signals	1073
Stop lights	1073
Center stop light	168
Tail lights	67
Back-up Lights	1073
License plate lights	1816
Interior light	211
Luggage compartment light	211

86636206

LIGHT BULB APPLICATION CHART

1985-1989 Scirocco	
Light Bulbs	**Bulb No.**
Headlights	
Inner	4651
Outer	4656
Front turn signal/parking lights	1034
Rear side marker lights	1816
Rear turn signals	1073
Stop lights	1073
Center stop light	168
Tail lights	67
Back-up Lights	1073
License plate lights	1816
Interior light	211
Luggage compartment light	211

86636207

LIGHT BULB APPLICATION CHART

1985-1989 Golf	
Light Bulbs	**Bulb No.**
Headlights	
Golf	H6054
GTI	9004
Front turn signal/parking lights	2057
Side marker lights	194
Rear turn signals	1073
Tail/stop lights	2057
Center stop light	W10/5
Back-up lights	1073
License plate lights	194
Interior light	-
Luggage compartment light	-

86636208

LIGHT BULB APPLICATION CHART

1985-1989 Jetta

Light Bulbs	Bulb No.
Headlights	9004
Front turn signal/parking lights	1034
Side marker lights	194
Rear turn signals	1073
Stop lights	1073
Center stop light	168
Tail lights	67
Back-up Lights	1073
License plate lights	1816
Interior light	211
Luggage compartment light	211

86636209

FUSE APPLICATION CHART

1981 Westmoreland built Rabbit

Fuse Identification	Amps
1-Radiator fan	30
2-Parking lamps	15
3-Horn	20
5-Dash illumination lamps	4
6-Fuel pump relay	30
9-Rear window wiper	10
10-Turn signals	15
11-Radio	5
12-Back-up lights	10
19-Heater blower motor	25
20-Rear defogger	25
21-Windshield wiper motor	20
24-Stop lamp/hazard flashers	15
25-Dome, clock and glove box lamps	15
26-Cigarette lighter	10
27-Horn relay	4

86636210

FUSE APPLICATION CHART

Rabbit, except 1981 Westmoreland built

Fuse Identification	Amps
1-Left low beam	8
2-Right low beam	8
3-Left high beam/high beam indicator light	8
4-Right high beam	8
5-Rear window defogger	16
6-Stop lights/emergency flasher system	8
7-Interior light/cigarette lighter/clock	8
8-Turn signals and indicator light	8
9-Back-up lights/horn	8
10-Fresh air fan	16
11-Windshield wiper and washer/rear window washer	8
12-License plate lights	8
13-Right side parking, tail and side marker lights	8
14-Left side parking, tail and side marker lights	8
15-Radiator fan	25
16-Glow plugs (in engine compartment)	50
17-Fuel pump (on relay or inline)	16
18-Rear wiper	8
19-Radio	5

86636211

FUSE APPLICATION CHART

1978-1981 Dasher

Fuse Identification	Amps
1-Left low beam	8
2-Right low beam	8
3-Left high beam/high beam warning	8
4-Right high beam	8
5-Rear window defogger	16
6-Stop lights/emergency flasher system	8
7-Interior light/cigarette lighter/clock/radio	8
8-Turn signals, including indicator light	8
9-Back-up lights/horn/shift console	8
10-Fresh air fan	16
11-Windshield wiper/washer system	8
12-License plate lights	8
13-Right side parking light, tail light, marker light	8
14-Left side parking light, tail light, marker light	8
15-Radiator fan	16
31-Electric fuel pump (on fuel pump relay)	16

86636212

FUSE APPLICATION CHART

Fox

Fuse Identification	Amps
1-Vacant	-
2-Emergency flasher	15
3-Brake lights/horn	25
4-Clock/radio/interior dome and luggage compartment lights	5
5-Radiator fan	30
6-Right side marker, tail light, parking and turn signal lights	3
7-Left side marker, tail light, parking and turn signal lights	3
8-Right side high beam and indicator light	10
9-Left side high beam	10
10-Right side low beam	10
11-Left side low beam	10
12-Back-up lights/turn signal lights/instrument cluster lights	10
13-Main and auxiliary fuel pumps/auxiliary air regulator	15
14-License plate light/glove box light	3
15-Windshield wiper motor/rear window washer	25
16-Rear window defogger	25
17-Heating/ventilation blower	25
18-Cigarette lighter/rear window wiper motor	15
19-Radiator fan	25
20-Heating/ventilation blower	30
21-Radiator fan	30
22-Vacant	-
23-Electronic control unit/seat belt indicator system	5
24-Instrument illumination	3
25-Reading lamp	5
26-Vacant	-
27-Vacant	-
28-Vacant	-

86636213

WIRING DIAGRAMS

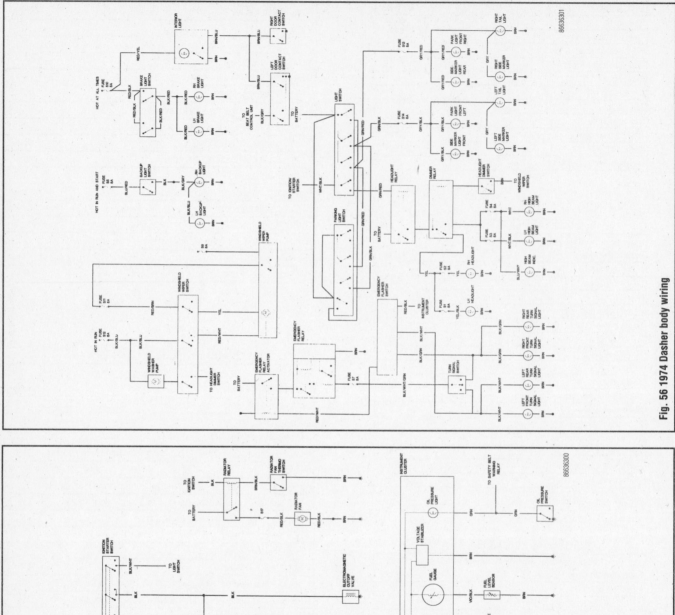

Fig. 56 1974 Dasher body wiring

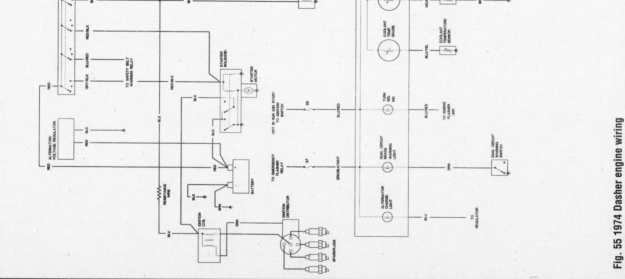

Fig. 55 1974 Dasher engine wiring

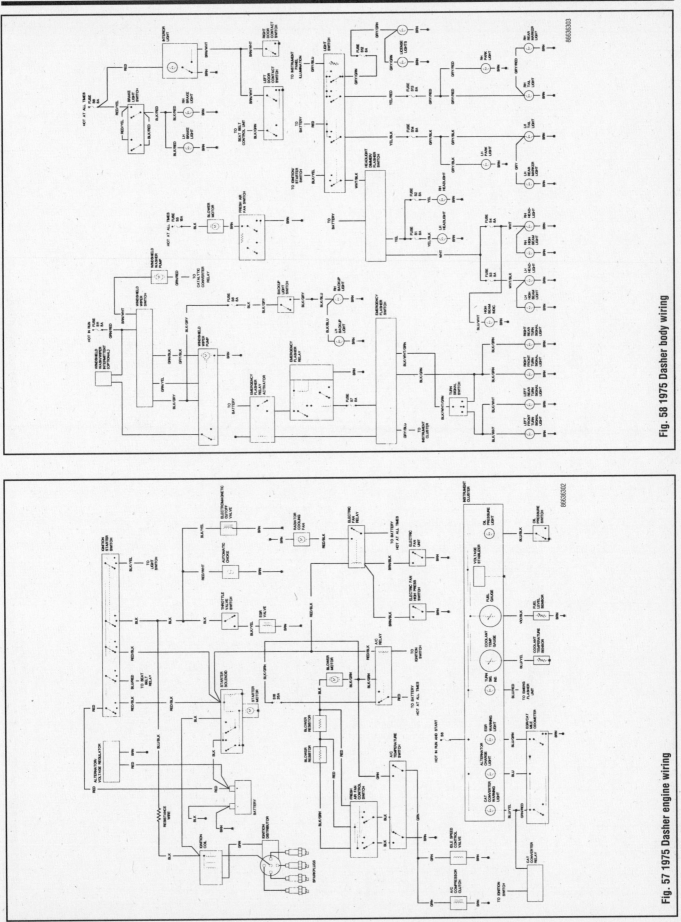

Fig. 58 1975 Dasher body wiring

Fig. 57 1975 Dasher engine wiring

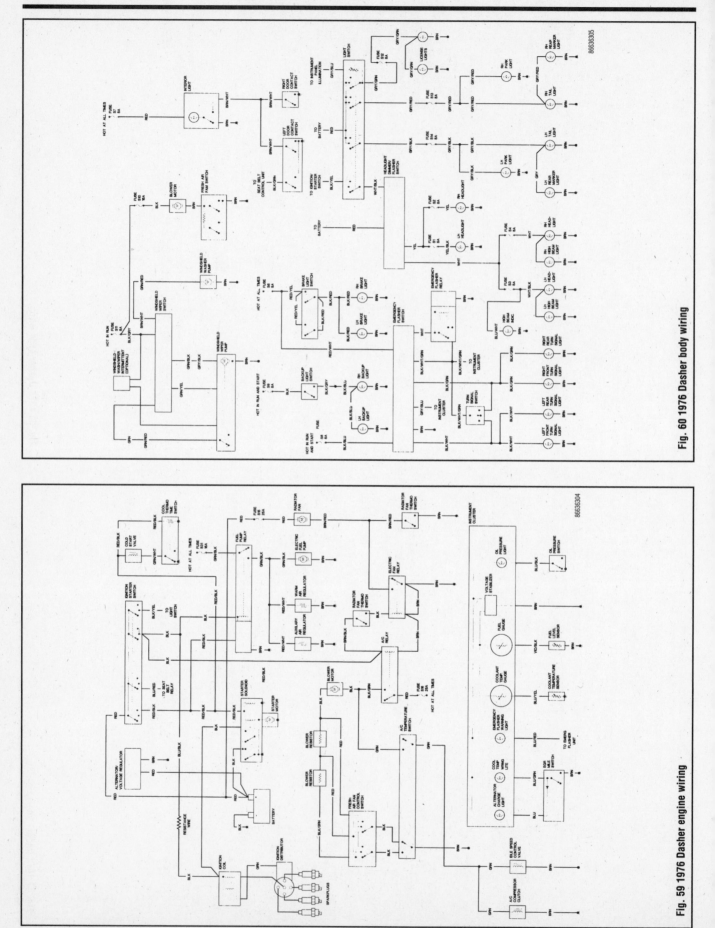

Fig. 60 1976 Dasher body wiring

Fig. 59 1976 Dasher engine wiring

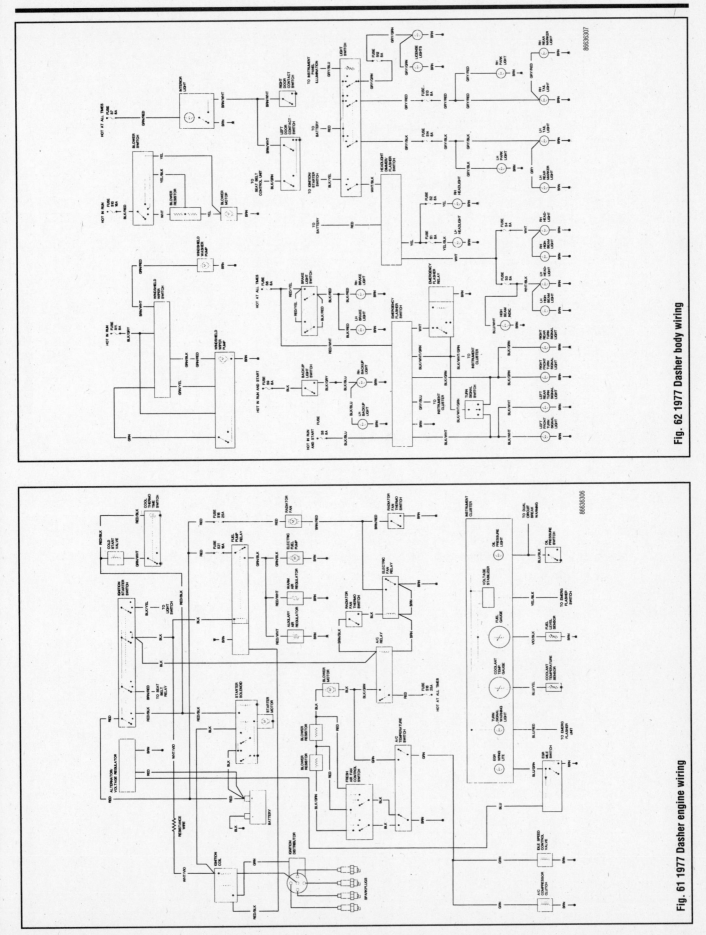

Fig. 62 1977 Dasher body wiring

Fig. 61 1977 Dasher engine wiring

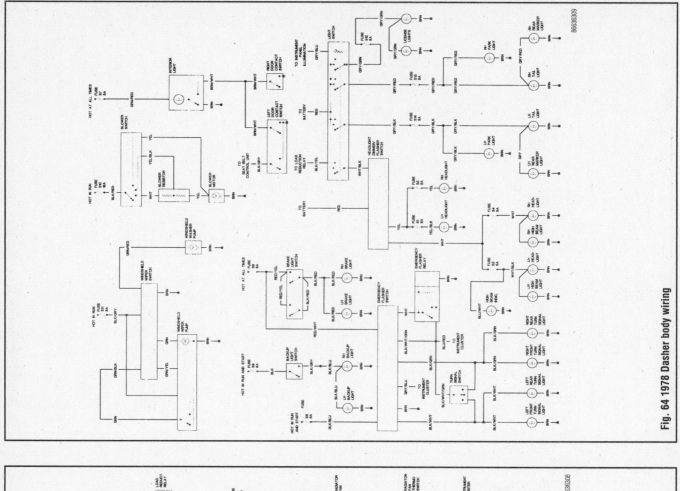

Fig. 64 1978 Dasher body wiring

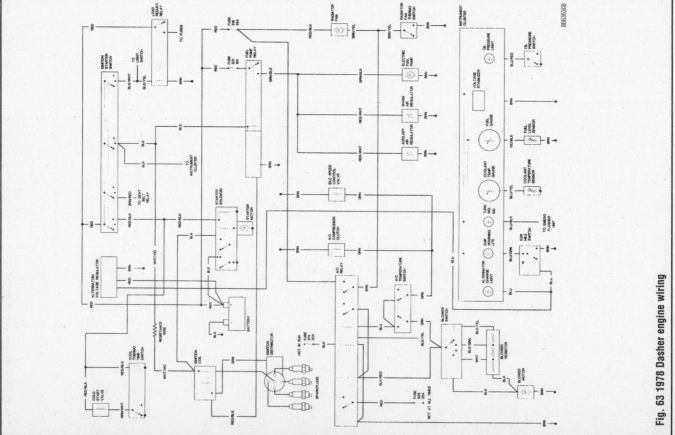

Fig. 63 1978 Dasher engine wiring

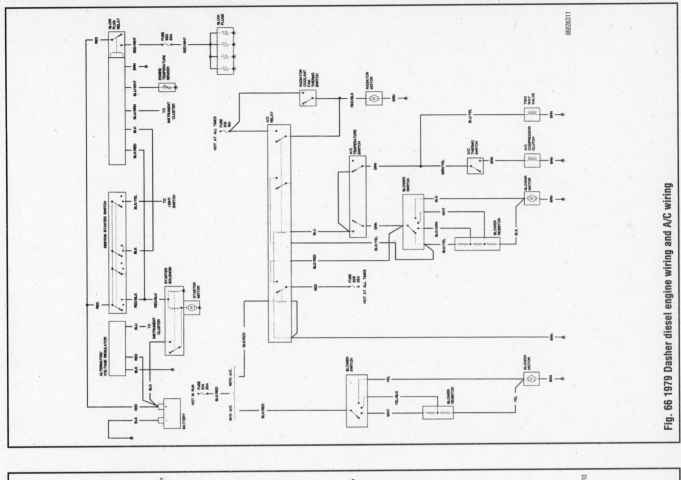

Fig. 66 1979 Dasher diesel engine wiring and A/C wiring

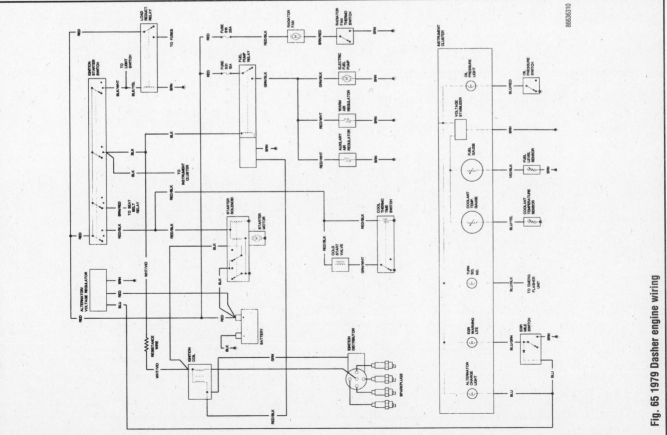

Fig. 65 1979 Dasher engine wiring

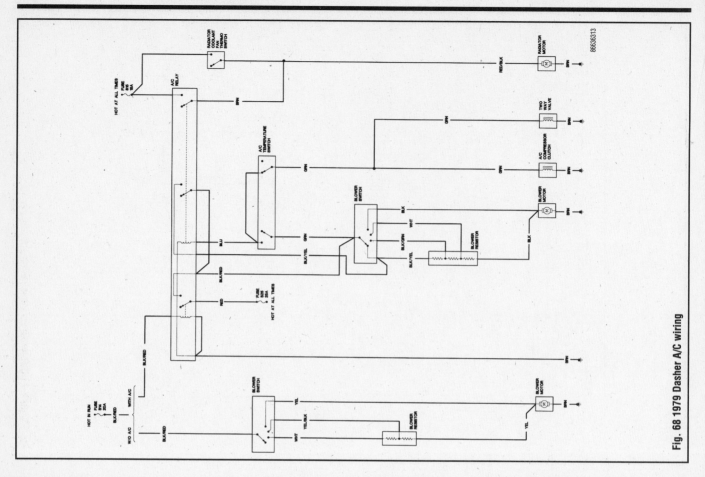

Fig. 68 1979 Dasher A/C wiring

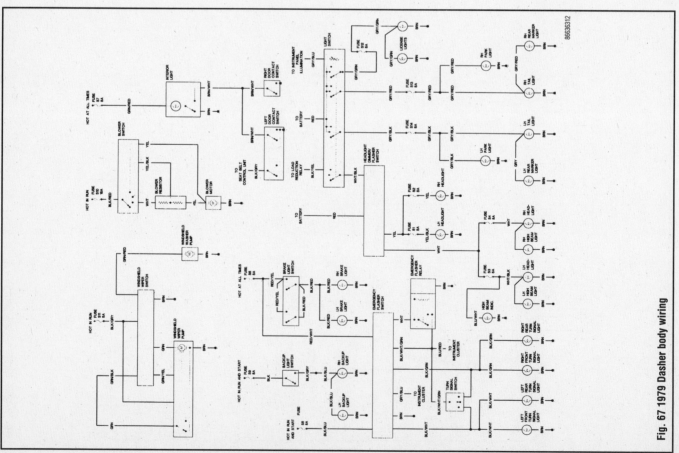

Fig. 67 1979 Dasher body wiring

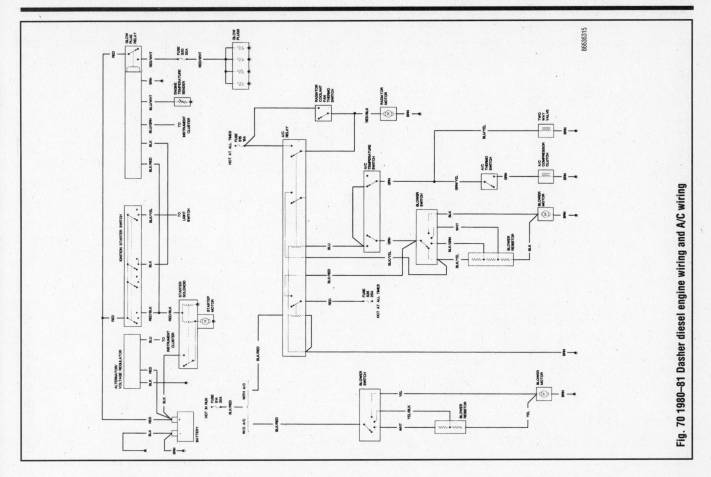

Fig. 70 1980–81 Dasher diesel engine wiring and A/C wiring

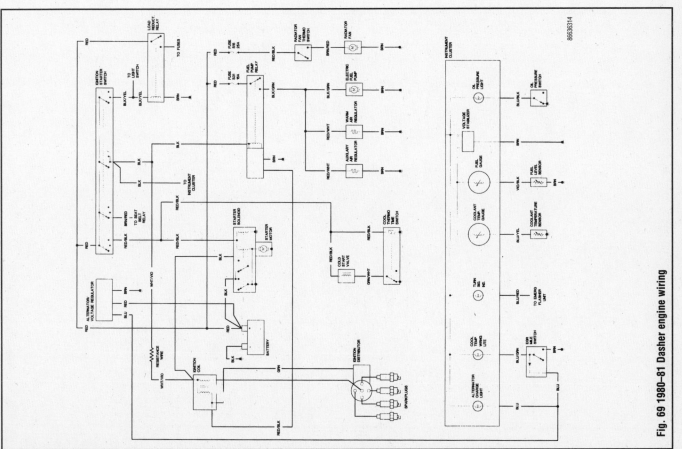

Fig. 69 1980–81 Dasher engine wiring

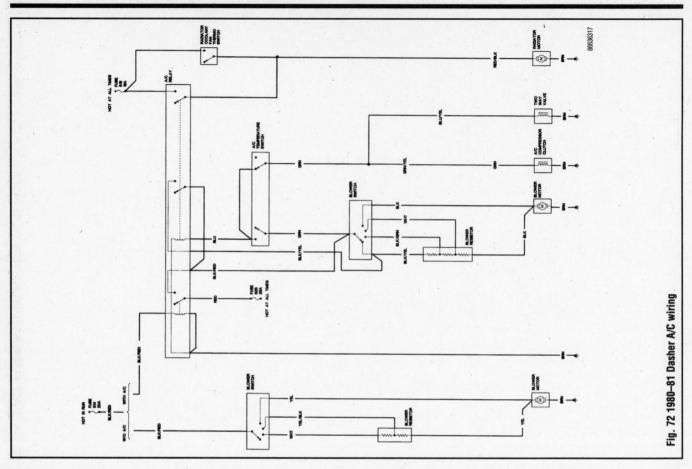

Fig. 72 1980–81 Dasher A/C wiring

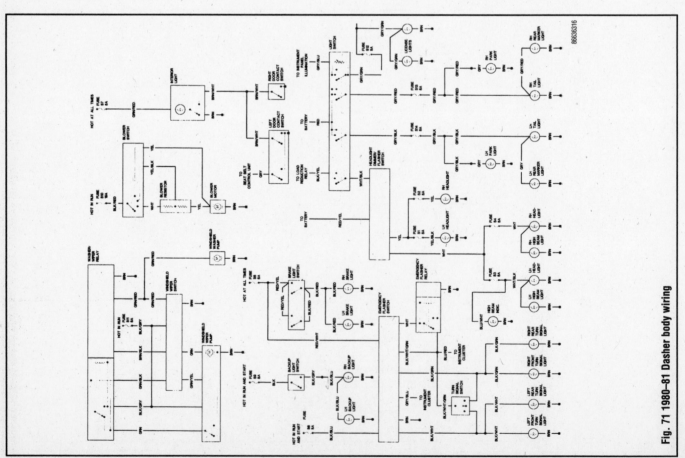

Fig. 71 1980–81 Dasher body wiring

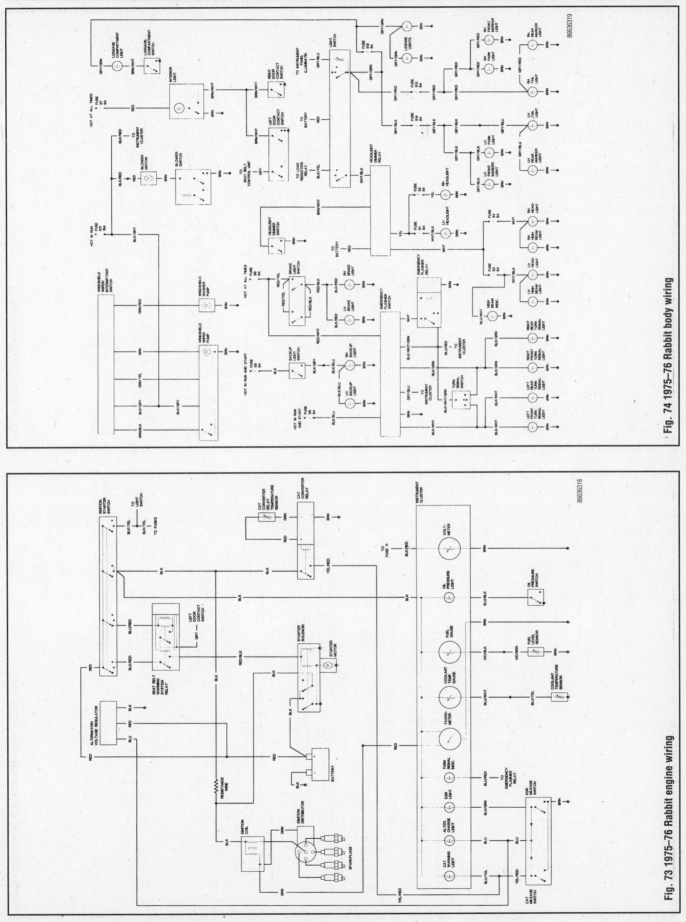

Fig. 74 1975–76 Rabbit body wiring

Fig. 73 1975–76 Rabbit engine wiring

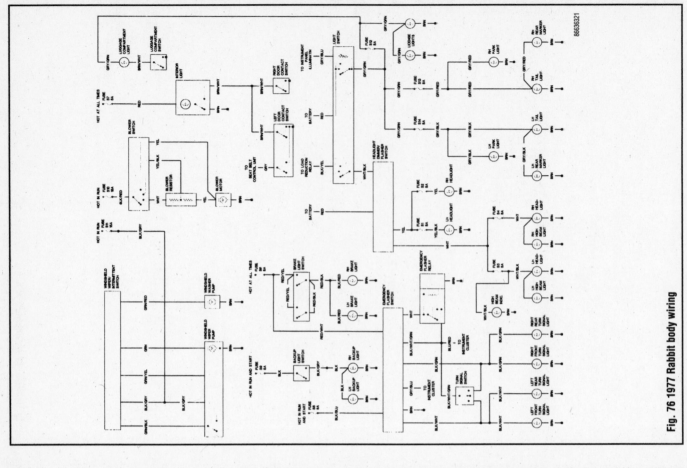

Fig. 76 1977 Rabbit body wiring

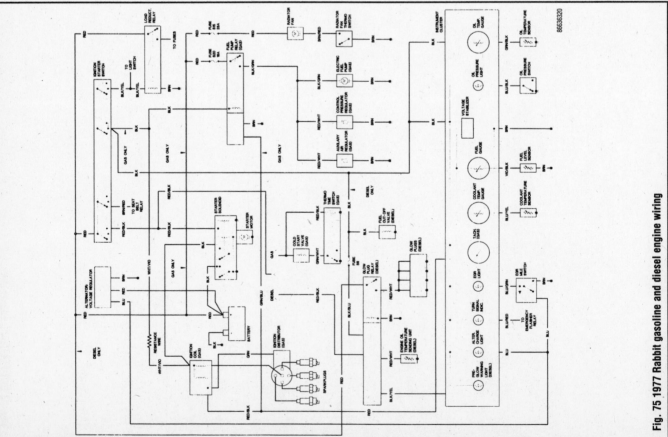

Fig. 75 1977 Rabbit gasoline and diesel engine wiring

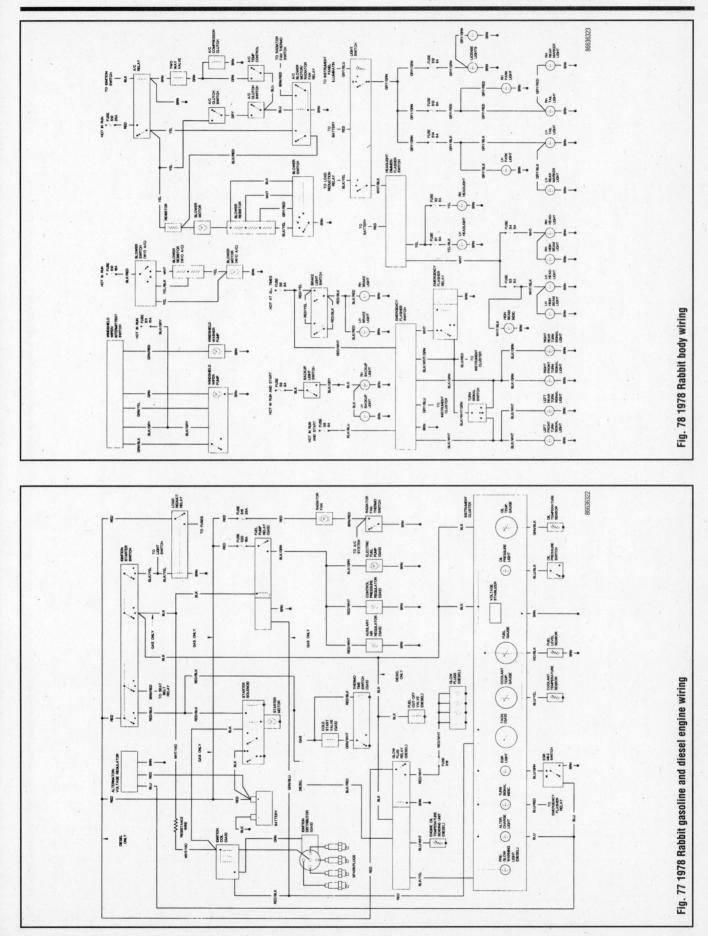

Fig. 78 1978 Rabbit body wiring

Fig. 77 1978 Rabbit gasoline and diesel engine wiring

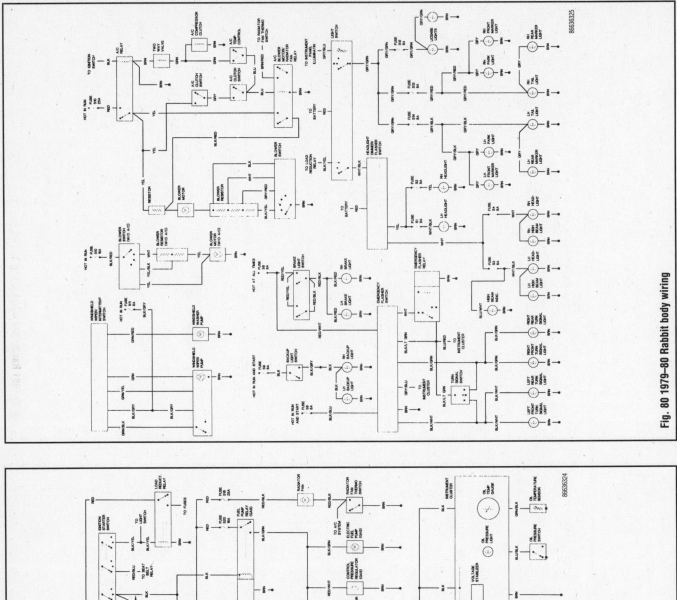

Fig. 80 1979-80 Rabbit body wiring

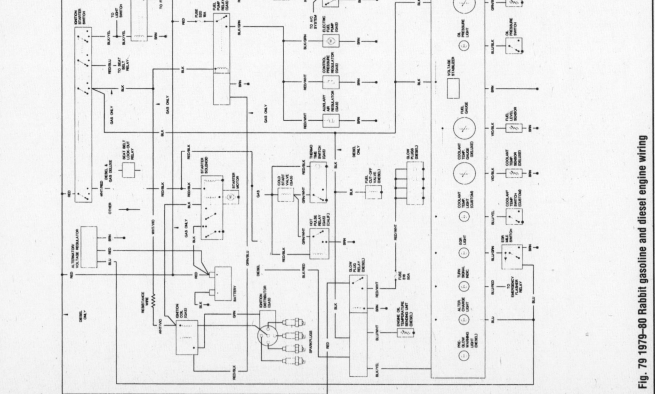

Fig. 79 1979-80 Rabbit gasoline and diesel engine wiring

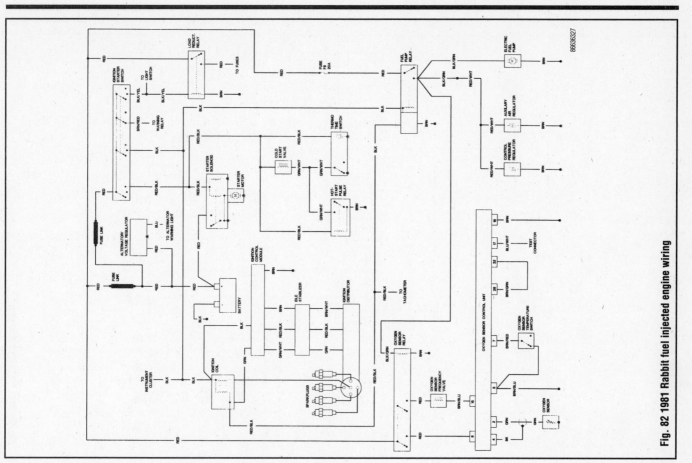

Fig. 82 1981 Rabbit fuel injected engine wiring

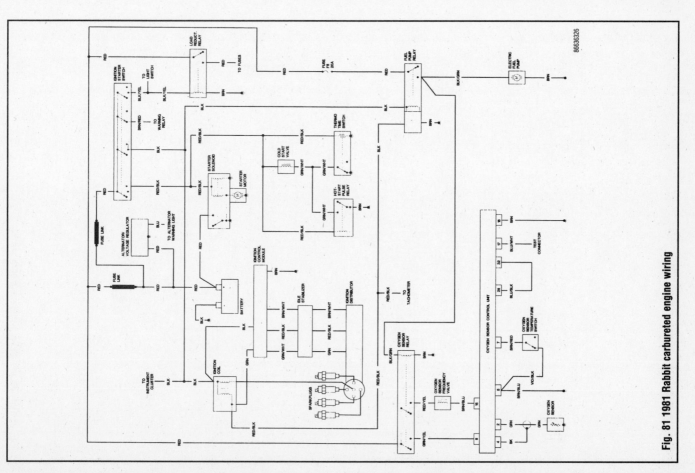

Fig. 81 1981 Rabbit carbureted engine wiring

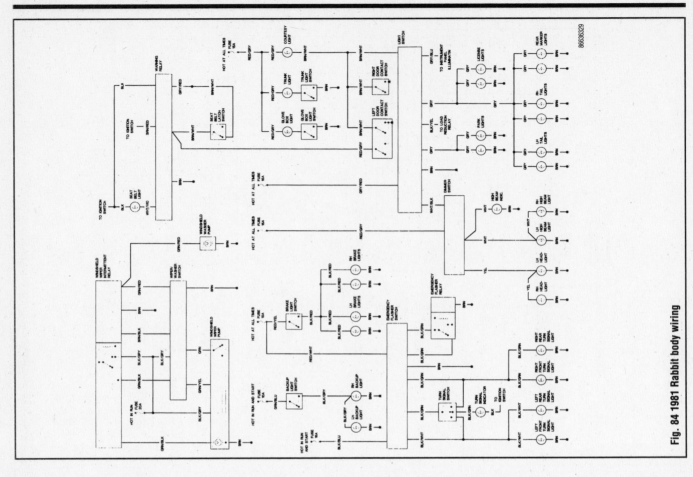

Fig. 84 1981 Rabbit body wiring

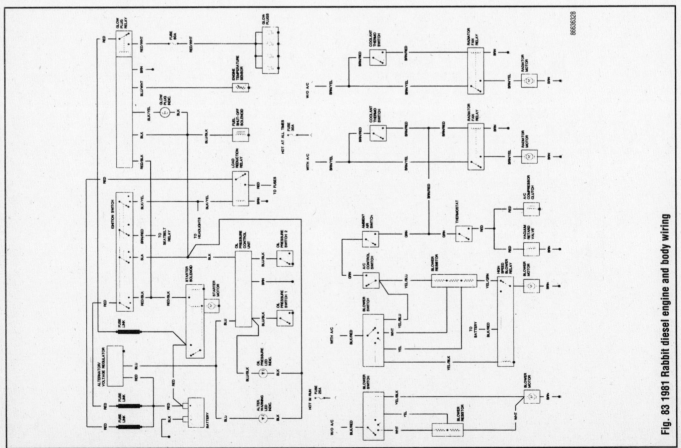

Fig. 83 1981 Rabbit diesel engine and body wiring

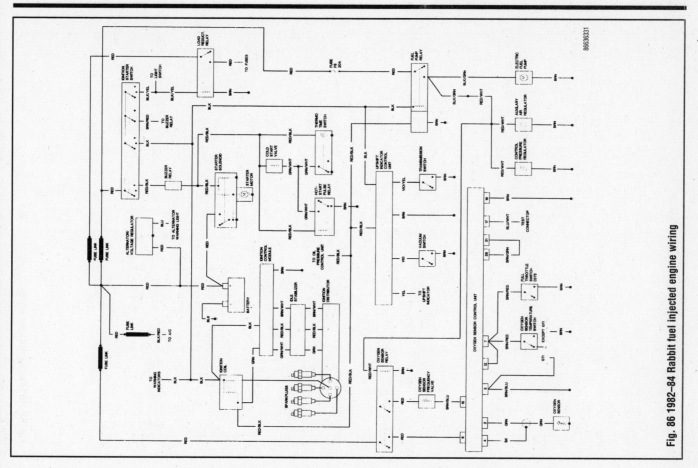

Fig. 86 1982–84 Rabbit fuel injected engine wiring

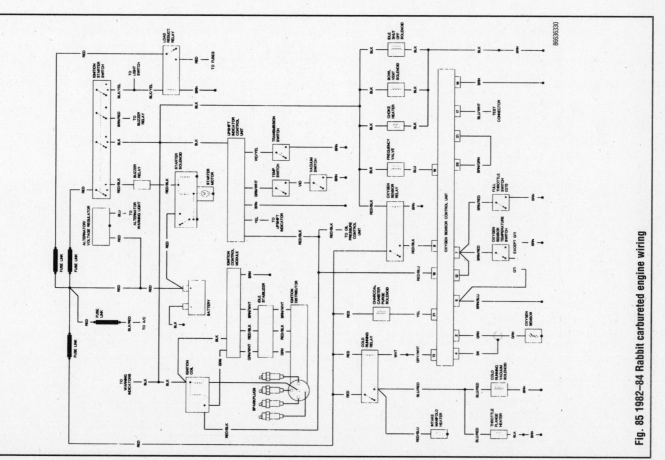

Fig. 85 1982–84 Rabbit carbureted engine wiring

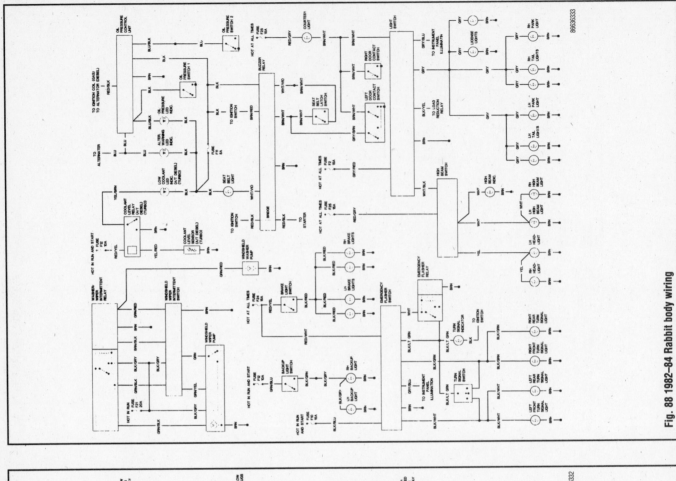

Fig. 88 1982–84 Rabbit body wiring

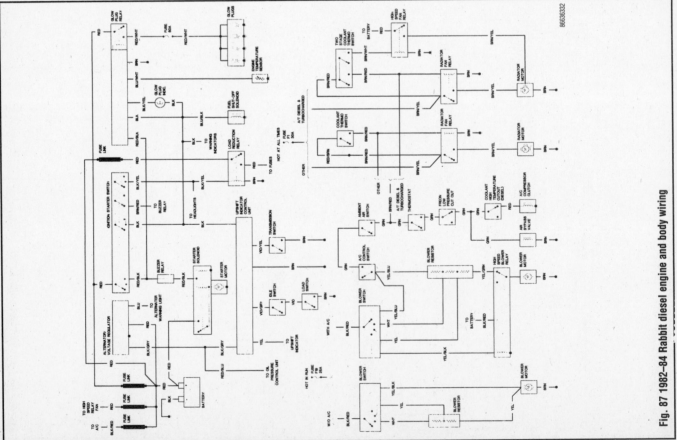

Fig. 87 1982–84 Rabbit diesel engine and body wiring

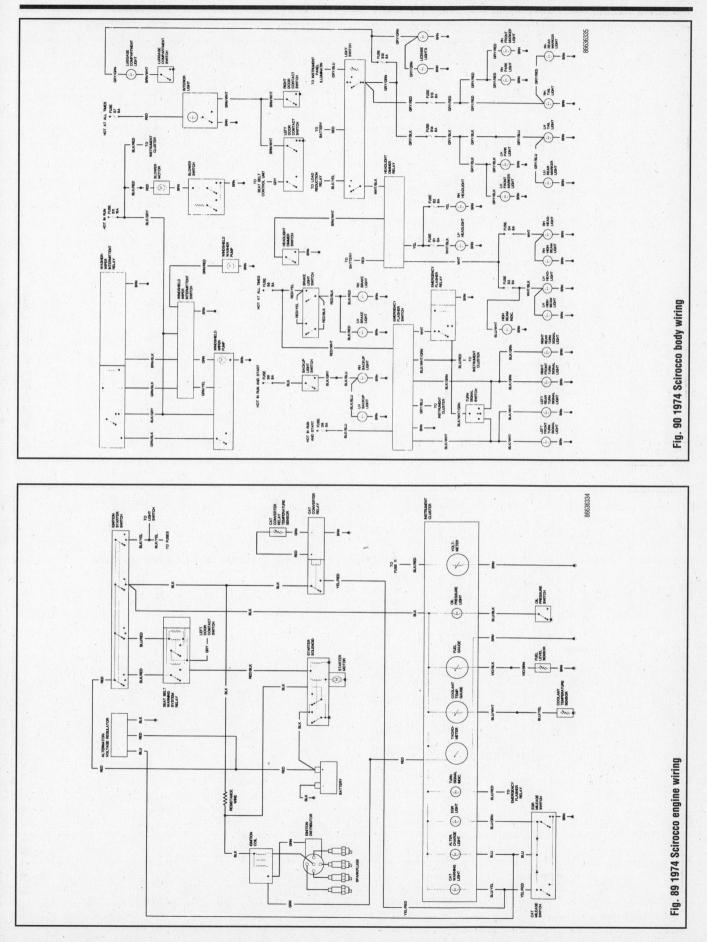

Fig. 90 1974 Scirocco body wiring

Fig. 89 1974 Scirocco engine wiring

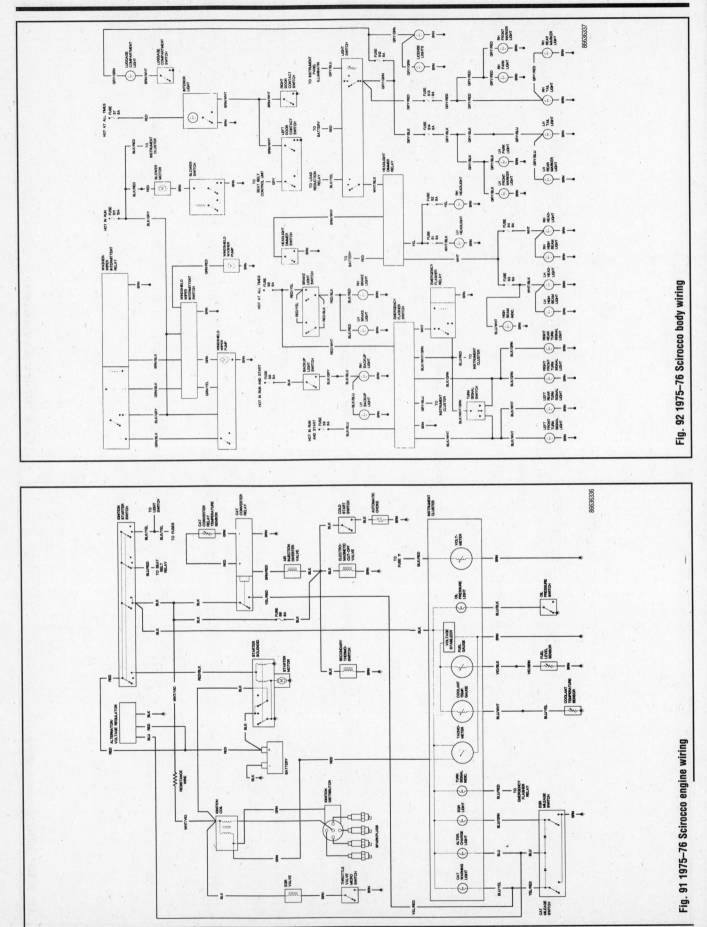

Fig. 92 1975–76 Scirocco body wiring

Fig. 91 1975–76 Scirocco engine wiring

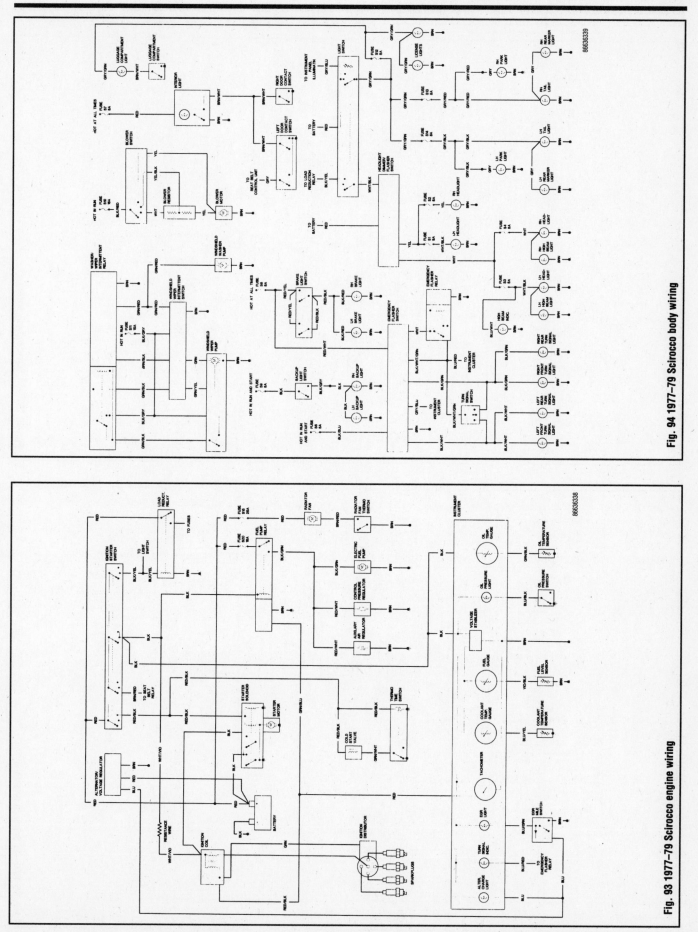

Fig. 94 1977–79 Scirocco body wiring

Fig. 93 1977–79 Scirocco engine wiring

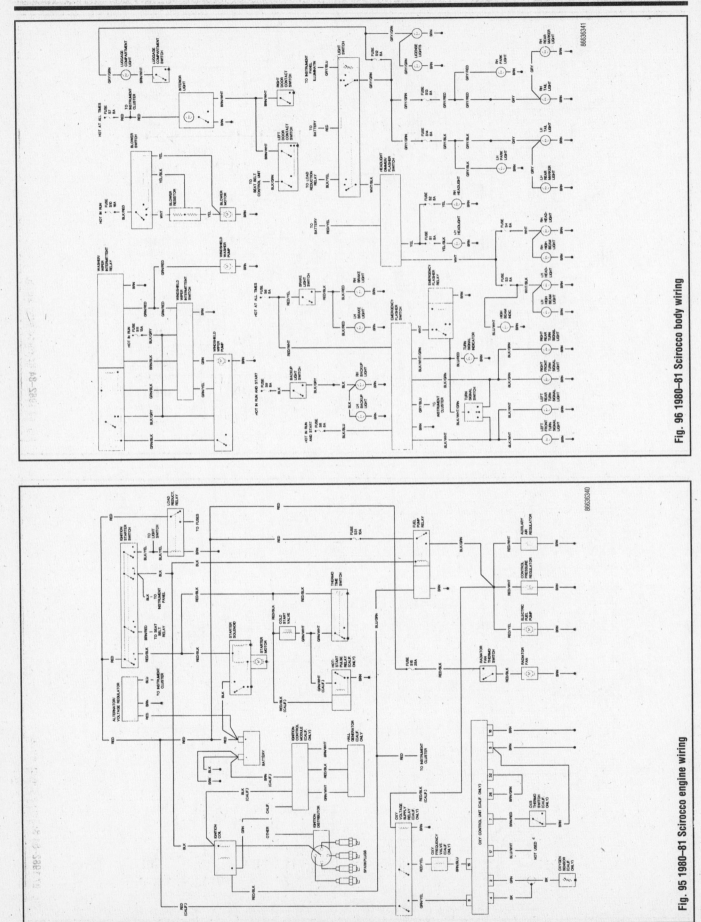

Fig. 96 1980–81 Scirocco body wiring

Fig. 95 1980–81 Scirocco engine wiring

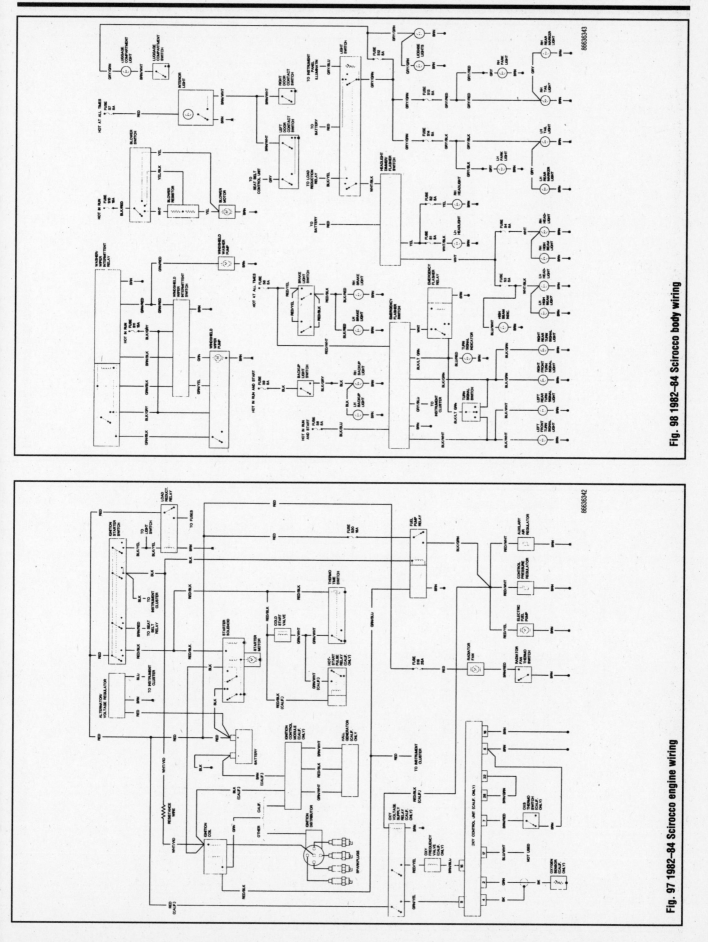

Fig. 98 1982–84 Scirocco body wiring

Fig. 97 1982–84 Scirocco engine wiring

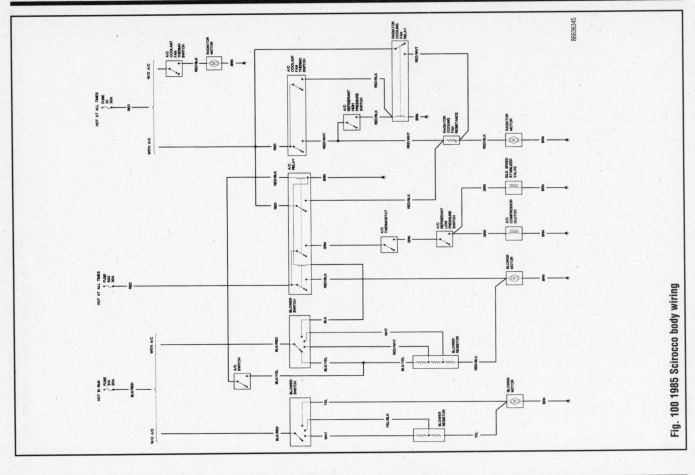

Fig. 100 1985 Scirocco body wiring

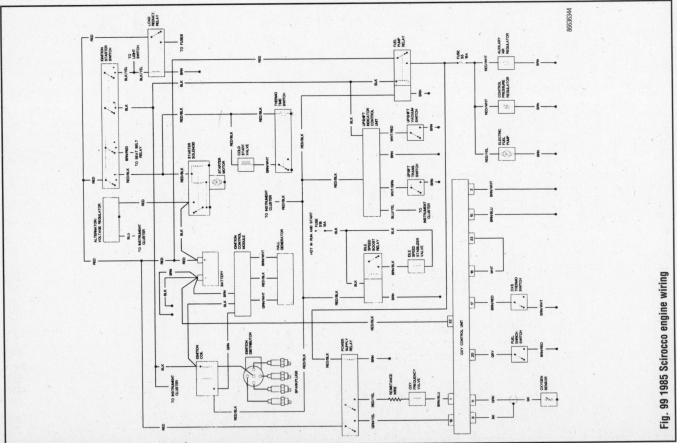

Fig. 99 1985 Scirocco engine wiring

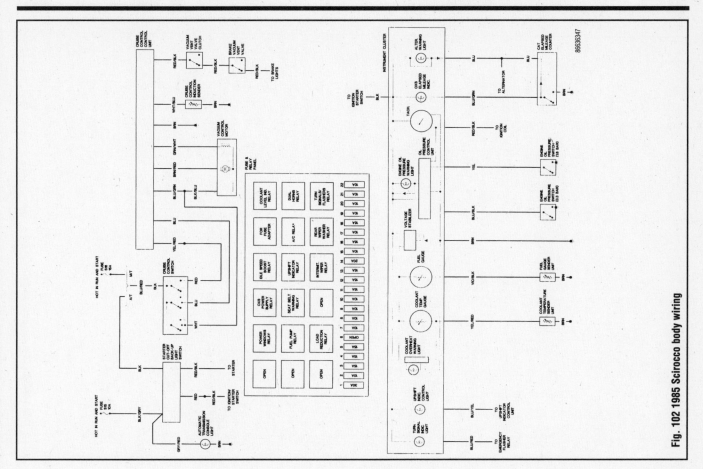

Fig. 102 1985 Scirocco body wiring

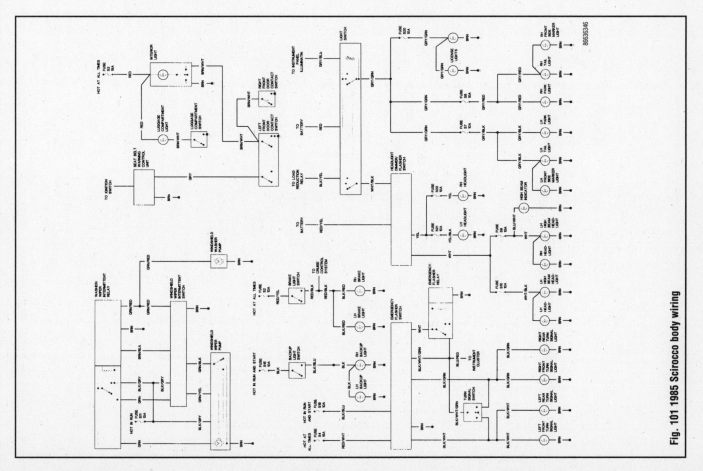

Fig. 101 1985 Scirocco body wiring

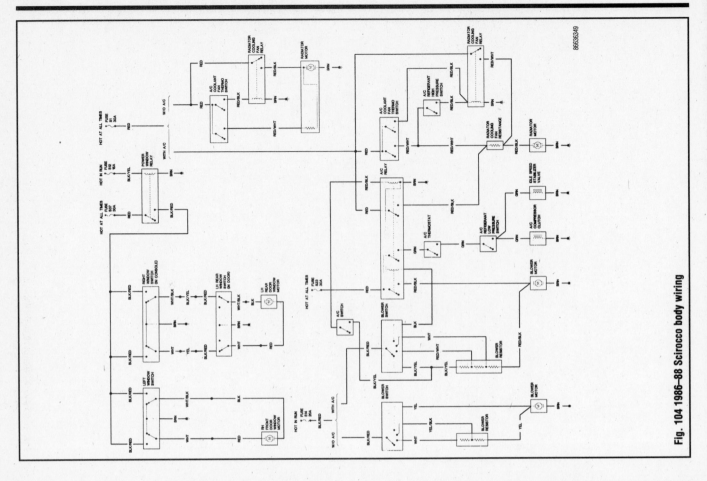

Fig. 104 1986–88 Scirocco body wiring

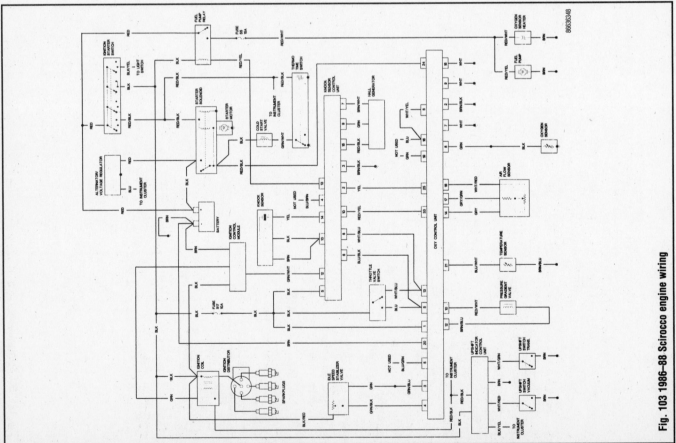

Fig. 103 1986–88 Scirocco engine wiring

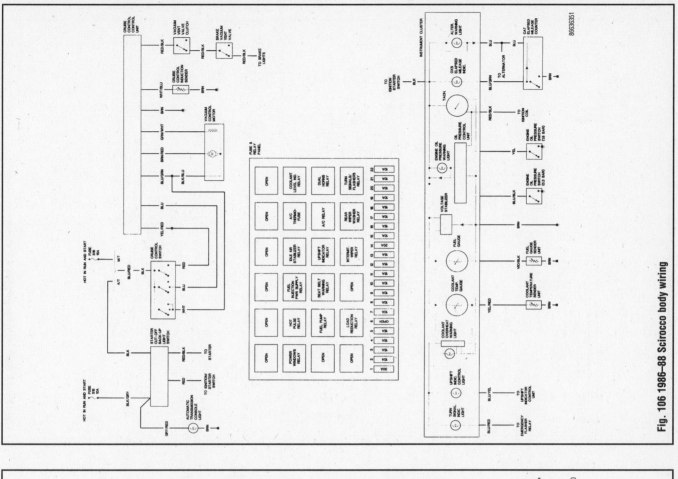

Fig. 106 1986-88 Scirocco body wiring

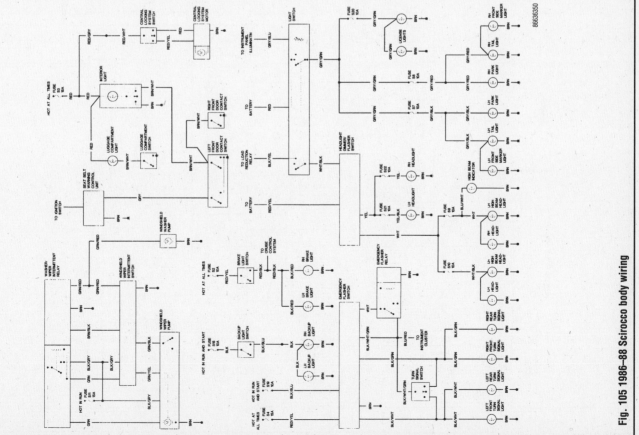

Fig. 105 1986-88 Scirocco body wiring

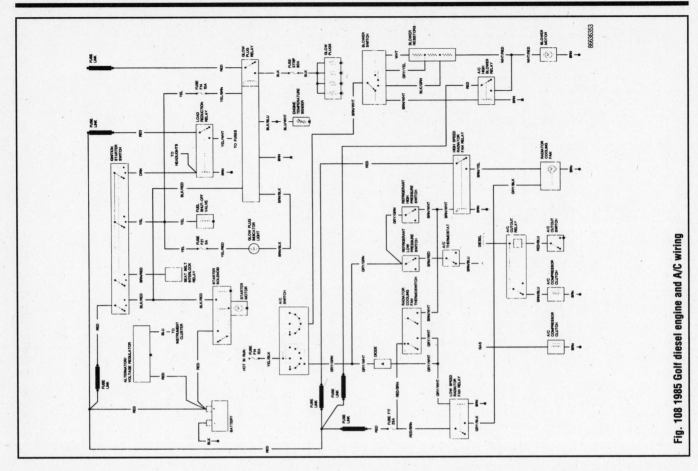

Fig. 108 1985 Golf diesel engine and A/C wiring

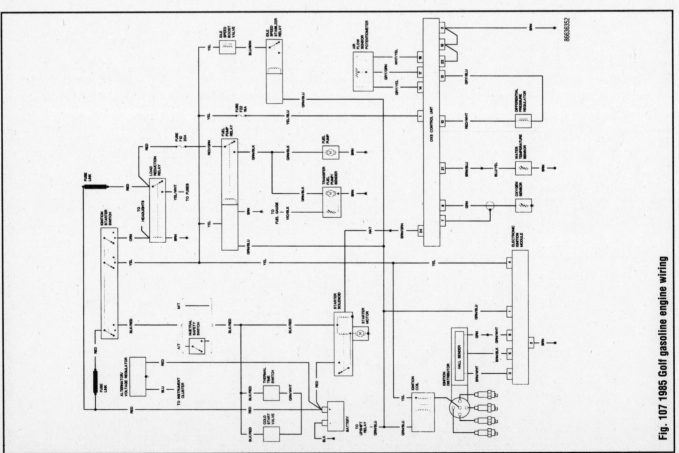

Fig. 107 1985 Golf gasoline engine wiring

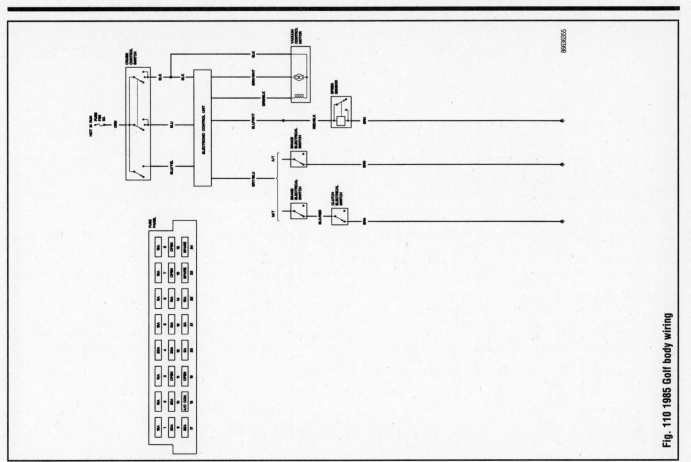

Fig. 110 1985 Golf body wiring

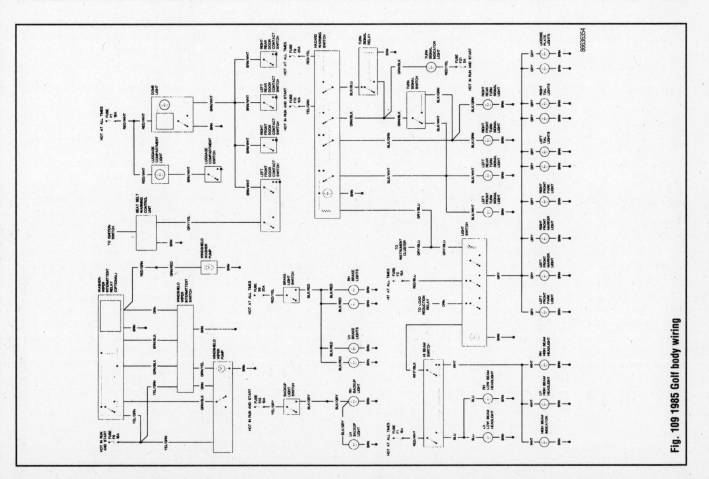

Fig. 109 1985 Golf body wiring

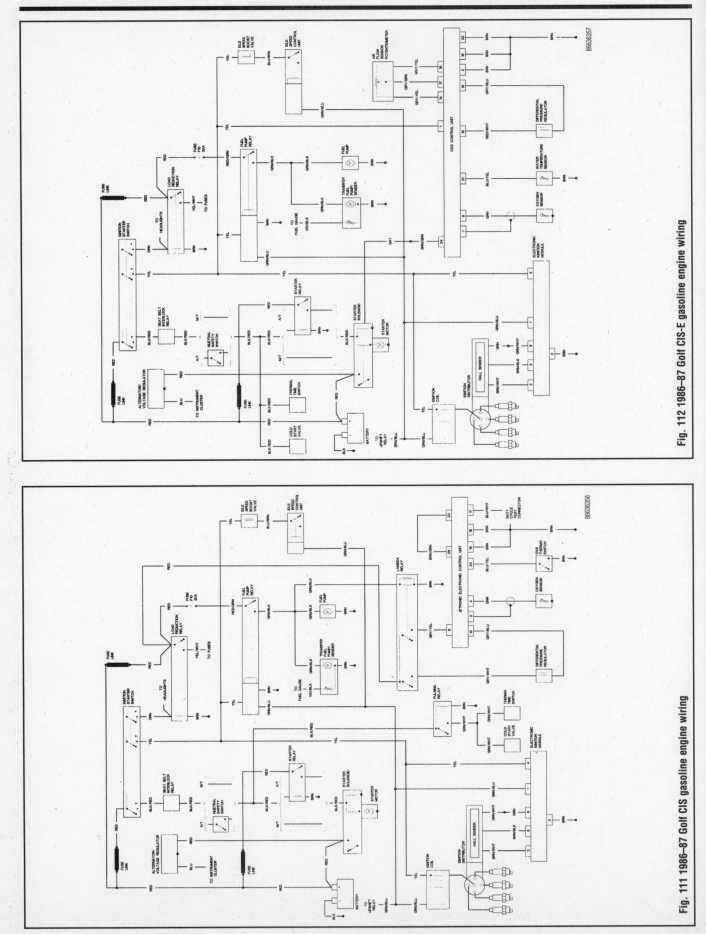

Fig. 112 1986–87 Golf CIS-E gasoline engine wiring

Fig. 111 1986–87 Golf CIS gasoline engine wiring

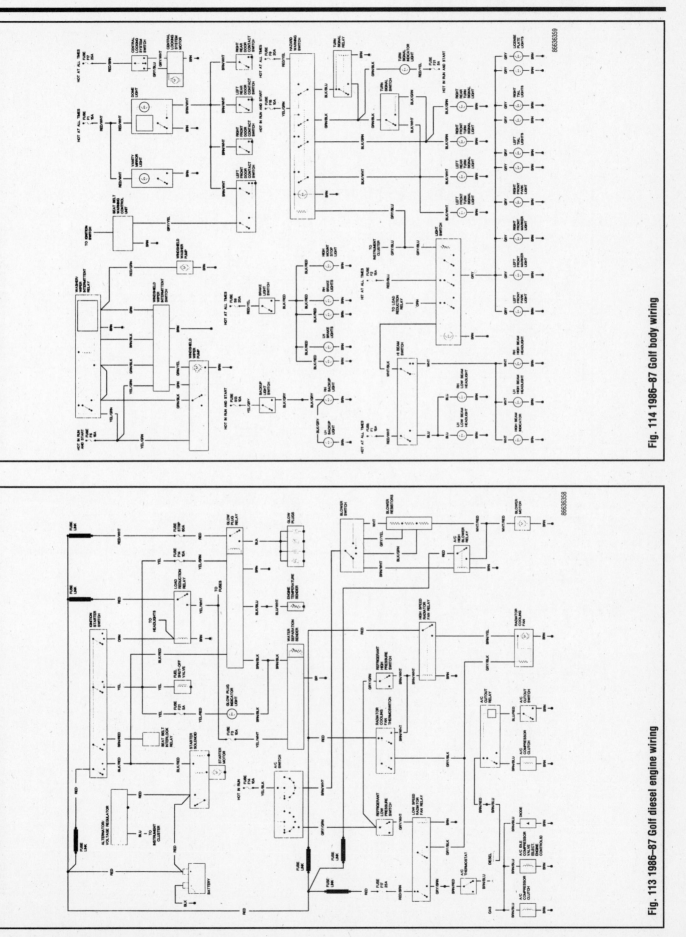

Fig. 114 1986–87 Golf body wiring

Fig. 113 1986–87 Golf diesel engine wiring

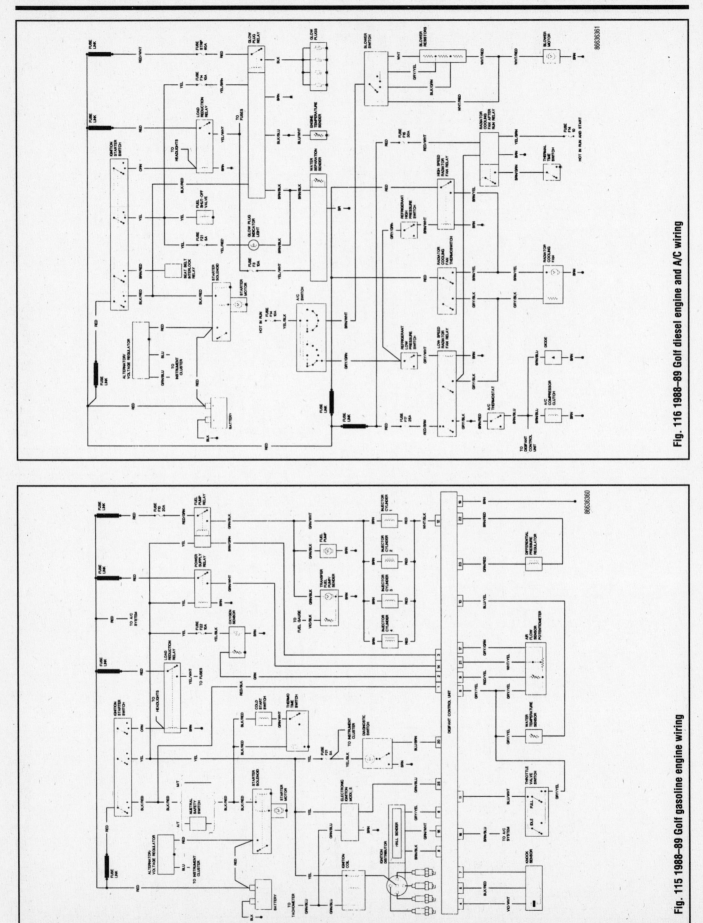

Fig. 116 1988–89 Golf diesel engine and A/C wiring

Fig. 115 1988–89 Golf gasoline engine wiring

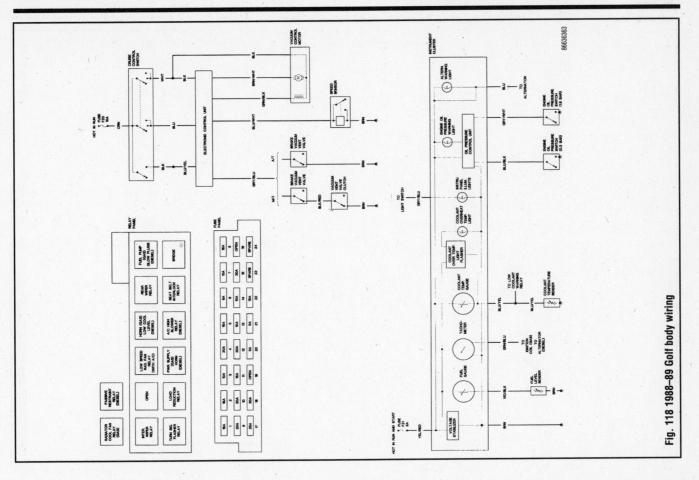

Fig. 118 1988–89 Golf body wiring

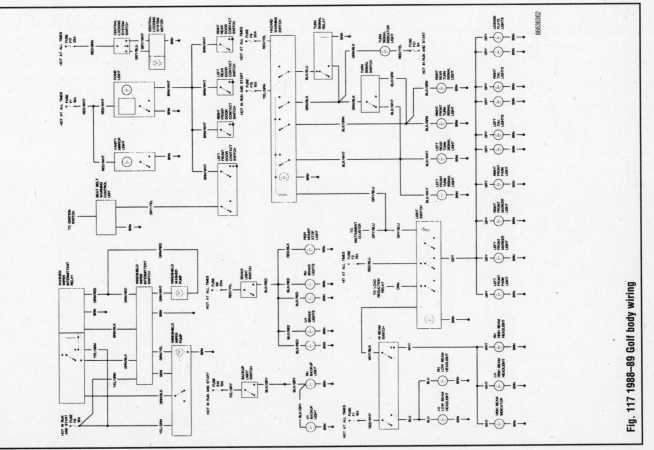

Fig. 117 1988–89 Golf body wiring

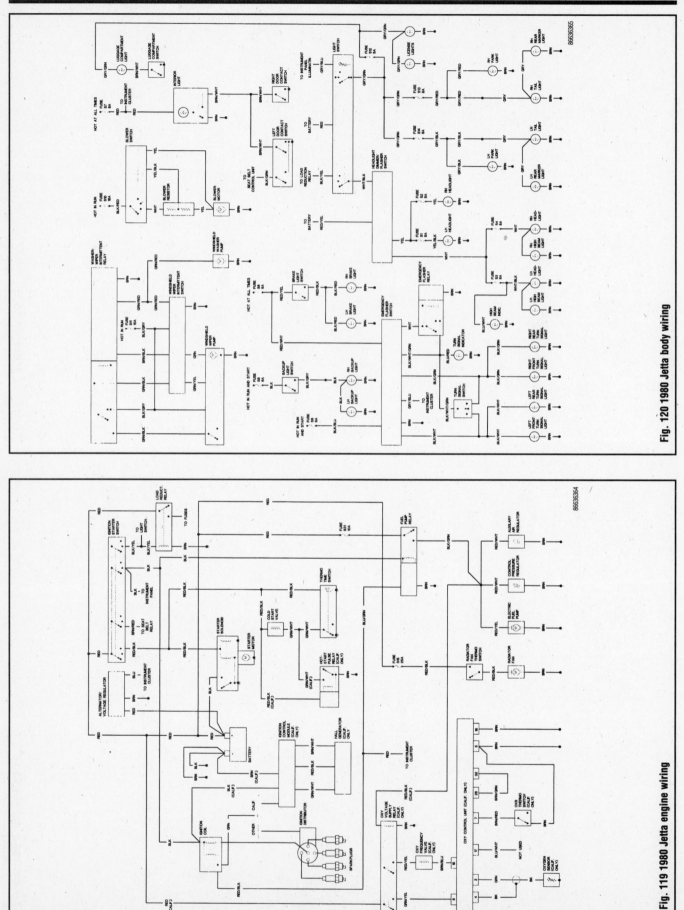

Fig. 120 1980 Jetta body wiring

Fig. 119 1980 Jetta engine wiring

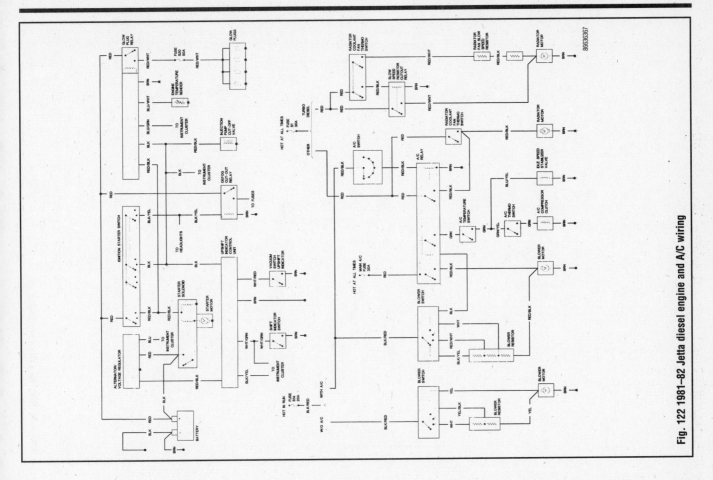

Fig. 122 1981–82 Jetta diesel engine and A/C wiring

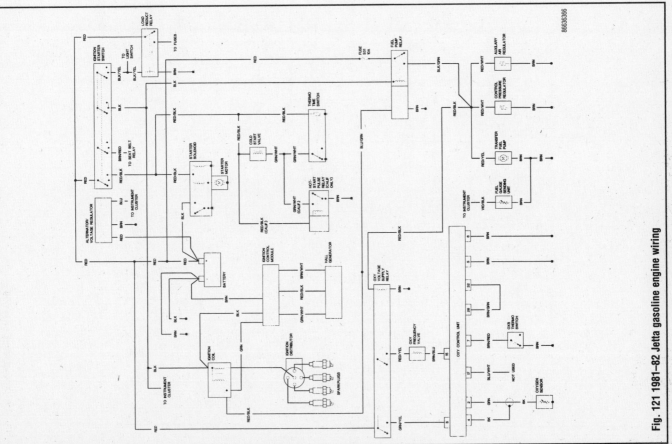

Fig. 121 1981–82 Jetta gasoline engine wiring

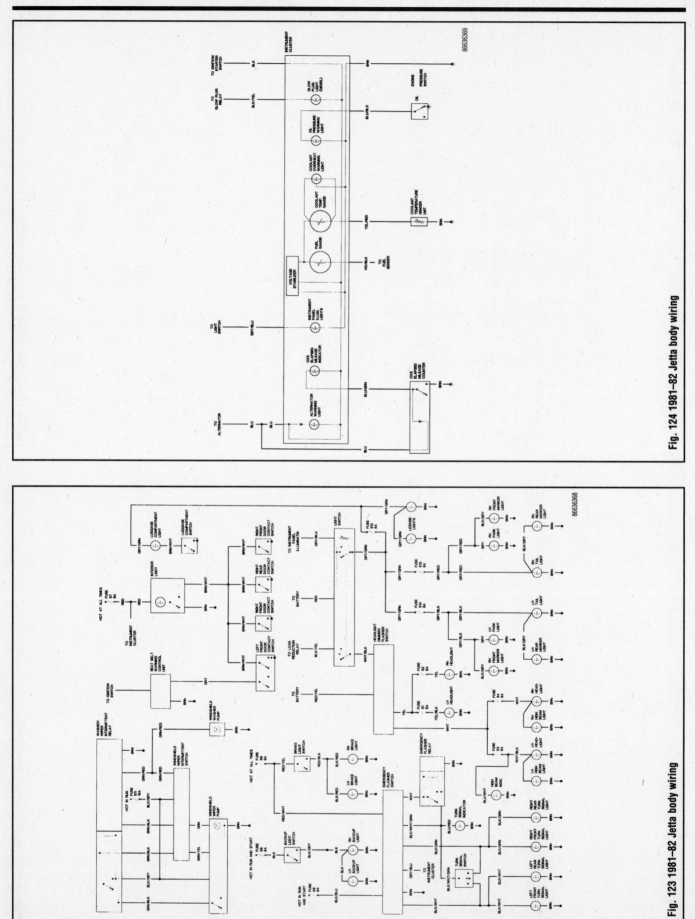

Fig. 124 1981–82 Jetta body wiring

Fig. 123 1981–82 Jetta body wiring

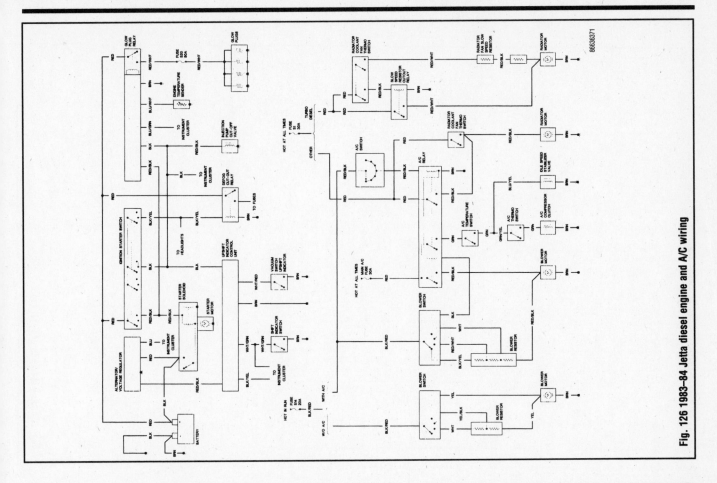

Fig. 126 1983–84 Jetta diesel engine and A/C wiring

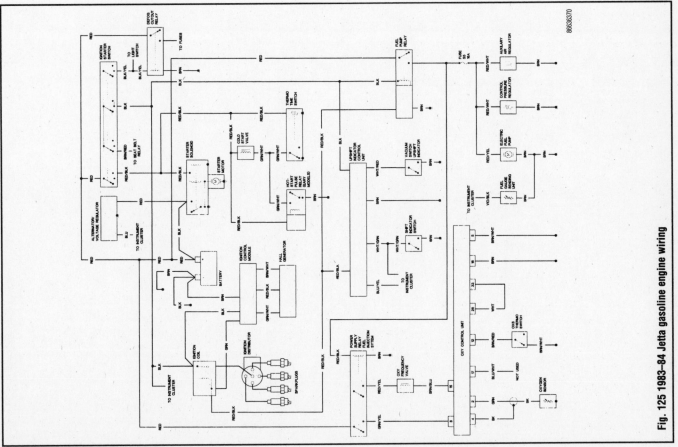

Fig. 125 1983–84 Jetta gasoline engine wiring

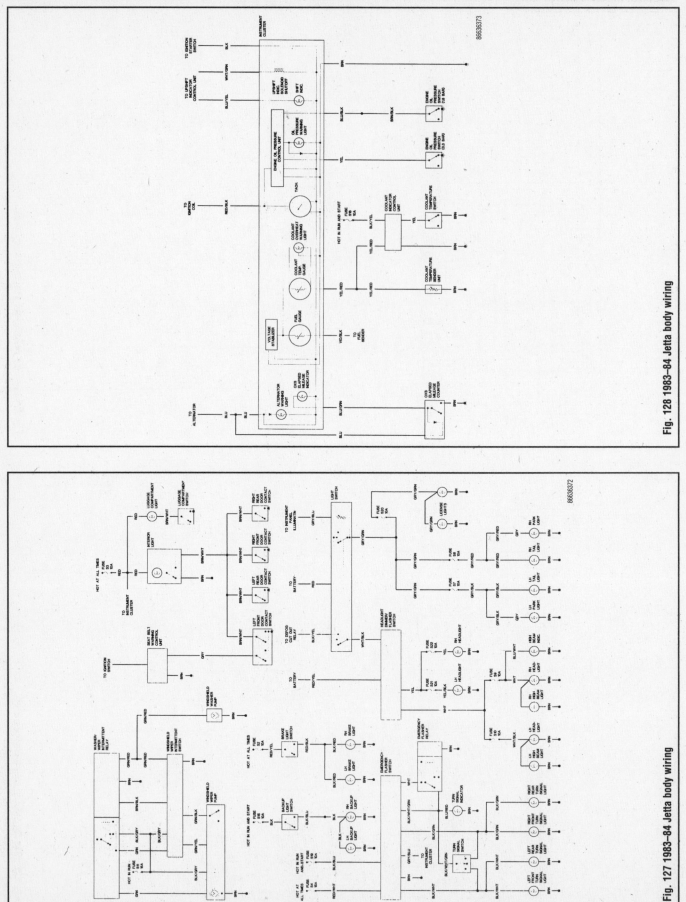

Fig. 128 1983–84 Jetta body wiring

Fig. 127 1983–84 Jetta body wiring

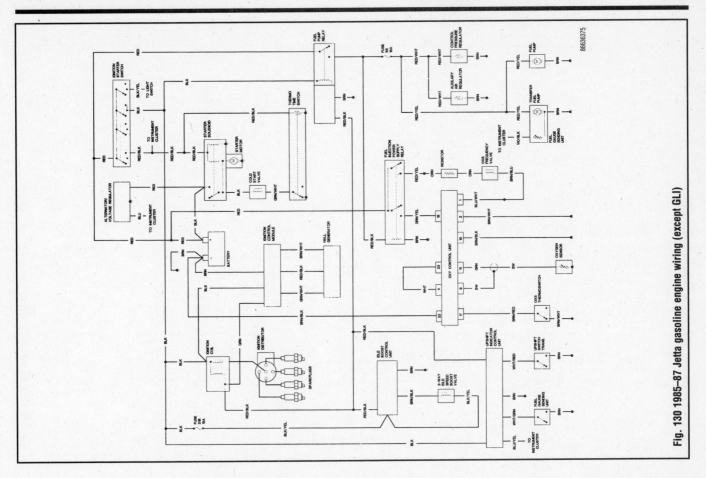

Fig. 130 1985-87 Jetta gasoline engine wiring (except GLI)

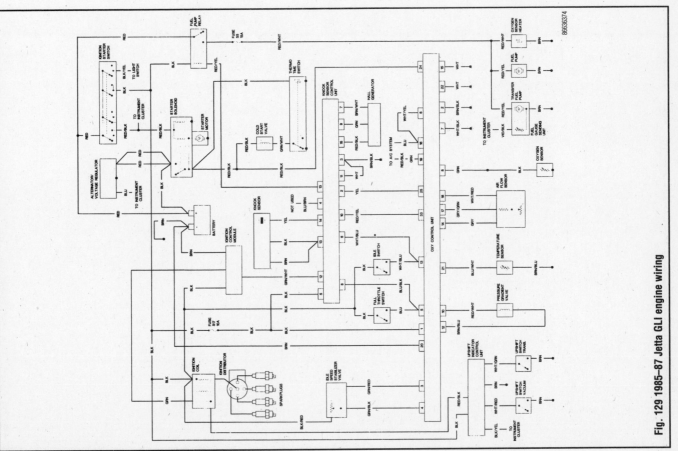

Fig. 129 1985-87 Jetta GLI engine wiring

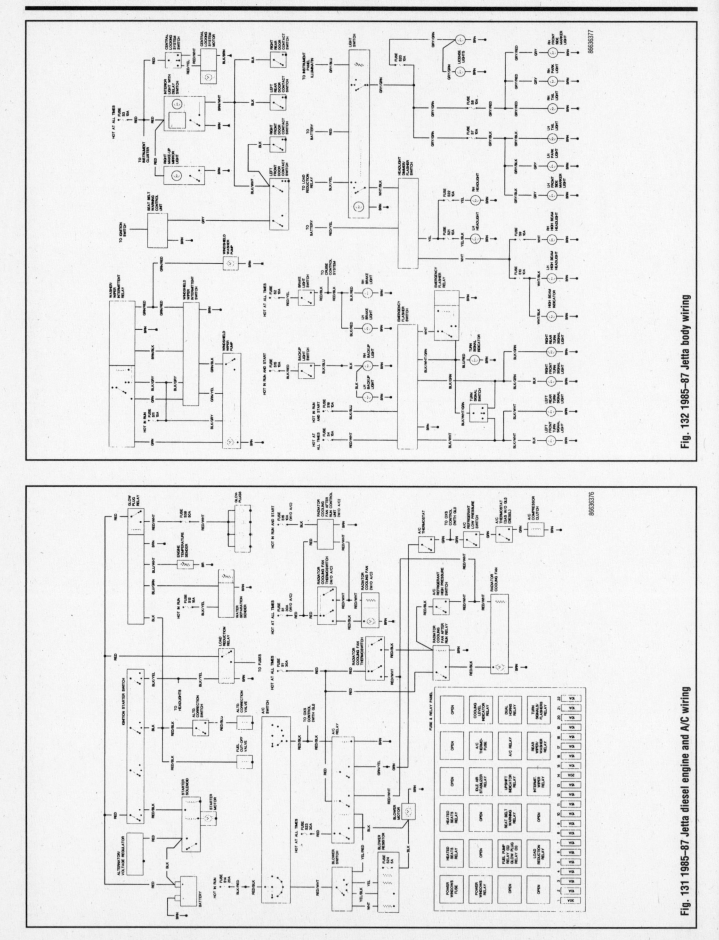

Fig. 132 1985–87 Jetta body wiring

Fig. 131 1985–87 Jetta diesel engine and A/C wiring

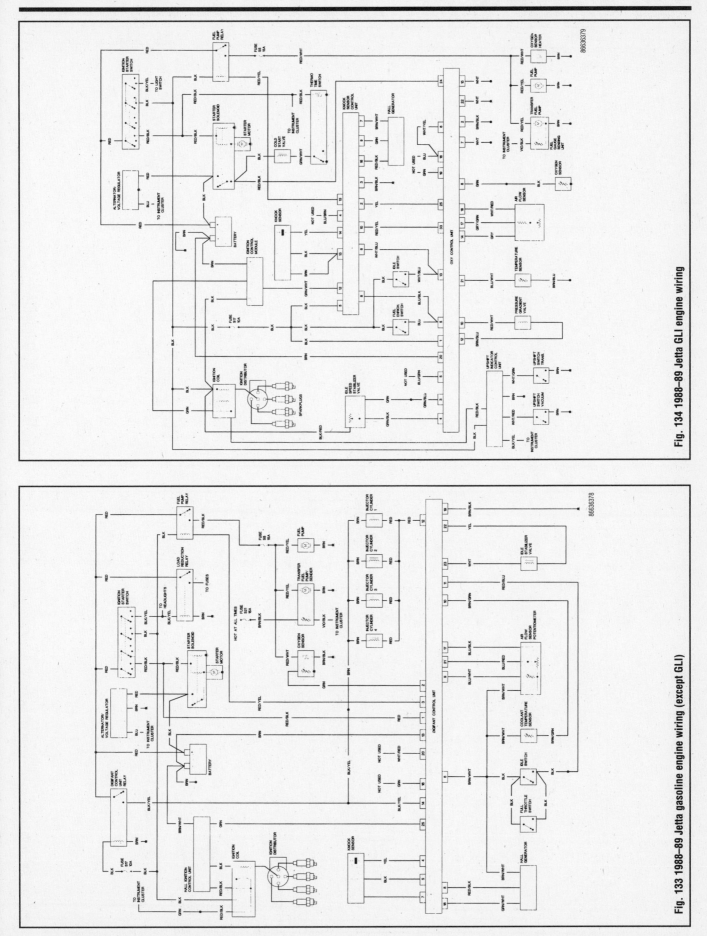

Fig. 134 1988–89 Jetta GLI engine wiring

Fig. 133 1988–89 Jetta gasoline engine wiring (except GLI)

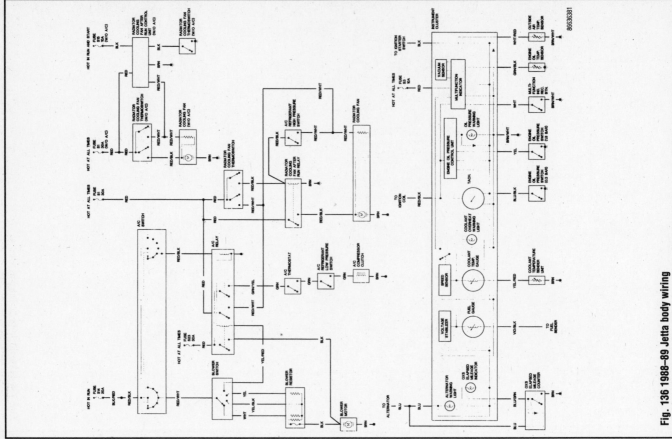

Fig. 136 1988–89 Jetta body wiring

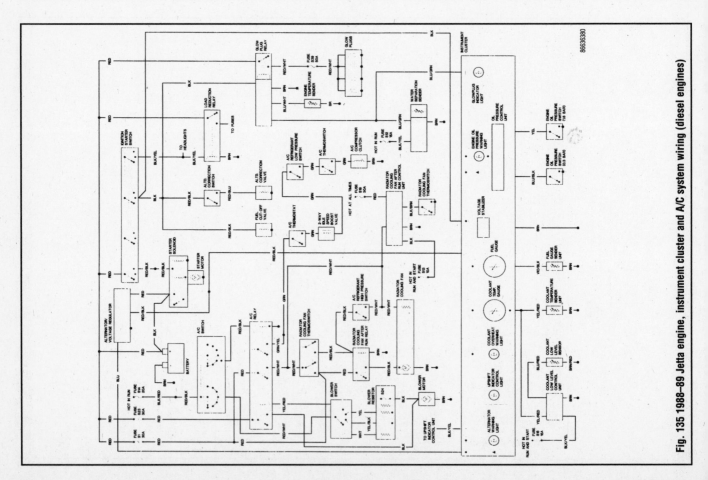

Fig. 135 1988–89 Jetta engine, instrument cluster and A/C system wiring (diesel engines)

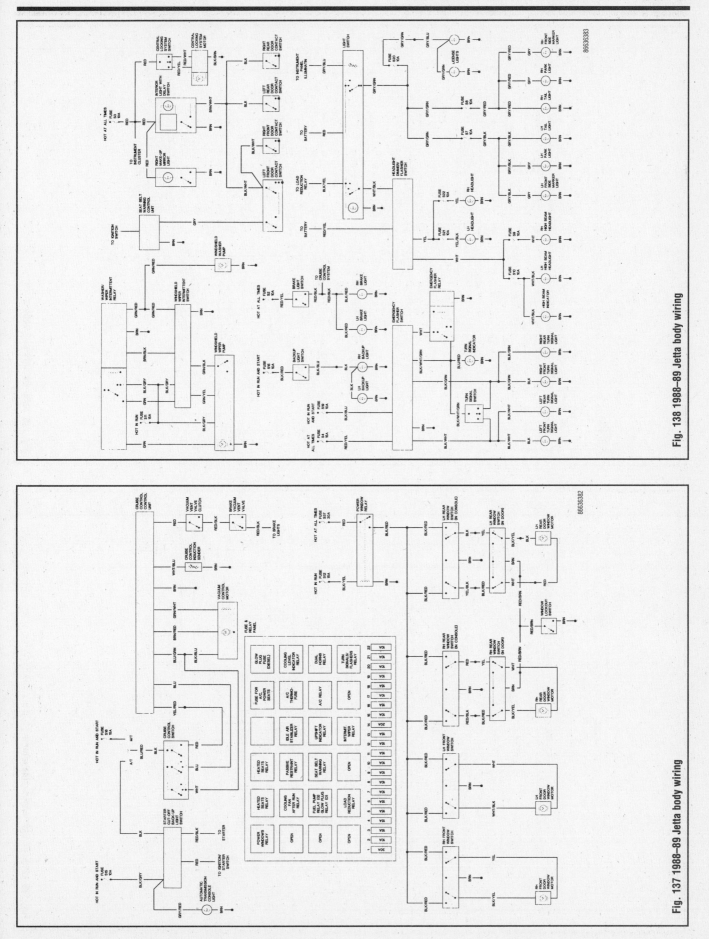

Fig. 138 1988–89 Jetta body wiring

Fig. 137 1988–89 Jetta body wiring

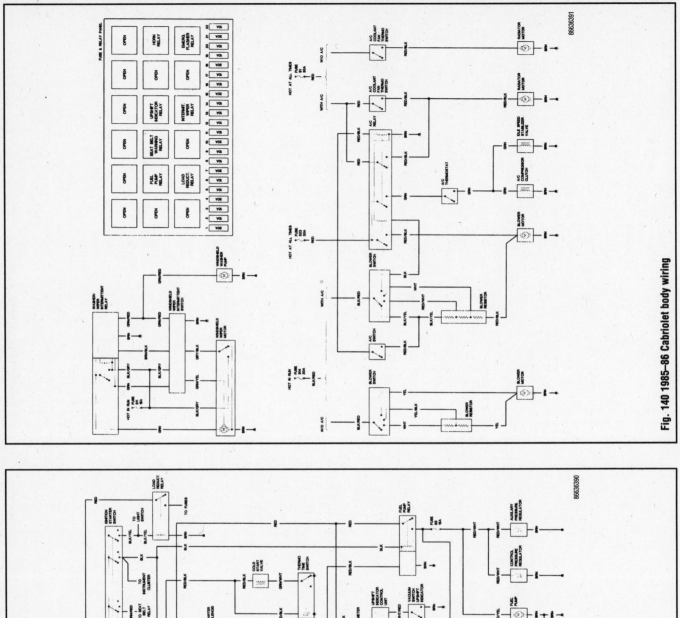

Fig. 140 1985–86 Cabriolet body wiring

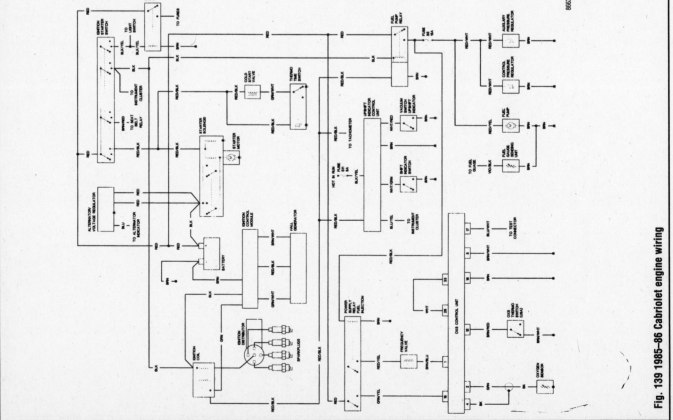

Fig. 139 1985–86 Cabriolet engine wiring

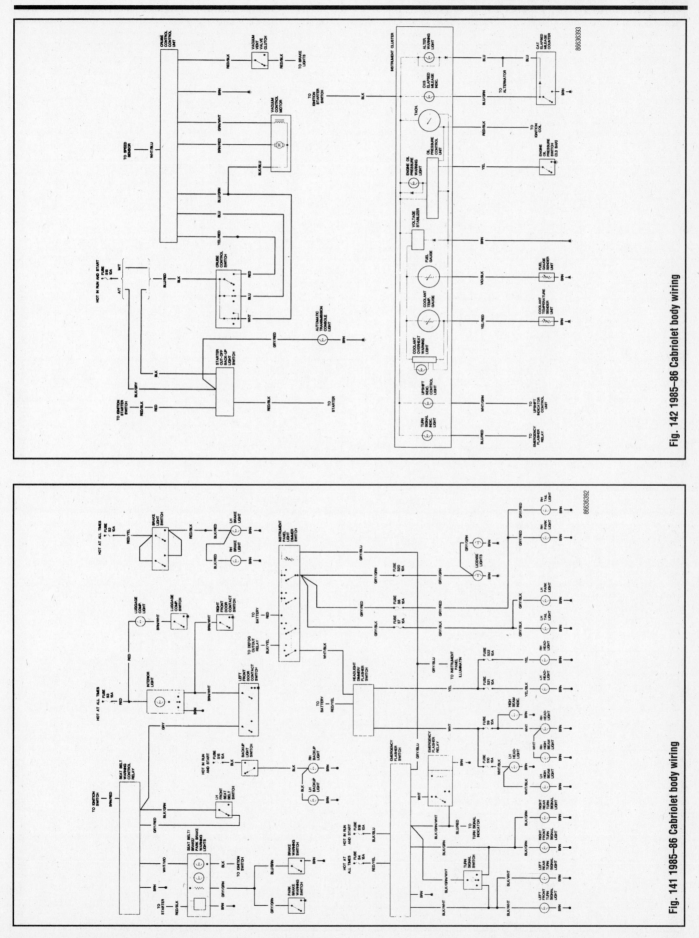

Fig. 142 1985-86 Cabriolet body wiring

Fig. 141 1985-86 Cabriolet body wiring

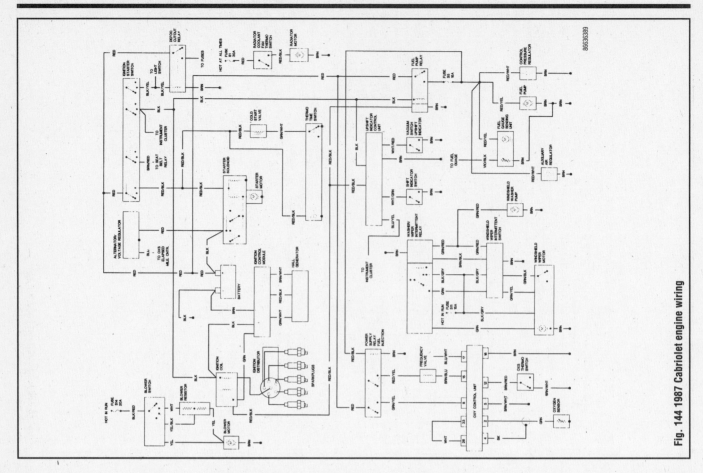

Fig. 144 1987 Cabriolet engine wiring

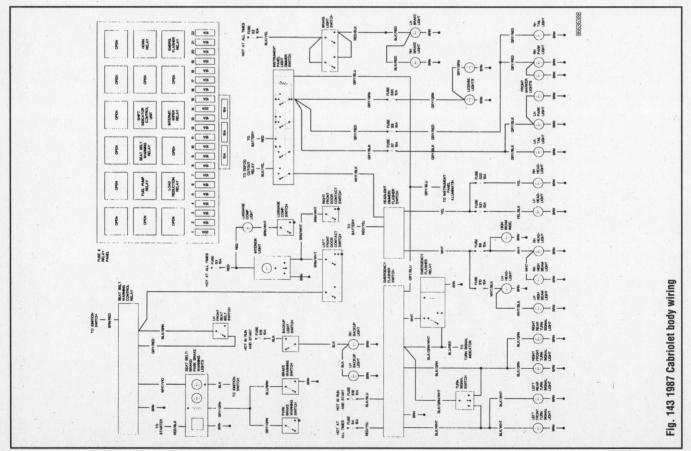

Fig. 143 1987 Cabriolet body wiring

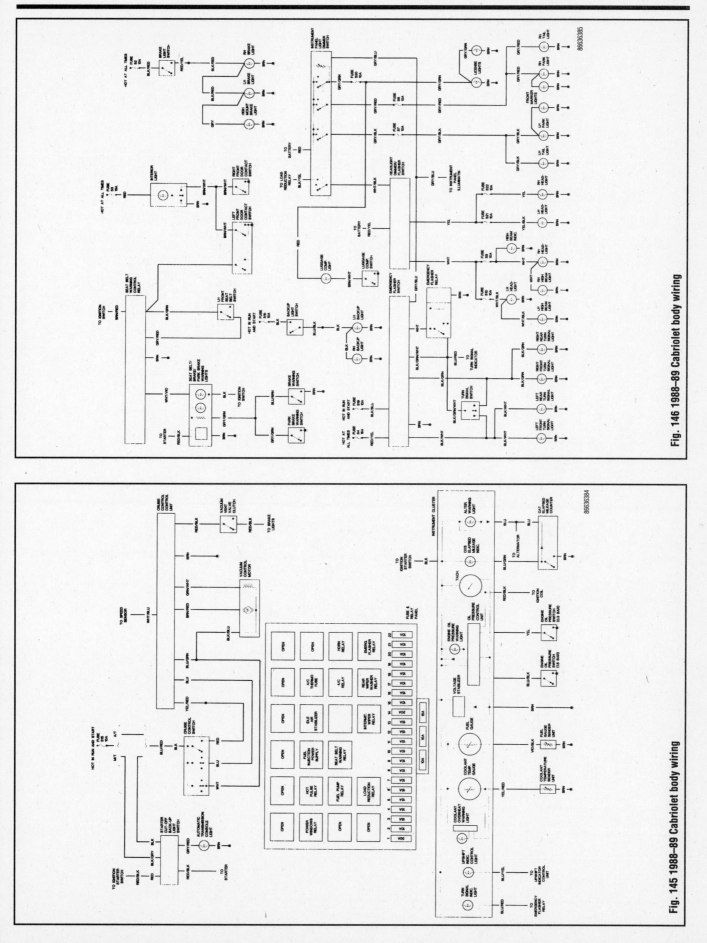

Fig. 146 1988-89 Cabriolet body wiring

Fig. 145 1988-89 Cabriolet body wiring

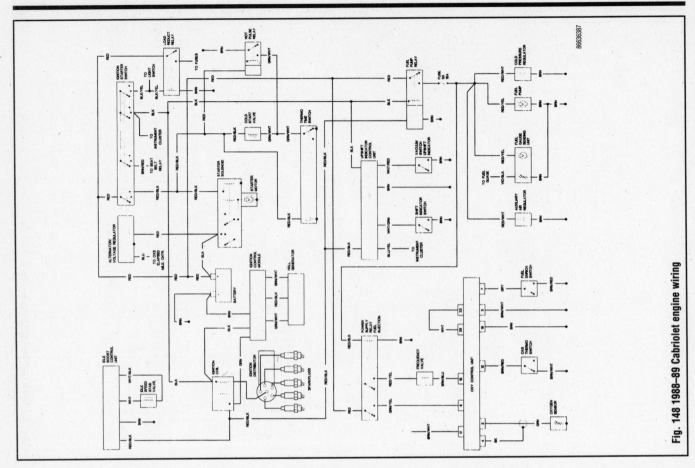

Fig. 148 1988–89 Cabriolet engine wiring

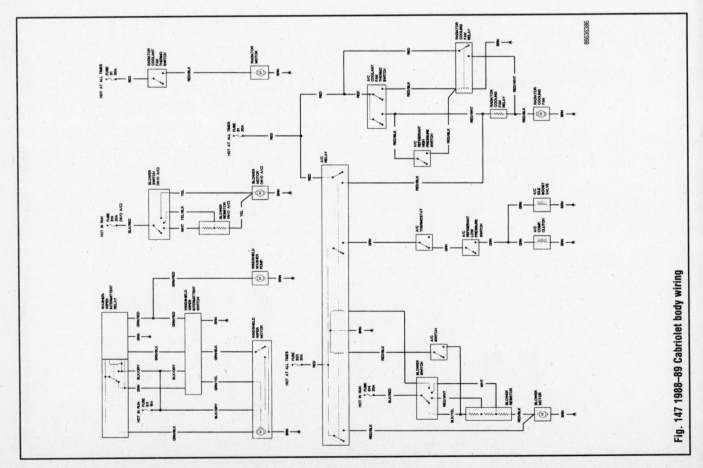

Fig. 147 1988–89 Cabriolet body wiring

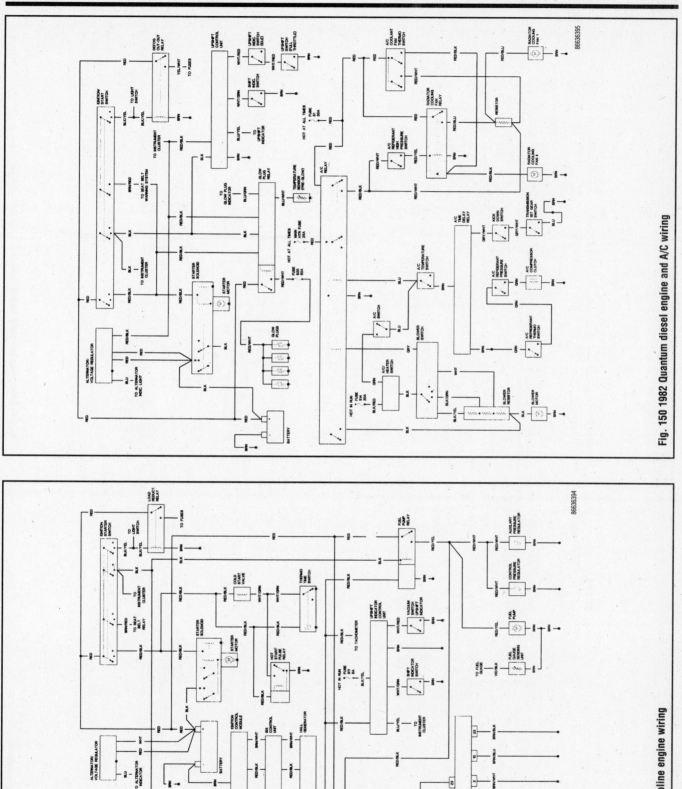

Fig. 150 1982 Quantum diesel engine and A/C wiring

Fig. 149 1982 Quantum gasoline engine wiring

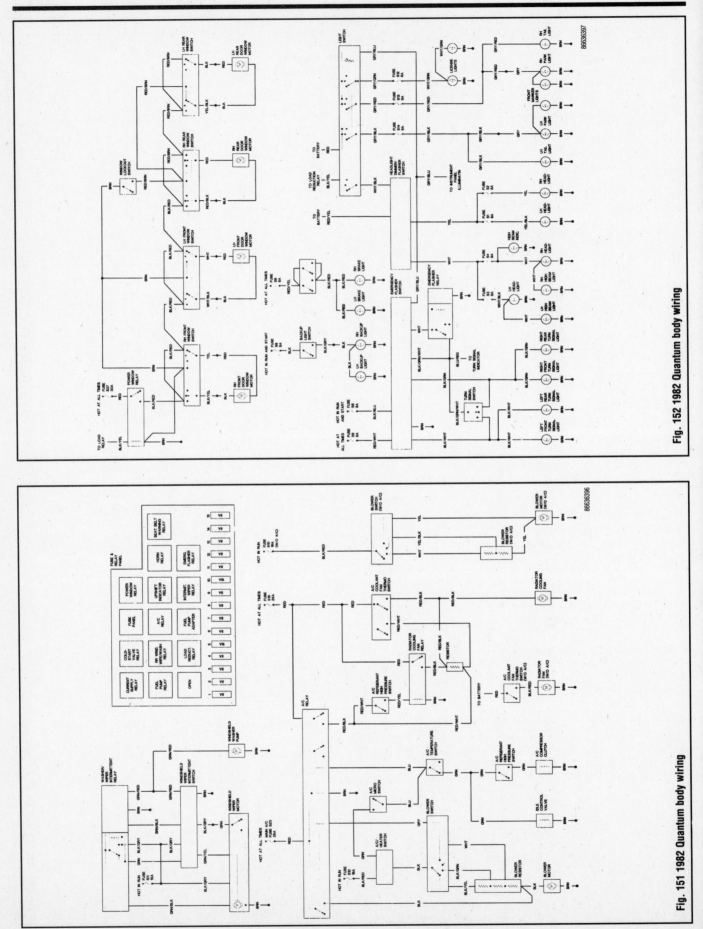

Fig. 152 1982 Quantum body wiring

Fig. 151 1982 Quantum body wiring

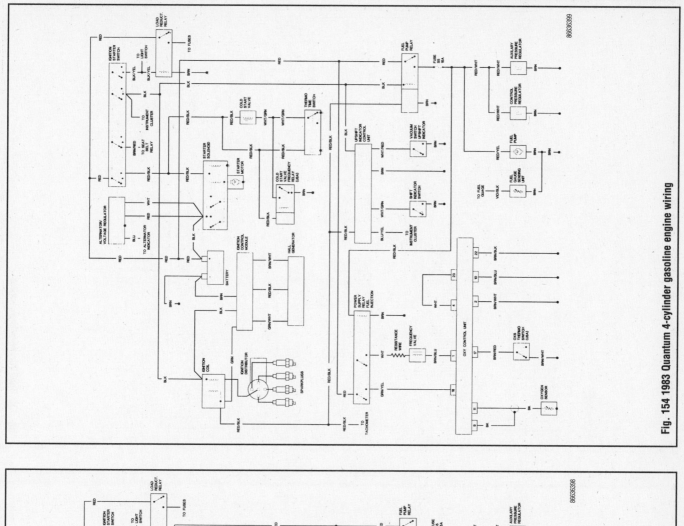

Fig. 154 1983 Quantum 4-cylinder gasoline engine wiring

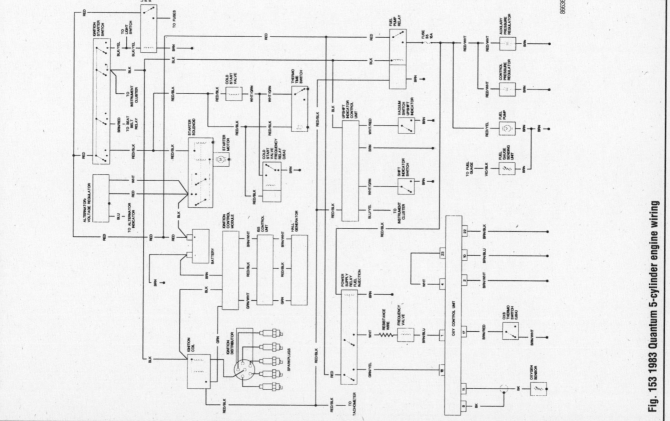

Fig. 153 1983 Quantum 5-cylinder engine wiring

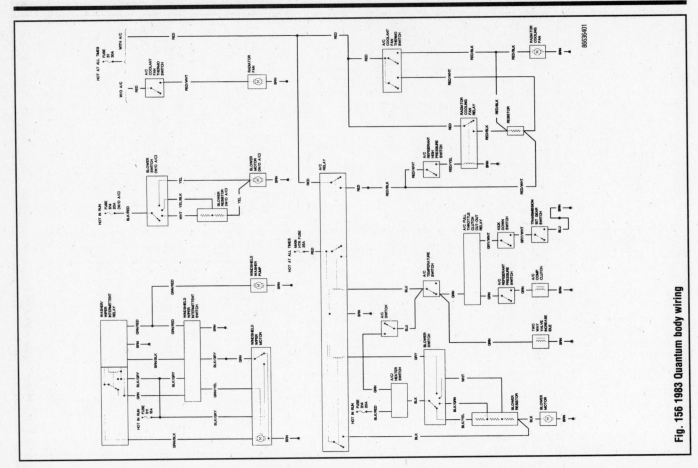

Fig. 156 1983 Quantum body wiring

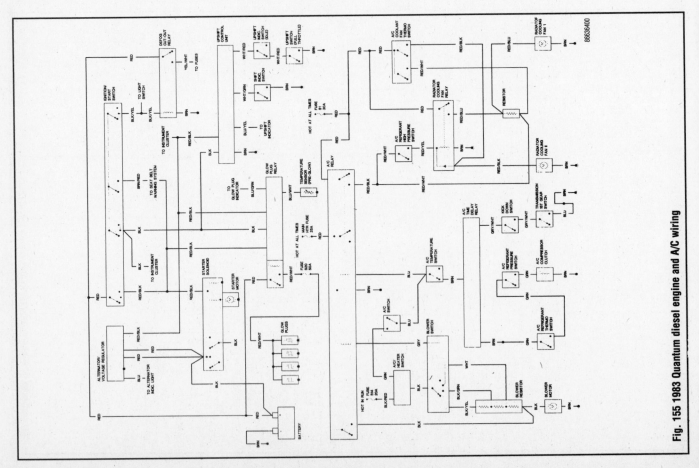

Fig. 155 1983 Quantum diesel engine and A/C wiring

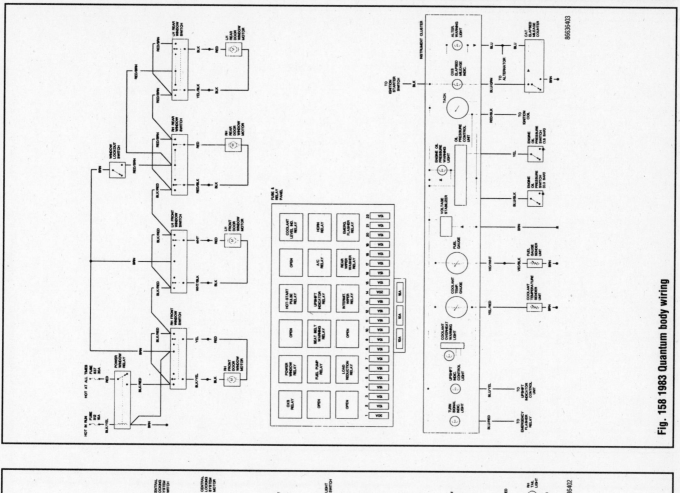

Fig. 158 1983 Quantum body wiring

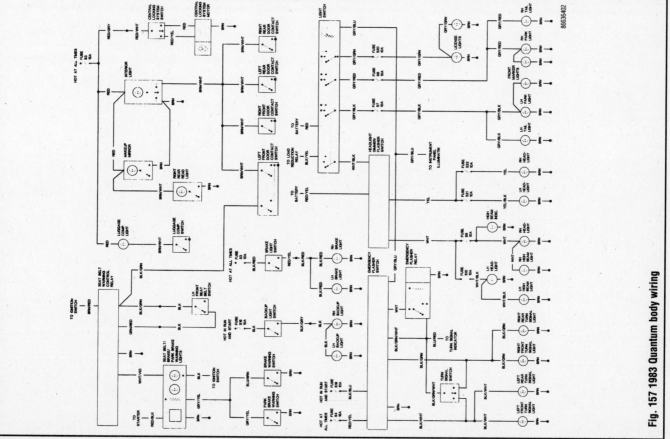

Fig. 157 1983 Quantum body wiring

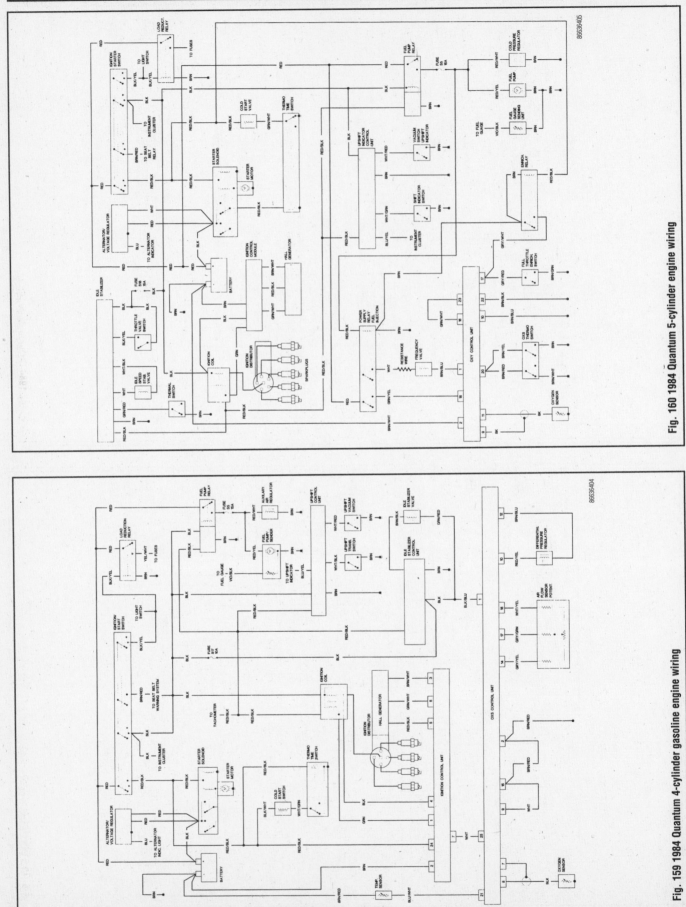

Fig. 160 1984 Quantum 5-cylinder engine wiring

Fig. 159 1984 Quantum 4-cylinder gasoline engine wiring

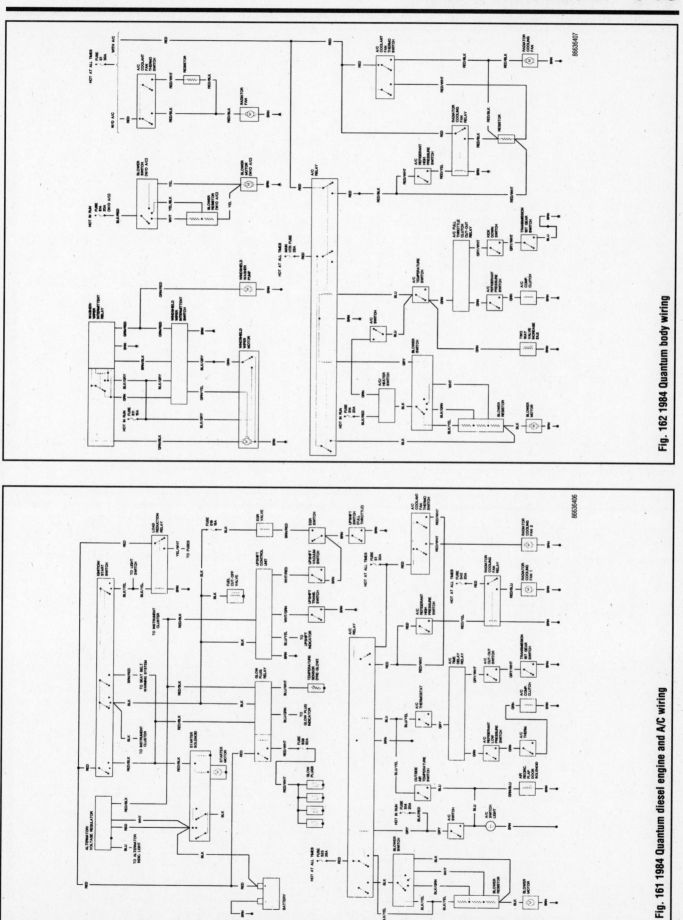

Fig. 162 1984 Quantum body wiring

Fig. 161 1984 Quantum diesel engine and A/C wiring

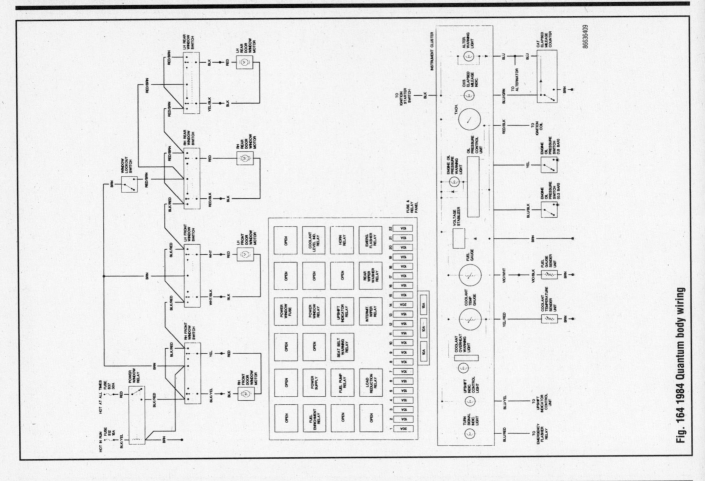

Fig. 164 1984 Quantum body wiring

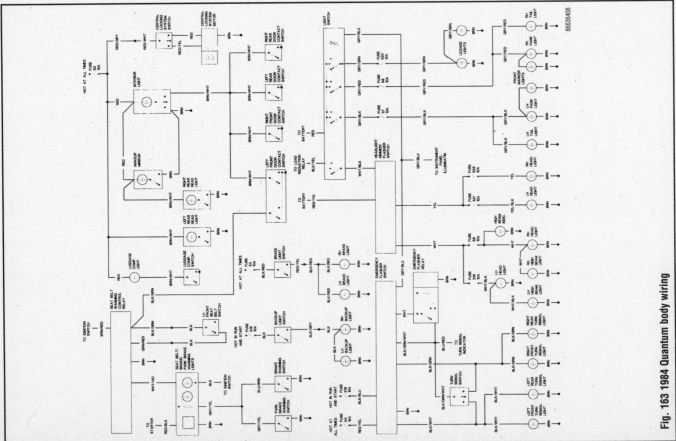

Fig. 163 1984 Quantum body wiring

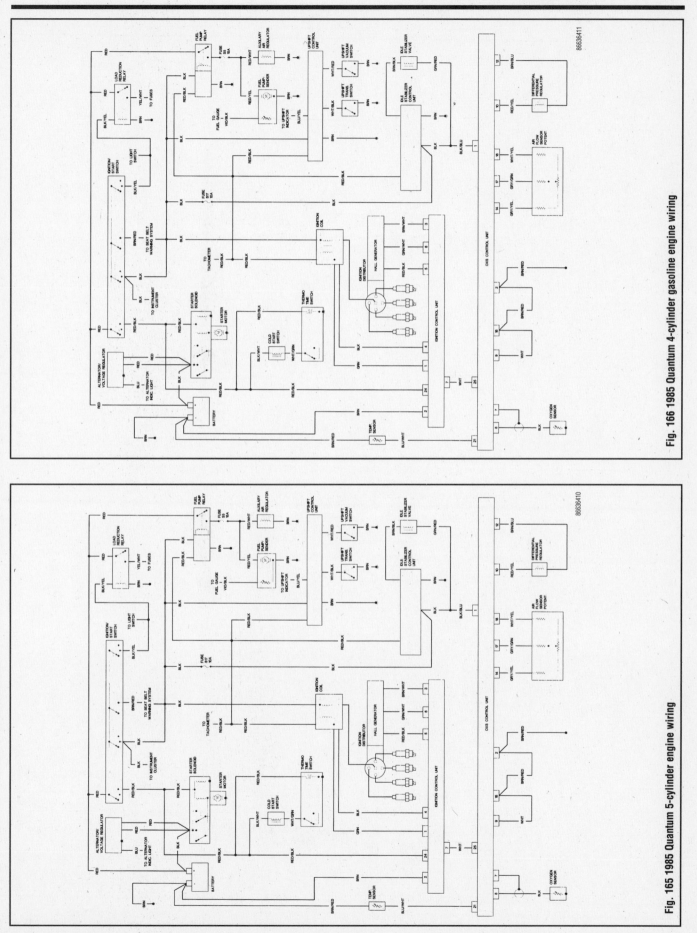

Fig. 166 1985 Quantum 4-cylinder gasoline engine wiring

Fig. 165 1985 Quantum 5-cylinder engine wiring

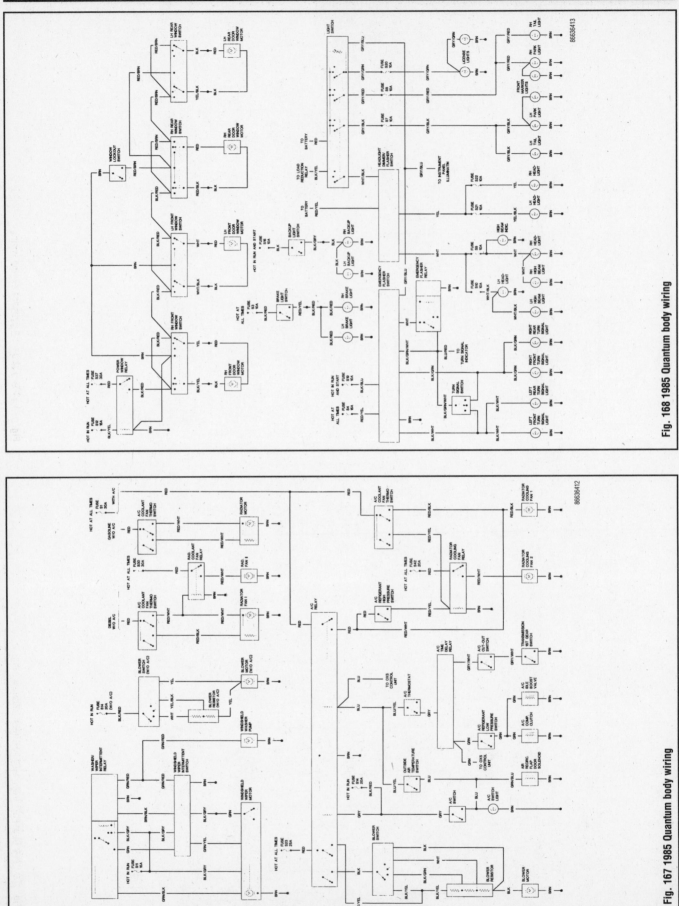

Fig. 168 1985 Quantum body wiring

Fig. 167 1985 Quantum body wiring

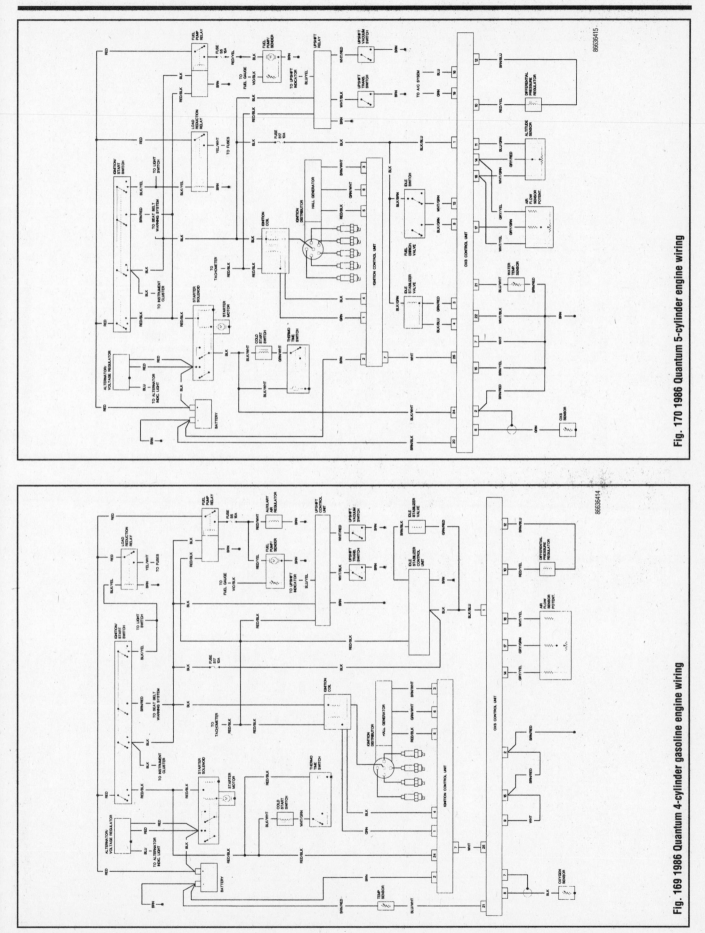

Fig. 170 1986 Quantum 5-cylinder engine wiring

Fig. 169 1986 Quantum 4-cylinder gasoline engine wiring

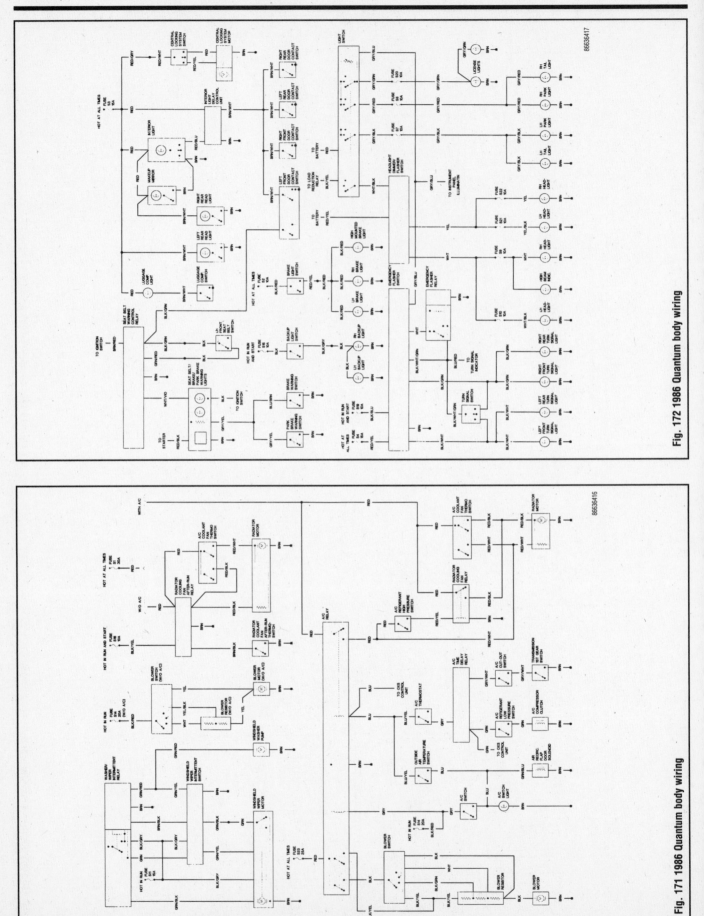

Fig. 172 1986 Quantum body wiring

Fig. 171 1986 Quantum body wiring

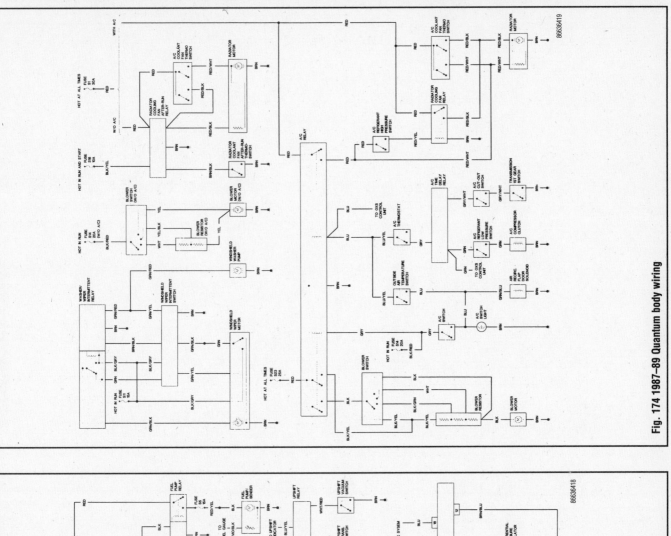

Fig. 174 1987–89 Quantum body wiring

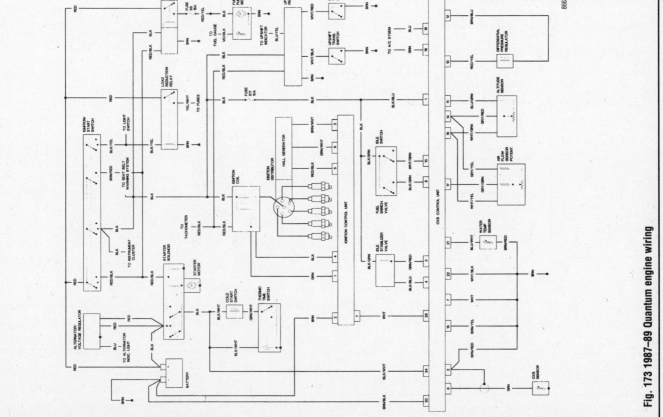

Fig. 173 1987–89 Quantum engine wiring

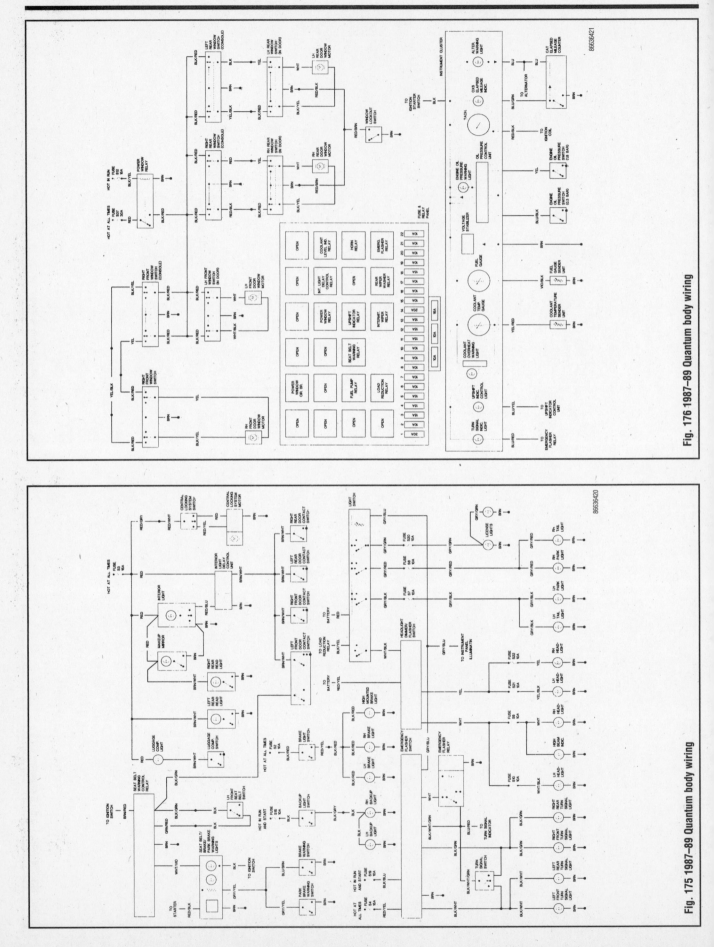

Fig. 176 1987–89 Quantum body wiring

Fig. 175 1987–89 Quantum body wiring

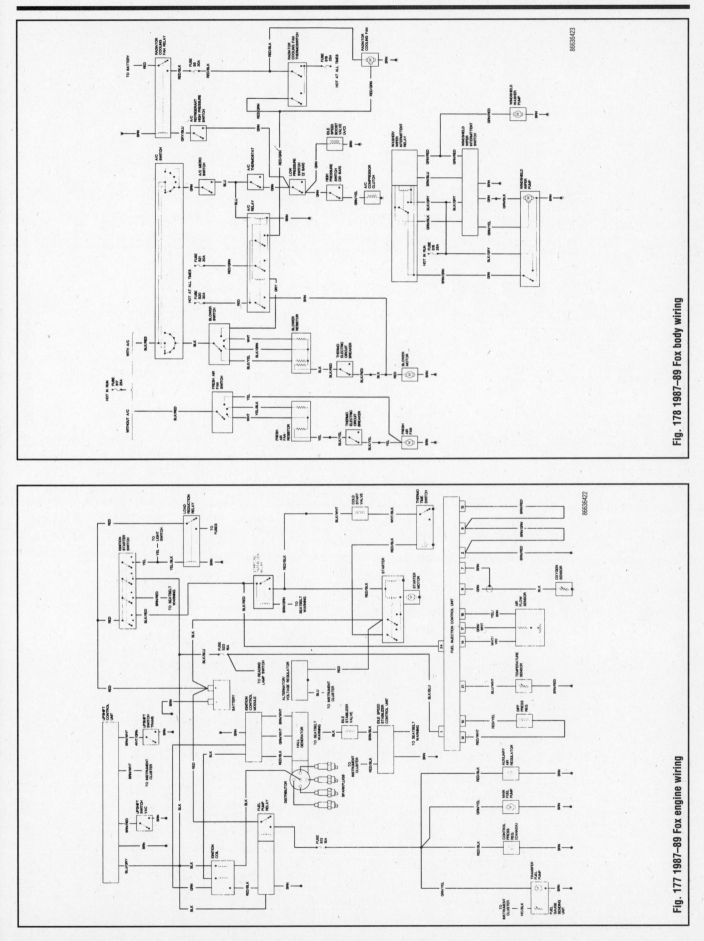

Fig. 178 1987–89 Fox body wiring

Fig. 177 1987–89 Fox engine wiring

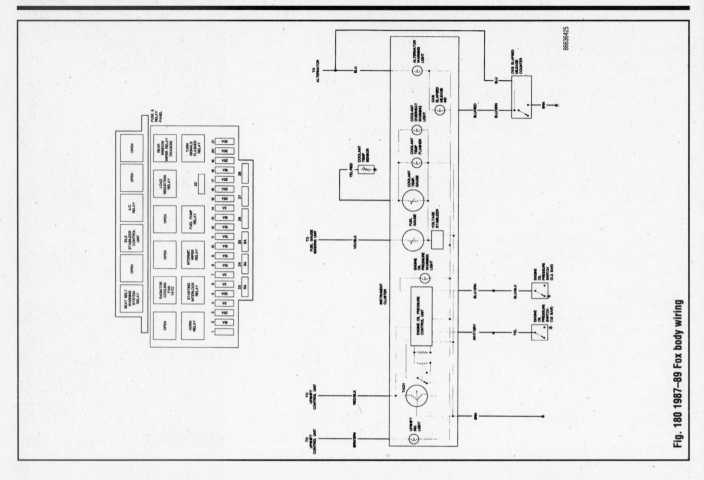

Fig. 180 1987-89 Fox body wiring

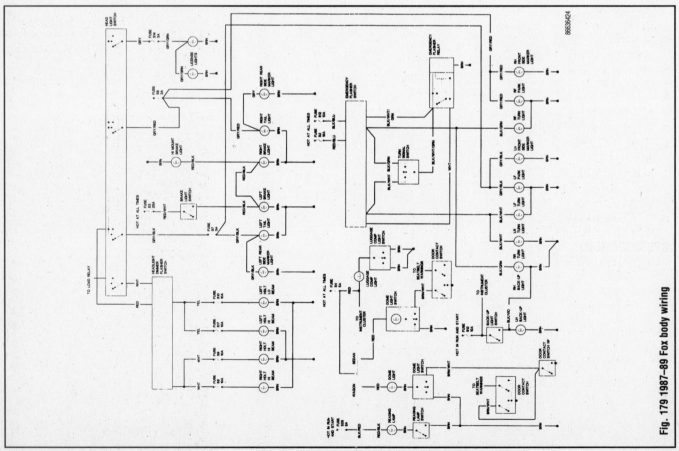

Fig. 179 1987-89 Fox body wiring

7

DRIVE TRAIN

MANUAL TRANSAXLE

Understanding the Manual Transaxle

Because of the way an internal combustion engine breathes, it can produce torque, or twisting force, only within a narrow speed range. Most modern, overhead valve pushrod engines must turn at about 2500 rpm to produce their peak torque. By 4500 rpm they are producing so little torque that continued increases in engine speed produce no power increases. The torque peak on overhead camshaft engines is generally much higher, but much narrower.

The manual transaxle and clutch are employed to vary the relationship between engine speed and the speed of the wheels so that adequate engine power can be produced under all circumstances. The clutch allows engine torque to be applied to the transaxle input shaft gradually, due to mechanical slippage. Consequently, the vehicle may be started smoothly from a full stop. The transaxle changes the ratio between the rotating speeds of the engine and the wheels by the use of gears. The gear ratios allow full engine power to be applied to the wheels during acceleration at low speeds and at highway/passing speeds.

In a front wheel drive transaxle, power is usually transmitted from the input shaft to a mainshaft or output shaft located slightly beneath and to the side of the input shaft. The gears of the mainshaft mesh with gears on the input shaft, allowing power to be carried from one to the other. All forward gears are in constant mesh and are free from rotating with the shaft unless the synchronizer and clutch is engaged. Shifting from one gear to the next causes one of the gears to be freed from rotating with the shaft and locks another to it. Gears are locked and unlocked by internal dog clutches which slide between the center of the gear and the shaft. The forward gears employ synchronizers; friction members which smoothly bring gear and shaft to the same speed before the toothed dog clutches are engaged.

Transaxle Identification

The transaxle is identified by a letter code that is stamped into the case near the top of the bellhousing. The first two or three digits are the transaxle code and the remaining numbers are the build date: day, month and year. The letter code indicates details about the transaxle such as the engine it goes with and the gear ratios. This code should also appear on the model identification label in the luggage compartment.

Adjustments

SHIFT LINKAGE

Dasher—Through Chassis No. 3–5 2 044 764

▶ See Figures 1 and 2

1. Shift into Neutral.
2. Remove the round floor cover.
3. Loosen the nuts and move the bearing housing so that the shift lever inclines approximately 5 degrees to the rear.

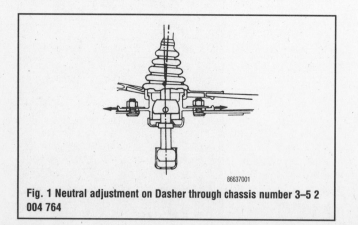

Fig. 1 Neutral adjustment on Dasher through chassis number 3–5 2 004 764

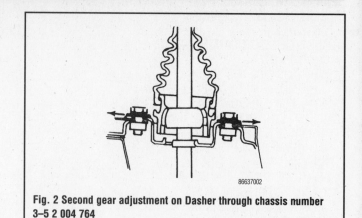

Fig. 2 Second gear adjustment on Dasher through chassis number 3–5 2 004 764

4. Tighten the nuts.
5. Shift into 2nd gear.
6. Loosen the stop plate bolts.
7. Adjust the plate so that the shift lever has 10–16mm lateral movement at the shift knob.

➡**Moving the plate to the right increases play; moving the plate to the left decreases play.**

8. Tighten the bolts. Check the shift pattern and make sure that reverse engages easily.

Dasher—From Chassis No. 3–5 2 044 765, and Quantum

An adjusting tool, VW 3014 or 3057, must be used on these models.
1. Place the lever in Neutral.
2. Working under the car, loosen the clamp nut.
3. Inside the car, remove the gear lever knob and the shift boot. It is not necessary to remove the console. Align the centering holes of the lever housing and the lever bearing housing.
4. Install the tool with the locating pin toward the front. Push the lever to the left side of the tool cutout. Tighten the lower knurled knob to secure the tool.
5. Move the top slide of the tool to the left stop and tighten the upper knurled knob.
6. Push the shift lever to the right side of the cutout. Align the shift rod and shift finger under the car, and tighten the clamp nut. Remove the tool.
7. Place the lever in 1st. Press the lever to the left side against the stop. Release the lever: it should spring back 0.24–0.47 in. (6–12mm). If not, move the lever housing slightly sideways to correct. Check that all gears can be engaged easily, particularly reverse.

Fox

1. Shift into Neutral.
2. Remove the gear shift lever knob and shift boot.
3. Loosen the clamp nuts and check that shift finger slides freely on the shift rod.
4. Move the gear shift lever to the right side, between 3rd and 4th gear position. The gear shift lever should remain perpendicular to the ball housing.
5. With the inner shift lever in neutral and the gear shift lever between 2nd and 3rd gear, tighten the clamp nut.
6. Check the engagement of all gears, including reverse, and make sure that the gear shift lever moves freely.

1975–76 Rabbit and Scirocco

➡**These procedures do not apply to some late 1976 models. Rabbits from chassis no. 176 3 000 001 and Sciroccos from chassis no. 536 2 000 001 are covered under the procedure for 1977 and later models.**

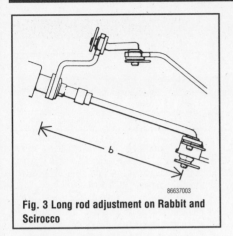

Fig. 3 Long rod adjustment on Rabbit and Scirocco

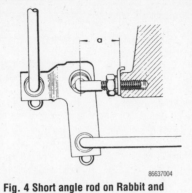

Fig. 4 Short angle rod on Rabbit and Scirocco with adjustable linkage

Fig. 5 Adjusting the shift lever on Rabbit and Scirocco

WITH ADJUSTABLE LINKAGE

▶ **See Figures 3, 4 and 5**

1. Adjust the long rod over the left driveshaft coupling to a length of 6.4–6.5 in. (163–165mm).
2. Adjust the short angle rod that attaches to the final drive housing to a length of 1.18–1.26 in. (30–32mm).
3. Make the lower part of the floorshift lever vertical (in the side to side plane) in the 1st gear position by loosening the bearing plate that supports the end of the long shift rod that connects to the bottom of the floorshift lever. Tighten the mounting nuts when the lever is vertical.
4. Make the lower part of the floorshift lever vertical (in the fore and aft plane) in the Neutral position by pulling up the boot and loosening the two lever plate bolts. Move the plate until the lever is vertical.

WITH NON-ADJUSTABLE LINKAGE

1. Make the lower part of the floorshift lever vertical (in the side to side plane) in the 1st gear position by loosening the bearing plate that supports the end of the long shift rod that connects to the bottom of the floorshift lever. Tighten the mounting nuts when the lever is vertical.
2. Make the lower part of the floorshift lever vertical (in the fore and aft plane) in the Neutral position by pulling up the boot and loosening the two lever plate bolts. Move the plate until the lever is vertical.

1977 and Later Rabbit and Scirocco; 1980–84 Jetta; 1985–89 Cabriolet

▶ **See Figures 6 and 7**

➡This category also includes some late 1976 models. It covers Rabbits from chassis no. 176 3 000 001, Sciroccos from chassis no. 536 2 000 001, all 1980–84 Jettas, and all 1985–89 Cabriolets.

1. Align the holes of the lever housing plate with the holes of the lever bearing plate. With the shifter in neutral.
2. Loosen the shift rod clamp so that the selector lever moves easily on the

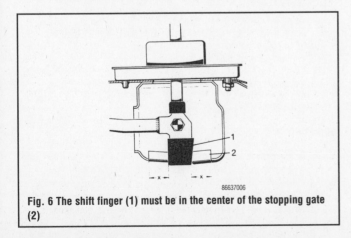

Fig. 6 The shift finger (1) must be in the center of the stopping gate (2)

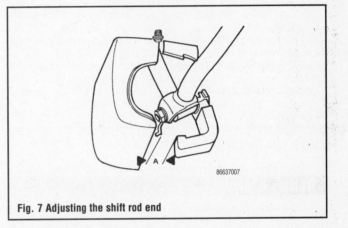

Fig. 7 Adjusting the shift rod end

shift rod. On 4-speed transaxles, pull the boot off the lever housing under the car and push it out of the way. It may be necessary to loosen the screws in the coverplate to free the boot.
3. Check that the shift finger (the rubber covered protrusion at the bottom of the shifter) is in the center of the stopping plate.
4. Adjust the shift rod end so that (A) is 0.80 in. (20mm) for 4-speed transaxles, or 21/32 in. (15mm) for 5-speed transaxles. Tighten the shift rod clamp and check the shifter operation.

1985–89 Golf and Jetta

1. Place the shifter lever into the Neutral position.
2. Under the vehicle, loosen the clamp on the shifter rod.

➡The shifter lever MUST move freely on the shifter rod.

3. Remove the shifter knob and the boot.
4. Position the gauge alignment tool VW 3104 on the shifting mechanism (lock it in place).
5. Place the transaxle selector lever in the Neutral position.
6. Align the shift rod with the selector lever and torque the clamp to 19 ft. lbs. (25 Nm).

➡The shifter linkage MUST NOT be under load during the adjustment.

7. Reverse the removal procedures. Check the shifting of the gears.

SELECTOR SHAFT LOCKBOLT

Rabbit, Scirocco, and Jetta

These selector shaft lockbolt adjustments are for Rabbits, Sciroccos and Jettas only. The adjustments are the same for both 4 and 5-speed manual transaxles.

➡For 5-speed transaxle 5th gear lockbolt adjustment, see the appropriate procedure.

Make this adjustment if, after completing the linkage adjustment, the linkage still feels spongy or jams. There are 2 kinds of lockbolts: those with plastic caps (1975), and those with lockrings (1976 and later). The lockbolt is located on the top of the transaxle.

1975 MODELS

▶ See Figure 8

1. Remove the linkage from the selector shaft lever and put the transaxle in Neutral.
2. Turn the slotted plunger until the plunger hits bottom. The nut will start to move out.
3. From here, turn the plunger back ¼ turn and install the plastic cap.
4. Reconnect the linkage.

1976 AND LATER MODELS

▶ See Figure 9

1. Disconnect the shift linkage and put the transaxle in Neutral.
2. Loosen the locknut and turn the adjusting sleeve in until the lockring lifts off the sleeve.
3. Turn the adjusting sleeve back until the lockring just contacts the sleeve. Tighten the locknut.
4. Turn the shaft slightly. The lockring should lift as soon as the shaft is turned.
5. Reconnect the linkage.

5th GEAR LOCKBOLT

Rabbit, Scirocco and Jetta

This adjustment is made with the transaxle in Neutral. The 5th gear lockbolt is located on top of the transaxle, next to the selector shaft lockbolt. It has a large protective cap over it.

1. Remove the protective cap.

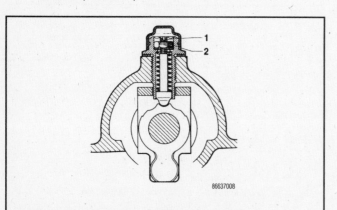

Fig. 8 Selector shaft lockbolt adjustment on 1975 models

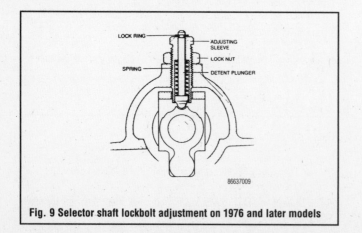

Fig. 9 Selector shaft lockbolt adjustment on 1976 and later models

2. Loosen the locknut, then tighten the adjusting sleeve until the detent plunger in the center of the sleeve just begins to move up.
3. Loosen the adjusting sleeve ⅓ of a turn and tighten the locknut. Make sure the transaxle shifts in and out of 5th gear easily. Replace the protective cap.

Back-up Light Switch

REMOVAL & INSTALLATION

The Dasher and Quantum back-up light switch is screwed into the rear of the gear shift housing above the shift lever. The Fox back-up light switch is screwed into the rear of the transaxle housing. The Jetta back-up light switch is screwed into the top of the transaxle case to the left of the shift linkage.

The back-up light switch on the Rabbit, Scirocco and Cabriolet is mounted in one of three positions: screwed into the front face of the transaxle beside the oil filler plug, screwed into the top of the transaxle case to the left of the shift linkage, or mounted as a microswitch on top of the transaxle with a lever that is activated by the external shift linkage.

ADJUSTMENT

The Rabbit and Scirocco microswitch can be adjusted by bending the bracket. No other back-up light switch can be adjusted.

Transaxle

REMOVAL & INSTALLATION

Dasher

1. Disconnect the exhaust pipe from the manifold and its bracket on the transaxle.
2. Remove the square-headed bolt on the shift linkage. Later models have a hex head bolt.
3. Press the shift linkage coupling off.
4. Disconnect the clutch cable.
5. Disconnect the speedometer cable.
6. Detach the axle shafts from the transaxle.
7. Remove the starter.
8. Remove the inspection plate.
9. Remove the engine-to-transaxle bolts.
10. Remove the transaxle crossmember.
11. Support the transaxle with a jack.
12. Pry the transaxle out from the engine.
13. Lift the transaxle out of the car with an assistant.
   To install:
14. Connect the transaxle to the engine. Tighten the bolts to 40 ft. lbs. (55 Nm).
15. Install the transaxle crossmember. Do not fully tighten the bolts until the transaxle is aligned and fully installed in the vehicle. On models with the rubber core rear transaxle mount, the rubber core must be centered in its housing.
16. Install the starter and inspection plate.
17. Install the axle shafts. Tighten the bolts to 33 ft. lbs. (45 Nm).
18. Connect the speedometer and clutch cables.
19. Connect the shift linkage.
20. Connect the exhaust pipe to the manifold.
21. If necessary, refill the transaxle. Refer to Section 1 for procedures.
22. Adjust the clutch.
23. Connect the negative battery cable.

Quantum

1. Disconnect the negative battery cable.
2. Disconnect exhaust pipe from the manifold and its bracket.
3. Unhook the clutch cable.
4. Detach speedometer cable.
5. Remove upper engine/transaxle bolts.
6. Remove engine support bolts on both sides of the engine block (front).

7. Remove front muffler and exhaust pipe.

8. Unbolt both driveshafts (halfshafts) at the transaxle.

➡ **On Quantum Syncro models, the driveshaft connected to the rear axle assembly will also have to be removed, in order to remove the transaxle.**

9. Disconnect back-up light wiring.

10. Remove the inspection plate on bottom of transaxle case.

11. Remove starter bolt.

12. Remove shift rod coupling bolt. Pry off the shift rod coupling ball with a prybar.

13. Pull off shift rod coupling from shift rod.

14. Place a jack under the transaxle and lift slightly.

15. Remove the transaxle support bolts and the transaxle rubber mounts.

16. Remove the front transaxle support bolts and the lower transaxle/engine support bolts.

17. Slowly pry the transaxle from the engine.

18. Lower the transaxle out of the car.

To install:

19. Make sure mainshaft splines are clean and lubricated with a molybdenum disulfide grease.

20. Connect the transaxle to the engine. Tighten the bolts to 40 ft. lbs. (55 Nm).

21. Install the transaxle support mounts. Make sure that all transaxle mounting bolts are aligned and free of tension (holes lined up) before tightening. Tighten the front transaxle support to 18 ft. lbs. (25 Nm) and the transaxle-to-body bolts to 80 ft. lbs. (108 Nm).

22. Connect the shift rod coupling.

23. Install the starter bolt and the inspection plate.

24. Connect the back-up light wiring.

25. Connect the halfshafts to the transaxle. Tighten the bolts to 33 ft. lbs. (45 Nm).

26. Install the front muffler and exhaust pipe, then install the engine support bolts.

27. Connect the speedometer and clutch cables.

28. Connect the exhaust pipe to the manifold.

29. If necessary, refill the transaxle. Refer to Section 1 for procedures.

30. Connect the negative battery cable.

Fox With 4-Speed Transaxle

1. Disconnect the negative battery cable.

2. Disconnect the exhaust pipe from the manifold and its bracket on the transaxle.

3. Remove the square-headed bolt on the shift linkage. Later models have a hex head bolt.

4. Press the shift linkage coupling off.

5. Disconnect the clutch cable.

6. Disconnect the speedometer cable.

7. Detach the halfshafts from the transaxle.

8. Remove the starter.

9. Remove the inspection plate.

10. Remove the engine-to-transaxle bolts.

11. Remove the transaxle crossmember.

12. Support the transaxle with a jack.

13. Pry the transaxle out from the engine.

14. Lift the transaxle out of the car with an assistant.

To install:

15. Connect the transaxle to the engine. Tighten the bolts to 40 ft. lbs. (55 Nm).

16. Install the transaxle crossmember. Do not fully tighten the bolts until the transaxle is aligned and fully installed in the vehicle. On models with the rubber core rear transaxle mount, the rubber core must be centered in its housing.

17. Install the starter and inspection plate.

18. Install the axle shafts. Tighten the bolts to 33 ft. lbs. (45 Nm).

19. Connect the speedometer and clutch cables.

20. Connect the shift linkage.

21. Connect the exhaust pipe to the manifold.

22. If necessary, refill the transaxle. Refer to Section 1 for procedures.

23. Adjust the clutch.

24. Connect the negative battery cable.

Fox With 5-Speed Transaxle

1. Disconnect the negative battery cable.

2. Remove the upper engine-to-transaxle bolts.

3. Disconnect the clutch cable from the clutch lever and route the cable off to the side and out of the way.

4. Disconnect the speedometer cable from the transaxle.

5. Disconnect the exhaust pipe from the manifold and its bracket on the transaxle.

6. Remove the engine stop bolts from the block.

7. Disconnect the front exhaust pipe from the catalytic converter.

8. Unbolt the exhaust pipe support from the transaxle.

9. Unbolt the axleshafts from the transaxle flanges. Tie the shafts up and out of the way.

10. Unplug the back-up switch wire.

11. Unbolt and remove the cover plate.

12. Remove the starter.

13. Remove the bolt from the shift rod coupling and pry the linkage from the coupling.

14. Pull the shift rod coupling from the shift rod.

15. Support the transaxle with a jack or support tool 2071 and raise the transaxle slightly.

16. Remove the transaxle support bar bolts and pivot the support to the rear. Remove the support bar mount.

17. Remove the lower engine/transaxle bolts.

18. Using a large prybar, separate the transaxle from the engine and lower it from the vehicle using the jack.

To install:

19. Make sure the mainshaft splines are clean, then lightly lubricate them with molybdenum disulfide grease or spray.

20. Raise the transaxle onto the engine and install the lower engine/transaxle bolts. Torque the bolts to 40 ft. lbs. (55 Nm).

21. Install the mounts and mounting support brackets. Torque the transaxle mounting fasteners to the following specifications:

    a. Subframe support-to-body—40 ft. lbs. (55 Nm).

    b. Mount-to-bracket—18 ft. lbs. (25 Nm).

    c. Mount-to-body—80 ft. lbs. (108 Nm).

    d. Front bracket-to-transaxle —40 ft. lbs. (55 Nm).

➡ **Make sure the engine/transaxle mounts are aligned and free of tension before tightening the fasteners. All the mount rubber cores should be centered in the mount.**

22. Connect the shift rod coupling to the shift rod.

23. Connect the shift rod linkage to the shift rod coupling. Torque the shift rod bolt to 14 ft. lbs. (19 Nm).

24. Install the starter. Torque the starter mounting bolts to 14 ft. lbs. (19 Nm).

25. Install the cover plate and torque the bolts to 7 ft. lbs. (10 Nm). Make sure the cover plate is properly seated.

26. Plug in the back-up switch wire.

27. Connect the axleshaft to the transaxle. Torque the flange bolts to 30 ft. lbs. (40 Nm).

28. Attach the exhaust pipe support to the transaxle.

29. Connect the front exhaust pipe to the catalytic converter.

30. Install the engine stop bolts and torque them to 18 ft. lbs. (25 Nm).

31. Connect the exhaust pipe to the bracket and manifold. Torque the manifold nuts to 22 ft. lbs. (30 Nm).

32. Connect the speedometer and clutch cables.

33. Install the upper engine/transaxle bolts. Torque the bolts to 40 ft. lbs. (55 Nm).

34. Connect the negative battery cable.

1975–84 Rabbit, Scirocco, Pick-up and Jetta

▶ **See Figure 10**

The engine and transaxle may be removed together as explained under engine removal and installation procedures in Section 1, or the transaxle may be removed alone, as explained here.

1. Disconnect the negative battery cable.

2. Support the left end of the engine at the lifting eye with the appropriate VW support tool.

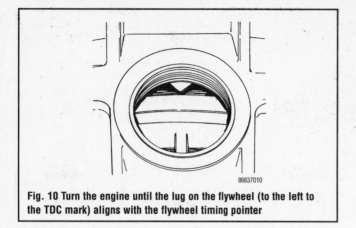

Fig. 10 Turn the engine until the lug on the flywheel (to the left to the TDC mark) aligns with the flywheel timing pointer

3. Remove the left transaxle mount bolts (between the transaxle and the firewall and ground strap.)

4. Turn the engine until the lug on the flywheel (to the left to the TDC mark) aligns with the flywheel timing pointer. The transaxle/engine must be in this position to be separated.

5. Detach the speedometer drive cable, back-up light wire, and clutch cable.

6. Remove the engine-to-transaxle bolts.

7. Disconnect the shift linkage.

8. Detach the transaxle ground strap.

9. Remove the starter.

10. Remove the engine mounting support near the starter.

11. Remove the rear transaxle mount.

12. Unbolt and hang the driveshafts with wire.

13. From underneath, remove the bolts for the large cover plate, but don't remove it. Unbolt the small cover plate on the firewall side of the engine. Remove the engine to transaxle nut immediately below the small plate.

14. Press the transaxle off the dowels and remove it from below the car.

To install:

15. The recess in the flywheel edge must be at 3 o'clock (facing the left end of the engine). Connect the transaxle to the engine. Tighten the engine-to-transaxle bolts to 47 ft. lbs. (64 Nm).

16. Install the cover plates.

17. Connect the driveshafts. Tighten the bolts to 33 ft. lbs. (45 Nm).

18. Install the rear transaxle mount. Tighten the bolt to 47 ft. lbs. (64 Nm).

19. Install the starter and connect the transaxle ground strap.

20. Connect the speedometer cable, back-up light wire and the clutch cable.

21. Install the left transaxle mounting bolts. Tighten them to 47 ft. lbs. (64 Nm).

22. Connect the negative battery cable. If necessary, refill the transaxle fluid. Refer to Section 1 for procedures.

1985–89 Scirocco and Cabriolet

1. Disconnect and remove the battery.

2. Unplug the back-up light switch connector and the speedometer cable from the transaxle. Plug the speedometer cable hole.

3. Turn the crankshaft to align the timing marks to TDC.

4. To disconnect the shift linkage, pry open the ball joint ends and remove both selector rods. Remove the pin, disconnect the relay rod and put the pin back in the hole on the rod for safe keeping.

5. Raise and safely support the vehicle and remove the front wheels. Connect the engine sling tool VW–10–222A or equivalent, to the loop in the cylinder head and just take the weight of the engine off the mounts. Do not try to support the engine from below.

6. Remove the drain plug and drain the oil from the transaxle.

7. Detach the clutch cable from the linkage and remove it from the transaxle case.

8. Remove the starter and front engine mount. On 16-valve engines, remove the engine damper.

9. Remove the small cover behind the right halfshaft flange and remove the clutch cover plate.

10. Disconnect the halfshafts from the drive flanges and hang them up with wire. Do not let them hang by the outer CV-joint or the joint may come apart.

11. Remove the long center bolt from the left-side transaxle mount.

12. Remove the entire rear mount assembly from the body and differential housing.

13. Lower the engine hoist enough to let the left mount free of the body and remove the mount from the transaxle.

14. Place a support jack under the transaxle, remove all the transaxle-to-engine bolts and carefully pry the transaxle away from the engine. Lower the transaxle from under the vehicle.

To install:

15. Coat the input shaft lightly with molybdenum grease and carefully fit the transaxle onto the engine. If necessary, put the transaxle in any gear and turn an output flange to align the input shaft spline with the clutch spline.

16. Install the engine-to-transaxle bolts and torque to 55 ft. lbs. (75 Nm).

17. When installing the mounts to the transaxle, torque the bolts to 33 ft. lbs. (45 Nm). Install but do not torque the bolts that go into the rubber mounts.

18. Install the starter and front mount.

19. With all mounts installed and the transaxle safely in the vehicle, allow some slack in the lifting equipment. With the vehicle safely supported, shake the engine/transaxle as a unit to settle it in the mounts. Torque all mounting bolts, starting at the rear and working forward. Torque the rubber mount bolts to 25 ft. lbs. (35 Nm). Torque the front mount bolts to 38 ft. lbs. (52 Nm).

20. Install the halfshafts and torque the bolts to 33 ft. lbs. (45 Nm). Install the clutch cover plates.

21. Connect the shift linkage and clutch cable, and adjust as required.

22. Complete the remaining installation and refill the transaxle with oil.

1985–89 Golf and Jetta

▶ **See Figures 11 thru 19**

1. Remove the left axle shaft nut with the vehicle on the ground.

2. Disconnect and remove the battery.

3. Disconnect the back-up light switch connector and the speedometer cable from the transaxle; plug the speedometer cable hole.

4. Remove the upper engine-to-transaxle bolts.

5. Remove the three right-side engine mount bolts, between the engine and firewall.

Fig. 11 Unplugging the back-up light switch connector

Fig. 12 Disconnect the speedometer cable from the transaxle

Fig. 13 Remove the upper engine-to-transaxle bolts

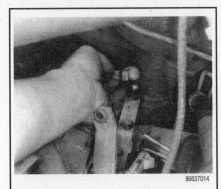

Fig. 14 Disconnecting the shift linkage ball joint

Fig. 15 Disconnect the clutch cable, then remove it from the transaxle

Fig. 16 Remove remaining transaxle mount bolts . . .

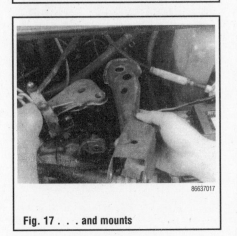

Fig. 17 . . . and mounts

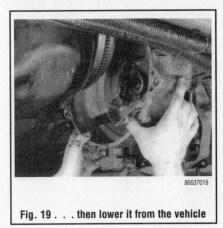

Fig. 18 Carefully pry the transaxle away from the engine . . .

Fig. 19 . . . then lower it from the vehicle

6. To disconnect the shift linkage, pry open the ball joint ends, then remove the shift and relay shaft rods.

7. Remove the center bolt from the left transaxle mount.

8. Raise and safely support the vehicle, then remove the front wheels.

9. Connect the engine sling tool VW–10–222A (or an equivalent that allows you to raise or lower the engine as needed) to the loop in the cylinder head, then take the weight of the engine off the mounts. On the 16-valve engine, the idle stabilizer valve must be removed to attach the tool. Do not try to support the engine from below.

10. Remove the drain plug and drain the oil from the transaxle.

11. Remove the left inner fender liner.

12. Disconnect the halfshafts from the inner drive flanges. Hang the right halfshaft and remove the left halfshaft.

13. Remove the clutch cover plate and the small plate behind the right half-shaft flange.

14. Remove the starter and front engine mount.

15. Disconnect the clutch cable and remove it from the transaxle housing.

16. Tilt the engine downward and remove the remaining transaxle mount bolts and mounts.

17. Place a jack under the transaxle and remove the last bolts holding it to the engine. Carefully pry the transaxle away from the engine and lower it from the vehicle.

➡Rotate the transaxle to allow clearance for removal.

To install:

18. Coat the input shaft lightly with molybdenum grease and carefully fit the transaxle in place. If necessary, put the transaxle in any gear and turn an output flange to align the input shaft spline with the clutch spline.

19. Install the engine-to-transaxle bolts and torque to 55 ft. lbs. (75 Nm).

20. When installing the mounts to the transaxle, torque the rear bracket–to–engine bolts and the transaxle support bolts to 18 ft. lbs. (25 Nm). Torque the left bracket–to–transaxle bolts to 25 ft. lbs. (35 Nm) and the remaining mounting bolts to 44 ft. lbs. (60 Nm). Install but do not torque the bolts that go into the rubber mounts.

21. Install the starter and front engine mount.

22. With all mounts installed and the transaxle safely in the vehicle, allow some slack in the lifting equipment. With the vehicle safely supported, shake the engine/transaxle as a unit to settle it in the mounts. Torque all mounting bolts, starting at the rear and working forward. Torque the bolts that go into the rubber mounts to 44 ft. lbs. (60 Nm).

23. Install the halfshafts and torque the bolts to 33 ft. lbs. (45 Nm). Install the clutch cover plates.

24. Connect the shift linkage and clutch cable, and adjust as required.

25. Install the inner fender liner, then complete the remaining installation in reverse order of removal. Be sure to refill the transaxle.

Axle Shaft (Halfshaft)

REMOVAL & INSTALLATION

✳✴ WARNING

When loosening or tightening an axle nut, make sure the vehicle is on the ground. The amount of torque required could cause the vehicle to fall off jackstands.

Dasher, Fox and Quantum

➡When removing the right axle shaft, you must detach the exhaust pipe from the manifold and the transaxle bracket. Be sure to buy a new exhaust flange gasket.

1. With the car on the ground, remove the front axle nut.

➡If necessary, use a long breaker bar with a length of pipe as an extension.

2. Disconnect the negative battery cable.

3. Raise and support the front of the vehicle.

4. Remove the socket head bolts retaining the axle shaft to the transaxle.

5. Pull the transaxle side of the driveshaft out and up and place it on the top of the transaxle.

6. Pull the axle shaft from the steering knuckle.

To install:

7. Installation is the reverse of removal. Tighten the axle shaft flange bolts to 33 ft. lbs. (45 Nm). The axle nut should be tightened to 145 ft. lbs. (198 Nm) for M18 nuts, or 170 ft. lbs. (231 Nm) for M20 nuts.

Except Dasher, Fox and Quantum

▶ **See Figures 20 thru 25**

1. With the vehicle on the ground, remove the front axle nut.
2. Disconnect the negative battery cable.
3. Raise and safely support vehicle and remove the front wheels.
4. Remove the ball joint clamping bolt and push the control arm down, away from the ball joint.
5. If necessary, carefully loosen the halfshaft in the hub using a brass drift and hammer.
6. Remove the socket head bolts from the transaxle drive flange.
7. Remove the halfshaft from the drive flange and support it below the flange. Do not let it hang by the outer CV-joint, or the joint may fall apart.
8. Remove the assembly from the vehicle.

To install:

9. Fit the halfshaft to the drive flange and install the bolts. It is not necessary to torque them yet.
10. Apply a thread locking compound to the outer ¼ inch of the spline. Slip the spline through the hub and loosely install a new axle nut.
11. Assemble the ball joint and torque the nut and bolt to 37 ft. lbs. (50 Nm).
12. Install the wheel and hold it to keep the axle from turning. Torque the drive flange bolts to 33 ft. lbs. (45 Nm).
13. With the vehicle on the ground, torque the axle nut to 195 ft. lbs. (265 Nm) on Golf and Jetta, or 175 ft. lbs. (240 Nm) on other models.
14. Connect the negative battery cable.

CV-JOINT AND BOOT OVERHAUL

The constant velocity joints (CV-joints) can be disassembled for cleaning and inspection, but they cannot be repaired. All parts are machined to a matched tolerance, so the entire CV-joint must be replaced as a unit.

1. With the car on the ground, remove the front axle nut.
2. Raise and safely support the vehicle.
3. Remove the halfshaft, as described earlier in this section.
4. Pry open and remove the boot clamps with a pair of wire cutters.
5. With the halfshaft securely clamped in a vise, the outer CV-joint can be removed by sharply rapping on the joint with a plastic hammer. The joint will snap off of the circlip and slide off the axle.
6. To remove the inner CV-joint, remove the circlip from the center and slide the joint off the axle.
7. Both boots can be removed after removing the CV-joint.

To install:

8. Always replace both circlips and make sure the CV-joint is clean before installation. Wrap a piece of black electrical tape around the shaft splines and slip the inner clamp and the boot onto the shaft.
9. Remove the tape and install the dished washer with the concave side out so it acts as a spring pushing the CV-joint out. On the outer joint, install the thrust washer and a new circlip.
10. To install the outer CV-joint, place it onto the spline and carefully tap straight in on the end with a plastic hammer. The joint will click into place over the circlip.
11. To install the inner CV-joint, slide it onto the spline and push in enough to allow the circlip to fit into the groove in the axle shaft.
12. Pack the CV-joint with special CV-joint grease. DO NOT use any other type of grease.
13. Pack any remaining grease into the boot and install the clamps on the outer boot.
14. Install the halfshaft, as previously described.
15. Lower the car, then tighten the front axle nut.

Fig. 20 Remove the front axle nut with the vehicle on the ground

Fig. 21 Removing the ball joint clamping bolt

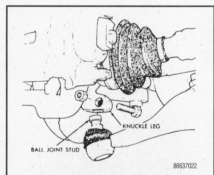

Fig. 22 Push the control arm down, away from the ball joint, after removing the clamping bolt

Fig. 23 If necessary, carefully loosen the halfshaft in the hub using a brass drift and hammer

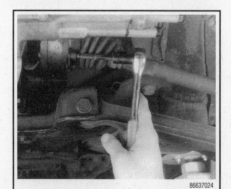

Fig. 24 Removing the socket head bolts from the drive flange

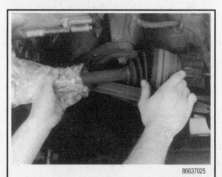

Fig. 25 The halfshafts can be wrapped in plastic to prevent damage to the boots and joints

CLUTCH

※※ CAUTION

Some clutch driven discs contain asbestos, which has been determined to be a cancer causing agent. Never clean clutch surfaces with compressed air! Avoid inhaling dust from any clutch surface! When cleaning clutch surfaces, use a commercially available brake cleaning fluid.

Understanding the Clutch

The purpose of the clutch is to disconnect and connect engine power at the transaxle. A vehicle at rest requires a lot of engine torque to get all that weight moving. An internal combustion engine does not develop a high starting torque (unlike steam engines) so it must be allowed to operate without any load until it builds up enough torque to move the vehicle. Torque increases with engine rpm. The clutch allows the engine to build up torque by physically disconnecting the engine from the transaxle, relieving the engine of any load or resistance.

The transfer of engine power to the transaxle (the load) must be smooth and gradual; if it weren't, drive line components would wear out or break quickly. This gradual power transfer is made possible by gradually releasing the clutch pedal. The clutch disc and pressure plate are the connecting link between the engine and transaxle. When the clutch pedal is released, the disc and plate contact each other (the clutch is engaged) physically joining the engine and transaxle. When the pedal is pushed inward, the disc and plate separate (the clutch is disengaged) disconnecting the engine from the transaxle.

Most clutches utilize a single plate, dry friction disc with a diaphragm-style spring pressure plate. The clutch disc has a splined hub which attaches the disc to the input shaft. The disc has friction material where it contacts the flywheel and pressure plate. Torsion springs on the disc help absorb engine torque pulses. The pressure plate applies pressure to the clutch disc, holding it tight against the surface of the flywheel. The clutch operating mechanism consists of a release bearing, fork and cylinder assembly.

The release fork and actuating linkage transfer pedal motion to the release bearing. In the engaged position (pedal released) the diaphragm spring holds the pressure plate against the clutch disc, so engine torque is transmitted to the input shaft. When the clutch pedal is depressed, the release bearing pushes the diaphragm spring center toward the flywheel. The diaphragm spring pivots the fulcrum, relieving the load on the pressure plate. Steel spring straps riveted to the clutch cover lift the pressure plate from the clutch disc, disengaging the engine drive from the transaxle and enabling the gears to be changed.

The clutch is operating properly if:
1. It will stall the engine when released with the vehicle held stationary.
2. The shift lever can be moved freely between 1st and reverse gears when the vehicle is stationary and the clutch disengaged.

Adjustments

➡ **On some 1986–89 models with 5-speed transaxles, a self-adjusting clutch cable is used. The cable incorporates an adjustment mechanism on the transaxle side of the cable which automatically adjusts to compensate for normal clutch disc wear.**

CHECKING TOTAL CLUTCH PEDAL TRAVEL

Prior to free-play adjustment, check total pedal travel as follows:
1. Hook a tape measure to the top of the clutch pedal. Measure distance between the top of the pedal and the centerline of the steering wheel.
2. Depress the pedal and measure the total distance again. If the difference between the measurements exceeds 4.7 in. (119mm), the floor covering may be interfering with pedal travel.

PEDAL FREE-PLAY

▶ **See Figure 26**

Clutch pedal free-play should be 0.59 in. (15mm) for all Dashers and pre-1979 Rabbits and Sciroccos. On 1979 and later models, there should be 0.85–0.98 in. (21.5–25mm) of free-play.

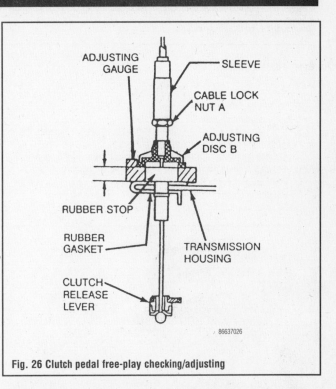

Fig. 26 Clutch pedal free-play checking/adjusting

Clutch pedal free-play is the distance the pedal can be depressed before the linkage starts to act on the throwout bearing. Clutch free-play insures that the clutch plate is fully engaged and not slipping. Clutches with no or insufficient free-play often wear out quickly and give marginal power performance.

1. Adjust the clutch pedal free-play by loosening or tightening the two nuts (or locknut and threaded sleeve) on the cable near the oil filter on Fox, Dasher and Quantum. On the Rabbit, Jetta, GTI, Scirocco and Cabriolet, it is on the left side at the front of the transaxle.

➡ **Correct free-play cannot be measured correctly if the floor covering interferes with clutch pedal travel.**

2. Loosen the locknut and loosen or tighten the adjusting nut or sleeve until desired play is present. Depress the clutch pedal several times and recheck free-play. Readjust if necessary. Tighten locknut.
3. On late models, VW recommends that a special tool (US5043) be used to determine proper adjustment. The procedure for adjustment is as follows:
   a. Depress the clutch pedal several times.
   b. Loosen the locknut and insert the tool.
   c. Adjust the sleeve until zero clearance between sleeve and tool is reached. Tighten locknut.
   d. Remove tool and depress clutch pedal at least five times. Check free-play at the clutch pedal.

Clutch Pedal

REMOVAL & INSTALLATION

➡ **With turbo-diesel and 16-valve engines, the clutch pedal has an over-center spring. A special tool is required to hold the spring for removal and installation.**

1. If only the over-center spring is to be removed, do not loosen the steering column. If the pedal is being removed, loosen the steering column and move it to the side.
2. Press the pedal and install the special retaining tool, 3113A.
3. Remove the clip to disconnect the cable from the pedal.
4. Remove the pin and remove the pedal from the bracket.
5. Installation is the reverse of removal. Remove the tool after installing the over-center spring.

Clutch Cable

REMOVAL & INSTALLATION

Except Self-Adjusting Cable

♦ **See Figure 27**

1. Loosen the adjustment.
2. Disengage the cable from the clutch arm.
3. Unhook the cable from the pedal. Remove the threaded eye from the end of the cable. Remove the adjustment nut(s).
4. Remove the C-clip which holds the outer cable at the adjustment point. Remove all the washers and bushings, first noting their locations.
5. Pull the cable out of the firewall toward the engine compartment side.
6. Install and connect the new cable. Adjust the pedal free-play.

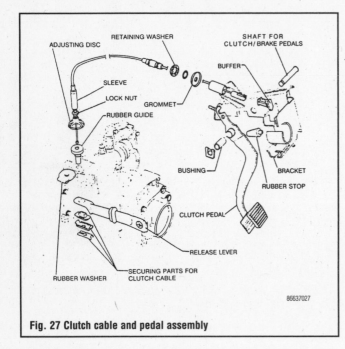

Fig. 27 Clutch cable and pedal assembly

Self-Adjusting Cable

1. Depress the pedal and release several times.
2. Compress the spring located under the boot at the top of the adjuster mechanism and remove the cable at the release lever.
3. Unhook the eye from the clutch pedal and remove the cable.
4. Install the new cable onto the pedal. Compress the spring and have a helper pull the cable down and install to the release lever.
5. If the adjuster spring is retained by a strap, remove the strap after cable installation.
6. Depress the clutch pedal several times to adjust the cable.

Driven Disc and Pressure Plate

REMOVAL & INSTALLATION

> ✳✳ **CAUTION**
>
> The clutch driven disc may contain asbestos, which has been determined to be a cancer causing agent. Never clean clutch surfaces with compressed air! Avoid inhaling any dust from any clutch surface! When cleaning clutch surfaces, use a commercially available brake cleaning fluid.

Except Dasher, Fox and Quantum

♦ **See Figures 28 thru 33**

➥You'll need special tool VW 547, VW 3190 or similar clutch pilot tool to center the clutch disc.

These cars use a type of clutch more common to motorcycles than to cars. The pressure plate is bolted to the crankshaft and the flywheel is bolted to the pressure plate; in other words, these two parts have switched places. The clutch release lever and bearing are in the left end of the transaxle. The clutch is actuated by a release rod which passes through a hollow transaxle shaft. The throwout bearing is in the transaxle and is lubricated with transaxle oil.

1. Remove the transaxle, as described earlier in this section.
2. Attach a toothed flywheel locking device and gradually loosen the flywheel to pressure plate bolts one or two turns at a time in a crisscross pattern to prevent distortion.

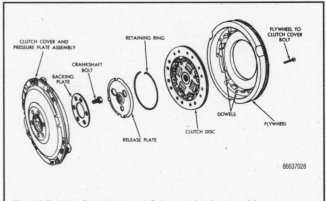

Fig. 28 Rabbit, Golf, Jetta and Scirocco clutch assembly

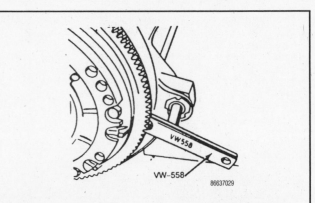

Fig. 29 Attach a flywheel locking tool to prevent the flywheel from turning

Fig. 30 Remove the flywheel and clutch disc after removing the retaining bolts

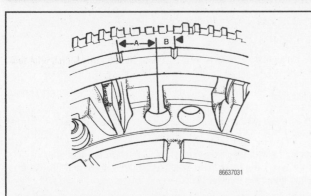

Fig. 31 Some new flywheels must have an additional timing mark cut into them

Fig. 32 Use a small prybar to remove the retaining ring

3. Remove the flywheel and the clutch disc.

4. If replacing the flywheel, some new ones haves only a TDC mark. Additional timing marks must be cut into the flywheel. Refer to the illustration. Dimension "A" is ⅝ in. (16mm) and "B" is ³⁄₃₂ in. (2.5mm). Timing mark "A" is 7½ degrees BTDC and "B" is 3 degrees ATDC.

5. Use a small prybar to remove the release plate retaining ring. Remove the release plate.

6. Lock the pressure plate in place and unbolt it from the crankshaft. Loosen the bolts one or two turns at a time in a crisscross pattern to prevent distortion.

To install:

7. Use new bolts to attach the pressure plate to the crankshaft, and be sure to use a thread locking compound. Torque the bolts in a diagonal pattern to 54 ft. lbs. (73 Nm) on pre-1985 models, or 74 ft. lbs. (100 Nm) on 1985 and later models.

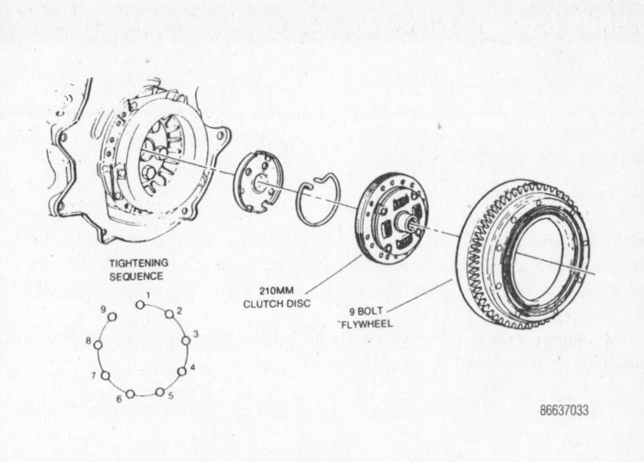

Fig. 33 Flywheel tightening sequence

8. Lubricate the clutch disc splines, release plate contact surface, and pushrod socket with multi-purpose grease. Install the release plate, retaining ring, and clutch disc.

9. Use special tool VW 547 or equivalent clutch pilot tool to center the clutch disc.

10. Install the flywheel, tightening the bolts one or two turns at a time in a crisscross pattern to prevent distortion. Torque the bolts to 14 ft. lbs. (20 Nm).

11. Install the transaxle, as described earlier in this section. Adjust the clutch free-play.

Dasher, Fox and Quantum

1. Remove the transaxle, as described earlier in this section.

2. Matchmark the flywheel and pressure plate if the pressure plate is being reused.

3. Gradually loosen the pressure plate bolts one or two turns at a time in a crisscross pattern to prevent distortion.

4. Remove the pressure plate and disc.

5. Check the clutch disc for uneven or excessive lining wear. The rivets in the plate should be tight and indented in the mating surface, not level with it.

6. Examine the pressure plate for cracking, scorching, or scoring. Replace any questionable components.

To install:

7. Install the clutch disc and pressure plate. Use a pilot shaft (available at most auto parts stores) or an old transaxle shaft to keep the disc centered.

➡ **The use of the proper pilot shaft is a necessity; if you can't obtain one, don't use "dead reckoning" to line up the clutch. You'll spend a long, sweaty time trying to force the transaxle spline into the misaligned clutch.**

8. Gradually tighten the pressure plate-to-flywheel bolts in a crisscross pattern. Tighten the bolts to 18 ft. lbs. (25 Nm).

9. Install the throwout bearing, if removed.

10. Apply a light film of grease to the input spline on the transaxle to aid in inserting it into the clutch. Don't go overboard with the amount of grease.

11. Install the transaxle, as described earlier in this section.

AUTOMATIC TRANSAXLE

Understanding the Automatic Transaxle

The automatic transaxle allows engine torque and power to be transmitted to the front wheels within a narrow range of engine operating speeds. It will allow the engine to turn fast enough to produce plenty of power and torque at very low speeds, while keeping it at a sensible rpm at high vehicle speeds (and it does this job without driver assistance). The transaxle uses a light fluid as the medium for the transmission of power. This fluid also works in the operation of various hydraulic control circuits and as a lubricant.

Identification

The first two or three letters on the number stamped into the torque converter housing are the transaxle code. This code describes the torque converter, gear ratios and valve body. The code also appears on the model identification label and describes the unit that is correct for that engine and body.

Fluid Pan and Strainer

REMOVAL & INSTALLATION

Dasher and Quantum

▶ **See Figure 34**

➡**As of transaxle no. 13 03 8, an additional oil strainer is installed between the oil pump and the valve body inside the transaxle. When installing it, be sure it fits into the locating lug of the transfer plate.**

1. Slide a drain pan under the transaxle. Raise the front of the car and safely support it with jackstands.
2. Remove the drain plug and allow all the fluid to drain. If the transaxle's fluid pan has no drain plug, loosen the pan bolts until a corner of the pan can be lowered to drain the fluid.
3. Unfasten the pan bolts and remove the fluid pan.
4. Discard the old gasket and clean the pan out. Be very careful not to get any threads or lint from rags in the pan.
   To install:
5. Install the strainer, but don't tighten the bolt too much. The specified torque is only 48 inch lbs. (5 Nm).
6. Replace the pan with a new gasket and tighten the bolts, in a crisscross pattern, to 14 ft. lbs. (19 Nm). If so equipped, reinstall the drain plug.
7. Refill the transaxle with about 2¾ qts. (2.5L) of fluid. Check the level with the dipstick. Run the car for a few minutes and check again. Add fluid as necessary.

Golf, Rabbit, Scirocco, Cabriolet and Jetta

▶ **See Figure 34**

➡**As of transaxle No. 09096, a new, cleanable oil filter is used which requires a deeper oil pan. Also beginning with transaxle number EQ-15 106, the drain plug was no longer installed in the oil pan.**

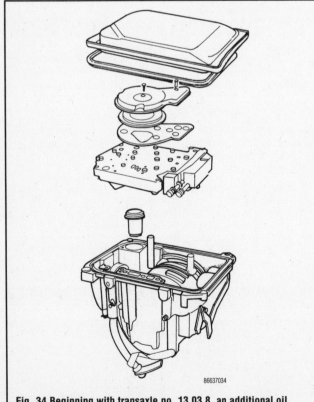

Fig. 34 Beginning with transaxle no. 13 03 8, an additional oil strainer is installed between the oil pump and the valve body. It cannot be installed on earlier models

1. Slide a drain pan under the transaxle. Remove the drain plug and let the fluid drain. If the transaxle's fluid pan has no drain plug, loosen the pan bolts until a corner of the pan can be lowered to drain the fluid.
2. Unfasten the pan bolts and remove the fluid pan.
3. Discard the old gasket and clean the pan out. Be very careful not to get any threads or lint from rags in the pan.
   To install:
4. The manufacturer recommends that the filter needn't be replaced unless the fluid is very dirty and burnt smelling. When replacing the strainer be careful, as the specified torque for the strainer screws is only 24 inch lbs. (3 Nm).

➡**Beginning with transaxle number 13 03 8, there is an additional strainer under the valve body. When installing it, be sure it fits into the locating lug of the transfer plate.**

5. Replace the pan with a new gasket and tighten the bolts, in a crisscross pattern, to 14 ft. lbs. (19 Nm). If so equipped, reinstall the drain plug.
6. Using a long-necked funnel, pour in 2½ qts. (2.3L) of Dexron®II automatic transaxle fluid through the dipstick tube. Start the engine and shift through all the transaxle ranges with the car stationary. Check the level on the dipstick with the lever in Neutral. It should be up to the lower end of the dipstick. Add fluid as necessary. Drive the car until it is warmed up, then recheck the level.

Adjustments

SHIFT LINKAGE

▶ **See Figure 35**

Check the cable adjustments on all models as follows:
1. Run the engine at 1,000–1,200 rpm with the parking brake on and the wheels blocked.
2. Select the Reverse gear. A drop in engine speed should be noticed.
3. Select the Park position; engine speed should increase. Pull the shift lever against the stop in the direction of Reverse. The engine speed should not drop (because reverse gear has not been engaged).
4. Move the shift lever to engage the Reverse. Engine speed should drop as the gear engages.
5. Move the shift lever into Neutral. An increase in engine speed should be noticed.
6. Shift into Drive. A noticeable drop in engine speed should result.
7. Shift into 1. The lever must engage without having to overcome any resistance.

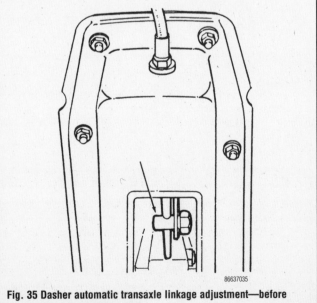

Fig. 35 Dasher automatic transaxle linkage adjustment—before chassis number 3-5 2 044 957

8. To adjust the cable, shift into Park, then proceed as follows:

9. On Dashers before chassis no. 3-5 2 044 957, remove the cover from the bottom of the shift lever case under the car and loosen the cable clamp. Using pliers, press the lever on the transaxle to the rear (against spring tension) until it hits the stop, then tighten the clamp.

10. On Dashers with chassis no. 3-5 2 044 957 and later, as well as Quantums, the shift cable clamp is loosened from inside the passenger compartment. Have an assistant under the car press the transaxle lever toward the Park position and tighten the clamp.

11. On all models except Dasher and Quantum, loosen the cable clamp at the transaxle end of the cable. Press the transaxle lever all the way to the left, then tighten the cable clamp.

THROTTLE CABLE

Except 1985–89 Golf and Jetta

▶ See Figure 36

➡️**Early Dashers with the type 003 automatic transaxle (identified by the modulator hose attached to the driver's side front of the transaxle above the pan) have a kickdown switch rather than a throttle cable. See the appropriate procedure for the switch test.**

1. Make sure the throttle is closed. On carbureted models, the choke and fast idle cam must be off.
2. Detach the cable end at the transaxle.
3. Press the lever at the transaxle into its closed throttle position.
4. You should be able to attach the cable end onto the transaxle lever without moving the lever.
5. Adjust the cable length to the correct setting.

1985–89 Golf and Jetta

1. Warm up the engine and move the gearshift lever to Park.
2. Loosen the adjusting nuts and remove the accelerator cable.
3. Remove the nuts on the throttle cable support bracket.
4. Grasp the throttle cable by the sleeve and push it way from the lever until all play is removed from the cable. While doing this, make sure the throttle valve and the accelerator/transaxle linkage remain in the closed position.
5. When all slack is removed from the cable, hold it and tighten the adjusting nut until it contacts the support bracket. Tighten the locknut to 7 ft. lbs. (10 Nm).
6. Install and connect the accelerator cable.

➡️**At this point an assistant will be needed to complete the adjustment procedure.**

7. Have an assistant press the gas all the way down until it hits the stop.
8. Move the transaxle operating lever against the kickdown stop and remove all the slack from the cable by turning the adjusting nut.

9. Let up on the gas pedal and push it all the way down again. Make sure the operating lever rests against the kickdown stop and tighten the locknut.

KICKDOWN SWITCH CHECK

➡️**Early Dashers with the type 003 automatic transaxle (identified by the modulator hose attached to the driver's side front of the transaxle above the pan) are the only VWs equipped with kickdown switches. All other models have throttle cable kickdowns.**

1. Turn the ignition switch **ON**.
2. Floor the accelerator. You should hear a click from the solenoid on the transaxle.
3. Replace the solenoid if no sound is heard. The solenoid is housed in the valve body and is accessible only by removing this unit from the transaxle; this job is best performed by a qualified mechanic.

FRONT AND REAR BANDS

▶ See Figure 37

➡️**These adjustments apply to Dashers with the 003 transaxle only. The type 003 transaxle is identified by the modulator hose attached to the driver's side front of the transaxle above the pan.**

The adjustment screws are located at the top of the transaxle housing, with the 1st gear (front) band being closest to the front of the unit on the passenger's side of the car. The 2nd gear (rear) band adjustment screw is located toward the rear of the unit on the driver's side of the vehicle.

➡️**The transaxle must be horizontal when the band adjustments are performed.**

1. To adjust the 1st gear band, loosen the locknut and tighten the adjusting screw to 84 inch lbs. (10 Nm).
2. Loosen the screw and retighten it to 42 inch lbs. (5 Nm).
3. Turn the screw out 3¼–3½ turns, then tighten the locknut.
4. To adjust the 2nd gear band, repeat Steps 1–2, then turn the screw out exactly 2½ turns before tightening the locknut.

Neutral Safety/Back-up Light Switch

REMOVAL & INSTALLATION

The combination neutral start and back-up light switch is mounted inside the shifter housing. It can be replaced after its retaining screws have been removed and the electrical connection unplugged.

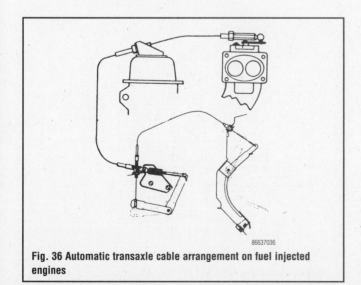

Fig. 36 Automatic transaxle cable arrangement on fuel injected engines

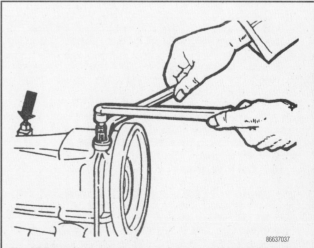

Fig. 37 Transaxle band adjustment. Front band (first gear) is shown being adjusted. The arrow indicates the second gear band adjustment location

ADJUSTMENT

The starter should operate in Park or Neutral only. Adjust the switch by moving it on its mounts. The back-up lights should only come on when the shift selector is in the Reverse position.

Transaxle

REMOVAL & INSTALLATION

Dasher and Quantum

The following procedures are for both types of Dasher automatic transaxles (003 and the 089). The model designation numbers are visible on the top of the automatic transaxle unit (as opposed to the differential unit of the transaxle). Another way to identify the transaxle is that type 003 has a vacuum modulator hose coming from the driver's side front of the transaxle above the pan, while type 089 does not. Do not confuse the transaxle fluid filler pipe with the above mentioned hose.

1. Disconnect the negative battery cable.
2. Raise the car and safely position support stands so that you will have free access to the transaxle and axle shafts.
3. Disconnect the speedometer cable.
4. On the 089 transaxle, remove the accelerator cable from the throttle valve housing.
5. Remove two of the upper engine/transaxle bolts. On the 089 transaxle, support the engine with either VW special tool 10–222 or an appropriate jack.
6. Disconnect the exhaust pipe.
7. Remove the torque converter cover plate. On the 003 transaxle, remove the vacuum modulator hose.
8. Remove the circlip holding the selector lever cable to the lever, then remove the cable.
9. Remove the starter.
10. On the 003 disconnect the kickdown switch wires.
11. The torque converter is mounted to the flywheel by three bolts. The bolts are accessible through the starter hole. You'll have to turn the engine over by hand to remove all three.
12. Remove the axle shaft to transaxle socket head bolts.
13. Matchmark the position of the ball joint on the left control arm and remove the ball joint from the arm. Hold the wheel assembly out away from the arm to provide clearance between the axle shaft and the transaxle.

➡ **On Quantum Syncro models, the driveshaft connected to the rear axle assembly will also have to be removed in order to remove the transaxle.**

14. Remove the exhaust pipe from the transaxle bracket.
15. Disconnect the remaining transaxle controls. Those you cannot reach can be removed when the transaxle is lowered a little.
16. Unbolt the transaxle crossmember and remove it from the transaxle.
17. Support the transaxle on a jack and loosen the lower engine/transaxle bolts.
18. On the 089 transaxle, remove all engine/transaxle bolts. Have an assistant pull the left wheel out as far as it will go and slowly lower the transaxle, making sure the torque converter does not fall off.
19. On the 003 transaxle, loosen the union nut on the ATF filler pipe so that the pipe can be swivelled. Remove the engine/transaxle bolts and lower the unit. You may have to pull the left wheel out a little so that the axle shaft clears the transaxle case. Make sure the torque converter does not fall off.

To install:
20. Installation is the reverse of removal. Be sure to observe the following:
   • The torque converter nipple must be about 21mm from the bellhousing face surface. If it sticks out further than this, the oil pump shaft has pulled out. To correct this, realign the converter and shaft.
   • Tighten the engine/transaxle bolts to 40 ft. lbs. (55 Nm) and the torque converter bolts to 23 ft. lbs. (31 Nm). New torque converter bolts should be used. Torque the axleshaft bolts to 33 ft. lbs. (45 Nm) and the ball joint-to-control arm bolts to 45 ft. lbs. (61 Nm).
   • Check the shift linkage adjustment.

1975–84 Rabbit, Scirocco and Jetta

♦ **See Figures 38 and 39**

The engine and transaxle may be removed together, as explained under the engine removal and installation procedure in Section 3, or the transaxle may be removed alone, as explained here.

1. Disconnect both battery cables.
2. Disconnect the speedometer cable at the transaxle.
3. Support the left end of the engine at the lifting eye. Attach a hoist to the transaxle.
4. Unbolt the rear transaxle carrier from the body, then from the transaxle. Unbolt the left-side carrier from the body.
5. Unbolt the driveshafts and wire them up.
6. Remove the starter.
7. Remove the three converter to drive plate bolts.
8. Shift into Park and disconnect the floorshift linkage at the transaxle.
9. Remove the accelerator and carburetor cable bracket at the transaxle.
10. Unbolt the left-side transaxle carrier from the transaxle.
11. Unbolt the front transaxle mount from the transaxle.
12. Unbolt the bottom of the engine from the transaxle. Lift the transaxle slightly, swing the left driveshaft up, remove the rest of the bolts, pull the transaxle off the mounting dowels, and lower the transaxle out of the car. Secure the converter so it doesn't fall out.

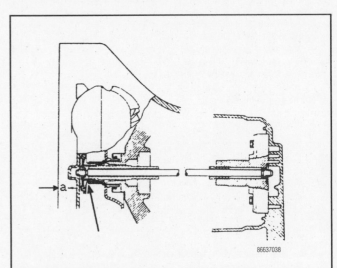

Fig. 38 Make sure the converter is fully seated on the one-way clutch support

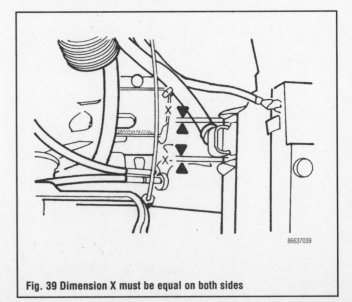

Fig. 39 Dimension X must be equal on both sides

➡**Don't tilt the torque converter! Fluid will spill out.**

To install:

13. Push the transaxle onto the mounting dowels and install two bolts. Be sure the torque converter is fully seated on the one-way clutch support (indicated by the longer arrow). Distance "a" should be 1.18 in. (30mm). Lift the unit until the left driveshaft can be installed, then install and torque the remaining bolts to 39 ft. lbs. (53 Nm). Align the transaxle so that the left mount is in the center of the body mount. Both sides' dimension ``X'' should be equal.

14. Tighten the front transaxle mount bolts to 39 ft. lbs. (53 Nm). Install the left-side transaxle carrier to the transaxle.

15. Connect the accelerator and carburetor cable bracket. Connect the floor-shift linkage.

16. Tighten the torque converter to drive plate bolts to 22 ft. lbs. (30 Nm). Torque the driveshaft bolts to 33 ft. lbs. (45 Nm).

17. Connect the speedometer cable and battery cables.

1985–89 Golf, Jetta, Scirocco and Cabriolet

1. Disconnect both battery cables.

2. Withdraw the speedometer drive gear, then plug the hole in the transaxle.

3. With the vehicle on the ground, remove the front axle nuts.

4. Raise and safely support the vehicle, then remove the front wheels. Connect the engine sling tool VW–10–222A or equivalent sling, to the cylinder head and just take the weight of the engine off the mounts. On 16-valve engines, the idle stabilizer valve must be removed to attach the tool. Do not try to support the engine from below.

5. Remove the driver's side rear transaxle mount and support bracket.

6. On Golf and Jetta, remove the front mount bolts from the transaxle and from the body and remove the mount as a complete assembly.

7. Remove the selector and accelerator cables from the transaxle lever but leave them attached to the bracket. Remove the bracket assembly to save the adjustment.

8. Remove the halfshafts.

9. Remove the heat shield and brackets and remove the starter. On Scirocco and Cabriolet, the front mount comes off with the starter.

10. Remove the bellhousing lower cover and turn the engine as needed to remove the torque converter-to-flywheel bolts.

11. Remove the remaining transaxle mounts and, on Golf and Jetta, the subframe bolts and allow the subframe to hang free.

12. Support the transaxle with a jack and remove the remaining engine-to-transaxle bolts. Be careful to secure the torque converter so it does not fall out of the transaxle.

13. Carefully lower the transaxle from the vehicle.

To install:

14. When reinstalling, make sure the torque converter is fully seated on the pump shaft splines. The converter should be recessed into the bell housing and turn by hand. Keep checking that it still turns while drawing the engine and transaxle together with the bolts.

15. Install the engine–to–transaxle bolts and torque to 55 ft. lbs. (75 Nm).

16. Install all mount and subframe bolts before tightening any of them. Tighten the bolts starting at the rear and work forward. Torque the smaller bolts to 25 ft. lbs. (34 Nm) and the larger bolts to 58 ft. lbs. (80 Nm). Remove the lifting equipment when all mounts are installed.

17. Install the torque converter–to–flywheel bolts and torque them to 26 ft. lbs. (35 Nm).

18. Install the starter and torque the bolts to 14 ft. lbs. (20 Nm). Install the heat shields.

19. Make sure the halfshaft splines are clean and apply a thread locking compound to the splines before sliding it into the hub. Connect the halfshafts to the drive flanges and torque the bolts to 33 ft. lbs. (45 Nm). Install new axle nuts, but do not fully torque them until the vehicle is on the ground.

20. If removed, fit the ball joints to the control arm and torque the clamping bolt to 37 ft. lbs. (50 Nm).

21. Connect and adjust the shift linkage as required.

22. When assembly is complete and the vehicle is on its wheels, torque the axle nuts to 195 ft. lbs. (265 Nm) on Golf and Jetta, or 175 ft. lbs. (240 Nm) on Scirocco and Cabriolet.

23. Unplug the hole in the transaxle, and insert the speedometer drive gear.

24. Connect the battery cables.

Axle Shaft (Halfshaft)

The axle shaft procedures are identical for manual and automatic transaxle equipped models. Refer to the procedures outlined in the manual transaxle portion of this section.

TORQUE SPECIFICATIONS

Component	US	Metric
Manual Transaxle		
Dasher		
Engine-to-transaxle bolts	40 ft. lbs	55 Nm
Quantum		
Engine-to-transaxle bolts	40 ft. lbs.	55 Nm
Transaxle-to-body bolts	80 ft. lbs.	108 Nm
Front transaxle support	18 ft. lbs.	25 Nm
Fox		
Engine-to-transaxle bolts	40 ft. lbs.	55 Nm
Subframe support-to-body	40 ft. lbs.	55 Nm
Mount-to-bracket	18 ft. lbs.	25 Nm
Mount-to-body	80 ft. lbs.	108 Nm
Front bracket-to-transaxle	40 ft. lbs.	55 Nm
Shift rod bolt	14 ft. lbs.	19 Nm
Cover plate bolts	7 ft. lbs.	10 Nm
Engine stop bolt	18 ft. lbs.	25 Nm
1975-84 Rabbit, Scirocco and Jetta		
Engine-to-transaxle bolts	47 ft. lbs.	64 Nm
Left/rear transaxle mounts	47 ft. lbs.	64 Nm
1985-89 Scirocco and Cabriolet		
Engine-to-transaxle bolts	55 ft. lbs.	75 Nm
Mount-to-transaxle bolts	33 ft. lbs.	45 Nm
Rubber mount bolts	25 ft. lbs.	25 Nm
Front mounts	38 ft. lbs.	38 Nm
1985-89 Golf and Jetta		
Engine-to-transaxle bolts	55 ft. lbs.	75 Nm
Right bracket-to-engine bolts	18 ft. lbs.	25 Nm
Left bracket-to-transaxle bolts	25 ft. lbs.	35 Nm
Transaxle support bolts	18 ft. lbs.	25 Nm
Rubber mount bolts	44 ft. lbs.	60 Nm
Automatic Transaxle		
Dasher and Quantum		
Engine-to-transaxle bolts	40 ft. lbs.	55 Nm
Torque converter bolts	23 ft. lbs.	31 Nm
1975-84 Rabbit, Scirocco and Jetta		
Engine-to-transaxle bolts	39 ft. lbs.	53 Nm
Front transaxle mount bolt	39 ft. lbs.	53 Nm
Torque converter	22 ft. lbs.	30 Nm
1985-89 Golf, Jetta, Scirocco and Cabriolet		
Engine-to-transaxle bolts	55 ft. lbs.	75 Nm
Mount and subframe bolts		
Smaller bolts	25 ft. lbs.	34 Nm
Larger bolts	58 ft. lbs.	80 Nm
Torque converter	26 ft. lbs.	35 Nm
Halfshafts		
Drive flange bolts	33 ft. lbs.	45 Nm
Axle nuts		
Dasher, Fox and Quantum		
18mm nuts	145 ft. lbs.	198 Nm
20mm nuts	170 ft. lbs.	231 Nm
1985-89 Golf and Jetta	195 ft. lbs.	265 Nm

86637400

TORQUE SPECIFICATIONS

Component	Others	US	Metric
Clutch			
Dasher, Fox and Quantum			
Pressure plate-to-flywheel		175 ft. lbs.	240 Nm
Other models			
Pressure plate-to-flywheel		18 ft. lbs.	25 Nm
Pressure plate-to-crank			
Pre-1985		54 ft. lbs.	73 Nm
1985 and later		74 ft. lbs.	100 Nm
Flywheel		14 ft. lbs.	20 Nm

86637401

8

SUSPENSION AND STEERING

WHEELS

Wheel Assembly

REMOVAL & INSTALLATION

1. Loosen the lug bolts of the wheel to be removed. If they are seized, one or two heavy hammer blows directly on the end of the bolt head usually loosens the rust. Be carefully as continued pounding will likely damage the brake drum or rotor.
2. Raise and safely support the vehicle on jackstands. There are small indentations in the rocker panels to indicate jacking points.
3. Remove the lug bolts and remove the wheel.

FRONT SUSPENSION

MacPherson Strut

REMOVAL & INSTALLATION

Dasher, Fox and Quantum

♦ **See Figure 1**

1. Disconnect the negative battery cable.
2. With the car on the ground, remove the front axle nut. Loosen the wheel bolts.
3. Raise and support the front of the car. Use jackstands. Remove the wheels.
4. Remove the brake caliper from the strut and hang it with wire. Detach the brake line clips from the strut.
5. At the tie rod end, remove the cotter pin, back off the castellated nut, and pull the tie rod end from the strut with a puller.
6. Loosen the stabilizer bar bushings and detach the end from the strut being removed.

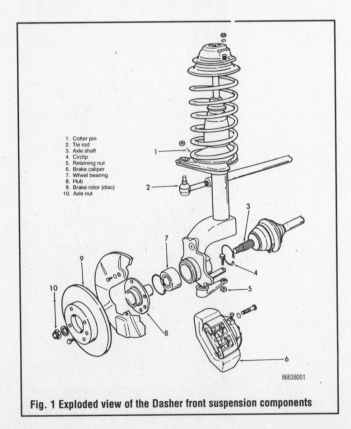

1. Cotter pin
2. Tie rod
3. Axle shaft
4. Circlip
5. Retaining nut
6. Brake caliper
7. Wheel bearing
8. Hub
9. Brake rotor (disc)
10. Axle nut

86638001

Fig. 1 Exploded view of the Dasher front suspension components

4. Installation is the reverse of removal. If desired, apply just a drop of oil to the threads to avoid seizing. DO NOT apply oil to the tapered head of the bolt or it will loosen when the vehicle is driven.
5. Torque the lug bolts to 81 ft. lbs. (110 Nm).

INSPECTION

Before installing the wheels, check for cracks or enlarged bolt holes. Replace any wheels as necessary. Remove any corrosion on the mounting surfaces with a wire brush. Installation of the wheels without proper metal-to-metal contact can cause the wheel lugs to loosen.

7. Remove the ball joint from the strut.
8. Pull the axle driveshaft from the strut.
9. Remove the upper strut-to-fender retaining nuts located under the engine hood.
10. Pull the strut assembly down and out of the car.
11. Installation is the reverse of removal. Observe the following torque specifications:
   - Axle nut—145 ft. lbs. (195 Nm) for M18 nuts or 175 ft. lbs. (238 Nm) for M20 nuts
   - Ball joint-to-strut nut—25 ft. lbs. (34 Nm) for M8 nuts or 36 ft. lbs. (49 Nm) for M10 nuts
   - Caliper-to-strut bolts—44 ft. lbs. (60 Nm)
   - Stabilizer-to-control arm bolts: 7 ft. lbs. (10 Nm).

Except Dasher, Fox and Quantum

♦ **See Figures 2, 3, 4, 5 and 6**

The upper strut-to-steering knuckle bolt may have an eccentric washer for adjusting wheel camber. Use a wire brush to clean the area, then mark a fine line on the washer and the strut together. This matchmark may be enough to preserve the front wheel camber adjustment. It will at least be accurate enough to allow you to drive the vehicle to a shop for a proper front wheel alignment. If there is no eccentric washer, a new bolt and eccentric washer can be substituted. The parts are available through the dealer.

A special tool is required to remove the upper strut nut on the Golf and Jetta. If necessary, it can be made by cutting away part of a 22mm socket.

1. Disconnect the negative battery cable.
2. Raise and safely support the vehicle, then remove the front wheels.
3. Detach the brake line from the strut and remove the caliper. DO NOT let the caliper hang by the hydraulic line, hang it from the body with wire.
4. Clean and matchmark the position of the strut-to-steering knuckle bolt.
5. Remove the bolts and push the steering knuckle down away from the strut. Support the knuckle so it is not hanging on the outer CV-joint.
6. Remove the rubber cap covering the upper strut attaching nut(s).
7. On Rabbit, Scirocco and pre-1985 Jetta, remove the nuts holding the rubber strut bearing to the body and lower the strut from the vehicle. On Golf and 1985–89 Jetta, use a hex wrench to hold the shock absorber rod and use the cut-away socket to remove the upper nut. Lower the strut from the vehicle.

   To install:
8. Place the strut into the fender and install the nuts. On Golf and 1985–89 Jetta, install a new center nut and torque it to 44 ft. lbs. (60 Nm). On Rabbit, Scirocco and pre-1985 Jetta, torque the 3 nuts to 14 ft. lbs. (20 Nm).
9. Fit the knuckle into the strut and install the bolts. Make sure the matchmarks are aligned and install the nuts.
   a. Tighten the strut-to-knuckle bolts. On 1985–89 Golf and Jetta, torque the 19mm bolts to 70 ft. lbs. (95 Nm) and the 18mm bolts to 59 ft. lbs. (80 Nm). On Rabbit, Scirocco and pre-1985 Jetta, torque the bolts to 70 ft. lbs. (95 Nm).
10. Install the brake caliper and torque the bolts to 44 ft. lbs. (60 Nm).
11. Install the wheels, then lower the vehicle.
12. Connect the battery cable. Have the front alignment checked and adjusted, as necessary.

Fig. 2 Matchmark the position of the strut-to-steering knuckle bolt

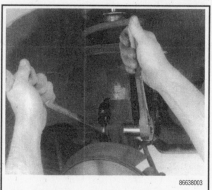

Fig. 3 Remove the bolts securing the strut to the steering knuckle

Fig. 4 Remove the rubber cap covering the upper strut attaching nut

Fig. 5 The hex wrench can be inserted either in the cut-away or through the top of the socket

Fig. 6 Removing the strut from the vehicle

STRUT OVERHAUL

♦ See Figures 7 thru 12

✳✳ CAUTION

The coil spring is very strong and under considerable pressure. If the correct tools and techniques are not available, do not attempt this job. Improper handling of coil springs can cause serious or fatal injury.

➡You must obtain a spring compressor, either the Volkswagen type (VW 340/5 and VW 340) or an equivalent.

1. Remove the strut from the vehicle.

2. Anchor the strut in a vise so it cannot move and attach the spring compressor. Be sure to follow the compressor instructions to the letter. The coil spring is under considerable pressure and has the potential to seriously harm you.

3. Compress the spring and loosen the center nut at the top of the strut assembly. To aid in removing the nut, fit an Allen wrench in the top of the shock absorber rod and loosen the nut with a closed end wrench. Some models use a threaded spacer which can be removed using a pair of needle-nose pliers.

4. Remove the collar parts from the top of the spring and arrange the parts in the order of removal to aid you in reassembly.

5. Slowly release the pressure on the spring and remove the spring from the strut.

➡The springs are color coded. When replacing them, make sure both replacement springs have the same color code.

Fig. 7 Some models use a threaded spacer

Fig. 8 Slowly release the spring pressure, then remove the coil from the strut

Fig. 9 Remove the round, threaded retaining cap on the shock tube. . .

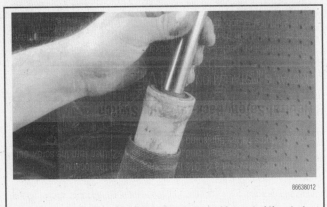

Fig. 10 . . . then pull the shock absorber cartridge out of the strut

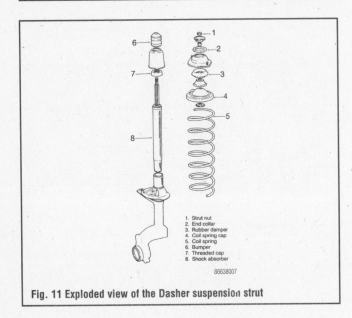

1. Strut nut
2. End collar
3. Rubber damper
4. Coil spring cap
5. Coil spring
6. Bumper
7. Threaded cap
8. Shock absorber

Fig. 11 Exploded view of the Dasher suspension strut

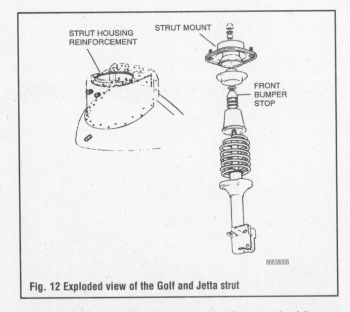

STRUT HOUSING REINFORCEMENT

STRUT MOUNT

FRONT BUMPER STOP

Fig. 12 Exploded view of the Golf and Jetta strut

6. To replace the removable shock absorber cartridge, proceed as follows:
    a. Remove the round, threaded retaining cap on the shock tube. There is a special VW tool (40 201) for this job, but you should be able to loosen the cap with a pipe wrench. Be careful not to bend or dent the cap during removal.

b. Pull the shock absorber cartridge out of the strut. You may have to put the nut back on the shock absorber rod and use it as a stop-point to tap the cartridge out of the strut. When installing, the threaded retaining cap should be tightened to 108 ft. lbs. (148 Nm).
    7. Installation of the coil spring is the reverse of removal. Tighten the coil spring retaining nut to 44 ft. lbs. (60 Nm) on the Dasher, Fox and Quantum, 58 ft. lbs. (80 Nm) on the Rabbit, Golf, Jetta and Scirocco.

➡**Make sure the coil spring fits into its grooves in the strut. If the strut has been replaced, the camber must be adjusted.**

Lower Ball Joint

INSPECTION

1. To check the ball joint, raise and safely support the vehicle. Let the front wheels hang free.
2. Insert a prybar between the control arm and the ball joint clamping bolt. Be careful to not damage the ball joint boot.
3. Measure the play between the bottom of the ball joint and the clamping bolt with a caliper. Total must not exceed 0.100 inch (2.5mm).

REMOVAL & INSTALLATION

◆ **See Figures 13 and 14**

1. Disconnect the negative battery cable.
2. Jack up the front of the vehicle and support it on jackstands.
3. Matchmark the ball joint-to-control arm position on the Dasher, Fox and Quantum.
4. Remove the retaining bolt and nut from the hub (wheel bearing housing).
5. Pry the lower control arm and ball joint down and out of the strut.
6. Remove the two ball joint-to-lower control arm retaining nuts and bolts

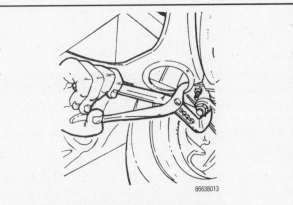

Fig. 13 Aligning the ball joint on Dasher and Quantum

Fig. 14 On the Golf, Rabbit, Jetta and Scirocco, bolt the new ball joint in place

on the Dasher, Fox or Quantum. Drill out the rivets on the Rabbit, Jetta, Golf and Scirocco, then enlarge the holes to 3mm.

7. Remove the ball joint assembly.

To install:

8. Install the Dasher, Fox or Quantum ball joint in the reverse order of removal. If no parts were installed other than the ball joint, align the match-marks made earlier. No camber adjustment is necessary if this is done. Pull the ball joint into alignment with pliers. Observe the following torques:

- Control arm-to-ball joint bolts—47 ft. lbs. (65 Nm)
- Strut-to-ball joint bolt—25 ft. lbs. (34 Nm) for M8 bolts or 36 ft. lbs. (48 Nm) for M10 bolts

9. On the Golf, Rabbit, Jetta and Scirocco, bolt the new ball joint in place (bolts are provided with the replacement ball joint), and tighten them to 18 ft. lbs. (25 Nm). Tighten the retaining bolt holding the ball joint to the hub to 21 ft. lbs. (28 Nm).

Sway Bar

REMOVAL & INSTALLATION

1. Disconnect the negative battery cable.
2. Raise the front of the vehicle and support it with jackstands. Remove the front wheels.
3. Remove the bolts/nuts securing the outer ends of the sway bar, then remove the bolts/nuts securing the brackets.
4. Remove the sway bar.

To install:

5. Position the sway bar in the vehicle.
6. Install the bolts/nuts securing the brackets. Tighten them until just snug (they will be fully torqued later).
7. Install the bolts/nuts securing the outer ends of the sway bar. Tighten until just snug (they will be fully torqued later).

➡**On Golf and Jetta models, the collars of the washers face away from the bushings. The conical side of the bushings face the washers.**

8. Install the wheels, then lower the vehicle.
9. Bounce the vehicle several times and allow the vehicle to stabilize.
10. On Quantum, Jetta and Golf models, tighten the bolts/nuts to 18 ft. lbs. (25 Nm). On other models, tighten the bolts/nuts to 15 ft. lbs. (20 Nm).
11. Connect the battery cable.

Lower Control Arm

REMOVAL & INSTALLATION

▶ **See Figure 15**

➡**When removing the left side (driver's side) control arm on the Rabbit, Jetta, Golf and Scirocco equipped with an automatic transaxle, remove the front left engine mounting, the nut for the rear mounting, the engine mounting support, then raise the engine to expose the front control arm bolt.**

1. Disconnect the negative battery cable.
2. Raise the vehicle and support it on jackstands. Remove the wheels.
3. Remove the nut and bolt attaching the ball joint to the hub (wheel bearing housing), then pry the joint down and out of the hub.
4. Remove the stabilizer bar.
5. Unbolt and remove the control arm-to-subframe (crossmember) mounting bolts on the Dasher and Quantum. On the Golf, Rabbit, Jetta and Scirocco, remove the control arm mounting bolts from the frame.
6. Remove the bolts securing the control arm, then remove the arm.

To install:

7. Installation is the reverse of removal. Observe the following torques:

- Dasher, Fox or Quantum control arm-to-subframe bolts—50 ft. lbs. (37 Nm).
- Rabbit, Jetta, Golf and Scirocco control arm-to-frame front bolt—43 ft. lbs. (57 Nm).
- Rabbit, Jetta, Golf and Scirocco control arm-to-frame rear bolts—32 ft. lbs. (44 Nm).

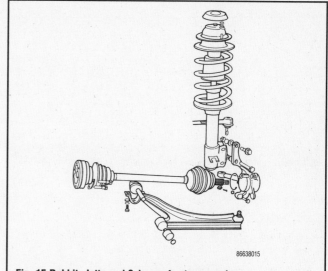

Fig. 15 Rabbit, Jetta and Scirocco front suspension

- Rabbit, Jetta, Golf and Scirocco ball joint-to-hub bolt—21 ft. lbs. (28 Nm).
- Dasher, Fox and Quantum ball joint-to-hub bolt—25 ft. lbs. (34 Nm) for M8 nuts or 36 ft. lbs. (49 Nm) for M10 nuts.
- Stabilizer bar link rods—18 ft. lbs. (25 Nm).
- Stabilizer bar bushing clamp bolts—32 ft. lbs. (43 Nm).

BUSHING REPLACEMENT

1. Remove the control arm.
2. Position the control arm on a press. Carefully push the bushing out of the control arm using the press.

To install:

3. Lightly lubricate, then position the bushing on the control arm. On Golf and Jetta models, align one arrow with the dimple on the control arm (the kidney shaped opening in the bushing must face the center of the vehicle when the control arm is installed).
4. Carefully press the bushing into the control arm.
5. Install the control arm.

Steering Knuckle

REMOVAL & INSTALLATION

✳✳ CAUTION

The torque required to loosen the front axle nut is high enough to make the vehicle fall off of jackstands. Make sure the vehicle is on the ground when loosening or tightening the front axle nut.

1. Disconnect the negative battery cable.
2. With the vehicle on the ground, remove the front axle nut.
3. Raise the vehicle and support with jackstands.
4. Remove the front wheels.

➡**The strut assembly does not have to be removed on all models except the Dasher. The Dasher's strut and knuckle is one assembly.**

5. Mark the knuckle-to-strut housing for installation alignment.
6. Remove the brake caliper and hang it from the frame using a piece of wire. DO NOT allow the caliper to hang from the brake hose.
7. Remove the tie rod nut and cotter pin. Disconnect the tie rod using a separator.
8. Disconnect the lower control arm from the knuckle.
9. Remove the two strut-to-knuckle bolts.
10. Slide the axle shaft out of the bearing and remove the knuckle.

To install:

11. Install the knuckle onto the vehicle and slide the axle shaft into the bearing.

12. Reconnect the lower ball joint, tie rod end, strut and caliper.

13. Torque the axle nut. On Dasher, Fox and Quantum, torque the M18 nut to 145 ft. lbs. (197 Nm) and the M20 nut to 170 ft. lbs. (231 Nm). On 1985–89 Golf and Jetta torque to 195 ft. lbs. (265 Nm). On other models, torque to 173 ft. lbs. (235 Nm).

14. Install the tire and lower the vehicle.

15. Connect the battery cable.

Front Hub and Wheel Bearing

REMOVAL & INSTALLATION

▶ **See Figures 16 and 17**

➡ **The hub and bearing are pressed into the knuckle and the bearing cannot be reused once the hub has been removed.**

Without Anti-Lock Brakes (ABS)

1. Disconnect the negative battery cable.

2. With the vehicle on the ground, remove the front axle nut. Raise and safely support the vehicle.

3. Remove the steering knuckle.

4. To remove the hub, support the knuckle assembly in an arbor press with the hub facing down.

5. Use a proper size arbor that will fit through the bearing and press the hub out.

6. If the inner bearing race stayed on the hub, clamp the hub in a vise and use a bearing puller to remove it.

7. On the knuckle, remove the splash shield and internal snaprings from the bearing housing.

8. With the knuckle in the same pressing position, press the bearing out.

9. Clean the bearing housing and hub with a wire brush, then inspect all parts. Replace parts that have been distorted or discolored from heat. If the hub is not absolutely perfect where it contacts the inner bearing race, the new bearing will fail quickly.

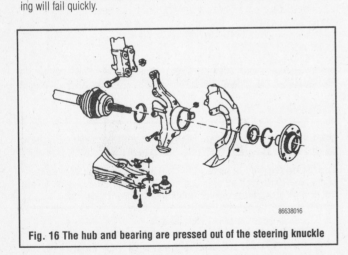

Fig. 16 The hub and bearing are pressed out of the steering knuckle

To install:

10. The new bearing is pressed in from the hub side. Install the snapring and support the steering knuckle on the press.

11. Using the old bearing as a press tool, drive the new bearing into the housing up against the snapring. Make sure the press tool contacts only the outer race of the bearing.

12. Install the outer snapring and splash shield.

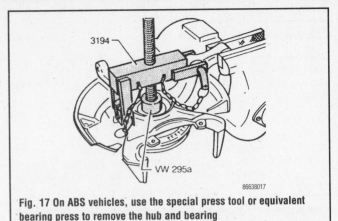

Fig. 17 On ABS vehicles, use the special press tool or equivalent bearing press to remove the hub and bearing

13. Support the inner race on the press and drive the hub into the bearing. Make sure the inner race is supported or the bearing will fail quickly.

14. Install the steering knuckle, then carefully lower the vehicle. BE SURE to torque the axle nut correctly before allowing the vehicle to roll.

15. Connect the battery cable.

With Anti-Lock Brakes (ABS)

1. Disconnect the negative battery cable.

2. With the vehicle on the ground, remove the front axle nut. Raise and safely support the vehicle.

3. Remove the steering knuckle.

4. Clamp the upper knuckle–to–strut bolt boss in a vice.

5. Install the special press tool onto the hub (as shown in the illustration) and press the hub out of the bearing.

6. If the inner bearing race stayed on the hub, clamp the hub in a vise and use a bearing puller to remove it.

7. On the knuckle, remove the splash shield and internal snaprings from the bearing housing.

8. After removing the snapring, the same press tool can be used to push the bearing out of the knuckle.

9. Clean the bearing housing and hub with a wire brush, then inspect all parts. Replace parts that have been distorted or discolored from heat. If the hub is not absolutely perfect where it contacts the inner bearing race, the new bearing will fail quickly.

To install:

10. The new bearing is pressed in from the hub side using a regular arbor press. Install the snapring and support the steering knuckle on the press.

11. Using the old bearing as a press tool, drive the new bearing into the housing up against the snapring. Make sure the press tool contacts only the outer race of the bearing.

12. Install the outer snapring and splash shield. If removed, install the speed sensor rotor onto the hub.

13. Support the inner race on the press and drive the hub into the bearing. Make sure the inner race is supported or the bearing fail quickly.

14. Install the steering knuckle and carefully lower the vehicle. BE SURE to torque the axle nut correctly before allowing the vehicle to roll.

15. Connect the battery cable.

Front End Alignment

If the tires are worn unevenly, if the vehicle is not stable on the highway or if the handling seems uneven in spirited driving, wheel alignment should be checked. If an alignment problem is suspected, first check tire inflation and look for other possible causes such as worn suspension and steering components, accident damage or unmatched tires. Repairs may be necessary before the wheels can be properly aligned. Wheel alignment requires sophisticated equipment and can only be performed at a properly equipped shop.

CASTER

▶ **See Figure 18**

Wheel alignment is defined by three different adjustments in three planes. Looking at the vehicle from the side, caster angle describes the steering axis rather than a wheel angle. The steering knuckle is attached to the strut at the top and the control arm at the bottom. The wheel pivots around the line between these points to steer the vehicle. When the upper point is tilted back, this is described as positive caster. Having a positive caster tends to make the wheels self-centering, increasing directional stability. Excessive positive caster makes the wheels hard to steer, while an uneven caster will cause a pull to one side. On all Volkswagens, caster is fixed by body geometry and it is not adjustable.

CAMBER

▶ **See Figure 19**

Looking at the wheels from the front of the vehicle, camber adjustment is the tilt of the wheel. When the wheel is tilted in at the top, this is negative camber.

In a turn, a slight amount of negative camber helps maximize contact of the outside tire with the road. Too much negative camber makes the vehicle unstable in a straight line.

TOE-IN

▶ **See Figure 20**

Looking down at the wheels from above the vehicle, toe alignment is the distance between the front of the wheels relative to the distance between the back of the wheels. If the wheels are closer at the front, they are said to be toed-in or to have a negative toe. A small amount of negative toe enhances directional stability and provides a smoother ride on the highway. On most front wheel drive vehicles, standard toe adjustment is either zero or slightly positive. When power is applied to the front wheels, they tend to toe-in naturally.

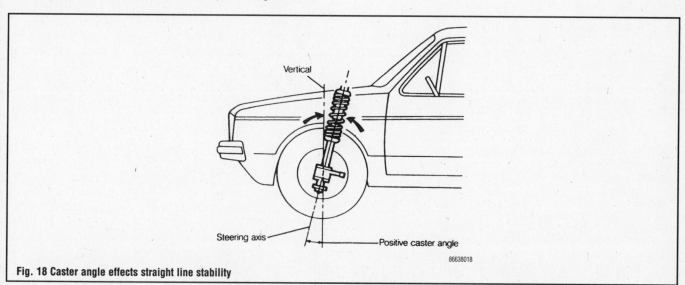

Fig. 18 Caster angle effects straight line stability

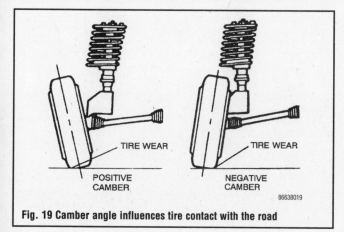

Fig. 19 Camber angle influences tire contact with the road

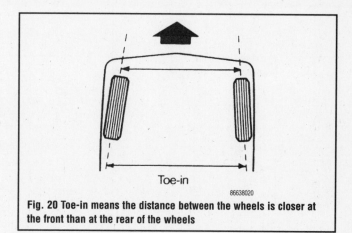

Fig. 20 Toe-in means the distance between the wheels is closer at the front than at the rear of the wheels

WHEEL ALIGNMENT (1987–1989)

Year	Model	Caster Range (deg.)	Caster Preferred Setting (deg.)	Camber Range (deg.)	Camber Preferred Setting (deg.)	Toe-in/out (In.)
1987	Golf	1P-2P	1 1/2P	13/16N-3/16N	1/2N	0
	Jetta	1P-2P	1 1/2P	13/16N-3/16N	1/2N	0
	GTI	1 1/16P-2 1/16P	1 9/16 P	7/8N-1/4N	9/16N	0
	GLI	1 1/16P-2 1/16P	1 9/16 P	7/8N-1/4N	9/16N	0
	Quantum	0-1P	1/2P	1 5/32N-5/32N	21/32N	5/64 in
	Quantum Syncro	11/16P-1 5/16P	1P	27/32N-5/32N	11/32N	13/64 in
	Fox	1 11/16P-2 5/16P	2P	13/16N-3/16N	1/2N	5/64 out
	Fox Wagon	1 7/16P-2 1/16P	1 3/4P	13/16N-3/16N	1/2N	5/64 out
	Scirocco	1 5/16P-2 5/16P	1 13/16P	3/16N-13/16P	5/16P	1/8 out
	Cabriolet	1 5/16P-2 5/16P	1 13/16P	3/16N-13/16P	5/16P	1/8 out
1988	Golf	1P-2P	1 1/2P	13/16N-3/16N	1/2N	0
	Jetta	1P-2P	1 1/2P	13/16N-3/16N	1/2N	0
	GTI 8-Valve	1 1/16P-2 1/16P	1 9/16 P	7/8N-1/4N	9/16N	0
	GTI 16-Valve	1 1/16P-2 1/16P	1 9/16 P	1N-3/4N	11/16N	0
	GLI 8-Valve	1 1/16P-2 1/16P	1 9/16 P	7/8N-1/4N	9/16N	0
	GLI 16-Valve	1 1/16P-2 1/16P	1 9/16 P	1N-3/4N	11/16N	0
	Quantum Syncro	11/16P-1 5/16P	1P	27/32N-5/32N	11/32N	13/64 in
	Fox	1 11/16P-2 5/16P	2P	13/16N-3/16N	1/2N	5/64 out
	Fox Wagon	1 7/16P-2 1/16P	1 3/4P	13/16N-3/16N	1/2N	5/64 out
	Scirocco	1 5/16P-2 5/16P	1 13/16P	3/16N-13/16P	5/16P	1/8 out
	Cabriolet	1 5/16P-2 5/16P	1 13/16P	3/16N-13/16P	5/16P	1/8 out
1989	Golf	1P-2P	1 1/2P	13/16N-3/16N	1/2N	0
	Jetta	1P-2P	1 1/2P	13/16N-3/16N	1/2N	0
	GTI 8-Valve	1 1/16P-2 1/16P	1 9/16 P	7/8N-1/4N	9/16N	0
	GLI 8-Valve	1 1/16P-2 1/16P	1 9/16 P	7/8N-1/4N	9/16N	0
	GLI 16-Valve	1 1/16P-2 1/16P	1 9/16 P	1N-3/4N	11/16N	0
	Fox	1 11/16P-2 5/16P	2P	13/16N-3/16N	1/2N	5/64 out
	Fox Wagon	1 7/16P-2 1/16P	1 3/4P	13/16N-3/16N	1/2N	5/64 out
	Scirocco	1 5/16P-2 5/16P	1 13/16P	3/16N-13/16P	5/16P	1/8 out
	Cabriolet	1 5/16P-2 5/16P	1 13/16P	3/16N-13/16P	5/16P	1/8 out

86638301

WHEEL ALIGNMENT (1974–1986)

Year	Model	Caster Range (deg.)	Caster Preferred Setting (deg.)	Camber Range (deg.)	Camber Preferred Setting (deg.)	Toe-in/out (In.)
1974	Dasher	0-1P	1/2P	0	1/2P	3/32 in
1975	Dasher	0-1P	1/2P	0	1/2P	3/32 in
	Scirocco	1 5/16P-2 5/16P	1 13/16P	3/16N-13/16P	5/16P	1/8 out
	Rabbit	1 5/16P-2 5/16P	1 13/16P	3/16N-13/16P	5/16P	1/8 out
1976	Dasher	0-1P	1/2P	0	1/2P	3/32 in
	Scirocco	1 5/16P-2 5/16P	1 13/16P	3/16N-13/16P	5/16P	1/8 out
	Rabbit	1 5/16P-2 5/16P	1 13/16P	3/16N-13/16P	5/16P	1/8 out
1977	Dasher	0-1P	1/2P	0	1/2P	5/64 in
	Scirocco	1 5/16P-2 5/16P	1 13/16P	3/16N-13/16P	5/16P	1/8 out
	Rabbit	1 5/16P-2 5/16P	1 13/16P	3/16N-13/16P	5/16P	1/8 out
1978	Dasher	0-1P	1/2P	0-1P	1/2P	5/64 in
	Scirocco	1 5/16P-2 5/16P	1 13/16P	3/16N-13/16P	5/16P	1/8 out
	Rabbit	1 5/16P-2 5/16P	1 13/16P	3/16N-13/16P	5/16P	1/8 out
1979	Dasher	0-1P	1/2P	0-1P	1/2P	5/64 in
	Scirocco	1 5/16P-2 5/16P	1 13/16P	3/16N-13/16P	5/16P	1/8 out
	Rabbit	1 5/16P-2 5/16P	1 13/16P	3/16N-13/16P	5/16P	1/8 out
1980	Dasher	0-1P	1/2P	0-1P	1/2P	5/64 in
	Scirocco	1 5/16P-2 5/16P	1 13/16P	3/16N-13/16P	5/16P	1/8 out
	Rabbit	1 5/16P-2 5/16P	1 13/16P	3/16N-13/16P	5/16P	1/8 out
	Jetta	1 5/16P-2 5/16P	1 13/16P	3/16N-13/16P	5/16P	1/8 out
1981	Dasher	0-1P	1/2P	0-1P	1/2P	5/64 in
	Scirocco	1 5/16P-2 5/16P	1 13/16P	3/16N-13/16P	5/16P	1/8 out
	Rabbit	1 5/16P-2 5/16P	1 13/16P	3/16N-13/16P	5/16P	1/8 out
	Jetta	1 5/16P-2 5/16P	1 13/16P	3/16N-13/16P	5/16P	1/8 out
1982	Quantum	0-1P	1/2P	1 5/32N-5/32N	21/32N	5/64 in
	Scirocco	1 5/16P-2 5/16P	1 13/16P	3/16N-13/16P	5/16P	1/8 out
	Rabbit	1 5/16P-2 5/16P	1 13/16P	3/16N-13/16P	5/16P	1/8 out
	Jetta	1 5/16P-2 5/16P	1 13/16P	3/16N-13/16P	5/16P	1/8 out
1983	Quantum	0-1P	1/2P	1 5/32N-5/32N	21/32N	5/64 in
	Scirocco	1 5/16P-2 5/16P	1 13/16P	3/16N-13/16P	5/16P	1/8 out
	Rabbit	1 5/16P-2 5/16P	1 13/16P	3/16N-13/16P	5/16P	1/8 out
	Jetta	1 5/16P-2 5/16P	1 13/16P	3/16N-13/16P	5/16P	1/8 out
1984	Quantum	0-1P	1/2P	1 5/32N-5/32N	21/32N	5/64 in
	Scirocco	1 5/16P-2 5/16P	1 13/16P	3/16N-13/16P	5/16P	1/8 out
	Cabriolet	1 5/16P-2 5/16P	1 13/16P	3/16N-13/16N	1/2N	1/8 out
	Golf	1 5/16P-2 5/16P	1 1/2P	13/16N-3/16N	1/2N	0
	Jetta	1 1/16P-2 1/16P	1 1/2P	-13/16N-3/16N	1/2N	0
	GTI	0-1P	1 1/2P	7/8N-1/4N	9/16N	5/64 in
1985	Quantum	0-1P	1/2P	1 5/32N-5/32N	21/32N	5/64 in
	Scirocco	1 5/16P-2 5/16P	1 13/16P	3/16N-13/16P	5/16P	1/8 out
	Cabriolet	1 1/16P-1 15/16P	1 1/2P	7/8N-1/4N	1/2N	1/8 out
1986	Quantum	0-1P	1/2P	1 5/32N-5/32N	21/32N	5/64 in
	Quantum Syncro	11/16P-1 5/16P	1P	27/32N-5/32N	11/32N	13/64 in
	Scirocco	1 5/16P-2 5/16P	1 13/16P	3/16N-13/16P	5/16P	1/8 out
	Cabriolet	1 5/16P-2 5/16P	1 13/16P	3/16N-13/16P	5/16P	1/8 out

86638300

REAR SUSPENSION

♦ See Figure 21

The Dasher rear suspension has a rear axle beam tube on each side. Trailing arms mount to the unit body in rubber bushings. A coil spring and shock absorber are located at each wheel. A Panhard rod locates the axle against side forces.

The Golf, Rabbit (except the Pick-up), Jetta and Scirocco rear suspension includes a torsion beam which connects the two trailing arms. On these models, the coil spring and the shock absorber are combined into a strut. The Quantum rear axle assembly is similar to this type, but uses different axle bushings.

The Rabbit Pick-up has leaf springs mounted on a simple axle beam with conventional shock absorbers mounted at each side of the beam.

The Fox rear suspension has a rear axle beam tube on each side. The trailing arms mount to the unit body in rubber bushings. The coil spring and the shock absorber are combined into a strut.

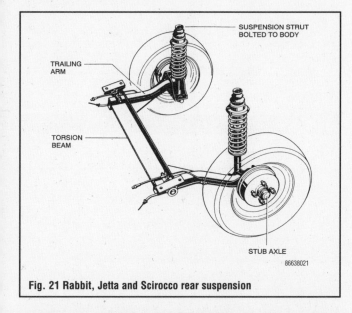

Fig. 21 Rabbit, Jetta and Scirocco rear suspension

Coil Springs

REMOVAL & INSTALLATION

➡This procedures is applicable to Dashers only and requires the use of either special tool VW 655/3 or a suitable spring compressor.

1. Disconnect the negative battery cable.
2. Raise the car and support it on jackstands. Do not place the jackstands under the axle beam.
3. Remove the wheel(s).
4. Attach special tool VW 655/3 between the axle beam and a prefabricated hook hung on the body frame above the beam. Use the special tool or a suitable spring compressor to compress and hold the spring.
5. Unbolt the shock absorber from the axle beam. Lower the axle beam just enough to remove the spring.

To install:

6. If necessary, transfer the compressor to a new spring. Remember, the compressed spring is under considerable pressure. Relieve the tension slowly, according to the tool manufacturer's instructions.
7. Install the spring.
8. Connect the shock absorber to the axle beam. Carefully remove the spring compressor.
9. Install the wheels, then lower the car to the ground.
10. Connect the battery cable.

Leaf Springs

REMOVAL & INSTALLATION

➡This procedure is applicable to the Rabbit Pick-Up only.

1. Disconnect the negative battery cable.
2. Jack up the rear of the vehicle and support it with jackstands placed under the frame. Remove the wheel(s).
3. Remove the parking brake cable from the spring and cut the tie-wrap.
4. Support the rear axle on a jack. Do not put pressure on the spring.
5. Remove the bottom shock absorber mount bolt.
6. Remove the U-bolts and their spring plates. Loosen the upper and lower shackle bolts.
7. When removing the left side spring, perform these additional steps:
   a. Remove the three bolts from the exhaust system flange on the flex pipe.
   b. Unhook the exhaust system hangers.
   c. Remove the exhaust system.
8. Remove the lower shackle bolt.
9. Remove the front spring bolt and remove the spring.

To install:

10. Install the spring. Tighten the bolts until just snug. The weight of the vehicle must be on the rear wheels before the leaf spring and shock absorber attaching bolts are fully tightened.
11. If necessary, install the exhaust system.
12. Connect the parking brake cable to the spring.
13. Install the wheels, then lower the vehicle on the ground.
14. Tighten the rear shackle bolts to 45 ft. lbs. (61 Nm), and the front bolt to 68 ft. lbs. (90 Nm). Tighten the U-bolt nuts and the lower shock absorber bolt to 29 ft. lbs. (40 Nm).
15. Connect the battery cable.

Shock Absorbers

REMOVAL & INSTALLATION

Dasher

➡Only remove one shock absorber at a time. Do not allow the rear axle to hang by its body mounts only, as it may damage the brake lines.

This operation requires the use of either special tool VW 655/3 or a suitable spring compressor and floor jack.

1. Disconnect the negative battery cable.
2. Raise the car and support it on jackstands. Do not place the jackstands under the axle beam.
3. Remove the wheel.
4. Attach special tool VW 655/3 between the axle beam and a prefabricated hook hung on the body frame above the beam. Jack the tool until you can see the shock absorber compressing. If you are using a spring compressor and a floor jack, compress the springs little and, placing the floor jack under the beam below the spring, jack it up until you see the shock absorber compress.
5. Unbolt and remove the shock absorber.
6. Installation is the reverse of removal. Tighten the shock absorber bolts to 43 ft. lbs. (58 Nm).

Rabbit Pick-Up

1. Disconnect the negative battery cable.
2. Jack up the rear of the vehicle and support the axle on jackstands.
3. Unbolt and remove the shock absorber, taking care to notice the direction of the mounting bolts for installation.
4. Installation is the reverse of removal. Tighten the mounting bolts to 29 ft. lbs. (40 Nm).

TESTING

The function of a shock absorber is to dampen harsh spring movement and provide a means of dissipating the motion of the wheels. This is done so that the roughness encountered by the wheels is not totally transmitted to the body and, therefore, to you and your passengers. As the wheel moves up and down, the shock absorber shortens and lengthens, thereby imposing a restraint on movement by its hydraulic action.

A simple way to see if your shock absorbers are functioning correctly is to push one corner of the car down a few times. This will compress the spring on that side of the car as well as the shock absorber. If the shock absorber is functioning properly, it will control the spring's tendency to remain in motion. Thus the car will level itself almost instantly when you release the downward pressure. If the car continues to bounce up and down several times, the shock absorber is worn out and should be replaced. Examine the strut body for heavy oil streaking, which would indicate shock leakage. Replace a leaky shock absorber.

Strut Assembly

REMOVAL & INSTALLATION

Fox, Rabbit (Except Pick-Up), Scirocco, Jetta and Golf

▶ **See Figures 22, 23 and 24**

1. Disconnect the negative battery cable.
2. Raise the car and support it on jackstands. Support the axle with a floor jack, but do not put any pressure on the springs.
3. Remove the cap/rubber guard from inside the trunk/hatch area of the car.
4. Remove the nut, washer and mounting disc.
5. Unbolt the strut assembly from the rear axle and remove it.

To install:

6. Position the strut assembly on the car. On Fox models, use a new top mount bolt. Tighten the top mount bolt to 14 ft. lbs. (20 Nm) on Fox, 11 ft. lbs. (15 Nm) on 1985–89 Golf and Jetta and 23 ft. lbs. (29 Nm) on other models. Tighten the bottom bolt to 43 ft. lbs. (59 Nm) on Fox, 52 ft. lbs. (70 Nm) on 1985–89 Golf and Jetta and 32 ft. lbs. (43 Nm) on other models.
7. Install the cap/rubber guard.
8. Lower the vehicle.
9. Connect the battery cable.

Quantum

1. Disconnect the negative battery cable.
2. Raise the car and support it on jackstands. Support the axle with a floor jack, but do not put any pressure on the springs.
3. Remove strut cover from inside the car.
4. Using tool 3017A, remove the self-locking nut securing the strut to the body.

5. Unbolt the strut from the axle, then remove it from the vehicle.

To install:

6. Position the strut assembly on the car. Use a new self-locking nut. Tighten it to 26 ft. lbs. (35 Nm). Tighten the bottom bolt to 52 ft. lbs. (70 Nm).
7. Install the strut cover from inside the car.
8. Lower the vehicle.
9. Connect the battery cable.

OVERHAUL

▶ **See Figures 25 and 26**

A spring compressor is necessary for this operation.

1. Clamp the strut in a vise. Do not overtighten, as this could damage the strut.
2. Attach the spring compressor, then carefully use it to compress the spring.
3. Remove the slotted nut at the top of the strut, then remove the protective collar and the spring.

To assemble:

4. If necessary, transfer the compressor to a new spring. Remember, the compressed spring is under considerable pressure. Relieve the tension slowly.
5. Install the spring and protective collar on the strut.
6. Tighten the slotted nut to 14 ft. lbs. (19 Nm), then carefully remove the spring compressor.

Stub Axle

REMOVAL & INSTALLATION

1. Disconnect the negative battery cable.
2. Raise and safely support the vehicle with jackstands, then remove the rear wheels.
3. With disc brakes, remove the caliper and hang it from the spring with wire. Do not let the caliper hang by the hydraulic line.
4. Remove the brake drum or rotor.
5. With drum brakes, disconnect the brake line and plug it. Unbolt, then remove the brake backing plate and stub axle complete with brake assembly.

To install:

6. Install the backing plate/brake assembly and stub axle. Make sure the axle mounting surface is clean, then torque the nuts/bolts to 44 ft. lbs. (60 Nm) on Dasher and Quantum or 52 ft. lbs. (70 Nm) on other models.
7. With drum brakes, install the brake drum.
8. Install the rotor and caliper on disc brakes.
9. Install the wheels, then lower the vehicle. If necessary, bleed the brake system.
10. Connect the battery cable.

Fig. 22 Remove the rubber cap from the trunk area

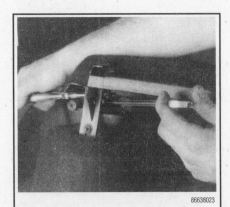

Fig. 23 Removing the nut and washer

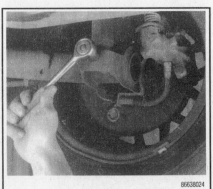

Fig. 24 Unbolt the strut assembly from the rear axle

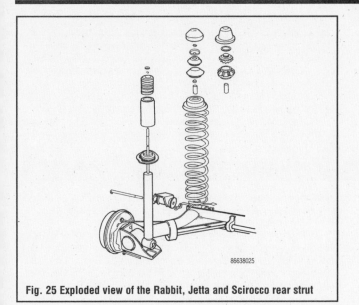

Fig. 25 Exploded view of the Rabbit, Jetta and Scirocco rear strut

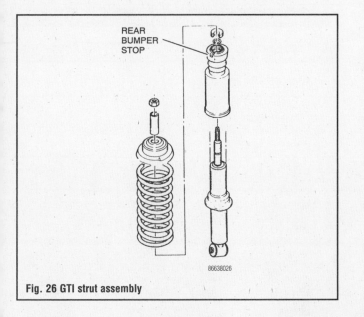

Fig. 26 GTI strut assembly

Axle Assembly

REMOVAL & INSTALLATION

1. Disconnect the negative battery cable.
2. Raise the vehicle and support with jackstands.
3. Remove the rear wheels. Remove the brake drums or the caliper and rotor depending on the vehicle.
4. Disconnect the brake hoses and parking brake cables. Plug the hydraulic hoses after disconnecting. Disconnect the ABS wheel sensors if so equipped.
5. Use a jack to support the axle.
6. Remove the strut-to-axle bolts and allow the axle to rest on the jack.
7. Remove the bolts at the axle bushing and lower the axle using the jack.

To install:

8. Install the axle, but do not tighten the bushing bolts yet. They should be torqued with the vehicle on the ground to properly align the bushings.
9. Connect the brake lines, cables and wires.
10. Install the brake drums or calipers.
11. Bleed the brake system, install the rear wheels and lower the vehicle.
12. With the vehicle on the ground, torque the right side axle bushing bolt first. Pry the left side bushing slightly towards the center of the vehicle, then tighten the left side. Torque the bolts to 52 ft. lbs. (70 Nm) on the Quantum and Dasher or to 44 ft. lbs. (60 Nm) on other models.
13. Connect the battery cable.

Rear Wheel Bearings

REPLACEMENT

▶ **See Figures 27, 28 and 29**

➡ **Do not use old bearings with new races or vise versa. Only use bearings in a matched set.**

1. Disconnect the negative battery cable.
2. Raise and safely support the vehicle, then remove the rear wheels.
3. On drum brakes, insert a small pry tool through a wheel bolt hole and push up on the adjusting wedge to slacken the rear brake adjustment.
4. On disc brakes, remove the caliper.
5. Remove the grease cap, cotter pin, locking ring, axle nut and thrust washer. Carefully remove the bearing and put all these parts where they will stay clean.
6. Remove the brake drum or rotor and pry out the inner seal to remove the inner bearing.
7. Clean all the grease off the bearings using solvent. If the bearings appear worn or damaged, they must be replaced.

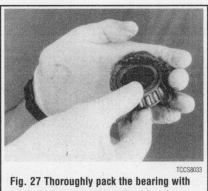

Fig. 27 Thoroughly pack the bearing with fresh, high temperature wheel bearing grease before installation

Fig. 28 Apply a thin coat of fresh grease to the new axle seal

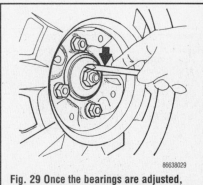

Fig. 29 Once the bearings are adjusted, the thrust washer must still move slightly without prying

8. To remove the bearing races, support the drum or rotor and carefully drive the race out with a long drift pin. They can also be removed on a press.

To install:

9. Carefully press the new race into the drum or rotor. The old race can be used as a press tool but make sure it does not become stuck in the hub.

10. Pack the inner bearing with clean wheel bearing grease and fit it into the inner race. Press a new axle seal into place by hand.

11. Lightly coat the stub axle with grease and install the drum or rotor. Be careful not to damage the axle seal.

12. Pack the outer bearing, then install the bearing, thrust washer and nut.

13. To adjust the bearing pre-load:

  a. Begin tightening the nut while turning the drum or rotor.

  b. When the nut is snug, try to move the thrust washer with a screwdriver.

  c. Back the nut off until the thrust washer can be moved without prying or twisting the screwdriver.

14. Without turning the nut, install the locking ring so a new cotter pin can be installed through the hole in the stub axle. Bend the cotter pin.

15. Pack some grease into the cap and install it.

16. Connect the battery cable.

STEERING

Steering Wheel

REMOVAL & INSTALLATION

▶ **See Figures 30, 31, 32, 33 and 34**

➡ **Beginning in August 1988, the steering wheels with modified inner splines were introduced into production on some models. The column remains unchanged except for the addition of a short splined adapter sleeve pressed onto the splines of the steering column. The short splined adapter was replaced by the longer sleeve starting in January 1989.**

1. Grasp the center cover pad and pull it from the wheel. (Cover varies depending on model).

2. Loosen and remove the steering shaft nut, then the washer.

3. Matchmark the steering wheel position in relation to the steering shaft so that when you install it, the wheel is perfectly level when the tires are straight ahead.

4. Pull the steering wheel off the shaft. You may need a puller to perform this operation. Under no circumstances should you bang on the shaft to try to free the wheel, or you may damage the collapsible steering column.

5. Disconnect the horn wire.

6. Replace the wheel in the reverse order of removal. On the Rabbit, Jetta and Scirocco, install the steering wheel with the tires straight ahead and the canceling lug pointing to the left. On the Fox, Dasher and Quantum with the tires straight ahead, the canceling lug on the steering wheel must point to the right and the turn signal lever must be in the neutral position. Tighten the steering shaft nut to 36 ft. lbs. (48 Nm).

Turn Signal (Combination) Switch

REMOVAL & INSTALLATION

1. Disconnect the battery ground cable.
2. Remove the steering wheel.
3. Remove the switch retaining screws.
4. Pry the switch housing off the column.
5. Disconnect the electrical plugs at the back of the switch.

Fig. 30 Remove the center cover pad

Fig. 31 Loosen and remove the shaft nut. . .

Fig. 32 . . . then remove the washer

Fig. 33 Matchmark the position of the wheel on the shaft

Fig. 34 Pull the steering wheel off the shaft

6. Remove the switch housing.

7. Install in the reverse order of removal.

➡**On the Rabbit, Jetta and Scirocco, tap the spacer sleeve into column (carefully) until there is 0.08–0.16 in. (2–4mm) clearance between the wheel and the hub.**

Ignition Switch

REMOVAL & INSTALLATION

The ignition switch is located at the bottom of the ignition key cylinder body. To remove the ignition switch, first remove the ignition lock cylinder. On all models except Dashers made before 1978, remove the switch by unfastening the screw at the bottom of the switch, then pull it out. On Dashers made before 1978, the screw is located on the side of the cylinder body. Installation is the reverse of removal.

Ignition Lock Cylinder

REMOVAL & INSTALLATION

▶ **See Figures 35 and 36**

1. Disconnect the negative battery cable.
2. Remove the steering wheel, then remove the steering column covers.
3. Remove the turn signal and wiper switches.
4. Disconnect the ignition switch wiring.
5. On some models, the hole in the lock body for removing the ignition lock cylinder was not drilled by Volkswagen. To make the hole, use the following measurements in conjunction with the illustrations. Drill the hole where "a" and "b" intersect on the lock body. The hole should be drilled 0.19 in. (3mm) deep.

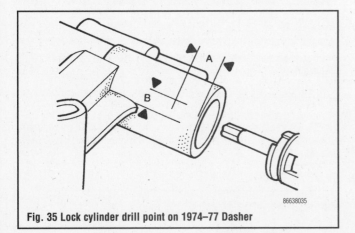

Fig. 35 Lock cylinder drill point on 1974–77 Dasher

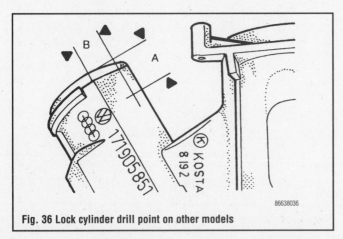

Fig. 36 Lock cylinder drill point on other models

- 1974–77 Dasher—a= 0.45 in. (11.5mm) b= 0.32 in. (8mm)
- 1975–76 Rabbit, Scirocco—a= 0.43 in. (11mm) b=0.43 in. (11 mm)
- 1977–89 Rabbit, Jetta, Scirocco and 1978 and later Dasher, Quantum and Fox—a= 0.47 in. (12mm) b= 0.39 in. (10mm)

6. Remove the lock cylinder by pushing a small drill bit or piece of wire into the hole and pulling the cylinder out. It might be easier to insert the ignition key, turn it to the right a little and pull on it.

To install:

7. Insert the lock cylinder into the housing with the key in the cylinder.
8. While gently turning the key side-to-side, press the cylinder in to the stop. It should click into place.
9. Temporarily fit the steering wheel onto the splines, then make sure the column locks and unlocks smoothly.
10. Install the switches, column covers, wiring and the steering wheel.
11. Connect the battery cable.

Steering Column

REMOVAL & INSTALLATION

▶ **See Figure 37**

1. Disconnect the negative battery cable.
2. Working from the inside of the vehicle, remove the steering wheel as previously described.
3. Remove the turn signal/headlight/wiper switches.
4. Remove the ignition switch and the ignition lock cylinder.
5. Carefully pry off the bearing support ring.
6. Remove the shear bolt cover, then drill out the shear bolt(s). Remove the steering shaft support bolts and lower the steering column.
7. Working from under the hood of the car, lower the dust boot and remove the bolt which secures the steering column to the universal joint shaft. On the Fox, the steering column is connected to a flange tube. Remove the retainer which holds the steering shaft to the flange tube.
8. Working from inside the vehicle, remove the steering column.

To install:

9. Position the steering column in the vehicle. On Fox models, hold the flange tube and the steering column together with pliers, then install the retainer.

➡**Do not push the steering column into the universal joint using excessive force.**

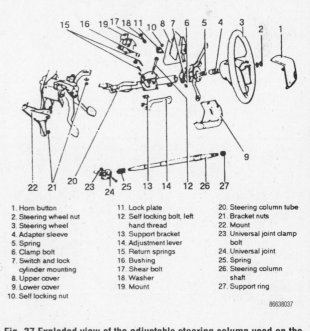

1. Horn button	11. Lock plate	20. Steering column tube
2. Steering wheel nut	12. Self locking bolt, left hand thread	21. Bracket nuts
3. Steering wheel	13. Support bracket	22. Mount
4. Adapter sleeve	14. Adjustment lever	23. Universal joint clamp bolt
5. Spring	15. Return springs	24. Universal joint
6. Clamp bolt	16. Bushing	25. Spring
7. Switch and lock cylinder mounting	17. Shear bolt	26. Steering column shaft
8. Upper cover	18. Washer	27. Support ring
9. Lower cover	19. Mount	
10. Self locking nut		

Fig. 37 Exploded view of the adjustable steering column used on the Golf and Jetta

10. Torque the universal shaft bolt to 22 ft. lbs. (30 Nm).
11. Torque the steering shaft support bolt to 14 ft. lbs. (20 Nm).
12. Install new shear bolts and tighten until the heads shear off.
13. Install the remaining components in the reverse of their removal.
14. Make sure that the tires are straight ahead when the steering wheel is installed.
15. Torque the steering wheel retaining bolt to 36 ft. lbs. (50 Nm).
16. Connect the battery cable.

Steering Linkage

REMOVAL & INSTALLATION

Tie Rod Ends

▶ See Figures 38 and 39

DASHER, FOX AND QUANTUM

1. Disconnect the negative battery cable.
2. Raise the front of the car, then support it with jackstands. Remove the front wheels.
3. Disconnect the outer end of the steering tie rod from the steering knuckle by removing the cotter pin and nut, then pressing out the tie rod end. A small puller or tie rod separator is required to free the tie rod.
4. Under the hood, pry off the lock plate and remove the mounting bolts from both tie rod inner ends. Pry the tie rod out of the mounting pivot and remove.

To install:

5. If you are replacing an adjustable tie rod, adjust the new tie rod to the same length.
6. Install the tie rod on the mounting pivot. Tighten the pivot bolts to 40 ft. lbs. (54 Nm). Install a new lock plate.

Fig. 38 Removing the nut on the tie rod end

Fig. 39 A puller is used to separate the tie rod end from the steering knuckle

7. Connect the tie rod to the steering knuckle. Tighten the tie rod-to-steering knuckle nut to 22 ft. lbs. (30 Nm). Install a new cotter pin.
8. Install the front wheels, then lower the vehicle. Have the alignment (toe) checked.
9. Connect the battery cable.

EXCEPT DASHER, FOX AND QUANTUM

➡**On some models, only the right side tie rod end is removable. The entire left tie rod must be replaced if the end joint is worn.**

1. Disconnect the negative battery cable.
2. Raise and safely support the vehicle on jackstands, then center the steering wheel.
3. Remove the wheels.
4. Remove the cotter pin and nut on the tie rod end. Use a ball joint separator/puller to disconnect the tie rod end from the steering knuckle.
5. Mark or measure the length of the right tie rod so it can be installed with the correct toe adjustment.
6. On the right side tie rod, hold the rod with a wrench and loosen the lock nut. Count and record the number of turns required to remove the tie rod end.
7. To remove the left tie rod, disconnect the rubber boot from the end of the steering rack and turn the steering wheel all the way to the right.
8. Loosen the lock nut and unscrew the tie rod from the steering rack.

To install:

9. Make sure each tie rod is the original length before installing. On the right side, thread the rod end into the tie rod the appropriate number of turns, then tighten the lock nut.
10. On the left side tie rod, thread the tie rod into the steering rack, then tighten the lock nut. Connect the rubber boot to the end of the steering rack.
11. Connect the tie rod end into the steering knuckle, then torque the nut to 26 ft. lbs. (35 Nm). Install a new cotter pin.
12. Install the wheels, then lower the vehicle.
13. Connect the battery cable.

Manual Steering Rack

ADJUSTMENTS

➡**On Dashers before chassis number 4 2 186 215, the rack is not adjustable.**

The adjusting screw is on the rack housing and adjusts pinion gear-to-rack clearance. Turning the screw clockwise tightens the clearance. Turn the adjusting screw no more than 20 degrees and test drive the vehicle after each adjustment. If the adjustment does not improve steering response or feel, return the screw to its original position and look for worn or damaged steering or suspension parts.

REMOVAL & INSTALLATION

▶ See Figures 40 and 41

Dasher, Fox and Quantum

1. Disconnect the negative battery cable.
2. Pry off the lock plate and remove both tie rod mounting bolts from the steering rack (inside the engine compartment). Carefully pry the tie rods out of the mounting pivot.
3. Remove the lower instrument panel trim.
4. Remove the shaft clamp bolt. Pry off the clip, then drive the shaft toward the inside of the car with a brass drift.
5. Remove the steering rack mounting bolts.
6. Turn the wheels all the way to the right and remove the steering rack through the opening in the right wheel housing.

To install:

7. Position the rack in the vehicle. Tighten the mounting bolts to 15 ft. lbs. (19 Nm).
8. Temporarily install the tie rod mounting pivot to the rack with both mounting bolts. Remove one bolt, install the tie rod, and reinstall the bolt. Do the same on the other tie rod. Tighten the pivot bolts to 40 ft. lbs. (54 Nm). Make sure to install a new lock plate.

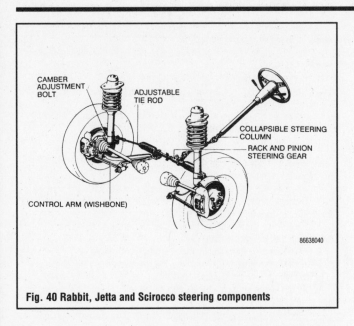

Fig. 40 Rabbit, Jetta and Scirocco steering components

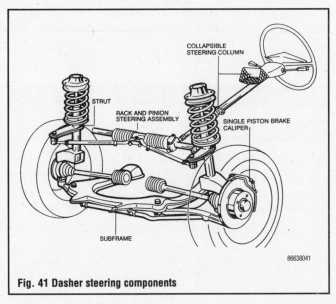

Fig. 41 Dasher steering components

9. Install the clip, then tighten the clamp bolt. Install the lower instrument panel trim.

10. Connect the battery cable.

Except Dasher, Fox and Quantum

1. Disconnect the negative battery cable.

2. Raise and safely support the vehicle on jackstands. Remove the ignition key to lock the steering wheel.

3. Remove the bolt from the steering shaft universal joint. Matchmark the universal joint to the pinion shaft.

4. Disconnect the tie rod ends from the steering knuckles.

5. Remove the mount nuts, then remove the steering rack as an assembly.

To install:

6. Fit the pinion shaft into the universal joint while fitting the steering rack into place on the body.

7. Torque the steering rack mount nuts and the universal joint bolt to 22 ft. lbs. (30 Nm).

8. After inserting the tie rod ends into the steering knuckle, torque the nut to 26 ft. lbs. (35 Nm). Install a new cotter pin.

9. Connect the battery cable.

Power Steering Rack

ADJUSTMENT

ZF Steering Rack

▶ See Figure 42

1. This job requires 2 people. With the vehicle on the ground and the wheels straight ahead, turn the steering wheel back and forth about 30 degrees with the engine not running.

2. If the steering feels loose or makes noise, have an assistant turn the adjusting bolt clockwise until the noise stops. The noise may not stop completely so do not continue tightening the adjustment.

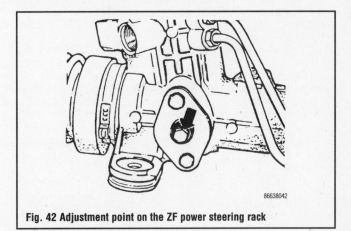

Fig. 42 Adjustment point on the ZF power steering rack

TRW Steering Rack

▶ See Figure 43

1. Remove the steering rack from the vehicle.

2. Loosen the lock nut and use the special pin wrench to turn the adjuster until the rack can be moved by hand without binding or excessive free play.

3. Install the steering rack.

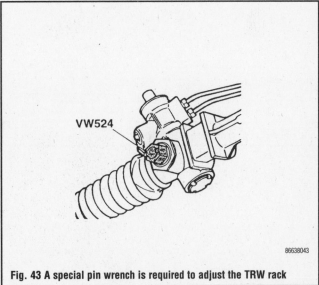

Fig. 43 A special pin wrench is required to adjust the TRW rack

REMOVAL & INSTALLATION

▶ See Figure 44

Dasher, Quantum and Fox

1. Disconnect the negative battery cable.
2. Pry off the lock plate and remove both tie rod mounting bolts from the steering rack (inside the engine compartment). Carefully pry the tie rods out of the mounting pivot.
3. Remove the lower instrument panel trim.
4. Remove the shaft clamp bolt. Pry off the clip, then drive the shaft toward the inside of the car with a brass drift.
5. Disconnect the power steering hoses. Place a pan under the steering rack to catch any fluid.
6. Remove the steering rack mounting bolts.
7. Turn the wheels all the way to the right and remove the steering rack through the opening in the right wheel housing.

To install:

8. Position the rack in the vehicle. Tighten the mounting bolts to 15 ft. lbs. (19 Nm).
9. Temporarily install the tie rod mounting pivot to the rack with both mounting bolts. Remove one bolt, install the tie rod, and reinstall the bolt. Do

the same on the other tie rod. Tighten the pivot bolts to 40 ft. lbs. (54 Nm). Make sure to install a new lock plate.

10. Install the clip, then tighten the clamp bolt. Install the lower instrument panel trim.
11. Connect the power steering lines, then refill the fluid reservoir.
12. Connect the battery cable and properly bleed the power steering system as described in this section.

Except Dasher, Fox and Quantum

1. Disconnect the negative battery cable.
2. Raise and safely support the vehicle on jackstands. Remove the ignition key to lock the steering wheel.
3. Place a catch pan under the power steering rack to catch the fluid.
4. Disconnect the suction hose and the pressure lines, then drain the fluid into the catch pan (properly discard the fluid).
5. Remove the bolt from the steering shaft universal joint. Matchmark the universal joint to the pinion shaft.
6. Disconnect the tie rod ends from the steering knuckles.
7. Remove the mount nuts to remove the steering rack as an assembly.

To install:

8. Fit the pinion shaft into the universal joint while fitting the steering rack into place on the body.
9. Torque the steering rack mount nuts and the universal joint bolt to 22 ft. lbs. (30 Nm).
10. After inserting the tie rod ends into the steering knuckle, torque the nut to 26 ft. lbs. (35 Nm) and tighten as required to install a new cotter pin.
11. Connect the power steering lines, then refill the fluid reservoir.
12. Connect the battery cable and properly bleed the power steering system as described in this section.

Power Steering Pump

REMOVAL & INSTALLATION

1. Disconnect the negative battery cable.
2. Place a catch pan under the power steering pump to catch the fluid.
3. Remove the suction hose and the pressure line from the pump, then drain the fluid into the catch pan (discard the fluid).
4. Loosen the tensioning bolt at the front of the tensioning bracket and remove the drive belt from the pump pulley.
5. Remove the pump mounting bolts and lift the pump from the vehicle.
6. To install, reverse the removal procedures. Torque the mounting bolts to 15 ft. lbs. (20 Nm) and adjust the drive belt. Fill the reservoir with approved power steering fluid and bleed the system.

BLEEDING

1. Fill the reservoir to the MAX level mark with approved power steering fluid.
2. With the engine idling, turn the wheels from the right to the left side as far as possible, several times.
3. Refill the reservoir to the MAX level and repeat the procedure until the level does not change.

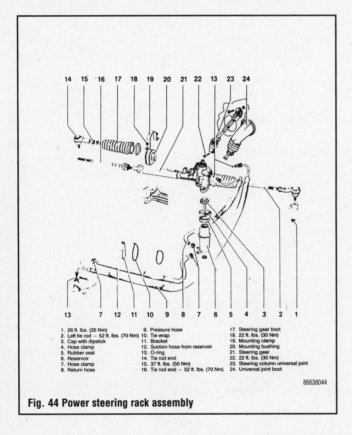

14 15 16 17 18 19 20 21 22 13 23 24

13 7 12 11 10 9 8 7 6 5 4 3 2 1

1. 26 ft. lbs. (35 Nm)
2. Left tie rod – 52 ft. lbs. (70 Nm)
3. Cap with dipstick
4. Hose clamp
5. Rubber seal
6. Reservoir
7. Hose clamp
8. Return hose
9. Pressure hose
10. Tie wrap
11. Bracket
12. Suction hose from reservoir
13. O-ring
14. Tie rod end
15. 37 ft. lbs. (50 Nm)
16. Tie rod end – 52 ft. lbs. (70 Nm)
17. Steering gear boot
18. 22 ft. lbs. (30 Nm)
19. Mounting clamp
20. Mounting bushing
21. Steering gear
22. 22 ft. lbs. (30 Nm)
23. Steering column universal joint
24. Universal joint boot

86638044

Fig. 44 Power steering rack assembly

TORQUE SPECIFICATIONS

Component	US	Metric
Front Strut		
Dasher, Fox and Quantum		
Ball joint-to-strut		
M8	25 ft. lbs.	34 Nm
M10	175 ft. lbs.	238 Nm
Caliper-to-strut	44 ft. lbs.	60 Nm
Stabilizer-to-control arm	7 ft lbs.	10 Nm
Other models		
Center nut	44 ft. lbs.	60 Nm
3 nuts	14 ft. lbs.	20 Nm
Strut-to-knuckle		
Except 1985- 89 Golf/Jetta	70 ft. lbs.	95 Nm
1985- 89 Golf/Jetta		
18mm	59 ft. lbs.	80 Nm
19mm	70 ft. lbs.	95 Nm
Lower Ball Joint		
Dasher, Fox and Quantum		
Control arm-to-ball joint	47 ft. lbs.	65 Nm
Strut-to ball joint		
M8	25 ft. lbs.	34 Nm
M10	36 ft. lbs.	48 Nm
Other models		
Retaining bolts	18 ft. lbs.	25 Nm
Hub retaining bolt	21 ft. lbs.	28 Nm
Sway Bar		
Quantum, Jetta and Golf	18 ft. lbs.	25 Nm
Other models	15 ft. lbs.	20 Nm
Lower Control Arm		
Dasher, Fox and Quantum		
Control arm-to-subframe	50 ft. lbs.	37 Nm
Ball joint-to-hub		
M8	25 ft. lbs.	34 Nm
M10	36 ft. lbs.	49 Nm
Other models		
Control arm-to-frame		
Front bolts	43 ft. lbs.	57 Nm
Rear bolts	32 ft. lbs.	44 Nm
Ball joint-to-hub	21 ft. lbs.	28 Nm
Leaf Springs		
Rear shackle bolts	45 ft. lbs.	61 Nm
Front bolt	68 ft. lbs.	90 Nm
U-bolt nuts	29 ft. lbs.	40 Nm
Shocks		
Dasher	43 ft. lbs.	58 Nm
Rabbit Pick-up	29 ft. lbs.	40 Nm
Rear Strut		
Top mount bolt		
Quantum	26 ft. lbs.	35 Nm
Fox	14 ft. lbs.	20 Nm
1985-89 Golf and Jetta	11 ft. lbs.	15 Nm
Others	23 ft. lbs.	29 Nm

86638303

TORQUE SPECIFICATIONS

Component	US	Metric
Bottom mount bolt		
Quantum	52 ft. lbs.	70 Nm
Fox	43 ft. lbs.	59 Nm
1985-89 Golf and Jetta	52 ft. lbs.	70 Nm
Others	23 ft. lbs.	43 Nm
Stub Axle		
Dasher and Quantum	44 ft. lbs.	60 Nm
Others	52 ft. lbs.	70 Nm
Axle Assembly		
Dasher and Quantum	52 ft. lbs.	70 Nm
Others	44 ft. lbs.	60 Nm
Steering Wheel		
Shaft nut	36 ft. lbs	48 Nm
Steering Column		
Universal shaft bolt	22 ft. lbs.	30 Nm
Steering shaft support bolt	14 ft. lbs.	20 Nm
Steering Linkage		
Tie rod ends		
Dasher, Fox and Quantum		
Pivot bolts	40 ft. lbs.	54 Nm
Tie rod-to-steering knuckle	22 ft. lbs.	30 Nm
Other models		
Tie rod end nut	26 ft. lbs.	35 Nm
Steering Gear		
Mounting bolts		
Dasher, Fox and Quantum	15 ft. lbs.	19 Nm
Other models	22 ft. lbs.	30 Nm
Power Steering Pump		
Mounting bolts	15 ft. lbs.	20 Nm

86638304

9

BRAKES

BRAKE OPERATING SYSTEM

General Description

The base model 1975–78 Rabbit is equipped with front and rear drum brakes. Some 1976–78 Rabbits, most 1979 and later Rabbits, and all Quantums, Dashers, Jettas, Foxes and Sciroccos are equipped with front disc brakes and rear drum brakes. Some models may also be equipped with front and rear disc brakes. Some late model Jettas are equipped with anti-lock brakes as an option.

The hydraulic system is a dual circuit type that has the advantage of retaining 50 percent of braking effectiveness in the event of failure in one system. The circuits are arranged so that you always have one front and one rear brake for a more controlled emergency stop (the right front and left rear are in one circuit; the left front and right rear are in the second circuit).

There is also a brake failure switch and a proportioning valve. The brake failure unit is a hydraulic valve/electrical switch which warns of brake problems by means of a warning light on the instrument panel. A piston inside the switch is kept centered by one brake system pressure on one side and the other system pressure on the opposite side. Should a failure occur in one system, the piston would go to the failed side and complete an electrical circuit to the warning lamp. This switch also functions as a parking brake reminder light and will go out when the parking brake is released. The proportioning valve (actually two separate valves on manual transaxle equipped Dasher sedans) provides balanced front-to-rear braking during hard stops. Extreme brake line pressure will overcome the spring pressure on the piston within the valve causing it to proportionately restrict pressure to the rear brakes. In this manner, the rear brakes are kept from locking. The proportioner doesn't operate under normal braking conditions.

The Anti-lock Brake System (ABS) available on some Jettas, is a three-channel system. It includes a hydraulic modulator, a pressure accumulator, speed sensors at each wheel and an electronic control unit. The control unit is equipped with a self-diagnostic program and is capable of storing fault codes. The code memory can only be accessed with the dealer's diagnostic equipment. The system operates at very high pressure and is capable of generating these pressures even when the engine is not running. Because of the need for special equipment and the dangerous pressures involved, owner service to this brake system is very limited.

Adjustments

DRUM BRAKES

▶ **See Figures 1 and 2**

Front

1. Raise and safely support the front of the car with jackstands. Block the rear wheels.

2. Remove the rubber plugs from the brake backing plate, which cover the adjusters.
3. Insert a small prytool through the hole and turn the adjuster clockwise until the wheel locks.
4. Back off the adjuster until the wheel can be turned. The shoes should drag lightly.
5. Back off the adjuster two notches. The wheel should spin without brake drag. Install the rubber plugs.

Rear

➡**On most models, it is necessary to push the brake pressure regulator lever toward the rear axle to relieve the pressure in the rear brake line.**

1. Raise the rear of the car and safely support it on jackstands.
2. Block the front wheels and release the parking brake. Step on the brake pedal hard to center the linings.
3. Remove the rubber plug from the rear of the backing plate on each wheel.
4. Insert a brake adjusting tool or a small prytool and turn the adjuster wheel clockwise until the brakes drag as you turn the wheel in the forward direction.
5. Turn the adjuster in the opposite direction until you just pass the point of drag.
6. Repeat on the other wheel.
7. Lower the car and road test. Readjust, if necessary.

Brake Light Switch

REMOVAL & INSTALLATION

Pedal Mounted Switch

▶ **See Figure 3**

The brake switch is mounted on the brake pedal support bracket. Disconnect and remove the switch by pulling the switch from the adjusting clip. To adjust, depress the brake pedal and push in the switch as far as it will go. Pull the pedal back by hand as far as it will go. The switch is adjusted after no clicks are heard.

Master Cylinder Mounted Switch

▶ **See Figure 4**

Disconnect the switch from the master cylinder, then remove using an appropriate sized wrench or socket. Lubricate the switch with brake fluid and torque to 18 ft. lbs. (25 Nm). Connect the wire and bleed the system as outlined in this section.

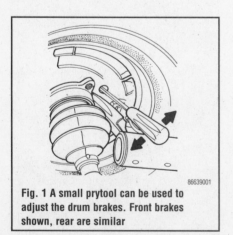

Fig. 1 A small prytool can be used to adjust the drum brakes. Front brakes shown, rear are similar

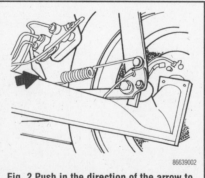

Fig. 2 Push in the direction of the arrow to relieve pressure at the brake pressure regulator valve—Dasher shown

Fig. 3 Pedal mounted brake light switch (black plunger). The threaded switch is for cruise control

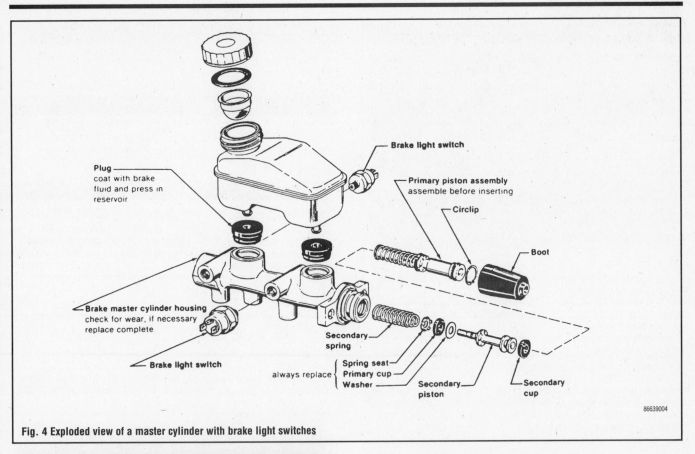

Fig. 4 Exploded view of a master cylinder with brake light switches

Plug —
coat with brake
fluid and press in
reservoir

Brake light switch

Primary piston assembly
assemble before inserting

Circlip

Boot

Brake master cylinder housing
check for wear, if necessary
replace complete

Secondary
spring

Brake light switch

always replace — Spring seat
Primary cup
Washer

Secondary
piston

Secondary
cup

86639004

Brake Pedal

REMOVAL & INSTALLATION

1. Disconnect the negative battery cable.
2. If applicable, disconnect the clutch cable at the transaxle end.
3. Remove the clip and remove the brake/clutch pedal pivot pin.
4. Installation is the reverse of removal. Lightly lubricate the pin with white grease.

Master Cylinder

REMOVAL & INSTALLATION

Standard (Non-ABS) Brakes

▶ **See Figures 5 and 6**

1. Disconnect the negative battery cable.
2. To prevent brake fluid from spilling out and damaging the paint, place a protective cover over the fender.
3. Disconnect and cap the brake lines to keep dirt out. Use flare nut or line wrenches.
4. Disconnect the wiring from the switches.
5. Remove the two master cylinder mounting nuts and pull the master cylinder away from the booster.

➡**Do not depress the brake pedal while the master cylinder is removed.**

To install:

6. Position the master cylinder and reservoir assembly onto the studs and install the washers and nuts. Torque the nuts to 10 ft. lbs. (14 Nm) on Dashers and 15 ft. lbs. (20 Nm) on other models.

7. Remove the plugs and connect the brake lines.
8. Bleed the brake system.
9. Connect the battery cable.

ABS Brakes

Volkswagen refers to the master cylinder on ABS systems as the hydraulic modulator. For removal and installation, follow the procedure outlined later in this section.

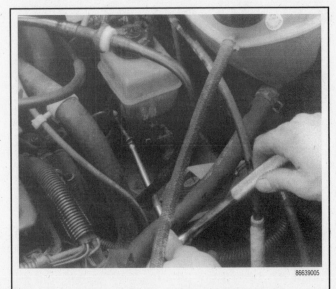

86639005

Fig. 5 An extension is helpful for reaching the mounting nuts

Fig. 6 Make sure the reservoir is capped to prevent dirt entry when removing the master cylinder

OVERHAUL

Volkswagen does not recommend rebuilding master cylinders; service parts are not available from the dealer network.

Power Brake Booster

REMOVAL & INSTALLATION

1. Disconnect the negative battery cable.
2. Remove the master cylinder from the booster.
3. At the pedals, remove the clevis pin on the end of the booster pushrod by unclipping it and pulling it from the clevis.
4. Disconnect the vacuum hose from the booster.
5. Unbolt the booster; remove the 2 nuts under the dashboard or the 4 nuts holding the booster to its bracket. Remove the booster.
6. Installation is the reverse of removal. Install the master cylinder and bleed the system.

Diesel Engine Vacuum Pump

REMOVAL & INSTALLATION

▶ See Figure 7

1. Disconnect the negative battery cable.
2. Disconnect both vacuum lines from the pump.

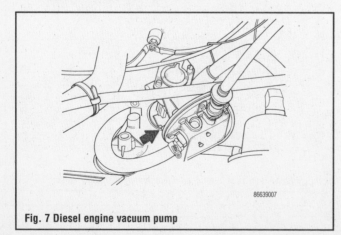

Fig. 7 Diesel engine vacuum pump

3. Remove the hold-down clamp and remove the pump.
4. The diaphragm and valves inside the pump can be replaced. A pump rebuild kit is available through the dealer.
5. Installation is the reverse of removal. Torque the hold-down bolt to 15 ft. lbs. (20 Nm).

Pressure Regulating Valve

REMOVAL & INSTALLATION

▶ See Figure 8

✳✳ CAUTION

The ABS hydraulic modulator is capable of self-pressurizing and can generate pressures above 3000 psi anytime the ignition switch is turned ON. Relieve the system pressure before testing or repairing the hydraulic system. Improper repair or test procedures can cause serious or fatal injury.

1. Disconnect the negative battery cable.
2. Raise and safely support the rear of the vehicle on jackstands.
3. If equipped with ABS, make sure the ignition switch stays **OFF** and pump the brake pedal 25–35 times to relieve the system pressure.
4. At the rear axle beam, disconnect the spring and relieve the pressure by pushing the lever towards the axle.
5. Using a line wrench, disconnect the lines from the valve.
6. Remove the retaining nuts and remove the valve from the frame.
7. Installation is the reverse of removal. Bleed the brake system.

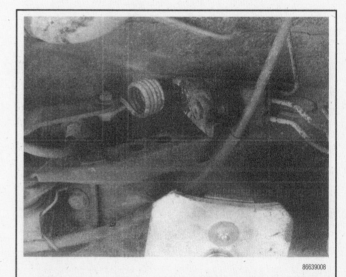

Fig. 8 The brake pressure regulating valve is located near the rear axle beam

Brake Lines

REMOVAL & INSTALLATION

Flexible Hoses

✳✳ CAUTION

The ABS hydraulic modulator is capable of self-pressurizing and can generate pressures above 3000 psi anytime the ignition switch is turned ON. Relieve the system pressure before testing or repairing the hydraulic system. Improper repair or test procedures can cause serious or fatal injury.

➥When removing any brake line or hose, always use a flare nut wrench to prevent damage to the soft metal fittings.

1. Disconnect the negative battery cable.
2. If equipped with ABS, make sure the ignition switch stays **OFF** and pump the brake pedal 25–35 times to relieve the system pressure.
3. Using a flare nut wrench, remove and plug the brake hose from the caliper.
4. Remove the brake hose from the holding bracket on the strut.
5. Using a flare nut wrench to hold the steel brake line, remove the brake hose with a suitable flare nut wrench.
6. Plug the steel brake line after removal.
7. Installation is the reverse of removal. Torque the fittings to 20 ft. lbs. (27 Nm).

Steel Lines

Loosen the steel brake line fittings using flare nut wrenches only. If the steel line starts to twist, stop and lubricate with penetrating oil. Move the wrench back and forth until the fitting turns freely. A backup wrench should be used when loosening steel-to-rubber brake hoses. Steel brake lines can be repaired by installing a double flare after the damaged portion has been removed. The tools needed for this procedure may be purchased at a local hardware or auto parts store. Steel brake lines MUST be double flared.

BRAKE PIPE FLARING

Flaring steel lines is a skill which needs to be practiced before it should be done on a line which is to be used on a vehicle. A special flaring kit with double flaring adapters is required. It is essential that the flare is formed evenly to prevent any leaks when the brake system is under pressure. Only steel lines, not copper lines, should be used. It is also mandatory that the flare be a double flare. With the supply of parts available today, a pre-flared steel brake line should be available to fit your needs. Due to the high pressures in the brake system and the serious injuries that could occur if the flare should fail, it is strongly advised that pre-flared lines should be installed when repairing the braking system. If a line were to leak brake fluid due to a defective flare, and the leak were to go undetected, brake failure would result.

✳✳ WARNING

A double flaring tool must be used, as single flaring tools cannot produce a flare strong enough to hold the necessary pressure.

1. Determine the length of pipe needed. Allow ⅛ in. (3.2 mm) for each flare. Cut using an appropriate tool.
2. Square the end of the tube with a file and chamfer the edges. Remove any burrs.
3. Install the required fittings on the pipe.
4. Install the flaring tool into a vice and install the handle into the operating cam.
5. Loosen the die clamp screw and rotate the locking plate to expose the die carrier.
6. Select the required die set and install in the carrier.
7. Insert the prepared line through the rear of the die and push forward until the line end is flush with the die face.
8. Make sure the rear of both halves of the die are resting against the hexagon die stops. Then rotate the locking plate to the fully closed position and clamp the die firmly by tightening the clamp screw.
9. Rotate the punch turret until the appropriate size points towards the open end of the line to be flared.
10. Pull the operating handle against the line resistance in order to create the flare, then return the handle to the original position.
11. Release the clamp screw and rotate the locking plate to the open position.
12. Remove the die set and the line then separate by gently tapping both halves on the bench. Inspect the flare for proper size and shape.

Brake System Bleeding

◆ See Figures 9 and 10

➥Use only new DOT 3 or 4 brake fluid in all Volkswagen vehicles. Do not use silicone (DOT 5) fluid. Even the smallest traces can cause severe corrosion to the hydraulic system. All brake fluids are corrosive to paint.

1. The procedure described here is for non-ABS brakes only. For ABS brakes, refer to the procedure outlined later in this section. Bleed the brakes with the engine off and booster vacuum discharged; pump the pedal with the bleeders closed about 20 times until the pedal effort gets stiff.
2. Fill the fluid reservoir.
3. On vehicles with a rear brake pressure regulator, press the lever towards the rear axle when bleeding the brakes.
4. Connect a clear plastic tube to the bleeder valve at the right rear wheel. Place the other end in a clean container.
5. Have an assistant pump the pedal to build pressure in the system, then hold pressure.
6. Open the bleeder slowly. When the pedal is all the way to the floor, close the bleeder before releasing the pedal.
7. Repeat this procedure until there are no air bubbles in the fluid stream. Be careful not to let the reservoir run out of brake fluid.
8. Repeat the procedure in sequence at the left rear, right front and left front: working farthest from the master cylinder to the nearest.

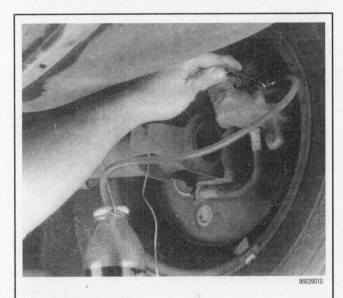

Fig. 9 Brake bleeding setup

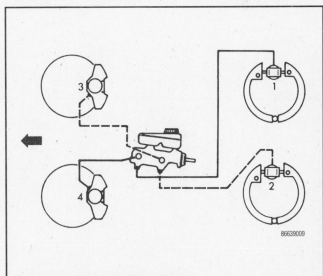

Fig. 10 Proper brake bleeding sequence

FRONT DRUM BRAKES

☀ CAUTION

Some brake pads may contain asbestos, which has been determined to be a cancer causing agent. Never clean the brake surfaces with compressed air! Avoid inhaling any dust from any brake surface! When cleaning brake surfaces, use a commercially available brake cleaning fluid.

Brake Drums

REMOVAL & INSTALLATION

1. Disconnect the negative battery cable.
2. Raise and safely support the front of the vehicle with jackstands. Remove the wheels.
3. Remove the rubber plug and back off the brake adjuster.
4. Remove the screw securing the drum to the hub. Pull off the drum.
5. Installation is the reverse of removal. Adjust the brakes.

INSPECTION

1. Check the drum for scoring or warping.
2. Check for signs of heat cracking or discoloring.
3. Check the maximum inside diameter after resurfacing. It must be no more than the figure listed in the Brake Specification Chart, at the end of this section.

Brake Shoes

INSPECTION

1. Check the shoes for contamination from brake fluid or axle grease.
2. Minimum allowed lining thickness is 0.098 in. (2.5mm).

REMOVAL & INSTALLATION

1. Disconnect the negative battery cable.
2. Raise the vehicle and safely support it with jackstands.
3. Remove the front wheel and brake drum assembly. The adjuster may have to be loosened to remove the brake drum.
4. Use a pliers to unlock the lower return springs.
5. Pull the lower part of the shoes over the wheel hub and unhook the upper return springs.
6. Remove the adjuster and locating spring.
To install:
7. Hook the upper return spring into the brake shoes.
8. Slide the adjuster into the shoes.
9. Push the lower ends of the brake shoes over the wheel hub.

10. Hook the lower return springs into the brake shoes and install the retaining springs.
11. Hook the upper return springs into the bracket on the backing plate.
12. Install the brake adjuster and locating spring.
13. Install the brake drum and adjust the shoes.
14. Install the front wheels and lower the vehicle.
15. Check the brake fluid and pump the pedal. Road test.

Wheel Cylinders

REMOVAL & INSTALLATION

1. Disconnect the negative battery cable.
2. Raise the front of the vehicle and safely support it with jackstands.
3. Remove the front wheels and brake drums.
4. Remove the brake shoes and move out of the way to access the wheel cylinders.
5. Using a flare nut wrench, disconnect the brake hose from the wheel cylinder. Plug the line.
6. Remove the two retaining bolts and wheel cylinder.
To install:
7. Install the cylinder and torque the bolts to 15 ft. lbs. (20 Nm).
8. Install the brake hose and torque to 15 ft. lbs. (20 Nm).
9. Install the brake shoes and drum. Bleed both wheel cylinders as outlined in this section.

OVERHAUL

♦ **See Figures 11 thru 20**

Wheel cylinder overhaul kits may be available, but often at little or no savings over a reconditioned wheel cylinder. It often makes sense with these components to substitute a new or reconditioned part instead of attempting an overhaul.

If no replacement is available, or you would prefer to overhaul your wheel cylinders, the following procedure may be used. When rebuilding and installing wheel cylinders, avoid getting any contaminants into the system. Always use clean, new, high quality brake fluid. If dirty or improper fluid has been used, it will be necessary to drain the entire system, flush the system with proper brake fluid, replace all rubber components, then refill and bleed the system.

1. Remove the wheel cylinder from the vehicle and place on a clean workbench.

2. First remove and discard the old rubber boots, then withdraw the pistons. Piston cylinders are equipped with seals and a spring assembly, all located behind the pistons in the cylinder bore.

3. Remove the remaining inner components, seals and spring assembly. Compressed air may be useful in removing these components. If no compressed air is available, be VERY careful not to score the wheel cylinder bore when removing parts from it. Discard all components for which replacements were supplied in the rebuild kit.

TCCA9P13

Fig. 11 Remove the outer boots from the wheel cylinder

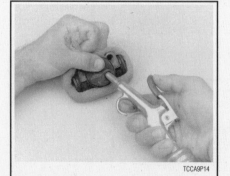

TCCA9P14

Fig. 12 Compressed air can be used to remove the pistons and seals

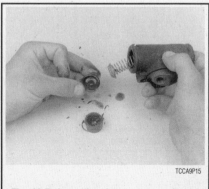

TCCA9P15

Fig. 13 Remove the pistons, cup seals and spring from the cylinder

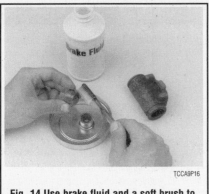

Fig. 14 Use brake fluid and a soft brush to clean the pistons . . .

Fig. 15 . . . and the bore of the wheel cylinder

Fig. 16 Once cleaned and inspected, the wheel cylinder is ready for assembly

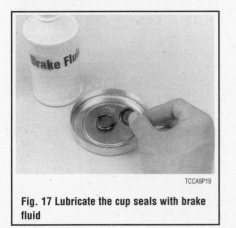

Fig. 17 Lubricate the cup seals with brake fluid

Fig. 18 Install the spring, then the cup seals in the bore

Fig. 19 Lightly lubricate the pistons, then install them

Fig. 20 The boots can now be installed over the wheel cylinder ends

4. Wash the cylinder and metal parts in denatured alcohol or clean brake fluid.

✳✳ WARNING

Never use a mineral-based solvent such as gasoline, kerosene or paint thinner for cleaning purposes. These solvents will swell rubber components and quickly deteriorate them.

5. Allow the parts to air dry or use compressed air. Do not use rags for cleaning, since lint will remain in the cylinder bore.

6. Inspect the piston and replace it if it shows scratches.
7. Lubricate the cylinder bore and seals using clean brake fluid.
8. Position the spring assembly.
9. Install the inner seals, then the pistons.
10. Insert the new boots into the counterbores by hand. Do not lubricate the boots.
11. Install the wheel cylinder.

Brake Backing Plate

REMOVAL & INSTALLATION

1. Disconnect the negative battery cable.
2. Raise the front of the vehicle and safely support it with jackstands.
3. Remove the front wheels and brake drums. Remove the brake shoe assembly.
4. Using a flare nut wrench, disconnect the brake hose from the wheel cylinder. Plug the line.
5. Remove the steering knuckle/hub assembly.
6. Remove the hub from the knuckle assembly.
7. Remove the bolts securing the backing plate to the knuckle.

To install:

8. Install the backing plate to the knuckle assembly. tighten the bolts to 43 ft. lbs. (59 Nm).
9. Install the hub to the knuckle assembly, then install the assembly on the vehicle.
10. Connect the brake hose and torque to 15 ft. lbs. (20 Nm).
11. Install the brake shoe assembly, then install the drum. Bleed the system as outlined in this section.
12. Connect the battery cable.

FRONT DISC BRAKES

❋❋ CAUTION

Some brake pads may contain asbestos, which has been determined to be a cancer causing agent. Never clean the brake surfaces with compressed air! Avoid inhaling any dust from any brake surface! When cleaning brake surfaces, use a commercially available brake cleaning fluid.

There are four types of disc brake calipers used on these Volkswagens. Refer to the illustrations to help identify the type used on your car.

➥**Some 1985 and later Golf and Jettas use a Mark II front brake caliper. The wheel bearing housing is designed to form an integral part of the brake assembly, thus making removal and replacement of the brake pads simpler. Removal and installation of the Mark II style caliper and the brake pads are similar to the procedure for the Kelsey-Hayes floating type caliper.**

Brake Pads

REMOVAL & INSTALLATION

❋❋ CAUTION

The ABS hydraulic modulator is capable of self-pressurizing and can generate pressures above 3000 psi anytime the ignition switch is turned ON. Relieve the system pressure before testing or repairing the hydraulic system. Improper repair or test procedures can cause serious or fatal injury.

Kelsey-Hayes Floating Caliper

◗ **See Figure 21**

This unit is a single piston, one piece caliper which floats on two guide pins screwed into the adapter (anchor plate). The adaptor, in turn, is held to the steering knuckle with two bolts. As the brake pads wear, the caliper floats along the adapter and guide pins during braking.

1. Disconnect the negative battery cable.
2. Raise the front of the vehicle and safely support it with jackstands. Remove the wheel.
3. Siphon some brake fluid from the master cylinder reservoir to prevent its overflowing when the piston is retracted into the cylinder bore.
4. Disconnect the brake pad warning indicator if so equipped.
5. Using a pair of needlenose pliers or the like, remove the anti-rattle springs.
6. Using an Allen wrench, back out the two guide pins that attach the caliper to the anchor plate.

➥When replacing pads only, it is not necessary to remove the guide pins completely from the rubber bushings, as they may be difficult to reinstall.

7. Lift off the caliper and position it out of the way with some wire. You need not remove the brake lines.

❋❋ WARNING

Never allow the caliper to hang by its brake lines.

8. Slide the outer pad out of the anchor plate and then remove the inner pad. Check the rotor as detailed in this section. Check the caliper for fluid leaks or cracked boots. If any damage is found, the caliper will require overhauling or replacement.
To install:
9. Carefully clean the anchor plate with a wire brush or some other abrasive material. Install the new brake pads into position on the anchor plate. The inner pad usually has chamfered edges.

➥When replacing brake pads, always replace both pads on both sides of the vehicle. Mixed pads may cause uneven braking.

10. Slowly and carefully push the piston into its bore until it is bottomed, then position the caliper onto the anchor plate. Install the guide pins and tighten them to 25–30 ft. lbs. (34–41 Nm).

➥The upper guide pin is usually longer than the lower one. Use extreme care so as not to cross-thread the guide pins when tightening!

11. Install the anti-rattle springs between the anchor plate and brake pads ears. The loops on the springs should be positioned inboard.
12. Fill the reservoir with brake fluid and pump the brake pedal several times to set the piston. It should not be necessary to bleed the system. However, if a firm pedal cannot be obtained, the system must be bled.
13. Install the wheel and lower the vehicle.
14. Connect the battery cable.

Girling Floating Caliper

◗ **See Figures 22, 23, 24 and 25**

Although similar in many respects to a sliding caliper, this single piston unit floats on guide pins and bushings which are threaded into a mounting bracket. The mounting bracket is bolted to the steering knuckle.

Variations in pad retainers, shims, anti-rattle and retaining springs will be encountered but the service procedures are all basically the same. Note the position of all springs, clips or shims when removing the pads. Work on one side at a time and use the other side for reference.

1. Disconnect the negative battery cable.
2. Raise and safely support the front of the vehicle on jackstands. Remove the wheel.
3. Siphon a sufficient quantity of brake fluid from the master cylinder

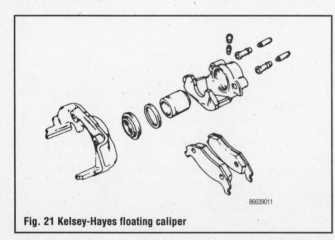

Fig. 21 Kelsey-Hayes floating caliper

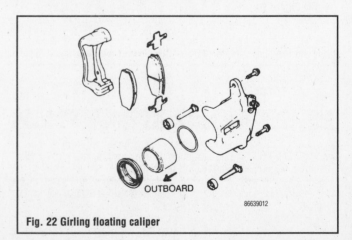

Fig. 22 Girling floating caliper

Fig. 23 Remove the caliper guide pins, then position the caliper aside and support it with wire

Fig. 24 Removing the inboard and outboard pads

Fig. 25 Be sure to install the anti-rattle hardware

reservoir to prevent the brake fluid from overflowing the master cylinder when removing or installing new pads. This is necessary as the piston must be forced into the cylinder bore to provide sufficient clearance to remove the pads.

4. Grasp the caliper from behind and pull it towards you. This will push the piston back into the cylinder bore.

5. Disconnect the brake pad lining wear indicator, if so equipped. Remove any anti-rattle springs or clips.

➡ **Depending on the model and year of the particular caliper, you may not have to remove it entirely to get at the brake pads. If the caliper is the swing type, remove the lower guide bolt, pivot the caliper on the upper bolt and swing it upward exposing the brake pads.**

6. Remove the caliper guide pins.

7. Remove the caliper from the rotor by slowly sliding it out and away from the rotor. Position the caliper out of the way and support it with wire so that it doesn't hang by the brake line.

8. Slide the outboard pad out of the adapter.

9. Remove the inboard pad. Remove any shims or shields behind the pads and note their positions.

To install:

10. Install the anti-rattle hardware, then the pads in their proper positions.

11. Install any pad shims or heat shields.

12. Reposition the caliper and install the guide pins.

➡ **If the caliper is the swing type, you need only pivot it back into position and install the lower guide pin.**

13. Refill the master cylinder with fresh brake fluid.

14. Install the tire and wheel assembly and then pump the brake pedal several times to bring the pads into adjustment. If a firm pedal cannot be obtained, the system must be bled. Road test the vehicle.

15. Connect the battery cable.

Sliding Yoke Caliper

▶ **See Figure 26**

This unit is a single piston, two piece caliper. It has a fixed mounting frame which is bolted to the steering knuckle. The pads are retained in the fixed frame. A floating frame, or yoke, slides on the fixed frame. The cylinder attaches to this yoke, creating a caliper. Braking pressure forces the piston against the inner pad. The reaction causes the yoke to move in the opposite direction, applying pressure to the outer pad.

1. Disconnect the negative battery cable.

2. Raise the front of the vehicle and safely support it with jackstands. Remove the wheel.

3. Siphon a sufficient quantity of brake fluid from the master cylinder reservoir to prevent the brake fluid from overflowing the master cylinder when removing or installing new pads. This is necessary as the position must be forced into the cylinder bore to provide sufficient clearance to remove the pads.

4. If equipped, disconnect the wire connector leading to the brake pad wear indicator.

5. Remove the brake pad retaining clips on the inside of the caliper and then drive out the retaining pins. Don't lose the pad positioner (spreader) that is held down by the pins.

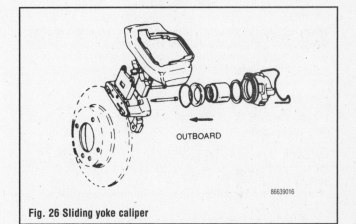

Fig. 26 Sliding yoke caliper

6. Pull out the inner brake pad.

7. The outer pads are secured by a notch at the top of the pad. Grasp the caliper assembly from the inside and pull it toward yourself. Remove the pad and detach the wear indicator.

8. Check the brake disc (rotor) as detailed in this section.

9. Inspect the caliper and piston assembly for breaks, cracks or other damage. Overhaul or replace the caliper as necessary.

To install:

10. Use a C-clamp and press the piston back into the cylinder bore.

11. Install the wear indicator on the outer pad, then install both pads.

12. Installation of the remaining components is the reverse order of removal.

13. Top off the master cylinder with fresh brake fluid.

14. Pump the brake pedal several times to bring the pads into adjustment. Road test the vehicle. If a firm pedal cannot be obtained, bleed the brakes as detailed in this section.

15. Connect the battery cable.

Girling Sliding Yoke Caliper

▶ **See Figure 27**

This unit is a double piston, one-piece caliper. The cylinder body contains two pistons, back-to-back, in a through-bore. The cylinder body is bolted to the steering knuckle, with both pistons inboard of the rotor. A yoke, which slides on the cylinder body, is installed over the rotor and the caliper.

When the brakes are applied, hydraulic pressure forces the pistons apart in the double ended bore. The piston closest to the rotor applies force directly to the inboard pad. The other piston applies force to the yoke, which transmits the force to the outer pad, creating a friction force on each side of the rotor.

One variation has a yoke that floats on guide pins screwed into the cylinder body.

1. Disconnect the negative battery cable.

2. Raise and safely support the front of the vehicle on jackstands. Remove the wheel.

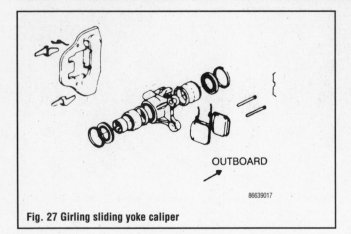

Fig. 27 Girling sliding yoke caliper

3. Siphon a sufficient quantity of brake fluid from the master cylinder reservoir to prevent the brake fluid from overflowing the master cylinder when removing or installing new pads. This is necessary as the piston must be forced into the cylinder bore to provide sufficient clearance to remove the pads.

4. Disconnect the brake pad lining wear indicator if so equipped.

5. Remove the dust cover and/or anti-rattle (damper) clip.

6. Lift off the wire clip(s) which hold the guide pins or retaining pin in place.

7. Remove the upper guide pin and the two hanger springs. Carefully tap out the lower guide pin.

➡ **The lower guide pin usually contains an anti-rattle coil spring. Be careful not to lose this spring. If a retaining pin is used, pull the pin out and remove the two hanger springs.**

8. Slide the yoke outward and remove the outer brake pad and the anti-noise shim (if so equipped).

9. Slide the yoke inward and repeat the previous step.

10. Check the rotor as detailed in the appropriate section.

11. Inspect the caliper and piston assembly for breaks, cracks or other damage. Overhaul or replace the caliper as necessary.

To install:

12. Push the piston next to the rotor back into the cylinder bore until the end of the piston is flush with the boot retaining ring. If the piston is pushed further than this, the seal will be damaged and the caliper assembly will have to be overhauled.

13. Retract the piston farthest from the rotor by pulling the yoke toward the outside of the vehicle.

14. Install the outboard pad. Anti-noise shims (if so equipped) must be located on the plate side of the pad with the triangular cutout pointing toward the top of the caliper.

15. Install the inboard pad with the shims (if so equipped) in the correct position.

16. Replace the lower guide pin and the anti-rattle coil spring.

17. Hook the hanger springs under the pin and over the brake pads.

18. Install the upper guide pin over the ends of the hanger springs.

➡ **If a single two-sided retaining pin is used, install the pin and then install the hanger springs.**

19. Insert the wire clip locks into the holes in the guide pins or retaining pin.

20. Refill the master cylinder with fresh brake fluid.

21. Install the tire and wheel assembly. Pump the brake pedal several times to bring the pads into adjustment. Road test the vehicle. If a firm pedal cannot be obtained, bleed the brakes as described in this section.

22. Connect the battery cable.

INSPECTION

1. The brake pad wear limit is 0.080 in. (2.0mm).

2. If the pads show signs of heat cracks or if they are worn unevenly, check the caliper for a sticking piston or guides.

3. Check the caliper for signs of fluid leakage or damage to the dust seal.

4. Check the rotor for signs of heat cracks or discoloration.

5. Check thickness of the rotor. Compare to the figure listed in the Brake Specification Chart, at the end of this section.

6. Check the run-out. Maximum allowed is 0.002 in. (0.06mm).

Brake Caliper

REMOVAL & INSTALLATION

▶ **See Figures 28, 29, 30 and 31**

✳✳ CAUTION

The ABS hydraulic modulator is capable of self-pressurizing and can generate pressures above 3,000 psi anytime the ignition switch is turned ON. Relieve the system pressure before testing or repairing the hydraulic system. Make sure the ignition switch stays OFF and pump the brake pedal 25–35 times to relieve the system pressure. Improper repair or test procedures can cause serious or fatal injury.

1. Disconnect the negative battery cable.

2. Raise and safely support the vehicle on jackstands, then remove the wheels.

3. Clean around the fittings to prevent entry of dirt into the lines.

4. On some models, use a pair of pliers to remove the lock spring from the fittings.

5. Disconnect the fittings, then cap the line to prevent fluid loss.

6. Loosen the guide pins, then remove the caliper from the carrier.

7. The carrier can be removed by removing the bolts.

To install:

8. If removed, install the carrier. On standard brakes, torque the carrier bolts to 52 ft. lbs. (70 Nm). On ABS brakes, torque the carrier bolts to 92 ft. lbs. (125 Nm).

9. Fit the caliper into place on the carrier.

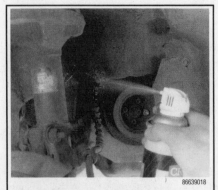

Fig. 28 Clean around the fittings to prevent entry of dirt into the lines

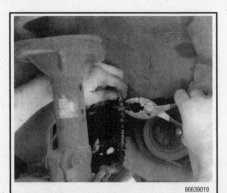

Fig. 29 A pair of pliers can be used to remove the lock spring

Fig. 30 Loosen the guide pins . . .

Fig. 31 . . . then remove the caliper from its carrier

Fig. 32 Removing the piston dust seal

Fig. 33 Use air pressure to remove the piston from the bore

Fig. 34 A small pick can be used to remove the seal from the bore

Fig. 35 Lubricate the piston and bore with brake fluid

Fig. 36 Remove the screw . . .

Fig. 37 . . . then slide the rotor off

10. On calipers with guide pins, torque the bolts to 25 ft. lbs. (35 Nm). On calipers with sleeves and bushings, torque the bolts to 18 ft. lbs. (25 Nm).

11. Tighten the hydraulic line and bleed the brakes. If applicable, install the lock spring.

12. Connect the battery cable.

OVERHAUL

▶ **See Figures 32, 33, 34 and 35**

1. Make sure the bleeder screw will loosen. If the screw breaks off, the caliper will have to replaced.

2. Remove the piston dust seal.

3. Place a wooden block in the caliper to prevent damage to the piston. Carefully force the piston out by blowing compressed air into the hydraulic line fitting. Use only as much pressure as required and keep tools or fingers out of the way.

4. Remove the piston seal from the bore. Be careful not to damage the finished bore surface.

5. Clean all components with denatured alcohol that leaves no residue and dry with compressed air.

6. If the guide sleeves and bushings do not move freely, remove the dust seals and remove the sleeves. On calipers with guide pins, the pins are part of the carrier and usually not available separately.

7. Remove any rust or corrosion from the piston and bore with very fine emery paper and clean again. Excessive corrosion will cause the caliper to leak. Replace caliper if the corrosion can not be removed with fine emery paper.

8. Install the piston seal into the groove and make sure it is not twisted.

9. Lubricate the piston and bore with new brake fluid. Anything else may cause damage to the rubber.

10. Install the piston and insert the inner lip of the dust seal into the groove in the brake caliper. The outer lip must slip into the groove in the piston. Make sure the dust seal is secure before installing the caliper.

Brake Disc (Rotor)

REMOVAL & INSTALLATION

▶ **See Figures 36 and 37**

1. Disconnect the negative battery cable.

2. Raise and safely support the vehicle, then remove the wheel.

3. Remove the brake caliper, pads and the pad carrier.

4. With the wheel removed, the rotor is held in place only with a countersunk screw threaded into the hub. Remove the screw and slide the rotor off.

To install:

5. Install the rotor screw, clean the screw threads with a wire brush and install the screw. Torque the screw to 15 ft. lbs. (20 Nm).

6. Reinstall the caliper and pump the brake pedal several times to bring the pads into adjustment. Road test the vehicle.

INSPECTION

Brake rotors may be checked for lateral run-out while installed on the car. This check will require a dial indicator gauge and stand to mount it on the caliper. VW has a special tool for this purpose which mounts the dial indicator to the caliper, but it can also be mounted on the shaft of a C-clamp attached to the outside of the caliper.

REAR DRUM BRAKES

✳✳ CAUTION

Some brake shoes may contain asbestos, which has been determined to be a cancer causing agent. Never clean the brake surfaces with compressed air! Avoid inhaling any dust from any brake surface! When cleaning brake surfaces, use a commercially available brake cleaning fluid.

Brake Drums

REMOVAL & INSTALLATION

1. Disconnect the negative battery cable.
2. Raise and safely support the vehicle, then remove the rear wheels.
3. Insert a small prytool through a wheel bolt hole and push up on the adjusting wedge to slacken the rear brake adjustment.
4. Remove the grease cap, cotter pin, locking ring, axle nut and thrust washer. Carefully remove the bearing and put all these parts where they will stay clean.
5. Carefully remove the drum.
To install:
6. Before installing, if any brake dust has fallen onto the axle, wipe off all the grease and apply a coat of new high temperature bearing grease. Install the parts in the reverse order of removal.

➡**When tightening the axle nut, the thrust washer must still be movable with a small screwdriver. Spin the drum and check that the thrust washer can still be moved.**

7. When installing the locking ring, keep trying different positions of the ring on the nut until the cotter pin goes into the hole. Don't turn the nut to align the locking ring with the hole in the axle. Use a new cotter pin.
8. Connect the battery cable.

INSPECTION

1. Check the drum for scoring or warping.
2. Check for signs of heat cracking or discoloring.
3. The maximum inside diameter after resurfacing must be no more than the figure listed in the Brake Specifications Chart, at the end of this section.

Brake Shoes

INSPECTION

1. Check the shoes for contamination from brake fluid or axle grease.
2. Minimum allowed lining thickness is 0.098 in. (2.5mm). This can be checked through the inspection plug on the backing plate without removing the drum.

REMOVAL & INSTALLATION

♦ **See Figures 38, 39 and 40**

1. Disconnect the negative battery cable.
2. Raise and safely support the vehicle, then remove the rear wheels.

1. Remove the wheel, then reinstall and tighten the wheel bolts to 65 ft. lbs. (88 Nm), in order to retain the rotor to the hub.
2. Mount the dial indicator securely to the caliper. The gauge stem should touch the rotor about 1/2 inch (13mm) from the outer edge.
3. Rotate the rotor and observe the gauge. Radial run-out (wobble) must not exceed 0.002 in. (0.06mm). A rotor which exceeds this specification must be replaced or refinished.
4. Brake rotors which have excessive radial run-out, sharp ridges, or scoring can be refinished. First grinding must be done on both sides of the rotor to prevent squeaking and vibrating. Rotors which have only light grooves and are otherwise acceptable can be used without refinishing.

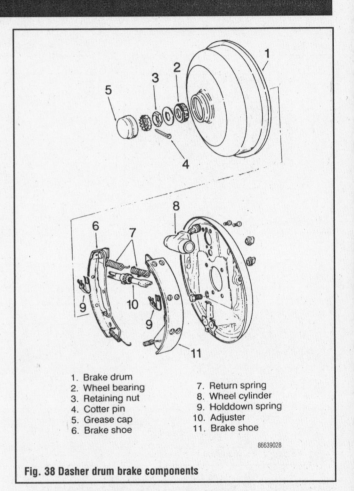

1. Brake drum
2. Wheel bearing
3. Retaining nut
4. Cotter pin
5. Grease cap
6. Brake shoe
7. Return spring
8. Wheel cylinder
9. Holddown spring
10. Adjuster
11. Brake shoe

86639028

Fig. 38 Dasher drum brake components

3. Remove the rear brake drum.
4. Remove the spring retainers by holding the pin behind the backing plate, while pushing on and turning the retainer ¼ turn.
5. Remove the shoes from the backing plate by first pulling one shoe, and then the other, against the upper spring, and detaching them from the wheel cylinder slot. Detach the parking brake cable from the brake lever. The entire shoe assembly should now be free of the vehicle.
6. Carefully note the position of each spring, as spring shapes and positions have varied from vehicle to vehicle and year to year.
7. Clamp the pushrod that holds the shoes apart at the top in a vise and begin removing the springs. Start with the lower return spring, adjusting wedge spring, upper return spring and then the tensioning spring and adjusting wedge.
8. On most vehicles, the parking brake lever must be removed from the old shoes and reused. When new parts are purchased, don't forget the clip that holds the parking brake lever pin in place.
To install:
9. Check the wheel cylinder for leaks. If any defects are found, replace the wheel cylinder.

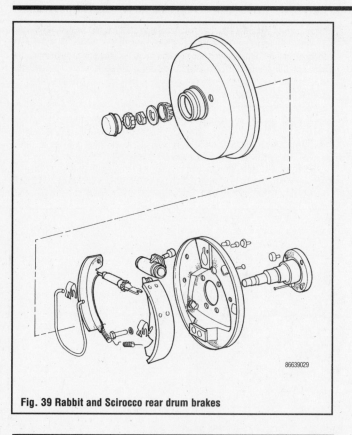

Fig. 39 Rabbit and Scirocco rear drum brakes

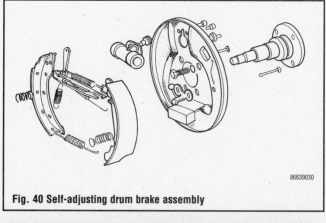

Fig. 40 Self-adjusting drum brake assembly

✳✳ WARNING

DO NOT step on the brake pedal while the drums are removed!

10. Inspect the springs. If the springs are damaged or show signs of overheating they should be replaced. Indications of overheated springs are discoloration and distortion.

11. Inspect the brake drum and recondition or replace as necessary.

12. Clean the backing plate and lubricate the shoe contact points with a suitable brake lubricant.

13. With the push rod clamped in a vise, attach the front brake shoe and tensioning spring.

14. Insert the adjusting wedge between the front shoe and pushrod so its lug is pointing toward the backing plate.

15. Remove the parking brake lever from the old shoe and attach it onto the new rear brake shoe.

16. Put the rear brake shoe and parking brake lever assembly onto the pushrod and hook up the spring.

17. Connect the parking brake cable to the lever and place the whole assembly onto the backing plate.

18. Install the hold-down springs.

19. Install the upper and lower return springs.

20. Install the adjusting wedge spring.

21. Center the brake shoes on the backing plate, making sure the adjusting wedge is fully released (all the way up) before installing the drum.

22. Install the drum and wheel assembly.

23. Apply the brake pedal a few times to bring the brake shoe into adjustment.

24. If the wheel cylinder was replaced, bleed the system.

25. Connect the battery cable.

26. Road test the vehicle.

Wheel Cylinders

REMOVAL & INSTALLATION

▶ **See Figure 41**

1. Disconnect the negative battery cable.

2. Raise and safely support the vehicle, then remove the wheel, brake drum and brake shoes.

3. Loosen the brake line on the rear of the cylinder but do not pull the line away from the cylinder or it may bend.

4. Remove the bolts and lockwashers that attach the wheel cylinder to the backing plate and remove the cylinder.

To install:

5. Position the new wheel cylinder on the backing plate and install the cylinder attaching bolts and lockwashers. Torque to 7.5 ft. lbs. (10 Nm).

6. Attach the brake line.

7. Install the brakes and bleed the system.

8. Connect the battery cable.

9. Road test the vehicle.

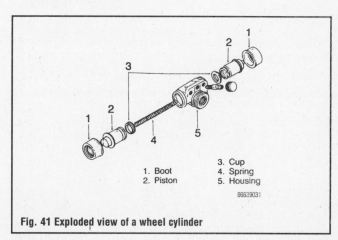

1. Boot	3. Cup
2. Piston	4. Spring
	5. Housing

Fig. 41 Exploded view of a wheel cylinder

OVERHAUL

Please refer to the front drum brake procedures in this section.

Brake Backing Plate

REMOVAL & INSTALLATION

The same bolts hold the brake backing plate and stub axle to the rear axle beam. The brake backing plate can be removed with the brakes and wheel cylinder still attached. Disconnect the hydraulic line from the wheel cylinder and remove the 4 bolts to remove the backing plate and stub axle. When installing, torque the bolts to 44 ft. lbs. (60 Nm).

REAR DISC BRAKES

♦ See Figure 42

※※ CAUTION

Some brake pads may contain asbestos, which has been determined to be a cancer causing agent. Never clean the brake surfaces
with compressed air! Avoid inhaling any dust from any brake surface! When cleaning brake surfaces, use a commercially available
brake cleaning fluid.

Brake Pads

REMOVAL & INSTALLATION

♦ See Figures 43, 44 and 45

1. Disconnect the negative battery cable.
2. Raise and safely support the vehicle, then remove the rear wheels.
3. Remove a sufficient quantity of brake fluid from the master cylinder

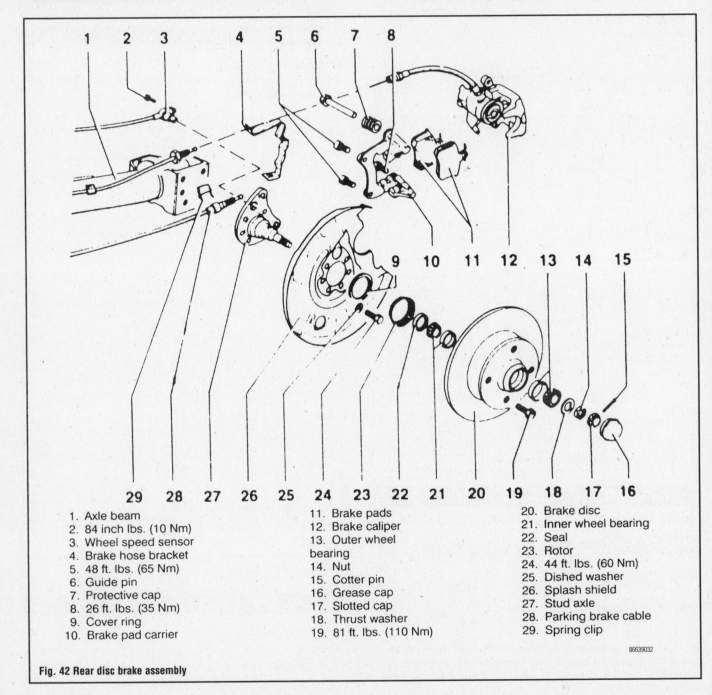

1. Axle beam
2. 84 inch lbs. (10 Nm)
3. Wheel speed sensor
4. Brake hose bracket
5. 48 ft. lbs. (65 Nm)
6. Guide pin
7. Protective cap
8. 26 ft. lbs. (35 Nm)
9. Cover ring
10. Brake pad carrier
11. Brake pads
12. Brake caliper
13. Outer wheel bearing
14. Nut
15. Cotter pin
16. Grease cap
17. Slotted cap
18. Thrust washer
19. 81 ft. lbs. (110 Nm)
20. Brake disc
21. Inner wheel bearing
22. Seal
23. Rotor
24. 44 ft. lbs. (60 Nm)
25. Dished washer
26. Splash shield
27. Stud axle
28. Parking brake cable
29. Spring clip

86639032

Fig. 42 Rear disc brake assembly

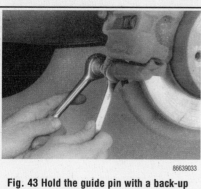

Fig. 43 Hold the guide pin with a back-up wrench and remove the mounting bolts from the caliper

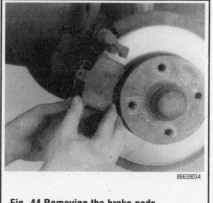

Fig. 44 Removing the brake pads

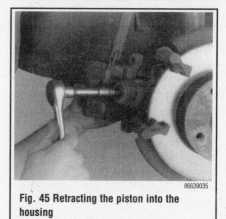

Fig. 45 Retracting the piston into the housing

reservoir to prevent it from over flowing when installing the pads. This is necessary as the caliper piston must be forced into the cylinder bore to provide sufficient clearance to install new pads.

4. Remove the parking brake cable clip from the caliper. Disconnect the parking brake cable.

5. Hold the guide pin with a back-up wrench and remove the mounting bolts from the brake caliper.

6. Remove the caliper and secure it to the side. Remove the brake pads.

7. Check the rotor for scoring and resurface or replace as necessary. Check the caliper for fluid leaks or a damaged dust seal. If any damage is found, the caliper will require overhauling or replacement.

To install:

8. Retract the piston into the housing by rotating the piston clockwise.

9. Carefully clean the anchor plate and install the new brake pads onto the pad carrier.

10. Install the caliper to the pad carrier using new self-locking bolts or a thread locking compound. Torque to 26 ft. lbs. (35 Nm).

11. Attach the hand brake cable to the caliper. It may be necessary to back off the adjustment nuts at the hand brake handle.

12. Fill the reservoir with brake fluid and pump the brake pedal about 40 times with the engine not running to set the piston. Setting the piston with the power assist could cause the piston to jam.

13. Check the parking brake operation, adjust the cable if necessary.

14. Connect the battery cable.

15. Road test the vehicle.

INSPECTION

1. The brake pad wear limit is 0.080 in. (2.0mm).

2. If the pads show signs of heat cracks or if they are worn unevenly, check the caliper for a sticking piston or guides.

3. Check the caliper for signs of fluid leakage or damage to the dust seal.

4. Check the rotor for signs of heat cracks or discoloration.

5. Minimum allowed thickness of solid brake rotors is 0.393 in. (10mm). Maximum allowed run-out is 0.002 in. (0.06mm).

Brake Caliper

REMOVAL & INSTALLATION

❋❋ CAUTION

The ABS hydraulic modulator is capable of self-pressurizing and can generate pressures above 3000 psi anytime the ignition switch is turned ON. Relieve the system pressure before testing or repairing the hydraulic system. Improper repair or test procedures can cause serious or fatal injury.

1. Disconnect the negative battery cable.

2. If equipped with ABS, make sure the ignition switch stays **OFF**, and pump the brake pedal 25–35 times to relieve the system pressure.

3. Raise and safely support the vehicle on jackstands. Remove the wheels.

4. Disconnect the parking brake cable.

5. Loosen the hydraulic line using a flare nut or line wrench.

6. Use a back-up wrench to hold the guide pins and remove the caliper bolts.

7. Lift the caliper off the carrier and unscrew it from the hydraulic line.

8. Installation is the reverse of removal. Use new caliper mount bolts or clean the old bolts and apply a thread locking compound. Torque the bolts to 26 ft. lbs. (35 Nm).

9. Bleed the brakes.

OVERHAUL

▶ **See Figure 46**

1. Place the caliper in a vise or holding fixture.

2. Make sure the bleeder screw will loosen. If the screw breaks off, the caliper will have to replaced.

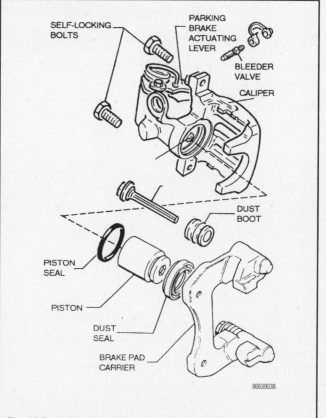

Fig. 46 Exploded view of the rear caliper assembly

3. Remove the piston dust seal.

4. Unscrew the piston from the caliper. Do not attempt to blow the piston out with compressed air.

5. Remove the piston seal from the bore. Be careful not to damage the finished bore surface.

6. Clean all components with denatured alcohol that leaves no residue and dry with compressed air.

➡**On calipers with guide pins, the pins are part of the carrier and are usually not available separately.**

7. Remove any rust or corrosion from the piston and bore with very fine emery paper and clean again. Excessive corrosion will cause the caliper to leak. Replace caliper if the corrosion can not be removed with fine emery paper.

➡**If the caliper is leaking at the parking brake lever, the caliper must be replaced.**

8. Install the piston seal into the groove and make sure it is not twisted.

9. Lubricate the piston and bore with new brake fluid. Any thing else may cause damage to the rubber.

10. Install the piston by screwing it onto the parking brake pushrod.

11. Insert the inner lip of the dust seal into the groove in the brake caliper. The outer lip must slip into the groove in the piston. Make sure the dust seal is secure before installing the caliper.

Brake Disc (Rotor)

REMOVAL & INSTALLATION

1. Disconnect the negative battery cable.
2. Raise and safely support the vehicle, then remove the rear wheels.
3. Remove the rear brake caliper and hang it from the rear spring with wire. Do not let the caliper hang by the hydraulic line.
4. Remove the grease cap, cotter pin, locking ring, axle nut and thrust washer. Carefully remove the bearing and put all these parts where they will stay clean.

PARKING BRAKE

Cables

REMOVAL & INSTALLATION

Rear Drum Brakes

1. Disconnect the negative battery cable.
2. Block the front wheels and release the hand brake.
3. Raise and safely support the rear of the vehicle.
4. Remove the rear brake shoes.
5. Remove the brake cable assembly from the backing plates.
6. Remove the cable adjusting nuts at the handle and detach the cable guides from the floor pan.
7. Pull the cables out from under the vehicle.
8. Installation is the reverse of removal. Adjust the parking brake and road test the vehicle.

Disc Brakes

1. Disconnect the negative battery cable.
2. Raise and safely support the vehicle.
3. Release the parking brake. It may be necessary to unscrew the adjusting nuts to provide slack in the brake cable.
4. At each rear wheel brake caliper, remove the spring clip retaining the parking brake cable to the caliper.
5. Lift the cable from the caliper mount and disengage it from the parking brake lever.
6. Pull the cables out from under the vehicle.
7. Installation is the reverse of removal. Adjust the parking brake.

5. Slip the rotor/hub off the axle.

To install:

6. Before installing, if any brake dust has fallen onto the axle, wipe off all the grease and apply a coat of new high temperature bearing grease. Install the parts in the reverse order of removal.

➡**When tightening the axle nut, the thrust washer must still be movable with a small screwdriver. Spin the rotor and check that the thrust washer can still be moved.**

7. When installing the locking ring, keep trying different positions of the ring on the nut until the cotter pin goes into the hole. Don't turn the nut to align the locking ring with the hole in the axle. Use a new cotter pin.

8. Connect the battery cable.

INSPECTION

Brake rotors may be checked for lateral run-out while installed on the car. This check will require a dial indicator gauge and stand to mount it on the caliper. VW has a special tool for this purpose which mounts the dial indicator to the caliper, but it can also be mounted on the shaft of a C-clamp attached to the outside of the caliper.

1. Remove the wheel and reinstall the wheel bolts (tightened to 65 ft. lbs.) to retain the rotor to the hub.

2. Mount the dial indicator securely to the caliper. The gauge stem should touch the rotor about 1/2 in. (13mm) from the outer edge.

3. Rotate the rotor and observe the gauge. Radial run-out (wobble) must not exceed 0.002 in. (0.06mm). A rotor which exceeds this specification must be replaced or refinished.

4. Brake rotors which have excessive radial run-out, sharp ridges, or scoring can be refinished. Initial grinding must be done on both sides of the rotor to prevent squeaking and vibrating. Rotors which have only light grooves and are otherwise acceptable can be used without refinishing. The standard solid rotor is 0.472 in. (12mm) thick. It should not be ground to less than 0.413 in. (10.5mm).

ADJUSTMENT

Rear Drum Brakes

◆ **See Figure 47**

1. Raise and safely support the rear of the vehicle on jackstands, so the rear wheels are free to turn.

2. With the parking brake handle down and the brake fully released, firmly apply the brake pedal once.

3. Pull the parking brake lever up 2–3 clicks. If the rear wheels cannot be turned by hand, no adjustment is required.

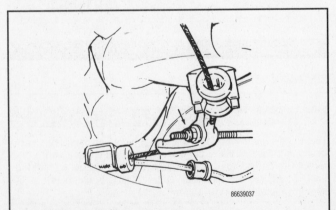

86639037

Fig. 47 Dasher parking brake adjusting nut (arrow)

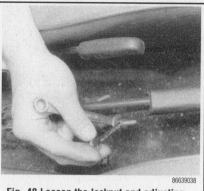

Fig. 48 Loosen the locknut and adjusting nut to relieve tension on the cables

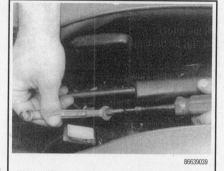

Fig. 49 Tighten the cable adjusting nut evenly until the actuating levers on the calipers just move off their stops

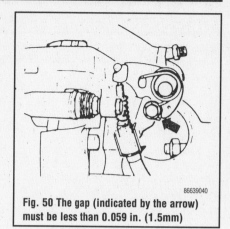

Fig. 50 The gap (indicated by the arrow) must be less than 0.059 in. (1.5mm)

4. If adjustment is required, lower the lever and pull it up again only 2 clicks.

5. Remove the brake handle cover and loosen the locknuts.

6. Turn the adjusting nuts as required until the rear wheels cannot be turned in either direction by hand. If the wheels never lock up, there is a problem with the cables or the brakes and the drums should be removed for inspection.

7. Release the handle and make sure the wheels turn freely. If they do, tighten the locknuts.

8. If the wheels do not turn freely, back off the adjusting nuts as required. If brake handle travel is more than 3–4 clicks, there is a problem with the cables or the brakes, and the drums should be removed for inspection.

Rear Disc Brakes

▶ **See Figures 48, 49 and 50**

➡**Parking brake adjustment is only necessary after replacing brake pads or other brake components. If the parking brake does not hold the vehicle, the rear calipers and brake pads must be removed for inspection.**

1. Raise and safely support the rear of the vehicle on jackstands, then remove the rear wheels.

2. With the parking brake handle down and the brake fully released, firmly apply the brake pedal once.

3. Pull the parking brake lever up 2–3 clicks. If the rear wheels cannot be turned by hand, no adjustment is required.

4. If adjustment is required, loosen the locknut and the adjusting nut to just relieve the tension on the cables.

5. Hold the release button on the handle and move the handle up and down 3 or more times to seat the cables and make sure they move freely, then leave the handle down.

6. Tighten the cable adjusting nut evenly until the actuating levers on the calipers just move off their stops. The gap must be less than 0.059 in. (1.5mm).

7. To check for correct adjustment:
   a. At the first click, the rotors should turn by hand with some drag.
   b. At the second click, the rotors should be difficult to turn.
   c. At the third click, it should not be possible to turn the rotors by hand.
   d. When the brake handle is released, the rotors should turn freely.

Brake Lever

REMOVAL & INSTALLATION

▶ **See Figures 51 and 52**

1. Make sure the vehicle will not roll, then remove the adjusting nuts from the brake cables under the parking brake handle.

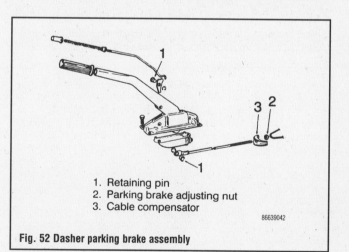

Fig. 51 Rabbit, Jetta and Scirocco parking brake handle assembly

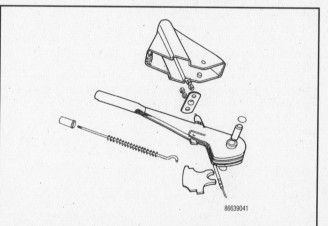

1. Retaining pin
2. Parking brake adjusting nut
3. Cable compensator

Fig. 52 Dasher parking brake assembly

2. Remove the spring clip from the guide pin and remove the pin. The lever will lift out when the button is pushed.

3. Installation is the reverse of removal. Push the button to fit the lever over the ratchet and insert the guide pin.

4. Adjust the parking brake as described at the beginning of this section.

ANTI-LOCK BRAKE SYSTEM

Description and Operation

Anti-lock Brake Systems (ABS) are designed to prevent locked-wheel skidding during hard braking or during braking on slippery surfaces. The front wheels of a vehicle cannot apply steering force if they are locked and sliding; the vehicle will continue in the previous direction of travel. The 4-wheel ABS system used on Volkswagen vehicles holds the wheels just below the point of locking, thereby allowing some steering response and preventing the rear of the vehicle from sliding sideways.

There are conditions for which the ABS system provides no benefit. Hydroplaning is possible when the tires ride on a film of water, losing contact with the paved surface. This renders the vehicle totally uncontrollable until road contact is regained. Extreme steering maneuvers at high speed or cornering beyond the limits of tire adhesion can result in skidding which is independent of vehicle braking. For this reason, the system is named anti-lock rather than anti-skid. Wheel spin during acceleration on slippery surfaces may also fool the system into detecting a system failure and entering the fail-safe mode.

Under normal conditions, the ABS system functions in the same manner as a standard brake system and is transparent to the operator. The system is a combination of electrical and hydraulic components, working together to control the flow of brake fluid to the wheels when necessary.

The Electronic Control Unit (ECU) is the electronic brain of the system, receiving and interpreting signals from the wheel speed sensors. The unit will enter anti-lock mode when it senses impending wheel lock at any wheel, and will immediately control the brake line pressures to the affected wheel(s) by issuing output signals to the hydraulic modulator assembly.

The hydraulic modulator contains solenoids which react to the signals from the ECU. Each solenoid controls brake fluid pressure to one wheel. The solenoids allow brake line pressure to build according to brake pedal pressure, hold (by isolating the system from the pedal and maintaining current pressure) or decrease (by isolating the pedal circuit and bleeding some fluid from the line).

The decisions regarding these functions are made very rapidly, as each solenoid can be cycled up to 10 times per second. Volkswagen employs a 3-channel control system; the front wheels are controlled separately, while the rear wheels are controlled together, based on the signal of the wheel with the greatest locking tendency.

The operator may feel a pulsing in the brake pedal and/or hear popping or clicking noises when the system engages. These sensations are due to the valves cycling and the pressures being changed rapidly within the brake system. While completely normal and not a sign of system failure, these sensations can be disconcerting to an operator unfamiliar with the system.

Although the ABS system prevents wheel lock-up under hard braking, as brake pressure increases, wheel slip is allowed to increase as well. This slip will result in some tire chirp during ABS operation. The sound should not be interpreted as lock-up but rather as an indication of the system holding the wheel(s) just outside the locking point. The final few feet of an ABS-engaged stop may be completed with the wheels locked, as the system is inoperative below 3 mph (5 kph).

When the ignition is **ON** and vehicle speed is over 3 mph (5 kph), the ECU monitors the function of the system. Should a fault be noted, such as loss of signal from a sensor, the ABS system is immediately disabled by the ECU. The ANTI-LOCK dashboard warning lamp illuminates to inform the operator. When the ABS system is disabled, the vehicle retains normal braking capacity without the benefits of anti-lock.

Relieving Anti-lock Brake System Pressure

With the ignition switch **OFF**, pump the brake pedal 25–35 times to depressurize the system. The system will recharge itself via the electric pump as soon as the ignition is turned **ON**. Disconnect the pump or the battery to prevent unintended pressurization. The system can then be serviced and bled.

Troubleshooting

GENERAL INFORMATION

Vehicles with anti-lock brake systems (ABS) have an electronic fault memory and an indicator light on the instrument panel. When the engine is first started,

the light will go on to indicate the system is pressurizing and performing a self-diagnostic check. After the system is at full pressure, the light will go out. If it remains lit, there is a fault in the system.

The fault memory can only be accessed with the VW tester VAG 1551 or VAG 1598, or equivalent. If this diagnostic equipment is not available, most of the system can still be tested with a volt/ohmmeter. Service for the system is quite limited. Most components cannot be repaired, only replaced.

Before diagnosing an apparent ABS problem, make absolutely certain that the normal braking system is in correct working order. Many common brake problems (dragging parking brake, seepage, etc.) will affect the ABS system. A visual check of specific system components may reveal problems creating an apparent ABS malfunction. Performing this inspection may reveal a simple failure, thus eliminating extended diagnostic time.

1. Inspect the tire pressures; they must be approximately equal for the system to operate correctly.
2. Inspect the wheels and tires on the vehicle. They must be of the same size and type to generate accurate speed signals.
3. Inspect the brake fluid level in the reservoir.
4. Inspect brake lines, hoses, master cylinder assembly and brake calipers for leakage.
5. Visually check brake lines and hoses for excessive wear, heat damage, punctures, contact with other parts, missing clips or holders, blockage or crimping.
6. Check the calipers for rust or corrosion. Check for proper sliding action if applicable.
7. Check the calipers for freedom of motion during application and release.
8. Inspect the wheel speed sensors for proper mounting and connections.
9. Inspect the sensor wheels (tone rings) for broken teeth or poor mounting.
10. Certain driver induced faults, such as not releasing the parking brake fully, spinning the wheels under acceleration, sliding due to excessive cornering speed or driving on extremely rough surfaces may fool the system and trigger the dash warning light. These induced faults are not system failures; they are examples of vehicle performance outside the parameters of the control unit.
11. Many system shutdowns are due to loss of sensor signals to or from the controller. The most common cause is not a failed sensor, but a loose, corroded or dirty connector. Check harness and component connectors carefully.
12. Check for correct battery voltage and inspect the condition of all ABS fuses.

SYSTEM TESTING

♦ **See Figures 53 thru 58**

✳✳ CAUTION

The hydraulic modulator is capable of self-pressurizing and can generate pressures above 3000 psi anytime the ignition switch is turned ON. Relieve the system pressure before testing or repairing the hydraulic system. Improper repair or test procedures can cause serious or fatal injury.

1. Make sure the ignition switch is **OFF**, then unplug the control unit connector. The control unit is in the right rear of the trunk.
2. Use a volt/ohmmeter and the following charts to test the system. Start at the beginning and work all the way towards the end before removing any components.
3. After repairs, make sure the warning light on the instrument panel operates properly. It should light when the ignition is first turned **ON**, then go out after the vehicle starts moving. If not, the system is still not repaired.

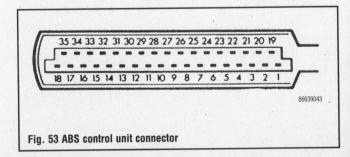

Fig. 53 ABS control unit connector

Test step	Connector terminals	Component to be tested	Testing requirements	Test results (specifications)	Additional steps (for test results NOT within specs)
8	5 + 23	Wheel speed sensor, left front (G47), voltage	• Switch ignition OFF • Raise vehicle with hoist; support • Rotate left front wheel, approximately 1 rotation per second	75 mV ac (minimum)	• Check installation of sensor • Check plug type terminal T2 • Perform Test step 19 • Perform Test step 23
9	1 + 3	ABS relay (J102), continuity	• Switch ignition OFF	1.5 Ohms (maximum) Note: Take reading on 200 Ohm scale	• Check circuit from terminal 3, via J102, to hydraulic unit ground • Check wire from terminal 1 to ground • If no open circuits exist, replace J102
10	1 + 20	ABS relay (J102), continuity	• Switch ignition OFF	1.5 Ohms (maximum)	• Check circuit from terminal 20, via J102, to hydraulic unit ground • Check wire from terminal 1 to ground • If no open circuits exist, replace J102
11	1 + 11	Inlet valve (N99), ground Outlet valve (N104), ground	• Switch ignition OFF	1.5 Ohms (maximum)	• Check circuit from terminal 11, via hydraulic unit to ground • Check wire from terminal 1 to ground
12	1 + 14	Hydraulic pump relay (J185), ground via high pressure switch (F109)	• switch ignition ON • press brake pedal to floor, 20 times	1.5 Ohms (maximum)	• Check circuit from terminal 14, to J185/186, and via F109, to ground • Check wire from terminal 1 to ground • Check continuity on F109
13	9 + 10	Low pressure warning switch (F116), continuity Brake fluid level warning contact (F117), continuity	• Check for correct brake fluid level • Switch ignition ON • Wait until pump switches OFF (reservoir filled)	1.5 Ohms (maximum)	• Check circuit from terminal 9, via F117 and F116, to terminal 10 • Perform Test step 14 • Perform Test step 15
14	9 + 10	Low pressure warning switch (F116), continuity	• Check for correct brake fluid level • Switch ignition ON • Press brake pedal to floor, 20 times (reservoir filled)	100 K Ohms (minimum) Note: Take reading on 200 K Ohm scale	• Check if F116 has continuity between terminals 3 and 5, of hydraulic unit's 5-pin terminal. If YES, F116 is defective. Replace • Perform Test step 15
15	9 + 10	Brake fluid level warning contact (F117)	• Switch ignition ON • Wait until pump switches OFF (reservoir filled) • Switch ignition ON • Remove warning contact from reservoir	2 M Ohms (minimum), when warning contact float has been removed from fluid (simulating level below minimum)	• Check F117, when removed, for continuity. If YES, F117 is defective. Replace

Fig. 55 Test steps 8 through 15

86639045

Test step	Connector terminals	Component to be tested	Testing requirements	Test results (specifications)	Additional steps (for test results NOT within specs)
1	2 + 1	ABS control unit (J104), voltage supply	• Switch ignition ON	Battery voltage (approximate) Note: Take reading on 20V scale	• Check wire from terminal 1 to ground • Check wire from terminal 2 to terminal D-7 (relay board)
2	3 + 1	ABS relay (J102), function	• Switch ignition ON • Remove fuse S16 • Bridge sockets 2 and 8 After testing: • Disconnect connections from sockets 2 and 8 • Install fuse S16	Battery voltage (approximate)	• Check wire from terminal 1 to ground • Check wire from terminal 3, via J102, to battery (+) • Perform Test step 9 • Perform Test step 24
3	12 + 1	Brake light switch, (F), function	• Switch ignition ON • Actuate brake pedal	Battery voltage (approximate)	• Check fuse S20 and brake light switch (F) • Check wire from terminal 1 to ground • Check wire from terminal 2 to terminal W-4 (relay board)
4	32 + 1	ABS relay for hydraulic pump (J185), function	• Switch ignition OFF • Pull plug terminal T2 from hydraulic pump (V64) • Press brake pedal to floor 20 times • Switch ignition ON After testing, reconnect plug terminal T2	Battery voltage (approximate)	• Check wire from terminal 1 to ground • Check wire from terminal 32, via J185 and fuse S53, to battery (+) • Perform Test step 12 • Perform Test step 32
5	4 + 22	Wheel speed sensor, right rear (G44), voltage	• Switch ignition OFF • Raise vehicle with hoist; support • Rotate right rear wheel, approximately 1 rotation per second	75 mV ac (minimum) Note: Take reading on 2V scale	• Check installation of sensor • Check plug type terminal T2 • Perform Test step 16 • Perform Test step 20
6	6 + 24	Wheel speed sensor, left rear (G46), voltage	• Switch ignition OFF • Raise vehicle with hoist; support • Rotate left rear wheel, approximately 1 rotation per second	75 mV ac (minimum)	• Check installation of sensor • Check plug type terminal T2 • Perform Test step 17 • Perform Test step 21
7	7 + 25	Wheel speed sensor, right front (G45), voltage	• Switch ignition OFF • Raise vehicle with hoist; support • Rotate right front wheel, approximately 1 rotation per second	75 mV ac (minimum)	• Check installation of sensor • Check plug type terminal T2 • Perform Test step 18 • Perform Test step 22

Fig. 54 Test steps 1 through 7

86639044

Test step	Connector terminals	Component to be tested	Testing requirements	Test results (specifications)	Additional steps (for test results NOT within specs)
16	4 + 22	Wheel speed sensor, right rear (G44), resistance	• Switch ignition OFF	0.8-1.4 K Ohms Note: Take reading on 2 K Ohm scale	• Check plug connector T2 • Check speed sensor resistance (0.8-1.4 K Ohms) • Check wire to wheel speed sensor • Perform Test step 20
17	6 + 24	Wheel speed sensor, left rear (G46), resistance	• Switch ignition OFF	0.8-1.4 K Ohms	• Check plug connector T2 • Check speed sensor resistance (0.8-1.4 K Ohms) • Check wire to wheel speed sensor • Perform Test step 21
18	7 + 25	Wheel speed sensor, right front (G45), resistance	• Switch ignition OFF	0.8-1.4 K Ohms	• Check plug connector T2 • Check speed sensor resistance (0.8-1.4 K Ohms) • Check wire to wheel speed sensor • Perform Test step 22
19	5 + 23	Wheel speed sensor, left front (G47), resistance	• Switch ignition OFF	0.8-1.4 K Ohms	• Check plug connector T2 • Check speed sensor resistance (0.8-1.4 K Ohms) • Check wire to wheel speed sensor • Perform Test step 23
20	1 + 4	Shielded wire to right rear wheel speed sensor (G44), insulator resistance	• Switch ignition OFF	2 M Ohms (minimum)	• Check wire for damaged insulation
21	1 + 6	Shielded wire to left rear wheel speed sensor (G46), insulator resistance	• Switch ignition OFF	2 M Ohms (minimum)	• Check wire for damaged insulation
22	1 + 7	Shielded wire to wheel speed sensor, right front (G45), insulator resistance	• Switch ignition OFF	2 M Ohms (minimum)	• Check wire for damaged insulation
23	1 + 5	Shielded wire to wheel speed sensor, left front (G47), insulator resistance	• Switch ignition OFF	2 M Ohms (minimum)	• Check wire for damaged insulation
24	1 + 8	ABS relay (J102), resistance	• Switch ignition OFF	50-100 Ohms Note: Take reading on 200 Ohm scale	• Check wire from terminal 8, via J102, to ground • Check coil resistance (50-100 Ohms). Replace J102, if necessary

Fig. 56 Test steps 16 through 24

Test step	Connector terminals	Component to be tested	Testing requirements	Test results (specifications)	Additional steps (for test results NOT within specs)
25	1 + 18	ABS main valve (N105), resistance	• Switch ignition OFF	2-5 Ohms	• Check wire from terminal 18, via N105, to ground • Check N105 coil resistance (2-5 Ohms). If defective, replace hydraulic unit • Perform test step 33
26	11 + 17	Inlet valve, rear (N103), resistance	• Switch ignition OFF	5-7 Ohms	• Check wire from terminal 17, via N103, to ground • Test N103 resistance (5-7 Ohms). If defective, replace hydraulic unit
27	11 + 15	Inlet valve, right front (N99), resistance	• Switch ignition OFF	5-7 Ohms	• Check wire from terminal 15, via N99, to ground • Check N99 resistance (5-7 Ohms). If defective, replace hydraulic unit
28	11 + 35	Inlet valve, left front (N101), resistance	• Switch ignition OFF	5-7 Ohms	• Check wire from terminal 35, via N101, to ground • Check N101 resistance (5-7 Ohms). If defective, replace hydraulic unit
29	11 + 33	Outlet valve, rear (N104), resistance	• Switch ignition OFF	3-5 Ohms	• Check wire from terminal 33, via N104, to ground • Check N104 resistance (3-5 Ohms). If defective, replace hydraulic unit
30	11 + 34	Outlet valve, right front (N100), resistance	• Switch ignition OFF	3-5 Ohms	• Check wire from terminal 34, via N100, to ground • Check N100 resistance (3-5 Ohms). If defective, replace hydraulic unit
31	11 + 16	Outlet valve, left front (N102), resistance	• Switch ignition OFF	3-5 Ohms	• Check wire from terminal 16, via N102, to ground • Check N102 resistance (3-5 Ohms). If defective, replace hydraulic unit

Fig. 57 Test steps 25 through 31

Test step	Connector terminals	Component to be tested	Testing requirements	Test results (specifications)	Additional steps (for test results NOT within specs)
32	2 + 14	ABS hydraulic pump relay (J185), resistance	• Switch ignition OFF	50–100 Ohms	• Check wire from terminal 2, via J185, to contact 14 • Check coil resistance (50–100 Ohms). If necessary, replace J185
33	Bridge 2–18	ABS main valve (N105), function	• Switch ignition OFF • Press brake pedal to floor and hold • Switch ignition ON	Pulsation from brake pedal should be felt at foot	For defective N105 • Replace hydraulic unit
34	—	ABS hydraulic pump (V64), function	• Switch ignition OFF • Pump brake pedal 20 times to discharge reservoir • Mark fluid level on reservoir • Switch ignition ON	Fluid level in reservoir drops approximately 1.0 cm (0.4 in.)	• Check wire from battery (+), via fuse S53 and components J185 and V64, back to battery. If no opens exist, replace V64
35	Bridge 2–17–33	Inlet and outlet valve, rear (N103, N104), function	• Raise/support vehicle • Switch ignition OFF • Depress brake pedal	Rear wheels must lock	• Replace defective hydraulic unit
			• Switch ignition ON • Depress brake pedal	Rear wheels must rotate freely	
36	Bridge 2–15–34	Inlet and outlet valve, right front (N99, N100), function	• Raise/support vehicle • Switch ignition OFF • Depress brake pedal	Right front wheel must lock	• Replace defective hydraulic unit
			• Switch ignition ON • Depress brake pedal	Right front wheel must rotate freely	
37	Bridge 2–16–35	Inlet and outlet valve, left front (N101, N102), function	• Raise/support vehicle • Switch ignition OFF • Depress brake pedal	Left front wheel must lock	• Replace defective hydraulic unit
			• Switch ignition ON • Depress brake pedal	Left front wheel must rotate freely	

86639048

Fig. 58 Test steps 32 through 37

Control Unit

REMOVAL & INSTALLATION

1. Disconnect the negative battery cable.
2. Make sure the ignition switch is **OFF**, then remove the right luggage compartment panel.
3. Remove the control unit and disconnect the wiring.
4. Installation is the reverse of removal. Make sure the warning light on the instrument panel goes out when the vehicle speed is above 3 mph.

Wheel Speed Sensor

REMOVAL & INSTALLATION

1. Disconnect the negative battery cable.
2. Raise and safely support the vehicle.
3. Remove the wheel and unbolt the sensor from the steering knuckle or stub axle.
4. The rotor portion of the sensor assembly is secured to the inside of the wheel hub. To remove the front rotor, the hub must be pressed out of the front wheel bearing.
5. On the rear wheels, the sensor is pressed into the brake rotor. To remove it:
   a. Remove the wheel bearing and the brake rotor.
   b. Insert a drift pin through the wheel bolt holes and gently tap the speed sensor rotor out a little bit at each hole, much like removing an inner wheel bearing race.

To install:

6. Use a suitable sleeve to drive the speed sensor rotor into the brake rotor evenly. When the cover ring is installed, the distance from the ring to the splash shield should be 0.375 in. (9.5mm).
7. Apply a dry lubricant on the sides of the sensor, then torque the retaining bolt to 7 ft. lbs. (10 Nm).
8. Connect the battery cable.

Modulator Assembly

REMOVAL & INSTALLATION

▶ See Figure 59

1. Disconnect the negative battery cable.
2. Turn the ignition **OFF** and depress the brake pedal 25–35 times to depressurize the modulator assembly. Disconnect the pump or battery to prevent unintended pressurization.
3. Inside the vehicle near the right tail light, locate and disconnect the ABS control unit and the ground connection.
4. Remove the brake fluid from the reservoir with a suction pump.
5. Disconnect the brake lines from the modulator assembly and protect the connections from contamination with suitable plugs.
6. Working inside the vehicle, remove the left shelf under the dash to gain access to the brake pedal linkage. Remove the clevis bolt and disconnect the pedal.
7. Unfasten the locknuts and remove the pressure modulator.
8. Installation is the reverse of removal. Use new locknuts and torque to 18 ft. lbs. (25 Nm). Refill the reservoir with new brake fluid and bleed the system, as described later in this section.

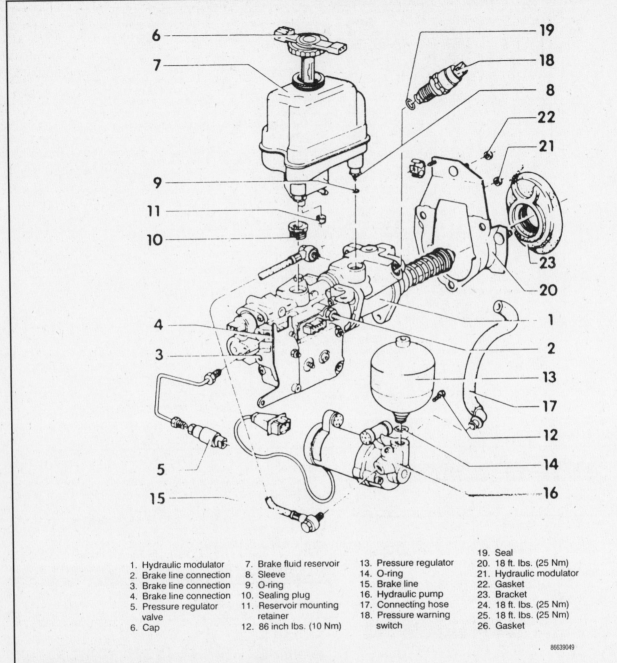

1. Hydraulic modulator
2. Brake line connection
3. Brake line connection
4. Brake line connection
5. Pressure regulator valve
6. Cap
7. Brake fluid reservoir
8. Sleeve
9. O-ring
10. Sealing plug
11. Reservoir mounting retainer
12. 86 inch lbs. (10 Nm)
13. Pressure regulator
14. O-ring
15. Brake line
16. Hydraulic pump
17. Connecting hose
18. Pressure warning switch
19. Seal
20. 18 ft. lbs. (25 Nm)
21. Hydraulic modulator
22. Gasket
23. Bracket
24. 18 ft. lbs. (25 Nm)
25. 18 ft. lbs. (25 Nm)
26. Gasket

86639049

Fig. 59 ABS modulator assembly

Filling and Bleeding

✻✻ CAUTION

The hydraulic modulator is capable of self-pressurizing and can generate pressures above 3000 psi anytime the ignition switch is turned ON. Relieve the system pressure before servicing the hydraulic system. Improper repair or test procedures can cause serious or fatal injury.

FILLING THE SYSTEM

The reservoir on the hydraulic modulator is filled in the usual manner with no special procedures being necessary. Always wipe the cap and surrounding area clean of dirt and debris before opening the reservoir; the smallest bit of dirt may impair the operation of the system. When adding fluid, fill the reservoir only to the MAX line on the reservoir; do not overfill.

Only DOT 4 brake fluid must be used; silicone or DOT 5 fluid is specifically prohibited. Do not use any fluid which contains a petroleum base; these fluids will cause swelling and distortion of the rubber parts within the system. Do not use old or contaminated brake fluid. Do not reuse fluid which has been bled from the system.

BLEEDING THE SYSTEM

Bleeding may be performed using either a pressure bleeder or the manual method. In either case an assistant will be required to depress the brake pedal. Extreme cleanliness must be observed at all times. If using the manual method, the fluid reservoir must be filled to the upper edge before bleeding begins. Do not allow the fluid level to drop below the MIN mark at any time. Do not reuse fluid released during bleeding.

Front Brakes

1. Turn the ignition switch **OFF**.
2. Relieve the brake system pressure, as described earlier in this section.
3. If using pressure bleeder equipment, connect it to the brake fluid reservoir and switch it on.
4. Connect a tight-fitting vinyl hose to the bleeder port of the caliper. If using pressure bleeding equipment, begin at the left front caliper. If using the manual method, begin on either side. Immerse the other end of the hose in a container of clean brake fluid.

➡**Use of a cap or cover on the container is recommended. The brake fluid may bleed with enough force to splash out of an open container.**

5. Open the bleeder screw. Have an assistant depress the brake pedal slowly until the fluid flows without bubbles.
6. Close the bleeder screw before the pedal is released.
7. Remove the vinyl tube from the caliper. Inspect and top off the fluid supply in the reservoir if necessary.
8. Repeat the procedure at the opposite wheel.

Rear Brakes

1. Turn the ignition switch **OFF**.
2. Relieve the brake system pressure, as described earlier in this section.
3. If using pressure bleeder equipment, connect it to the brake fluid reservoir and switch it on.
4. Connect a tight-fitting vinyl hose to the bleeder port of either caliper. Immerse the other end of the hose in a container of clean brake fluid.

➡**Use of a cap or cover on the container is recommended. The brake fluid may bleed with enough force to splash out of an open container.**

5. Open the bleeder screw. Have an assistant turn the ignition switch **ON**.
6. Press the lever of the proportioning valve towards the axle until brake fluid flows out without bubbles. Release the lever and close the bleeder screw.

➡**Running time of the ABS pump must not exceed 120 seconds at any one time. If this time is approached or exceeded, a minimum of 10 minutes cooling time is required before proceeding. Do not allow the fluid level to fall below the MIN line at any time.**

7. Switch the ignition **OFF** while transferring equipment. Remove the vinyl tube from the caliper. Inspect and top off the fluid supply in the reservoir if necessary.
8. Repeat the procedure at the opposite wheel.
9. Once both rear calipers are bled and the service equipment removed, switch the ignition **ON** until the pump shuts off.
10. Fill the brake fluid reservoir to the MAX line.

BRAKE SPECIFICATIONS
All measurements in inches unless noted

Year	Model	Brake Disc Minimum Thickness	Brake Disc Maximum Runout	Brake Drum Diameter Original Inside Diameter	Brake Drum Diameter Maximum Machine Diameter	Minimum Lining Thickness Front	Minimum Lining Thickness Rear
1986	Quantum	0.393 [5]	0.002	7.874	7.894	0.276 [6]	0.098
	Cabriolet	0.393	0.002	7.086	7.150	0.250 [6]	0.098
	Scirocco	0.709 [10]	0.002	7.087	7.106	0.276 [6]	0.098
	Jetta [7]	0.393	0.002	7.087	7.106	0.276 [6]	0.098
	Golf [8]	0.393	0.002	7.087	7.106	0.276 [6]	0.098
1987	Quantum	0.393 [5]	0.002	7.874	7.894	0.276 [6]	0.098
	Cabriolet	0.709	0.002	7.087	7.106	0.276 [6]	0.098
	Scirocco	0.709 [10]	0.002	7.087	7.106	0.276 [6]	0.098
	Jetta [7]	0.393	0.002	7.087	7.106	0.276 [6]	0.098
	Golf [8]	0.393	0.002	7.087	7.106	0.276 [6]	0.098
	Fox	0.393	0.002	7.087 [12]	7.106 [13]	0.276 [6]	0.098
1988	Quantum	0.393 [5]	0.002	7.874	7.894	0.276 [6]	0.098
	Cabriolet	0.709	0.002	7.087	7.106	0.276 [6]	0.098
	Scirocco	0.709 [10]	0.002	7.087	7.106	0.276 [6]	0.098
	Jetta [7]	0.393	0.002	7.087	7.106	0.276 [6]	0.098
	Golf [8]	0.393	0.002	7.087	7.106	0.276 [6]	0.098
	Fox	0.393	0.002	7.087	7.106	0.276 [6]	0.098
1989	Cabriolet	0.709	0.002	7.087 [12]	7.106 [13]	0.276 [6]	0.098
	Scirocco	0.709 [10]	0.002	7.087	7.106	0.276 [6]	0.098
	Jetta [7]	0.393 [9]	0.002 [11]	7.087	7.106	0.276 [6]	0.098
	Golf [8]	0.393 [9]	0.002	7.087	7.106	0.276 [6]	0.098
	Fox	0.393	0.002	7.087 [12]	7.106 [13]	0.276 [6]	0.098

1. Riveted. Bonded-0.059
2. Front drum brakes-9.059
3. Front drum brakes-9.079
4. Front drum brakes-0.040
5. 5-cylinder and Syncro-0.709. Rear disc-0.315
6. Measurement of lining and metal.
7. Includes GLI.
8. Includes GTI.
9. Solid front rotor. Vented rotor-0.709. Rear rotor-0.315
10. Rear disc-0.315
11. ABS-0.001
12. Fox wagon-7.874
13. Fox wagon-7.894

86639301

BRAKE SPECIFICATIONS
All measurements in inches unless noted

Year	Model	Brake Disc Minimum Thickness	Brake Disc Maximum Runout	Brake Drum Diameter Original Inside Diameter	Brake Drum Diameter Maximum Machine Diameter	Minimum Lining Thickness Front	Minimum Lining Thickness Rear
1974	Dasher	0.413	0.004	7.850	7.900	0.080	0.098 [1]
1975	Dasher	0.413	0.004	7.850	7.900	0.080	0.098 [1]
	Rabbit	0.413	0.004	7.086 [2]	7.105 [3]	0.080 [4]	0.098 [1]
	Scirocco	0.413	0.004	7.086	7.105	0.080	0.098 [1]
1976	Dasher	0.413	0.004	7.850	7.900	0.080	0.098 [1]
	Rabbit	0.413	0.004	7.086 [2]	7.105 [3]	0.080 [4]	0.098 [1]
	Scirocco	0.413	0.004	7.086	7.105	0.080	0.098 [1]
1977	Dasher	0.393	0.004	7.850	7.900	0.080	0.098 [1]
	Rabbit	0.413	0.004	7.086 [2]	7.105 [3]	0.080 [4]	0.098 [1]
	Scirocco	0.413	0.004	7.086	7.105	0.080	0.098 [1]
1978	Dasher	0.393	0.004	7.850	7.900	0.080	0.098 [1]
	Rabbit	0.413	0.004	7.086 [2]	7.105 [3]	0.080 [4]	0.098 [1]
	Scirocco	0.413	0.004	7.086	7.090	0.080	0.098 [1]
1979	Dasher	0.393	0.004	7.850	7.900	0.080	0.098 [1]
	Rabbit	0.413	0.004	7.086 [2]	7.105 [3]	0.080 [4]	0.098 [1]
	Scirocco	0.413	0.004	7.086	7.105	0.080	0.098 [1]
1980	Dasher	0.393	0.004	7.850	7.900	0.080	0.098 [1]
	Rabbit	0.393	0.004	7.086	7.105	0.080	0.098 [1]
	Scirocco	0.393	0.004	7.086	7.105	0.080	0.098 [1]
	Jetta	0.393	0.004	7.086	7.105	0.080	0.098 [1]
1981	Dasher	0.393	0.004	7.850	7.900	0.080	0.098 [1]
	Rabbit	0.393	0.004	7.086	7.105	0.080	0.098 [1]
	Scirocco	0.393	0.004	7.086	7.105	0.080	0.098 [1]
	Jetta	0.393	0.004	7.086	7.105	0.080	0.098 [1]
1982	Quantum	0.393 [5]	0.002	7.874	7.894	0.276 [6]	0.098
	Rabbit	0.393	0.002	7.086	7.105	0.250 [6]	0.098
	Scirocco	0.393	0.002	7.086	7.150	0.250 [6]	0.098
	Jetta	0.393	0.002	7.086	7.105	0.250 [6]	0.098
1983	Quantum	0.393 [5]	0.002	7.874	7.894	0.276 [6]	0.098
	Rabbit	0.393	0.002	7.086	7.105	0.250 [6]	0.098
	Rabbit GTI	0.709	0.002	7.086	7.150	0.375 [6]	0.098
	Scirocco	0.393	0.002	7.086	7.105	0.250 [6]	0.098
	Jetta	0.393	0.002	7.086	7.105	0.250 [6]	0.098
1984	Quantum	0.393 [5]	0.002	7.874	7.894	0.276 [6]	0.098
	Rabbit	0.393	0.002	7.086	7.105	0.250 [6]	0.098
	Rabbit GTI	0.709	0.002	7.086	7.150	0.375 [6]	0.098
	Scirocco	0.393	0.002	7.086	7.105	0.250 [6]	0.098
	Jetta	0.393	0.002	7.086	7.105	0.250 [6]	0.098
1985	Quantum	0.393 [5]	0.002	7.874	7.894	0.276 [6]	0.098
	Cabriolet	0.393	0.002	7.086	7.150	0.250 [6]	0.098
	Scirocco	0.393	0.002	7.086	7.150	0.250 [6]	0.098
	Jetta [7]	0.393 [9]	0.002	7.087	7.106	0.276 [6]	0.098
	Golf [8]	0.393 [9]	0.002	7.087	7.106	0.276 [6]	0.098

86639300

10

BODY AND TRIM

EXTERIOR 10-2
INTERIOR 10-8

EXTERIOR

Doors

REMOVAL & INSTALLATION

1. Open the door and support it securely with a floor jack or blocks. Remove the door check strap sleeve and remove the door check strap.
2. If necessary, remove the door panel to disconnect the wiring for speakers, electric windows, electric mirrors and the air line for power door locks.
3. Have an assistant steady the door, then remove the hinge bolts. Remove the door.

To install:

4. Position the door, the install the hinge bolts. Do not tighten them at this time.
5. Engage any electrical or vacuum connections, then install the door panel.
6. Adjust the door.

ADJUSTMENT

When checking door alignment, look carefully at each seam between the door and body. The gap should be even all the way around the door. Pay particular attention to the door seams at the corners farthest from the hinges; this is the area where errors will be most evident. Additionally, the door should push against the weatherstrip when latched to seal out wind and water. The contact should be even all the way around and the stripping should be about half compressed. The position of the door can be adjusted in three dimensions: fore and aft, up and down, in and out. The primary adjusting points are the hinge-to-body bolts.

1. Apply tape to the fender and door edges to protect the paint. Two layers of common masking tape works well.
2. Make sure the bolts are loosened just enough to allow the hinge to move. With the help of an assistant, position the door up and down as required, then snug the bolts.
3. Inspect the door seams carefully and repeat the adjustment until correctly aligned.
4. Inspect the front door seal and determine how much it is being crushed. If there is little or no contact in this area, or if the door is recessed into the body at the front when closed, loosen the hinge-to-door bolts and adjust the door in or out as needed. Don't worry about the latch yet.
5. Make sure the door moves smoothly on the hinges without binding. When the door fits the opening correctly, tighten the bolts securely.
6. To adjust the latch, loosen the large cross-point screw holding the striker on the door jam on the body. These bolts will be very tight; an impact screwdriver is the best tool for this job. Make sure you are using the proper size bit.
7. With the bolts just loose enough to allow the striker to move if necessary, hold the outer door handle in the released position and close the door. The striker will move into the correct location to match the door latch. Open the door and tighten the mounting bolts. The striker may be adjusted towards or away from the center of the car, thereby tightening or loosening the door fit. The striker can be moved up and down to compensate for door position, but if the door is correctly mounted at the hinges this should not be necessary.

➡**Do not attempt to correct height variations (sag) by adjusting the striker.**

8. After the striker bolts have been tightened, open and close the door several times. Observe the motion of the door as it engages the striker; it should continue its straight-in motion and not deflect up or down as it hits the striker.
9. Check the feel of the latch during opening and closing. It must be smooth and linear, without any trace of grinding or binding during engagement and release. It may be necessary to repeat the striker adjustment several times (and possibly re-adjust the hinges) before the correct door-to-body fit is achieved.

Hood

REMOVAL & INSTALLATION

▶ **See Figures 1, 2 and 3**

1. Raise the hood and support it securely. Cover the painted areas of the body to protect the finish from being damaged. Scribe the hood hinge-to-hood locations for installation.
2. If applicable, unplug the washer nozzle hoses.
3. While an assistant holds the hood, remove the hinge-to-hood retaining bolts.
4. Remove the hood from the vehicle.

To install:

5. Align the hood with the scribe marks, then tighten the bolts until snug. Check the position of the hood and adjust as necessary.
6. When adjustment is completed, torque the bolts to 15 ft. lbs. (20 Nm).

ALIGNMENT

Loosen the hinge to hood attaching bolts and move the hood from side to side until there is an equal amount of clearance on both sides of the hood and fender. Tighten the hood bolts.

Trunk Lid

REMOVAL & INSTALLATION

1. Open and support the trunk lid securely.
2. If necessary, remove the inner panel to disconnect any wiring or tubing.
3. Mark the position of the trunk lid hinge in relation to the trunk lid.
4. With an assistant, remove the two bolts attaching the hinge to the trunk lid. Remove the trunk lid from the vehicle.

86630001

Fig. 1 Scribe the hood hinge-to-hood locations

86630002

Fig. 2 Unplug the washer nozzle hoses

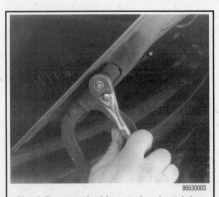

86630003

Fig. 3 Remove the hinge-to-hood retaining bolts

To install:

5. Align the trunk lid with the scribe marks, then tighten the bolts until snug. Check the position of the trunk lid and adjust as necessary.

6. When adjustment is completed, torque the bolts to 18 ft. lbs. (25 Nm).

ALIGNMENT

To make the front-to-rear or side-to-side adjustment, loosen the trunk lid attaching bolts and move the trunk lid as necessary. Tighten the trunk lid attaching bolts. To make the up-and-down adjustment, loosen the hinge-to-hinge support attaching bolts and raise or lower the hinge as necessary. The trunk lid is at the correct height when it is flush with the trunk deck.

Rear Hatch

REMOVAL & INSTALLATION

♦ See Figure 4

1. Open the rear hatch fully and support it in place.
2. Carefully remove the trim fasteners with a flat screwdriver and remove the trim.
3. Disconnect the wiring and any tubing.
4. Remove the ball studs from both the upper and lower ends of the struts and remove them.

✳✳ CAUTION

Never disassemble the support strut, as it is filled with high pressure gas. Do not turn the piston rod and the cylinder when the piston rod is extended. When discarding the strut, drill a 0.08–0.12 in. (2–3mm) hole in the bottom of the damper or use a hack saw to release the gas. Make sure to protect yourself against any metal particles that may be thrown into the air by the compressed gas during drilling.

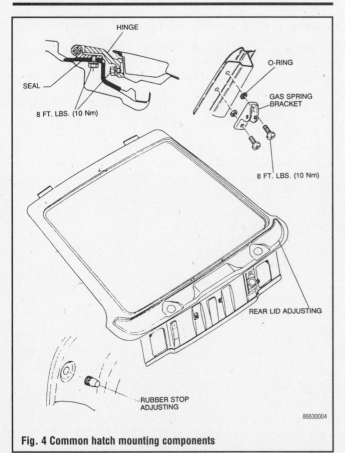

HINGE

O-RING

SEAL

GAS SPRING BRACKET

8 FT. LBS. (10 Nm)

8 FT. LBS. (10 Nm)

REAR LID ADJUSTING

RUBBER STOP ADJUSTING

86630004

Fig. 4 Common hatch mounting components

5. Mark the position of the hinge on the hatch, then remove the nuts/bolts.
6. Remove the rear hatch.

To install:

7. Align the hatch with the scribe marks made earlier and loosely install the bolts/nuts.
8. Connect the struts to the hatch. Engage any electrical wiring.
9. If necessary, adjust the hatch, then tighten the nuts/bolts securely.

ALIGNMENT

1. To align the front-to-rear position of the hatch, loosen the hinge attaching bolts on both the hatch and the body.
2. Position the hatch so the gap is even all the way around the hatch.
3. To adjust the hatch closing position, loosen both the lock and striker bolts.

Bumpers

REMOVAL & INSTALLATION

♦ See Figure 5

✳✳ CAUTION

Use extreme caution when working on a vehicle which has been involved in a collision. Some models may be equipped with a shock-type energy absorber which may not rebound immediately after a collision. The absorber may suddenly rebound to its original length at any time. It could cause serious or fatal injury if it were to contact you.

Front

FOX

1. Disconnect the negative battery cable.
2. Remove the air intake hose, bracket and air duct box cover.
3. From inside the engine compartment, remove the upper bumper bracket bolts.
4. Disconnect the turn signal wiring and remove the bumper.

To install:

5. Position the bumper and install the bolts. Tighten the bolts securely.
6. Connect the turn signal wiring.
7. Install the air intake hose, bracket and air duct.

DASHER

1. Raise the vehicle and support with jackstands.
2. Remove the bracket bolts or, on models with bumper covers, remove the bolts securing the bumper reinforcement to the brackets.
3. Remove the bumper.
4. Remove the bolts securing the brackets to the bumper, or on models with bumper covers, remove the screws securing the cover to the bumper reinforcement.
5. Installation is the reverse of removal. Tighten all bolts securely.

QUANTUM AND 1975–84 RABBIT, SCIROCCO AND JETTA

1. Unbolt the impact absorbers from the frame rails.
2. Pull the bumper out parallel to the guide brackets.
3. Remove the bumper cover and/or impact absorbers from the bumper reinforcement as necessary.
4. Installation is the reverse of removal. Tighten the bolts securely.

1985–89 GOLF AND JETTA

1. Raise the vehicle and support with jackstands.
2. Remove the bracket on both body long members and bolts from underneath the vehicle.
3. Remove the small grille under the apron. Remove bumper bracket bolts and remove the bumper from the vehicle.
4. Install the bumper and torque the bolts to 59 ft. lbs. (83 Nm).

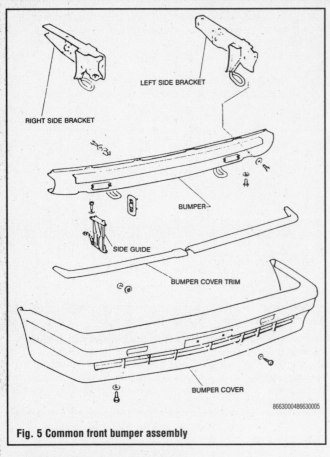

Fig. 5 Common front bumper assembly

1985–89 SCIROCCO AND CABRIOLET

1. Raise the vehicle and support with jackstands.
2. If necessary, drill out the rivets holding the bumper cover to the body inside the front wheel well.
3. Disconnect the parking light wiring.
4. Remove the bolts and slide the bumper out of the brackets.
5. Installation is the reverse of removal. Torque the bolts to 66 ft. lbs. (90 Nm).

Rear

FOX

1. Remove the bolts securing the bumper cover brackets, then remove the brackets.
2. Remove the bolts securing the bumper brackets.
3. Pull the bumper out parallel to the guide brackets.
4. Remove the bumper cover from the bumper reinforcement as necessary.
5. Installation is the reverse of removal. Tighten the bolts securely.

DASHER

1. Open the hatch.
2. Remove the side bolts securing the bumper to the frame rail.
3. From under the car, remove the through bolts securing the bumper.
4. Pull the bumper out parallel to the guide brackets.
5. Remove the bumper cover and/or brackets from the bumper reinforcement as necessary.
6. Installation is the reverse of removal. Tighten the bolts securely.

QUANTUM AND 1975–84 RABBIT, SCIROCCO AND JETTA

The rear bumpers on these vehicles are removed using the same procedure as the front bumpers.

1985–89 GOLF AND JETTA

1. Raise and support the vehicle with jackstands.
2. Working under the car, remove the bolts from both sides of the bumper.

3. Remove the bolts from each side of the luggage compartment.
4. Slide the bumper assembly away from the body.
5. Installation is the reverse of removal. Torque the inside bolts to 29 ft. lbs. (40 Nm) and the other four bolts to 51 ft. lbs. (70 Nm).

1985–89 SCIROCCO AND CABRIOLET

1. Raise the vehicle and support with jackstands.
2. Drill out the rivets holding the bumper cover to the body inside the rear wheel well.
3. Remove the bolts inside the luggage compartment and slide the bumper out of the brackets.
4. Installation is the reverse of removal. Torque the bolts to 66 ft. lbs. (90 Nm).

Grille

REMOVAL & INSTALLATION

1. Open the hood.
2. If necessary, remove the screws attaching any trim panels which may interfere with grille removal.
3. Remove any screws securing the grille.
4. Unclip the radiator grille at the lock carrier and remove upward. Check the rubber supports for damage.

To install:

5. Engage the grille into the retaining clips.
6. Install any screws which secure the grille.
7. If necessary, install the trim panels.

Outside Mirrors

REMOVAL & INSTALLATION

Sail Mount

♦ See Figure 6

➡ If equipped with electric mirrors, remove the door trim panel and disconnect the wiring harness before removing mirror assembly.

1. Disconnect the negative battery cable.
2. Remove the remote knob and unscrew the control lever.
3. Remove the trim cover, retaining screws and clamps.
4. Remove the mirror and outer shim.

To install:

5. Position the mirror with the outer shim, then tighten the retaining screws.

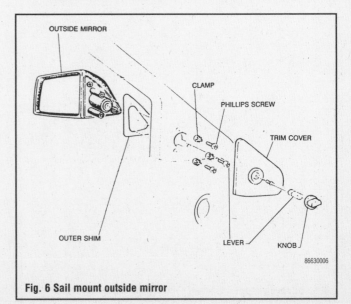

Fig. 6 Sail mount outside mirror

6. Install the trim cover with the retaining screws/clamps.
7. Install the remote knob or connect the wiring.

Door Mount

▶ **See Figure 7**

1. Remove the door trim panel.
2. Remove the adjusting knob, bezel and locking nut.
3. Remove the mirror trim cover, retaining screws and mirror.
To install:
4. Install the mirror, screws, trim cover and remote wire.
5. Install the locking nut, bezel and adjusting knob.
6. Install the trim panel.

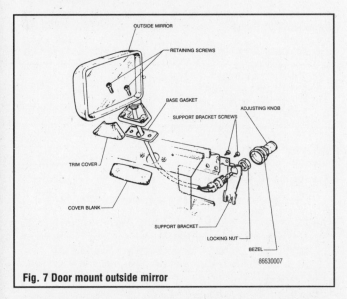

Fig. 7 Door mount outside mirror

Antenna

REMOVAL & INSTALLATION

Fender Mount

1. Disconnect the negative battery cable.
2. Remove the radio and the instrument cluster.

3. Remove the drip tray above the firewall under the hood and pull the antenna cable from the foam tube. Note the routing for installation.
4. Remove the rubber grommet and unclip the antenna cable from the water tray.
5. Remove the inner wheelhouse liner.
6. Remove the mast retainer nut from the top of the fender.
7. Pull the assembly downward into the inner wheelhouse and remove the lower mounting bracket.
To install:
8. Install the antenna and route the wire through the vehicle. Keep the cable away from the heater control cables.
9. Tighten the mast nut.
10. Install the remaining components in the reverse of removal.

Roof Mount

1. Remove the radio.
2. Remove the headliner, as outlined later in this section.
3. Remove the screws securing the antenna, then remove it from the vehicle.
To install:
4. If necessary, route a new antenna cable to the radio, then secure the antenna to the roof.
5. Install the headliner.
6. Install the radio.

Fenders

REMOVAL & INSTALLATION

▶ **See Figure 8**

1. Open the hood.
2. Tape the edges of the fender and door to prevent damage to the paint finish.
3. If necessary, use a heat gun and razor blade to soften and cut the PVC bead where the fender meets the A-pillar. Be careful not to use too much heat.
4. Remove the front bumper.
5. Remove any screws securing the inner fender liner to the fender.
6. Remove the bolts securing the fender, then remove it from the vehicle.
To install:
7. Position the fender on the vehicle. Be sure the zinc foil plates are in place at the bolt holes on the body, as these prevent corrosion between the metal body parts. Carefully lower the hood and be sure it does not rub on the fender (there should be an equal gap on both sides of the hood).
8. When the fender is correctly positioned, tighten the retaining bolts securely.
9. If necessary, attach the inner fender liner to the fender.

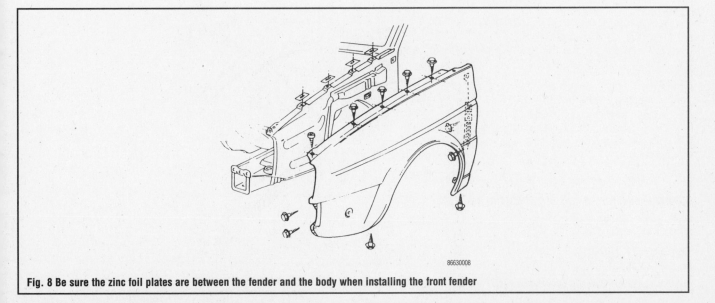

Fig. 8 Be sure the zinc foil plates are between the fender and the body when installing the front fender

10. Install the front bumper.
11. Apply a new bead of body (PVC) sealer where the fender meets the A-pillar.
12. Remove the tape from the edges of the door and fender. Close the hood.

Convertible Top

REMOVAL & INSTALLATION

▶ See Figures 9 and 10

Removing and installing the convertible top from the frame requires special tools and adhesives, and also requires cutting the top fabric. The job is best left to a well equipped body shop with convertible top experience. The procedure described here is for removing the top and frame together as an assembly. Installation requires two people.

1. Open the top to release the tension, but don't fold it back yet.
2. Bend open the metal tabs under the luggage compartment lining and pull the headliner off the tabs.
3. Pull the rear window defogger wiring out of the window seal.
4. Remove the window frame hinges and pull the cover off.
5. Remove the trim pieces at the rear corner of the rear windows.
6. On manual tops, remove the bolt to release the tension on the gas pressurized strut. Remove the clip at the other end and remove the strut.
7. If equipped with a power top, disconnect the cylinder from the top frame.
8. Disconnect the tensioning wire from its anchor on each side. A 4mm open end wrench can be used to prevent the wire from twisting.
9. Peel the top cover and tensioning wire out of the channels on the sides, then out of the rear channel.
10. Remove the headliner at the rear corners and remove the belt fastening bracket.
11. Remove the trim pieces covering the main bearing hinge. Remove the three bolts on each side and remove the top as an assembly.

To install:

12. Fit the top into place and start all the main bearing hinge bolts. When they are all started, tighten them.
13. Attach the belt at the rear corners.
14. Secure the tensioning wire to the anchors at each side and have a helper and top cover into the channel with a wooden drift.
15. Carefully align the beading and drive that into place with the drift.
16. Install the gas strut and try closing the top to make sure it fits properly and operates smoothly.
17. Install the rear window frame.
18. Attach the headliner and install the remaining trim pieces.

MOTOR REPLACEMENT

➡**The top can be operated by hand, if necessary, by opening the valve on the pump. Turn the valve counterclockwise until it stops.**

1. Disconnect the negative battery cable.
2. Unclip and remove the left side luggage trim panel.
3. Disconnect the motor wiring.
4. Loosen the filler plug to relieve the pressure. Have a rag handy to catch any fluid that may spill.
5. Disconnect the hydraulic fittings that are accessible. Make sure the fittings are clean before disconnecting them and cover them with plastic or paper to keep dirt out. Do not use rags because the lint is enough to cause problems with the hydraulic system.
6. Remove the mount bolts and remove the pump and disconnect the remaining hydraulic fittings.

To install:

7. Connect any hydraulic fittings to the motor which will not be accessible when the pump is mounted.
8. Connect the remaining hydraulic lines.
9. Connect the motor wiring.
10. Fill and bleed the hydraulic system.
11. Install the luggage trim panel.
12. Connect the negative battery cable.

POWER TOP CYLINDERS

▶ See Figures 11, 12 and 13

1. Unclip and remove the left side luggage compartment trim.
2. Bend the metal tabs and pull the top material up until the cylinders are visible.
3. Remove the lockring and pin to disengage the pushrod from the frame.
4. Unfasten the bracket nuts to remove the cylinder from the frame.
5. Disconnect the hydraulic line and remove the cylinder. Make sure no dirt or lint gets into the hydraulic system. Use plastic or paper covers to protect the fittings.

To install:

6. Secure the cylinder to the frame with the bracket nuts.
7. Connect the hydraulic line to the cylinder.
8. Engage the pushrod to the frame, then install the lockring and pin.
9. Secure the top material.
10. Fill and bleed the system.
11. Install the luggage trim panel.

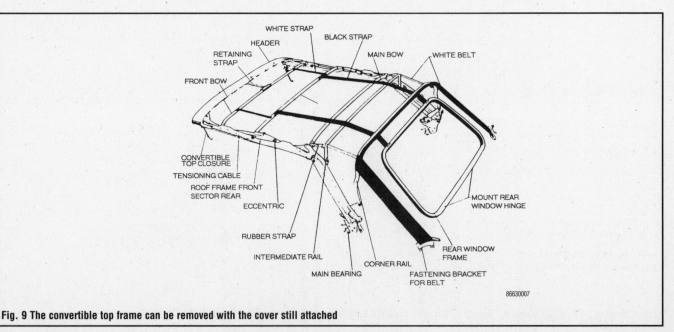

Fig. 9 The convertible top frame can be removed with the cover still attached

86630007

1
2
3
X
x Body
1 Top cover
2 Plastic bead
3 Tensioning wire
86630010

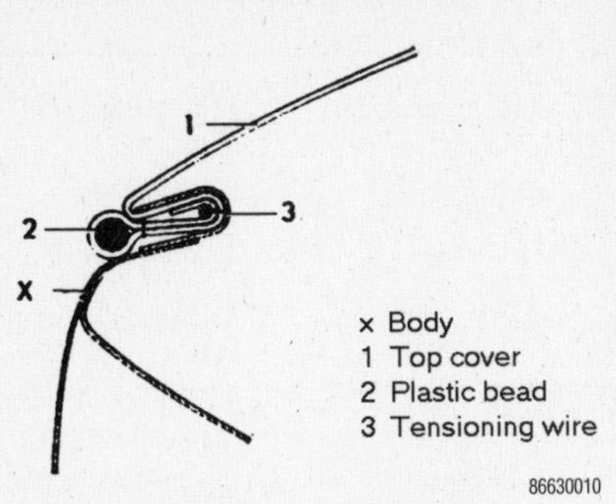

Fig. 10 Cross-sectional view of how the top cover is fastened to the body

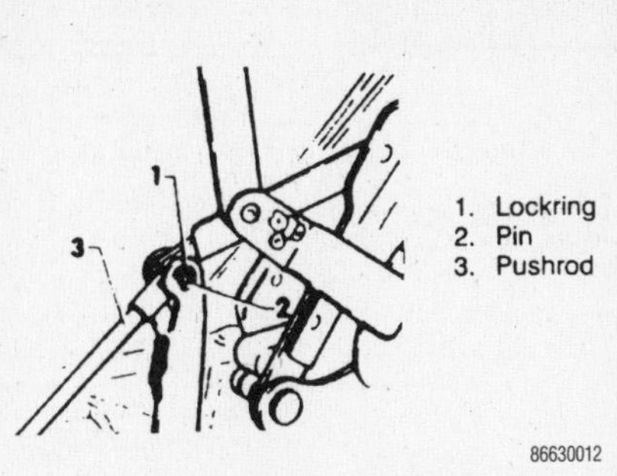

1
2
3
1. Lockring
2. Pin
3. Pushrod
86630012

Fig. 11 Disengage the pushrod after removing the lockring and pin

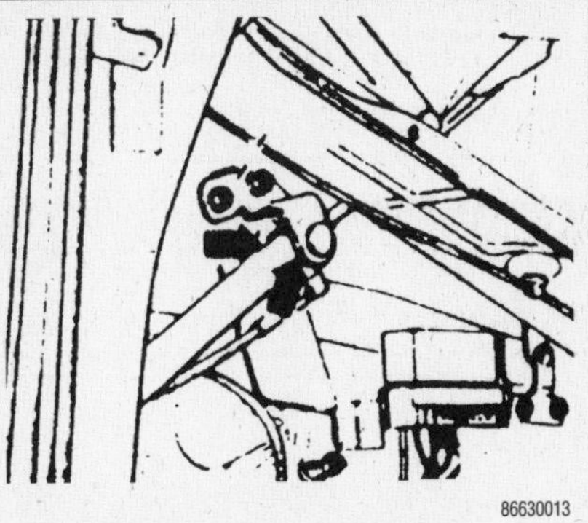

86630013

Fig. 12 Unfasten the bracket nuts to remove the cylinder from the frame

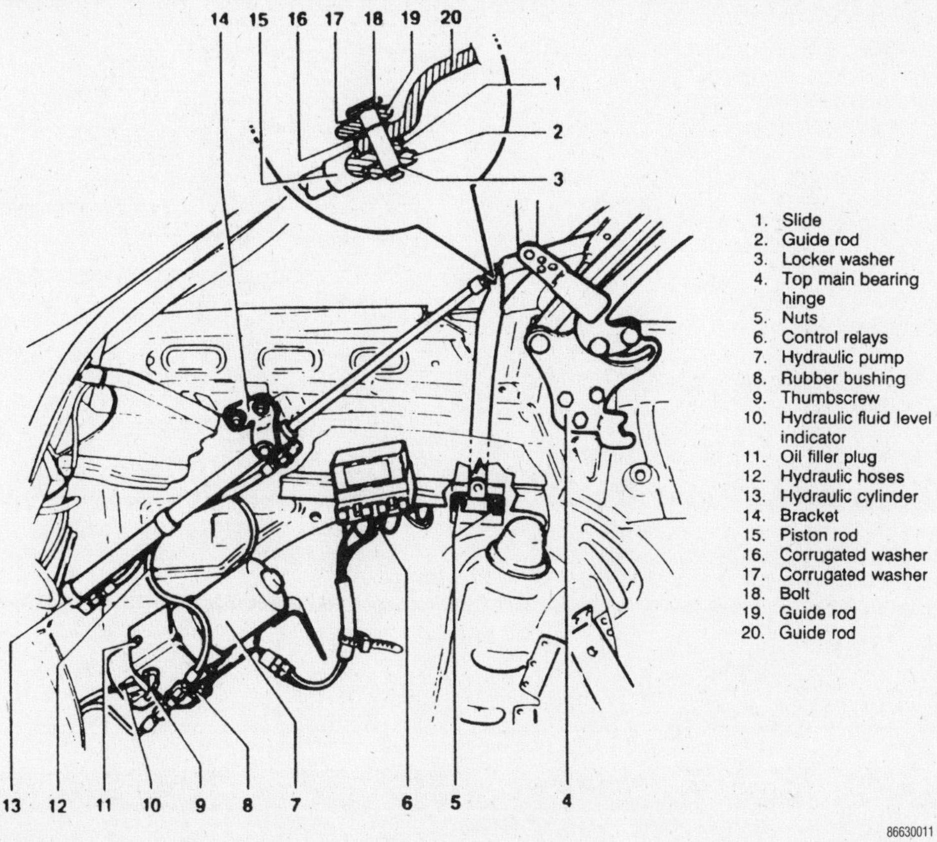

14 15 16 17 18 19 20
1
2
3
13 12 11 10 9 8 7 6 5 4
1. Slide
2. Guide rod
3. Locker washer
4. Top main bearing hinge
5. Nuts
6. Control relays
7. Hydraulic pump
8. Rubber bushing
9. Thumbscrew
10. Hydraulic fluid level indicator
11. Oil filler plug
12. Hydraulic hoses
13. Hydraulic cylinder
14. Bracket
15. Piston rod
16. Corrugated washer
17. Corrugated washer
18. Bolt
19. Guide rod
20. Guide rod
86630011

Fig. 13 Power top hydraulic system

BLEEDING THE SYSTEM

See Figure 14

1. Remove the left side luggage compartment trim panel.
2. Turn the valve on the pump to the left (counterclockwise) until it stops.
3. Open and close the top by hand twice, then open the top and leave it open.
4. Close the valve (fully clockwise).
5. Remove the filler plug and add hydraulic fluid as needed. Do not overfill.

The hydraulic fluid level must be checked with the top open. The level must be between the MIN and MAX marks.

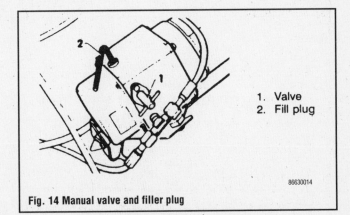

1
2
1. Valve
2. Fill plug
86630014

Fig. 14 Manual valve and filler plug

Sunroof

REMOVAL & INSTALLATION

▶ **See Figure 15**

1. Open the sunroof halfway, then remove the steel clips at the front edge using a plastic wedge tool.

2. Close the sunroof and push the interior panel back all the way.
3. Remove both front guides from the outer panel.
4. Slide the springs at the rear guide in towards the center.
5. Unfasten the screws, then remove the rear support plates in towards the center. Lift the sunroof cover out.
6. Installation is the reverse of removal.

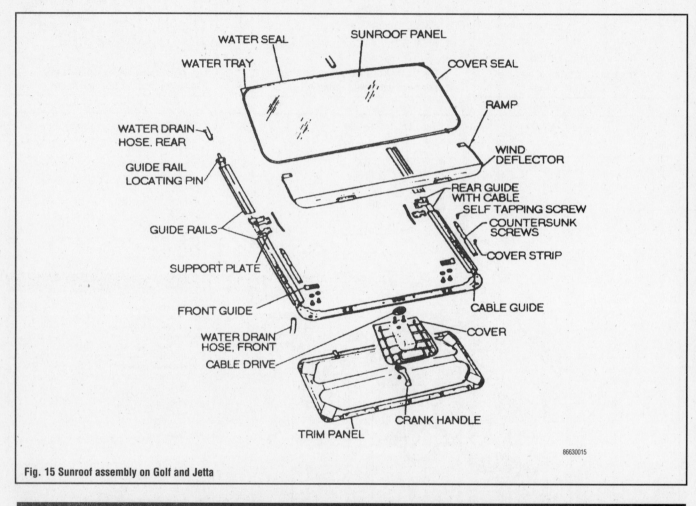

Fig. 15 Sunroof assembly on Golf and Jetta

INTERIOR

Instrument Panel

REMOVAL & INSTALLATION

Dasher

1. Disconnect the negative battery cable.
2. Remove the screws securing the center cover under the dash, then remove the cover. Disconnect the cigarette lighter.
3. Remove the nuts securing the glove box, then remove it from the vehicle.
4. Remove the screw securing the right side cover.
5. Remove the screws securing the cover and shelf.
6. Remove the screws securing the right and left sides of the dash.
7. Remove the nuts securing the dash below the cowl panel.
8. Disconnect the hoses from the air vents.
9. Disconnect the speedometer and all electrical terminals.
10. Remove the dashboard.

To install:
11. Position the dashboard in the vehicle.
12. Connect the electrical terminals and speedometer cable.
13. Connect the hoses to the air vents.
14. Install the nuts securing the dash below the cowl panel.
15. Install the screws securing the right and left sides of the dash.
16. Install the screws securing the cover and shelf.
17. Install the screw securing the right side cover.
18. Install the glove box in the vehicle.
19. Position the center cover under the dash, then connect the cigarette lighter. Install the screws securing the center cover.

Quantum

1. Disconnect the negative battery cable.
2. Remove the steering wheel.
3. Remove the screws securing the center cover under the dash, then remove the cover. Disconnect the cigarette lighter.
4. Remove the screws securing the trim panel (below the dash air vent) on

the passenger side. Carefully pull the trim out of its retaining clips. Do the same for the driver's side.

5. Carefully pry the lever switch trim of the dash.
6. Detach the shelf.
7. Pull off the heater and fresh air control knobs. Press out the trim and remove the controls.
8. Remove the screws securing the dash, then pull the instrument panel trim slightly.
9. Unplug all electrical connections and disconnect the speedometer cable.
10. Remove the dashboard.

To install:
11. Position the dashboard in the vehicle.
12. Connect the electrical terminals and speedometer cable.
13. Install the screws securing the dash.
14. Install the heater/fresh air control and knobs.
15. Install the shelf.
16. Carefully push the lever switch trim into the dash.
17. Install the driver's and passenger's side trim panel. Install the retaining screws.
18. Position the center cover under the dash and connect the cigarette lighter. Install the retaining screws.
19. Install the steering wheel.
20. Connect the negative battery cable.

Fox

1. Disconnect the negative battery cable.
2. Remove the console.
3. Tip the vent grilles in at the top, then remove the screws.
4. Tip the vent grilles in at the bottom. Pry up on the release tabs and remove the vent assembly.
5. Pull off the heater control knobs, then remove the face plate. Unplug the light.
6. Remove the screws securing the fan switch, then remove the switch and unplug.
7. Unplug the cigarette lighter wiring.
8. Remove the air duct to heater housing.
9. Remove the radio.
10. Remove the screws on the bottom of the instrument panel.
11. Remove the steering wheel.
12. Carefully pry the covers from the vacant switch positions.
13. Insert a small thin-bladed prytool behind the switches to the release the spring, then pull the switch from the instrument panel. Unplug the connection.
14. Remove the screws securing the instrument cluster trim, then remove the trim.
15. Remove the screws securing the turn signal switches, then disconnect the wiring.
16. Remove the instrument cluster.
17. Remove the screw at the back of the glove box and disconnect the lamp wiring.
18. Open the hood. From inside the engine compartment, remove the two nuts securing the dash to the cowl panel.
19. Drill out the rivets on both sides of the instrument panel.
20. Remove the instrument panel by pulling firmly on both side of the panel.
To install:
21. Position the instrument panel in the vehicle.
22. Properly position all wiring harnesses.
23. Connect the cigarette lighter and blower motor wiring.
24. Install the heater control assembly.
25. Install the radio.
26. Install the screws on the bottom of the instrument panel and the screw at the back of the glove box.
27. From inside the engine compartment, install the two nuts securing the dash to the cowl panel.
28. Install new rivets or screws on both sides of the instrument panel.
29. Install the center air vent assembly.
30. Install the instrument cluster.
31. Connect the turn signal wiring and secure the switches with screws.
32. Install the lever switches in the dash.
33. Install the instrument cluster trim.

34. Install the steering wheel.
35. Connect the negative battery cable.

Rabbit, Golf, Jetta, Scirocco

1. Disconnect the negative battery cable.
2. If applicable, remove the gear shift boot and the center console.
3. Remove the steering wheel.
4. Remove the trim panels from below the dashboard.
5. Remove the steering column support bracket and lower the column.
6. Pull the knobs off the heater controls and remove the control assembly and the radio.
7. Remove the headlight switch and switch blanks to gain access to the screws. Remove the instrument cluster and trim panel around the cluster.
8. Remove the glove compartment.
9. At the firewall, remove the plastic tray and remove the nuts holding the top of the dashboard.
10. Remove the main fuse panel and disconnect the plugs at the back. Disconnect the ground wires.
11. Disconnect any remaining wiring from the dashboard and remove the last screws securing the dash. Remove the dashboard.
To install:
12. Fit the dashboard into place and start all screws, then tighten them.
13. Install the fuse panel and connect the wiring.
14. Secure the steering column into place.
15. Install the switches and instrument cluster.
16. Install the heater controls and radio.
17. Install the console and connect all wiring.
18. Install the steering wheel and all other remaining components.
19. Connect the negative battery cable.

Console

REMOVAL & INSTALLATION

♦ **See Figures 16 and 17**

Consoles are usually removed by loosening the mounting screws and disengaging the retaining clips. Many of these screws are concealed by plastic covers which may be popped off with a small prybar or similar tool. The console can be lifted over the shifter handle and removed from the car. Be very careful not to lose any small parts between the floor pan and carpet while the console is out.

Once the console is removed, take an extra moment to clean it thoroughly and apply a vinyl protectant. You can now get all the crevices that have been blocked by the seats and hidden by the carpet. When the console is reinstalled, make sure that any wires in the area are not pinched by the console or pierced by the mounting screws.

86630016

Fig. 16 Most consoles are secured by several mounting screws and clips

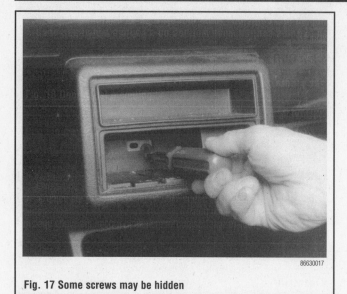

Fig. 17 Some screws may be hidden

Door Panels

REMOVAL & INSTALLATION

▶ **See Figure 18**

1. Remove the window regulator handle.
2. Remove the arm rest.
3. Remove the door lock knob.
4. Remove the inner door handle cover.

5. Using a flat prytool, gently separate the door trim panel clips from the door.
6. Lift the panel to remove it and disconnect the speaker or mirror wires as required.

To install:

7. Make sure the sheet of plastic behind the panel is properly sealed against the metal to keep drafts out of the interior.
8. Place the door trim panel into position on the door.
9. Apply pressure to the trim panel in the areas where the trim panel clips attach to the door.
10. Install the inner door handle cover, door lock knob and the arm rest.

Headliner

REMOVAL & INSTALLATION

Vehicles Without a Sunroof

1. Remove the rear view mirror, sun visors, sun visor holders and assist grip.
2. Separate the lens from the interior light and remove the screws.
3. Disconnect the interior lamp harness coupler.
4. Remove the weatherstrip.
5. Remove the seaming welt.
6. Remove the front door trim with a flat prytool.
7. Remove the center pillar trim.
8. Remove the weatherstrip and fasteners, then remove the rear pillar trim.
9. Remove the fasteners from the roof lining.
10. Remove the headliner rear end plate.

➡**On some models, remove the plate while pushing the weatherstrip away from the end plate.**

11. Remove the rear of the roof lining by pulling it free from the corners.

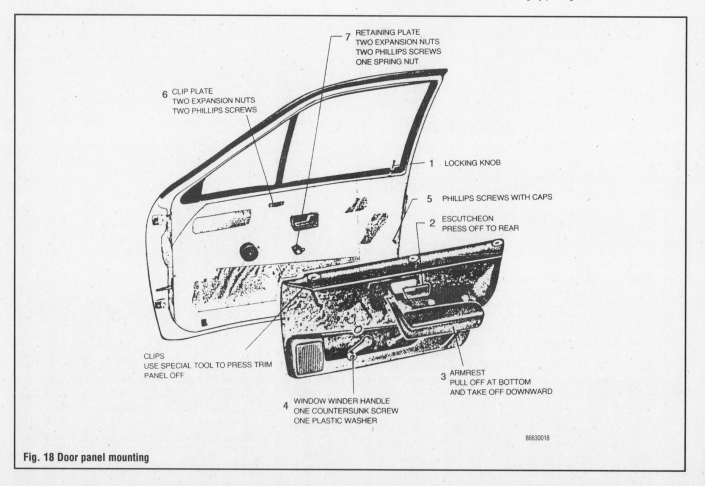

7 RETAINING PLATE
TWO EXPANSION NUTS
TWO PHILLIPS SCREWS
ONE SPRING NUT

6 CLIP PLATE
TWO EXPANSION NUTS
TWO PHILLIPS SCREWS

1 LOCKING KNOB

5 PHILLIPS SCREWS WITH CAPS

2 ESCUTCHEON
PRESS OFF TO REAR

3 ARMREST
PULL OFF AT BOTTOM
AND TAKE OFF DOWNWARD

CLIPS
USE SPECIAL TOOL TO PRESS TRIM
PANEL OFF

4 WINDOW WINDER HANDLE
ONE COUNTERSUNK SCREW
ONE PLASTIC WASHER

Fig. 18 Door panel mounting

12. Move the roof lining brace rearward and remove the front part of the roof lining.

To install:

13. Position the headliner in the vehicle. Install the fasteners to the roof lining.
14. Install the headliner rear end plate.
15. Install the rear pillar trim and weatherstrip.
16. Install the front door trim.
17. Install the seaming welt and weatherstrip.
18. Connect the interior lamp wiring and install the lens.
19. Install the sun visors, rear view mirror and assist grip.

Vehicles With a Sunroof

1. Remove the rear view mirror, sun visors, sun visor holders and assist grip.
2. Separate the lens from the interior light and remove the screws.
3. Disconnect the interior lamp harness coupler and remove the interior lamp.
4. Remove the seaming welt from the sunroof opening.
5. Remove the front of the door opening seaming welts.
6. Remove the front pillar trims.
7. Remove the roof lining front lace.
8. Remove the rear of the door opening seaming welts.
9. Remove the rear pillar trim.
10. Remove the roof lining rear lace.
11. Remove the side pillar trim.
12. Remove the attaching screws of the roof lining side lace and remove the side lace.
13. Remove the fasteners at the side of the roof lining and remove the roof lining.

To install:

14. Position the headliner in the vehicle. Install the fasteners to the roof lining.
15. Install the side pillar trim and the roof lining rear lace.
16. Install the rear pillar trim.
17. Install the seaming welts and weatherstrip. Install the front pillar trims.
18. Connect the interior lamp wiring and install the lens.
19. Install the sun visors, rear view mirror and assist grip.

Air Conditioner Vents

REMOVAL & INSTALLATION

The ducts are held into the dashboard with barbed clips on the sides of the vent. They can be pried out and pushed in easily. Some may also be secured by screws. Be careful not to damage the dashboard pad. Place a clean rag on the pad and pry carefully with a small prytool. If the pad is dented without breaking the "skin", gently warm the pad with a heat gun and it should regain most of its original shape.

Manual Door Locks

REMOVAL & INSTALLATION

♦ **See Figure 19**

1. Set the door lock in the locked position with either the lock knob or the key.
2. Remove both of the door lock retaining screws, and pull the lock approximately ⅜–½ in. (10–12mm) away from the door.
3. Insert a screwdriver into the access hole at the bottom of the lock mechanism and hold the remote control lever in the pulled out position.
4. Detach the remote control lever from the pull rod.
5. Pull the locking lever, at the top of the mechanism, out of the sleeve.
6. Remove the lock from the door.
7. Close the rotary latch and lock it with the locking lever.
8. Insert a screwdriver into the access hole at the bottom of the lock mechanism and hold the remote control lever in the pulled out position.
9. Insert the locking lever into the sleeve and attach the remote control lever to the pull rod.
10. Pull the screwdriver out of the access hole.
11. Mount the door lock to the door, insert the retainer screws and tighten securely.

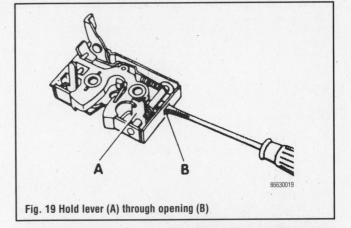

Fig. 19 Hold lever (A) through opening (B)

86630019

Central Locking System

TESTING

♦ **See Figure 20**

The heart of the pneumatic central locking system is the bi-pressure pump mounted in the luggage compartment. The pump runs both ways to provide vacuum or pressure as required for locking or unlocking. There are lock actuators at each door, the rear hatch or trunk and at the fuel filler door. The master actuator at the driver's door includes the switch that activates the pump. In normal operation, the pump runs for about 2 seconds and will build enough pressure or vacuum to operate all locks and activate an internal shut-off switch. If the pump runs for more than 5 seconds, a leak in the system is preventing shut-off switch operation and an automatic shut-off will occur in about 35 seconds. If the pump does not run at all, the problem is most likely electrical.

1. Open the luggage compartment and remove the left side interior trim. Unhook the strap, remove the pump cover and pull the pump out of the housing.
2. Install a small clamp on the hose before the first branching tee and turn the key in the driver's door lock. If the pump does not run at all, go to Step 7.
3. If the pump runs for more than 5 seconds, the shut-off switch inside is faulty and the pump must be replaced. If the pump stops in less than 5 seconds, the pump is good and there is a leak somewhere in the system.
4. Move the clamp to the upper branch of the tee and turn the driver's door lock again. If the pump runs too long, the leak is at the left rear door actuator or the hose.
5. If the pump stops in less than 5 seconds, move the clamp to the next hose junction at the right rear of the luggage compartment and test again. The hose that branches to the right supplies the fuel filler door and trunk or hatch actuator. The hose branching down supplies the right door actuators.
6. Continue moving the clamp towards the actuators until the pump does not stop within 5 seconds. This means the clamp is now past the leak and the previous section of hose or actuator is leaking.
7. If the pump does not run at all, disconnect the wiring and connect a voltmeter or test light to the center and right terminals on the connector. There should be 12 volts when the driver's door is unlocked.
8. Move the tester to the center and left terminals. There should be 12 volts when the driver's door is locked.
9. If the voltages appear as specified, the pump is faulty and must be replaced. If there is no voltage in either or both tests, the lock switch, wiring or fuse is faulty. The switch is part of the master actuator and cannot be replaced separately.

REMOVAL & INSTALLATION

♦ **See Figures 21 and 22**

1. To replace the pump, remove the left luggage compartment interior panel and remove the pump cover and the pump. Test the new pump before completing the installation.
2. To replace the actuator, remove the door panel. Follow the hose to the actuator and disconnect the hose and the linkage at the actuator. On the driver's door, disconnect the wiring.

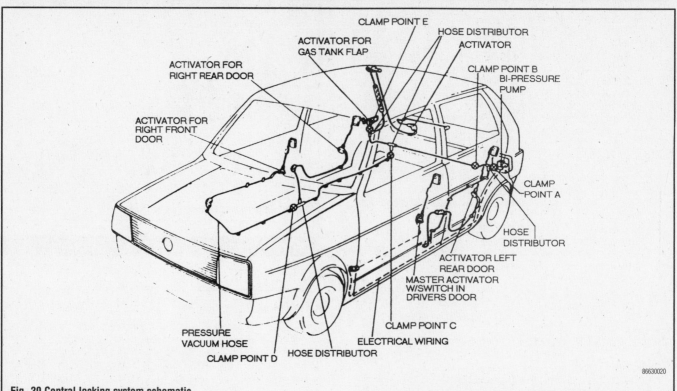

Fig. 20 Central locking system schematic

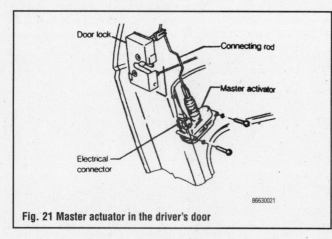

Fig. 21 Master actuator in the driver's door

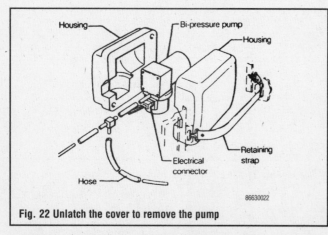

Fig. 22 Unlatch the cover to remove the pump

3. Remove the screws and remove the actuator. Connect the hose to the new actuator and test the system before installing it.

Hatch Lock

REMOVAL & INSTALLATION

♦ See Figure 23

1. Using a flat screwdriver, gently remove the trim fasteners, then remove the trim from inside the hatch.
2. Disconnect the rod for the push button release.
3. Remove the push button securing clip and remove the push button.
4. Remove the lock attaching bolts, then remove the lock.
5. Installation is the reverse of the removal procedure. If necessary, adjust the hatch.

Door Glass and Regulator

REMOVAL & INSTALLATION

♦ See Figure 24

1. Lower the window glass and remove the inner handle cover, door lock knob, the window regulator handle and the door trim panel.
2. On vehicles with power windows, disconnect the wiring coupling.
3. Carefully peel off the door screen so that it can be reused.
4. On convertible models remove the seven screws attaching the window regulator to the door and one screw from the winder.

➡**The window regulator may be riveted to the door on later model vehicles. Drill the rivets out to remove and use nuts, bolts and lock washers for installation.**

5. Temporarily install the window regulator handle and position the door glass so that the bolts can be removed from the service hole. Remove the door glass installation bolts.
6. On convertible models, remove the door glass and take out the window regulator through the large access hole. On other models, remove the door glass. Disconnect the retainer clips from the window winder, then remove the winder through the service access hole.

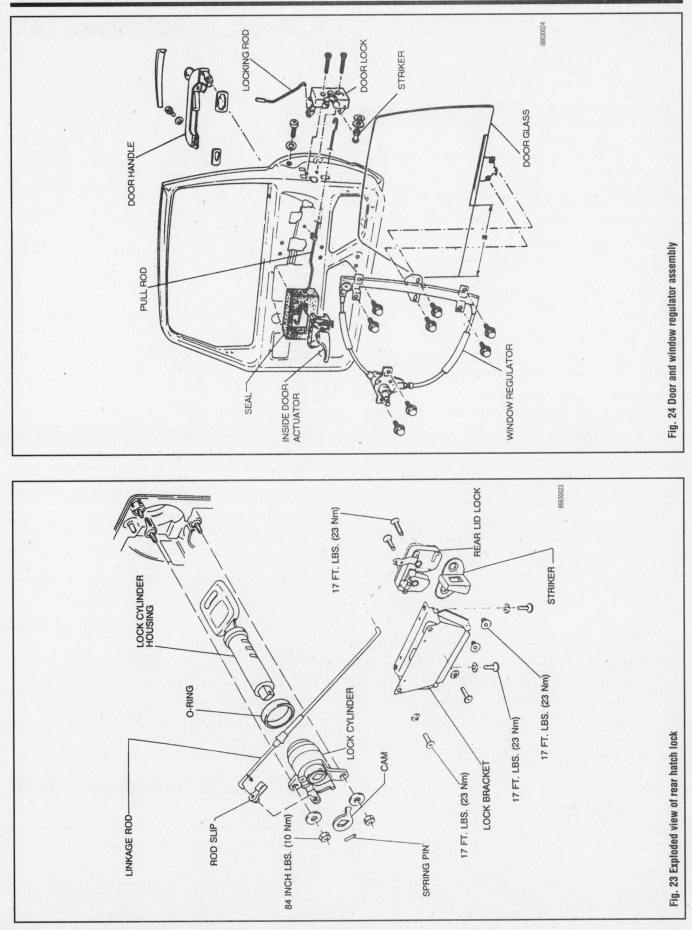

86630024

LOCKING ROD

DOOR LOCK

STRIKER

DOOR HANDLE

DOOR GLASS

PULL ROD

SEAL

INSIDE DOOR ACTUATOR

WINDOW REGULATOR

Fig. 24 Door and window regulator assembly

86630023

LOCK CYLINDER HOUSING

O-RING

LINKAGE ROD

ROD SLIP

LOCK CYLINDER

CAM

SPRING PIN

84 INCH LBS. (10 Nm)

17 FT. LBS. (23 Nm)

17 FT. LBS. (23 Nm)

LOCK BRACKET

17 FT. LBS. (23 Nm)

17 FT. LBS. (23 Nm)

REAR LID LOCK

STRIKER

17 FT. LBS. (23 Nm)

Fig. 23 Exploded view of rear hatch lock

To install:

7. Position and install the window regulator in the door.
8. Install the glass.
9. Install the door screen.
10. On models with power windows, engage the wiring.
11. Install the trim panel and all other remaining components.

Electric Window Motor

REMOVAL & INSTALLATION

▶ **See Figure 25**

1. Lower the window glass and remove the inner handle cover, door lock knob (if necessary), the window regulator handle and the door trim panel.
2. Disconnect the wiring coupling. Carefully peel off the door screen so that it can be reused.
3. Pull the glass run channel out of the window guide. Remove the retaining screws that secure the front and rear window guides and remove the window guides. Then remove the front quarter window glass from the vehicle.

➡**The window regulator may be riveted to the door on later model vehicles. Drill the rivets out to remove and use nuts, bolts and lock washers for installation.**

4. On the convertible models remove the six bolts attaching the window regulator to the door.
5. Temporarily install the window regulator handle, then position the door glass so that the door glass installation bolts can be removed from the service hole.
6. Remove the door glass installation bolts.
7. On the convertible models, remove the door glass and take out the window regulator through the large access hole.
8. On all other models, remove the door glass. Remove the winder cable installation clips, then remove the window winder through the service access hole.
9. Unfasten the window motor mounting bolts, then remove the motor from the regulator/winder cable.
10. Lubricate the front quarter window glass gasket.

To install:

11. Install the motor in the door and connect the winder cable.
12. Position and install the window regulator in the door.
13. Install the glass.
14. Install the glass run channel.
15. Install the door screen.
16. Engage the wiring.
17. Install the trim panel and all other remaining components.

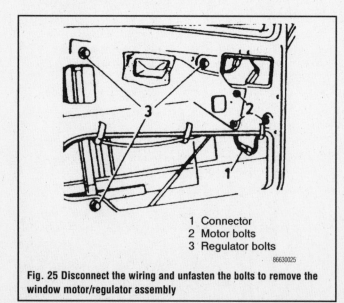

1	Connector
2	Motor bolts
3	Regulator bolts

86630025

Fig. 25 Disconnect the wiring and unfasten the bolts to remove the window motor/regulator assembly

Windshield and Fixed Glass

REMOVAL & INSTALLATION

If your windshield, or other fixed window, is cracked or chipped, you may decide to replace it with a new one yourself. However, there are two main reasons why replacement windshields and other window glass should be installed only by a professional automotive glass technician: safety and cost.

The most important reason a professional should install automotive glass is for safety. The glass in the vehicle, especially the windshield, is designed with safety in mind in case of a collision. The windshield is specially manufactured from two panes of specially-tempered glass with a thin layer of transparent plastic between them. This construction allows the glass to "give" in the event that a part of your body hits the windshield during the collision, and prevents the glass from shattering, which could cause lacerations, blinding and other harm to passengers of the vehicle. The other fixed windows are designed to be tempered so that if they break during a collision, they shatter in such a way that there are no large pointed glass pieces. The professional automotive glass technician knows how to install the glass in a vehicle so that it will function optimally during a collision. Without the proper experience, knowledge and tools, installing a piece of automotive glass yourself could lead to additional harm if an accident should ever occur.

Cost is also a factor when deciding to install automotive glass yourself. Performing this could cost you much more than a professional may charge for the same job. Since the windshield is designed to break under stress, an often life saving characteristic, windshields tend to break VERY easily when an inexperienced person attempts to install one. Do-it-yourselfers buying two, three or even four windshields from a salvage yard because they have broken them during installation are common stories. Also, since the automotive glass is designed to prevent the outside elements from entering your vehicle, improper installation can lead to water and air leaks. Annoying whining noises at highway speeds from air leaks or inside body panel rusting from water leaks can add to your stress level and subtract from your wallet. After buying two or three windshields, installing them and ending up with a leak that produces a noise while driving and water damage during rainstorms, the cost of having a professional do it correctly the first time may be much more alluring. We here at Chilton, therefore, advise that you have a professional automotive glass technician service any broken glass on your vehicle.

WINDSHIELD CHIP REPAIR

▶ **See Figures 26 thru 40**

➡**Check with your state and local authorities on the laws for state safety inspection. Some states or municipalities may not allow chip repair as a viable option for correcting stone damage to your windshield.**

Although severely cracked or damaged windshields must be replaced, there is something that you can do to prolong or even prevent the need for replacement of a chipped windshield. There are many companies which offer windshield chip repair products, such as Loctite's® Bullseye™ windshield repair kit. These kits usually consist of a syringe, pedestal and a sealing adhesive. The syringe is mounted on the pedestal and is used to create a vacuum which pulls the plastic layer against the glass. This helps make the chip transparent. The adhesive is then injected which seals the chip and helps to prevent further stress cracks from developing. Refer to the sequence of photos to get a general idea of what windshield chip repair involves.

➡**Always follow the specific manufacturer's instructions.**

Hatchback Window Glass

REMOVAL & INSTALLATION

1. Remove the wiper arm, wiper motor, back door trim and defogger connector.
2. Remove the rear window molding.
3. Use an awl to make a hole in the sealant.
4. Pass a piece of piano wire, about ⅛ in. (3mm) in diameter, through the hole, and attach wood bars to both ends.

Fig. 26 Small chips on your windshield can be fixed with an aftermarket repair kit, such as the one from Loctite®

Fig. 27 To repair a chip, clean the windshield with glass cleaner and dry it completely

Fig. 28 Remove the center from the adhesive disc and peel off the backing from one side of the disc . . .

Fig. 29 . . . then press it on the windshield so that the chip is centered in the hole

Fig. 30 Be sure that the tab points upward on the windshield

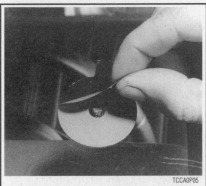

Fig. 31 Peel the backing off the exposed side of the adhesive disc . . .

Fig. 32 . . . then position the plastic pedestal on the adhesive disc, ensuring that the tabs are aligned

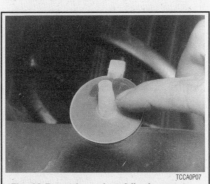

Fig. 33 Press the pedestal firmly on the adhesive disc to create an adequate seal . . .

Fig. 34 . . . then install the applicator syringe nipple in the pedestal's hole

5. Two people should hold the bars, one inside and one outside the vehicle, and then "saw" the sealant from around the glass, cutting along the border between the glass and the sealant.

6. Then, with the help of an assistant, remove the glass from the vehicle. Note the location of the spacers and clips, and make sure that none of them are lost during windshield removal.

To install:

7. Use a knife to smoothly trim the sealant on the body. Leave a layer about 0.04–0.08 in. (1–2mm) thick.

➡ **If there are small gaps or flakes in the sealant use new sealant to patch it.**

8. Carefully clean and remove any dirt or grease from a 1.97 in. (50mm) wide area around the circumference of the glass and the remaining bond of the body.

9. Bond a dam along the circumference of the glass 0.31 in. (8mm) from the edge.

➡ **Securely bond the dam and allow it to dry before proceeding to the next step.**

10. Apply primer with a brush to the circumference of the glass and the body, and allow it to naturally dry for 20 to 30 minutes.

➡ **Be sure not to allow dirt, water, oil, etc. to come in contact with the coated surfaces, and do not touch it with your hand!**

11. Install the spacers in their original positions. Replace any clips with flaws.

12. When the primer has dried, cut the nozzle of the sealant cartridge on an angle, then apply a 0.43 in. (11mm) thick bead of repair seal 0.28 in. (7mm) from the frame of the glass. If necessary, smooth the repair seal to correct any irregularities.

13. Attach the back door glass to the body. Fully lower the side windows to prevent any pressure from being exerted on the back door glass should the doors be closed suddenly. Keep the side windows open until the repair seal dries to some degree.

TCCA0P09

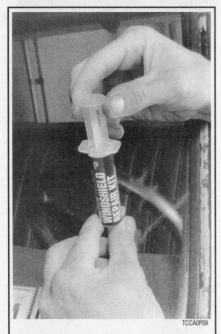

Fig. 35 Hold the syringe with one hand while pulling the plunger back with the other hand

TCCA0P10

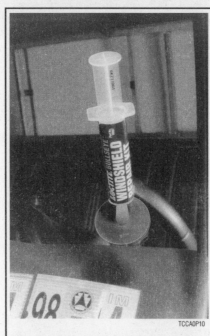

Fig. 36 After applying the solution, allow the entire assembly to sit until it has set completely

TCCA0P11

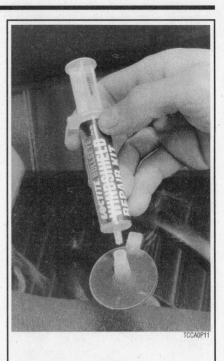

Fig. 37 After the solution has set, remove the syringe from the pedestal . . .

TCCA0P12

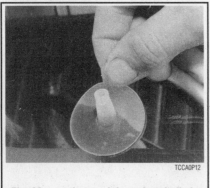

Fig. 38 . . . then peel the pedestal off of the adhesive disc . . .

TCCA0P13

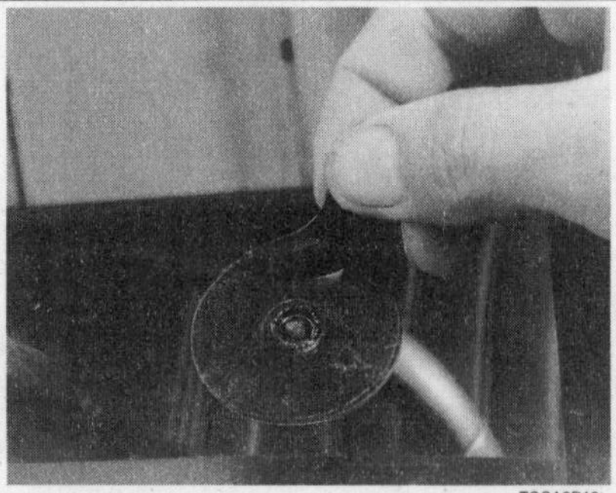

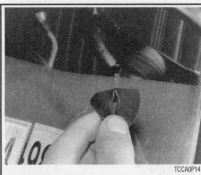

Fig. 39 . . . and peel the adhesive disc off of the windshield

TCCA0P14

Fig. 40 The chip will still be slightly visible, but it should be filled with the hardened solution

14. Remove any excess, or add repair seal where necessary.
15. Check the back door glass for water leaks. If a leak is found, wipe off the water and add repair seal.
16. After checking for water leaks, install the molding.
17. Install the wiper arm, wiper motor door trim and defogger connector.

Side Quarter Glass

REMOVAL & INSTALLATION

The procedure for removing and installing stationary side windows is the same as for the windshield. Please refer to the windshield removal and installation procedure as a guide when completing this repair.

Inside Rear View Mirror

REMOVAL & INSTALLATION

The break-away safety mirror can be removed by rotating the mounting stalk to the left or right.

Seats

REMOVAL & INSTALLATION

Front Seats

1. Slide the seat forward to the stop and remove the track cover beside the tunnel.
2. Remove the acorn nut, washer and bolt at the front of the center seat rail.
3. Pull the seat release handle and push the seat back and out of the tracks. Lift the seat out of the vehicle.

To install:

4. Slide the seat assembly into the tracks and install the bolt, washer and nut.
5. Install the track cover and check operation.

Rear Seat

1. On Fox, Golf, Jetta and Quantum models, lift the seat cushion up and pull forward to remove it.

2. On other models, remove the two screws at the front of the seat cushion and pull forward and up.

3. Release the seat backrest and fold forward.

4. Release the locking lug in the mounting and pull the backrest out of the mounting.

To install:

5. Install the seat and fold back.

6. Install and tighten the retaining bolts.

Seat Belts

REMOVAL & INSTALLATION

1. Disconnect the belt from the door mount, then remove the front seat.

2. Remove the screw and bolt, then release the spring loop to remove the belt retractor from the seat.

3. Open the door and unfasten the countersunk screws to remove the latch from the door.

4. Installation is the reverse of removal. Torque the countersunk screws to 11 ft. lbs. (15 Nm) and the retractor bolt to 30 ft. lbs. (40 Nm).

TORQUE SPECIFICATIONS

Component	US	Metric
Hood		
Retaining bolts	15 ft. lbs.	20 Nm
Trunk		
Retaining bolts	18 ft. lbs.	25 Nm
Bumpers		
Front		
1985-89 Golf and Jetta	57 ft. lbs	83 Nm
1985-89 Scirocco and Cabriolet	66 ft. lbs	90 Nm
Rear		
1985-89 Golf and Jetta	29 ft. lbs.	40 Nm
1985-89 Scirocco and Cabriolet	66 ft. lbs.	90 Nm
Seat Belts		
Counter sunk screws	11 ft. lbs.	15 Nm
Retractor bolt	30 ft. lbs.	40 Nm

86630300

GLOSSARY

AIR/FUEL RATIO: The ratio of air-to-gasoline by weight in the fuel mixture drawn into the engine.

AIR INJECTION: One method of reducing harmful exhaust emissions by injecting air into each of the exhaust ports of an engine. The fresh air entering the hot exhaust manifold causes any remaining fuel to be burned before it can exit the tailpipe.

ALTERNATOR: A device used for converting mechanical energy into electrical energy.

AMMETER: An instrument, calibrated in amperes, used to measure the flow of an electrical current in a circuit. Ammeters are always connected in series with the circuit being tested.

AMPERE: The rate of flow of electrical current present when one volt of electrical pressure is applied against one ohm of electrical resistance.

ANALOG COMPUTER: Any microprocessor that uses similar (analogous) electrical signals to make its calculations.

ARMATURE: A laminated, soft iron core wrapped by a wire that converts electrical energy to mechanical energy as in a motor or relay. When rotated in a magnetic field, it changes mechanical energy into electrical energy as in a generator.

ATMOSPHERIC PRESSURE: The pressure on the Earth's surface caused by the weight of the air in the atmosphere. At sea level, this pressure is 14.7 psi at 32°F (101 kPa at 0°C).

ATOMIZATION: The breaking down of a liquid into a fine mist that can be suspended in air.

AXIAL PLAY: Movement parallel to a shaft or bearing bore.

BACKFIRE: The sudden combustion of gases in the intake or exhaust system that results in a loud explosion.

BACKLASH: The clearance or play between two parts, such as meshed gears.

BACKPRESSURE: Restrictions in the exhaust system that slow the exit of exhaust gases from the combustion chamber.

BAKELITE: A heat resistant, plastic insulator material commonly used in printed circuit boards and transistorized components.

BALL BEARING: A bearing made up of hardened inner and outer races between which hardened steel balls roll.

BALLAST RESISTOR: A resistor in the primary ignition circuit that lowers voltage after the engine is started to reduce wear on ignition components.

BEARING: A friction reducing, supportive device usually located between a stationary part and a moving part.

BIMETAL TEMPERATURE SENSOR: Any sensor or switch made of two dissimilar types of metal that bend when heated or cooled due to the different expansion rates of the alloys. These types of sensors usually function as an on/off switch.

BLOWBY: Combustion gases, composed of water vapor and unburned fuel, that leak past the piston rings into the crankcase during normal engine operation. These gases are removed by the PCV system to prevent the buildup of harmful acids in the crankcase.

BRAKE PAD: A brake shoe and lining assembly used with disc brakes.

BRAKE SHOE: The backing for the brake lining. The term is, however, usually applied to the assembly of the brake backing and lining.

BUSHING: A liner, usually removable, for a bearing; an anti-friction liner used in place of a bearing.

CALIPER: A hydraulically activated device in a disc brake system, which is mounted straddling the brake rotor (disc). The caliper contains at least one piston and two brake pads. Hydraulic pressure on the piston(s) forces the pads against the rotor.

CAMSHAFT: A shaft in the engine on which are the lobes (cams) which operate the valves. The camshaft is driven by the crankshaft, via a belt, chain or gears, at one half the crankshaft speed.

CAPACITOR: A device which stores an electrical charge.

CARBON MONOXIDE (CO): A colorless, odorless gas given off as a normal byproduct of combustion. It is poisonous and extremely dangerous in confined areas, building up slowly to toxic levels without warning if adequate ventilation is not available.

CARBURETOR: A device, usually mounted on the intake manifold of an engine, which mixes the air and fuel in the proper proportion to allow even combustion.

CATALYTIC CONVERTER: A device installed in the exhaust system, like a muffler, that converts harmful byproducts of combustion into carbon dioxide and water vapor by means of a heat-producing chemical reaction.

CENTRIFUGAL ADVANCE: A mechanical method of advancing the spark timing by using flyweights in the distributor that react to centrifugal force generated by the distributor shaft rotation.

CHECK VALVE: Any one-way valve installed to permit the flow of air, fuel or vacuum in one direction only.

CHOKE: A device, usually a moveable valve, placed in the intake path of a carburetor to restrict the flow of air.

CIRCUIT: Any unbroken path through which an electrical current can flow. Also used to describe fuel flow in some instances.

CIRCUIT BREAKER: A switch which protects an electrical circuit from overload by opening the circuit when the current flow exceeds a predetermined level. Some circuit breakers must be reset manually, while most reset automatically.

COIL (IGNITION): A transformer in the ignition circuit which steps up the voltage provided to the spark plugs.

COMBINATION MANIFOLD: An assembly which includes both the intake and exhaust manifolds in one casting.

COMBINATION VALVE: A device used in some fuel systems that routes fuel vapors to a charcoal storage canister instead of venting them into the atmosphere. The valve relieves fuel tank pressure and allows fresh air into the tank as the fuel level drops to prevent a vapor lock situation.

COMPRESSION RATIO: The comparison of the total volume of the cylinder and combustion chamber with the piston at BDC and the piston at TDC.

CONDENSER: 1. An electrical device which acts to store an electrical charge, preventing voltage surges. 2. A radiator-like device in the air conditioning system in which refrigerant gas condenses into a liquid, giving off heat.

CONDUCTOR: Any material through which an electrical current can be transmitted easily.

CONTINUITY: Continuous or complete circuit. Can be checked with an ohmmeter.

COUNTERSHAFT: An intermediate shaft which is rotated by a mainshaft and transmits, in turn, that rotation to a working part.

CRANKCASE: The lower part of an engine in which the crankshaft and related parts operate.

CRANKSHAFT: The main driving shaft of an engine which receives reciprocating motion from the pistons and converts it to rotary motion.

CYLINDER: In an engine, the round hole in the engine block in which the piston(s) ride.

CYLINDER BLOCK: The main structural member of an engine in which is found the cylinders, crankshaft and other principal parts.

CYLINDER HEAD: The detachable portion of the engine, usually fastened to the top of the cylinder block and containing all or most of the combustion chambers. On overhead valve engines, it contains the valves and their operating parts. On overhead cam engines, it contains the camshaft as well.

DEAD CENTER: The extreme top or bottom of the piston stroke.

DETONATION: An unwanted explosion of the air/fuel mixture in the combustion chamber caused by excess heat and compression, advanced timing, or an overly lean mixture. Also referred to as "ping".

DIAPHRAGM: A thin, flexible wall separating two cavities, such as in a vacuum advance unit.

DIESELING: A condition in which hot spots in the combustion chamber cause the engine to run on after the key is turned off.

DIFFERENTIAL: A geared assembly which allows the transmission of motion between drive axles, giving one axle the ability to turn faster than the other.

DIODE: An electrical device that will allow current to flow in one direction only.

DISC BRAKE: A hydraulic braking assembly consisting of a brake disc, or rotor, mounted on an axle, and a caliper assembly containing, usually two brake pads which are activated by hydraulic pressure. The pads are forced against the sides of the disc, creating friction which slows the vehicle.

DISTRIBUTOR: A mechanically driven device on an engine which is responsible for electrically firing the spark plug at a predetermined point of the piston stroke.

DOWEL PIN: A pin, inserted in mating holes in two different parts allowing those parts to maintain a fixed relationship.

DRUM BRAKE: A braking system which consists of two brake shoes and one or two wheel cylinders, mounted on a fixed backing plate, and a brake drum, mounted on an axle, which revolves around the assembly.

DWELL: The rate, measured in degrees of shaft rotation, at which an electrical circuit cycles on and off.

ELECTRONIC CONTROL UNIT (ECU): Ignition module, module, amplifier or igniter. See Module for definition.

ELECTRONIC IGNITION: A system in which the timing and firing of the spark plugs is controlled by an electronic control unit, usually called a module. These systems have no points or condenser.

END-PLAY: The measured amount of axial movement in a shaft.

ENGINE: A device that converts heat into mechanical energy.

EXHAUST MANIFOLD: A set of cast passages or pipes which conduct exhaust gases from the engine.

FEELER GAUGE: A blade, usually metal, or precisely predetermined thickness, used to measure the clearance between two parts.

FIRING ORDER: The order in which combustion occurs in the cylinders of an engine. Also the order in which spark is distributed to the plugs by the distributor.

FLOODING: The presence of too much fuel in the intake manifold and combustion chamber which prevents the air/fuel mixture from firing, thereby causing a no-start situation.

FLYWHEEL: A disc shaped part bolted to the rear end of the crankshaft. Around the outer perimeter is affixed the ring gear. The starter drive engages the ring gear, turning the flywheel, which rotates the crankshaft, imparting the initial starting motion to the engine.

FOOT POUND (ft. lbs. or sometimes, ft.lb.): The amount of energy or work needed to raise an item weighing one pound, a distance of one foot.

FUSE: A protective device in a circuit which prevents circuit overload by breaking the circuit when a specific amperage is present. The device is constructed around a strip or wire of a lower amperage rating than the circuit it is designed to protect. When an amperage higher than that stamped on the fuse is present in the circuit, the strip or wire melts, opening the circuit.

GEAR RATIO: The ratio between the number of teeth on meshing gears.

GENERATOR: A device which converts mechanical energy into electrical energy.

HEAT RANGE: The measure of a spark plug's ability to dissipate heat from its firing end. The higher the heat range, the hotter the plug fires.

HUB: The center part of a wheel or gear.

HYDROCARBON (HC): Any chemical compound made up of hydrogen and carbon. A major pollutant formed by the engine as a byproduct of combustion.

HYDROMETER: An instrument used to measure the specific gravity of a solution.

INCH POUND (inch lbs.; sometimes in.lb. or in. lbs.): One twelfth of a foot pound.

INDUCTION: A means of transferring electrical energy in the form of a magnetic field. Principle used in the ignition coil to increase voltage.

INJECTOR: A device which receives metered fuel under relatively low pressure and is activated to inject the fuel into the engine under relatively high pressure at a predetermined time.

INPUT SHAFT: The shaft to which torque is applied, usually carrying the driving gear or gears.

INTAKE MANIFOLD: A casting of passages or pipes used to conduct air or a fuel/air mixture to the cylinders.

JOURNAL: The bearing surface within which a shaft operates.

KEY: A small block usually fitted in a notch between a shaft and a hub to prevent slippage of the two parts.

MANIFOLD: A casting of passages or set of pipes which connect the cylinders to an inlet or outlet source.

MANIFOLD VACUUM: Low pressure in an engine intake manifold formed just below the throttle plates. Manifold vacuum is highest at idle and drops under acceleration.

MASTER CYLINDER: The primary fluid pressurizing device in a hydraulic system. In automotive use, it is found in brake and hydraulic clutch systems and is pedal activated, either directly or, in a power brake system, through the power booster.

MODULE: Electronic control unit, amplifier or igniter of solid state or integrated design which controls the current flow in the ignition primary circuit based on input from the pick-up coil. When the module opens the primary circuit, high secondary voltage is induced in the coil.

NEEDLE BEARING: A bearing which consists of a number (usually a large number) of long, thin rollers.

OHM: (Ω) The unit used to measure the resistance of conductor-to-electrical flow. One ohm is the amount of resistance that limits current flow to one ampere in a circuit with one volt of pressure.

OHMMETER: An instrument used for measuring the resistance, in ohms, in an electrical circuit.

OUTPUT SHAFT: The shaft which transmits torque from a device, such as a transmission.

OVERDRIVE: A gear assembly which produces more shaft revolutions than that transmitted to it.

OVERHEAD CAMSHAFT (OHC): An engine configuration in which the camshaft is mounted on top of the cylinder head and operates the valve either directly or by means of rocker arms.

OVERHEAD VALVE (OHV): An engine configuration in which all of the valves are located in the cylinder head and the camshaft is located in the cylinder block. The camshaft operates the valves via lifters and pushrods.

OXIDES OF NITROGEN (NOx): Chemical compounds of nitrogen produced as a byproduct of combustion. They combine with hydrocarbons to produce smog.

OXYGEN SENSOR: Use with the feedback system to sense the presence of oxygen in the exhaust gas and signal the computer which can reference the voltage signal to an air/fuel ratio.

PINION: The smaller of two meshing gears.

PISTON RING: An open-ended ring with fits into a groove on the outer diameter of the piston. Its chief function is to form a seal between the piston and cylinder wall. Most automotive pistons have three rings: two for compression sealing; one for oil sealing.

PRELOAD: A predetermined load placed on a bearing during assembly or by adjustment.

PRIMARY CIRCUIT: the low voltage side of the ignition system which consists of the ignition switch, ballast resistor or resistance wire, bypass, coil, electronic control unit and pick-up coil as well as the connecting wires and harnesses.

PRESS FIT: The mating of two parts under pressure, due to the inner diameter of one being smaller than the outer diameter of the other, or vice versa; an interference fit.

RACE: The surface on the inner or outer ring of a bearing on which the balls, needles or rollers move.

REGULATOR: A device which maintains the amperage and/or voltage levels of a circuit at predetermined values.

RELAY: A switch which automatically opens and/or closes a circuit.

RESISTANCE: The opposition to the flow of current through a circuit or electrical device, and is measured in ohms. Resistance is equal to the voltage divided by the amperage.

RESISTOR: A device, usually made of wire, which offers a preset amount of resistance in an electrical circuit.

RING GEAR: The name given to a ring-shaped gear attached to a differential case, or affixed to a flywheel or as part of a planetary gear set.

ROLLER BEARING: A bearing made up of hardened inner and outer races between which hardened steel rollers move.

ROTOR: 1. The disc-shaped part of a disc brake assembly, upon which the brake pads bear; also called, brake disc. 2. The device mounted atop the distributor shaft, which passes current to the distributor cap tower contacts.

SECONDARY CIRCUIT: The high voltage side of the ignition system, usually above 20,000 volts. The secondary includes the ignition coil, coil wire, distributor cap and rotor, spark plug wires and spark plugs.

SENDING UNIT: A mechanical, electrical, hydraulic or electro-magnetic device which transmits information to a gauge.

SENSOR: Any device designed to measure engine operating conditions or ambient pressures and temperatures. Usually electronic in nature and designed to send a voltage signal to an on-board computer, some sensors may operate as a simple on/off switch or they may provide a variable voltage signal (like a potentiometer) as conditions or measured parameters change.

SHIM: Spacers of precise, predetermined thickness used between parts to establish a proper working relationship.

SLAVE CYLINDER: In automotive use, a device in the hydraulic clutch system which is activated by hydraulic force, disengaging the clutch.

SOLENOID: A coil used to produce a magnetic field, the effect of which is to produce work.

SPARK PLUG: A device screwed into the combustion chamber of a spark ignition engine. The basic construction is a conductive core inside of a ceramic insulator, mounted in an outer conductive base. An electrical charge from the spark plug wire travels along the conductive core and jumps a preset air gap to a grounding point or points at the end of the conductive base. The resultant spark ignites the fuel/air mixture in the combustion chamber.

SPLINES: Ridges machined or cast onto the outer diameter of a shaft or inner diameter of a bore to enable parts to mate without rotation.

TACHOMETER: A device used to measure the rotary speed of an engine, shaft, gear, etc., usually in rotations per minute.

THERMOSTAT: A valve, located in the cooling system of an engine, which is closed when cold and opens gradually in response to engine heating, controlling the temperature of the coolant and rate of coolant flow.

TOP DEAD CENTER (TDC): The point at which the piston reaches the top of its travel on the compression stroke.

TORQUE: The twisting force applied to an object.

TORQUE CONVERTER: A turbine used to transmit power from a driving member to a driven member via hydraulic action, providing changes in drive ratio and torque. In automotive use, it links the driveplate at the rear of the engine to the automatic transmission.

TRANSDUCER: A device used to change a force into an electrical signal.

TRANSISTOR: A semi-conductor component which can be actuated by a small voltage to perform an electrical switching function.

TUNE-UP: A regular maintenance function, usually associated with the replacement and adjustment of parts and components in the electrical and fuel systems of a vehicle for the purpose of attaining optimum performance.

TURBOCHARGER: An exhaust driven pump which compresses intake air and forces it into the combustion chambers at higher than atmospheric pressures. The increased air pressure allows more fuel to be burned and results in increased horsepower being produced.

VACUUM ADVANCE: A device which advances the ignition timing in response to increased engine vacuum.

VACUUM GAUGE: An instrument used to measure the presence of vacuum in a chamber.

VALVE: A device which control the pressure, direction of flow or rate of flow of a liquid or gas.

VALVE CLEARANCE: The measured gap between the end of the valve stem and the rocker arm, cam lobe or follower that activates the valve.

VISCOSITY: The rating of a liquid's internal resistance to flow.

VOLTMETER: An instrument used for measuring electrical force in units called volts. Voltmeters are always connected parallel with the circuit being tested.

WHEEL CYLINDER: Found in the automotive drum brake assembly, it is a device, actuated by hydraulic pressure, which, through internal pistons, pushes the brake shoes outward against the drums.

MASTER
INDEX